1 MONTH OF
FREE
READING

at
www.ForgottenBooks.com

By purchasing this book you are eligible for one month membership to ForgottenBooks.com, giving you unlimited access to our entire collection of over 1,000,000 titles via our web site and mobile apps.

To claim your free month visit:

www.forgottenbooks.com/free931820

ISBN 978-0-260-16294-6
PIBN 10931820

REPORTS OF CASES

ARGUED AND DETERMINED

IN THE

𝔖upreme 𝔠ourt of 𝔑ew 𝔖outh 𝔚ales,

WITH

TABLES OF THE CASES AND PRINCIPAL MATTERS,

AND

AN·APPENDIX

CONTAINING DECISIONS BY THE JUDICIAL COMMITTEE OF THE PRIVY
COUNCIL FROM APPEAL, AND A SELECTION FROM THE FORMER
DECISIONS OF THE COURT.

BY

W. H. WILKINSON, Esq., and J. S. PATERSON, Esq.,

BARRISTERS-AT-LAW.

VOL. IV.

SYDNEY:

J. J. MOORE, BOOKSELLER AND PUBLISHER,

GEORGE-STREET, OPPOSITE ST. ANDREW'S CATHEDRAL.

1866.

224516

F. CUNNINGHAME,
STEAM MACHINE PRINTER,
146 PITT STREET.

TABLE OF CASES

REPORTED IN THE FOURTH VOLUME.

CASES AT LAW.

CASES IN EQUITY.

APPENDIX.

CASES

ARGUED AND DETERMINED

IN

THE SUPREME COURT

OF

NEW SOUTH WALES,

AT LAW.

The QUEEN *against* COUSINS (a).

*I*SAACS, on the 27th of February, obtained a rule calling on *Richard Wilmot Cousins*, to show cause why the Court should not grant leave for an information in the nature of a *quo warranto*, to be exhibited against him—to show by what authority he claimed to be councillor for the municipality of Newtown, on the following grounds :—1. That the names of persons were improperly inserted in the electoral list, for the purpose of the election of a councillor for Enmore Ward, in the Municipality of Newtown, on the 14th of February instant, after the said list had been passed by the Council and published. 2. That the votes of persons

Persons whose names are on the electoral roll, and also entered as having a free-hold, lease-hold, and household qualification, are prima facie rate-payers, and entitled to vote at the election of councillors for a municipality.

An application for a *quo warranto* information will not be granted on the ground of the badness of some of the votes given in favor of the defendant, unless it is shown by the relator that if the votes complained of are rejected, the defendant would be in a minority.

Persons assessed for rates are entitled to pay the amount at any moment ; and, therefore, the proper officer is justified in receiving the rates of such persons on the day of the poll, although the Municipal Council has resolved that rates should not be received on that day.

The ballot boxes had been opened, and the poll declared by the Chairman before the time directed by the 24th section of the Act. *Held*, that although such opening and declaration were clearly illegal –yet, as the Chairman believed that he acted with the assent of all parties, and was not shown to have acted from improper motives—the Court would not, on this ground, make absolute a rule for a *quo warranto* information.

(a, Before *Stephen*, C.J., *Milford*, J., and *Wise*, J.

VOL. 4—A

were received at the election who had not duly paid
their rates. 3. That the votes of persons were received
at the election who were not ratepayers, liable to be
assessed for the payment of some rate within the meaning of the Municipalities Act of 1858. 4. That the
election of *R. W. Cousins* was not duly declared pursuant to the 24th section of the statute. 5. That the
ballot boxes used at the election were improperly opened
in contravention of the 24th section of the statute.

By the affidavit of the relator it appeared that an
election of one councillor for Enmore Ward, and one for
O'Connell Ward, took place on the 14th of February,
1865, pursuant to a notice issued by order of the returning officer. The notice contained the following paragraph—"No person will be allowed to vote, any portion
of whose rates are in arrear. For the purposes of this
election no rates will be received after Monday, the 13th
instant." The relator and the defendant were opposing
candidates for election as councillors for Enmore Ward.
At a meeting of the Council of the municipality on the
31st of January, objection was taken by the relator (then
a councillor) to the names of *M. Hurley* and *J. Vanson*
being on the list of ratepayers, on the ground that they
were servants of Mr. *Josephson*, and resided in small
tenements on his property, for which they paid no rent,
and the assessment on which was included in the assessment at £300 per annum, with the rate on which Mr.
Josephson was charged ; and after some discussion a
majority of the council resolved that *Hurley* and *Vanson*
were not qualified ratepayers, and their names were
struck out. The electoral list so passed by the council
was printed and published. At the polling for the
election of councillors on the 14th of February, when the
relator attended at the polling places, the council clerk
thrust into his hands a copy of the electoral list for
Enmore Ward, having interlined in writing the names
of *Hurley* and *Vanson*, stating also that some persons
whose names were erased with a blue line on the list
were not entitled to vote, as not having paid their rates.
Vanson afterwards entered the polling place and voted.

While the polling was going on, the returning officer
and the council clerk received payment of rates from
persons whose names were on the electoral list, notwithstanding the notice that such rates would not be
received, and although their names had been erased
with a blue line. At the close of the poll the ballot
boxes were opened, and a rough state of the poll
declared, " when," the relator's affidavit stated, " I
again verbally protested against the legality of the
proceedings. On the next day, at noon, a rough state
of the poll was declared; and on the following day, at
noon, the final state of the poll was declared, to the
effect that the said *R. W. Cousins* was duly elected as
councillor for the Enmore Ward, in the said municipality; and I then handed to the said chairman, as
such returning officer, a written protest."

The written protest was said to be " in consequence
of the illegality of the election; the said election not
having been carried out under the proper list of ratepayers appointed for that purpose by the council at
their meetings."

Mr. *Josephson* was assessed as the owner and occupier
of Enmore House and grounds at £300 a year. *Hurley,
Vanson,* and one *Broadfoot* were servants in his employ,
as coachman and gardeners respectively, and lived in
cottages on Mr. *Josephson's* property, which were not
separately assessed, but included in the assessment of
£300, the rate on which was alone paid by Mr. *Josephson.*

There were affidavits in reply; one by the returning
officer at the recent election (Mr. *Kingsbury*), which
stated that *Hurley, Vanson* and *Broadfoot* were named
on the electoral roll for the electoral district of Newtown,
for 1864 and 1865, in respect of the tenements they
occupied, and had voted in respect of such properties
and qualifications at the election of a councillor for
Enmore Ward, in February, 1864, and that the relator
acted as returning officer at such election.

It appeared that an application had been made to
him (Mr *Kingsbury*) as the returning officer, to allow
these persons to vote at the then coming election,

and notice given that he would be held responsible if he refused, and that he accordingly inserted their names in the list as above mentioned, and at the election he allowed them to vote after they had made the necessary declaration. The affidavit continued, "after the close of the poll I was requested by (amongst others) Mr. *Munro*, on behalf of the said *F. W. Holland*, to open the ballot boxes and declare the rough state of the poll that evening, which I declined to do, unless the same were consented to by all the then councillors of such municipality, the candidates for election at such election held that day, and the various scrutineers. Afterwards, 1 was informed that all the said parties had so consented, whereupon I opened the boxes." This statement was confirmed by the affidavit of *Munro*, the chairman of the municipality for the present year.

The affidavits in answer (*a*), which were filed by leave of the Court, stated the facts to be as follows :—That *Munro* came to *Holland* and said, "I have been going round to some of the candidates; have you any objection to knowing the state of the poll this evening ?" *Holland* replied, "let the returning officer do just as he likes." *Holland* also said to the bystanders, "if he puts the ballot boxes on his kitchen fire it would not concern me ; he has the Act to guide him, and if he tampers with the ballot boxes he will have to take the consequences." *Munro* afterwards met *Teeson* (*Holland's* scrutineer), and said that he had been round to the candidates, and that they wished to know the state of the poll that evening, if the returning officer would declare it. *Teeson* asked if *Holland* wished to know the state of the poll, and *Munro* said yes ; and *Teeson* said, in that case he would not stand in the way.

Isaacs (*b*) in support of the rule. Any illegality, by the wrong reception of votes, especially where, as here,

---

(*a*) See note (*b*).

(*b*) When *Salomons*, who showed cause against the rule, read the affidavits tending to show that the relator consented to the irregularity complained of.

the electoral roll had been altered, and also by the premature opening of ballot boxes, vitiates the election. It is clear that names were improperly inserted in the list of ratepayers after they had been finally prepared and published. The 10th section provides that "for all future electiohs all such persons (that is persons named on the electoral roll), being also ratepayers as herein-after mentioned, shall be and be deemed to be electors" of such municipality. The 11th section enacts that " ratepayers, for the purposes of this Act, shall be per-sons who are liable to be assessed for the payment of some rate, or who are at the time of claiming to vote assessed for the payment of some rate—no portion where-of shall at that time be in arrear ; and every person named in the electoral roll, having a freehold, leasehold, or household qualification, shall *prima facie* be deemed a ratepayer." The first part of the 10th section shows that the electoral roll was only to be the guide in the first election; but that for all future elections ratepayers, whose names appeared on the roll for the municipality, were to be the electors. After the first election lists were to be prepared, containing the names of the rate-payers, and such persons, even although their names might be omitted from the electoral roll, were entitled to vote. ·

Salomons contra. Mere irregularities will not entitle the relator to have the rule made absolute. The title of *Hurley* and *Vanson* to have their names on the electoral roll cannot be questioned in this proceeding. It is sufficient that their names were on the roll. The authorities are clear that the title of the electors will not be enquired into in an information against the elected ; *R.* v. *Hughes* ˈ(a). *Bayley*, J., in giving judgment, says, " In *R* v. *Mein* (b), Lord *Kenyon* held, that

Isaacs asked leave to file affidavits in answer, as the affidavits just read were only filed this morning and not served. He referred to *Cole* on Criminal Informations.*

Per Curiam. On this point the defendant may have time to reply. Affidavits in answer were consequently filed and read during the argument.

* p. 178.

(a) 4 B. & C. 377.   (b) 3 T. R. 597.

where the electors do not fill a corporate office, it is allowable to enter into their titles, in questioning that of the elected, because there is no other mode of doing it. But a distinction has long been recognised between such cases and those of corporators; the title of the latter must be impeached in a different mode." In *R.* v. *Mein,* Lord *Kenyon* recognised the authority of *Symmers* v. *The King* (a), in which Lord *Mansfield* held that the titles of persons who were *de facto* members of a corporation, admitted, sworn, and in the actual enjoyment of their offices, could not be impeached upon the trial of a *quo warranto* information against a person elected by them. *Tancred* on *Quo Warranto* (b), and *Cole* on Criminal Informations (c) were also referred to.

But it is submitted that these persons are electors. The 10th section enacts, that all persons named on any electoral roll for the time being, and having a freehold, leasehold, or household qualification, being also ratepayers, shall be deemed to be electors. The 11th section describes ratepayers as "persons liable to be assessed for the payment of some rate;" and the 79th section directs that "the rate so assessed shall be payable by the tenant or other person occupying or in possession of the premises, for which such rate is payable." The electoral roll referred to, is not a distinct roll for the municipality, but the electoral roll for the parliamentary district within which the municipality is situated. Persons resident within the municipality, whose names are on such roll and are ratepayers, are entitled to vote, if only they have no rates in arrear.

But even if these votes are invalid, it is submitted that the Court will not dispossess the party who has been declared elected, unless it can see a clear right in some other; *R.* v. *Mushiter* (d). *R.* v. *Jefferson* (e) is a distinct authority that to impeach the election of a party returned as elected, it is not sufficient to allege that

(a) Cowp. 507.   (b) p. 184.
(c) p. 139.   (d) 6 A. & E. 161.
        (e) 2 N. & M. 487; S. C., 3 B. & Ad. 855.

many of his votes are bad and fictitious, without showing that some other candidate had a majority of legal votes. And it is not shown that *Holland* would have been returned, even if all the votes objected to by him had been refused. Illegalities do not necessarily vitiate an election. At all events a *quo warranto* will not be granted at the suit of a person not ousted, and therefore for whom judgment cannot be given.

The relator has assented (personally, or by his scrutineer) to the opening of the ballot boxes; and also on a former occasion he has allowed persons to vote on qualifications to which he now objects. The Court also will not entertain this application, which is made at the instance of one who is now attempting to impeach the defendant's title on account of an irregularity in which he concurred; *R.* v. *Mortlock (a)*, *R.* v. *Stacey (b)*, *R.* v. *Symmons (c)*. In *R.* v. *Trevenen (d)*, the Court would not listen to a relator who was present and concurred at the time of the objectionable election, even although he was then ignorant of the objection; for a corporator, it was said, must be taken to be cognisant of the contents of his own charter, and of the law arising therefrom. In *R.* v. *Slythe (e)* the rule is qualified by *Abbott*, C.J., who says, "that if a person should concur in an election in ignorance of some fact making it invalid, and should afterwards come before the Court and show the objection, and that it has come to his knowledge since the election, and that it is a matter which ought to be inquired into, I would by no means have it inferred that such an application ought not to be heard." He also referred to *R.* v. *Parkyn (f)*, and *R.* v. *Cudlipp (g)*.

There is no statutory limit as to the time when a defaulting elector should pay his rates; and he may pay them to the proper officer on the polling pay as well as at any other time, and being then a ratepayer, "no portion of whose rates are in arrear," he is entitled to vote.

(a) 3 T.R. 300. (b) 1 T.R. 1.
(c) 4 T.R. 223. (d) 2 B. & A. 339.
(e) 6 B. & C. 243. (r) 1 B. & Ad. 690.
(g) 6 T. R. 508; See also *R.* v. *Green*, 2 Q. B. 463.

Isaacs replied. It is contended that these electors could not be proceeded against by *quo warranto*. But assuming that they could, it is clear that they have no title—first, because their names were not on the electoral list of the municipality [*Wise*, J. The statute does not require an electoral list for the municipality]; and also because they were not entitled to be·on such list, as being mere servants of Mr. *Josephson* and living on his premises. *R. v. Smith* (a) shows that if specially questioned on the record, the title of the electors can be impeached. If sufficient cause for interference be shown the Court will, as a matter of discretion, allow the matter to be tried whether the names of these persons were struck off by the proper tribunal and after a sufficient investigation. It is immaterial whether the relator, who was the opposing candidate, would or would not have been returned, if these vicious votes had been rejected. It is also submitted that the returning officer was not the proper person to receive these rates, and that the receipt of them under such circumstances is not a good discharge; and for this reason also their vote was invalid. As to the alleged acquiescence in opening the ballot box, it is submitted that the scrutineer was not the relator's agent for any such purpose. The affidavits show that the relator did not acquiesce. And as to his having formerly received these votes which he now objects to, the circumstances may have since changed, or the objection may not have been known. A relator is not disqualified by the mere circumstance of having formerly taken part in other elections, when the same irregularity existed, if it was not noticed; *R. v. Benney* (b), *R. v. Morris and Stewart* (c). On the question of costs, the Court generally discharges the rule without costs, *R. v. Wardroper* (d), unless the application is, as it was in that case, "very unreasonable and groundless." On this question, *R. v. Orde* (e) was also referred to. [*Salomons* referred to *R. v. Hartley* (f).]

(a) 5 M. & S. 271.   (b) 1 B. & Ad. 684.
(c) 3 East 213.   (d) 4 Burr. 1963.
(e) 8 A. & E. 420, in nota.   (f) 3 E. & B. 143.

STEPHEN, C.J. The writ of *quo warranto* issues in order to obtain substantial justice ; and the Court, therefore, does not allow the information to be filed, if thereby irreparable injury is likely to arise. The law also requires that a person claiming the assistance of the Court, should come into Court with clean hands; and that it should appear that such person has not been an assenting party to the irregularity complained of, or been himself guilty of any such irregularity on any former occasion. In the present case, it is said in the first place that three persons, whose votes were received, were not entitled to vote, because their names were not on the municipal list. I cannot see very clearly whether these persons had or had not a right to vote ; but on the whole, I think that they had no such right, and that the reception of their votes was a mistake. This Municipality Act is very full of defects, and it ought to be amended. His Honor then read the 9th, 10th, and 11th sections. The first thing to discover is, what is the electoral roll. If it is intended to refer to the roll of electors for members of parliament, an Act altering the qualifications of these electors had been passed since the Municipalities Act, and all property qualifications have been thereby abolished, and it is only necessary now that a man to be an elector should have been a resident for six months. But the Municipalities Act has been allowed to remain as it was. It seems to me that although a person is not on the roll he may be yet entitled to vote. But if he is on the roll, that is *prima facie* evidence that such person is a ratepayer, and therefore entitled to vote, provided he is stated to have a freehold, leasehold, and household qualification. Although the names of these persons were not on the municipal roll, they were on the electoral roll. It seems to me that if the names of these voters were on the electoral roll, and also entered as having a freehold, leasehold, or household qualification, they were *prima facie* ratepayers and entitled to vote. It seems that they were not in fact ratepayers. It is clear that they had not paid rates. But it is sufficient under the statute that they should be liable to assessment. For it says that if a person is assessed or liable to be assessed as having a freehold, leasehold, or household qualification, he is *prima facie* to be deemed a ratepayer. I do not decide whether these persons were liable to be assessed ; but if they were so liable, and the Municipal Council has not thought fit to assess them, they cannot be said to be persons whose rates are in arrear. If I am liable to be assessed, I am not to be deprived of my franchise, because the Council has not assessed me. So a man's rates cannot be said to be in arrear, if he has not been called on to pay them, or has not been assessed. It would be a different question if these persons were shown not to be liable to be assessed. I am inclined to think that they were not so liable; but there is no evidence to show this, and therefore I must take it for granted that they were ratepayers, and then the objection fails. In receiving the votes of these persons, it does not seem clear to me that the returning officer has done wrong.

The relator also says—the returning officer has done this in contravention of the regulation of the majority of the Municipal Council. The returning officer replies, I thought that the Council had no power to make such a resolution; I received these votes because I thought that these persons were entitled to vote. On this part of the question I conclude that we ought not to grant the application asked for, because the defendant has only received the votes of persons on the electoral roll who were *prima facie* ratepayers, and were liable to be assessed, even although they were not assessed. But, further, I think the rule ought not to be made absolute, even assuming that all these votes were wrong, and that the conduct of the returning officer was injudicious, because it is the duty of the relator to show that he is injured by what has been done—not conclusively, it may be—but he must suggest that he was injured by it to some extent. There is no doubt about the law that an application of this kind cannot be made by a person not interested in the result. The relator must be able to say that A. has been returned, whereas B. ought to have been returned.

So I am clearly of opinion against making this rule absolute on both grounds.

It is also said that some persons were allowed to pay rates on the day of the poll, in order that they might be able to vote, although the Council had resolved that rates should not be received on that day. The chairman acting, I suppose, under advice, says, " I thought that I had no right to refuse to receive these rates at the last moment." It may be that if he had refused the vote he would have been liable to an action, as the defendant was in the case of *Ashby* v. *White*. It seems to me that a person assessed for rates is entited to pay the amount at any moment, and the chairman is bound to receive it, and at all events that such receipt is not illegal. If the chairman had refused to receive the vote of such persons, I am not sure that the refusal would not have been actionable. It is also said that there was great irregularity as to the opening of the ballot boxes. The opening of the ballot boxes prematurely was clearly illegal, and a violation of the statute —the provisions of which the officer is bound to follow. But it does not follow that in consequence of this irregularity the election is void, or that we are to help the relator to make it void. The chairman says, "I did it at the request of, and with the assent of, all parties." That is no justification or excuse for the misconduct ; but it is an answer to the application by this relator. There is a conflict of testimony as to what occurred, on which it is not necessary for me to come to a conclusion. I am inclined to think that the relator did not assent, because he says that he never did assent to this being done; but it is not clear that he did not lead the chairman to suppose that he had assented. It may be that he did not intend to assent; but he should have protested at once when he was asked to assent. On this ground, too, I think we ought to refuse the rule. I do not think we ought to assist in setting aside this election under these circumstances. It would be our duty to do so under circumstances clearly blameable, and where the parties had acted from improper motives. But in the present case I do not think that we ought to interfere, because the defendant did not act from a bad intention, but supposing that he acted with the assent of all parties. I also think that the rule must be discharged without costs, because it has been shown that the defendant acted illegally, and has been elected after irregularities contributing to his return ; and the relator had good ground for supposing that the election was bad, because an illegal act, namely, the opening the ballot boxes, had certainly been committed.

MILFORD, J.   The Chief Justice has gone fully into the case, and I concur to all that he has said.   I am of opinion that a *quo warranto* ought not to issue to set aside this election.   It is doubtful whether these three persons were entitled to vote or not; but however that may be, it appears that the exclusion of these votes would not affect the result of the election.   With regard to the receipt of the rates on the day of the election, the statute says nothing to prevent the payment up to the time of the election ; and the clerk of the Council is, I should think, the proper person to receive them, and to give a valid discharge.   As to the opening of the ballot boxes, the election was over when this occurred, and all the parties had given their votes   It is not suggested that there had been any tampering with the votes ; and if this be so, why should the irregular conduct of the returning officer vitiate the election? I do not think that if the question were to be decided by strict law, that this would be a sufficient ground for setting aside the election ; but certainly not on an application for leave to file a *quo warranto* information, which is a matter of discretion.   But as such irregularities occurred, I think the rule should be discharged without costs.

WISE, J.   I am of the same opinion.   The first four points can be dealt with generally.   Whatever be the right construction of the 10th and 11th sections, it would be contrary to law to initiate a long and expensive proceeding, involving a trial by jury, without some glimmering of light as to what the result of that proceeding would be. The relator asks that there may be a trial whether these persons are entitled to vote, and he does not show that as the result of the trial the defendant would be ousted. The cases show that on an application to set aside an election for defects in the title of the electors, you must shew that the result of the enquiry would be that such election would be set aside. In the present case, it was necessary to show that there was ground for supposing that the reception of these votes turned the election in favour of the elected, that is, the defendant.

My impression is, that any person named on the electoral roll, and also having a freehold, leasehold, or household qualification, would be entitled to vote, provided he had paid the rates for which he had been assessed; and that it would be illegal to refuse the rates on the day of election. As it appears that there were persons willing to pay, and also other persons willing to receive the rates, the natural inference is that the proper person received them. As money was tendered and received, it must be taken that it was received by the proper person. Under the 11th section, the being on the electoral roll, and having a freehold, leasehold, or household qualification, is not conclusive evidence in favour of a person being an elector; and if it can be shown that such person is not a ratepayer, and does not possess the qualification, an enquiry might take place as to what title to vote he possessed. I am inclined to think that the natural inference, from what appears on the affidavits, is, that it is not shown that the relator did not assent; and I am inclined to think that whether he assented or not in his own mind, he led the other side to think that he had assented (a).

Rule discharged without costs.

(a) In *R. v. Parry** the rule was discharged without costs.
* 6 A. & E. 823.

March 14.

The QUEEN *against* NORTH (a).

The chairman of a Municipal Council, who by sect. 35 of the Municipalities Act of 1858, is the returning officer at the election of councillors, is disqualified as returning officer from being elected a councillor at the election where he presides; and sect. 34, which provides that every retiring councillor may, if otherwise qualified, be re-elected, does not qualify the chairman, being a retiring councillor, to act as returning officer; and, therefore, if he be returned, the election is void.

Quœre, whether the chairman, if a candidate for election as councillor, can, under sect. 16, appoint a substitute to act for him as returning officer.

SALOMONS, on the 14th of March, obtained a rule calling on *Samuel Charles Valentine North* to show cause why the Court should not grant leave for an information in the nature of a *quo warranto,* to be exhibited against him—to show by what authority he claimed to use, have, and occupy the office of an alderman for the municipality of Albury—upon the grounds, first, that being the Mayor for the city of Albury for the municipal year, commencing in 1864, and acting by virtue of that office as the returning officer at the election of aldermen on the 7th of February, 1865, in accordance with the Municipalities Act of 1858, his election and return as an alderman whilst so acting, and his subsequent election as Mayor, were illegal and void; and secondly, that being at the said election in February, 1865, the Mayor, &c., he was disqualified by the 39th section of the Act from being an alderman, and therefore his election as such, and subsequent election as Mayor for the municipal year, commencing in 1865, were illegal and void.

The following facts appeared by the affidavits in support of the rule :—*North,* against whom the present application was made, was elected an alderman in February, 1862; and in February, 1864, he was elected Mayor. In February, 1865, he retired, having completed his term of office in accordance with the 34th section of the Act. Mr. *North,* as such Mayor and returning officer, presided over the meeting of ratepayers, &c., on the 7th of February (of which due notice had been given), when seven candidates were duly nominated. A poll having been demanded on the 14th, he (*North*) " duly took his seat at the Court House, Albury, as presiding and returning officer, at nine o'clock in the forenoon, and remained there until four o'clock in the afternoon, when the poll was duly closed, and during that time took the

(a) Before *Stephen,* C.J., and *Wise,* J.

votes of all persons who tendered their votes at such
election. On the following day, *North*, as such Mayor
and returning officer, officially declared the state of the
poll, when it appeared that he (*North*), *L. Jones*, and
T. Field were at the head of the poll ; and on the next
day (the 16th) he officially declared these gentlemen
duly elected. *North* duly made the necessary declaration of office, in accordance with the 44th section of
the Act; and on the 17th of February, at a meeting of
the aldermen he was nominated as a candidate to fill
the office of Mayor, as also Mr. *Blackmore*, and *North*
was by a majority chosen Mayor for the ensuing year.

Salomons in support of the rule. The objection
chiefly relied on is, that the defendant being returning
officer returned himself as councillor. The 16th section
of the Municipalities Act of 1858 (*a*) enacts, that " in
case the returning officer, or any other presiding officer,
shall be prevented from attending any of his duties by
illness or other sufficient cause, he may, by writing
under his hand, appoint a substitute to act for him."
It is submitted that being a candidate is a sufficient
cause, and that the defendant should have availed himself of the power given by this section. The 39th
section provides that the " holding any office or place
of profit under or in the gift or disposal of the Council,"
shall be disqualified from being a councillor. The
office of chairman is, it is submitted, included in this
limitation. In the corresponding section of the Imperial Act, the 28th section of the 5 and 6 Vic., c. 76,
there are the additional words, "other than the Mayor."
It has been recently held in *R.* v. *Owens* (*b*), that notwithstanding these words the Mayor cannot act as
returning officer, although he is rendered eligible for
election ; and as he had acted as returning officer, the
election was held to be void.

Martin, Q.C., contra. There are no sections in the
Imperial Act like the 31st and 34th sections of the

(*a*) 22 Vic., No. 13.   (*b*) 2 E. & E. 93 ; 28 L. J. Q. B. 316.

Colonial Act. The 31st section provides that the chairman "shall go out of office at the next annual election of councillors, but may then be re-elected;" and the 34th section, after providing that one-third of the Council shall retire on the 1st Tuesday in February, in each and every year, enacts that "the councillors longest in the Council shall first retire, and every retiring councillor may, if otherwise qualified, be re-elected." This latter section renders every retiring councillor, not otherwise disqualified, eligible for re-election; and as the 35th section directs that the chairman for the time being shall be the returning officer, the sections taken together are a legislative declaration that the chairman, when a retiring councillor, is eligible for election, although he must *ex officio* act as returning officer. The 16th section, which empowers the chairman to appoint a substitute if prevented from attending any of his duties " by illness or other sufficient cause," was never intended to apply to cases like this. The word " prevented," must mean by some power superior to himself, and cannot be understood to refer to a case where a man creates the impediment himself (*a*). Neither for the same reason could the councillors, under the 57th section, appoint one of themselves to perform his duty. In *Owens'* case, *Crompton*, J., expressed his opinion that the power to appoint a substitute did not exist in a case like this. The chairman could not retire from his duties, and he had no power to appoint a substitute; and so being expressly made eligible, and being necessarily the returning officer, he had no alternative to the course of still acting. He could not resign without exposing himself to a fine of £50 under the 45th section, neither could he appoint a substitute.

The case of *R.* v. *Owens* decides merely that, under the language of the Imperial Act, the Mayor is not eligible; but the words of the colonial statute direct that the chairman shall be the returning officer, and provide also that he is eligible for re-election. As to the

(*a*) On this point see *R.* v. *Thurlow* (15th October, 1851).

decision of this Court in *R.* v. *Hill* (*a*), that case was decided merely on the ground of the *knowledge*, by the electors, of the disqualification of Mr. *Hill* (the Mayor), and on the authority of *Gosling* v. *Veley* (*b*), and has no application to the present case. The following passage from the judgment of the Chief Justice rather supports the argument now advanced—" Had we found an express enactment that the Mayor might be again elected, and no enactment providing a substitute for the discharge, in such case, of his official duties, we might have been led to hold, notwithstanding their apparent incompatibility, that the two characters of declaring or returning a candidate were sustainable by him, by reason of the necessity of the thing, lest the intention of the legislature should be frustrated."

On the question of costs, it will be contended on the other side that the Court has no discretion, but that under the 9 Ann, c. 20, s. 5 (*c*), the relator, if successful, is entitled to his costs. It is submitted, however, that that statute, not being a statute of the realm, but limited by the first section to that part of Great Britain called England and Wales (excluding, therefore, Berwick upon Tweed), is not in force in this colony. As municipal institutions did not exist in this colony at the time of the passing of the 9 G. IV., c. 83, statutes regulating them cannot be held to be applicable under the 24th section of that statute ; *Whicker* v. *Hume* (*d*).

Salomons, in reply, on the question of costs. The Court will not deprive the relator of the costs to which, under the 9 Ann, c. 20, he is entitled. *Crompton, J.,* in *R.* v. *Hartley* (*e*), says, " we have no power to deprive the relator, who has committed no fault, of the costs which the law gives him. The office being full, there must be a formal information and ouster to set the

1865.

The QUEEN
v.
NORTH.

(*a*) December, 1850.   (*b*) 7 Q. B. 439.
(*c*) The words of the section are—" It shall and may be lawful to and for the said Courts respectively to give judgment. that the relator or relators, in such information named, shall recover his or their costs of such prosecution."
(*d*) 14 Beav. 526 ; 7 H. L. Ca. 153.   (*e*) 3 E. & B. 143.

corporation right; and then the costs of an information and ouster are regulated by the statute."

STEPHEN, C. J.   In accordance with first principles the defendant cannot act as a Judge in his own case.   It cannot be supposed that the legislature intended, unless the words are clear and unmistakeable, that he should so act.   There may be some difficulty in the case, on the assumption that he cannot appoint a substitute. But I think that he could appoint a substitute under such circumstances, and that his being a candidate would be a sufficient cause under the 16th section.   It is a legal or moral incapacity which prevents him from discharging his duty as returning officer in an election at which he is a candidate.

We make the rule absolute without saying anything as to costs.   The reason assigned in *R*. v. *Hartley*, is that the office being full, though wrongly, there must be a judgment to make it void.   We both think that the defendant ought to pay these costs.   But it is a possible case that the relator might eventually fail in the case.

WISE, J.   The defendant cannot fill two inconsistent offices; he cannot be judge and suitor in the same cause; but he has, as returning officer, acted as a judge in his own cause.   It is not necessary to decide whether, under the 16th section, he can appoint a substitute under such circumstances.

The rule is made absolute.   On the question, whether making the rule absolute entitles the relator to his costs, I give no opinion.

The QUEEN *against* MOON (a).

STEPHEN, on the 27th of February, obtained a rule calling on *Thomas Moon* to show cause why an information in the nature of a *quo warranto* should not issue—calling on him to show by what authority he claimed to hold the office of councillor of the municipality of Waterloo—upon the ground that he was, at the time of his election, and is, an infant under the age of twenty-one years, and, therefore, disqualified by law from holding such office.

An infant is not eligible to be elected councillor for a municipality under the 22 Vic., No. 13. Semble, an infant named on the electoral roll, and being a ratepayer, is competent to vote.

To the affidavit in support of the application was attached a certificate of the defendant's baptism, from which it appeared that he was born in April, 1845.

Stephen in support of the rule. An infant does not possess the qualification of an elector, for part of that qualification is being of mature years, and therefore an infant cannot be elected chairman, councillor, or auditor, under the 9th section of the Municipalities Act (b). If an infant is eligible for election as councillor, he can by the 31st section be elected chairman; and by the 32nd section the chairman is made *ex officio* a justice of the peace. But it is clear that an infant cannot be a justice of the peace, for he cannot generally do an act which requires an oath, as he cannot do fealty, *Com. Dig.* (c); and the same authority says he cannot be a mayor of a corporation, nor elected a burgess of one. In *R.* v. *Carter* (d), it appeared by the pleadings on the record that the defendant, when an infant under six years of age, had been elected a burgess of the borough of Portsmouth, and sworn in after he had attained the age of twenty-one; and the election was held bad, on the ground that the person elected must at the time of the election possess a present legal capacity of being sworn.

March 8.

(a) Before *Stephen*, C. J., and *Wise*, J.   (b) 22 Vic., No. 13
(c) Enfant (C. 1.), citing Co. Lit. 65 b.   (d) Cowp. 220.

He also referred to *R. v. White*, cited in *Selwyn's Nisi Prius* (a). [*Stephen*, C. J., referred to *Bacon's* Abridgement, Offices 1 (b).]

Salomons showed cause. The affidavit shows that the respondent is on the electoral roll and a ratepayer, and therefore by s. 10 he is an elector, and is eligible to be a councillor; and the Court cannot enquire, because it is not the proper tribunal for that purpose, into the question of the respondent's qualification. *Martin* v. *Nicholson* (c) was decided on this ground. But if he is an elector, he might clearly be a councillor, unless disqualified by the 39th section. This alleged defect is a defect in the defendant's title as an elector, and therefore ought to have been questioned in an information against him in that capacity, and not indirectly in a proceeding against him as the elected; *R.* v. *Hughes* (d), cited in *Tancred* on Informations (e). In *R.* v. *Carter* this point was taken; but the Court, declining to decide the case on this ground, decided it on the construction of the charter. The question as to the capacity of an infant to be an elector, or elected for parliament, which is raised in *Coke's* Institutes (f), was considered so doubtful that it was thought proper to settle it by the 7 & 8 W. III., c. 25. The Court will refuse also to make the rule absolute, on the ground of convenience; and at all events will allow the defendant to disclaim, as was done in *R.* v. *Morton* (g). *R.* v. *Harvey* (h), and *R.* v. *Quayle* (i) were referred to.

Stephen in reply. The relator is not questioning the title of the electors as was sought to be done in *R.* v. *Hughes*, but the title of the elected, because he is himself ineligible; no other or earlier application could have been made, for there is nothing to show that he claimed to vote as an elector.

(a) 2 Vol. 1068 (h.) ; see Harr. Dig. 3274.
(b) And see Corporations (E) s. 6.   (c) 27th September, 1850.
(d) 4 B. & C. 368.   (e) p. 198.   (f) 4 Inst. 47.
    (g) 4 Q. B. 146 ; but see *R.* v. *Hartley*, 3 E. & B. 143.
(h) 3 Q. B. 475.   (i) 11 A. & E. 508.

STEPHEN, C. J.   I am of opinion that this rule must be made absolute.   But the defendant has leave to disclaim within twenty-four hours, otherwise the information may be filed.   The Court has a discretion in granting applications of this kind, and will refuse them, either if the relator has been a partaker in, or has acceded to, the irregularity complained of—or if the corporation will, by the proceeding, be destroyed.   Such applications are also refused where it appears that there is the same defect in the title of the relator as there is in the title of the other side ; in other words, the applicant must show a better title.

I have no doubt that an infant cannot be elected a councillor.   I am inclined to think that he may vote ; but it is not necessary to decide the point ; for assuming that he can vote, I am of opinion that he cannot be elected a councillor.   If he could be, he might be elected chairman, and would be, therefore, *ex officio* a justice of the peace.   But an infant could not be a justice of the peace.   The authorities, as cited in *Comyn's* Digest, and *Bacon's* Abridgement, show that an infant cannot be a burgess.   He may possess in fact every natural qualification.   But the line must be drawn somewhere, and the law of England has drawn the line at the age of twenty-one.   In America, no one can be a member of the house of representatives unless he is twenty-five.   Neither does it follow that, because the statute says that a councillor must possess certain qualifications, those are the only qualifications which he must possess.   The office of councillor is an office of trust, and there is attached to it a power to tax and also to expend.   Such an office should be held by persons of skill and discretion ; and it is presumed that persons not of the age of twenty-one do not possess these qualifications.   An infant can hold some ministerial offices.   It is said that an infant can sit in the House of Commons ; and no doubt they were elected till the statute of 7 & 8 W. III., c. 25.   *Coke* says an infant cannot be an elector or elected, yet he may have property and may be taxed, and process to enforce payment may go against him.   The same

authority shows that he may not sit in the House of
Lords, but he may be a peer ; he may have an inchoate,
but not a perfect right.

WISE, J. The argument derived from the maxim
expressio unius est exclusio alterius, is unfounded ; for
it is not necessary that the statute should say that every
baby in arms is not qualified ; neither does it follow,
because some disqualifications are specified, that all pre-
existing disqualifications are got rid of. Infants are not
capable of holding offices which require discretion. The
line limiting the age must be drawn somewhere, and
when drawn it must be kept ; and an enquiry cannot be
made as to the capacity of any particular person. An
arbitrary rule must be followed. The office of councillor
is an office of trust. A councillor may be a chairman ;
he may indirectly affect the property of others ; he has
to determine the appropriation of taxes and to manage
public money ; and, therefore, according to the principle
recognised in *Claridge* v. *Evelyn* (a), an infant is
ineligible for such an office. In that case it was held
that an infant could not be appointed to the office of
clerk of a Court of Requests, because it was part of the
duty of that officer to receive the money of suitors, and
the office was therefore one of pecuniary trust. If the
statute had said that every one on the electoral roll, being
a ratepayer, should be eligible to be elected councillor,
the argument would have been stronger ; but the words
are, no person shall be eligible unless he shall hold a
qualification as an elector. I am inclined to think,
although I give no opinion on the point, that an infant
whose name is on the roll, and who is a ratepayer, has a
right to vote. Another reason why an infant is incapable of
being a councillor, is the existence of a clause (b) imposing
a fine for refusing to accept the office ; for an infant is not
liable to a penalty for non-feasance under ordinary circumstances. This question was much discussed in *R.* v.
Sutton (c), in which case the defendant, who was only

(a) 5 B. & A. 81.   (b) s. 45.
            (c) 3 A. & E. 597.

eleven years old, had inherited land charged with the repair of a bridge. His guardian in socage resided on the property; but the infant was being educated from home, although passing his vacations there, and occasionally residing there; and the Court held that he was not chargeable by indictment for the non-feasance of not repairing the bridge. The rule will be absolute, or, on the defendant's counsel in Court undertaking to disclaim, the rule will be discharged without costs.

Judgment accordingly.

1865.

The QUEEN
v.
MOON.

Ex parte HICKEY (a).

March 14.

THIS was a rule calling on *E. A. Hickey* to show cause why an order made at his instance by *Milford*, J., in Chambers, directing a prohibition to issue, to restrain the District Court Judge of the Hunter River district from proceeding on a judgment against *Hickey* by default, should not be set aside.

It appeared from the affidavits that the applicant (Mr. *Hickey*) was sued in the Hunter River District Court, holden at East Maitland, in February, 1865, and that when the cause was called on, on the sixth of that month, the defendant did not appear, but an affidavit by *John Mackinlay*, head bailiff of the Sydney District Court, was handed in by the plaintiff, which stated that the deponent, on the 25th of January, 1865, served the summons, "by delivering the same to a waiter at the Union Club, Bligh-street, Sydney, who said that the defendant would be in the Club House in the course of the day, when he would give him the summons." It also appeared from the affidavit of Mr. *O'Meagher*, who was the applicant's attorney in the present motion, that when the cause was called on in the District Court, he stated to his Honor, as *amicus curiæ*, "that the Court had no jurisdiction, and that the affidavit of the bailiff who served the summons was not sufficient to warrant his Honor proceeding *ex parte*, &c.;" he said also that

The 64th section of the District Court Act provides that if the defendant shall not appear, "the Judge, upon due proof of service of the summons, may proceed to the trial of the cause." *Held* that the mode and sufficiency of the proof of the service of the summons, is in the discretion of the District Court Judge; and the Court will not interfere with the exercise of that discretion by prohibition.

(a) Before *Stephen*, C. J., and *Wise*, J.

he did not appear for the defendant, lest he should prejudice any right of Mr. *Hickey*, to take any ulterior objection to the proceeding, and handed in two affidavits —one by Mr. *Hickey*, which was sworn at Maitland, on the 6th of February, which stated, "I, on Saturday last, for the first time, saw by the *Maitland Mercury* that I was being sued in this Court. I have not been served with a summons either personally nor at my residence, nor has the service of the same come to my knowledge in any way." The other affidavit stated his residence to be in Hunter-street, Sydney, and not at the Union Club. The learned Judge stated that he was satisfied that the service of the summons had come to the defendant's knowledge, and ultimately gave a verdict for the plaintiff for £69 9s. 6d.

Salomons in support of the rule. *Robinson* v. *Lenaghan* (a) is a distinct authority that the mode of proof of the service of the summons, under the 64th section of the District Court Act, is in the discretion of the Judge; and that as he has held the evidence before him on affidavit sufficient proof, this Court has no power to interfere by prohibition. In *Robinson* v. *Lenaghan* the summons had been served in the wrong place, where the defendant had never resided, and he had no knowledge of the proceedings until his goods were taken in execution. But as the County Court Judge was satisfied that the summons had been served as required by the statute, the Court of Exchequer held that prohibition would not lie, as the matter was within the jurisdiction of the Judge. *Pollock*, C. B., in giving judgment, says—"the words in the 80th section, 'the Judge, upon due proof of the service of the summons,' do not require to be understood as meaning that such service has been *absolutely* proved, but that there has been such proof as satisfied the mind of the Judge that service of the process has been made. When he is so satisfied, he has jurisdiction; and by the provisions of the statute, our right to interfere is at an end." The language of the

(a) 2 Exch. 333.

64th section of the District Courts Act is precisely the same as that of the Imperial Act. [*Stephen*, C. J. In cases where title to land comes in question, it has been held that the District Court Judge cannot, by deciding that point in the negative, give himself jurisdiction, if the Court see that such decision is wrong.] The same decision was arrived at in *The Guardians of the Lexden Union* v. *Southgate* (a), although the Court thought the County Court Judge wrong. *Joseph* v. *Henry* (b), *Ex parte Rayner* (c), *In re Bowen* (d), and *Ellis* v. *Watt* (e) were referred to.

Stephen showed cause. The rules are to be taken as part of the Act; and by the 46th rule, in all cases where the summons has not been served under the provisions of the four last rules (neither of which embraces this case), and the defendant does not appear in person, &c., at the return day, the cause may proceed, if the Judge be satisfied by evidence on oath before him that the service of such summons has come to the knowledge of the defendant before the return day. It is submitted that evidence on affidavit is not evidence on oath before him, and that therefore the Judge had not jurisdiction in this case. If the affidavit of the bailiff is sufficient, the evidence on oath may not be necessary. But if, as in this case, the affidavit is clearly insufficient, the rule requires evidence on oath that the service of the summons has come to the defendant's knowledge. [*Stephen*, C. J. If the Judge may take proof by affidavit of the service of the summons, why may he not take proof by affidavit of the cause of action?]

Salomons in reply. The 20th rule directs that the evidence of service by the bailiff of a foreign district should be by affidavit; and if it were not so, such bailiff would be obliged to attend the Court which issued the summons, to prove its service in pursuance of the 38th section. [*Stephen*, C. J. The common law says that a

(a) 10 Exch. 201 ; 23 L. J. Ex. 316. (b) 19 L. J. Q. B. 365.
(c) 5 C. B. 162 ; 17 L. J. C. P. 16. (d) 15 Jur. 1196.
(e) 19 L. J. C. P. 113.

man cannot be duly adjudicated against unless he has been summoned; and in accordance with that principle the 64th section requires, where the defendant does not appear, "due proof of the service." If there was no proof at all, has the Court below jurisdiction at all?] It is altogether a matter for the Judge; and if the defendant is aggrieved, he can apply for a new trial.

STEPHEN, C. J. I am compelled by the authority of *Robinson* v. *Lenaghan* to hold that it is within the power of the District Court Judge to decide what shall be the mode of service, and what shall be sufficient proof of service; and, therefore, if he should take an affidavit and should say that was sufficient proof of service, which was not sufficient proof of service, the remedy would not be by prohibition. The 64th section says that the Judge, upon due proof of service of the summons, may proceed to the trial of the cause; that must mean, upon such proof as the Judge shall think to be due proof. I have been much pressed by the consideration that if proof by affidavit is not sufficient, the bailiff of a foreign district might be obliged to travel five hundred miles to prove the service. Sir *John Jervis'* Act (a) enacts that the constable or other person who shall have served him with the summons, shall declare on oath in what manner he served the summons; and although this mode of proof may involve the inconvenience of travelling five hundred miles, yet, until it is so proved, a warrant cannot be issued. It was to obviate this difficulty that, in the Deserted Wives and Childrens Act (b), the legislature provided that such proof might be by affidavit. I entertain much doubt as to the correctness of this conclusion; but on the authority of *Robinson* v. *Lenaghan* I agree that this rule must be discharged, but without costs. The plaintiff must be put in the same position as if he had succeeded in Chambers; but I think that he ought not to have the costs of this motion, as the defendant has a right to appear to support the decision of the Judge in Chambers in his favor.

(a) 11 & 12 Vic., c. 43, s. 13.   (b) 22 Vic., No. 6, s. 2.

WISE, J. I agree that the rule must be made absolute. Whether the decision of the District Court Judge
was right or wrong, this Court cannot interfere by prohibition. The District Court Judge has not an arbitrary
power of deciding what he pleases; but the law does not
invest this Court with the power of interfering by prohibition with his decision, as to the sufficiency of the
evidence of service of the summons. My present impression is in favor of the practice of taking the evidence
of the bailiff by affidavit. The difficulty is caused by
the colonial statute omitting the section contained in the
English statute (a); which expressly enacts that the
service of any summons, which shall require to be served
out of the district, may be proved by affidavit. On the
question of costs, I think it is a wholesome rule which
has been adopted by the Privy Council, that a party
compelled to apply to the Court for justice should have
his costs, and that an unsuccessful litigant should pay
costs.

1865.

Ex parte
HICKEY.

SADDINGTON *against* BYRNE and others.

DECLARATION against the executors of one
Andrew Byrne, for that the deceased (on July
14, 1862) made, signed, and delivered to the plaintiffs
a guarantee in the words and figures following, that is
to say—

"Sydney, July 14, 1862.
Messrs. *Saddington & Sons*,
Wynyard Square.

DEAR SIRS,—I beg to request that you will supply
goods to Mr. *William Andrew Byrne*, of George-street,
or to his father, also of George-street, to an amount not
exceeding at any one time £150, for the due payment of
which I do hereby make myself responsible. I reserve
due, and giving notice to that effect." *Held* a continuing guarantee.

"I request
that you will
supply goods
to W. A. B. to
an amount
not exceeding
at any one
time £150, for
the due pay-
ment of which
I hereby
make myself
responsible.
I reserve to
myself the
liberty to re-
lease myself
of this re-
sponsibility
on paying up
the amount

(a) 9 & 10 Vic., c. 95, s. 62.

to myself the liberty to relieve myself of this responsibility upon paying up the amount due, and giving you notice to that effect."

Averment of delivery of goods to *William Andrew Byrne*, and non-payment.

Plea (1) traversing the delivery of the goods in pursuance of, and in accordance with, the terms of the alleged guarantee ; and (2) payment. Issue thereon.

The case came on for trial before *Wise*, J., in the November sittings, when the learned Judge ruled that the instrument declared on was a continuing guarantee. A verdict accordingly was found for the plaintiffs for a certain amount, by consent. But execution was stayed in order to give the defendants an opportunity of moving for a rule *nisi*, on the ground of misdirection.

November 30.   *Isaacs* now, for the defendants, moved accordingly. The question is whether this instrument was a continuing guarantee of unlimited duration, or a guarantee for a certain amount and time only.   In *Kirby* v. *The Duke of Marlborough* (a), where A. and B. executed a bond to the plaintiff, to enable A. to carry on business, conditioned for the payment of all such sums not exceeding £3,000, which the plaintiff should at any time thereafter advance to A., the Court say, in giving judgment, "this is a bond given by the surety as an indemnity for advances to a definite amount ; it is the same as if the surety had expressed that the bankers might lend to the amount of £3,000 ; and when an advance was made to that amount the guarantee became *functus officio*, and was not a continuing guarantee." It is submitted that the rule of construction laid down by *Bayley*, J., in *Nicholson* v. *Paget* (b), that such instruments ought to be construed liberally in favor of the person giving the guarantee, is more reasonable than that laid down in *Mason* v. *Pritchard* (c), and recognised in *Mayer* v. *Isaac* (d).   *Melville* v. *Hayden* (e) was referred to.

(a) 2 M. & S. 19.   (b) 1 C. & M. 68.
(c) 12 East 227.   (d) 6 M. & W. 608.
              (e) 3 B. & A. 593.

STEPHEN, C. J.   I am of opinion that this is a continuing guarantee, and that as the testator never gave to the plaintiff the stipulated notice, his executors are bound to pay for the goods supplied to the amount limited.   It is unnecessary to express any opinion as to which rule of construction is correct, for I think that according to either construction this is a continuing guarantee.   The rule, therefore, must be refused.

1864.
SADDINGTON
v.
BYRNE
and others.

MILFORD, J., and WISE, J., concurred.

Rule refused.

WOOLFE against BURKE (a).

March 17,
1865.

MOTION to review the Prothonotary's taxation. The first count was for a breach of warranty, that certain tobacco was undamaged; the second was for a breach of warranty, that the tobacco was free of stems.   The third count was for default in doing his duty as the plaintiff's agent, in the purchase of tobacco. And there were counts for money lent, money had and received, and on accounts stated.   The particulars under the common counts were, "amount received by defendant, £438 16s. 4d.; amount received by defendant being part of price of tobacco, £164 6s. 8d.; amount received by defendant for tobacco not delivered, £7; amount paid by plaintiff for survey, £6 6s."

There were pleas traversing the breaches in the first two counts, and the promise in the third count, and to the common counts never indebted and set off.   Issue was joined on the several pleas.

After issue had thus been joined, a commission issued to examine witnesses in Melbourne.   The evidence under this, however, did not appear to have touched the two items of £7 and 6 guineas mentioned in the particulars to the common counts; and after the return of the commission the defendant obtained leave to pay £13 6s. into Court.   The pleadings were thereupon

When money is paid into court after issue joined, and the plaintiff elects to go on with the action for the residue of his claim, and fails at the trial, the defendant is entitled to all his costs (except as to any which affect the items covered by the plea of payment into court), from the time of his giving instructions for pleading to the causes of action on which he succeeded.

(a) Before *Stephen*, C. J., and *Wise*, J.

amended. The pleas to the common counts being—as to the residue of the declaration, except as to £13 6s., never indebted and set off; and as to so much of the residue as claims £13 6s., payment into Court of that amount. Issue was joined on the pleas of never indebted and set off; and as to the last plea the plaintiff accepted the sum paid into Court, in satisfaction and discharge of the causes of action in respect of which it had been paid in. The case went on to trial, when the defendant obtained a verdict on all the issues.

On the taxation of the defendant's costs, the prothonotary decided that under rule 37 (a) the defendant was only entitled to his costs as costs in the cause from the time of plea of payment into Court, and accordingly disallowed all the previous costs (including the costs of the commission) which were incurred before such payment.

Darley, for the plaintiff, moved on notice to make absolute a rule calling on the defendant to show cause why the prothonotary should not review his taxation. It is submitted that this case is not within the 37th rule on which the prothonotary relied, but is governed by the 12th rule of Hil. T. 1853 (b). The ruling of the prothonotary, therefore, cannot be supported, and directly conflicts with the decision in *Harold* v. *Smith* (c) ; in which it was held that when money is paid into Court after issue joined, and the plaintiff elects to go on with the action for the residue of his claim, and fails at the trial, he is not entitled, on taxation of costs, to the costs of preparations for trial, even although partly incurred before the payment into Court, as the taxation ought then to be considered as taxation of the costs on amendment of pleading, and not, under the 12th rule of Hil. T., 1853, as a payment into Court. If a defendant pay money into Court upon some of the counts only, the

(a) Sup. Ct. Pr. 70. The rule is—"A defendant succeeding on the issue of no debt or damages *ultra*, shall be entitled to costs from the time of plea pleaded only ; or where leave to pay the money into Court was necessary, from the time of applying for such leave ; and, in either case, the plaintiff's costs, up to that time, shall be deducted from the defendant's costs."

(b) Ch. Arch Pr. 1358.   (c) 29 L. J. Ex. 141.

plaintiff is entitled to the costs of that count; *Baillie* v. *Cazelet* (a), *Skarrott* v. *Vaughan* (b). So here the plaintiff is entitled to the costs of this particular issue; but as the case went to the jury, all the other costs in the case ought to go to the defendant.

Isaacs for the plaintiff. The plaintiff ought not to be deprived of his costs up to the time of paying money into Court; for by paying the money into Court, the defendant admits that the plaintiff was right.

STEPHEN, C. J. In this case the plaintiff sued the defendant for neglecting his duty as agent in the purchase of some tobacco; and the plaintiff also alleged that the defendant was indebted to him for £7, on account of an overpayment to that extent, and also six guineas which were paid for a survey of this same tobacco. The defendant traversed the alleged breach of duty, and also denied the alleged debt. A commission was, at this stage of the proceedings, issued to examine witnesses at Melbourne; and after the return of that commission, the defendant was advised to pay £18 6s. into Court. The defendant paid this amount into Court, and it was taken out by the plaintiff. The cause went on to trial, when the defendant succeeded on every issue. Under these circumstances, on the authority of *Harold* v. *Smith*, the defendant is entitled to the costs of the trial. Not a scintilla of the evidence taken on commission touched the part of the case on which the money was paid into Court. I am clearly of opinion that the defendant is entitled to all his costs, except as to any which affect the items covered by the plea of payment, from the time of his giving instructions for pleading to the causes of action, on which he succeeded. The taxation must be reviewed on the principle laid down, without costs.

WISE, J., concurred.

Order accordingly.

(a) 4 T. R. 579.   (b) 2 Taunt. 266.

March 3. GRAINGER *against* VINDIN (a).

·A. wrote to B., "could you supply me with ten tons of flour at £16 per ton, three months credit, but 'paid for before removed." B. replied, "we are willing to supply you with ten tons of flour on the terms named by you, viz., promissory note three months from present date, and the flour not to be delivered until paid for. We enclose invoice and promissory note for your signature." *Held*, that B.'s letter introduced a new term into the proposed contract, and, therefore, that there was not a complete contract when that letter was posted.

APPEAL from the Hunter River District Court, holden at West Maitland.

The particulars of demand were for the non-delivery of ten tons of flour, at the price of £16 a ton, under a contract dated 22nd February, 1864, which, the plaint alleged, were to be delivered "in three months then next following, and to be paid for by the plaintiff before delivery." The defendant pleaded, *inter alia*, that he did not contract as alleged. At the trial before Mr. District Court Judge Purefoy, it appeared that the alleged contract was contained in the following correspondence. The plaintiff wrote to the defendant from Singleton, on February 20, " could you supply me with ten tons of the same quality of flour as the one ton I have had at £16, three months credit, but paid for before removed. I have no room to store it for three or four months." To which the plaintiff replied from East Maitland, on February 22, "in reply to yours of 20th instant, we beg to say that we are willing to supply you with ten tons of flour as before, on the terms named by you, viz., promissory note at three months from present date, and the flour not to be delivered until paid for. We enclose invoice and promissory note for your signature." The appeal case then stated, that " it was proved that one day was sufficient time for the transmission and delivery of letters in due course between Singleton and Maitland." The plaintiff stated that he was prevented by the floods from sending to the Post Office till March 9th; and that on that day he went there and found no letter. On the following day (the 10th) he called at the defendant's stores in West Maitland, and asked whether his letter about the flour had been received. He was told by Mr. *Vindin* that the defendant had written on the 22nd February, in answer to

(a) Before *Stephen*, C. J., and *Milford*, J.

his letter of February 20th; but that so long a time had now elapsed without plaintiff taking any notice of the matter that they did not consider themselves bound by that letter of theirs—that they no longer adhered to their intention expressed therein, and that they would have nothing more to do with the affair. Plaintiff, on his return home, called at Falbrook—a post-office nine miles from Singleton—where he found, as he alleged, the defendants' letter.

On finding this letter, "notwithstanding the intimation of the defendants above stated, plaintiff wrote to defendants as follows:—

Glennies Creek, Post Office,
March 14th, 1864.

Messrs. *Solomon Vindin & Co.*

GENTLEMEN,—I have this morning received your invoice of bill of sale for the ten tons of flour, ordered by me on the 18th February. I beg by return of post to forward the bill of sale signed by me and made payable at the Bank of New South Wales.

Yours obediently,
John Grainger.

Enclosing the promissory note above mentioned, signed.

This was immediately refused, and returned to him by the defendants on their receiving it.

The plaintiff afterwards offered the defendants the price of the flour at £16 per ton, and demanded delivery, which was refused by the defendants, on the grounds that the bargain was off, and that there never had been a complete contract. It was proved that flour of the quality in question had risen £10 per ton between the date of the defendants' letter (February 22nd, 1864) and the 10th March following, when the defendants refused to have anything more to do with the affair.

The plaintiff refused to be nonsuited. No evidence was called for the defence.

Upon these facts the Judge told the jury that there was a contract for the sale of the flour complete from the moment that the defendants posted their letter, dated February 22nd, enclosing the promissory note and invoice; and that no subsequent repudiation of that letter by the defendants, though before the said letter came to

c—4

the possession or knowledge of the plaintiff, could alter the case.

The questions for the opinion of the Supreme Court are—First, whether the Judge was not wrong in ruling that there was a contract of sale complete from the moment that the letter, dated February 22nd, was posted? Secondly, whether the Judge was not wrong in ruling that the subsequent repudiation by the defendants, before the letter came to the possession or knowledge of the plaintiff, would not alter their liability."

Simpson for the respondent. The ruling of the Judge, that the contract was complete when the letter in reply was posted, is now admitted by the appellant to have been right, and that is the only point which was raised at the trial, or intended to be raised on the appeal. The point then taken, and which was intended to be submitted by the case, was only this—that until the actual receipt of the defendants' letter by the plaintiff, the defendants were at liberty to retract; and that as they did really retract before such receipt, there was no complete contract. [*Stephen*, C. J. Is there not a variance between the letter making the proposal and the reply?] The point now raised as to the variation between the terms of the acceptance and the terms of the offer was not taken in the Court below, and is a mere afterthought. *Watson* v. *Ambergate Railway Company* (a) is an authority that on these appeals objections cannot be raised which were not taken at the trial. *Yorke* v. *Smith* (b) is to the same effect (c). [*Stephen*, C. J. We must answer categorically the questions submitted to us, even although we may see that another question was intended to have been submitted.]

Faucett, S. G., for the appellant. The plaintiff's letter of the 20th February was a mere negotiation and proposal, and the offer might have been retracted until it was accepted, as in *Cooke* v. *Oxley* (d); at all events it was

(a) 15 Jur. 488.   (b) 21 L. J. Q. B. 53.
    (c) But see *Stancliffe* v. *Clarke*, 21 L. J. Ex. 129.
                    (d) 3 T. R. 653.

not binding on the plaintiff, unless the answer of the defendants was a simple acceptance without the introduction of any new term. But here the first letter proposed a credit for three months; whereas the reply requested the plaintiff's signature to a promissory note payable at three months. It is admitted that where a contract is made by letter between A. and B.—A. making an offer, and B. accepting that offer *unconditionally*—the contract is complete when B.'s letter is posted, even although it may chance not to reach its destination; *Dunlop* v. *Higgins* (a). *Routledge* v. *Grant* (b), *Adams* v. *Lindsell* (c), *Payne* v. *Cave* (d), and *Duncan* v. *Topham* (e) were referred to.

1865.

GRAINGER
v.
VINDIN.

STEPHEN, C. J. The objection as to the omission to take the point in the Court below is put an end to by the terms of the two questions stated in the case; because there is no way of answering them except in favour of the appeal. The question is whether the contract of sale was completed? The plaintiff's letter of the 20th February enquired whether the defendant could let him have certain goods at a certain price, on a certain credit; and the defendants replied, accepting the offer, but sending up for the plaintiff's signature a promissory note payable at the expiry of the agreed period. I think this letter introduced a new term into the proposed contract; for if a promissory note were given, it might have been circulated, and the plaintiff might have been obliged to pay it in the hands of third persons. The contract, therefore, was not completed by the posting of this letter of the defendants, and the defendants could withdraw from it at any time before the actual receipt of it by the plaintiff. The contract would not have been completed until the plaintiff had assented to the giving of the promissory note, and had in fact actually signed it.

MILFORD, J., concurred.

Judgment for the appellant, with costs.

(a) 1 H. L. Oa. 881.
(c) 1 B. & A. 681.
(b) 4 Bing. 653.
(d) 8 T. R. 148.
(e) 8 O. B. 225.

1864.

November 30,
1864.

BROWN *against* THE MELBOURNE AND NEWCASTLE MINMI COLLIERY COMPANY (LIMITED).

The provisions of the Absent Defendants' Act apply to the case of a foreign corporation.

*S*TEPHEN appeared in support of an application under the sixth section of the Absent Defendants' Act (*a*). It appeared that the summons had issued and been returned *non est inventus*, on the 1st November, and that the writ of Foreign Attachment issued on the 4th, and was made returnable on the 22nd of the same month. There had been the usual publications of notice; and the bond, duly executed, had been filed on the 12th November. The defendants were a mining corporation created in Victoria, but having property in this colony under the control of the garnishee. He referred to *Grant* on Corporations (*b*), the decision of this Court in *Ex parte Harwood* (*c*), *Corbett* v. *General Steam Navigation Company* (*d*), and *Adams* v. *The Great Western Railway Company* (*e*).

Darley asked, and was allowed, to be heard on behalf of the garnishee. The terms of the various sections of this Act show that its provisions were not intended to apply to the case of foreign corporations. The affidavit in support of this application states that the contract sued upon arose in this colony, and it must therefore be presumed that they reside here. *Ingate* v. *The Austrian Lloyd's Company* (*f*) decides that the sections of the Common Law Procedure Act, as to service, do not apply to foreign corporations resident abroad.

Per Curiam. We think the words of the Absent Defendants' Act embrace the case of foreign corporations.

> Order made attaching the property in the hands of the garnishee.

(*a*) 4 Vic., No. 6.   (*b*) p. 339.   (*c*) 24 October, 1858.
(*d*) 4 H. & N. 482; 28 L. J. Ex. 214.   (*e*) 30 L. J. Ex. 124.
          (*f*) 27 L. J. C. P. 323.

1865.

March 10, 14,
and 17.

RUSSELL and another *against* ROBINSON.

THE first count of the declaration stated, that whereas the plaintiffs, at the time of committing the grievances by the defendant hereinafter mentioned, were, and theretofore had been, the proprietors of the American Tannery, in or near the town of Yass, in the colony, &c., and carried on business therein as tanners, and thereby made large gains and profits; and whereas at the time aforesaid there was and had been a flood in and around the said town of Yass, whereby much property had been swept away and destroyed, the defendant well knowing the premises, but contriving, and falsely, fraudulently, and maliciously intending, to injure the plaintiffs in their business, and to deprive them of the gains so derived and derivable therefrom, and to induce the belief that the tannery of the plaintiffs had been swept and carried away in and by the flood, falsely, fraudulently, and maliciously spoke and published of the plaintiffs and their tannery and business, in the presence of one *Milne* and one *Foster*, and of divers other persons, to all of whom the real facts were unknown, the false and malicious words following, that is to say, "the whole of the pits and sheds of *Russell's*" (meaning thereby the pits and sheds of the said tannery of the plaintiffs) "are swept away, and there are neither tops nor bottoms left" (meaning that the said tannery was wholly swept away and destroyed).

The second count, after stating the same prefatory averments as the first count, alleged that the defendant wrote and published of the plaintiffs and their tannery and business a certain telegram, and sent and directed to be sent the same to a person in Sydney afore-

Declaration for maliciously circulating a false statement that the whole of the pits and sheds of the plaintiff's tannery had been swept away, by stating that such was the case to B., who forwarded a telegram to a person in Sydney to that effect, whereby the plaintiff was put to great loss, inconvenience and delay in carrying on the tannery and business, and lost great gains which he would otherwise have made; and also was put to great loss, &c., in this, that one F. L. who had, on the order of the plaintiff, dispatched from Sydney certain galvanized iron roofing for the sheds of the tannery, on hearing the report so circulated by the

defendant, stopped the roofing, and directed the same to be brought back to Sydney, whereby the tannery and sheds were greatly injured from being left without the roofing; and also in this—that a certain bark mill, constructed for the plaintiff, on the order of one H., by R. and Co. of Sydney, was detained for a long time, to wit, until the falsity of the report was known to H., and R. and Co., whereby the plaintiff sustained great loss and damage. *Held*, on demurrer, to disclose no cause of action.

said, in the words and figures following, that is to say—
" it is reported that *Russell's* American tannery (meaning
the said tannery of the plaintiffs) has been swept away ; "
the said defendant well knowing that the said tannery
had not been swept away, but contriving, and falsely,
fraudulently, and maliciously intending, to injure the
plaintiffs in respect of their said business and tannery,
by creating the belief that the said tannery had been
swept away.

The third count alleged that the defendant had said
to one *Buckle*, the telegraph master stationed at Yass,
the following words, " the whole of the pits and sheds
of *Russell's* (meaning thereby the pits and sheds of the
tannery of the plaintiffs) are swept away, and there are
neither tops nor bottoms left " (meaning that the tannery
was wholly swept away and destroyed)—he, the defendant, knowing the same to be false, but contriving,
and falsely, fraudulently, and maliciously intending
thereby, to injure the plaintiffs in and in regard to their
said tannery and business ; and thereupon, and acting
upon the said information of the defendant, and believing
the same to be true, the said *John Buckle* sent and forwarded to Sydney aforesaid, a telegram to the following
effect—" It is reported that *Russell's* American tannery
(meaning the said tannery of the plaintiffs) has been
swept away.". By means of which several grievances the
plaintiffs were put to great loss, inconvenience, and
delay, in carrying on the said tannery and business, and
lost great gains and profits, which, but for the committing of the said grievances, they might and would
have made and obtained ; and were also put to great
loss, inconvenience, delay, and expense, in this, that one
Frederick Lasseter, who, on the order of the plaintiffs,
had dispatched from Sydney certain galvanized iron
roofing for the sheds of the said tannery, upon learning
the said report so circulated by the defendant, stopped
the said roofing, and directed the same to be brought
back to Sydney aforesaid, whereby the said tannery and
sheds were greatly injured from being left without the
said roofing ; and also in this—that a certain bark mill,

constructed for the plaintiffs, on the order of one *W. R.*
Hall, by Messieurs *Russell and Company* of Sydney
aforesaid, was detained for a long time, to wit, until the
falsity of the said report was and became known to the
said *W. R. Hall*, and the said Messieurs *Russell and
Company*, whereby the plaintiffs sustained great loss and
damage.

Demurrer and joinder.

Butler in support of the demurrer. It is submitted
that the alleged slander, being in the nature of slander
of title, is not actionable without an allegation of special
damage; *Malachy* v. *Soper* (a). The report complained
of was not calculated to prejudice the plaintiff in the
way of his trade, but rather to throw doubts on the
nature or rather existence of his tannery; *Evans* v.
Harlow (b). At all events, the special damage alleged
is too remote, and is damage for which the defendant
is not responsible. The acts of *Lasseter* and *Russell
and Co.* were a breach of contract, for which they may
be liable; but they are no ground of action against the
defendant. In *Allsop* v. *Allsop* (c), illness caused by
the slanderous charge was held not to be such special
damage as could be recovered in an action, as not being
the natural and immediate result that would flow from
the slander. It is submitted that only the legitimate
and natural damage can be regarded, and that the inconvenience here alleged is not such special damage.

The repetition of the defamatory matter by *Buckle*
was his own unlawful act, for which the defendant is
not responsible. In *Ward* v. *Weeks* (d) the declaration
stated the defendant to have said of the plaintiff, "he is
a rogue and swindler; I know enough about him to
hang him;" in consequence of which, *Buyer* refused to
sell the plaintiff certain goods. It appeared that the
words were spoken to *Bryce*, and communicated by him
to *Buyer*, who thereupon refused to trust the plaintiff.
And the Court held, that under these circumstances the

(a) 3 B. N. C. 380.
(c) 29 L. J. Ex. 315.

(b) 5 Q. B. 624.
(d) 7 Bing. 211.

action would not lie. *Parkyns* v. *Scott* (a) was an
action for slander by husband and wife, against a husband and wife. The words declared on, imputing
adultery to the female plaintiff, had been addressed to
her by the female defendant, in the presence of other
persons, but in the absence of the male plaintiff, and
were repeated without the authority of the female defendant by the female plaintiff to her husband, who, for
this reason, refused to continue to cohabit with her;
and the loss by the female plaintiff of the consortium of
her husband was alleged as special damage. The Court
held, on the authority of *Ward* v. *Weeks*, that the defendants were not liable for the unauthorized repetition
of the slanderous matter by the female plaintiff to her
husband. In giving judgment, *Pollock*, C. B., says—
"*Ward* v. *Weeks* decides that to make the original
utterer of a slander liable, either the person affected by
it should have been present and have heard it uttered,
or that the utterer should have authorized its repetition."
He also referred to *Allsop* v. *Allsop* (b), and the notes to
Vicars v. *Willcox* (c).

Isaacs in support of the declaration. It is submitted
that the special damage is sufficiently alleged, and that
the loss of gains by diminished custom is a natural
result of the defendant's wrongful act. Greater particu-
larity is not necessary; *Hartley* v. *Herring* (d), *Rodgers*
v. *Nowell* (e). It will be a question for the jury whether
the words were spoken by the defendant to *Buckle* with
the intention and desire of their being repeated. It is
also submitted that *Ward* v. *Weeks* is no authority that
the defendant is not responsible, when the slander is
promulgated by the voluntary and unauthorized agency
of a third person. The decision in that case is only that
the evidence did not support the allegation in the declaration. The declaration alleged the special damage to
have arisen from *Buyer*, in consequence of words spoken
by the defendant; and the Court held that this allegation

(a) 31 L. J. Ex. 331.   (b) 29 L. J. Ex. 315.
(c) 2 Sm. L. C. 425.   (d) 8 T. R. 130.
            (e) 5 C. B. 109; 17 L. J. C. P. 52.

could not be supported by proof, that the defendant had spoken the words to *Bryce*, and that the damage accrued in consequence of *Bryce's* improperly repeating them as the words of the defendant. "We think," says Lord Chief Justice *Tindal*, "that as each count alleges as the only ground, the original false speaking of the words, the allegation that by means of the committing of such grievance *Buyer* refused to give the plaintiff credit, is not made out by the evidence; and on that ground we think the nonsuit right." The proper inference from that decision is, that if the declaration had gone on to allege the intermediate agency, it would have coincided with the proof, and the plaintiff might have succeeded. The authority of *Vicars* v. *Willcox* has been questioned in *Knight* v. *Gibbs* (a) and *Green* v. *Button* (b), and in *Starkie* on Libel (c); and it is submitted that according to the existing authorities it is immaterial whether or not the plaintiff has any right of action against *Lasseter*, or *Russell and Co.*, and that he is entitled to cover full compensation against the author of the slander.

Butler in reply. *Rodgers* v. *Nowell*, which has been relied on, is irrelevant; and in that case the thing complained of—namely, the imitation by the defendant of the plaintiff's trade mark—was actionable *per se*, without any averment of special damage, and is merely an authority that an averment of special damage does not vitiate a count otherwise good. It is submitted that the special damage is not the natural consequence of the report complained of. And that it is not sufficiently alleged, because it is not stated to have been spoken to a customer of the plaintiffs, or in the neighbourhood of plaintiff's tannery. Lastly, the remarks made do not tend to the prejudice of the plaintiff in his business, as in *Irwin* v. *Brandwood* (d); but the injury is rather like that complained of in *Evans* v. *Harlow* (e), where the Court held that the imputation on the plaintiff's

1865.

RUSSELL
and another
v.
ROBINSON.

(a) 1 A. & E. 48.   (b) 2 C. M. & R. 707.
(c) p. 205.   (d) 33 L. J. Ex. 257.
          (e) 5 Q. B. 631.

lubricators, that they wasted tallow, was only on the goods, and formed no ground of action.

STEPHEN, C. J. I am of opinion that this action will not lie. It is a startling proposition that the defendant should be liable, because he said that the plaintiff's tannery was burnt down or washed away. Assuming that there is no cause of action, unless the damage alleged is the damage which would naturally flow from the words complained of, I think no such damage is here alleged. It appears that the defendant went to the telegraph station, and said that the plaintiff's tannery had been swept away. In my opinion, the plaintiff has no cause of action against the defendant on account of this. If the law were otherwise, no one could ever communicate any intelligence of the mischief done by floods, fire, or other destructive agents. I know of no authority to support the position that such an injury is actionable.

WISE, J. This case is like that of *Evans* v. *Harlow*, and the injury alleged is a false statement as to the plaintiffs' goods. But the statement is not as to the character of the goods, but as to their existence. It is not a statement as to the plaintiff's character, but only that particular goods are not now in his shop; and I am of opinion that under such circumstances an action will not lie by the owner of the goods. If another person had been thereby prevented from going to the plaintiff's shop and taking his goods there, perhaps that person being so prevented might have a cause of action. No doubt in cases of libel general averments of damage can be eked out; but here there is no imputation upon the plaintiff's character; and even if there had been such an imputation, I should have still doubted whether the action would have lain. The strongest authority in favor of such a position is *Barley* v. *Walford* (a); but there the special damage to the plaintiff arose from the plaintiff's confidence in the defendant's false assertion.

Judgment for the defendant.

(a) 9 Q. B. 207.

BLACKMAN *against* MYLECHARANE.

TRESPASS for breaking and entering the plaintiff's close, called Gungalma, and depasturing it with cattle. The particulars of trespass filed with the declaration stated that the trespasses complained of were committed upon a tract of country lying to the south-west of Nedgra Creek, as shown in the plan which was annexed.

The defendant pleaded—(1) not guilty; (2) not possessed; (3) that the land was Crown land, and that no lease from the Crown of the land was in force at the time of the several alleged trespasses; that *George Barney*, Chief Commissioner of Crown Lands, being then an agent of the Crown lawfully authorised for the granting, under the Orders of Council referred to in the Crown Lands Occupation Act of 1861, a lease of Crown lands for a term unexpired, did (as such agent on behalf of the Crown) duly promise, engage, and contract with one *William Morris*, to grant a lease for a term unexpired to the said *William Morris*, of the land under the name of West Gungalma—and the land being such Crown land has ever since been known by and occupied under

The 28th section of the Crown Lands Occupation Act of 1861, provides that it shall be lawful for any party to an action of trespass upon Crown lands, of which no lease from the Crown shall be in force, "to plead and put in evidence any promise, engagement, or contract from or with the Crown, or its agents lawfully authorized, for the granting under the Orders in Council, or under this Act, for any term unex-

pired, of a lease of such lands; and such promise, &c., shall, as between the parties in such action, have the same effect as if a lease from the Crown of such lands had been duly issued, in pursuance of such promise, &c., to the party entitled thereunder to such lease." *Held*, that this section gives effect only to promises, &c., made after the Orders in Council came into operation.

In a squatting action it was proved that A. occupied 68,500 acres of land, called by the general terms of G., from 1838 to 1848, when he applied in the usual way for a lease of G. by the ascribed limits, and stating in his application that the quantity of land was only 16,000 acres. This application was advertised in the *Gazette*. A license in the usual form, to occupy certain lands "known as G.," was afterwards issued, and rent was for several years paid by A. as for 16,000 acres. After some years, the Government discovered that the quantity of land actually occupied was much larger than 16,000 acres, and thereupon, in 1856, it promised a lease of about 30,000 acres out of the entire area to B. In an action of trespass by A. against B., for trespasses on the land included in the promise to B., the latter pleaded a promise of a lease under the 28th section of the Crown Lands Occupation Act of 1861, and A. replied a previous promise under the same section. *Held*, that even assuming that the application for a lease, and its publication in the *Gazette* in 1848, coupled with the subsequent licenses and payments of rent, were unitedly some evidence of a promise to A. as to 16,000 acres—that they were no evidence of such a promise as to 68,500 acres; and a verdict which had been found in favor of A. was set aside.

the said name; and that during the unexpired term,
William Morris duly sold and transferred to one *John
Andrew Gardner* all his right, title, and interest in and
to the unexpired term, and in and to the land, and in
and to the lease; and that *John Andrew Gardner* duly
sold and transferred all his right, title, and interest in
and to the unexpired term, and in and to the land, and
in and to the lease, to the defendant and *John Ford*, junr.,
jointly; and that the several sales and transfers were
duly authorised, and ratified by and on behalf of the
Crown by such duly authorised agent as aforesaid; and
that before and at the time of the alleged trespasses he
was in occupation of the land jointly with *John Ford*,
junr., under and by virtue of the promise, engagement,
and contract for a lease; and relying upon the same,
and acting on behalf of himself and *John Ford*, junr.,
jointly, he committed, as he lawfully might, the several
alleged trespasses therein complained of.

There was a fourth plea in the same terms as to the
residue of the plaintiff's alleged close, which was another
piece of contiguous country called East Gungalma.

The plaintiff joined issue upon the various pleas; and
also replied to the third and fourth pleas, that before
George Barney promised, engaged, and contracted with
William Morris as in those pleas alleged, the Crown,
by its agent lawfully authorised for the granting, under
the Orders in Council referred to in the Crown Lands
Occupation Act of 1861, of leases of Crown land, promised, engaged, and contracted with *William Blackman*
to grant a lease to him for a term unexpired at the time
of the trespasses upon the said portions of land in the
pleas mentioned respectively; and that before and at
the said times when, &c., the interest in the said term
became and was vested in the plaintiff, *Samuel Alfred
Blackman*. Issue thereon.

The cause was tried before *Wise*, J., and a jury of
four, in August, 1864, when it appeared that the father
of the plaintiff had 68,500 acres of land in his occupation, called by the general term of Gungalma; this

68,500 acres included the land in controversy. The father had thus occupied from about the year 1838 up to 1848, when he applied in the usual way for a lease of Gungalma by the ascribed limits, and stating in his application (dated the 28th February, 1848), that the quantity of land included in the application was only 16,000 acres. This application of the father was advertised in the *Government Gazette* (a), and the father, and his son (the present plaintiff), after his death, occupied the land under licenses in the usual form. But there was no actual acceptance or notification of acceptance by the Government; nor had it been the usage to accept formally, or publish, or send any notification of such acceptance. It was proved that the course of proceeding in the Crown Lands office had been, when a tender was accepted—first, to write a letter to the applicant to pay the rent within sixty days; secondly, to write to the Colonial Treasurer to receive the money; thirdly, to write to the Auditor-General that the tender was accepted; fourthly, to write to the District Commissioner to the same effect; fifthly, to note upon the documents the word " accepted." At length the Government discovered, a few years ago, that the quantity actually occupied was much larger than 16,000 acres; and thereupon, in 1856, it promised and accepted the tenders for about 30,000 acres out of the entire area, including this particular land in question—of *Morris*, the

(a) The notice in the *Gazette* was dated the 20th September, 1848, which, after notifying that certain persons (whose names were given) had demanded leases of the several runs particularised in connection with their names, and inviting caveats from persons who objected to these claims, continued as follows;—" It is to be distinctly understood that the Government does not pledge itself to the issue of a lease in any case, until due enquiry has been made into the validity of the claim; and whether or not it may be necessary to reserve any portion of the land claimed for any of the public purposes, as contemplated in the Order in Council."

The licenses to the plaintiff after the promulgation of the Orders in Council, were in the usual form, stating that whereas the plaintiff had made application for a license to occupy certain waste lands of the Crown, situate in the district of Bligh, &c., and known as Gungalma, "now I, the Governor aforesaid, do hereby authorise the said *William Blackman*, upon payment by him of the sum of £10 into the hands of the Colonial Treasurer, on or before, &c., and upon the due acknowledgment, &c., to occupy the said waste lands for the term hereinafter mentioned. Upon the issue of the license by the said Colonial Treasurer, the same is to operate and be in force from, &c., until, &c."

person through whom the present defendant claimed. This land was tendered for in two blocks, of about 16,000 acres a piece, which were called respectively East and West Gungalma. It was admitted that these two blocks were included in the defendant's promise of a lease. But the plaintiff contended that he had a previous promise, including the same land; and as evidence of this promise, showed his father's application for and the promise to him of a tract of land containing 16,000 acres, bounded, as the application said, "on the west by pine and sand ridges." But the evidence clearly showed that if this application extended to the particular pine and sand ridges that they insisted upon, that it would embrace about 68,000 acres, and the particular land now in dispute. It was contended, therefore, on behalf of the defendant, that these pine and sand ridges could not have been the pine and sand ridges referred to by the plaintiff's father in his application, or by the Government when they accepted that tender. And this argument was strengthened by the fact which also appeared in evidence, that the plaintiff or his father had for some years paid rent or assessment only on 16,000 acres. But on the other hand evidence was given to show that there were only a few pine trees, scarcely amounting to a ridge of pines, at or near the spot where the 16,000 acres or thereabouts should terminate.

The jury found that the defendant, and those through whom he claimed, received a promise of a lease of this land; but that the plaintiff's father had obtained a previous promise of a lease of the same land, and also a renewal of such promise. The verdict, therefore, was entered for the plaintiff.

A rule *nisi* for a new trial was obtained on behalf of the defendant, on the grounds—first, that the verdict was against evidence, as the jury found a promise of a lease to the plaintiff, and that there was a renewal of such promise by the Government, and also as the plaintiff's promise or licensed occupation, if under the Crown, did not embrace the land licensed and promised to be leased to the defendant. Secondly, that having regard to the provisions of the Orders in Council of 1847, and the Assessment Act of that year, independently of the general rules of law, the Judge ought to have ruled that the plaintiff's title extended only to 16,000 acres, or thereabouts. Thirdly, that the notification by the Government, in the *Gazette* of 20th September, 1848 (a), was no evidence of a promise of any lease to the plaintiff as to the land in question. Fourthly, that the licenses put in by the plaintiff, respecting land "called Gungalma," were inadmissible in evidence.

1865.

BLACKMAN
v.
MYLE-
CHARANE.

Sir *W. Manning*, Q. C. (*Stephen* and *Salomons* with him), showed cause. The jury have found that the plaintiff's father was in licensed occupation of the locus when he applied for the lease of it. Up to 1848, when the Orders in Council came into operation, he was in licensed occupation—and thereupon, under the Orders of 9th March, 1847, he was entitled to a lease of all the land he then occupied, provided he made an application within six months from their publication; Ch. 2, sect. 11; he did make the application within that period, and in such application he described this land as Gungalma, and by metes and bounds; and that description includes the land in dispute. The evidence showed that the usual course of proceeding was, when a tender was sent in, for the Chief Commissioner to refer it to the local Commissioner for his report; and when that report was received, to publish the tender in the *Gazette* and invite caveats. It was proved that after such publication the father of the plaintiff continued in occupation of the entire area, and paid rent—holding a license for the run known as Gungalma. It is submitted that this evidence shows acquiescence on the part of the Government, which is equivalent to, or rather evidence of, a promise; and that even if the *Gazette* is not by itself evidence of a promise, yet, that, taken with all the other circumstances, it is evidence for the jury. The defendant's plea alleges a promise to his predecessor of this land in 1857. But the plaintiff's replication meets, or

March 13, 15

(a) See note (a), p. 45.

rather overcomes this, by setting up his previous promise of a lease for fourteen years, which would not expire till 1861 or 1862, or rather till January, 1864, according to the Governor General's regulation of 28th October, 1851 ; which says, that "in regard to all leases to be issued, both for lands held under licensed occupation, previously to the promulgation of the Order in Council of 9th March, 1847, and for runs hitherto acquired by tender, the maximum terms of eight years and fourteen years shall commence from a future certain day, namely, 1st January, 1852, without reference to the actual date on which the leases may issue." This term of fourteen years had not expired when *Morris'* tender was accepted in 1857. And, moreover, if the plaintiff had a subsisting lease, the land was not open to tender, as the Orders in Council give a right of renewal. *Morris'* tender also was under the 13th section of the Orders ; but that section, which provides for applications for leases of new runs, would not apply. It is also a rule of law that the Crown cannot grant a reversion. [*Stephen*, C. J. Are the statutes, under which the Crown can only grant leases to take effect at once, applicable ?] It is further submitted that the promise is of the same effect as a lease. But a lease of land described by boundaries, would pass all the land by those boundaries. In *Sheppard's* Touchstone (a), it is said that if one grant in this manner all my meadow in D., containing ten acres, whereas in truth his meadow there doth contain twenty acres, it seems this is a good grant for the whole twenty acres. *Llewellyn* v. *Earl of Jersey* (b), and *Barton* v. *Dawes* (c) are authorities to the same effect, and show that the calling the quantity 16,000 acres amounts to a mere *falsa demonstratio*, which would not vitiate the instrument. [*Stephen*, C. J. But the rent is in all cases in proportion to the quantity; and moreover the Crown, from the years 1847 to 1857, received rent for 16,000 acres only. Can it then be said that it promised an area more than four times as large ?]

(a) p. 248.   (b) 11 M. & W. 190.
                 (c) 10 C B. 261 ; 19 L. J. C. P. 302.

It is also contended, that assuming that the plaintiffs' father was limited to 16,000 acres, he might take them anywhere within the area.

Martin, Q. C. (*Butler* with him), contra. The first section of the Assessment Act of 1847 authorises the collection of an assessment. The second section directs that certain returns should be made in the form provided by the Act. Among other items contained in this form is the estimated extent of the run to be furnished for purposes of assessment. The plaintiff's father signed and sent in as his return of this run, dated 1st January, 1848, that its estimated extent was twenty-five square miles, or 16,000 acres; and he made the same return in many succeeding years. Under these circumstances, and remembering that under the second section of the Order in Council of March, 1847, the rent to be paid was to be proportioned to the number of sheep or cattle which the run should be estimated as capable of carrying, it is submitted that the evidence relied on is utterly insufficient to show any promise, engagement, or contract for a lease of 68,000 acres. *Blackman* may have had a right to demand a lease; but there is nothing to show that he was entitled to or had a lease of any particular land, or for any particular period; but these were matters to be determined by the Governor. But even if it be conceded that the parties were entitled to a lease of 68,000 acres, the question would still remain whether he or the plaintiff had obtained it. The promise is, under the Act, equivalent to a lease; but it is submitted that a promise of 16,000 acres cannot be deemed to be a promise of 68,000 acres. But if not, how has the plaintiff shown a promise of a lease of this particular piece of land? It is also contended that the application and the publication of it cannot amount to a contract between these parties; and, if not a contract, it was not a promise; and there was, therefore, no contract or promise by the Crown with or to the plaintiff's father of 68,000 acres.

STEPHEN, C. J. I am of opinion that the verdict was demonstrably wrong, both in point of fact and in point

D—4

of law. The defendant has clearly proved that he held a license and a promise with respect to this specific piece of land, and the plaintiff has utterly failed to prove that it forms part of the 16,000 acres to which alone he had a prior promise. Assuming that the application and publication in 1848, coupled with the subsequent licenses and payments of rent, amount to, or unitedly were evidence of, a promise to the plaintiff as to 16,000 acres, to what particular 16,000 acres did it relate? It is clear that the Crown neither promised nor meant to promise 68,500 acres. But I am of opinion that there was no contract or promise shown as to any quantity of land, or for any term of lease. There was only, at the most, a promise conditional on various things not shown to have been done. And if the licensed occupation of 68,500 acres, in and before 1847 and up to 1848, entitles the plaintiff in law to a lease to that land, the answer is that the right was existing at or before the time of the Order in Council. But the statute gives effect only to promises or contracts that have been made under the Orders in Council.

MILFORD, J. I concur with the judgment, just delivered as to the construction of the 28th section, that the promise must be made subsequent to the Orders in Council; and that the Orders in Council cannot be considered as creating any contract, engagement, or promise on the part of the Crown. The question, therefore, is whether there has been a promise since the promulgation of these Orders? It has been contended that the application, and its publication in the *Gazette*, show such a promise. But it seems to me that the publication in question is not a promise, but rather avoids making a promise. But even assuming it to be a promise of a lease, what kind of lease would it be? It cannot be a lease from year to year, when the power conferred is a power to lease for fourteen or eight years; and therefore such a lease would seem to me to be void for uncertainty; but this point it is not necessary to decide.

WISE, J. I am of the same opinion. At the trial I thought that the defendant had made out his case, and expected that the verdict would have been in his favor; but I did not see how .the question could be withdrawn from the jury. It seems to me that the 28th section only applies to promises made since the Orders in Council came into existence. In the present case, I see no evidence of any *aggregatio mentium.* What is the evidence that the Crown did assent to any promise? The evidence is simply that the Crown received an annual rent of £10 for 16,000 acres. This being the case, it is not necessary to consider the authorities cited with regard to misdescription in a grant.

1865.
BLACKMAN
v.
MYLE-
CHABANE.

Rule absolute for a new trial.

Ex parte OGILVIE (a).

March 8, 10.

MARTIN, Q. C. (*Darley* with him), moved to make absolute a rule granted in the last term of 1864, calling on *Walker* to show why an award made under the Crown Lands Occupation Act of 1861 should not be set aside, on the grounds—

First, of misconduct of one of the arbitrators under the following circumstances. The arbitrators appointed were one *Lardner* on behalf of *Walker*, and one *Fisher* on behalf of *Ogilvie.* The question in dispute was as to a boundary line, and the controversy between the parties whether a line drawn in a particular direction from a

The sixth section of the Crown Lands Occupation Act of 1861 enacts, that where two or more persons entitled to leases claim the same land, "the lease shall be granted to the person whose right thereto may have been or may be established.

after due inquiry, to the satisfaction of the Governor or the Minister;" and where the right shall not have been so established, "it shall be lawful for the Minister to require such right to be inquired into and determined by arbitration, and the lease may be granted in accordance with the award of such arbitration." The fourth paragraph of the twenty-third section says, that "the award of any arbitrators appointed in pursuance of the Act, shall be binding, final, and conclusive upon all parties to the arbitration, for all intents and purposes whatever." *Held*, that it is discretionary with the Crown to issue a lease to the party in whose favor the award is made or not.

The eleventh and fourteenth paragraphs of the twenty-third section provide that any submission to arbitration under the provisions of the Act, may be made a rule of the Supreme Court on the application of either party, and that no award shall be set aside for irregularity or error in matter of form. *Held*, that such Court has jurisdiction to set aside such award, but that a merely wrong description of a boundary in an award is not a sufficient ground for setting it aside.

(a) Before *Stephen*, C. J., and *Wise*, J..

certain point fell above or below the confluence of two creeks. Both sides produced, before the arbitrators, maps of the district, between which a great discrepancy existed. According to the affidavits of *Ogilvie*, it was intimated by *Ogilvie's* advocate that unless the arbitrators would resolve to visit the place, and determine from actual inspection the relative correctness of the two maps, he should require to call further evidence to establish the correctness of the map he produced. The arbitrators promised that they would not make any decision without seeing the land. But these allegations were denied by the other side. There was a conflict of evidence as to whether the arbitrators did or did not promise to view the ground. But it is certain and not denied that they were told of *Ogilvie's* intention to call witnesses, if they did not view it; and yet the award was made the next day without any notice to *Ogilvie*. In *Earl* v. *Stocker* (a) it is laid down that if an arbitrator promise to have witnesses, and afterwards make an award before he has done so, the award shall be set aside. And the same rule has been held to apply if he declares that he will suspend further proceedings in the reference till some books of account have been referred to, and afterwards make an award without examining such books, or giving notice to the parties that he has found the inspection of the books unnecessary; *Pepper* v. *Gorham* (b). And in *In re Peterson* v. *Ayre* (c) the award was set aside, because the arbitrators had not given the plaintiff notice that they were about to make their award, and thus given him an opportunity of examining his witnesses.

Secondly, on the ground of partiality and corruption in the same arbitrator. It appeared that some days before the making the award *Fisher* asked *Ogilvie* whether it was true, as he had been informed, that he (*Ogilvie*) was the cause of his (*Fisher's*) having been struck off the Commission of the Peace that had been lately issued. *Ogilvie* replied, that he had been consulted

(a) 2 Vern. 250.
(b) 4 Moore 148; cited in *Russell*, Part II., ch. 4, s. 1.
(c) 23 L. J. C. P. 129.

by the Government as to the propriety of his *(Fisher's)* name remaining on the Commission, and that he had expressed his opinion to the contrary, alleging, as his reasons for such opinion, his concurrence with the rule laid down by the Government that no person in active business should be on the Commission, adding that it was no reflection on his *(Fisher's)* personal character; and that if he *(Ogilvie)* did not consider him competent to be a magistrate, he would not have appointed him as a judge in a case where his own interests were so heavily at stake. It also appeared that *Fisher* had at first obtained the information as to *Ogilvie's* recommendation to the Government from *Walker*, pending this enquiry, or rather from one *Greaves* in whom *Walker's* interest at that time had vested. What could have been *Greaves'* object in telling *Fisher* that *Ogilvie* had recommended his name to be left out of the new Commission? The only object must have been a corrupt one, namely, to prejudice *Fisher* against *Ogilvie* in the arbitration then being carried on. And why does *Fisher* at that time enquire of *Ogilvie* on the matter? The denials by *Fisher* in his affidavit, that his mind was influenced by what had occurred, are of no value.

And thirdly, this award is bad for incompleteness *(a)*. No boundary can be collected from this award. What " range " is intended? There is no direct reference to any map. The supplement to the award, consisting of a description, is as unintelligible as the award itself.

Darley applied to be allowed time to file affidavits in reply to the arbitrators' statement, that a view was not necessary, because of the alleged admissions of a certain line by *Ogilvie*—denying, first, his assent to the running

(a) The award was as follows:—" We declare our award to be as follows—that the land south of the range, forming the northern watershed of the Hanging Rock Creek, belongs to the Newbold run; and that the boundary between Mr. *Ogilvie's* cattle run on the east, and Newbold on the west, is the range dividing the waters of the south river and those of the Clarence in a north and north-westerly direction, to the forge on the Clarence River." And after the signatures of the arbitrators there followed the words—" Description of boundaries between *Ogilvie's* cattle station on the south river, and Newbold cattle run, as fixed by us the arbitrators, commencing, &c.;" and the signatures of the two arbitrators were again added.

of any such line; and secondly, the accuracy of *Walker's* map; and thirdly, that there was not any agreement in fact by the arbitrators to view the land. He referred to *Pritchard* v. *Leech* (a), and *Wood* v. *Cox* (b).

Isaacs contra.

Per Curiam. We will reserve our decision until we have heard the case.

Isaacs showed cause. The fourth paragraph of the 23rd section of the Crown Lands Occupation Act (c). enacts, that the "award appointed in pursuance of this Act shall be binding, final, and conclusive upon all parties," and the Court, therefore, has no jurisdiction over the award. [*Stephen*, C. J. If manifestly corrupt, no Court would let the award stand if it could be avoided; but this Act provides that it shall be made a rule of Court.] That may be merely to enforce the payments of costs; but the statute makes it final, for the purposes for which the arbitration takes place; at all events the Court will only interfere in case of the grossest fraud. It is provided by the 6th section that " the lease shall be granted to the person whose right thereto may have been or may be established, after due enquiry, to the satisfaction of the Governor or the Minister;" and when the right shall not have been so established, "it shall be lawful for the Minister to require such right to be inquired into and determined by arbitration, and the lease may be granted in accordance with the award of such arbitration." The language of the latter clause shows that, notwithstanding the result of the arbitration, the power of the Crown is altogether discretionary. [*Stephen*, C. J. I am inclined to think that we ought not to interfere, assuming that we have power to do so, on account of any uncertainty or incompleteness in the description; for in such case the award cannot prejudice the other side.] •

Martin, Q. C., in reply. Nothing can be more dangerous than that the Minister of Lands should

(a) 2 Jur. N. S. 475.   (b) 24 L. J. C. P. 155.
(c) 25 Vic., No. 2.

possess the large powers which the construction of the
6th section, contended for by the other side, would place
in his hands. It is submitted that, by the reference to
arbitration, the Crown admits that one or other of the
parties is entitled, and, there being no right of the
Crown in question, the award is absolutely binding.
The 23rd section of the Crown Lands Occupation Act
prescribes the manner in which the arbitration shall be
conducted ; and the fourth paragraph enacts that the
award of the arbitrator shall be binding, final, and conclusive upon all parties, for all intents and purposes
whatsoever. [*Wise*, J. The 6th section enacts that the
lease may be granted in accordance with the award, and
by the eighth section of the Acts Shortening Act (*a*)
the word "may" imports a discretion.] The 6th section must be taken with the 23rd, and the .proper construction then is that the Crown may refuse altogether
to refer the matter ; but if it be referred, the action
of the Crown must be in accordance with the award.
But at all events the Court has complete jurisdiction
over these arbitrations; for even assuming a discretion
to exist in the Minister for Lands, yet, as the award must
be assumed to operate to some extent on the Minister's
mind, the Court would control such arbitrations.

The award is uncertain and not final. For if this
award be allowed to stand good, it will require some
other person or tribunal to do something to carry it out.
A survey will be necessary in order to find out this line,
and then a further proceeding to enquire whether such
survey is correct.

STEPHEN, C. J. We are prepared to give judgment
on two points, in order that, if it be considered necessary,
the legislature may alter the law. On the first point,
whether the award is binding on the Government, I am
still of opinion, notwithstanding Mr. *Martin's* argument,
that it is entirely discretionary whether the Crown will
issue a lease in accordance with the award or not. I
admit that it is dangerous to give to the Crown a power

(*a*) 22 Vic., No. 12.

to issue leases according to its discretion, after an award
has been given.   It might seem inexpedient and unwise.
On the other hand, there might be cases in which no
Government could give as bad a decision as arbitrators
might do; and, therefore, it may not be desirable that a
Government should be bound by a grossly erroneous
decision.   I do not entertain any doubt that there is a
discretion in the Government, notwithstanding the award,
to do what it thinks right.   The first clause of the 6th
section provides that the lease *shall be* granted to the
person whose right thereto may be established after due
inquiry to the satisfaction of the Governor or Minister;"
but the following clause uses the language, "the lease
may be granted in accordance with the award."   Without reference to the section of the Acts Shortening Act,
I cannot understand why the Legislature should have
altered the phrase, unless there was some reason for the
change, and it was intended that there should be a difference in the two cases.   The reason may be, that it was
thought proper that the Government should be allowed
to say—"we are not satisfied ; we do not like the people
you have appointed as arbitrators, or the way in which
they have acted."   If the award was strictly binding, it
might also have been contended that where the award
gave a bad description the Government must have
adopted it; and therefore the present enactment was
passed, it may be, to avoid difficulties of this kind, which
might have arisen, if the award had been imperative.
But whatever the reason may have been, it is sufficient
to say that in one place the Legislature has used the
word "may," and in the other "shall."   The Acts
Shortening Act, moreover, was passed before this Act,
and puts an end to all doubt on the point.

I am also of opinion that we have power under this
Act to set aside an award.   The eleventh and fourteenth
paragraphs of the 23rd section enact, that any submission to arbitration under the provisions of the Act,
may be made a rule of this Court; and that no award
shall be set aside for irregularity or error in matter of
form.   This shows that it may be set aside for sufficient

reason. Could this Court grant an attachment for the non-payment of the costs of a grossly foolish award? But I am, also, of opinion that the Court would not set aside an award for a merely wrong description of the boundary, if it was proved what was meant; for the Government is not bound to adopt an unintelligible description; and as the Government can, under such circumstances, do justice, the Court ought not to interfere on such a ground.

We will take time to consider on one point. It is objected that the arbitrators said that they would see the land, if they thought it necessary. I wish to see what the facts are, and whether, if they did not see the land, Mr. *Ogilvie* ought to have had an opportunity of giving additional evidence.

WISE, J. I am of the same opinion. As to the construction of the statute, it seems to me that under the sixth section of the Crown Lands Occupation Act, and the eighth section of the Acts Shortening Act, the Governor and the Executive Council, but not the Minister for Lands, have power, if they choose, to refuse to grant a lease to A., notwithstanding the award may be in his favor. The policy or expediency of this state of things is a delicate question, on which I need not offer an opinion. But it seems to me to be discretionary with the Governor and the Executive Council—that is the majority of the Council—to grant or not to grant a lease according to the award. If the power be discretionary, it is a reason why the Court should not lightly interfere to set aside the award. But it does not follow as a correlative of this position that the Court will enforce it by attachment, or that the Court will consider it binding.

The 27th section may have some bearing on the question of the sufficiency of the description, as it may be that a less minute description will be sufficient than would be necessary under ordinary circumstances.

I think that the Court has power over these awards, because no precedent can be found of a statute declaring that a Court of justice shall be an instrument of injustice, by enacting that it shall not interfere under any

circumstances.   It seems contrary to first principles to
give any such construction, by implication, to the words
of the Legislature.   It must be presumed, when parties
are made to come to the Court to enforce an award, that
such award must be subject to the ordinary rules of that
Court.   On the other point,

Cur. ad. vult.

March 18.   STEPHEN, C. J., gave judgment on the point on which
judgment was reserved, as follows:—
    I have looked through the affidavits, and I think that
the motion must fail, and that there is no necessity to
give the applicant further time to file affidavits in reply.
It seems clear to me that if Mr. *Ogilvie* had produced
all the evidence in his power, it would not and ought
not to have affected the award.   If it had appeared that
he had lost an opportunity of calling fresh evidence, or
that he would have called it but for what the arbitrators
said, I should have been inclined to grant the application.   But it seems to me that if he had supplemented
his case, it would have been of no use.   The affidavits
filed on behalf of the arbitrators show what the issues
were, and that the evidence of Mr. *Ogilvie* is incorrect.
It is sworn most positively that no opportunity of calling
additional evidence was lost by Mr. *Ogilvie*, and that the
arbitrators promised to see the land only, if it was found
to be necessary, and that it was entirely unnecessary.
They do not say that they communicated to Mr. *Ogilvie*
that it was not necessary; but they say that no opportunity of calling such evidence was lost, and that no
intention was expressed by them of calling new evidence.

    WISE, J.   I desired to look into the affidavits to satisfy
my own mind.   It is the duty of the Court to set aside an
award, if satisfied that unfairness has been used—that is,
if both sides have not been properly heard, or if the
arbitrators have made a mistake in deciding without hearing both sides.   Mr. *Ogilvie's* affidavits are answered by
the affidavits on the other side.   I see an affidavit of the

attorney stating the grounds of the decision of the arbitrators. The attorney has no right to state on affidavit the grounds on which the arbitrators told him they based their award. My impression is, that the Court will not hear the reasons which, the arbitrators say, guided them.

1865.

Ex parte
OGILVIE.

Rule discharged.

THE QUEEN *against* WILLIS.

December 17,
1864.

SPECIAL.case stated for the opinion of the Judges, under the 13 Vic., No. 8.

"The prisoner was indicted for that he did commit an assault upon one *Margaret Ann Wilson*, with intent to commit a rape upon her. The prosecutrix was nearly fifteen years of age; her testimony was clear besides being confirmed.

A boy under
the age of
fourteen can-
not be con-
victed of an
assault with
intent to com-
mit a rape.

"For the defence two witnesses were called, who proved that the prisoner was a native of the colony, and at the time of the commission of the offence was under fourteen years of age.

"The advocate for the prisoner contended that a boy, according to the English cases, under fourteen years of age, could not in law be guilty of such an offence.

"The Crown prosecutor denied that these cases could be recognised as law in this colony, regarding its climate and its effect upon human beings. After some reluctance, and with a view of obtaining the decision of their Honors the Judges of the Supreme Court upon the point, I refused to stop the case, intimating that if the Jury should be of opinion that the prisoner in point of fact did commit the offence, and at the time of its commission was under fourteen years of age, I would reserve the point. The jury found the prisoner guilty, stating at the same time that they believed that the prisoner was under fourteen years of age at the time of its commission. He received a sentence of three months hard labor in Darlinghurst Gaol. I reserved, therefore, the following question for the consideration of their Honors the Judges of the Supreme Court, viz., whether a boy under fourteen years of age, a native of the colony, can in point of law commit the crime set forth in the information.

(Signed)   *JAMES S. DOWLING,*

D. C. J. and Chairman, &c."

Windeyer for the prisoner. As matter of law a boy under the age of fourteen cannot be guilty of rape, except as a principal in the second degree, and therefore cannot be guilty of the attempt; *R.* v. *Eldershaw* (a), *R.* v. *Jordan* (b), *R.* v. *Phillips* (c).

Butler, for the Crown, referred to *Best* on Presumptions (d).

STEPHEN, C. J. The law is settled, and the conviction cannot be sustained.

WISE, J. In *Bishop* on Criminal Law (e) it is said, " According to the English doctrine, a boy under the age of fourteen years is conclusively presumed to be incapable, whatever be the real facts of the case. The reason is, that puberty does not often develope itself at an earlier period ; and so this rule works justice in most cases, while its conclusive nature prevents those indecent disclosures which tend to the corruption of public virtue. In this country (America) the rule has been little discussed, but some Courts have held that it is to be received only to establish a *prima facie* case, which may be overthrown by actual testimony. We can hardly suppose the instances of physical capability, exhibited at an earlier age than fourteen years in a boy, sufficiently numerous to call for the abolition of a technical rule so well adapted as this, to prevent those particular statements of indecent things which wear away the nice sense of the refined, placed, by the Maker, in the human mind as one of the protections of its virtue." (f)

(a) 3 C. & P. 396.   (b) 9 C. & P. 118.
(c) 8 C. & P. 736.   (d) p. 23.   (e) 2 Vol., p. 936.
(f) An attempt to commit an offence is clearly distinguishable from an intent or intention to commit it. The attempt must be the taking some step towards the offence, so that, if it had succeeded, the whole offence would have been committed. (Per *Cockburn*, C. J., in *R.* v. *McPherson*,[*] affirmed in *R.* v. *Collins.*[†]

[*] Dear. & B. 197; 26 L. J. M. C. 134.   [†] 33 L. J. M. C. 177.

1865.

WOLFE and another *against* BLICK (a).

March 10.

THIS was an appeal from the District Court, holden at East Maitland.

It appeared from the appeal case that the plaintiffs had sued the defendant, "for that the latter, on or about the 15th day of February last, bargained and sold to the plaintiffs, and the plaintiffs bought from the defendant ten tons of potatoes, belonging to the defendant then at Belmont, &c., described as black Derwent and according to sample exhibited, for six pounds per ton, to be delivered by the defendant to the plaintiffs within one week from the 15th of February last, and the plaintiffs gave the defendant twelve bags on account of the said potatoes." General averment of the fulfilment of all conditions precedent, and that the plaintiffs were always ready and willing to receive the same. Breach, that although the defendant tendered potatoes to the plaintiffs, it was not in accordance with the contract, and she has failed to carry out her undertaking; whereby, &c.

The defendant pleaded—(1) that she did not sell ten tons of potatoes as alleged; (2) that she tendered one ton, but the plaintiffs refused delivery thereof.

The case was tried in May, 1864, before his Honor Mr. District Court Judge *Purefoy*, without a jury.

The appeal case continued—"It appeared the alleged contract was not in writing, and I found that the plaintiffs failed to prove the contract for the sale of ten tons of potatoes, and I stated so in summing up the evidence, upon which I founded my final judgment, adding that my judgment would be substantially for the defendant; but as the defendant admitted she had contracted to sell one ton of potatoes, and to deliver the same in one week

In an action for the non-delivery of ten tons of potatoes, where the plaintiff failed to prove the contract, but the defendant admitted a contract for one ton, the District Court Judge gave a verdict for the plaintiff with damages for the breach of the contract for one ton. The Court on appeal held, that on the contract declared on, and without amendment of the pleadings, the verdict was wrong; and a verdict was directed to be entered for the defendant.

If the appeal case is signed by the District Court Judge, the Court of Appeal will presume that the parties differed as to its statement.

Semble, that the District Court Judge has no power to sign a case for appeal, unless the parties so differ.

If a plaintiff in a District Court *bona fide* claimed and could have recovered £30, an appeal lies, although less than that amount may have been recovered in the action.

(a) Before *Stephen*, C. J., and *Wise*, J.

from the date of the contract, and that she also admitted she did not tender the one ton of potatoes until two days after the week had expired, I found for the plaintiffs £6, as damages for the breach of the contract for the non-delivery of one ton of potatoes within the week as agreed on.

"It did appear in evidence that when defendant tendered the one ton of potatoes, the plaintiffs refused to accept same, alleging the contract was for ten tons, that one ton would be of no use to them."

The defendant contended at the trial that the plaintiffs could not succeed, as they had failed to prove the contract declared on.   The question was, whether, under the circumstances, the verdict could stand.   At the end of the appeal case the learned Judge said—"Having, since this case was tried, looked into the authorities on the subject of contracts, I consider it is due to myself to state that upon the first point I am now of opinion that I was wrong."

When the case was called on, *Salomons*, for the plaintiffs, moved on- notice to strike out the case, and referred to *Stone* v. *Dean* (a).

Martin, Q. C., objected that the affidavits in support of the objection had not been filed before one o'clock in the afternoon of the preceding day, as required by Rule 6 (b).

Per Curiam.   The objection is fatal.   The case must go on.

Martin, Q. C., for the appellant.   The evidence for the plaintiffs showed a contract (which was not in writing) for ten tons of potatoes, at £6 a ton, and no contract for any less contract.   The evidence for the defendant proved a contract for one ton only.   The learned Judge thereupon gave a verdict for £6, as damages for the breach of the contract proved by the defendant.   It is submitted that this cannot be done, for it amounts to a substitution of one contract for another.

(a) 27 L. J. Q. B. 319.   (b) Sup. Ct. Pr. 22.

Salomons for the respondent. The Judge may have believed the witnesses of the defendant; at all events, it is a question of fact upon which his decision is final, and from which no appeal will lie; *East Anglian R. Co.* v. *Lythgoe* (a). The learned Judge had power to amend the plaint, and it must be presumed in favor of the verdict that he did so, or the Court will now amend it. [*Wise*, J. Could the District Court Judge have amended, unless the party asked him to amend?] He also referred to *Cawley* v. *Furnell* (b). He also argued that the learned District Court Judge had no jurisdiction to sign the appeal case, as there had been no disagreement between the parties, as required by the 94th section of the Act.

1865.
WOLFE
and another
v.
BLICK.

Martin, Q. C., in reply. *Cawley* v. *Furnell* shows that though questions of fact as well as of law are before a Judge without a jury, an appeal will lie if the Court of Appeal can see from the facts stated that the Judge, in order to arrive at his judgment, must have decided a question of law in a particular way. [*Wise*, J. Does an appeal lie in this case where the damages are only £6?] The plaintiff was entitled to recover the difference between the contract price and the market value; and the damages might have been more than £30; in fact, it appeared in evidence that the price of potatoes had risen £6 a ton. In *Mayer* v. *Burgess* (c), which may be relied on as an adverse authority, it appears that, in the words of Lord *Campbell*, "so much as £20 could not have been recovered."

STEPHEN, C. J. The first question is whether £30 was really claimed—that is, not merely claimed as damages, but whether the plaintiffs *bona fide* claimed £30. Could they have sworn that they had a cause of action to that amount, in order to obtain the defendants arrest under the 3 Vic., No. 15? I do not see whether they really claimed that amount or not; but it appears

(a) 20 L. J. C. P. 84.   (b) 20 L. J. C. 197.
      (c) 4 E. & B. 659; 24 L. J. Q. B. 67.

that the learned Judge has given £6 damages for the non-delivery of one ton; and further, the point has not been taken by the other side. It is admitted that if £30 might have been recovered, an appeal lies; and therefore we cannot get rid of the appeal on that ground.

A second point has been taken. It is alleged that the appeal case was signed by the learned Judge, without any disagreement between the parties. If we saw clearly that the fact was as alleged, we must have dismissed the appeal on that ground. But in the absence of information, one way or the other, we cannot refuse to entertain the appeal on that ground.

I am of opinion that the appellant must have judgment in his favor. The plaintiffs say, we entered into a contract for ten tons; the defendant says, I never made such a contract. That was the issue the parties went down to try. The plaintiffs fail to prove the contract they relied on; but the defendant admitted that she sold one ton, although denying that she sold ten tons. On these pleadings, and on this contract, and without any amendment, I am of opinion that the plaintiffs were not entitled to a verdict. But the learned Judge believed the evidence of the defendant, and yet gave a verdict for the plaintiffs. I give no opinion whether, at this stage of the proceedings, we have power to amend; but it could only be on very strict terms, and I think we ought not to do so in this case. There ought not to be a new trial, for in this state of the pleadings the verdict ought to have been entered for the defendant; and I see no reason why the party who ought to have succeeded at the trial should not have the costs of the appeal.

WISE, J. I am of opinion that the District Court Judge was wrong; for I think he was not entitled to give a verdict for the plaintiffs on the contract declared on, although, if he had thought fit to mend the plaint upon the plaintiffs' application, he might then have found such a verdict. In *Cooper* v. *Blick* (a), where

(a) 2 Q. B. 922.

the question was, what was the effect of payment of money into Court as an admission of the contract declared on ? *Patteson, J.*, says, "the amount of salary is laid under a videlicet. As to the effect of that averment, the true test is whether, if *non assumpsit* had been pleaded, the plaintiff would have been bound to prove the amount as laid." He then adds, "had the videlicet been omitted, the same test would have applied; the plaintiff would have been bound to the precise statement, and the defendant's admission by payment into Court would have bound him in the same manner." Here, the precise statement is " ten tons," and the plaintiffs were bound to prove a contract for ten tons. If they failed to prove that agreement, they should have asked for an amendment; and the Judge was wrong in thinking that without an amendment he could give a verdict for the plaintiffs.

I had some doubt whether this was a case for appeal at all. To give a right of appeal, £30 must be substantially in issue; and a plaintiff cannot by claiming £200 give himself a right of appeal. If it had been distinctly shown that the matter in issue was less than £30, we should not have allowed an appeal (*a*).

Judgment for the appellant.

1865.

WOLFE and another v. BLICK.

(*a*) As to the signing an appeal case being a ministerial act, see *Paley* on Convictions 17 ; 4 Bac. Ab. 619 ; 4 Com. Dig. 656 ; 2 Hawk. P. C. 47.

E—4

1865.

FULLER *against* GOODWIN.

The non-registration of a conveyance makes it void, as against a subsequent purchaser for value, under a deed duly registered, whether from the transferor himself, or from his assignee.

EJECTMENT for certain land at Kiama. The defendant was the tenant in possession at the time of the service of the summons. His landlord, *James Irving*, appeared and defended as landlord. It appeared at the trial before *Stephen*, C.J., that one *William Irving* had been seized of the land in question, and that on 1st May, 1861, he executed a mortgage of it to his brother, *James Irving*; but this conveyance was not registered. On the 4th of the following July, on the petition of a creditor, an order *nisi* for the sequestration of *William Irving's* estate was granted, which was made absolute on the 12th of the same month, and an official assignee appointed. On the 20th October, 1863, the official assignee conveyed the premises to the plaintiff for valuable consideration, and this conveyance was registered on the 7th March, 1865. On proof of these facts, the learned Judge being of opinion that under the 11th section of the Registration Act (*a*) the deed of 20th October, 1863, had priority, and that the plaintiff was therefore entitled to recover, directed the jury accordingly, reserving leave to the defendant, to move to enter a verdict for him, if the Court should consider such direction wrong.

June 7.

Stephen now, for the defendant, moved accordingly. The question is whether this section applies to a deed executed by the assignee of an insolvent, conveying the same property which the insolvent himself had before his sequestration conveyed, but by an unregistered deed? It is submitted that under such circumstances no estate and no potentiality whatever passed to the assignee, and

(*a*) 7 Vic., No. 16. The eleventh section enacts, that "all deeds and other instruments (wills excepted) affecting any lands or hereditaments, or any other property which shall be executed or made, *bonâ fide*, or for valuable consideration, and which shall be duly registered under the provisions of this Act, shall have and take priority, not according to their respective dates, but according to the priority of the registration thereof only."

so that the Registration Act does not apply. It applies only to cases where the same individual executes two conveyances, and not where one conveyance is executed by an insolvent and the other by his assignee. It is submitted that the statute only applies in cases where the intention or *bona fides* of the conveying party is material. [*Wise*, J. If so, an insolvent can keep all his real property from his creditors, by secret conveyances.] He referred to *Sugden's* Vendors and Purchasers (a), *Warburton* v. *Loveland* (b), and *Doe* v. *Rusham* (c).

1865.
FULLER
v.
GOODWIN.

Cur. ad. vult.

The judgment of the Court was now delivered by

June 12.

STEPHEN, C.J. In this case a person seized of certain land, executed a mortgage of it, and afterwards became insolvent. His assignee having (it would seem) no knowledge of that transaction—although whether he had such knowledge or not is, we conceive, immaterial —executed a conveyance of the same land, for valuable consideration, to the plaintiff. The latter instrument was registered immediately; and it is conceded, or the fact must be taken to have been found, that the plaintiff purchased the property innocently, and in good faith. The first instrument was not registered at all. The question is, under these circumstances, whether the plaintiff's conveyance shall or not prevail over that of the mortgagee?

The Registration Act of 1843, following the words of the old enactment in 6 G. 4, No. 22, gives "priority" to all deeds affecting property, if executed *bona fide*, according to the time of their registration. But section 18 of the Titles to Land Act, passed in 1858 (extended by the 24 Vic., No. 7), enacts that no instrument shall, by reason of bad faith in the conveying party, lose any "priority" to which it might be entitled by registration, if the party beneficially taking under it acted in good faith, and there was valuable consideration for the same.

(a) Ch. 22, s. 44.   (b) 2 Dow & Cl. 480.
(c) 17 Q.B. 732.

No amount of fraud, therefore, or bad faith, in a conveying party, will affect the efficacy or operation of a registered deed, where the taker is himself innocent, as here, and gives value for the property. The question is, in what manner does registration operate; for where there is no conflict as to priority—in other words, where there arises no question between two or more deeds, executed by the same transferor, or some person in his right, and conveying or purporting to convey the same property—registration is of no value. Registration is, at any rate not necessary (certain special cases excepted), to give efficacy to any deed. It appears clearly to us, that, in favour of an innocent taker for value who registers his deed, the statute confers on the conveying party, notwithstanding his previous inconsistent conveyance, if not registered, a title as against the transferee named therein; and thus enables the person secondly taking, immediately upon registration, to acquire that title.

Whether the first transferee, therefore, shall afterwards register his conveyance or not, the second deed will operate effectually against him. If he does so register, the words of the statute will be strictly applicable. There will then be "priority" in registration; and, each deed taking effect according to such priority, not according to its date, the second taker's will prevail. But it would be an absurd construction, that, because the Legislature has indiscreetly used this word "priority" in the enactment, a different result could be attained by the first taker's omitting to register at any time. This would be to give effect to the letter, in utter disregard of the substance and evident object of the statute; and to enable every transferee of an estate, concealing his title—created possibly for purposes of fraud—to defeat a subsequent meritorious purchaser at pleasure. By never registering the first conveyance, such a transferee would obtain more than impunity for his neglect; and no man could ever safely purchase property, whatever might be the precautions adopted.

But the objection was taken for the defendant, that the enactment applied only to cases of double transfer by

the same individual; since, although bad faith in the
conveying party was immaterial against an innocent
purchaser for value, yet the question of its existence is
still a matter for inquiry in every case—and there can
be no such question, as affecting a second conveyance
in disparagement of the first, where the second is by a
different person.   The assignee of the transferor, moreover, after the latter's insolvency, could not (it was
urged) have any estate to convey as his: for no estate
or title, after the conveyance, remained in the insolvent
—and none descended to the assignee, therefore, in his
right.

If the law were as thus contended for, it would follow
that persons taking property by deed, from a transferor
subsequently becoming insolvent, would be in a wholly
different position as to registration—or the security to
be gained by registering—from all other parties similarly acquiring property.   The transferees would enjoy
complete immunity from molestation, as to their titles;
for, as these need not be registered, the transactions
would rarely, if ever, be known.   The insolvent, on the
other hand, would be enabled to escape the consequences
of making such transfers, however fraudulent; while the
assignee, tracing title by the registry alone, would incur
the risk in all cases of conveying, or assuming to convey
property, which the purchasers might eventually not be
able to retain.   The Registration Acts, in short, or at
least their priority clauses, would not apply at all to
conveyances executed, under any circumstances, by men
who afterwards, at any time, are declared insolvent.
We are of opinion that such is not the law; and that,
as in the case of the English Registry Acts, although
the language certainly is different—see *Warburton* v.
Loveland (a)—the non-registration of a conveyance
makes it (in effect) void, as against a subsequent purchaser for value, under a deed duly registered, whether
from the transferor himself, or from his assignee.   The
Insolvent Act, sections 53 and 54, and the Amending
Act of 1843, section 14, vest in the assignees of an in-

(a) 2 Dow & Cl. 480.

1865.

FULLER
v.
GOODWIN.

solvent all his estates and rights of every kind; and it is declared that all powers vested in him, which he might have legally executed for his benefit, may be executed after sequestration by such assignees. The question of " bad faith " in an assignee, we conceive, in executing the conveyance of a property previously transferred by the insolvent, would not necessarily be excluded—in considering the validity or operation of the second conveyance. For the case, in that respect, is not analogous to the execution of a conveyance, for value, by a man's heir or devisee, of land conveyed voluntarily and without value, by the testator, as in *Doe* v. *Rusham* (a).

In the latter case, the execution by devisees was relied on, as operating under the statute 27 Eliz., c. 4 ; by which, conveyances to purchasers for value are made (constructively) to indicate fraud, in the execution of any previous transfer of the same property without value. But it was held, first, that devisees were clearly not purchasers for value; and secondly, that no act by these living persons could—by any construction whatever—be taken to show fraud, in the execution of a deed by their testator. Here, however, the only question of fraud would be as to the party himself (the assignee), in executing the second deed.

For these reasons we hold that the plaintiff claiming for value under the assignee is entitled to recover in this action ; and there will be no rule, therefore, to set aside the verdict.

Rule discharged.

(a) 17 Q.B. 732.

Ex parte ASHER.

W INDEYER moved to make absolute a rule calling on the District Court Judge of the South Western District Court, holden at Albury, and the Registrar of the said Court, and *George Adams* and *Henry Brooke*, to show cause why a writ of prohibition should not issue to restrain them, severally, from further proceeding in an action now pending in the District Court of Albury— on the ground that the said Court had no jurisdiction to hear and determine the said action; because, at the time the alleged cause of action accrued, and at the time of the issuing and service of the plaint and summons, the applicant did not reside within the jurisdiction of the Court; and that the applicant had been for six years and upwards a permanent resident at Sydney, and did not give any engagement or promise in writing to pay the alleged claim of the plaintiff, at any place specified within the jurisdiction of the said Court.

It appeared by the affidavit in support of the application that the applicant had been summoned, at his residence in Sydney, to appear at the Albury District Court, on 13th March instant; that at the time of the service of the summons, and for the previous six years, he had resided in Sydney with his wife and family; that about the 18th November, 1864, he went to Albury as a candidate for election to the Legislative Assembly; that for that purpose he was absent from Sydney till about December 30th; that he merely visited Albury for the purpose of contesting the election; and that the greater part of the alleged claim, which was for printing and advertisements, accrued before he left Sydney; and that he had not given the plaintiff, or any other person,

The defendant, residing and carrying on business in S., but who had contracted a debt while living temporarily at A., was sued for the amount in the District Court of the latter place, he being described in the plaint and summons as being of S. *Held*, that the defendant could at once apply for a prohibition, and was not bound first to raise the objection in the District Court where he sued.

The proviso of the sixth section of the District Court Act enacts, that "if any party after having in one place contracted a debt, or become liable for any damages recoverable in any District Court, shall, by removal, become resi-

dent within the jurisdiction of any other such Court, &c.," he may be sued in the Court of the district within the jurisdiction of which such debt or liability for damages arose. *Held*, that a District Court has no jurisdiction under this section in respect of the contracting of a debt within the creditor's district, unless the defendant at that time resided in that district.

The defendant, it appeared, remained at A. for six weeks, having visited the place for the purpose of contesting an election. *Held*, that he had not become resident there within the meaning of the sixth section.

any engagement or promise in writing to pay any debt or sum of money at any place specified within the jurisdiction of the said District Court of Albury.

The summons in the action was " Between *George Adams* and *Henry Brooks*, plaintiffs, of Albury, and *Morris Asher*, defendant, of Hunter-street, Sydney."

Windeyer in support of the application. The first question is whether, under these circumstances, *Asher* was resident at Albury ? It is submitted that it sufficiently appears on the affidavits that he was not resident ; for he was only there about six weeks at the time of the contracting of the debt. He referred to *Turner* v. *Nicholson* (a), *Ex parte Pollard* (b), and *Foster's* District Court Act (c). It is also submitted that *Sewell* v. *Jones* (d) shows that the defendant was not bound to wait till the District Court had proceeded to hear the case ; but, as it appeared on the face of the proceedings that he resided out of the jurisdiction of the Albury District Court, he was bound immediately, on being served with the plaint, to make the present application, and not take the chance of the District Court Judge's decision being in his favour; *De Haber* v. *The Queen of Portugal* (e).

Darley showed cause. On the first point it is contended that, under the sixth section (*f*) of the District Court Act, the mere contracting of a debt in Albury, and then " removing " to Sydney, is sufficient to give the Albury District Court jurisdiction. The defendant contracted

(a) 1 Sup. Ct. R., C. L. 171, in *nota*.
(b) 2 Sup. Ct. R., C. L. 192.   (c) p. 4.
(d) 19 L. J. Q. B. 372.   (e) 20 L. J. Q. B. 394.
(*f*) This section provides, " that in case the defendant in any action shall have given an engagement or promise in writing to pay any debt or sum, at a particular place specified, the plaintiff may, if he shall think fit, cause such defendant to be summoned to the Court within the jurisdiction of which the place so specified shall be: Provided that if any party after having in one place contracted a debt, or become liable for any damages recoverable in any District Court, shall, by removal, become resident within the jurisdiction of any other such Court, previously to the issuing of a summons for the recovery of such debt or damages, it shall be lawful for the plaintiff, if he shall think fit, to cause such defendant to be summoned to the Court holden for the district, within the jurisdiction of which such debt or liability for damages arose."

a debt in Albury, and he afterwards, " by removal, became resident" in Sydney. [*Wise*, J. The beginning of the section is wholly independent of the question of residence.] If a man goes into a district and there contracts a debt, and afterwards removes to another district, it is submitted that justice requires that, if possible, such a construction should be put upon these words as would enable the defaulting debtor to be sued in the district where the liability was incurred, rather than compel the creditor with his witnesses to go into another district—it may be, the other end of the colony—to prove his claim. The cases which may be relied on, on the other side, are all cases under the English County Court Act (*a*), where the words are, " where the plaintiff dwells more than twenty miles from the defendant ;' and such cases like that of *Butler* v. *Ablewhite* (*b*), therefore, have no application to cases under the local Act.

The defendant, moreover, should have pleaded in the District Court to the jurisdiction, and he is premature in making the present application before that Court has adjudicated on such pleading. Prohibition is granted on the ground that the inferior Court is assuming jurisdiction; but such Court cannot assume jurisdiction until it hears the case. It is for the District Court Judge to interpret the language of the Act ; and also to decide, in the first place, whether the case was within his jurisdiction. The Court is now asked to decide a matter of fact—the duty of deciding which is cast by law upon the District Court Judge. The question under the sixth question, whether the engagement sued upon was given by the authorised agent of the defendant—or whether a particular promise in writing to pay a debt was signed by the defendant—ought to be tried by the District Court Judge upon evidence, and not upon affidavit. *Marsden* v. *Wardle* (*c*) shows that a prohibition can be obtained after judgment. In *Sewell* v. *Jones* (*d*), where a prohibition was granted before the action was tried, the defect in the jurisdiction appeared on the face of the

1865.

Ex parte
ASHER.

(*a*) 9 & 10 Vic., c. 95, s. 128. (*b*) 28 L. J. C. P. 292.
(*c*) 23 L. J. Q. B. 263. (*d*) 19 L. J. Q. B. 372.

proceedings. So also in *De Haber* v. *The Queen of Portugal*, it appeared on the face of the proceedings that the defendant was an independent sovereign. In *Nicholson* v. *Turner* the District Court Judge had assumed jurisdiction, by wrongly deciding that the defendant lived at Maitland. He also referred to *McAllum* v. *Cookson* (a), and the judgment of *Wise*, J., in *Ex parte Grover* (b).

Windeyer replied.

STEPHEN, C. J. We are not at present agreed on the question, whether the present application is premature; but I will make one or two observations on the point. If this application is premature, I do not understand on what ground the Courts have granted prohibitions to the Vice Admiralty Courts in certain well known cases. The Vice Admiralty is not a national, but a European, or rather an international Court. It has jurisdiction over cases in respect of sailors' wages, foreign as well as domestic; but where the contract is special—as for instance, where the wages are to be paid by a proportion of the oil procured from the whales caught during the voyage—in such cases it has been held that the Vice Admiralty Court has no jurisdiction. It seems to me that, according to the arguments advanced by the plaintiff, the question whether the contract is special, ought first, in such cases, to be decided by the Vice Admiralty Court. But Courts of law have been accustomed to interpose at once, as soon as it appeared that the contract was special—on the ground that the jurisdiction of the Vice Admiralty Court was thereby ousted (c). It has been contended, also, there may be a difficulty in deciding, in cases under the sixth section, whether there is a written contract to pay at a particular place specified or not; in deciding, for instance, whether such contract was signed by an authorised agent, or whether the signature is or not a forgery. It seems to me that in cases of great difficulty a pro-

(a) 28 L. J. C. P. 1   (b) 1 Sup. Ct. R., C. L. 168.
(c) See *Howe* v. *Nappier*; Burr. 1944.

hibition might be refused, on the ground that the applicant has not made out his case.

In this case the defendant resides, and has always resided, in Sydney; he went down to Albury on an electioneering canvass. I do not say that the time might not have arrived when he would have become a resident there. But it seems as absurd to say that he became a resident there, because he stayed there six weeks, as it would to say that a Judge who might remain in a town six weeks on circuit, would thereby become resident in such town.

On the question raised as to the construction of the fifth and sixth sections of the District Courts Acts, I am prepared at once to give my judgment. I am of opinion that a District Court has no jurisdiction in respect of the contracting of a debt within the creditor's district, unless the defendant at that time resided there; for if not, he cannot be said to have "removed" or "become resident" in another district. And were this not so, a written promise to pay in the creditor's district would never be necessary (unless, indeed, in the case of a debt contracted by an agent) to give jurisdiction to a District Court out of the defendant's district; but every resident in a district, passing into or merely through a second district, and contracting a debt in the latter district, might be sued in the latter so soon as he removed therefrom, or passed on to his own district. On the question, whether the present application is premature, we will take time to consider the authorities.

I am further of opinion that the case of *Ex parte Grover*, in effect, has decided that section 6 must thus be construed. For, if not, the prohibition in that case would have been refused; inasmuch as it was clearly proved, that the defendant there contracted the debt in question in Maitland, and from thence went on (or, according to the plaintiff's argument here, *removed*) to his home at the Namoi. The defendant, moreover, had, on former occasions, paid the plaintiff claims of exactly the same character, and contracted under precisely the same circumstances, in Maitland. So that, if the con-

struction now contended for be the right one, the Maitland District Court had jurisdiction in *Grover's* case,
and the decision there by this Court was wrong. For
the reasons now given, therefore, and on the authority
of *Ex parte Grover*, I am clearly of opinion that a
District Court has no jurisdiction, under the sixth
section, in respect of the contracting of a debt within
the creditor's district, unless the defendant at that time
resided in that district. Such residence, doubtless,
might be a temporary one ; but there can be no "removal" to a second, unless there was a first, residence—
and here we both agree that *Asher*, the contracting
party, was not in the true sense ever a "resident" in
Albury.

WISE, J.   On one point we are prepared to give judgment ; and I am of opinion that a person is not liable
to be sued in a District Court for a debt contracted
within the district over which that Court has jurisdiction, unless he has been resident in the place where the
debt was contracted.   On the question of residence, I
refer to the language used by me in *Ex parte Grover;*
for I purposely used those words, because I do not wish
to decide that the defendant must ordinarily reside in
the place where he is sued.   The question must be
decided by the circumstances of each particular case.
The proviso of the sixth section says, that " if any party
after having in one place contracted a debt, or become
liable for any damages, recoverable in any District Court,
shall, by removal, become resident within the jurisdiction of any other Court," he shall be suable in the
former District Court.   A debt cannot be said to be
" recoverable in any District Court," unless the debtor
is *quoad* that Court resident ; and the proviso does not
apply, unless the debtor was liable to be sued in the
District Court of the place from which he has removed.

On the question of policy, I see danger in allowing
defendants to be sued in the place where the plaintiff
resides ; such a provision might confer great powers of
extortion.   As the law is, the plaintiff can protect him-

self; he is subject to no abuse, but what he brings on himself by his own act.

Cur. ad. vult.

Their Honors delivered judgment in this case as follows :—

STEPHEN, C. J. The defendant, a merchant residing and carrying on business in Sydney, but who had contracted a debt while living temporarily at Albury, was sued for the amount in the District Court of that place. He thereupon applied for a prohibition—on an affidavit that he had never resided (except for a short time as a visitor) in the district, and had never given any promise in writing to pay the debt there. In the plaint and summons, the defendant was described as being of Sydney ; so that *prima facie* the want of jurisdiction appeared, in the Court itself, on the face of the proceedings. There was a contest, whether the case did not after all come within the Act, if not by reason of residence, yet because of the writing of a certain letter. These points, however, we decided in the defendant's favour—reserving judgment on the question, only, whether the motion for this prohibition was premature.

I have, since the argument, fully considered the matter, and looked into the authorities ; and I am of opinion that the writ asked for ought to be granted.

The cases most relied on for the plaintiff were— *Kimpton* v. *Willey* (a), and *Lilley* v. *Harvey* (b). In the latter, the motion for the prohibition was, as here, before trial; the objection being, that the jurisdiction of the County Court was ousted, by title to land coming in question. But the Queen's Bench held, that the assertion of that fact could not avoid the jurisdiction—and that the County Court had authority to inquire whether title really did come in question. Had that fact been disclosed on the pleadings, however, Mr. Justice *Wightman* intimates that the prohibition must have issued ; since there would, in such case, have been nothing on the point to try. There is a recent decision to the same

(a) 1 L.M. & P. 281 ; 19 L.J.Q.B. 269.   (b) 17 L.J.Q.B. 357.

effect in the *Skipton Industrial Society* v. *Prince* (a).
By statute, certain societies (that at Skipton being one)
may refer disputes between them and their members to
arbitration ; and County Courts are empowered to enforce the award.   On motion for a prohibition (the
action being on an award made ostensibly under such a
reference, against a person alleged to be a member) the
Queen's Bench held that whether there was such a dispute, within the meaning of the statute, must in the
first instance be determined by the County Court.

The case of *Kimpton* v. *Willey* is less to the point—
the prohibition there having been applied for after verdict, and the contest being, whether the want of jurisdiction had been shown in fact, and on which side the
onus of proof lay.

The cases abstracted are, in my opinion, distinguishable from the present, on the ground that here the want
of jurisdiction is apparent, until new facts be shown on
the face of the plaintiff's own proceedings—and that the
question is not, as to the exclusion of jurisdiction, in
a case ordinarily or presumably within it, but whether
the defendant (on the description in the plaint) ever was
personally amenable to that jurisdiction.   Thus, in
Sewell v. *Jones* (b), where the pleading in the County
Court itself disclosed the objection relied on (namely,
that title to land would come in question), the Queen's
Bench granted a prohibition before trial.   Mr. Justice
Wightman, in delivering judgment, comments on the
inconvenience which would result from delay, in case
the local Court decided that no question of title did
arise.   In that event, he observes, an application for the
writ would certainly be made, which, nevertheless, the
defendant might not be able for some time to procure.
If this afforded a reason for immediate interposition, in
the case of an English County Court, how much more
force is there in the argument applied to suits in the
District Courts of this colony, some of which may be
distant from a defendant's residence three hundred miles
or more.   The distinction, however, between cases where

(a) 11 Jur. N. S. 12 ; 33 L.J.Q.B. 323.   (b) 19 L.J.Q.B. 372.

the inferior Court has, ordinarily, jurisdiction over the subject matter or the defendant, but either exceeds or is by some special circumstance ousted of that jurisdiction —and cases where the subject itself, or the party sued, is *prima facie* altogether outside the jurisdiction—may be collected from all the decisions. *Wadsworth* v. *The Queen of Spain* (a), and the numerous cases in which prohibitions have been granted, against suits in the Ecclesiastical and Admiralty Courts, are instances.

The defendant here is in effect described, as in *Ex parte Grover* (b) (where, however, the prohibition was after judgment), as residing out of the district to which he was summoned. Living in Sydney, he was sued at Albury where the debt was contracted, distant from Sydney 350 miles and upwards. Now the District Courts Act, section 5, gives a District Court jurisdiction only over persons resident within its own district. There the enactment stops. Clearly, therefore, (or at least presumably so), this defendant never was subject to the Albury Court. And section 46 directs—perhaps for the very purpose of indicating the jurisdiction—that the last known place of abode of the defendant shall be stated in the plaint. But, possibly (it was urged) by some fact or matter not alleged, the defendant may— under the provisions of some other clause—be amenable to the Albury Court. The sixth section, no doubt, contains two provisos, under one or the other of which, it was said, the defendant might have been shown to come. I conceive that this possibility is no answer to the application. If the plaintiff had alleged on oath that in fact the defendant was within one of the categories, stating which, a question of more difficulty would have existed.

The defendant, when moving for the prohibition, denied specifically (and I think that he was bound to deny) the existence of all matters, which would have made this sixth section applicable. On that denial, a serious conflict of allegation might have arisen; and I am not prepared to say, that in such a case this Court would feel called on, at that stage, to interfere further.

(a) 17 Q.B. 218.   (b) 1 Sup. Ct. R., C.L. 168.

Yet, it is certain, that after a verdict in the District
Court on the controverted points, affirming the jurisdiction, we should on a similar motion be compelled to
decide ; since a wrong finding on the facts, by a subordinate tribunal, cannot in any case give it jurisdiction.
It is sufficient to say, however, that there arose here no
conflict of allegation ; the only questions raised being
questions of law.   The one most debated was, whether
the defendant—by lodging for a few weeks at Albury,
and within that period contracting the debt sued for—
had in respect of that debt subjected himself to the
local Court.   On that question, we were, on the construction of the Act, in the defendant's favour.

I am, therefore, of opinion that the prohibition asked
for in this case ought to issue ; and I see no sufficient
reason, although it may press hardly on the plaintiff,
for refusing to the defendant his costs of the motion.

WISE, J.   The question remaining for our decision
in this case is, whether a defendant sued in a District
Court, within the jurisdiction of which he never was a
resident, can at once apply to this Court for a prohibition, or whether he must first raise the objection in
the District Court itself.

This argument is founded upon the enactment in the
sixth section, which gives jurisdiction to the District
Court in several cases, notwithstanding the defendant's
non-residence within the local limits of the Court.   And
it was contended by Mr. *Darley* that, as in these cases,
the jurisdiction would depend upon a question of fact;
it could not be anticipated that the District Court
Judge would come to a wrong decision upon the facts
before him, and that, therefore, it was premature for
this Court to interfere.   I was certainly much struck
with the argument ; but I am now satisfied that this
Court must interpose by prohibition as soon as it is
judicially satisfied that the suit is not within the jurisdiction of the Court, whether by reason of the subject
matter, or of the non-residence of the defendant, and the
non-existence of any of the conditions required by the

sixth section to give the District Court jurisdiction, not-withstanding the non-residence of the defendant within its limits. In addition to the cases referred to in the judgment of his Honor the Chief Justice, I would refer to *Re Walsh* (a). Prohibition was there granted before any appearance in the inferior Court, on the ground that the cause of action was not one of those which could be brought against a resident out of the jurisdiction, inasmuch as it arose out of the local limits of the Court. The present is the. converse; the subject matter being within the jurisdiction, but the person not. The principle is, however, I think, the same, and falls within what is laid down by Lord *Coke* (b), that the King's Courts may award prohibition, being informed that any Court, temporal or ecclesiastical, doth hold plea of that whereof they have not jurisdiction, as well after judgment and execution as before.

If this were not so, great injustice and hardship might arise; for, according to the decision of the Court of Exchequer in *Lawford* v. *Partridge* (c), the inferior Court, in the absence of any special enactment, has no jurisdiction to award costs where the suit abates by reason of the want of jurisdiction. It would, therefore, be a strange anomaly if a person sued in a Court without jurisdiction should be without a remedy, except upon the condition of appearing in Court at his own cost to resist such illegal assumption of jurisdiction. I am aware of the case of the *Skipton Industrial Society* v. *Prince;* but even assuming that decision to be right upon some special ground, it does not affect to overrule the previous cases in which prohibitions have been granted before appearance in the inferior Court. If, indeed, the want of jurisdiction is not clear upon the affidavits, the Court would, I apprehend, direct the applicant to declare in prohibition, and the final decision would depend upon the result of the trial. Thus, for instance, there might, upon the affidavits, be a direct conflict of evidence as to his residence or any other fact

(a) 1 E. & B. 383.   (b) 2 Inst. 602.
                    (c) 20 L. J. Ex. 147.

F—4

involving the question of jurisdiction; and in such a
case the Court would direct the applicant to declare in
prohibition.   I agree, therefore, that in this case the
rule must be absolute, and I see no reason for exempting
the plaintiff below from the payment of the costs.

It may be convenient for me here to mention that the
whole question of the right to issue prohibition was recently argued before me by Mr. *Darley* and Mr. *Salomons*, and after examining all the authorities, I decided
that if a defendant is sued for a cause of action within
the jurisdiction of the Court, and is duly served with a
summons, he cannot, after the cause has been tried in
the District Court, obtain a prohibition, on the ground
of his residence beyond the local limits of the Court, if
the District Court Judge came to a right conclusion
upon the evidence then before him.   In the words of
Lord *Mansfield*, in *Buggin* v. *Bennet* (a):—" If it appears
upon the face of the proceedings that the Court below
have no jurisdiction, a prohibition may issue at any
time, either before or after sentence, because all is a
nullity; it is *coram non judice*.   But where it does not
appear upon the face of the proceedings, if the defendant
below will lie by, or suffer that Court to go on under
an apparent jurisdiction as upon a contract made at sea,
it would be unreasonable that this party, who, when
defendant below, has thus lain by and concealed from
the Court below a collateral matter, should come hither
after sentence against him there, and suggest that
collateral matter as a cause of prohibition, and obtain
a prohibition upon it, after all this acquiescence in the
jurisdiction of the Court below.   It is to be remembered,
however, that if the subject matter of the suit is not
within the jurisdiction, a prohibition may be applied for,
whether before or after appearance in the inferior Court,
and even after judgment."

(a) 4 Burr. 2087.

1865.

THE QUEEN *against* CORCORAN.   June 5.

SPECIAL case reserved for the consideration of the Judges, under the 13 Vic., No. 8.

"This prisoner was tried and convicted before me at Goulburn, of a robbery with arms, and wounding a person in the prosecution of that crime. During the trial discussions arose, on an objection to the receipt of any evidence of belief as to the prisoner's identity. I held that such evidence was admissible—although a belief on insufficient grounds, I observed, would be of little, and might be of no value.

Evidence of belief as to a prisoner's identity is admissible, although a belief on insufficient grounds would be of little, and might be of no, value.

"Several questions were then put and answered in succession, as nearly as I could write them down as follows :—' Have you any grounds for a belief as to the person? I have. What are they? His make, and his height. From this I think that it was the prisoner. I was too much excited to observe more. Which of the three do you believe that it was? The tallest. Did you think so at the time? I did. I do believe it to be the prisoner.'

"The point reserved is, on the demand of prisoner's counsel, whether any part of those questions, or of the answers to them, ought to have been rejected.

"There was other evidence given against the prisoner, however, of a positive nature, as to his identity, in the course of the trial.

ALFRED STEPHEN."

2nd June, 1865.

No counsel appeared for the prisoner.

Per Curiam. The evidence is clearly admissible, and the conviction must be sustained (a).

Conviction sustained.

(a) *R.* v. *Hodges.* 30th December, 1853. (Before *Stephen*, C. J., *Dickinson*, J., and *Therry*, J.) It was decided that a witness clearly may be asked as to, and may state his belief as to, the identity of a person, or of property. And the Court thought the point clear, but added that such testimony would be of no value, unless there are probable grounds stated for it. See Tayl. Ev., 4th Ed., ss. 1272, 1273.

1865.

March 24.   THE QUEEN *against* GEORGE LAUNT and others.

Where the deposition of a deceased witness, taken in accordance with the provisions of Sir *John Jervis'* Act, contained hearsay evidence, the Judge directed the whole of the deposition to be read, but told the jury not to pay any attention to the hearsay testimony. *Held*, that this was the proper course to be pursued.

SPECIAL case for the consideration of the Judges, under 13 Vic., No. 8.

"The prisoners were indicted and tried before me, as Chairman of Quarter Sessions at Mudgee, in the colony of New South Wales, on the 15th March, 1865, for feloniously stealing (with second count for receiving), on the 19th February, 1864, at Yaminbar, in the said colony, one horse and twenty-six oxen, the property of *Ebenezer Orr*.

"The Crown prosecutor having given the necessary proofs for the admission of the depositions of *John Ward*, a constable then dead, the same depositions were read to the jury, and are as follows:"

The depositions were then set out at length, and contained in parts some hearsay evidence—as for instance, "from information I received, I was led to believe that the prisoners, with four or five others, were riding about Mr. *Orr's* run, driving horses and cattle for some illegal purpose;" and again, "we knew it would be of no use to try and apprehend them at that time, as they knew the country better than us, and had better horses than we had;" and further on, "Mr. *Orr* said to us it was all right, he was perfectly satisfied they were the parties he had spoken to me about;" and again, "I thought it advisable not to try and apprehend the prisoners till they were all fairly inside the tent;" and there were other portions of the depositions of the same kind.

The special case then stated " that the counsel for the prisoners objected to these portions of the deposition being read to the jury, on the ground that they were hearsay evidence. or evidence of facts unconnected with the issue or statements made not in the presence or hearing of the prisoners.

"I directed the jury to exclude from their consideration those portions of the depositions which were objected to.

" It was elicited on the cross-examination of Mr. *Orr*, that he (Mr. *Orr*) did tell constable *Ward* that he (Mr. *Orr*) was perfectly satisfied the *Launts*, meaning the prisoners, were the parties he (Mr. *Orr*) had spoken to constable *Ward* about, and were the parties driving the cattle.

" The prisoners were found guilty.

" It was reserved for the consideration of the Supreme Court whether such portions of the above depositions, as were objected to, ought to have been read.

HENRY CARY,
Chairman of Q. S."

March 17th, 1865.

Isaacs for the prisoner. The 17th section of *Jervis'* Act (a) provides that, under certain circumstances, it shall be lawful to read the deposition of a witness who is dead, as evidence in the prosecution; but the evidence thus rendered admissible must, it is submitted, be legal evidence. Mr. *Taylor* (b), in his work of Evidence, says, " when depositions are tendered in evidence as secondary proof of oral testimony, they are, of course, open to all the objections which might have been raised, had the witness himself been personally present at the trial. Leading and other illegal questions are, therefore, constantly suppressed, together with the answers to them; and this, too, whether the testimony has been taken *viva voce*, or by written interrogatories; " and he cites *Hutchinson* v. *Bernard* (c), where that course was pursued by *Patteson*, J. In *Scarfe's* case (d), where three prisoners were indicted for felony, and a witness for the prosecution was proved to be absent through the procurement of one of them, the Court held that his deposition might be read in evidence as against the prisoner who had kept him out of the way, but that it could not be received as against the other two; and the Court granted a new trial, because the Judge had left such evidence generally to the jury, and had not pointed out that it applied only to such prisoner.

(a) 11 & 12 Vic., c. 42.   (b) s. 493.
(c) 2 M. & R. 1.   (d) 17 Q. B. 238; 2 Den. 281.

SUPREME COURT REPORTS.

Pell, for the Crown, relied on the words of the 17th section, and contended that it must be left to the discretion of the presiding Judge to order how much of the deposition should be read, and to direct the jury as to its effect, as it was inconvenient and almost impossible for the Judge to eliminate, usefully and effectually, all the inadmissible matter, until the rest of the deposition had been read.

STEPHEN, C. J. The words in the 17th section of the 11 and 12 Vic., c. 42, being, " it shall be lawful to read such deposition as evidence," I am of opinion that the whole of this deposition was rightly read. It might have been safer and better if the words had been, as in 1 W. IV., c. 22, that the deposition or examination should be read, "saving all just exceptions."

WISE, J. The prisoner, when on his examination before the justices, might get on the depositions some evidence which he might then think favorable to him ; shall he afterwards be allowed to object to such evidence being read, because it is in strictness legally inadmissible ?

Conviction confirmed.

THE QUEEN *against* LOTZE.

June 13, 30.

An informa-
tion charged
L. with falsely
pretending
" that he had
good right
and full power
and authority
to sell and

SPECIAL case stated under the 13th Vic., No. 8, s. 2. " The defendant was indicted and tried before me at the last Sydney gaol delivery, for obtaining a promissory note from *Edward Flood,* in part payment of 1000 head of cattle.

dispose of" certain cattle, by means of which he obtained a certain promissory note, the property of *Flood,* whereas, in truth and in fact, he had not "good right and full power and authority to sell and dispose of" the said cattle. It appeared that a treaty was pending between the agent employed by *L.* and *Flood,* and at *Flood's* request *L.* was asked whether he was selling as a principal or as agent for the previous owner. *L.* replied that he was selling as a principal, and added, " we had a mortgage over the station (on which the cattle were depastured), but foreclosed it, and are now in possession." *Held,* that this was evidence to support the finding that *L.* did make the representation charged.

Held also (*Wise,* J., *dissentient*), that the representation was not sufficient in law to support the charge of a false pretence within the meaning and intent of the statute.

" The information stated that *Edward Lotze*, on the &c., at &c., unlawfully, knowingly, and designedly, did falsely pretend to one *John Brewster* that he the said *Edward Lotze*, and one *James Macdonald Larnach*, then trading under the name of *Lotze* and *Larnach*, were then possessed of a certain cattle station called Southgate Station, and certain cattle, to wit, 1000 head of cattle upon the said station, and had good right and full power and authority to sell and dispose of the said cattle, by means of which said false pretences he, the said *Edward Lotze*, did then and there unlawfully obtain from the said *John Brewster* a certain valuable security, to wit, a promissory note for the sum of £333 6s. 8d., of the property of one *Edward Flood*, with intent thereby then to defraud, whereas, in truth and in fact, the said *Edward Lotze* and *James Macdonald Larnach*, so trading under the name of *Lotze* and *Larnach* as aforesaid, were not then possessed of a certain cattle station called Southgate Station, and were not then possessed of the said 1000 head of cattle upon the said station, and had not good right and full power and authority to sell and dispose of the said cattle, as he, the said *Edward Lotze*, then well knew.

" The facts of the case appeared to be these :—The defendant was in partnership, in Sydney, with one *Larnach*, and the firm (some time before the transaction with *Flood*) had become owners of the station and cattle in question, under an assignment or transfer from a Mr. *Sharp*, the former holder. They mortgaged it, however, together with all the cattle thereon, to the Bank of New South Wales—and afterwards, being in want of money, employed Mr. *John Brewster* as their agent to sell 1000 of the same cattle for them; but the only partner who actually instructed, or ever saw this agent on the subject, was the defendant. Negotiations having commenced in August last, between Mr. *Brewster* and Mr. *Flood*, it appears that the latter wished (for some reason not disclosed) to ascertain if the cattle were still *Sharp's* — or, in other words, whether *Lotze* and *Larnach* were selling as his agents, or on their own account as principals. *Flood* therefore made the specific inquiry from *Brewster*, and the latter saw the defendant accordingly, and put the question to him; to which, the defendant answered that they were principals, adding, ' we had a mortgage over *Sharp's* station, but foreclosed it, and are now in possession.' Mr. *Brewster* repeated this to Mr. *Flood*, and almost immediately afterwards the purchase was completed—the latter relying on this assurance, and declaring at the trial that but for his belief in the statement, he would not have made the bargain. Mr. *Flood* had no suspicion whatever, nor had *Brewster*, that the bank or any other claimant had at the time a mortgage over the property.

"This representation through Mr. *Brewster* was relied on as evidence of the pretence charged—that the defendant was then possessed of the 1000 cattle, and had good right and full power to sell the same. It was submitted, however, for the defendant—first, that the fact of the pretence alleged was not shown by that evidence; and secondly, that a representation of that kind amounted to no more than a warranty of title—the breach of which could not support the charge of a false pretence within the meaning of the statute. On the latter of these points I had so much doubt that it at first occurred to me to direct an acquittal; but, after conferring with Mr. Justice *Wise*, I resolved on sending the case to the jury, reserving the point for the opinion of the Court, in case of a conviction—and in the meantime, according to the invariable practice under such circumstances, holding the defendant to bail. On the first point I felt less difficulty; but this also I reserved, at the demand of the defendant's counsel.

"Of the fact that Mr. *Flood* gave to *Lotze* and *Larnach*, through their agent Mr. *Brewster*, the promissory note in question (being the amount of the first instalment of the purchase), and that Mr. *Flood* thereupon sent to the station to obtain delivery of the cattle, but was prevented from receiving any by the bank, there can be no doubt. The fact is, that, either having heard of the transaction with *Flood*, or finding that *Lotze* and

Larnach had got into irretrievable embarrassment, the
bank early in October—the sale by *Brewster* having
been closed on the 25th August—sent up an agent to
the station, who took possession of it and the cattle. In
the month of December, the firm was declared insolvent.
The promissory note had previously been negotiated,
and at maturity it was paid.

"The defence set up was simply this—that the defendant in concert with his partner really believed,
notwithstanding the mortgage, that they were entitled
to sell the 1000 head of cattle. As evidence of this,
the defendant produced two letters, dated in April, 1863,
pending the negotiations for the mortgage, in one of
which the bank consented to allow *Lotze* and *Larnach* to
sell all 'surplus' stock on the station, and to pay themselves the working expenses out of the proceeds, handing
over to the bank the balance. At that time there was
considerable litigation between the parties as to the
property. The mortgage deed itself was not executed
until April 1864, and that contained most stringent
provisions in direct conflict with any such power. But
their solicitor, Mr. *Robberds*, swore (his evidence on this
point being strongly objected to, but received by me
after argument) that he advised them afterwards, that
they had still the right to surplus stock. Messrs. *Lotze*
and *Larnach* consulted him on the question, in reference
apparently to the very negotiation which *Flood* now
impeached, saying that they wanted cash for station
expenses. Mr. *Robberds* thereupon told the defendant
that they could so sell for that purpose; giving it as
his reason, on cross-examination, that the mortgage was
subject to the arrangement previously made, because the
deed was founded on it. I told the jury as to this—that
if the defendant asked and obtained that advice *bona
fide*, and really believed that he had power to sell the
stock in question, he could not be guilty of this charge,
whether the advice given was correct or not.

"The question still remained, however, whether the
defendant believed that the 1000 head came in fact
within the description? Was that number of cattle

really believed by him to be 'surplus' stock within the
true meaning of that expression in the letters of 1863?
To show that they were (or probably might have been)
so deemed, a good deal of evidence was given by the
superintendent, and adduced from the station books and
returns, showing the number of cattle on the station at
different periods, their increase from time to time, the
grazing capabilities of the property, and the probable
number for disposal, or which ought in due course to
be got rid of as in excess, at the time of the sale. It
was shown that the station expenses were, throughout
1864, unusually heavy, and that some previous sales had
been at a serious loss to the partnership. But the jury
found specially, that the defendant did not believe himself entitled to sell the 1000 head. Four jurors thought
that his belief might have extended to 600 head, but
eight were of opinion that he fraudulently sold the
whole. All, therefore, found the defendant guilty; and
I sentenced him accordingly (as the law requires) upon
the verdict—but having reference to the point reserved
by me, admitted him to bail as already intimated.

"The questions for the opinion of the Judges are the
following :—First, whether there was evidence to go to
the jury to support the allegation that the defendant in
fact represented or pretended that he had 'good right
and full power' to sell the cattle in question? Second,
whether for the making of such a representation, although
false and with intent to defraud, an indictment will lie
as for a false pretence within the statute?

ALFRED STEPHEN." (a).

Martin, Q. C. (Windeyer with him), for the Crown.
It is contended that the evidence did not make out
the pretence alleged in the information. There is no
evidence of any representation by the defendant of his
having the right or power to sell these cattle. The

(a) This case was twice argued—on the first occasion, on June
9th (before Stephen, C. J., and Wise, J.), by Martin, Q. C., for the
prisoner, and the Attorney-General (Darvall) for the Crown ; on the
second occasion, on June 30th (before Stephen, C. J., Wise, J., and
Hargrave, J.), by Martin, Q. C., for the prisoner, and Sir W. Manning,
Q. C., for the Crown.

evidence is, that on enquiry whether they were selling as agents or principals, the defendant said as principals. He might have sold as a principal, and yet not have asserted or meant to assert that he had power to sell.

It is also submitted that the representation charged is no false pretence within the statute. In order to come within the statute, there must be a statement that some particular thing is a fact, which is not a fact; and a statement of an erroneous conclusion from certain facts is not sufficient. In *Rex.* v. *Codrington*, in 1825 (a), the defendant was charged with obtaining £29 3s., by falsely pretending to a person named *Varlow* that he was entitled to a reversionary interest in one-seventh share of a sum of money left by his grandfather. It appeared that the defendant had, by means of the representation alleged, induced the prosecutor to purchase it, on the 22nd of December, for £29 3s.—the defendant having in fact sold all his interest in it to one *Pick*, on the 18th of the previous September. To prove the pretence a deed, in which was the usual covenant for title, assigning the defendant's interest to *Varlow*, was tendered, and rejected by *Littledale*, J., on the ground that a covenant in a deed cannot be taken to be a false pretence. The prosecutor then proved the pretence, and the previous sale to *Pick*; and *Littledale*, J., held, with regard to this parol evidence, that it was only a ground for a civil action. "The doctrine contended for, on the part of the prosecution," says that learned Judge, "would make every breach of warranty or false assertion, at the time of a bargain, a transportable offence." The next case in which *Codrington's* case is noticed, *R.* v. *Crossley*, in 1837 (b), where the indictment stated that the prisoner, by falsely pretending that he was then provided with sufficient funds to pay the full amount of a particular bill of exchange, excepting £300, obtained the last mentioned sum. When the *R.* v. *Codrington* was cited, *Patteson*, J., said, "in that case it does not appear that the prisoner did distinctly allege that he had a good title to the estate he was selling." This remark shows that

(a) 1 C. & P. 661. (b) 2 Mood. R. 17.

Patteson, J., thought that, on this defect of proof, *Codrington's* case could be maintained; and, therefore, his dictum is in favor of the defendant, as he did not allege anything about warranty of title, but only that he was selling as principal. The next case is *Reg.* v. *Adamson*, in 1843 (a), in which the prisoner was charged with falsely pretending to one *H.* that he had obtained the appointment of emigration agent at Port Phillip, which was worth £600 a year, and that for £200 he would give *H.* one-third of the emigration agentship, and that he would be sure to have back his £200 out of the emigration agentship the first year. The evidence showed that the prisoner obtained the money by means of the alleged pretences, and that the latter were false. It also showed that the prisoner proposed to *H.* to become his partner, and promised—if the proposal were accepted, and the £200 advanced as a bonus—that *H.* should have a third share of the emigration agentship. Before the money had been obtained a partnership deed was executed by the prisoner and *H.* The consideration of the partnership was stated in the deed to be £200, and no mention was made of the emigration agency in respect thereof. It was objected that as the deed did not contain the pretences stated in the indictment, but on the contrary represented the £200 to be given in consideration of a general partnership, the parol evidence of the false pretences ought to be rejected, and the prisoner acquitted; and *R.* v. *Codrington* was cited in support of this argument. But it was held that parol evidence was admissible of the false pretences laid in the indictment, although a deed between the parties stating different considerations for parting with the money be put in evidence. But no such point as that for which it was cited was decided in *R.* v. *Codrington*, and its authority remains, therefore, untouched by *R.* v. *Adamson*. It follows, therefore, that the remark made in *R.* v. *Kenrick* (b), as to *R.* v. *Codrington* having been doubted, is erroneous. In *Kenrick's* case there were three counts charging a conspiracy, and two (which were

(a) 2 Mood. C. C. 286.   (b) 5 Q. B. 49.

abandoned) charging the obtaining money by falsely pretending that certain horses were the property of a private person, and not of a horse dealer. But the Court gave its opinion on them (as it would seem, unnecessarily, and therefore extrajudicially) as follows:—"A general question seems here to be raised, whether, if money be obtained through the medium of a contract between the defendant and the party defrauded, the charge of false pretences can be sustained. Questions approaching this have been raised in the Criminal Courts. With some plausibility, the thing obtained through the false pretence may be said to be the contract, and not the money which is paid in fulfilment of it, and which the party is probably by its terms liable to pay. This was the ground on which his brother *Littledale* directed an acquittal in *R.* v. *Codrington*." It is submitted that the case cited seems to have been misunderstood; and at all events, neither this nor the preceding case show that a false warranty of title is a fraud, for in both cases the warranty was of a distinct fact, and the two cases are authorities only for the position that there may be a false pretence made in the course of a written contract. *R.* v. *Codrington* is also cited in *Reg.* v. *Abbott* (a), in which it is decided that a false pretence knowingly made to obtain money is indictable, although the money be obtained by means of a contract, which the prosecutor was induced by the falsehood to make. In that case the main false pretence was that a certain sample of cheese, which the prisoner had given the prosecutor to taste, was taken from a cheese offered for sale, whereas, in truth, it was taken from a cheese of very superior quality, and the money was thus obtained. This was a clear false pretence; but the case is no authority to the effect that a false warranty of title is a crime. It affirms the three preceding cases, but does not overrule *Codrington's* case more than they do. So also *Reg.* v. *Bates*, in 1848 (b), calls in question *Codrington's* case, but only in the same way as the preceding cases, without deciding that a false warranty of title is indictable. The

(a) 1 Den. 273; 2 Cox C. C. 430.　　(b) 3 Cox C. C. 201.

1865.

The Queen
v.
Lotze.

next case is *Reg.* v. *Eagleton* (a), which clearly shows that the Court did not consider *Abbott's* case and *Kenrick's* case decisive. The point in these cases is there stated to be, whether the statute against obtaining money under false pretences applies where there was some bargain or consideration for giving the money, and so some cause for the giving other than the false pretence —and not whether a false warranty of title is within the statute; and, therefore, *Codrington's* case is untouched by this judgment as to the point in controversy here. In *Oates'* case, in 1855 (b), the indictment charged that the prisoner falsely pretended that he having executed certain work there was a certain sum of money "due and owing" to him on account of the work, whereas there was not "due and owing" such amount; and the Court held the indictment bad, inasmuch as a false pretence of an existing fact was not sufficiently alleged, and it could be proved by evidence of a mere wrongful overcharge. It is submitted that there is no difference in principle between the assertion of a right to demand 6s. 6d. and a right to sell. *Pollock*, C. B., in giving judgment, says, " considering this as an allegation, merely that so much was 'due and owing,' it may involve many questions both of law and fact. The allegations of a false pretence should be clear and precise, in order that you may see on the face of the indictment whether it discloses a false statement of an existing fact. The statute was never intended to extend to cases where the transaction between the parties is really one of buying and selling, although there may be a degree of fraud in the representations made by the vendor." *Burgon's* case (c), in 1856, was a case where a party obtained an advance of money upon a representation that a house had been built upon some land which he proposed to mortgage, when in fact there was no such house. It is submitted that the pretence here alleged was of an existing fact. In the course of the argument, *Codrington's* case was improperly relied on as an authority that a

(a) Pearce & Dears. 515 ; 24 L. J. M. C. 164.
(b) Pearce & Dears. 469.   (c) Dears. & B. 11 ; 25 L. J. M. C. 105.

pretence forming a constituent part of a written contract was not indictable; and the decision, therefore, does not affect the present argument. In *Roebuck's* case (*a*), in 1856, which was twice argued, *Abbott's* case and *Kenrick's* case, although acted upon, were doubted by almost every member of the Court. In giving judgment, Lord *Campbell* says, " I think it right to say that, although the doctrine seems to me to be untenable, that there can be no false pretence within the statute if it be made in the course of a contract, I should have been very loath to concur in the doctrine which was laid down in *Reg.* v. *Kenrick*, and was acted upon in *Reg.* v. *Abbott*, and I should have been inclined to adhere to the decision of *Littledale*, J., in *R.* v. *Codrington.*" In *Bryan's* case (*b*), in 1857, the pretence was that certain spoons had as much silver on them as *Elkington's* A., and that the foundations were of the best material; and it was held by a large majority of the Court, that as it was a mere misrepresentation of the quality of the commodity during a bargain for the purchase of it, it was not within the statute. The dicta of the various Judges are very applicable to this case; and very great doubt is thrown upon *Abbott's* and *Kenrick's* case in the judgment of *Creswell*, J. In *Sherwood's* case (*c*) the conviction was supported, on the ground that the prisoner, having sold the article and delivered it, when there came to be a question about the price, represented as a fact the quantity to be more than it really was. The same principle was applied in the cases of *Reg.* v. *Goss* and *Ragg* (*d*), in 1860, where the false representation by the prisoner in the latter case was, that he had delivered 15 cwt. of coal, when he knew that he had only delivered 8 cwt. ; and in the former, that a taster of a different and superior cheese produced as a sample, had formed part of, and been taken out of, the cheese sold. He also referred to *Reg.* v. *Evans* (*e*). It is submitted that in all the cases referred to, the distinction is recog-

(*a*) Dears. & B. 24; 25 L. J. M. C. 101.
(*b*) 1 Dears. & B. 265; 26 L. J. M. C. 84.
(*c*) 1 Dears. & B. 251; 26 L. J. M. C. 217.
(*d*) 1 Bell 215; 29 L. J. M. C. 86.
(*e*) Leigh & Cave 252; 32 L. J. M. C 38.

nised between statements of matters of fact known to be
false, and a false assertion of a mere matter of opinion.
Can it be maintained that the prisoner's guilt or innocence can depend on the view which may be taken by a
jury as to his right to sell a larger or smaller number of
cattle? There must be an affirmation of a fact, a definite and simple fact, and not as in this case, a compound
proposition made up of fact and inference.

The *Attorney General* for the Crown (a). The representation was substantially the one charge against the
prisoner. He said, in answer to enquiry, that their firm
had foreclosed, and were selling as principals, and were
in possession. What could that mean, if not that they
were the owners and had power to sell?

It is also submitted that if there be a false assertion
leading to a contract, and by which a contract is induced, an indictment lies, although there may have been
a contract entered into respecting or warranting the
assertion. The question will be, whether the money
was obtained by the representation? What is a representation that the speaker had full right, power, and
authority to sell, but a representation of a matter of fact?
In *Reg.* v. *Maria Giles* (b), an indictment charging the
prisoner with obtaining monies from a wife, whose husband had run away, by falsely pretending to her that
she, the prisoner, had power to bring him back over
hedges and ditches, was held to be good. *Erle, C. J.,*
in his judgment, says, "the pretence is of a power either
physical, moral, or supernatural; and obtaining money
by the false assertion of such a power, whatever it may
be, is, in our opinion, an indictable offence within the
letter of the statute, and within the mischief intended to
be prevented by it." The case shows that where a deliberate fraud is practised by the assertion of what is
untrue, it is within the statute. It also shows that the
information need not allege the precise statement of the
defendant, for not one word is stated in the indictment
which was used by the witch, but only what amounted

(a) See note (a), p. 90.   (b) 34 L. J. M. C. 50.

to the same thing. In *Codrington's* case the prosecutor relied on the warranty or covenant alone. The money was not obtained on the faith of the representation in that case, and the assertion was of a future right. It is clear that the prosecutor did not give up his money, because of the tittle tattle as to the reversionary interest, but on the faith of the covenant. But in this case the information was asked to guide *Flood* in making his purchase; it was given to mislead him, and it did mislead him. So in *Oates'* case the assertion was merely as to the value of the work; that was not matter of fact, but of opinion only. And *Parke*, B., says, therefore, " if the prisoner had said that so much work had been done, when it had not, the case might have been like *Reg.* v. *Leonard,* being a false statement of a fact, and not a false estimate." In *West's* case (*a*), a fraudulent misrepresentation of an existing matter of fact, accompanied by an executory promise to do something at a future period, as that the prisoner had bought certain skins and would sell them to the prosecutor, is a false pretence within the statute, although it appears that the promise, as well as such misrepresentation of fact, induced the prosecutor to part with the money. In this case *Flood* parted with his money, because of the sale note as well as the false assertion; and had it not been for the false assertion, the second step would not have been taken. The test is whether an action for tort would or would not lie for such a misrepresentation as this.

Cur. adv. vult.

Their Honors now gave judgment in this case as follows :—

STEPHEN, C. J. In this case, the two representations charged as pretences are, that the prisoner and his partner were then possessed of the cattle which, through their agent, they then offered for sale, and that the firm had a right to sell them. It is material to bear this in mind, because confusion, not infrequently, arises from inattention to the exact frame of the charge. In some instances the decision has been on the sufficiency of the

(*a*) 1 Dears. & B. 575; 27 L. J. M. C. 227.

G—4

indictment, and in others of the evidence to sustain it; but the distinction between these two things, in every case, is not at first sight apparent. We are not to consider whether the evidence might have supported a more specific charge, or a differently framed allegation; but whether the charge, as it stands, can be maintained.

As to the first of the representations alleged, there has been no dispute. The prisoner did state that he and his co-partner were in possession; and it cannot be denied, that this is a matter of existing .or non-existing fact, simple and definite. Such an assertion, therefore, confessedly, may be a pretence indictable under the statute. But then, upon the evidence, that assertion was strictly true. The firm had never ceased to have possession; and their contract of sale to *Flood* was on the 25th of August, whereas the mortgagees had no right of possession until default, which could not happen before the 30th of September. The contest is solely as to the other pretence charged; namely, the right of *Lotze* and his partner to sell the offered portion. I think that there was evidence to support the finding, that the prisoner did—in effect, though not in the exact words—make that representation. But I am of opinion that the representation itself, true or false, is not sufficient in law to support the charge of a pretence, within the meaning or intent of the statute.

The opinion thus expressed, after consideration of all the authorities, is founded mainly on this; that the assertion or pretence must be as to some matter of fact, *simply*—definite, and not matter of opinion, warranty, or inference; still less, matter partly of fact and partly of law. I venture to say that in no case has a conviction been sustained, where the representation charged was not of this character. And it seems clear to my apprehension, that the assertion by a vendor, in reference to property offered by him for sale, that he has a right or power to sell that property, cannot be within the category.

The strongest case relied on for the Crown—certainly, in some respects a startling one—is that of *Maria*

1865.

The QUEEN
v.
LOTZE.

Giles (a). A swindling fortune-teller obtained some money from a woman, whose husband had deserted her, by pretending that the assertor had power, by means of some "stuff" in her possession, to bring him back. The Judges held that this was a false pretence within the statute, because the representation was in respect of a supposed present fact—that is to say, according to Mr. Justice *Mellor*, the prisoner represented herself (in effect) as having "efficient means" to fulfil her promise.

It was asked on the argument before us, why the assertion of a "right to sell property" was not equally a supposed present fact. The difficulty of distinguishing, in terms, between the two cases, may be admitted. Yet the difference is felt to be a marked one. A question as to the existence of title in property, or the right under given circumstances to sell it, is in the nature of things a question of law, more than of fact. The assertion of such a right, therefore, is rather the expression of an opinion. It is not the representation of matter of fact, exclusively; nor, indeed, of a fact at all, except in a very qualified and limited sense. But, with respect to the pretended power in the fortune-teller's case, the representation that she possessed such a power, *i.e.* had means—by stuff in her possession, or otherwise—to accomplish the stated object, was either an assertion of matter of fact, or of nothing.

I come now to the cases cited on behalf of the prisoner. Of these, the first is *The King* v. *Codrington* (b), in which the facts were the following. The prisoner, as stated in the indictment, represented that he was entitled to a certain "reversionary" interest. According to the evidence, the prisoner offered the property in question for sale—representing that he would be entitled to it, on the death of a relation, under the will of his grandfather. On the faith of that allegation, the prosecutor bought the reversion; and thereupon a conveyance of it was executed, in which the prisoner entered into (according to the report) the "usual" covenant for title. In other words, that, notwithstanding any act done by him, he

(a) 34 L. J. M. C. 52.   (b) 1 C. & P. 662.

(the vendor) had a title to and good right to convey the property. Under this deed, relying either on the covenant, or on the oral representation, the prosecutor paid his purchase money. It was proved, however, that the prisoner had conveyed the same reversionary interest, three months previously, to another person.

On this statement of the facts (assuming always that the prisoner's representation induced the purchase, and consequent payment), the charge seems clearly to have been established. For, that a man is entitled to a reversion, or that he " will be " entitled to the property on the happening of the stated event, is manifestly the same thing. Two objections, nevertheless, were made. First, as to the covenant, that it was no evidence of a pretence. Secondly, as to the oral representation, that it was (as I understand the objection) merged in the covenant—upon which, and not on the faith of that representation, the prosecutor paid his money. It was answered, that the pretence consisted in *Codrington's* assertion, that he had a title to the interest which he sold ; and that the prisoner's reiteration of that assertion in a deed, covenanting that he had such title, could not affect the question. But Mr. Justice *Littledale* held, that a covenant cannot be taken to be a false pretence—and he adds these words : " the doctrine contended for would make every breach of warranty, or false assertion at the time of a bargain, a transportable offence. Here the party bought the property, and took as his security a covenant that the vendor had a good title ; and if the vendor has not one, the purchaser must resort to the covenant." An acquittal was accordingly directed.

The effect of that decision is, it seems to me, that no allegation of title by a seller, however false, is indictable as a false pretence under the statute. One ground of the Judge's direction certainly may have been (although this was a question for the jury), that the prosecutor had not paid his money, in reliance on the oral representation. That, however, does not invalidate the other portions of the judgment ; and Mr. Justice *Littledale* lays it down as law, that a covenant for title cannot amount to a false pretence. If so, then by reasonable inference, as applied to that case, the prisoner's oral assertion of title could not. On the faith of that assertion, although the money may not have been paid until the conveyance, the prosecutor made his purchase. But, as it was unanswerably urged, the repetition of that assertion in a covenant could not weaken, much less destroy, its effect.

It will be observed, that there was no charge in the indictment, in that case, of a pretence that the prisoner had not, in fact, already parted with his interest. The evidence, I conceive, might have sustained such a charge; and then there would have been no difficulty. Mr. Justice *Blackburn*, in the case of *Maria Giles*, referring to the *Queen* v. *Douglas* (a)—where the pretence stated was, that the prisoner would tell where the prosecutor's horses were—observes that *Douglas's* case turned on the sufficiency of the indictment; and suggests that the evidence might have supported the averment of a pretence, that the prisoner "could" tell (or in other words *knew*) where the horses were. So, in the present case. If the charge had been, that *Lotze* pretended some mere matter of fact, not involving matter of law, warranty, or opinion—such as, that the firm had not mortgaged the cattle, or the like—the indictment would have been sufficient. An extra-judicial opinion of Mr. Justice (now Chief Justice) *Erle* has been referred to, expressed in *Watts* v. *Porter* (b), that a knowingly false assertion as to an incumbered property, that it was unincumbered, would be indictable. Possibly so; for that may be deemed matter of fact, merely. But the representation charged in this case is not, even, that the partnership in fact owned the cattle. It is, merely, that they had the right to sell them; the existence of which right, although obvious in an unincumbered owner, may depend (as in this very case it did) on various questions.

Codrington's case, however, need not be relied on by me; and certainly no case has been more misquoted, or

(a) 1 Moody's C. C. 462.   (b) 3 El. & Bl. 760.

apparently less understood. The marginal note has been supposed to show, that the acquittal was solely on the ground, already noticed, of a covenant having been taken after the representation. I do not think so. But in *Crossley's* case, at *Nisi Prius* (a), Mr. Justice *Patteson* assumes the fact to be, that *Codrington* "did not distinctly allege that he had a good title to the estate" sold by him. This was of course a sufficient answer, to dispose of *Codrington's* case, for any purpose. And, for that very reason, the learned Judge's remark (so mistaken as to the fact) cannot be accepted as any authority, that the allegation itself, if made, would have sustained a conviction. In *Kenrick's* case (b), on the other hand, Lord *Denman* appears to have thought that *Codrington's* acquittal was directed, because the thing obtained by the pretence was the conveyance—and not the purchase money, which the prosecutor paid under it. Again, in *Adamson's* case (c), the *King* v. *Codrington* was relied on for the prisoner, as showing that a deed of co-partnership executed by him and the prosecutor, consequent on a pretence that the prisoner held a particular employment, got rid of that pretence. I cite *Codrington's* case, for the conclusion which seems inevitably to follow from the Judge's observations—the effect of which, according to my apprehension of them, has been already stated.

But all the cases show the distinction, on which my judgment in this case rests. In the *Queen* v. *Kenrick*, the representations were clearly as to simple and definite facts—namely, that the horses offered for sale were the property of a lady, and not of a horse dealer, and that they were quiet. Again, in the *Queen* v. *Adamson*, the representation was of a definite existing fact—namely, that the prisoner had obtained a certain appointment. On the faith of that allegation, as the prosecutor swore, he was induced to enter into a deed of co-partnership with the prisoner—and, under that deed, to pay him the stated consideration money. Again, in *Parker's* case (d),

(a) 2 M. & R. 19.   (b) 5 Q. B. 64.
(c) 2 Moody 287.   (d) 7 C. & P. 828.

a watch and chain were sold and delivered to the prisoner, on the faith of his representation that a check given
in payment (post-dated), was a good order for the
amount, and was of the stated value. The reasons of
the Judges are not given, but a majority thought the
conviction right. It will be seen that the assertion there
was of a fact, and nothing more. An allegation that a
worthless check was valuable; and that it was a genuine,
whereas it was a pretended order. Substantially, indeed,
the prisoner's representation was that he kept an account,
and had money at the bankers; and Lord C. J. *Tindal*
thought, accordingly, that the indictment ought so to
have charged.

A fraudulent representation as to quantity, stating
that an article sold weighs or contains so much, when
the quantity is less to the seller's knowledge, is a pretence within the statute; *Sherwood's* case (a). The
assertion there was plainly of a mere fact—a matter as-
certainable and definite. Yet even there, some of the
Judges doubted whether the pretence was within the
statute; observing that it was never intended to apply
at all, to frauds committed in the course of actual business transactions, but only to cases of pretended buying
or selling. In the present case, however, it is unquestionable that the sale by *Lotze* and *Larnach*—whatever else may have been its character—was no pretence.
It was a real transaction. The assertion of their right
or authority to sell, since the 'jury have so found, may
have been knowingly false: but, if so, it was the mortgagee, not the purchaser, that was meant to be defrauded.

In *Burgon's* case (b), after taking above twelve
months' time to consider, the Judges held that a misrepresentation inducing the loan of money might be,
and in that instance was, a false pretence within the
statute. But there the assertion was as to a definite and
simple fact; namely, the existence of a house on the
land mortgaged, whereas no house had ever been erected
on it. So, in the case of *Abbott* (o). There, the sale

(a) 1 Dears. & Bell 259.   (b) 1 Dears. & Bell 23.   (o) 1 Den. C. C. 273.

1865.

The QUEEN
v.
LOTZE.

was in truth a delusion throughout. The cheeses delivered were, in fact, not those represented to have been sold; the pretence being, that samples produced were taken out of those exhibited—whereas the samples were fraudulently abstracted from other cheeses, of a very different quality.

In *Roebuck's* case (a), after two arguments, and some months' deliberation, a representation that certain chains were of silver, whereas they were entirely of another and inferior metal, was holden to be a false pretence within the statute. And the same decision appears to have been previously arrived at in the *Queen* v. *Ball* (b). Lord *Campbell's* judgment shows the principle, on which both cases rest; namely, that the prisoner virtually stole the money obtained by him, under pretence of a contract for borrowing it on the articles—they being in no respect the things bargained for. His Lordship, however, referring to the decision in *Rex.* v. *Codrington*, expressly says that "warranties" are not within the statute. Baron *Parke* observes, that to hold that a man could be indicted for warranting a horse sound, which he knows to be unsound, would be going an "alarming" length. And that learned Judge, in reference to the conviction in *Copeland's* case (c)—where the prisoner had pretended that he was a single man, and entitled to sue for the breach of a promise of marriage, made to him by the prosecutrix—intimates an opinion that the latter pretence was not indictable. Nothing can well indicate, more plainly, the distinction on which I have insisted. For, as to the one matter, it was plainly the assertion of a fact; but the other related to a legal right, and so was matter of inference or opinion only.

In the same case of *Roebuck*, C. J. *Jervis* puts as an example of a false pretence, the representation by a man that he has in his possession a carriage, when in fact he has not got one. But this, obviously, is an instance within the admitted general rule. There would be in such a case the design to cheat, under the pretence of

(a) 1 Dears. & Bell 37.   (b) Car. & Marsh. 249.
(c) Car. & Marsh. 516.

dealing for a carriage. The representation concerning it, moreover, would be as to a matter of plain fact, simply and exclusively. But the fraudulent representation of warranty (for instance) that a horse is sound, although false to the assertor's knowledge, has been expressly holden not to be a pretence within the statute; *Pywell's* case (a). For, although such an assertion may in any given instance be on a bare matter of fact, yet it is in its nature the expression rather of a belief or opinion. And so in the present case. Whether the assertion was of a power, a right, or an authority, the same idea is conveyed—and the legal result must be the same. In each case, the allegation may really be confined to matter of fact. But, in all alike, it is of a compound or mixed character, involving necessarily in its terms matter of law.

On exactly this principle, I conceive, the cases of *Oates* (b) and of *Bryan* (c) were decided. In the latter, a representation that some spoons pledged by the prisoner—being plated, but in the slightest degree—were equal to and had as much silver on them as particular well known articles, of very superior quality, was there held not to be a pretence within the statute. An assertion, knowingly false, that the spoons were of the specified manufacture, it was conceded, would have been indictable. But a representation merely as to their quality, it was ruled, was not so. Mr. Justice *Erle* clearly rests his own judgment on the distinction pointed out; that the pretence was really one as to opinion—or, at least, more so than the assertion of a definite fact. He expressly says, that such a matter as the prisoner there had represented "could not be decidedly affirmed, or denied, in the same way as a past fact could be." It was not the affirmation of a definite and triable fact, such as all men can at once judge of, and decide upon. Mr. Justice *Willes*, who dissented from the majority of the Court, admits that no representation on a matter of opinion, unascertainable by inspection or calculation, would be within the statute. But, as he conceived, the

(a) 1 Stark. N. P. 403.   (b) Dears. 465.   (c) 1 Dears. & Bell 269.

assertion was as to the quantity of silver on the spoons ; and so, respecting a matter of fact. Baron *Channell* thought the conviction wrong, because the representation related to that which was matter of opinion.

The decision in this case of *Bryan*, and the principle on which it was determined by the Court, I may observe in passing, have been upheld after full consideration, in the cases of *Goss* and *Bagg* (a).

In *Oates's* case the indictment stated that the prisoner "knowingly and designedly did falsely pretend" to the prosecutor, his employer, that there was then due and payable to him (the prisoner) for the work which he had done, a certain sum—being an amount in excess of the real sum due. And the Court unanimously held, that a false and fraudulent overcharge, or over-estimate of the value of work done, was not a pretence within the statute. On the evidence there could be no doubt of the fraud, for the prisoner obtained the money by erasing and substituting figures in the books. But the decision (there being no other point reserved) was on the terms of the charge as laid, only. And the Court held it to be bad, as disclosing no matter of existing fact merely, but as involving also questions of law.

There is no foundation whatever for the supposition, that this case went off on some defect in form, or deficiency of allegation, in the indictment ; such as, that the prisoner might, for anything there appearing, not have known that his estimate or overcharge was false. No such point was taken, either on the bench or at the bar. The objection was exclusively that which I have stated, and it was sustained. It was assumed, throughout, that the overcharge was fraudulent—as to which, especially after verdict, the language of the indictment left no room for doubt. And, indeed, on this ground, Mr. Justice *Maule* appears at first to have thought that the allegation of the prisoner's fraudulent intent, and guilty knowledge (see his observations in p. 468), excluded the idea of any matter of law being involved in the representation. A consideration of what fell from

(a) 8 Cox's C. C. 267.

the Judges, in delivering separately their opinions, will show the correctness of the conclusion expressed by me.

Thus, *Pollock*, C. B.—"Considering this as an allegation, merely that so much was due and owing, it may involve many questions of law and fact; the price to be paid, the value of the work, the credit to be given, and the terms of payment. The allegation of a false pretence should be clear and precise, in order that you may see on the face of the indictment, whether it discloses a false statement of an existing fact." Baron *Parke* is to the same effect.—"In this case, there is merely a fraudulent claim in respect of the value of the prisoner's work; and the indictment would be supported, by evidence that he made a false estimate of the value of that work. I do not think that an indictable offence. The short ground of my judgment is, that the indictment contains no false statement of an existing fact." In other words, a knowingly false and fraudulent estimate, or claim founded on a knowingly false estimate, of the value of the amount payable for work, is not indictable; because the representation is in its nature, or may be, matter of opinion— not mere matter of existing fact. Again, Mr. Justice *Crompton*.—"The indictment avers no misrepresentation of an existing fact, but merely a false representation that a certain sum was due and payable; and that averment might be proved, by evidence of a wrongful overcharge, or a misrepresentation of a matter of law. The false statement that money is due and payable, does not necessarily involve a false pretence of an existing fact." Surely these observations cannot mean, that perhaps the prisoner only made a wrong estimate by mistake.

In *Witchell's* case (a), the pretence was that some workmen had "earned" a certain amount of money. This was, doubtless, thought equivalent to an assertion, that they had done work to that amount; whereas, some of the men had done much less work, and some no work at all. On this view of the charge, the assertion was simply respecting a matter of fact, and the conviction would be in harmony with the other authorities. But

(a) 2 East P. C. 830.

the question there reserved was, as to the credit obtained by the false pretence—not as to the nature of the pretence itself. If the assertion be regarded as the representation of a compound matter, partly fact and partly opinion or inference, the case is overruled by the *Queen* v. *Oates.*

Lord *Campbell's* dictum in *Woolley's* case (a), that it is an indictable false pretence for a tradesman to tell a customer, who owes nothing, that he owes the assertor several pounds, was cited on the argument. It may be sufficient to say, that *Woolley's* case—for the reasons given in the *Queen* v. *Oates*—is no authority on any such question. But it is quite possible to hold, that the assertion by a man of the existence of a debt, as owing to him by another, may be on a matter of definite and simply fact only, without conceding that the assertion of a right—which can mean only a right in point of law, although itself deducible from facts—can, under any circumstances, be so deemed.

The authorities, in short, seem abundantly to establish my conclusion—that the assertion or pretence by *Lotze,* in this case, of a "right," or power and authority, in him and his partner, to sell the cattle which formed the subject of their negotiation, cannot sustain an indictment for a false pretence within the statute; and no one contends that, if not, it is otherwise indictable as an offence.

The statement by a vendor, however fraudulently made, that he is or believes himself to be entitled, or authorised, to sell the property under negotiation, is no representation of a definite matter of fact, susceptible (in the language of C. J. *Erle*) of decided affirmation or denial, as ordinary facts are. But, if equivalent to an assertion of ownership, it would (see *Eicholtz* v. *Bannister*) (b) amount to a warranty; and so, it would seem, on that ground alone, not be indictable as a pretence. And who is certainly to ascertain, as you may respecting an ordinary fact, the falsehood or reality of such a representation? For it may depend, as already

(a) 1 Den. C. C. 559.   (b) 11 Jur. N. S. 16.

observed, on the simplest or on the most complicated matters; questions of lien, of agency, of powers under a settlement, and other points of much intricacy. It cannot be that a vendor's guilt or innocence, on a charge of false representation, should depend in any degree on such inquiries. And if, in particular instances, the charge may embrace an assertion rather of fact than of legal conclusion, a rule of law cannot be made to contract, or expand, with circumstances. Cases may with ease be put, in which the assertion could only be regarded in any fair sense, as the expression of an opinion on a matter of law.

The circumstance, merely, that the representation was in the course of, and related to, a real business transaction, would not alone prevent a false representation (if on a matter of fact simply) from being deemed a pretence within the statute. But my opinion on the whole case is, that the charge as laid cannot be supported in point of law; and that, upon its appearing at the trial that the prisoner's right to sell depended, in part, on a question of law, an acquittal should have been directed. I will add this—that, whatever the character of a business transaction, however fraudulent or tricky it may be, it is far safer and better that the guilty individual should escape, than that the criminal law should be strained to meet it—especially on a point of great and acknowledged difficulty, on which the ablest men may be permitted to doubt.

WISE, J. The indictment states that the defendant "unlawfully, knowingly, and designedly did falsely pretend to one *John Brewster* that he the said *Edward Lotze*, and one *James Macdonald Larnach*, then trading under the name of *Lotze* and *Larnach*, were then possessed of a certain cattle station called Southgate Station, and certain cattle, to wit, 1000 head of cattle upon the said station, and had good right and full power and authority to sell and dispose of the said cattle, by means of which said false pretences he, the said *Edward Lotze*, did then and there unlawfully obtain from the said *John*

Brewster a certain valuable security, to wit, a promissory note for the sum of £333 6s. 8d., of the property of one *Edward Flood*, with intent thereby then to defraud, whereas, in truth and in fact, the said *Edward Lotze* and *James Macdonald Larnach*, so trading under the name of *Lotze* and *Larnach* as aforesaid, were not then possessed of a certain cattle station called Southgate Station, and were not then possessed of the said 1000 head of cattle upon the said station, and had not good right and full power and authority to sell and dispose of the said cattle, as he, the said *Edward Lotze*, then well knew."

The prisoner was found guilty, but there were two points reserved, which have been argued first before his Honor the Chief Justice and myself, and subsequently before us and Mr. Justice *Hargrave*. The points reserved were, first, whether there was evidence to go to the jury to support the allegation that the defendant in fact represented or pretended that he had "good right and full power and authority" to sell the cattle in question. Second, whether, for the making of such representation, although false and with intent to defraud, an indictment would lie as for a false pretence within the statute. It was intimated on the first argument that there was evidence to go to the jury, and I will state my reason very shortly on this point.

A treaty was pending between the agent employed by the prisoner and Mr. *Flood*, and at Mr. *Flood's* request the prisoner was asked whether he and his partner were selling as principals or as agents for the previous owner. The defendant did not reply merely that they were selling as principals, though even that would, I think, have been evidence of the representation charged, but he added for the information of the purchaser, "We had a mortgage over *Sharp's* station, but foreclosed it, and are now in possession." In my opinion, the natural meaning of this language was that they had become and were the owners, in the ordinary sense of the word, by having foreclosed the mortgage and entered into possession. There was, therefore, evidence to go to the jury that the prisoner did pretend that he had full right and authority to sell the land in question.

The second question still remains for decision

The jury having found him guilty, it must be taken for the purpose of this argument, not merely that the defendant made representations not in accordance with the fact, which in one sense would be a false representation, but that he made such representations, well knowing that they were false, and with intent to defraud, and that by making such false representations he obtained the promissory notes in question.

I gave the utmost attention to the able arguments of Mr. Martin, and I have most carefully considered the judgment of his Honor the Chief Justice; but while concurring with much that is there stated, I am unable to arrive at the conclusion that, under the circumstances found by the jury, the prisoner was not guilty of an offence against the statute.

I entirely agree that, to constitute a false pretence, the representation must not be of a mere matter of opinion or inference; and further, that a false pretence as to a fact may be so mixed up with matter of law as not to be indictable. But the short ground upon which I hold that the conviction must be upheld is, that what took place here was, according to the finding of the jury, no assertion of opinion or inference, but an assertion of a fact—namely, that the firm had good right and full power and authority to sell the cattle, whereas they had no such right, power, and authority, and the prisoner well knew that they had none.

A man may be in possession under circumstances which leave it very uncertain whether he has power to sell or not—or he may honestly make a mistake as to his powers; in none of these cases could he be convicted of obtaining money by false pretences, although untruly representing that he had authority to sell, because there would be merely a misapprehension of legal right. But here the jury have expressly found that there was no misapprehension, but a wilful and fraudulent statement that the firm had an authority, which the prisoner knew they had not. It will not be denied that if a man professes to sell a carriage, which he fraudulently states he has in his possession, and thereby induces the purchaser to pay for it beforehand, and he has not in fact got one, he obtains the money by false pretences (see per *Jervis*, C. J., *Roebuck's* case) (a); and it would be strange indeed if the bare physical possession of a chattel, over which the possessor knows he has no legal control or power, should enable him to commit a fraud without the danger of punishment. Suppose, for instance, a man is asked by his friend to drive some cattle along the road, and whilst he is so engaged, a person says to him, have you authority to sell these cattle, to which he replies yes, and thereupon the price is named, and the cattle are handed over. Under these circumstances, it seems to me clear that the assertion as to his authority is the statement of an existing fact. Nor is it the less so, because circumstances might be put in which the same words would not amount to an indictable misrepresentation of a fact. For instance, in this very case the jury were rightly directed, that if they believed the prisoner acted on the advice, however wrong, given to him by his attorney, he could not be convicted.

Taking the view that I do of the meaning of the indictment and the finding of the jury, it is unnecessary for me to go through all the cases cited in the argument. I think, however, that *Reg.* v. *Giles* is an express authority for the principle upon which my judgment proceeds. There, upon an indictment charging that the prisoner falsely alleged she had the power to do a certain thing, it was held that it was a representation of an existing fact; and so here the allegation that the prisoner had authority to sell is, under the circumstances found by the jury, a representation of an existing fact. In like manner, a false representation that a person was an unmarried man was held to be a false pretence under the statute (*R.* v. *Copeland* (b), *R.* v. *Jennison* (c), and yet the status of marriage depends upon matter of law; and if, in the

(a) Dears. & Bell, p. 33.   (b) Car. & Marsh. 516.
(c) 31 L. J. M. C. 147.

particular case, it had been proved that the prisoner had *bona fide* made a mistake, supposing himself not to be married, I apprehend that he could not have been convicted; nor, on the other hand, could he have been convicted if he had represented himself as a single man, and in point of law the marriage was void, although he did not know it, and supposed at the time of making such representation that he was a married man.

In this case, no motion could be made in arrest of judgment; because, in form, the indictment is good, as it states that the prisoner alleged that he was possessed. On motion in arrest of judgment, the facts are not before the Court, only the mode of stating them; whereas, after a verdict, an ambiguity in the indictment is often cured.

It is for this reason that I do not consider that *Oates'* case is any authority against the present indictment. There the Court held in arrest of judgment, that an allegation of so much being " due and owing " was not sufficient, as it did not disclose a false statement of an existing fact. *Wightman*, J., on giving judgment, said " the facts are not before us, but merely the form of the indictment." The judgment of that Court must, of course, bind in a similar case, but it only decides in terms the effect of a particular form of indictment; and it seems to me that the language used by *Pollock*, C. B., clearly excludes its application as an authority in this case. He says, considering " this as an allegation merely, that so much was due and owing, it may involve many questions both of law and fact. It may involve the price to be paid, and the value of the work, the credit to be given, and the terms of payment." But the jury have by their finding, as already pointed out, cleared this case from any such difficulty. They have found in effect that the representation made by the prisoner included none of these questions, but was a deliberate assertion for a fraudulent purpose of a fact which he knew to be false.

It may be in arriving at this conclusion, that I decide against the judgment of Mr. Justice *Littledale* in *R.* v. *Codrington* (a), and if satisfied that that learned Judge

(a) 1 C. & P. 662.

H—4

was wrong, it would be my clear duty to do so, for it was
the decision of a single Judge only, and given on circuit,
without any time for consideration, and before the meaning of the statute had been so fully discussed as it has
been of late years by very able counsel, and before very
able Judges.   But, looking at that case and the various
observations upon it by counsel and Judges in the subsequent cases, I cannot avoid coming to the conclusion that
the report does not show clearly what the point decided
was; and my own view, founded chiefly on the marginal
note, and the observation of *Patteson, J.*, in *Crossley's*
case (a), is, that Mr. Justice *Littledale* considered that the
conversation preceding the conveyance was only a conversation between buyer and seller, not amounting to any
definite representation relied upon as the basis of the
contract, and that the inducement to the buyer was the
covenant for title, which gave him a remedy for damages;
in other words, that the false statement did not induce
the purchaser to part with his money, but that he relied
upon his claim to damages, if the covenant turned out to
be broken.

But assuming that Mr. Justice *Littledale* did hold
that there could be no indictment for false pretences,
where a vendor falsely and knowingly represented that
he was the owner of a reversion, and entitled to sell it,
notwithstanding that he had already sold it, as he well
knew, and could convey no right whatever to the purchaser, I should, notwithstanding my great respect for that
very learned Judge, feel myself bound to differ from him.
I should be prepared to hold, in the words of Mr. Justice
Erle (now the Chief Justice of the Common Pleas, whose
knowledge of the Criminal Law is not, I believe, sur-
passed by any living Judge), in a written judgment
delivered after the first argument in *Eagleton's* case (b),
" that if a dealer asserted expressly that stock which he
was selling was unencumbered, and obtained the advance
by that falsehood, he would be indictable for a false pretence " (c).   Falsehood, of course, here means that the
statement was to his knowledge false, as in the present case

(a) 2 M. & R. 19.   (b) Dears. 376.   (c) 3 E. & B. 761.

has been expressly found by the jury. So in *Butcher's* case (a), it seems to have been considered that a representation that a person had "authority" to receive money would be good in an indictment for false pretences. See also *Rex* v. *Parker* (b). Mr. *Martin*, in the course of the argument, cited many passages from the judgments of various Judges, as to the danger of allowing a disappointed buyer to turn round and charge the seller with a false pretence, and especially referred to language of *Pollock*, C. B., that he doubted whether any real dealing about buying and selling is within the statute. These doubts may still exist without touching the present case; for, as his Lordship added (see *Eagleton's* case (c) and *Evan's* case) (d), if the buying and selling are merely a pretence in order to cheat, it is a different thing, and this the jury have, in my opinion, found.

In conclusion, I wish to quote some passages from the elaborate judgment of Mr. Justice *Willes* in *Bryan's* case, because I think they throw great light on the construction of this statute, he says:—

"I am looking to the words of that section, and I am unable to bring myself to think that the Legislature was at all dealing with anything in the nature of a distinction between the case of property fraudulently obtained by a fraudulently obtained contract and goods obtained without any contract, but fraudulently obtained. I cannot help thinking that if the attention of the framers of the statute had been directed to any such possible operation of it, they would, in the spirit in which the section is framed, have enacted, in terms even more clear than those of the 53rd section, that that which is obtained by fraud shall not benefit the fraudulent person, and that the interposition of a contract also obtained by fraud ought not to make any difference in favour of the cheat. The section commences with the recital that 'a failure of justice frequently arises from the subtle distinction between larceny and fraud.' That

(a) Bell C. C. 18, 19.   (b) 7 C. & P. 825.
(c) Dears. 531; 24 L. J. M. C. 158.   (d) 32 L. J. M. C. 40.

is the recital, and I had on my mind an impression that the recital of a statute may have the effect of enlarging, but not of restraining, the operation of the subsequent enactment. The enacting part of the section is, 'If any person shall by any false pretence obtain from any other person any chattel, money, or valuable security, with intent to cheat or defraud any person of the same, every such offender shall be guilty of a misdemeanor.' And it appears to me that the only proper test to apply to any case is, whether it was a false pretence by which the property was obtained, and whether it was obtained with the intention to cheat and defraud the person from whom it was obtained."

After referring to the views of the other Judges that it was a mere matter of opinion, he proceeds—

"It appears that the persons who made the advances were thereby defrauded, and thereby induced to make the advances, and the jury have found that the statements were known to the prisoner to be untrue, and that in consequence of those statements he obtained the money mentioned in the indictment. It appears to me that for all practical purposes that ought to be taken for a sufficient fact, coming within the region of assertion and calculation, and not mere opinion, that it should be considered as a false pretence. Well, then the statute says—'obtain from any other person any chattel, money, or valuable security.' It is found in this case that the money was obtained. If the matter was a simple commendation of the goods, without any specific falsehood as to what they were; if it was entirely a case of one person dealing with another in the way of business, who might expect to pay the price of the articles which were offered for the purposes of pledge or sale, and knew what they were, I apprehend it would have been easily disposed of by the jury, who were to pass an opinion on the subject, acting as persons of common sense and knowledge of the world, and abstaining from coming to any such conclusion as that praise of that kind should have the effect of making the party resorting to it guilty of obtaining money on a false pretence.

I say nothing on the effect of a simple exaggeration, except that it appears to me it would be a question for the jury in each case whether the matter was such ordinary praise of the goods (*dolus bonus*) as that a person ought not to be taken in by it, or whether it was a misrepresentation of a specific fact material to the contract and intended to defraud, and did defraud, and by which the money in question was obtained. Well, then there is the latter part of the section—'With intention to cheat and defraud any person of the same.' It must be with intent to cheat and defraud the person of the same. I am unable to bring my mind to any anxiety to protect persons who make false pretences 'with intent to cheat and defraud.' It was stated in the evidence by the prosecutor, 'I would have advanced nothing but for the misrepresentation,' and it was found by the jury that the money was obtained by the misrepresentation.

"But it is said that the effect of establishing such a rule as that for which I contend, would be to interfere with trade; no doubt it would, and I think ought to, prevent trade being carried on in the way in which it is said to be carried on. I cannot help expressing any regret if trade is carried on, and I do not believe it is generally carried on, by persons making false pretences, with the intention to cheat or defraud persons of their money. I am far from wishing to interfere with the rule as to simple commendation or praise of the articles which are sold, on the one hand, or to fair cheapening on the other; those are things persons may expect to meet with in the ordinary and usual course of trade; but I cannot help thinking that people ought to be protected from any such acts as those I have referred to being resorted to for the purpose and with intent to cheat or defraud purchasers of their money, or tradesmen of their goods. If the result of it would be to multiply prosecutions, that must be because we live in an age in which fraud is multiplied to a great extent, and, amongst others, in this form. I agree in what the late Chief Justice *Jervis* said as peculiarly applicable to

such a supposed state, though I hope not to ordinary
trade, that if there be such a commerce as requires to be
protected by the statute being limited in the mode suggested, it ought to be made honest, and conform to the
law, and not the law bent for the purpose of allowing
fraudulent commerce to go on."

I have quoted from this judgment at length, because,
although Mr. Justice *Willes* dissented from the other
Judges in that particular case, this judgment was thus
spoken of by *Erle*, C. J., in *Bagg's* case (a)—"In *R.* v.
Byran, my brother *Willes,* who deserves well of all who
take interest in the administration of the law, differed
from the majority in the decision; he agreed in the
principles that ought to govern, but differed in the application of that principle to the facts of the case. The
Judges thought that the representation 'that the quality
of the plating of the spoons, and the quantity of silver-
ing laid on them by the electrotype process, was equal
to *Elkington's,* and that the material was the best,' was
exaggerated praise on a matter of opinion, and so not
indictable; opinion not being directly cognisable by the
senses. My brother *Willes* thought it a representation
on a matter of fact."

I am of opinion, therefore, for these reasons, that upon
the finding of the jury the defendant is liable, because
he did make a false representation, with intent to defraud, of a present fact, that is to say, that the firm had
authority to sell, which, as the indictment states, "he
well knew was false." I say "upon this finding," for it
is no part of our duty at this stage of the case to consider, nor have I considered, whether the verdict was
right or wrong. I think it right to add, after the
perusal of the judgments of my brother Judges, that I
do not understand the Court upon the present occasion
to decide that, upon a differently-framed indictment, a
person might not be found guilty, if he, well knowing
that he was not entitled in any way to dispose of or sell
property of which he was in ostensible possession, fraudulently obtained money from another person by represent-

(a) Bell's C. C. 219.

ing that it was his own property, which he had a right to sell.

HARGRAVE, J. The information in this case states that the defendant, on the 8th of September, 1864, unlawfully, knowingly, and designedly did falsely pretend to one *J. Brewster* that he, the said *Edward Lotze* and *J. M. Larnach*, then trading, &c., were then possessed of a certain cattle station, and certain cattle, to wit, one thousand head of cattle, upon the said station; and had good right and full power and authority to sell and dispose of the said cattle—by means of which said false pretence he, the said *Edward Lotze*, did then and there unlawfully obtain from one *E. Flood* a certain valuable security, &c., or promissory note, for £333 6s. 8d., &c., with intent to defraud, &c.—whereas in truth the said firm were not then possessed of the station, and were not then possessed of the said cattle upon the said station, and had not good right and full power and authority to sell the said cattle, as he, the said *E. Lotze*, then well knew, &c.

The two questions reserved for the opinion of the full Court were:—" 1st. Whether there was evidence to go to the jury to support the allegation that the defendant in fact represented or pretended that he had good right and full power and authority to sell the cattle in question? 2nd. Whether, for the making of such a representation, although false, and with intent to defraud, an indictment will lie as for a false pretence within the statute?"

With reference to the first of these questions, I understand the Court to have already held (previously to the argument on the 30th ultimo) that there was evidence to go to the jury to prove that the prisoner pretended he had good right and full power and authority to sell the thousand head of cattle; and the jury having found that the prisoner "did not believe himself entitled to sell, and that he fraudulently sold—and that he fraudulently pretended that he had good right, full power, and authority "—I am relieved from the necessity of considering the first of these questions. And I mention the matter here only to state that I consider the finding of the jury, according to the decision of my brother Judges, to be conclusive as to the fact of this alleged pretence having been made; and the only question now remaining for consideration is, whether the subject matter or words of such false pretence, being only as to a "right, power, and authority to sell," is within the statute.

It was argued on the one side, on behalf of the prisoner, that, inasmuch as the false pretence was as to a matter of right, power, and authority, the subject matter of the pretence was *per se* a mere matter of "opinion," "inference," or "law"—or, at least, of "mixed law and fact"—and therefore not of such then existing facts as to be comprised within the "false pretences" forbidden by the statute.

It was argued on the other side, on behalf of the Crown, that the statute makes no exception of any particular false pretences; and that the reported cases have not yet established as an universal and general rule that false pretences of any "right, power, or authority," when made and set up as matters of fact, are not to be *prima facie* included within the statute; and that the penalties of the statute are only to be avoided by establishing that such pretences, though false in fact, were not fraudulent or wilful within the meaning of the general Criminal Law.

The case is one of great difficulty, and I admit that, during the argument, my mind has fully felt the force of all the cogent reasons which have been advanced on each side of the question.

On the one hand it would be very dangerous to throw any doubt upon the clear rule of law, that the subject matter of a false pretence under the statute must not, as a general rule, be the statement of a mere opinion, inference, or matter of deduction from facts; because the lawful differences of opinion, not merely as to questions of law, professional topics, or questions of science, but also as to almost every other matter of in-

1865.

The QUEEN
v.
LOTZE.

ference or deduction from facts, are acknowledged *per*
se to entitle all persons to the benefit of such differences,
whatever criminal intention is under consideration.

The principle of this rule is also recognised in indictments for perjury, which seem to me very much to illustrate and aid our consideration of the present case.
Nothing can be clearer law than that matters of "opinion"
or inference cannot be made the subject of any indictment
for perjury; still, as Mr. *Roscoe* remarks (a), there are
exceptions to such general rule. For example—"If the
statement of opinion assert a fact or draw an inference
evidently false—as, if a medical attendant swear that a
person is unfit to travel who is in perfect health, or an
architect shall declare a tenement to be ruined which
is in good condition—certainly the gross falsehood of
such an assertion shall, in neither case, be protected by
the plea that it related to a matter of professional investigation."

Although these remarks are quoted by Mr. *Roscoe*
from *Alison's* Principles of the Criminal Law of Scotland, I apprehend there can be no doubt that these exceptions to the general rule prevail in every branch of
the English Criminal Law; and that the passage I have
quoted points out the true foundation both of the rule
and of the exceptions as applied to all persons, whether
professional or otherwise; and that the statute as to
false pretences ought to receive a construction by
analogy to the same rule and the same exception.

I confess myself unable to believe in the general and
universal exemption of matters of "opinion," "inference," or so called "mixed matters of opinion and fact,"
from the statute, otherwise than as removing the criminal intention; and I cannot concur in the opinion that
there can be no indictment whatever under any possible
circumstances for any false pretence under the statute, as
to such matters either simple or mixed; or that there is
a general protection or exemption incident and annexed
to these subject matters *per se*, and in their nature;

(a) Rosc. Cr. Ev 799.

otherwise, or in any different sense, than as in cases of perjury.

On the contrary, the conclusion of my own mind, to which I have arrived only after long reflection, is rather in accordance with Sir *William Manning's* argument that, since the words of the statute contain no such exception of any exempted subject matters of false pretence *per se*, and as all classes of false pretence are clearly within the mischiefs provided against, there cannot be any such general and protected class of false pretences different from other analogous branches of criminal law—except so far as express decisions have established actual exceptional cases; but that every false pretence proved to the satisfaction of a jury to be in all its incidents otherwise within the statute, may be made by its surrounding circumstances the subject of indictment under this statute; if such circumstances show that the party pretended, that is, held forth such " opinion " as a matter of fact, falsely, fraudulently, and knowingly, as an inducement to obtain money or other security, which in fact was obtained thereby contrary to the statute.

I am confirmed in this view of the construction of the statute by one of the most recent decisions, *Watts* v. *Porter* (a), in which the Chief Justice *Erle* says distinctly—" If he asserted expressly that it was unincumbered, and obtained the advance by that falsehood, he would be indictable for a false pretence." I confess that I cannot see how a false pretence as to an " authority to sell " when stated as a matter of fact, and so found by the jury, differs from a false pretence as to ownership when stated as a matter of fact. To put the case of most common occurrence at almost every Criminal Sittings, I cannot see why a person who draws and gives a cheque upon a bank from which he has no right, power, or authority to draw any money, should, by that conduct, be convicted (as is done at almost every session of our Criminal Court) of a false pretence; while another person who draws and gives a delivery order for cattle at a station where he has no right, power, or authority to sell any

(a) 3 E. & B. 760.

cattle, should be exempt from the statute. The circumstances which usually surround the former class of cases
may be, and usually are, very simple as compared with
the circumstances which usually surround the latter class
of cases; but, assuming these circumstances to be sufficient to satisfy the jury as to the false pretence and the
fraudulent intention, as in the case now before the Court,
I feel myself bound to state that my mind, as a lawyer,
is not satisfied by calling the latter transactions "warranties," or matters of opinion, and not within the
statute, and calling the former "false pretences" of facts,
and from their nature within the statute.

I have carefully considered all the reported decisions
upon this statute down to the case of *Maria Giles* in
1864, all of which were quoted during the argument of
this case, and have been commented upon by the two
judgments already delivered, and I have arrived at the
four following conclusions:—

First, that these decisions are characterised by an intricacy and guardedness of expression by almost all the
Judges, which show that the precise limits of the statute
are by no means yet so accurately defined by legal
boundaries as to meet all the frauds and false pretences
apparently within the general intention of the statute.

Secondly, that in no case which has arisen upon
this statute has any special verdict at all similar to that
now under consideration been given by a jury or brought
under judicial consideration.

Thirdly, that the words of this special verdict point so
obviously to a technical and formal assertion of a legal
right, legal power, and a legal authority—and to such
right and power and authority being good and full—
that I cannot consider these words as merely equivalent
to a simple assertion of the fact of "ownership" or of the
right, power, and authority as a matter of fact.

And, lastly, that as I am not convinced beyond all
doubt that this special verdict includes a finding of a
criminal intention within the law, as already laid down
by legal authorities superior to my own, I feel myself
bound to decline to carry the law beyond its present

1865.

The QUEEN
v.
LOTZE.

limits; as I fear that I should thereby endanger commercial and business transactions of almost daily occurrence by exposing parties to criminal prosecution who
have not been hitherto subjected thereto. Upon the
whole, therefore, though with hesitation, I concur in the
conclusion arrived at by the Chief Justice.

　　　　　　　　　　The prisoner was then discharged.

June 15.

PERRY and wife *against* HOSKINGS and wife (*a*).

The second
section of the
11 Vic., No.
13, provides
that, on the
trial of any
action for
defamatory
words not
imputing an
indictable
offence, it
shall be com-
petent to the
jury under
the plea of
not guilty to
consider
whether the
words com-
plained of
were spoken
on an occasion
when the
plaintiff's
character was
likely to be
injured there-
by; and if the
jury shall be
of opinion
that the words
were spoken
on an occasion
when the
plaintiff's

SLANDER. The first count of the declaration stated
that the female defendant, in a certain discourse
which she had had with one *Bynon*, had spoken of the
female plaintiff the words complained of. These words
which were set out conveyed in very gross and abusive
language a charge that the female plaintiff had committed adultery with *Bynon*. The second count complained of words conveying a similar imputation, which
were alleged to have been spoken to the female plaintiff
herself. Plea, not guilty. Issue thereon.

At the trial before *Stephen*, C. J., in November, 1864,
it appeared that the male plaintiff was coachman, and
Bynon was groom, in the defendant's service. The
words complained of were proved, but there was no evidence that any other persons were present, at the time
they were spoken, than the female plaintiff and *Bynon*.
The learned Judge left the case to the jury, telling them
that under the second section of the Defamation Act
(10 Vic., No. 13), they might, if they thought fit, find
a verdict for the defendants, on the objection (which in
his Honor's opinion was unanswerable) that the words
were spoken on an occasion when the plaintiff's character

character was not likely to be injured thereby, to find a verdict for the defendant.
In an action for slander by the defendant's wife imputing that the plaintiff's wife had
committed adultery with one *B*., it appeared that the words complained of were
spoken when the plaintiff's wife and *B*. only were present, who both denied the
truth of the imputation. The jury having given a verdict for the plaintiff with
substantial damages, the Court refused a new trial.

The second section of the 11 Vic., No. 13, commented on.

　　　　　(*a*) Before *Stephen*, C. J., and *Wise*, J.

was not likely to have been injured thereby. That, nevertheless, the Act left it to the jury to find for the plaintiff, even in such a case. But that then (if they thought the occasion such as he considered it) the difficulty was to say what damages, even the lowest, the plaintiffs could have sustained, or be likely to sustain. The jury, however, found for the plaintiffs, with £50 damages.

A rule *nisi* for a new trial having been obtained, on the ground that under the circumstances proved at the trial,. the words having been addressed to the female plaintiff and *Bynon*, who both knew that the imputation was false, the jury were not warranted in awarding any damages, or, at all events, more than nominal damages to the plaintiffs.

Salomons, for the plaintiffs, showed cause ; and *Isaacs* appeared in support of the rule. The arguments sufficiently appear in the judgments, which were as follows :—

STEPHEN, C. J. I am of opinion that the rule must be discharged. It is to be regretted that a matter of so much importance has not been discussed before the full Court ; but I think it desirable to express my opinion on the construction of this statute. The second section provides that, on the trial of any action for defamatory words, not imputing an indictable offence, it shall be competent to the jury under the plea of not guilty to consider whether the words complained of were spoken on an occasion when the plaintiff's character was likely to be injured thereby ; and if the jury shall be of opinion that the words were spoken on an occasion when the plaintiff's character was not likely to be injured thereby, to find a verdict for the defendant. In the first place, where words are spoken under circumstances when the plaintiff's character is not likely to be injured thereby, and the jury find otherwise, I am of opinion that the Court has power to grant a new trial. But secondly, the exercise of this power after a verdict for the plaintiff would, in any case, be practically useless; as even where they may think that the words were so spoken, it is not imperative on, but optional with, the jury to return a verdict for a defendant.

In this instance the speaking of the words was certainly not likely to, nor in my opinion is it possible that it could, have injured the plaintiff's character. For character can only be injured by the hearers thinking it possible that the slanderous charge may be true; as for example, if a man asserts of my servant, in the latter's and my presence (no other person but we three being in hearing), that the servant has stolen my watch, which watch has in fact to my knowledge never been out of my possession, and cannot have been stolen by the servant, how can the latter's character be, or be at any risk of being, injured by the speaking of such words?

The jury, however, having a right to give at all events (if I am right in my decision on the second point) nominal damages, ought we to disturb the verdict because they have given £50 damages? I am of opinion that we ought not to interfere. A right of action existing, the jury were entitled to consider the insult, and therefore the injury to the plaintiff's feelings; and the Court is not entitled to say that, for such words spoken by a person of fortune to her servant, such damages were outrageous.

WISE, J. It is with regret and diffidence that I feel myself obliged to dissent from the opinions expressed by his Honor the Chief Justice, as to the construction of the second section of the statute. I am clearly of opinion, however, that the Court is not deprived of its legitimate right to interfere with the verdict of a jury, where that verdict is manifestly wrong, by anything contained in that section. Statutes are passed with reference to a known system of law; and it seems to me that, as this statute does not take away from the Court its well known jurisdiction, that jurisdiction remains untouched. There are certain recognised legal principles, and an existing machinery, and the words of a statute must be construed with reference to such principles and machinery. Thus, for instance, it is a question entirely for the jury to say whether a particular publication is a libel; but in *Parmiter* v. *Coupland* (a), where the jury had returned a verdict for the defendant, the Court while thus laying down the law set aside the verdict, on the ground that it was wrong. It might have been argued in that case, that for the reasons assigned by the Court, where the jury had found that the publication was not a libel, such finding was conclusive. But the law is clear, that although the question whether the publication is libellous, is a question upon which a jury is to exercise their judgment, and to pronounce their opinion as a matter of fact, yet the jury have no power to say that that is not a libel which is a libel. For this reason, and following the authority of *Parmiter* v. *Coupland*, this Court granted a new trial in the case of *Holroyd* v. *Parkes* (b).

For these reasons I am of opinion that although the second section of the local statute gives a certain power to a jury in actions of slander, it is subject to the usual incidents of other powers exercised by a jury. Suppose, for instance, that a jury found that the defamatory matter was not likely to injure the plaintiff, when it clearly had injured him, when, for instance, ten witnesses who had heard it, proved that they in consequence of it had ceased to trust the plaintiff; and suppose, also, that the matter complained of was manifestly libellous; I should think such verdict ought to be set aside. If the Court can interfere with the verdict when it is in favor of the plaintiff, it seems to me that it can also do so when it is in favor of the defendant.

But in the present case I do not think the verdict ought to be set aside; because I do not see conclusively that it is wrong. The first section says that the right of action for oral slander shall extend to all defamatory words, for which an action might be maintained if the same were reduced into writing. Defamatory matter is matter tending to injure the reputation of another,

(a) 6 M. & W. 105.   (b) 15th November, 1856.

and thereby exposing him to public hatred, contempt, or ridicule. The language complained of in this action was of a most gross and insulting character, and was, in my opinion, calculated to bring the female plaintiff into ridicule, or contempt, or disgrace. The second section enacts that it shall be competent to the jury, if they are of opinion that the words were spoken on an occasion when the plaintiff's character was not likely to be injured, to find a verdict for the defendant. But if it is shown beyond doubt that the jury have come to a wrong conclusion, it seems to me that the verdict ought not to be allowed to stand; but that any interference with such verdict ought only to take place in an extraordinary case. In this case the charge is made by a married woman, that the plaintiff (who is a married woman) is a dirty old wretch, and has been locked up in a room with another man. Is it not derogatory to the character of a married woman to say that she has been shut up alone with another man under circumstances of suspicion, whether adultery is charged or not? Suppose that she is charged with disgraceful conduct, coupled with adultery with a particular man, and that she and that man alone are present when the charge is made, and that this man knows that she has not been guilty of such adultery, it seems to me that, notwithstanding, such a charge is libellous. It is libellous to tell the friend of A. that A. is dishonest, even although it can be shown that such friend did not believe the charge. If written, such charge would be actionable. As to the question whether the plaintiff's character is likely to be injured, it might be said that the party addressed knew that the charge was unfounded; but, on the other hand, it might be replied that this charge would not have been made, unless on some other occasion the plaintiff had acted improperly, or had been guilty of light conduct.

If I had been of opinion that the plaintiff was only entitled to recover nominal damages, I should have thought that £50 was excessive. But in my opinion, for the reasons I have given, the jury were entitled to find the verdict they have done (a).

(a) *Milford*, J., was suffering from indisposition.

JENKINS *against* HARRIS and wife (a).

EJECTMENT for 410 acres of land called Mount Ramsay, at North Harbour.

The case was tried before *Stephen*, C. J., in November, 1864, when the following facts were shown. The plaintiff's grandfather had been in possession of the land in question in 1829, and he remained in possession till his death in 1835. His eldest son, the father of the plaintiff, was shown to have been in possession till his death in 1855. It appeared, however, that the grandfather made a will, in which, after providing for the payment of his debts, he used the following words, " I give, devise and bequeath, unto my wife *Elizabeth Jenkins*, and unto my children (naming them), all the rest residue and remainder of my estate, both real and personal, &c., of what nature or kind, and wheresoever the same may be; and it is my will and desire that in case my wife shall be pregnant at the time of my decease, that the child or children which may be born after my decease shall participate in this my will, and that the whole of my property, both real and personal, after payment as aforesaid, shall be fairly and equally divided between my wife and the aforesaid children, &c.; and it is my will and desire that all or any part of my estate, real or personal, shall or may be sold at any time when my said wife shall think fit, in order to pay over to my children, as they shall arrive at age, the amount of their shares, and for which purpose I do empower my said wife to execute, seal, and deliver any conveyance for the sale of all or any part of my real estate; I do hereby nominate, constitute, and appoint my said wife, *Elizabeth Jenkins*, executrix of this my will, and guardian of my children. In testimony, &c." There were, it appeared, several children. In 1840, the widow

Where the guardian in socage has not entered, an infant under the age of fourteen years can maintain ejectment.

The testator after providing for the payment of his debts by will gave and devised unto his wife Elizabeth, and his children (naming them), all the rest of his real and personal estate, and declared it to be his desire that the whole of his property, both real and personal, should be equally divided between such wife and children, and that all or any part of his estate, real or personal, should be sold when his wife should think fit, in order to pay over to his children as they came of age the amount of their shares; and the will stated, " for which purpose

I do empower my said wife to execute seal and deliver any conveyance for the sale of all or any part of my real estate," and he appointed her executrix. *Held*, that by the will the wife had an interest in the estate, and not a mere power of sale.

(a) Before *Stephen*, C. J., and *Wise*, J.

I—4

married one *Burnicle*; and in 1843, shortly after the
plaintiff's father came of age, a family arrangement
took place. On the 15th of December in that year, in
pursuance of such arrangement, a deed was executed by
Burnicle and his wife, the grandfather's widow, and was
duly acknowledged by the latter. This deed—after reciting the will, and that the father's share thereunder
had been estimated at £1000, and that he had agreed
to accept the land conveyed as equivalent to such share
or sum of £1000, and release the estate, &c., from all
claims under such will—conveyed to the plaintiff's
father a certain portion of the grandfather's real estate,
including this land in dispute. The plaintiff was under
the age of fourteen years, and sued by his next friend,
his father's sister.

On the close of the plaintiff's case a nonsuit was
moved for, on the grounds—first, that under the grandfather's will the widow had no power to divide the
estate, as all the devisees were tenants in common, and
that, therefore, a less number than all such devisees
could not make a partition; secondly, that the plaintiff
could not rely on possession, as the grandfather's will
showed that nothing passed to the father; and thirdly,
that if it did, yet the legal estate of the grandfather and
father, as his heir was under the age of fourteen, passed
to his guardian in socage.

The learned Judge refused to nonsuit, but reserved
the last point.

The defendant's case was, that after the death of the
plaintiff's mother, the plaintiff's father married the
female defendant, and when he died he left a will under
which she claimed as testamentary guardian. But the
judgment of the Court has rendered it unnecessary to
consider the defendant's title.

His Honor directed the jury that (subject to the
question of the legal estate, until the plaintiff was fourteen years of age, being in the guardian in socage) if
the father and grandfather had possession of the
property, and if the plaintiff was the eldest son of
the father, the plaintiff was entitled to recover, even

although there might have been no legal title acquired
under the grandfather's will and the partition deed.
Because, according to the modern decisions, a possessory
title was not defeated by the disclosure of an imperfect
legal title by deed. The jury found a verdict for the
plaintiff.

Sheppard, for the defendant, obtained a rule to show
cause why a nonsuit should not be entered, or a new
trial granted, on the grounds—first, that the legal
estate was in the plaintiff's guardian in socage; and
secondly, that evidence of seisin, arising from the possession of the plaintiff's father, was rebutted by the
documentary evidence.

Butler showed cause. He contended, first, that there
cannot now be a guardian in socage, and referred to
Barnett v. *Earl of Guilford* (a); or, at all events, the
guardian's occupation is that of the heir; *R.* v. *Sutton* (b). In that case, where the respective interests of
an infant heir and his guardian in socage are much considered, and where all the authorities on the point are
collected, Lord *Denman* says, in giving judgment, "it
is clear that to some purposes the infant, whose guardian
in socage has entered and is in possession, is considered in
law as not merely the owner in right, but the owner in
actual seisin of the lands. This is so for the purpose of
transmitting land by descent, or excluding the half-
blood by a *possessio fratris*—Bro. Abr. Discent 19,
Good title dem. Newman v. *Newman* (c); in each of
which cases an actual entry and possession, at least by
construction of law, are necessary." For this reason,
therefore, an infant, although he is under the age of
fourteen, can maintain ejectment. The law is so laid
down in *Cole* (d), and *Adams* (e) on Ejectment.

On the question whether the title passed by the
grandfather's will to the plaintiff's father, or rather to
the grandfather's widow, it is submitted that the estate

(a) 11 Exch. 19.   (b) 3 A. & E. 597; S. C., 5 N. & M. 363.
(c) 3 Wils. 516; S. C., 3 Cruise 349.   (d) p. 584.   (e) p. 67.

passed to the widow. Mr. Justice *Williams* (a) says,
"It has been a subject of discussion in what cases
executors take a fee simple, in trust to sell, under a will,
or are invested merely with a power of disposition. The
distinction resulting from the authorities appear to be
this; that a devise of the land *to executors to sell*,
passes the interest in it; but a devise that *executors
shall sell the land*, or that *lands shall be sold by the
executors*, gives them but a power. An eminent writer (b)
has concluded from an examination of all the cases, that
even a devise of *land to be sold by the executors*, without
giving the estate to them, will invest them with a power
only, and not give them an interest." This case comes
within the former category; as it was necessary that the
estate should vest in the wife until the time had expired
wherein a posthumous child might be born, and also, it
is submitted, in order that she might pay the testator's
debts. The will also contemplates that as the children
come of age, she shall convey to them their respective
shares. The estate must, therefore, have passed to her
to enable her to carry out such intention of the testator.
It is admitted that if she had the legal estate, she passed
it to the plaintiff's father. [*Stephen*, C. J. The defendant asserts that the mother had, at all events, only
the power to sell; and that the conveyance to her son,
the plaintiff's father, is not in truth a sale.] Even
assuming the mother possessed a mere power to sell, the
conveyance to the plaintiff's father was a due execution
of such power. Although it is still undecided whether
a power of sale will authorise a partition, *Bradshaw* v.
Fane (c); yet, as is suggested by Lord *St. Leonards*,
the difficulty can be obviated by selling the undivided
estate, and expending the money received from such sale
in the purchase of the divided part of the estate. The
course pursued in this case was somewhat similar; the
father released his claim for £1000 against the estate,
and with that amount purchased the share containing the
land in dispute. He also contended that the plaintiff

(a) Wms. Executors 579.   (b) 1 Sugd. on Pow. 129.
(c) 25 L. J. Ch. 413; 2 Sugd. on Pow. 483.

must succeed on the twenty years' possession in the plaintiff's father, and that, therefore, it was not necessary to rely on the title from the grandfather.

Sheppard (*Rogers* with him) contra. The only possession proved was for thirteen years, for no possession was shown prior to 1843.

As to the grandfather's will there was only a bare power to sell, given to the mother, but there was no power to divide: and the conveyance is therefore void, as a partition is not a proper execution of a power to sell; *McQueen* v. *Farquhar* (a), *Sugden* on Powers (b). A mere executor has no implied power to sell or mortgage land for the payment of the testator's debts, charged by the will on the land; but the land descends to the heir charged simpliciter with the payment of debts; *Doe* v. *Hughes* (c). It is submitted that the legal estate was in the widow and children as tenants in common, with a power of sale in the former, and that under that power she could only sell the whole. [*Wise*, J. The same language is used as regards the realty and personalty; but it could not have been intended that there should be a tenancy in common of the personalty.]

Ejectment will only lie by the guardian in socage, that is, the next of the blood of the heir to whom the inheritance cannot descend; *Co. Litt* (d). [*Stephen*, C. J. But if such guardian be not in possession?] The authorities are clear that the whole estate and interest in the land is in the guardian in socage, who can maintain trespass and ejectment in his own name, or even make leases in his own name, until the infant comes to the age of fourteen; *Osborn* v. *Carden* (e), *Wade* v. *Baker* (f), *Shopland* v. *Ryoler* (g). *R.* v. *Sutton* shows that the seisin is in the infant, but the right to the possession in the guardian. The present plaintiff, therefore, cannot maintain this action. But if there be no guardian in socage, it is argued that the defendant, who was his

(a) 11 Ves. 474.
(c) 6 Exch. 223.
(e) Plowd. 293.
(b) 8th Ed., 856.
(d) 88 a.
(f) 1 Ld. Raym. 131.
(g) Cr. Jac. 99; and see 10 East 495, note (a).

1865.

JENKINS
v.
HARRIS
and wife.

stepmother, was his testamentary guardian; *Blackwell*
v. *Bull* (a).

STEPHEN, C. J.   As to the first point, whether by the
grandfather's will the estate passed to his widow, which
she has conveyed to the plaintiff's father, I am of opinion
that the estate did pass to his widow, and that by the
will it was intended that she should have the same power
over the real as over the personal estate.   The widow,
therefore, possessing the legal estate, conveyed it to the
plaintiff's father, and to this estate the plaintiff succeeded
as being his heir.   I need not, therefore, consider the
question of possession.

The next question is, whether this action ought not
to have been brought by the nearest blood relation who
could not inherit?   I shall assume that there can still
be a guardian in socage, and that the plaintiff's aunt is
entitled to be and is such guardian.   The question then
will be, whether, it appearing that she has never entered,
the infant can maintain ejectment.   There are authorities
to show that both the infant and his guardian in socage
can maintain ejectment; and it has been argued that it
is strange that this should be.   Both the text writers,
however, who have mentioned this point, seem to consider that it is settled law, and I do not think that *Rex*
v. *Sutton* is an authority against it, but rather in its
favor; for Lord *Denman* says, "It is clear from several
authorities that to some purposes the infant, whose
guardian in socage *has entered and is in possession*, is
considered in law as not merely the owner in right, but
the owner in actual seisin of the lands;" and in a subsequent part of the judgment, he says, "now it is clear
that the guardian in socage, *after entry*, has the legal
possession of the land to the use of the infant.   It is
observed by *Bayley*, J., in *Rex* v. *Oakley* (b), that the
form of pleading by a guardian in socage was, that *he
entered* as such, and was possessed."   The judgment
also states that where the guardian in socage has
entered and is in possession, there is by construction of

(a) 1 Keen 176.   (b) 10 East 495.

law an actual entry and possession by the heir. But in this case no guardian in socage has appeared; but the infant plaintiff is alone shown to be seized. If, however, he is the owner and actually seized, I see no reason why he should not be able to maintain ejectment.

WISE, J. I am of the same opinion. If the plaintiff's aunt be guardian in socage, she is not in possession. I am content to bow to the decision of the learned authorities whose opinions have been cited, and who say that an infant can maintain ejectment in his own name. Under the will it seems to me that it was intended that the widow should take the realty by the same title by which she took the personalty.

I was at first inclined to think that the case of *Forbes* v. *Peacock* (a) (which however is much modified by *Doe* v. *Hughes*) was an authority in favor of the defendant. But in that case the will disposed of realty in one clause and personalty in another; but here they both are mentioned in the same clause.

ATTORNEY GENERAL *against* JOSEPHSON.

INFORMATION filed by the Attorney General to recover certain arrears of rent.

The first count stated that whereas, heretofore to wit, on the 24th March, 1862, the Chief Commissioner for

The third paragraph of the 13th section of the Crown Lands Occupation Act of 1861,

enacts that "the rent (under leases of runs) shall be payable to the Colonial Treasurer, in Sydney, for each year after the first year, on or before the 31st day of December of the year preceding; provided that a fine shall be payable for the whole time during which any rent due shall remain unpaid after that date, at the rate of eight per centum on the amount, if not more than three months in arrear, and of ten per centum if more than three months. And if the rent be not paid at or before the end of six months after such date, together with such fine, the lease shall then become forfeited." To an information for a year's rent of a run, leased under the provisions of the above section, and also for the fine specified in the above section, the defendant pleaded that the run had become forfeited, in conformity with the condition and provision contained in the latter part of the section; and that Her Majesty the Queen, relying upon and recognising and adopting such forfeiture, took possession of the run, and offered and exposed the same for sale as forfeited, and the run was sold accordingly. *Held*, on demurrer, a bad plea.

(a) 11 M. & W. 637.

Crown Lands caused new leases for five years of certain
runs, and amongst them of the runs called "Banga" and
"Manwanga," in the unsettled districts of the colony,
which had been forfeited or vacated, to be advertised
in the *Government Gazette*, for sale by 'public auction,
at the rooms of Messieurs *W. Dean and Company*,
Government Auctioneers, on the 22nd May, 1862, upon
the terms and conditions prescribed by the Crown Lands
Occupation Act of 1861, and the regulations framed in
pursuance thereof; and afterwards, on the said 22nd
May, 1862, in accordance with the advertisement, the
leases of the runs so advertised were, under the direction
of the Colonial Treasurer acting for and on behalf of
her said Majesty the Queen, put up for sale by public
auction, at the said rooms, by the said Messieurs *W.
Dean and Company*, in conformity with existing regulations; and amongst the said conditions and regulations
were the following, viz. :—

That each lot would be put up for lease at the annual
rent stated in the advertisement, and the bidder of that
rent, or the highest bidder above it, would be declared
the purchaser, provided he should immediately pay down
the rent of the first year, computed from the first of
April to the thirty-first December, 1862, and sign the
sale list, thereby binding himself to the performance of
all the conditions of sale.

And also, that the rent should be payable to the
Colonial Treasurer in Sydney, for each year after the
first year, on or before the thirty-first day of December
of the year preceding; provided that a fine should be
payable for the whole time during which any rent due
should remain unpaid—after that date, at the rate of
eight per centum on the amount if not more than three
months in arrear, and of ten per centum if more than
three months.

It then averred that at the said sale the defendant
being the highest bidder for the said lease of the said
run called "Banga," became the purchaser thereof at
the yearly rent of £415, and also being the highest
bidder for the said lease of the said run called "Man-

wanga," became the purchaser thereof at the yearly rent of £410, and paid the rents of the first year of the said runs, computed as aforesaid, and signed the sale list, and thereupon entered into possession of the said runs; and although the 31st day of December, 1862, and a further period of more than three months, had elapsed long before the commencement of this suit, yet the defendant did not, on or before the said 31st December, 1862, or within the said further period of three months, pay the rent of the said runs called "Banga" and "Manwanga," or of either of them, for the year next ensuing the said 31st day of December, or any part thereof, and the said rent is still unpaid and in arrear; and by reason of the premises her said Majesty the Queen has been deprived of the said rents of the said runs for the said year, and a fine at the rate of ten per centum has also become payable to her said Majesty, which fine the defendant, although often requested, has not paid, but on the contrary wholly refused so to do.

There was also a count for use and occupation.

The defendant pleaded to the first count that the sale and purchase of the runs in the said count mentioned, was had and made under and by virtue of the Act and regulations in the information mentioned, and not otherwise; and that in and by and under and by virtue of the said Act and regulations, it is provided and prescribed that rent payable on any run purchased as in the said first count alleged, "shall be payable to the Colonial Treasurer in Sydney, for each year after the first year, on or before the 31st day of December of the year preceding—provided that a fine shall be payable for the whole time during which any rent shall remain unpaid after that date, at the rate of eight per centum on the amount if not more than three months in arrear, and of ten per centum if more than three months, and if the rent be not paid at or before the end of six months after such date, together with such fine, the lease shall become forfeited." Averment, that in conformity with such condition and provision the said runs were and became duly forfeited, and that Her Majesty the Queen,

acting upon and recognising and adopting such forfeiture, took possession of the said runs, and offered and
exposed the same for sale as forfeited, and the said runs
were sold accordingly.

Demurrer and joinder.

The office of Attorney General being vacant, and
there also being no Solicitor General, it was objected by
Isaacs, on behalf of the defendant, that the Court could
not proceed. He referred to Lord *Mansfield's* judgment
in *Wilkes'* case (a), and *R.* v. *Jones* (b).

Faucett, for the plaintiff, contended that the Queen
was the actual party to the record, and that the suit
does not abate by the vacancy of the office.

Isaacs replied.

STEPHEN, C. J. I am of opinion that the Attorney
General is the plaintiff in a suit of this kind, and if that
be so, that it is impossible for the Court this day to give
judgment in favor of, or against, a non-existing person.
The Crown is not the plaintiff in point of form. If there
be no plaintiff to appear here to day, how can the Court
proceed? I do not think that the suit abates, but I
am of opinion that it is suspended till a new Attorney
General shall have been appointed. I may add that
the first section of the Act (c), providing for the payment of costs in proceedings instituted by the Crown,
enacts that the Attorney General, and not the Crown,
shall be entitled to recover costs when the plaintiff re-
covers. The suggestion which must be filed in ordinary
cases is not necessary in suits on behalf of the Crown.

WISE, J. I understand the point that has been
argued is whether the Court is seized of the case. There
is no evidence before us that there is not an Attorney
General at present. There is no plea in abatement, but
a mere statement by counsel that such is the case, and
an objection taken to the jurisdiction of the Court,
because the plaintiff does not appear. I am of opinion

(a) 4 Burr. 2558.   (b) 2 Camp. 131.   (c) 20 Vic., No. 3.

that the defendant is entitled to argue this case, in which issue has been joined, in the absence of all evidence; that the Court has ceased to have jurisdiction over the case. Suppose, in a criminal case, the jury empannelled, and that then the Attorney General died, would there be an abatement under such circumstances? There having been a joinder in demurrer, the question is whether the Court is seized of the argument. If the objection was valid, should we not find some trace of an amendment of the proceedings when there is a change in the office of Attorney General. There is no trace of any such suggestion on the record as there is in cases of abatement. I shall be prepared to give judgment on this record as I find it, either for or against the Attorney General, in whose name the proceedings are filed. In the absence of any authority to the contrary, I am clearly of opinion that the suit does not abate, and that we can go on with this record. There being no suggestion that any other Attorney General is in office, we must assume that the same gentleman, whose name appears on the record, is Attorney General.

HARGRAVE, J. I regret that I must differ from the opinion of his Honor the Chief Justice. With reference to the case of death, *The Attorney General* v. *The Mayor of Galway* (a) shows that if the Attorney General dies the suit does not abate, and that his intervention is only with regard to costs. That principle is recognised by the practice in England. Her Majesty is sued before her Majesty's Court, in order that justice may be attained; and she appears by her Attorney General. The latter is only like counsel who signs the pleadings, and conducts the case for her. The death of counsel is not noticed on the proceedings, and it seems to me that the death of the Attorney General produces no more variation than the death of counsel. Further, a similar thing must often have occurred in England; but no procedure to remedy this alleged defect on the record can be found. I am of opinion that the objection is not valid (b).

(a) 1 Moll. 95. (b) See *Armagh (Archbishop)* v. *Att. Gen.*, 8 Br. P. C. 507.

1865.

ATTORNEY
GENERAL
v.
JOSEPHSON.

Fawcett in support of the demurrer. The Crown is clearly entitled to recover. It would not be so with respect to rent accruing after entry for the forfeiture. But here the Crown claims the amount due and payable before such entry. It is submitted that the penalties are cumulative; and the Crown, although availing itself of the forfeiture, is still entitled to recover the rent previously accrued. If there is a re-entry for a forfeiture, rent due before the entry is recoverable; *Hartshorne* v. *Watson* (a), *Doe* v. *Peck* (b), *Selby* v. *Browne* (c), *Lee* v. *Smith* (d), *Johns* v. *Whitley* (e), *Com. Dig. Dett* (A. 5), and *Franklin* v. *Carter* (f). It is the defendant's own fault if he does not choose to occupy.

Isaacs in support of the plea. The second year's rent is one entire thing, and is due for the whole year; and the Crown by entering, pending the year, as for a forfeiture, has prevented itself from recovering any portion of the year's rent. [*Stephen*, C. J. If that be so, a lessee by not paying during the half year will avoid the effect of a forfeiture for the whole year.] The remedies are not cumulative; and the Crown having adopted the remedy by forfeiture, cannot now sue for the rent. It could not have been intended that the Crown should receive rent from two people for the self-same period. [*Stephen*, C. J. If the forfeiture be the only penalty, the tenant would in every case occupy for six months for nothing.]

STEPHEN, C. J. The facts apparent on the pleadings are, that the defendant became tenant of the two runs which had become forfeited, he undertaking to pay the rent in advance, on or before the 31st December in the preceding year. After the first year there was to be a fine of eight per cent. if in arrears less than three months, and ten per cent. if more than three months; and if the rent was not paid at or before the end of six

(a) 4 B. N. C. 178. (b) 1 B. & Ad. 428.
(c) 7 Q. B. 620. (d) 9 Exch. 662.
(e) 8 Wils. 127, 140. (f) 1 C. B. 750; 14 L. J. C. P. 241.

months, together with such fine, the lease was then to become forfeited. The plea alleges that the Crown has taken advantage of the forfeiture, and entered on the demised premises. The ground of demurrer to this plea is, that it is no answer to the action for the rent thus payable in advance and for interest; and I am of opinion that the Crown, notwithstanding its having taken advantage of the forfeiture, is entitled to recover this rent and interest. I have some doubt whether the lease is not forfeited at the expiration of the six months *ipso facto*, although perhaps the Crown might condone the forfeiture. Parties have six months to pay the rent; and if it is not then paid the lease is forfeited, if the Crown thinks fit to enforce it. Suppose that at the end of three months the Crown had demanded the rent, the Crown could then distrain for the whole and sell, or could sue for it; and if the Crown did not recover the whole rent, the balance would still remain due with interest thereon at ten per cent. The language of the enactment, and of the agreement, is clear.

WISE, J. The words are quite plain. The defendant contracted to pay the rent at a given time; and if it was not paid, to pay a fine increasing in amount if the rent continued unpaid. If the rent were not paid at or before the end of six months, together with such fine, the lease should then become forfeited. The defendant, therefore, is bound to pay the rent and the fine. If he is not to pay the rent because of the forfeiture, he would for the same reason be entitled to get rid of the fine; in other words, he would be in a position to occupy the runs for six months, for nothing.

HARGRAVE, J., concurred, for the reasons already given.

Judgment for the plaintiff.

June 14.   CAMPBELL *against* THE QUEEN.

In a petition of right it appeared that tenders were invited by a notice in the *Gazette* of 12th March, 1851, for a block of land described as " Coonargo, block A, 48,000 acres," and bounded as therein mentioned ; and a tender by *D.* containing the same description and boundaries was accepted. Afterwards, an amended description of the same block, stating the area to be 80,000 acres, and giving new boundaries in accordance with such enlarged area, was sent by the Government to *D.*

THIS was a petition of right to the Queen's Most Excellent Majesty, under the provisions of the 24 Vic., No. 27, and was as follows :—

1. That A. D. 1852, to wit, in the month of August in that year, a certain run or tract of Crown land (hereinafter designated as " the said run "), situated in the unsettled districts of New South Wales—that is to say, the Murrumbidgee district—which run then was, and from thence hitherto has been, and now is, part of the waste lands of the colony belonging to your Majesty, in right of your Majesty's Royal Crown as Queen, &c., and which said run was then, and from thence hitherto has been, and now is, known as, and under the name of " Coonargo, block A," was, in due form of law, and in accordance with the laws in that behalf then existing and in force, duly contracted and promised to be leased by and on behalf of your Majesty, subject to the conditions and reservations specified in your Majesty's orders in Council, having reference to the occupation of Crown lands in New South Wales, to a certain subject of your Majesty (hereinafter designated as " the said original lessee "), in pursuance of a tender duly made by him, and duly accepted by and on behalf of your Majesty ; and the said original lessee duly paid the first and published in the *Gazette* of 11th August, 1852, and thereupon Government accepted the tender of *D.* by the new description. This run having been forfeited for non-payment of rent, tenders were again invited by a notice in the *Gazette* of 11th September, 1857, for the same run therein stated to have become vacant, giving it the same name, and describing it in the same terms and with the same boundaries as in the advertisement of 12th March, 1851. The tender of *H.*, which stated that he proposed to take a lease, &c., of the land " known as Coonargo, block A," and, in a schedule annexed to the tender, described in the same way as in the *Gazette* of 12th March, 1851, having been accepted, the Government put up to auction as a new run, under the name of " Coonargo D," the land included in the amended description, published in the *Gazette* of 11th August, 1852, but excluded from the description published in the *Gazettes* of 12th March, 1851, and of 11th September, 1857. *Held*, that under such circumstances the contract between the Government and *H.* only related to the land described in the *Gazette* of March, 1851, and September, 1857, and that the Government was entitled to sell the excess—that is, the land included in the larger, but excluded from the smaller area, as a new run, under the 13th section of the second chapter of the Orders in Council—and that the 12th section did not affect any such power.

year's rent for the said run to an officer of your Majesty, duly authorised to receive the same, and thereupon the occupation of the said run by the said original lessee was duly authorised by the proper authorities in that behalf, pending the preparation of the lease thereof, subject to all the conditions and reservations specified as aforesaid.

2. That afterwards and before the month of September, 1857, the said original lessee or his assigns made default in the performance of the conditions and reservations specified as aforesaid, or some of them, and he or they thereby forfeited the lease and the promise thereof, and he or they thereby forfeited their right to occupy the said run, and thereby under the laws then in force affecting the waste lands of your Majesty, the said run became and was a forfeited run within the meaning of the said laws.

3. That after the said run had so become a forfeited run as aforesaid, and before the month of September, 1857, application was duly made in pursuance of the laws for the purchase of a lease thereof; and afterwards, in 1857, to wit, in the month of September in that year, it was in pursuance of the laws duly notified in the New South Wales *Government Gazette*, that tenders in the proper form would be received by the proper officers of your Majesty in that behalf, up to the 7th day of December in the last-mentioned year, from the previous applicants, and from any other persons desirous to enter into competition with them for the purchase, under and in accordance with the said laws, of the lease of the said run, and thereupon and thereby the lease thereof then became, and was duly submitted, according to law and in pursuance of the laws aforesaid, for sale as a forfeited run.

4. That after the month of September, 1857, and before the 7th day of December in the last-mentioned year, the lease of the said run was duly tendered for by divers persons, and the tender of a certain other subject of your Majesty (hereinafter designated as "the said second lessee") being the highest of such tenders, was then and there duly accepted by or on behalf of your

Majesty, and thereupon a promise to him was duly made by and on behalf of your Majesty of the lease of the said run.

5. That the said second lessee thereupon duly entered into the occupation of the said run, and performed all matters and things on his part to be performed in reference thereto, and to the lease thereof so contracted and promised to be granted and given to him as aforesaid, and he became duly entitled to such lease under and by virtue of, and in accordance with, the laws at that time in force, in reference to such waste lands of the Crown as aforesaid.

6. That afterwards the right to the last-mentioned lease of the said run, and all the right and interest of the said second lessee therein and thereto, were, in accordance with the laws aforesaid, and with the consent and authority of your Majesty's proper officers in that behalf, duly transferred and assigned to your suppliant, and your suppliant thereupon duly entered into the occupation and possession of the said run, and has ever since been and now is in the actual lawful and exclusive possession thereof, by virtue of the aforesaid tender for the last-mentioned lease thereof, and of the acceptance thereof, and of the several other facts and circumstances hereinbefore set forth in that behalf; and your suppliant has paid all rent and other moneys, and performed all matters and things on his part to be paid and performed respectively, to entitle him to continue in the occupation of the said run, and to have granted and issued to him a lease thereof, in pursuance of and in accordance with the tender of the said second lessee, and the acceptance thereof, and all rights, benefits, and advantages arising or accruing therefrom, or incident thereto.

7. That the term for which the last-mentioned lease of the said run was so promised, and contracted to be granted as aforesaid, has not yet expired.

8. That, nevertheless, certain officers of your Majesty in New South Wales have, recently, unlawfully put up for sale by public competition an alleged right to grant a lease by and on behalf of your Majesty, during the

continuance of the term of the last mentioned lease of the
said run to which your suppliant was and is so entitled
as aforesaid, of a large portion of the lands comprised in
the said run so in the occupation of your suppliant, and
so under lease or promise of lease to him as aforesaid.

9. That in order to prevent your suppliant's rights
being prejudicially affected by the last aforesaid proceedings of the officers of your Majesty, your suppliant
attended at the time and place of the last mentioned
putting up for sale of the alleged right to grant such
lease as last aforesaid, of such portion as aforesaid of the
said run, and publicly protested against any such sale,
and the right of the officers of your Majesty to submit any
such right to sale as aforesaid, or to pledge your Majesty
to promise or grant any such lease as aforesaid of the
portion of the said run; but, notwithstanding such protest, and the facts hereinbefore set forth, your Majesty's
officers persisted in proceeding with the sale, and the
same was proceeded with accordingly; and divers persons
having bid for and made offers to purchase the lease of
the portion of the said run so put up for sale as last aforesaid, your suppliant in order to protect his own interests
from aggression by any pretended purchasers, and in
order to protect your suppliant's just and legal rights of
in to and in respect of the said run from being illegally
invaded or interfered with, and to prevent his lawful and
rightful possession of the said run being unlawfully in-
truded upon and interfered with, did, by his agent, nomi-
nally become the purchaser of the alleged right to such
last mentioned lease as aforesaid, of the portion of the said
run; and under cover of the illegal sale your Majesty's
last mentioned officers did, in the name and on behalf of
your Majesty, obtain from your suppliant, through your
suppliant's agent, the sum of £260, which sum of money
was so obtained from your suppliant as aforesaid, and is
now held by or on behalf of your Majesty, through your
Majesty's said officers in the said colony, without any
consideration whatever, and is, as your suppliant humbly
submits, so much money of your suppliant had and received by and on behalf of your Majesty, through your

K—4

Majesty's officers in the colony, to and for the use of your suppliant, and ought as your suppliant submits to be forthwith repaid to your suppliant.

10. That your suppliant has duly applied to the proper officers of your Majesty in that behalf, for the return to him of the said sum of £260; but your Majesty's officers have declined and refused to return or pay the same, or any part thereof, to him.

There were similar counts with regard to a sum of £212 10s., which had been paid for another block called "Coonargo, block C"; and there were counts for money had and received, money paid and interest.

The cause came on for trial before his Honor the Chief Justice, and a special jury of twelve, in the November sittings, in 1864, when the facts of the case were proved to be as follows:—About the year 1850, it appeared from a mass of correspondence which was in evidence, applications were made to the Government to put up for tender a large block of country, afterwards called the Murrumbidgee Plains, lying between the Murrumbidgee and Billibong Rivers—the former being to the north, and the latter to the south of these plains. At this time the country on the south bank of the Murrumbidgee and the north bank of the Billabong had already been taken up, and constituted a number of runs, having frontages to those rivers. These runs were called frontage runs; and the plains in question are situate between the northern boundary of the runs fronting the Murrumbidgee, and the southern boundary of the runs fronting the Billabong. The object of parcelling out these plains was to form back runs to these frontage runs. At this time, Mr. *Bingham* was the Crown Lands Commissioner of the district, and he accordingly plotted out this country; but he did it without actual survey. These back blocks were advertised in the *Gazette* of the 12th March, 1851, as adjusted new runs. This notice stated "that tenders having been received for the undermentioned new runs of Crown land, the boundaries of which required to be adjusted so as to exclude lands already under lease, or promise of lease,

or applied for by other parties, sealed tenders in the prescribed printed form will be received at this office until
noon of Monday, the second day of June next." In
that notice, the two blocks of land in question are
described as "Coonargo back run, block A, 48,000
acres, commencing at the north-east terminus of the
Wirkenbergil run, leased to *Walter Ogilvie*, and extending south for 10 miles, thence east by north 7½ miles,
thence north 10 miles, and thence west by south 7½
miles." "Coonargo back run, block C, 32,000 acres,
commencing at the north-east terminus of Coonargo,
block B, and extending south for 10 miles, thence east
by north 5 miles, thence north 10 miles, and thence west
by south 5 miles." There was an intermediate back run
called Coonargo back run, block B, with a similar
depth. Tenders for these runs were sent in, containing
the description as given in the *Gazette*, and shortly
afterwards were duly accepted; that for block A by
Mr. *Denny*, that for block B by Messrs. *Lang*, and that
for block C by Mr. *Keating*. Some time after the acceptance of these tenders, the descriptions were sent to
Mr. *Townshend*, the Government surveyor, who made
new and amended descriptions, giving a much larger area.
Block A was described by *Townshend* as containing
80,000 instead of 48,000 acres, and block C as containing
55,000 instead of 32,000 acres. These descriptions were
sent to the Chief Commissioner of Crown lands, by whom
they were supplied to the respective tenderers, as containing the descriptions of the land they might occupy;
and there was evidence that the map used in the local
Crown Lands Office was based upon this survey. In
the *Gazette* of the 11th August, 1852, there was the
following notification:—"It is hereby notified for general
information that the tenders of the undermentioned
parties having been accepted for the runs of Crown land
specified in connection with their respective names, &c.,
the occupation of the runs has been authorised, &c."
The description of block A is then given, as furnished
by *Townshend*, namely—"Name of run. Coonargo.
block A. Estimated area, 80,000 acres. Estimated

grazing capability, 4,000 sheep.   Bounded on the east
by a line bearing south 18 miles and 24 chains, commencing at the south-east corner of Burrabogu, block A,
on the south by a line bearing west 7 miles and 40
chains, on the west by a line bearing north 17 miles and
16 chains, and on the north by a line bearing east 7
degrees north, 7 miles and 48 chains." No such notification in the *Gazette* as the above appeared to have
been given with regard to block C.

In consequence of the non-payment of rent that
accrued after these dates, blocks A. and C. became forfeited.   Block B (with which, however, this case had
nothing to do) was not forfeited, but kept by Messrs.
Lang till 1858, when it was sold and transferred to
Reid, Brothers.

The following advertisement, dated 11th September,
1857, was published in the *Gazette* :—"It is hereby
notified, for general information, that application having
been made for the purchase of leases of the runs of
Crown land hereunder described, which have been
adjusted in consequence of conflicting tenders, or
after having been occupied have become vacant by
forfeiture or otherwise, tenders in the prescribed form
will be received at this office until noon of Monday, the
7th day of December, &c."   The runs in question are
described in this notice, in the same terms and with the
same boundary lines as in the advertisement of the 12th
March, 1851, except that the first block is called
"Coonargo, block A," instead of "Coonargo back run,
block A ;" and one boundary line is said to extend
"north 10 miles" instead of "south 10 miles." Various
tenders were received by the Government; and on 13th
April, 1858, the tender of *Charles Huon* for block A,
and that of *David Reid* for block C, were accepted.
The tenders stated that the party tendering did "hereby
propose to take a lease for fourteen years of the Crown
lands known as Coonargo back run, block C, in the district of Murrumbidgee, which lands are particularly
described in the schedule annexed to this tender." The
tender for Coonargo, block A, was in similar terms.   In

the schedules accompanying these tenders, the same descriptions and acreage were given as in the advertisement of the 16th September, 1857, calling for tenders. It was notified in the *Gazette* of 16th April, 1858, that the "tenders of the undermentioned parties have been accepted for the runs of Crown lands specified in connection with their respective names:—Name of tenderer, *C. Huon ;* name of run, Coonargo, block A. Name of tenderer, *D. Reid;* name of run, Coonargo back run, block C." The interests of *Reid* and *Huon* became vested in the suppliant in 1862.

The Government being of opinion that *Huon* and *Reid* were only entitled to occupy the land described in the notices in the *Gazette* of the 12th March, 1851, and the 11th September, 1857, notwithstanding their repeated protests, offered to public competition, under the names of Coonargo D and Coonargo E, the land included in the land contained in *Townshend's* amended description, but excluded from the land described in the notices of the 12th of March, 1851, and the 11th of September, 1857. Leases of the land in question, which was at the south of blocks A and C, were accordingly submitted to auction on the 1st July, 1863, as new runs; and although the suppliant protested in the sale room, they were sold, being purchased by Mr. *Chauvel* as his agent, who, in accordance with the conditions of sale, paid the rents thereof computed from 1st July to 31st December, 1863—that is to say, £260 for Coonargo D, and £212 10s. for Coonargo E. It was to recover these amounts that the present petition had been presented. There was also a mass of correspondence between the different officers of the Government, and also between those officers and the suppliant and those through whom he claimed, which was received in evidence.

At the trial it was contended for the suppliant that Coonargo, block A, and Coonargo, block C, were ascertained and known runs, and that the stated area and length of lines were a mere mistake and *falsa demonstratio ;* and that this, it was argued, was the more apparent, as under the 12th section of the second chapter of the Orders in Council the Crown had no power to divide a forfeited run. At the suggestion of the learned Judge, a verdict was taken for the plaintiff by consent for the amount claimed, subject to the opinion of the Court whether the plaintiff could retain such verdict. The question ·for the Court to be, whether the lands— the lease of which was sold by the Crown in 1863, and purchased then by the plaintiff under the circumstances stated in the petition—were, at the time of such sale, included in the runs purchased by him from the Messrs. *Reid* the previous year; in other words, whether the lands resold in 1863 were included within the blocks— the lease of which was purchased from the Crown by Mr. *Huon* and Mr. *Reid*, in 1857. The Court to have the same power to draw inferences from the evidence that the jury could have drawn.

A rule *nisi* having been obtained in the last term, 1864, on behalf of Her Majesty,

June 14.   Sir *W. Manning*, Q. C., and *Stephen*, on behalf of the suppliant, now showed cause. The correspondence shows that it was intended that the owners of the frontage runs should have the advantage of these plains as back runs ; and that it was supposed that the entire space would be occupied by giving each frontage run 10 miles in depth of back run. The advertisements, therefore, should be understood as indicating blocks, beginning where the ten miles from the respective rivers ended. The descriptions by *Bingham*, as adopted in the notices in the *Gazette* of 12th March, 1851, mention 10 miles to be the length of these runs ; but the acceptance of *Denny's* tender in 1852, mentions 18 miles as the actual depth of block A. In the enlarged descriptions in 1852, the self-same capability is attributed to the 80,000 acres as was assigned before to the 48,000 acres. It never could have been intended to leave these blocks, D and C, unoccupied, as the object was to lease the entire tract of country between the two rivers, and this could only be done by giving the whole 18 miles to blocks A and C. In offering these blocks, therefore, again in 1857, the Crown must have intended in fact to offer the same extent and area as before. The name, together with the known area occupied under it, and appearing by the local office map taken from *Townshend's* survey, was the test and guide, and conclusively shows what was purchased. It is submitted that when, in 1857, the advertisement appeared, respecting blocks A and C as " forfeited " runs, the 18 miles in depth was necessarily the extent offered to tenderers. For no run whatever, called Coonargo A and C, of 10 miles only, had been occupied and vacated. [*Stephen*, C. J. But this advertisement in 1857 distinctly specifies 10 miles only, as the depth for each block. Is the suppliant entitled to 18 miles in each case ?] The three Coonargo blocks were known as back runs to Coonargo, the frontage run on the Billabong—and as such blocks they were advertised and tendered for. *Reid's* tender was for a run known as " Coonargo back run," and this tender was accepted; but the acceptance was not according to the description in the *Gazette*. The suppliant is therefore entitled to hold all the 18 miles extent by the same name. [*Stephen*, C. J. Although *Denny's* and *Keating's* tenders were accepted as 18 miles in length, yet they each tendered only for the lands respectively as ten miles.] In conveyances, if the thing intended to be conveyed is sufficiently certain in itself, the addition of other circumstances (false or mistaken) will not frustrate the grant; *veritas nominis tollit errorem demonstrationis.* A description by name is sufficient, and the statement of the length of lines corresponding with ascribed boundaries, or of the occupation by a particular person, is of no importance. What is the length of a line, or the statement of an area, but a mere description? In *Manning* v. *Fitzgerald* (a), a lease of land described by admeasurement " with the houses now erected, or being erected thereon " (it being found as a fact that at the time the lease was executed, the foundations of the houses had been laid), was considered to be in effect the same as though it had been a

(a) 29 L. J. Ex. 24.

lease of these specific houses, and, the dimensions considerably exceeding those stated, the admeasurement was considered to be a mere false description. In *Llewellyn* v. *Earl of Jersey* (a), a deed conveyed a piece of land forming part of a close, by reference to a schedule annexed. The schedule described the land in a column headed " No. on the plan of the Briton Terry Estate," as " 153 b ;" in a second column headed " Description of premises," as " a small piece marked on the plan;" in a third column, as being in the occupation of *T. E.*; and in a fourth, as " 34 perches." At the time of the contract a line was drawn upon the plan as the boundary line, dividing the piece 153 b from the rest of the close of which it formed a part. The plan was upon actual measurement found to be incorrect; and 153 b contained, according to actual measurement, only 27 perches. And the Court held that the statement, that the piece of land conveyed contained 34 perches, was merely *falsa demonstratio*—the prior portion of the description being sufficient to convey it. *Parke*, B., says, " the portion conveyed is perfectly described and can be precisely ascertained, and no difficulty arises except from the subsequent statement, that it contains 34 perches. That, however, becomes merely a false description of that which is conveyed with convenient certainty before; and resembles the case in *Sheppard's* Touchstone, of the meadow in D. described as containing ten, when in fact it contained twenty, acres." The passage referred to is, " If one grant in this manner all my meadow in D., containing ten acres, whereas in truth his meadow there doth contain twenty acres, it seems this is a good grant for the whole twenty acres" (b). *Dowtie's case* (c), *Doe* v. *Hubbard* (d), *Wood* v. *Rowcliffe* (e), and *Broom's* Maxims (f) were referred to.

It is submitted also that the Orders in Council contemplate only the leasing of a forfeited run in its

---

(a) 11 M. & W. 183 ; see also *Barton* v. *Dawes*, 10 C. B. 261;
19 L. J. C. P. 302.
(b) p. 248.   (c) 2 Rep. 24.
(d) 15 Q. B. 241 ; 20 L. J. Q. B. 61.   (e) 6 Exch. 407.
(f) [4th Ed.,] p. 604.

entirety, and not the dividing them in any way. Sections 11, 12, and 13 of Chapter 11 were referred to. The 12th section confers a power to lease a run already described. It provides that it shall be competent for any person, &c., "to purchase anew the lease of such run ; " and sealed tenders are to be sent in by persons " disposed to enter into competition for the said lease; and every tender shall state the term of years for which it is proposed to take the said run," &c. The section clearly contemplates the reletting of the same runs that had become forfeited, and not any division of them. [*Wise*, J. Has it not been understood that that section applies only to cases of pre-emption ?]

It is also to be remembered that *Denny* and *Keating* occupied 18 miles, and so did *Reid* and the suppliant; and there have been expensive improvements on the portions afterwards sold as D and E; and that the Government always intended and announced that the entire block A and C, so occupied and forfeited, should be offered again.

The *Attorney General*, the *Solicitor General*, and *Butler*, who appeared for the Crown, were not called on.

STEPHEN, C. J. I am of opinion that the plaintiff's claim is unfounded, and that the verdict must be entered for the Crown. This case when looked at in all its circumstances is very plain ; but it has been complicated by small facts with which we have nothing to do. Where a person conveys a well known property as a farm, and describes it as containing a greater or less number of acres than it really does, such incorrect description of acreage can be rejected, and the property pass under the general description by which it is known. The application of this principle in the present case is, I think, as plain as possible, when the facts are properly understood.

The facts are as follows :—The two rivers, Murrumbidgee and Billabong, run somewhat parallel to each other—the former lying to the north, and the latter to the south.   There were a number of frontage runs on the northern side of the Billabong, and on the southern side of the Murrumbidgee.   The land between these two classes of runs is a large plain called the Murrumbidgee plains.   The Crown intended to lease out this intermediate country as back runs to these frontage runs already referred to.   It was thought that if the whole of this intermediate country were divided between them, each would obtain a back run of about the depth of ten miles.   It appears accordingly that the back runs of the runs fronting the Billabong are described as bounded on the north by the southern extremity of the back runs of the runs fronting the Murrumbidgee.   But it is quite plain that the Government only intended to give to either sets of frontage runs, blocks with a depth as was supposed of about ten miles.   Tenders therefore were in March, 1851, invited for this country, of which the land in dispute, called Coonargo, blocks A 'and C, formed a portion.

It appears that the two blocks were originally named Coonargo, block A and block C, respectively, by the Government itself; but in so naming them, the Government also in the same advertisement gave a description of those blocks; in other words, announced unmistakably that the land so named indicated a particular area and no more ; that is, as in every other instance, 10 miles long by a certain breadth.   Messrs. *Denny* and *Keating*, the original tenderers, adopted and repeated this description.   The land moreover was offered to the public by this description.   But after this, both after the advertisement and after the receipt of the tender, the Government received a description from its surveyor, by which it appeared that Coonargo, blocks A and C, as shown on the ground, were nearly twice as large, because the length of the side lines was really 18 instead of 10 miles, and thereupon Government accepted the tender for these runs by the new description—that is, for one described as containing 80,000 instead of 48,000 acres, and for the other as containing 55,000 instead of 32,000 acres.   A few years after this, however, Messrs. *Denny* and *Keating* (it not being clear that they even occupied the land by the new description) forfeited the blocks. The Government then advertised them as before, by the old description, giving the same names (Coonargo, blocks A and C), or with a slight and immaterial variation, but stating the length as ten miles and the area as originally mentioned. The suppliant, or rather Messrs. *Reid* and *Huon* from whom he claims, thereupon tendered for the blocks by that description. What was that, but admitting that "Coonargo, blocks A and C," as so described by the diminished length and area, was the land offered and which he sought to obtain? The Government finally accepted the tender by the self-same description; and these things being so, the undisturbed occupation afterwards of the blocks, to the enlarged extent by Messrs. *Reid* and *Huon*, proves nothing.

It seems to me that although the Government advertised the two blocks as "forfeited," the Crown cannot be held to have thereby meant the lands as occupied by Messrs. ·*Denny* and *Keating* ; nor even as held by them, under the descriptions furnished in the letter of the Chief Commissioner of Crown lands, and notified in the *Gazette* of the 11th August, 1852. For the reverse is shown by the new offer and tender, which described these blocks by the diminished areas and lengths. Nor does any argument arise from the fact that in *Townshend's* maps the two are represented by larger areas. It is a mere question, what was the contract and transaction between the suppliant or his predecessor, and the Government, as evidenced by the negotiations between them. The land in excess, in my opinion, was not included or intended to be included in the leases; and if the parties were before a Court of Equity, that Court would not cause the lease to be amended so as to include such excess, because no intention to include such excess existed either on the one side or the other.

I am of opinion, therefore, that the Crown, both in law and equity, had a right to sell the excess, called Coonargo, blocks D and E, and so that the verdict must be entered for the defendant.

As to block B, which has been always occupied since it was first offered, and the tender accepted in 1851, I doubt much whether, even in that case, the Government might not disturb the owner in the occupation of the country in excess of the ten miles.

WISE, J. I am of the same opinion. The contract relied on is in writing. It is the tender and acceptance of the 11th of September, 1857. It is headed, "Adjusted, Forfeited, and Vacated Runs," and is as follows:—[His Honor read the notice in the *Gazette* of that date.] That notice referred to a large number of runs. It did not define what was adjusted or forfeited; but all these runs were headed with this description; and, therefore, by a necessary rule of construction, the words adjusted and forfeited showed the purchasers what these runs were, and they purchased by the description and not by the name. It was not a private sale; but a public notice was given to all the world,—to persons who knew as well as those who did not know the subject matter. It is clear that persons competing for these runs would be guided by this description, and would tender accordingly. Shall a person who happened to know that previously the same description of 48,000 acres meant 80,000, therefore, become entitled to the latter quantity when the other competitors only supposed that the run contains 48,000 acres? If you look at the name only, there is evidence that at one time it had a depth of ten miles, at another of eighteen miles. The question is, what the one party tendered for, and the other party accepted. If there were a clear difference; if the one party meant one thing and the other party meant something else; I am at a loss to know how a Court of Law or of Equity could interfere. According to the argument for the plaintiff, because he knew in his mind that the Government ought to have described the land differently, he is to obtain something quite contrary to his contract. In strict law the plaintiff is not entitled to succeed. I trust it will not be considered that questions of this kind are to be considered as compound questions of law and equity. In questions of specific performance a Court of Equity can decree a performance of a contract with compensation. How can a Court of Law carry out such principles?

Judgment for the Crown.

THE QUEEN *against* DOUGLASS.

SPECIAL case reserved for the consideration of the Judges, under 13 Vic., No. 8.

An acquittal on a charge of feloniously assaulting and wounding with intent to murder, is not a bar to an information for a common assault and battery.

" This prisoner was tried before me at the late Goulburn Assizes, on a charge of felonious assault with intent to murder, by throwing down earth upon the prosecutor who was at the bottom of a gold shaft, and he was acquitted on a direction from me that it was essential to the felony that the prisoner should have actually meditated murder. He was then indicted for a common assault upon the same facts, and put in a plea of *autrefois acquit*, founded on his acquittal in the previous case. The Crown took issue on the plea, and a jury was sworn to try the question whether the offences in the two indictments were the same.

"There were two counts in the first indictment, to which I refer as part of this special case. But, at the time of both trials, only the first of those counts was adverted to; nor can I now state that I was aware of the existence of the second (*a*).

(*a*) The first count charged that the prisoner on the &c., at Young, &c., feloniously, unlawfully, and maliciously did assault one *Ah Look*, and by throwing earth and soil into a certain excavation in the ground, in which the said *Ah Look* then was, did attempt to suffocate the said *Ah Look*, with intent thereby then feloniously, wilfully, and of his malice aforethought, to kill and murder the said *Ah Look*.

The second count charged that the prisoner feloniously, wilfully, and maliciously, in and upon the said *Ah Look*, did make an assault, and him (the said *Ah Look*) did beat, wound, and illtreat, with intent thereby then feloniously, wilfully, and of his malice aforethought, to kill and murder the said *Ah Look*.

The second information charged that the prisoner, in and upon one *Ah Look*, did make an assault, and him (the said *Ah Look*) did then beat, wound, and illtreat, and other wrongs to the said *Ah Look* then did.

"I told the jury in my charge that the two offences were essentially different, and that the prisoner could not on the first indictment have been found guilty, merely on the evidence which would sustain a charge of assault, or assault and battery. The intention to kill in the former case being the main ingredient and consti-tuting a felony, whereas in the latter that intention was wholly immaterial, and that he could not in the first case, on any evidence, have been convicted of assault. Upon this charge the jury returned a verdict for the Crown.

"At the request of the prisoner's counsel I reserved the question, whether this charge was correct, and whether the verdict ought or not, under the circumstances, to have been in the prisoner's favor on the plea of *autrefois acquit*.

                                   ALFRED STEPHEN, C. J."

Sydney, 16th June, 1865.

Isaacs for the prisoner. The felony charged in the first information included an assault of which he might on that information have been convicted, and, therefore, on the second information he was entitled to judgment on the plea of *autrefois acquit*. He referred to *Bird's* case (a), *Elrington's* case (b), *Wright's* case (c), *Gray's* case (d), and *Archbold's* Criminal Pleading (e).

Windeyer, who appeared for the Crown, was not called upon.

STEPHEN, C. J. I am of opinion that our judgment must be for the Crown. The prisoner in the first count of the first information was charged with feloniously attempting to suffocate with intent to murder, which is made a felony by the 1 Vic., c. 85, sect. 3; in the second, with beating, wounding, and illtreating with the same intent. On this information there was an acquittal. The special case goes on to state that the prisoner was

(a) 2 Den. 94; 20 L. J. M. C. 70.   (b) 8 Jur. N. S. 97; 31 L. J. M. C. 14.
(c) 2 F. & F. 321.   (d) 33 L. J. M. C. 78.   (e) p. 529.

then charged in a second information with a common assault. Under such circumstances, it seems to me clear that he could not have been convicted on the first information, on the same evidence which would have sustained a conviction upon the second information; because, even if on the first trial it had been proved that he assaulted and beat the prosecutor, he could not have been convicted, unless it was also proved that he did so with intent to murder.

It is unnecessary to discuss the policy of repeating the very useful provisions contained in the eleventh section of the 1 Vic., c. 85, which remained in the statute book for thirteen years, and under which a person could have been convicted of an assault when the felonious crime charged included an assault, if the evidence warranted such finding. But as the law now is, I am of opinion that on the information for the felony the prisoner could not have been found guilty of the misdemeanor.

But a difficulty has suggested itself to me, which I think it right to mention. I have said that the second information contains a charge of a common assault; but on referring to that information, I find that the words used are "beat, wound, and illtreat." The second count of the first information, which is framed on the second section of the 1 Vic., c. 85, also uses the same words, "beat, wound, and illtreat." By the fifth section of the Better Prevention of Offences' Act (a), if on the trial of any information for any felony, except murder and manslaughter, where the information shall allege that the defendant did cut, stab, or wound any person, the jury shall be satisfied that the defendant is guilty of the cutting, stabbing, or wounding charged in such information, but are not satisfied that the defendant is guilty of the felony charged, the jury may acquit of the defendant of such felony, and find him guilty of unlawfully cutting, stabbing, or wounding. The doubt I have entertained is whether, as the second count of the first information charges a beating, wounding, and illtreating, the prisoner could not at the first trial have

(a) 16 Vic., No. 18.

been found guilty on such information of unlawfully wounding. If so, it would seem that he could have been found guilty on that count of the offence with which he is charged in the second information. This circumstance of the word wounding being inserted in the second information was not noticed at the trial, nor till now; and if it had been noticed, the word might have been struck out. It would be better if, in informations for an assault, the word wound were omitted. It will be found in the old precedents; but as the law has been so much altered, that word being now a word of substance should not be used. On the special case as stated, we are clearly of opinion that there must be judgment for the Crown.

WISE, J.   The last point mentioned in the judgment of his Honor the Chief Justice, was not taken at the trial. If it had been then taken, a *nolle prosequi* might have been entered as to this count; and, therefore, it being a technical difficulty (which, if then discovered, might have been cured), I do not think that the prisoner should have any benefit from it.

The second information seems to me to be good, and not to be vitiated by the addition of the word wounding.

HARGRAVE, J.   I am also of opinion that the prisoner could not have been convicted of an assault upon the second count of the first information, and that, therefore, the present conviction must be affirmed.

Conviction sustained.

HICKEY *against* THE QUEENSLAND SHEEP INVESTMENT
COMPANY (LIMITED) (*a*).

SIR *W. Manning*, Q. C., and *Milford* moved on
behalf of the defendants to make absolute a rule
to set aside an award in the above case.

By a contract dated the 22nd April, 1864, the
plaintiff sold to the defendants certain stock and stations
belonging to him, on the Darling Downs, in the colony
of Queensland. One clause of the contract provided
that "any matter in difference between the parties, and
any persons claiming or to claim under them respectively, respecting the construction of these presents, or
any act or default done or committed by virtue of or
under these presents, shall be referred to the arbitration of two persons, one to be named by the said *E. A.
Hickey*, and the other by the financial agent at Sydney
of the said Company, for the time being; and such
arbitrators shall have power to appoint an umpire, and
the costs, charges, and expenses of, and incident to,
the arbitration, shall be in the discretion of the arbitrators or umpire."

This clause was, on the 12th of September, 1864,
made a rule of Court on the application of the plaintiff.

A bill in Equity having been filed by the defendants
on their motion, an order was made on the 28th of
October by the Primary Judge, restraining *Hickey*
from appointing a sole arbitrator, and from proceeding
in such reference, unless he assented to the defendants
appointing an arbitrator to act on their behalf; and
upon such assent being given, the arbitration was to
proceed.

In pursuance of that order it was agreed, on the 4th
of November, between the parties to refer the matters in
dispute to certain specified arbitrators, and an umpire to
be appointed by them. The arbitration was proceeded

An agreement
to refer, not
naming the
referees, does
not amount
to a sub-
mission, and
cannot, there-
fore, be made
a rule of
Court.

(*a*) Before *Stephen*, C.J., and *Wise*, J.

L—4

1865.

HICKEY
v.
THE
QUEENSLAND
SHEEP
INVESTMENT
COMPANY
(LIMITED).

with ; and the award, which it was the object of the present motion to set aside, was made on the 1st of March, 1865.

Martin, Q. C. (*Darley* with him), took a preliminary objection, that the submission under which the award had been made, had never been made a rule of Court. The only thing made a rule of Court was the agreement to submit.   But this latter was so made a rule of Court before the actual submission existed.   For the rule of Court was obtained on the 12th of September.   But the submission and the appointment of the arbitrators and the umpire are in writing, dated the 4th of November, 1864.   In the very recent case of *Ex parte Glaysher* (a), it was held that the Court will not make a parol submission a rule of Court, although that parol submission is made in pursuance of a previous written agreement to refer.

Sir *W. Manning*, Q. C., and *Milford* contra.   As *Hickey* himself caused the original submission or contract to be made a rule of Court, he thereby misled the defendants, and cannot now be heard to take such an objection.   Although perhaps the Court ought to have refused to make such a document a rule of Court, yet having been so made, the Court has jurisdiction.   The Court will recognise their subsisting rule, unless, or until, it is set aside.   In *Ex parte Glaysher* (b) the agreement to recover was never, as here, made a rule of Court.   Mr. *Russell* (c), after stating that when the arbitrators are not named in the agreement to refer, it cannot be considered a complete submission, as, until the arbitrator is determined, there is no one who has the binding authority to decide the questions submitted, says, "when the agreement, though not naming the referees, provides for their appointment in a particular manner, and they are afterwards so appointed, though contrary to the will of one of the disputing parties, this has the same effect as if the referees were named in the clause itself.   And an award made by such referees will

(a) 34 L.J. Ex. 41.   (b) 9 Dowl. P.C. 539.
(c) On Arbitration, p. 62 (3rd Ed.)

be enforced." The authorities for this proposition are Haddon v. Roupell (a), and Woodcroft v. Jones (b).

1865.

HICKEY
v.
THE
QUEENSLAND
SHEEP
INVESTMENT
COMPANY
(LIMITED).

Martin, Q.C., in reply. The question is, what is the submission to arbitration; it is not the agreement to submit, but the submission that takes place under that agreement. The agreement cannot be made a rule of Court. [*Stephen*, C.J. In the rule the agreement is called an "agreement or submission."]

STEPHEN, C. J. I am of opinion that the mode in which the rule is drawn up does not affect the question. At all events there is no estoppel; and we are of opinion, both on principle and on the authority of *Ex parte Glaysher*, that unless the actual submission, as well as the agreement to submit, be made a rule of Court, we have no jurisdiction. As to *Haddon* v. *Roupell* it has no application. For, in that case, no point was taken as to the submission not having been made a rule of Court, and it did not appear that in fact the submission was not so made. Not to mention also, although this may not have been material on the question, that in that case there was a clause in the agreement making it expressly subject to the provisions of the Common Law Procedure Act. The agreement to refer cannot be treated as the submission; and it is necessary to make the submission a rule of Court before the Court can interfere.

WISE, J. I think the point is quite clear on principle, even without the authority of *Ex parte Glaysher*. The Court is to interfere on the submission being made a rule of Court; but there can be no submission, unless the parties are named to whom the matter is referred.

Rule discharged without costs.

(a) 9 C.B.N.S. 683.   (b) 9 Dowl. 538.

1865.

July 1.   *Ex parte* HAMILTON.

Where a
Court of Petty
Sessions un-
der the Small
Debts Act
made an order
against A. for
the payment
of rates due
upon certain
premises,
under the 81st
section of the
Municipali-
ties Act, the
Court refused
to interfere by
prohibition,
although
there was no
evidence to
show that A.
was a tenant,
proprietor, or
occupier of
the premises
at the time
the rate be-
came due.

STEPHEN moved to make absolute a rule *nisi* for
a prohibition at Common Law to restrain certain
justices sitting in Petty Sessions, under the Small Debts
Act (*a*), at Wollongong, and the Municipal Council of
central Illawarra, from proceeding upon and in respect
of a certain decision or order made by the justices.

The question sought to be raised was whether the
applicant coming into a house or lands, in respect of
which rates were due for past years, was liable for the
amount under the Municipalities Act as for a debt.
The justices had decided that he was ; but

Sir *W. Manning,* Q.C., who appeared for the Municipality, now objected that, as the Court of Petty Sessions
had jurisdiction over the person of the applicant, and
also over the subject matter, the Court would not interfere by prohibition, even although it were assumed that
the decision of the justices was wrong.

Stephen contra. The applicant is not a person over
whom jurisdiction is given by the Municipalities Act,
not being either " a tenant, proprietor, or occupier at
the time of the assessment," within the meaning of the
79th and 81st sections. His goods and chattels may be
liable to distress, or the rates may be a charge upon the
premises, but it is submitted that he cannot be sued for
the past rates. In *Ex parte Bailey* (*b*) the Court
allowed affidavits to be used for the purpose of showing
that there was no evidence before the justice from
which he could legally infer a contract creating the relation of master and servant between the parties, and
thus negativing jurisdiction. So also in *Ayrton* v.
Abbott (*c*), where the justices had jurisdiction to adjudicate in cases of " small tithes, offerings, oblations, and

(*a*) 10 Vic., No. 10.   (*b*) 3 E. & B. 607; 23 L.J.M.C. 161.
                            (*c*) 14 Q.B. 1.

obventions," evidence was received to show that the
subject matter of their adjudication was a mortuary,
and that, therefore, such adjudication was without
jurisdiction. So here, it is clear that the applicant
did not come within class, over which their jurisdiction
extended.

STEPHEN, C.J.   This Court of Petty Sessions has
jurisdiction over the subject matter as was decided in
Ex parte Blackhouse (a), and also over the person of
the applicant ; and therefore we cannot interfere by
prohibition.

WISE, J., and HARGRAVE, J., concurred.

Rule discharged.

1865.
Ex parte
HAMILTON.

RUDD and another *against* WILLANS.   June 21.

THE first count of the declaration stated that, in consideration that the plaintiffs would retain the
defendant as an attorney of the Supreme Court, &c., to
conduct the defence of the plaintiffs in an action in the
said Court, at the suit of *Osborne* and others, for reward
to the defendant in that behalf, the defendant promised
the plaintiffs that he would use due diligence about the
said defence, and on being thereunto required by the
plaintiffs would offer no improper obstacle to an order of
a Judge for a change of attorneys, by substituting some
other attorney for and in the place of the defendant as
such attorney for the plaintiffs in the action brought
against them.   Averment of the fulfilment of all conditions precedent.   Breach, that the defendant broke his
promise, in this, that he offered an improper obstacle to
an order of a Judge for a change of attorneys, by substituting another attorney named *W. M. Miller* for and in
the place of the defendant, as such attorney for the
plaintiffs in this action brought against them, whereby,

An action will
not lie by a
client against
his attorney
for taking a
futile or
vexatious ob-
jection, in
proceedings
taken by the
former
against the
latter to
change the
attorney.
An attorney
is responsible
for the act of
the managing
clerk of his
town agent in
the ordinary
course of
business as
such town
agent in the
cause or pro-
ceedings in
which he is
engaged.

(a) 3 Sup. Ct. R., C. L. 85.

&c., alleging, as special damage, that in consequence of the defendant's neglect and delay the plaintiffs were unable to go to trial at a certain sittings, and were compelled to pay heavy costs in endeavouring to get a postponement.

The second count alleged that the plaintiffs retained the defendant to conduct the defence in the action then pending and referred to in the first count, and on the revocation by the plaintiffs of their said retainer to deliver up the plaintiffs' papers connected with the suit to the attorney retained by the plaintiffs in the place and stead of the defendant, and to do all acts necessary for a change of attorneys, according to the practice of the Supreme Court, for reward to the defendant in that behalf ; and the defendant as and being such attorney accepted the said retainer on the terms aforesaid. And the plaintiffs afterwards gave due notice to the defendant that they desired to revoke their retainer, and to retain one *Miller* as their attorney to prosecute the defence of the said action. Yet the defendant, by himself and through his agents, without reasonable or lawful excuse, neglected within a reasonable time to deliver up to the attorney retained in the place of the defendant the papers connected with the suit, and negligently, improperly, and unskilfully, did certain acts, and negligently and improperly omitted to do certain other acts, which, according to the practice of the Supreme Court, were and are necessary for changing attorneys in an action. The special damage alleged, was that the plaintiffs were delayed in obtaining the change of attorneys, and by reason of such delay an application made by them to postpone the trial of the cause which was then at issue was unsuccessful, and they were cast in the costs of such application; and also, they incurred, which they would not otherwise have done, heavy expenses in preparing for the trial of the cause which became a remanet.

The defendant pleaded to the first count—1. *Non assumpsit;* 2. denying the breach of the alleged promise, and alleging that he was not guilty thereof. To

the second count—3. traversing the alleged retainer;
4. and the due notice of the desire to revoke the retainer; 5. not guilty. Issue thereon.

The facts as proved at the trial before *Stephen*, C.J.,
were as follows:—The defendant, who resided at Wagga
Wagga, had been the attorney of the present plaintiffs
in a squatting action brought against the latter by the
Messrs. *Osborne*, and had acted as such attorney up to
the short time after notice of trial had been given by
the Messrs. *Osborne*, for the November sittings, 1863.
The cause was set down for the 12th of November.
But after receiving notice of trial, namely, on the 28th
of October, the plaintiffs communicated to the defendant
that their chief witness, a Mr. *Berry*, the Government
surveyor, lived at Albury, and that he had said to them
that he could not get up their case unless they changed
their attorney and appointed Mr. *Miller*, of Albury, as
their attorney instead of the defendant. The latter at
once expressed his concurrence, and asked them to give
him a written authority to that effect. On the same
day the defendant wrote to Mr. *Miller*, asking him to
take the necessary steps to change the attorneys. He
also, on the same day, wrote to Mr. *Iceton*, his Sydney
agent, acquainting him with the circumstances, and
asking him to assent. Mr. *Levy*, the Sydney agent of
Mr. *Miller*, received from the latter a letter of instructions dated the 30th of October, to bring about the
change of attorneys. This letter enclosed the defendant's letter to *Miller* of the 28th of that month.
Levy thereupon saw *Iceton* and asked him to consent,
when the latter said that he must take his own course;
Levy thereupon took out a summons, returnable before
Milford, J., sitting in Chambers, on the 6th of November. When the summons was called on, *Iceton's*
managing clerk objected that it would have been more
satisfactory if the original letter from the defendant had
been attached to the affidavit in support of the summons.
The learned Judge thereupon dismissed the application
with costs, remarking that there was apparently no
authority from the clients themselves. This was the

1865.

RUDD
and another
v.
WILLANS.

grievance complained of in the present action. It appeared in evidence that a consent to change had subsequently, that is, on the 13th October, been given by Mr.
Iceton. This decision of *Milford*, J., was also reviewed
by the Court, who set aside the order with costs as
against the defendant. While Mr. *Iceton's* managing
clerk, who was called as a witness for the defendant,
was under examination, he was asked what instructions
he had received from Mr. *Iceton* with respect to the
summons by Mr. *Levy*. This evidence was objected to
and rejected.

It was contended for the defendant that there was no
such contract as alleged in the first, and still less such a
duty as alleged in the second count. That the damage
(whatever it might be) was the result of the Judge's
erroneous decision, for which no action would lie, and
that the objection was really one taken by the Judge
and not by the clerk. And also that any opposition
before the Judge was the act of *Iceton* and his clerk,
for which the defendant was not responsible, since
Iceton's agency ceased the moment that the defendant's
employment as the plaintiffs' attorney ceased.

The learned Judge directed a verdict for the de-
dendant on the second count, but was of opinion that
the plaintiff was entitled to recover in the first count.
He left to the jury the question, whether the defendant
did or not interpose an improper obstacle to the substitution of *Miller* for himself; and that, if so, the plaintiffs
were certainly entitled to nominal damages; but in his
opinion they were entitled also to substantial damages—
that is, to all expenses reasonably incurred by them in
consequence of the order to change not having been made
on the 6th of November. His Honor also ruled that the
defendant was responsible for the acts of *Iceton* and his
clerk, and that the objection taken was wrong, because
Iceton had at that time a similar letter in his own possession. His Honor reserved of the question the sufficiency of the first count, and of the defendant's liability
for the dismissal of the summons by the Judge; and
also whether the defendant was responsible for the act of

Iceton in violation of his instructions not to oppose or delay the changing of attorneys in the case.

The jury accordingly found a verdict for the plaintiff.

Salomons, for the defendant, now moved accordingly for a rule *nisi* to set aside the verdict and enter it for the defendant, or to enter a nonsuit, or for a new trial. It is submitted that what was said by Mr. *Iceton* to his clerk was admissible, as the country attorney cannot be considered to be bound by the clerk of his town agent when acting contrary to his instructions. How can he know the clerks whom his agent may employ? He referred to *Cornelius* v. *Harrison* (a), and *Malin* v. *Greenway* (b). He also argued that no such duty as was alleged in the first count existed; that the defendant was not responsible for the act of the Judge; and that the damages were excessive, and estimated on a wrong principle.

STEPHEN, C.J. On the question of the admissibility of the evidence of the instructions given by Mr. *Iceton* to his clerk, I am at once prepared to give judgment. I am most clearly of opinion that both the defendant and Mr. *Iceton* are responsible for the act of Mr. *Iceton's* clerk, and are estopped from disputing his authority. Evidence, therefore, of any instructions given by Mr. *Iceton* to his clerk, is utterly inadmissible for the purpose of exonerating the defendant. Any other doctrine must be fatal to the practice of allowing any business to be conducted by an attorney's clerk. I assent to the doctrine as laid down by Mr. *Pulling* (c). "The town agent in an action binds the client in every thing he does, in the ordinary course of business as such town agent in the cause or proceedings in which he is engaged;" and thus, for instance, where an attorney suffered judgment by default, the Court would not allow the matter to be questioned by the client. If the attorney acts contrary to the instructions of his client, the remedy of the latter is against the attorney. But a

1865.

RUDD
and another
v.
WILLANS.

November 29,
1864.

(a) 2 F. & F. 759.   (b) 10 L.J. Ch. 26.
(c) Law of Attorneys, p. 445.

rule will be granted on three grounds—first, that no
such duty or liability exists or arose out of the relation
of attorney and client, as is relied on in the first count;
secondly, that if it did arise, yet there was no evidence
of any breach of such duty or liability by the defendant, because the dismissal of the summons to change
attorneys was the act of the Judge, for which the defendant was not responsible, and because the defendant
was not bound to do more than he did, as the relation
of attorney and client at the time of the application
had ceased; thirdly, that no damage was shown to the
extent given by the jury.

MILFORD, J. No doubt ought to be allowed to be
thrown on the responsibility of the attorney for the act
of his clerk. The attorney is bound by the act of his
clerk; the country attorney by the act of his town
agent; and the client by the act of his attorney; and
all are bound by the act of the clerk of the town agent.

WISE, J. I am of the same opinion. In *Taylor* v.
Willans (a) it is said, " if the attorney leaves the conduct of a cause to his clerk, what the latter does therein
binds the party, as much as the act of the attorney himself." And in *Griffiths* v. *Williams* (b), which was an
action for unliquidated damages, the defendant had paid
money into Court. The plaintiff's attorney gave notice
that the payment was irregular, and that he should not·
take the money out of Court. But a few days afterwards the plaintiff's agent took the money out, and it
was held that the plaintiff was bound by the act of his
attorney's agent in town.

Rule *nisi* accordingly.

June 21, 1865.   *Isaacs*, for the plaintiff, showed cause (c). Admitting
that the defendant personally had not been to blame, it
is equally clear that the plaintiffs are in no degree to
blame. They are injured by the act of the defendant's
agent with whom they are not in privity, and of whom

(a) 2 B. & Ad. 856.   (b) 1 T. R. 710.
       (c) Before *Stephen*, C.J., and *Wise*, J.

in fact they knew nothing; *Pulling's* Law of Attorneys (*a*), *Robbins* v. *Fennell* (*b*), *Wildbore* v. *Bryan* (*c*), *Re Andrew* (*d*). The defendant must, therefore, be responsible for the act of such agent. Here the act of the agent is in violation of his instructions, but within the scope of his authority. He referred to *Griffiths* v. *Williams* (*e*), *Ex parte Jones* (*f*), *Frankland* v. *Cole* (*g*), and *Hoby* v. *Built* (*h*). The grievance complained of cannot be considered in point of law the act of the Judge, because he was moved thereto by the defendant's agent.

As to the damages, it is submitted that there was ample evidence before the jury to justify the verdict, and they have not proceeded upon any improper principle; *Creed* v. *Fisher* (*i*).

Sir *W. Manning*, Q.C., *Martin*, Q.C. (*Salomons* with them), for the defendant, in support of the rule. The full Court has decided that the summons to change the attorneys ought not to have been dismissed. If that be so, the objection taken by the defendant's agent was a frivolous, or at least a futile, one. How then will an action lie against the defendant for the mere taking by his agent of an objection of that character? It was the fault of the Judge; the agent putting him in motion. The defendant was only employed, and therefore his agent was only employed to conduct the defence, that is, until the action be at an end, and was not employed to manage matters between the client and the defendant himself. [*Stephen*, C.J. Is not the change of attorneys a proceeding in the action, and connected with the defence? Did not the retainer necessarily extend to the taking of such a step?] It is submitted that the dismissal of the summons was wholly the act of the Judge. [*Stephen*, C.J. But it was occasioned by the objection taken by the defendant or his agent.] The proceeding

(*a*) p. 446.
(*b*) 11 Q.B. 248.
(*c*) 8 Price 677.
(*d*) 30 L.J. Ex. 403.
(*e*) 1 T.R. 710.
(*f*) 2 Dowl. 601.
(*g*) 2 Cr. & J. 590.
(*h*) 3 B. & Ad. 350.
(*i*) 9 Exch. 472.

to change an attorney is one adverse to him; why is he not to show cause, even an insufficient cause. In *Davies* v. *Lowndes* (a) a most technical objection was taken; but the Court do not say that the attorney was wrong for taking it. *Archbold's* Practice and *Wynne* v. *Wynne* (b). [They were here stopped by the Court (c).]

STEPHEN, C. J. For the reasons just given, I think that a nonsuit must be entered. For although, for the purposes of the action, the relation of attorney and client continued, yet it ceased as between them by the dismissal. And the proceedings to change the attorney, although entitled in the cause, is one by the client against the attorney alone, not against the opposite party The latter need not even have notice of the application, although of course, after the change, the adverse party is entitled to notice of the change, and of the order making it. No action therefore will lie by the client against the attorney for taking a futile or vexatious objection—at all events as here, on a supposed implied contract between them, or on the subsisting duty arising out of the actual and terminated contract. The attorney when called on to show cause why he should not be changed, is entitled to make the best defence he can; at all events, the law does not render him liable to an action for trying to defend himself, even although such defence be groundless. Under such circumstances the attorney is liable to costs, which may be inflicted upon him for improperly resisting such an application. If the attorney resists the application, the Judge can make him pay the costs thereby occasioned, or the Court may interfere summarily; but the law does not make him liable to an action for defending himself, even in an improper manner, in a judicial proceeding to which he is a party. Here the defendant was entitled to appear before Mr. Justice *Milford*, and although liable to be mulcted

(a) 3 C. B. 808.   (b) 2 Sc. N. R. 278.
(c) As to the liability of an attorney for acts of tort, see *Williams.* v. *Smith,*[*] and *Purves* v. *Landell.*[†]

[*] 14 C. B. N. S. 596.   [†] 12 Cl. & F. 91.

in costs for objecting to the order, if the objection was
insufficient, he was not liable to an action.

WISE, J. I am of the same opinion. The out-going
attorney has a right to be heard, and may make the
best defence he can, without being liable to an action
in a Court of law.

Nonsuit.

RAPLEY against MARTIN.

TRESPASS for breaking and entering a close of the
plaintiff, situate at Theresa Park, and breaking
down fences, &c., whereby, &c.

Pleas.—1. not guilty; 2. not possessed; 3. plea of
public right of way; 4. that the close was the soil and
freehold of the Crown; and the defendant being duly
authorised by the Crown in that behalf entered on the
land, with servants, horses, cattle and drays, and because
the fences were on the land encumbering the same, the
defendant being duly authorised as aforesaid, did tear
up and break down the fences, doing no unnecessary
damage as he lawfully might, which are the alleged
trespasses. Issue thereon.

At the trial before Stephen, C.J., in November, 1864,
the following facts were proved:—In the year 1832, the
defendant's father purchased the farm now occupied by

In 1832, M.
obtained a
grant of land
therein de-
scribed as
640 acres,
bounded by
the Nepean
on the north,
commencing
at a certain
spot on the
east; extend-
ing westerly
43 chains, and
thence along
a due south
line 155
chains. This
land had been
previously
advertised,
and the adver-
tisement was
referred to in
M.'s grant;

but in neither was there a road mentioned, or a reservation of a road, on the western
boundary, indicated. In 1835, a portion of the unoccupied land to the west of M.'s
grant was advertised for sale, and purchased by H. This portion was described,
both in the advertisement and the deed of grant as 1180 acres, commencing at "M.'s
north-west corner;" and as being bounded on the east by a south line of 126 chains;
this south line divided M.'s and H.'s properties. The grant to H., after specifying
that the south boundary extended from the east 123 chains, "including one chain
for a road," added the following clause—" This lot is subject to a road, one chain
wide, commencing on the western boundary of lot 1, about fourteen chains south
from the river, extending thence in a direction about south 70 degrees east, to the
western line of M.'s purchase, and thence southward along that line." The advertisement which was referred to in the grant, announced the same reservation of a
road. In an action by H. against M. for trespasses committed by the latter on the
chain of land thus reserved, it being conceded that at the western continuation or
commencing point of this line there was no reserved or declared road, although
there had been formerly a way used to and from other property belonging to H.,
    Held that the land in question was a public highway; there having been, both
before and after the grant to H., a dedication to the public—effectuated by the terms
of the grant to H., at all events as against H.

the defendant, then vacant Crown land, from the Crown
agents ; and in the same year he obtained a grant of it.
The land was there described as 640 acres, bounded by
the Nepean River on the north, commencing at a certain
occupied spot on the east; extending westerly 43 chains,
and thence along a due south line 155 chains. The
southern boundary, with the eastern, was then given
in like manner, but on these nothing turned.

The land had been previously advertised, and the advertisement was referred to in *Martin's* grant ; but in
neither was there a road mentioned, or the reservation
(actual or intended) of a road, along his western
boundary, indicated. All the land to the west, however,
was then unoccupied —or, at all events, ungranted and
unsold ; so that the reservation or dedication of a road
along that boundary, if then contemplated by the Crown,
might have been thought unnecessary or premature.

In 1835, that unoccupied land or a portion of it was
put up for sale, and purchased by *John Terry Hughes*—
to whom it was accordingly soon afterwards granted.
The plaintiff was lessee, under the representatives of *John
Terry Hughes*, of a portion of the land contained in this
grant ; and the land in dispute formed a portion of the
land thus demised. The land purchased by *John Terry
Hughes* was described (*a*), both in the advertisement and
the deed of grant, as 1180 acres, commencing at "*Martin's*
north-west corner ;" and as being bounded on the west
(confessedly and palpably a clerical mistake for east), by
a south line of 126 chains. There could be no doubt,
therefore, and the fact was indeed admitted, that this

(*a*) The parcels were described as " commencing at the north-
west corner of *Alexander Martin's* purchase of 640 acres, bounded
on the west by a line south 126 chains, on the south by a line west
123 chains (including one chain for a road), on the west by a line
north 80 chains, on the north by a line east 80 chains, again on the
west by a line north 57 chains 50 links to the Nepean, and again on
the north by that river. This lot is subject to a road one chain
wide, commencing on the western boundary of lot No. 1, about 14
chains south from the river, extending thence in a direction about
south 70 degrees east to the western line of *Martin's* purchase, and
thence southward along that line, being the land sold as lot 11, in
pursuance of advertisement of 13th May, 1834, with all the appurtenances whatsoever, saving and reserving unto his Majesty, his
heirs and successors, all such parts of the said land as may be hereafter
set out for a way or ways by any person lawfully authorised in that
respect, &c."

south line—to the extent here mentioned—was identical with *Martin's* south line of 155 chains. In other words, that line divided the plaintiff's (*i.e. Hughes's*) and the defendant's properties. And the grant to *Hughes*, after specifying that the south boundary extended from the east 123 chains, "*including one chain for a road*," added the following clause—"This lot is subject to a road, *one chain wide*, commencing on the western boundary of lot one" (land admitted to be to the west of *Hughes's* purchase), "about 14 chains south from the river, extending thence in a direction about south 70 degrees east, *to the western line of Martin's purchase, and thence southward along that line*."

That is to say, a road or right of road was indicated, whether then existing or to exist across *Hughes's* land at its western boundary, running in an easterly direction up to *Martin's* boundary—and thence along the latter, southward, the entire remaining length of that boundary.

The advertisement for the sale of this land, as in the case of *Martin*, was referred to in the grant; and it announced the same reservation of a road, or right of road —except that, more accurately (there being again a mistake of the copyist), its commencing point on *Hughes's* land was mentioned as the eastern boundary of lot one. That land, in common with all the country westward of *Hughes's* in the district, was at that time unoccupied. So also, it seemed, was the country south of *Hughes's*. Hence, it was argued for the plaintiff, there could have been no farms or "locations" in either direction, as the terminating points for a road. On the other hand the fact was noticed, that although the quantity of land purchased by *Hughes*, and stated to be conveyed to him, was only 1180 acres, the described area according to his grant proved, on actual measurement, to include 1206. Except, however, as tending to show that the site of the indicated road was granted to *Hughes*, although a right of way for the public was reserved, or intended so to be, this circumstance did not appear to be material. The entire area of the roadway was about fifteen acres.

It was proved, that the only trespasses committed by

the defendant (or, at least, those complained of in this action) were along the roadway or chain of land, on his western boundary; and that they were necessary, in point of fact, for the exercise and enjoyment of his supposed right. On the other hand, it was conceded that at the western (or north-western) continuation or commencing point of this line—mentioned in the grant apparently as lot one—there was no reserved or declared road; although there was formerly a way used there by the neighbours, to and from a mill erected on other property belonging to *Hughes*.

The jury found a verdict for the plaintiff, damages £10—it being agreed between the parties that all questions were reserved for the Court in banc; the Court to have power to draw inferences as a jury might, and to order the verdict to be entered on the several issues, either for the plaintiff or for the defendant, as the law might require.

Darley now accordingly obtained a rule *nisi* to set aside the verdict and enter it for the defendant. On the grounds—1. That the words "subject to a road," contained in the grant, amounted to an exclusion of the area or site of the road from the subject matter of the grant. 2. That these words amounted to a dedication of the area or site of the road to the public as and for a public highway. 3. That the land whereon the trespasses were committed was Crown land, and the defendant entered thereon by the authority of the Crown.

Sir *W. Manning*, Q.C., and *Butler*, for the plaintiff, showed caused. The defendant's grant of his own contiguous land in 1838, mentions no roadway or right of road; neither has the Crown made any grant of this easement to him, or to the public. The plaintiff's grant, or rather in truth *Hughes's* grant (the plaintiff having been the latter's tenant), is made "subject to a road one chain wide," along the defendant's boundary or side line. But this reservation is in favour simply of the Crown itself. It is not a dedication of a road or high-

way to the public; still less was it a reservation in favor
of the defendant. In the *Durham and Sunderland*
Railway Company v. *Walker* (a) it is said, "It is to
be observed that a right of way cannot, in strictness, be
made the subject either of exception or reservation. It
is neither parcel of the thing granted, nor is it issuing
out of the thing granted ; the former being essential to
an exception, and the latter to a reservation. A right of
way *reserved* (using the word in a somewhat popular
sense) to a lessor is, in strictness of law, an easement
newly created by way of grant from the grantee or
lessee, in the same manner as a right of sporting or
fishing, which has been much considered in the cases of
Doe v. *Lock* (b), and *Wickham* v. *Hawker* (c)."

The so-called reservation is no reservation at all. The
land was purchased by the plaintiff, and, although he
might have been willing to buy, subject to the Crown's
own right to use this way, he might not have agreed to
let all the world, as in the case of a highway, use it
also. And by what did the Crown dedicate this right to
others ? It is submitted that even if intended to be a
road at a future period, there is no roadway there now.
The length of the ascribed lines proves conclusively that
the area or site was granted to *Hughes*. His land is
said to commence at the north-west corner of the defendant's 640 acres, bounded on the east by a line south
126 chains. But if the site of this road be excluded
from *Hughes'* grant, that description is incorrect. It is
submitted that the soil is in *Hughes*, subject only to
this right in favor of the Crown itself. It is admitted
that on two sides of the plaintiff's grant was vacant
Crown land at that time. It was merely a way between
these two farms for the benefit of the Crown, in facilitating a sale of other neighbouring lands. In any event
the site or area of the roadway was granted to the
plaintiff, " subject " only to this reservation. But what
had the public at large to do with this ? How had
there been a dedication to the public ? Even if intended
at a future period, there is no roadway now. [*Stephen*,

(a) 2 Q. B. 967.　　(b) 2 A. & E. 705.　　(c) 7 M. & W. 63.

M—4

1865.

RAPLEY
v.
MARTIN.

C. J.   The plea claims the roadway as a highway.] It is submitted that it is no highway; it goes from no place to no place, and it has not been used from 1835 to 1862.   The conduct of the defendant was a recognition by him that the land in dispute was not a highway, but formed a portion of the land granted to *Hughes.*   For having put up the boundary fence in the place where it now stands, he was paid for some portion of it by *Hughes*; but if this road existed the lands were not coterminous, and he would not have been entitled to such contribution.   [*Milford*, J.   If the Crown reserved a road to itself, could it have granted to another person the use of that road?]   *Rooke* v. *Lord Kensington* (a), and *Sheppard's* Touchstone (b) were referred to.

(c) As to the authority given by the Crown to the defendant to use the way, it was submitted that there was no authority in the Surveyor General to confer it, and no intention to confer it; and the mode of dedicating public roads, as given in the 4 W. IV., No. 11, was referred to.

Darley contra.   The area of this roadway never passed at all.   The plaintiff purchased by advertisement land " subject to a road "—that is, subject to a then existing way.   He bought and paid for 1184 acres only, and obtained a grant of the same quantity; but the stated boundary lines embrace 1206 acres.   The area of the entire road was proved to be fifteen acres, leaving to the plaintiff 1191 acres.   The grant is of so many chains— that is 126 chains on the south in length, plus one chain more for the road.   The intention clearly was to grant only 1184 acres, as advertised for sale and sold, and not to grant 1206 acres.   The Crown, however, might retain a right of highway.   For the benefit of the public the Crown might do this.   Where a subject claims a specific portion of land, the property of the Crown, even under a grant by letters patent, he must

(a) 25 L. J. Ch. 795.   (b) p. 80.
(c) On the question of authority as relied on in the fourth plea, the argument has been omitted, as the judgment of the Court rendered a decision on that point unnecessary.

show a specific description of the particular place as meant to be conveyed by the instrument, for he cannot avail himself of general words; *Parmeter* v. *Gibbs* (a). There a grant from the Crown was construed beneficially for the Crown, although for value. The area of this road must, therefore, be excluded from the grant, and be considered as Crown lands. The Crown, by advertisement in May, 1834, and in its grant to *Hughes*, recognised the existence of this road. For the grant to *Hughes*, being a grant from the Crown, is a matter of public record, and is, by letters patent, that is, exposed to view, with the great seal pendant at the bottom, and addressed by the Sovereign to all subjects of the realm (b). At all events the deed shows a dedication to the public; and if so dedicated, even the Queen has only a right of passage for herself and her people (*Burn's* Justice (c); Bac. Ab. Highways, tit. B.; Viner's Ab. Chemin, private); and cannot after such dedication close it up. Even assuming that the road in question is not a thoroughfare, it has been decided that there may be a public highway over a place where no thoroughfare exists; *Bateman* v. *Bluck* (d). The notes to *Dovaston* v. *Payne* (e) were referred to.

The letter of the Surveyor General, dated September, gave authority to the defendant to use the land. So that if the land be still the property of the Crown, the defendant was justified. But it is submitted that the defendant must succeed on the first issue as to the highway; for this area is a highroad, open to all her Majesty's subjects.

Cur. adv. vult.

The judgment of the Court was now delivered by STEPHEN, C.J. This was an action to recover damages, for trespassing on the plaintiff's land in the county of Camden, held by him under lease from the representatives of *John Terry Hughes*, by driving carts and cattle through it, and cutting down fences erected there. The

1865.

RAPLEY
v.
MARTIN.

August 18.

(a) 10 Price 412.　　　(b) 1 Step. Com. 616.
(c) 3 Vol., p. 511.　(d) 18 Q. B. 870.　(e) 2 Sm. L. C. 128.

defendant, who occupies a farm adjoining, justified these acts on the ground of the existence, as he alleges, of a public highway over the plaintiff's land—along the portion trespassed on. If not a public highway, the defendant insisted that it was Crown land; and averred, in his second plea, that he entered on it by license from the Crown. On each of these defences, at the trial before me, there was a good deal of evidence, terminating in a verdict for the plaintiff on both issues ; but, under my direction, and by consent, subject to the opinion of the Court (with power to draw inferences as to facts), whether the verdict ought not to have been for the defendant.

His Honor, after stating the facts of the case as above, continued—

We are of opinion, on this state of facts, that the verdict on the first issue must be entered for the defendant. There was here, we conceive, both before and at the time of the sale and grant to *Hughes*, a dedication of the road in question to the public, as a highway—effectuated by the terms of the grant, at all events as against *Hughes* and all claiming under him. There may be some uncertainty, as to the portion of this road described as commencing " about " fourteen chains from the river; but there is none respecting the part now in controversy. The actual user of the right, however, along a certain line, especially if uninterrupted and for a considerable period, might perhaps be sufficient to indicate that as the intended roadway. See observations of Sir *John Patteson*, in the judgment of the Judicial Committee, in *Doe d. Devine* v. *Wilson* (a). But, be this as it may, nothing can (we think) be clearer than that the Crown meant to confer—and did all in its power to confer—a general right of way to the public, along his entire eastern boundary, by the grant to *Hughes*. The granting of a right of way to *Martin*, or to any other individual or individuals specified, over then ungranted Crown land, would have been inconsistent with such an intention. So would the retention

(a) 10 Moore's P. C. 526-7.

(call it by what name you will) of such a right, in or for the benefit of the Crown itself. There was here either the dedication, to the public at large, of the described road as and for a highway, or there was nothing.

But *Hughes*, or persons claiming under him, can hardly be permitted to say that there was no such grant; for he purchased the land, and accepted the conveyance of it, subject to a declared general right of road. Not only so, but he obtained the site and soil of that road, in addition to his purchase—in consideration probably of the road's passing (partly) through his ground. At the moment of the conveyance, *Hughes* as grantee is apprised of the dedication; he takes his land, subject in express words to the right so given; *Campbell* v. *Dent*, in this Court (a), and the case of *Lord* v. *City Commissioners* (b) there cited. See also *Durham Railway Company* v. *Walker* (c). We need not inquire, therefore, whether the terms amounted technically and in strictness to an exception, or to a reservation; for the words might be taken to operate by way of grant (we think) or dedication, by *Hughes* himself.

The nature of the case being considered, the existence of direct authority on this question is hardly to be expected. Here is an enormous territory, ungranted, unoccupied—which the Crown, the trustee for its subjects, from time to time conveys in parcels for them, for purposes of colonisation and settlement. Roads through these granted lands, for the use of other existing or intending settlers, are indispensable. All such roads, if for the general benefit, are simply highways. The Crown, therefore, usually reserves in its grants the power of making such roads. We will assume that, if indefinite, such a reservation may be void. But why may not the Crown, as in this case, define a road in the first instance, and dedicate it at once to the public? And, if so, the form and mode of dedication adopted here, by declaration in letters patent—necessarily matters of re-

(a) 3 Sup. Ct. R., C. L. 62.   (b) 12 Moore's P. C. 499.
(c) 2 Q. B. 967.

cord—would seem on principle to be sufficient for the purpose. A private individual can effectually dedicate (and thereby irrevocably grant) a way to the public, without deed. See the numerous cases as to dedication, collected in *Woolrych* on Ways (a). It would seem to follow, that the Crown may do the same thing, by a declaration to that effect of record.

There is nothing in the objection, that possibly there was in this case no thoroughfare, in the strict sense of the word; for there can be legally a public way, although there be no outlet or entrance from or to it, except one only; *Bateman* v. *Bluck* (b), and *Willis* v. *Campbell*, in this Court (c).

As in our judgment the site of the road passed to *Hughes*, the road itself (in other words the right of passage therein) being dedicated to the public, the Crown could give no operative license afterwards to the defendant, or any other individual, to use that road, either as Crown land or otherwise. The verdict, therefore, on the second issue in this case, will stand for the plaintiff; the defendant succeeding on the first, and consequently in the action.

Judgment accordingly.

THE QUEEN *against* NORTH (d).

Costs are not recoverable upon a judgment of *quo warranto* (by *Wise*, J.)

THIS was a question as to the recovery of costs on a proceeding by *quo warranto*, under the Municipalities Act of 1858. The matter was argued before *Wise*, J., by *Salomons* on behalf of the real plaintiff, and by *Burton* for the defendant.

WISE, J., gave judgment in the following terms :—
This was a *quo warranto* against *Samuel V. North*, who had been elected alderman of the municipality of Aldbury, and allowed judgment to go by default, and

(a) Cap. 2.							(b) 18 Q. B. 876.
(c) 2nd June, 1856.						(d) In Chambers.

Mr. *Miller*, who had caused the proceedings to be instituted, included in the judgment the costs of the proceeding. The question for my decision was, whether any costs were recoverable in this colony upon a judgment of *quo warranto*.

The question turns, in my opinion, entirely on whether the 9th Anne, cap. 20, s. 5, is or is not applicable to a proceeding of this kind. I am of opinion that it is not.

The present proceeding is, in point of law, an information in the name of the Attorney-General, under the provisions of 9 George IV., cap. 83, sections 5 and 6, and rule 19 of the 29th April, 1856, which sections apply alike to all crimes, whether felonies or misdemeanours. No distinction is made between one kind of felony or misdemeanour and another; and it seems to me, therefore, that the rule as to costs must be alike in all—that is to say, the defendant pays no costs in any case.

It has long been well settled that no costs can be obtained in a *quo warranto*, except by force of 9 Anne, cap. 20, or some other statute; and that statute does not apply, in my opinion, to any case in which the Attorney-General is the officer in whose name and by whose authority the information is presented.

I am not aware of any rule now in force giving costs to the plaintiff in criminal informations, even supposing that a rule to that effect would be within the power of the Court. The 25th rule of April 29th, 1856, only states that the Court may on motion award costs to the defendant, if the prosecutor does not give notice of trial or bring the case on to trial.

This is a new question and one of considerable difficulty, and as the defendant escapes the payment of all costs, although the merits are against him, I think that the order should be granted without costs.

1865.

August 9.   SEMPILL *against* RASHLEIGH (*a*).

In ejectment by the official assignee of *R.* an order was made *ex parte,* allowing *R.* and his wife to appear and defend under the 123rd section of the Common Law Procedure Act of 1853 ; on motion to rescind the order, *held* (by *Hargrave,* J.), that such order was rightly granted *ex parte.* But it appearing by the affidavits that *R.'s* right to the order was abandoned, and no facts were shown from which the relation of landlord and tenant could be said to exist between the wife of *R.* and the defendant, the order was rescinded.

A second application having been made upon an affidavit that the legal estate had

A N action of ejectment had been brought by the plaintiff, as official assignee, against the defendant. An order had been made *ex parte* (by *Cheeke,* J.), to permit certain parties to come in and defend. The present proceeding was an application to rescind that order.

Darley appeared for the official assignee ; *Salomons* for the defendant.

HARGRAVE, J., gave judgment in the following terms :—

This is an application to rescind an order made *ex parte,* permitting *Stephen · Richardson* and *Martha Richardson* his wife, under the 123rd section of Common Law Procedure Act (1853), to appear as landlord and landlady of the abovenamed defendant, and to defend for the property claimed by the plaintiff in this action. It was objected that this order, though obtained *ex parte,* being obtained from a Judge at Chambers upon the usual affidavit that the applicants, or one of them, was landlord or landlady in possession of the property by the abovenamed defendant as his or her tenant, could not be rescinded by me under mere Chamber jurisdiction. It seems to me, however, to be an inherent right in the party to be affected by every *ex parte* order, and to be his proper and only course when desirous of remedying any mistake, fraud, or irregularity in the *ex parte* order, in the first place to bring the facts of the case before the same jurisdiction that issued the said order.

been conveyed to the wife of *R.* in fee simple from the Crown ; that she had resided with the defendant on the premises rented from her by him ; that the defendant about a week back had given up absolute possession to her as his landlady, and that she was now in actual possession, was refused with costs by *Hargrave,* J.

(*a*) In Chambers.

It is plain also by the practice as laid down in *Archbold* (a), that this application is quite regular, being made "on new matter now to be considered," and I have also to state that my learned brother, Mr. Justice *Cheeke*, states to me that the *ex parte* order was granted by him as a mere formal order, and that he quite concurs in my hearing this application.

Besides this reason for the plaintiff's right to be heard against the *ex parte* order, the 127th section of the Common Law Procedure Act (1853) seems to me expressly to require me to hear this application, by authorising " the Court, or a Judge," "to strike out or confine appearances and defences set up by persons not in possession by themselves or their tenants." I am aware of the dictum of *Pollock*, C. B., in *Butler* v. *Meredith* (b), to the effect that this 127th section does not apply to striking out the appearance of defendants, made so by order of the Court or a Judge under the 123rd section ; but in the first place I cannot concur in this limitation of the plain words of the 127th section; and in the second place, that learned Judge expressly limits his meaning to cases where the Court or a Judge "has been satisfied of the *bona fide* possession of the landlord defendant ; " and as this application is made for the purpose of ascertaining the *bona fides* of the matter and the real facts of the alleged tenancy, I do not think that the Chief Baron's dictum applies to this case.

The first objection made to the *ex parte* order sought to be set aside by the present notice of motion, is that this order ought not to have been granted *ex parte;* but although in *Cole* on Ejectment (c), it is said that the English practice is to grant " these orders only on rule *nisi*, or summons in the first instance," the present practice as laid down in *Archbold* (d), is to grant these orders *ex parte* in the first instance ; and the learned Prothonotary of this Court reports to me that the colonial practice here is to grant the *ex parte* order in the first instance, if so applied for.

(a) p. 1596 (Ed. 1862.)   (b) 11 Exch., p. 89.
(c) p. 124.   (d) p. 1022.

The other objections to the *ex parte* order are objections to the merits, viz., that *Richardson* demised the property to *Rashleigh* by two separate leases, for three years from 1861, both of which leases have expired, but under which *Rashleigh* obtained possession ; that all *Richardson's* estate and interest, including expressly the property in question, have been duly sequestrated, and are now vested in Mr. *Sempill* as Official Assignee ; that defendant *Rashleigh* has never paid any rent, either to *Richardson* or to his wife ; that the deponent does not believe that *Rashleigh* is tenant to either of them, and lastly, that *Richardson* is an uncertificated insolvent.

In reply to this affidavit, thus challenging the whole merits of the *ex parte* order, and the former affidavit on which it was obtained, *Richardson's* attorney has now filed an affidavit setting up a grant from the Crown to *Martha Richardson*, since her marriage, and a distinct claim by her to the property "as purchased by her, out of her own earnings entirely ;" and further stating that she was not aware of her husband's dealings with the land, either by the leases or assignments, and that her husband is merely joined with her in this application as a formal defendant ; she alleging herself to be the real landlady of the property in question.

Upon this affidavit it is plain that the husband's right to the *ex parte* order is now abandoned, and very properly so ; for it is impossible to allow an uncertificated insolvent to dispute this title in ejectment as against his own official assignee. With regard to Mrs. *Richardson's* right to this order, as the case is very peculiar in its circumstances, I have examined all the authorities on this subject, and find that the reported cases have clearly established—

Firstly, that a " liberal construction " is to be given to this 123rd section, per *Coleridge*, J., in *Doe* v. *Birchmore* (a). Secondly, that " nice questions " as to the applicant's right to defend are not to be considered, but left to the full Court or to the action itself, provided a clear *prima facie* case be *bona fide* shown ; *Croft* v.

(a) 9 A. & E. 663.

Lumley (a). And thirdly, the older cases also show that a mortgagee, *Doe* d. *Tillyard* v. *Cooper* (b), the heir or devisee of a deceased landlord, *Lovelock* v. *Doncaster* (c), though out of possession, may be admitted to defend.

On the other hand, the recent case of *Whitworth* v. *Humphrey* (d), the leading case in opposition to Mr. *Richardson's* application, shows that actual possession either by himself or his tenant must be shown by an applicant under this section. So also in *Butler* v. *Meredith* (e), it was held by *Pollock*, C. B., and Barons *Martin* and *Platt*, though Baron *Parke* doubted, firstly, that the Court or the Judge has a discretion; and secondly, that it is not sufficient merely to file "an affidavit which may be colourable, but that the party must satisfy the Judge that he is in actual possession by his tenant before he can be allowed to come in, and when he has done that, the leave or order of the Judge ought, as a matter of course, to be granted." And again, in *Thompson* v. *Tomkinson* (f), Barons *Alderson* and *Platt* refused to allow a person who had recovered in ejectment to come in as defendant until he had actually obtained possession.

After carefully considering these authorities, I am of opinion that as *Martha Richardson's* possession has been fairly challenged by the plaintiff's affidavits—and as she has failed to show any facts whatever from which the relation of landlord and tenant can be held in any sense to exist between her and *Rashleigh*, and from which I can be satisfied that *Rashleigh's* possession is in any sense her possession; and as she in no sense denies the facts of her husband's dealings as landlord and owner with the property, but only denies her knowledge of such dealings—I am bound to consider the formal affidavit under which the *ex parte* order was obtained as a mistake of the deponents thereto; and, consequently, that the *ex parte* order ought to be rescinded,

(a) 4 E. & B. 608 ; 24 L. J. Q. B. 78.   (b) 8 T. R. 645.
(c) 4 T. R. 122.   (d) 5 H. & N. 185 ; 29 L. J. Ex. 113.
(e) 11 Exch. 89.   (f) 11 Exch. 442.

and the names of Mr. and Mrs. *Richardson* struck out
of the record as not being landlord or landlady of the
defendant *Rashleigh* within the true intent and meaning
of the statute. But as the present application has challenged the *ex parte* order to be irregular in practice,
which I clearly think it is not—and as the real merits of
the case on all the facts are of considerable difficulty—I
do not think this is a case to give costs against Mr. and
Mrs. *Richardson*.

A second application was made upon further affidavits,
the facts contained in which sufficiently appear in the
following judgment delivered by

HARGRAVE, J. The present application differs only
from that dismissed by me on the 8th instant, by the
new allegations as to Mrs. *Richardson's* being in possession by herself, instead of by the defendant as her
tenant; and after carefully considering the affidavits
and the authorities, I do not see how I can lawfully
grant this application any more than the former.

The first objection to this application is, that it is an
attempt to introduce into the Common Law jurisdiction
the whole equitable doctrines and practice as to the
separate estates of married women. The Equity Courts
alone have acknowledged, and indeed alone created those
estates, and a Judge sitting at Common Law can only
recognise the rights and interests of married women
according to the long established principles and maxims
of the Common Law.

The intervention of trustees for the separate use of
married women, and the vesting of the legal estates in
such trustees, is the only legal mode by which the Common Law incidents of coverture will be prevented from
attaching to married women and to their property, and,
as in this case there has been no such conveyance to
trustees, I must consider the rights and interests of Mrs.
Richardson in relation to this property according to the
rules and maxims of the Common Law alone, leaving her
to maintain whatever equitable rights (if any) she may

possess, by proceedings in the ordinary jurisdiction of the Court of Equity.

Upon this part of the case, I should, however, remark that it is impossible, according to the clear law as to the disabilities of married women under coverture, to understand how the allegation that the purchase of this estate was made from moneys "earned" by Mrs. *Richardson* during coverture, and "belonging to herself," could constitute any quasi-separate estate in a Court of Common Law; nor, indeed, according to the widest interpretation of the decisions in Equity, any separate estate even in a Court of Equity.

The second and most important point for consideration is, as to the legal position of the parties, upon the admitted facts of these affidavits, viz.,—"That the legal estate has been in fact conveyed to Mrs. *Richardson* in fee simple from the Crown in the usual manner; that Mrs. *Richardson* has for twelve months resided with the defendant *Rashleigh* on the said premises, rented from her by him; that the said defendant about a week back gave up absolute possession to her as his landlady; and that she is now in possession of and living on the said premises." The precise point for my decision, therefore, is, whether such a state of circumstances constitutes in a married woman during coverture, and as against her husband's official assignee, a being "in possession by herself" within the intent and meaning of the 123rd section of the Common Law Procedure Act of 1853; and after carefully considering all the authorities on this section, and the principles and maxims of the Common Law as to such matters, I am not prepared to create a precedent which seems to me to be contrary to all legal principle applicable to such a state of circumstances. It is quite elementary law that wherever freeholds are vested in a married woman, as in this case, without any settlement to her separate use, the husband is by the Common Law entitled in right of his wife to the rents and profits during the coverture. It is an error, therefore, for Mr. *Richardson* to swear that he has received the rents as " agent for his wife;" and for me to recognise such an allegation as legal would be to create a quasi-separate estate in the wife at Common Law, which I am not prepared to do.

So, likewise, it is equally clear law that whatever estate or interest the husband has in his wife's lands, passes to his official assignee.   See *Comyn's* Digest "Bankrupt" D., *Polyblank* v. *Hawkins* (a), *Mace* v. *Cadell* (b) *Archbold's* Bankruptcy (c).   In *Michell* v. *Hughes* (d) it was also held that the husband was seised in right of his wife of her freehold lands for their joint lives, and that this life estate vested in the official assignee during the coverture.   The like was also held in *Robertson* v. *Norris* (e).

These authorities, and the statute 32 Hen. VIII., c. 28, enabling husbands seised in right of their wives to grant leases in the mode directed by that Act, completely illustrate the legal position of husband and wife in relation to the freehold lands of the latter during coverture ; and it is quite impossible for me now to overlook all these well-established principles and rules of the Common Law, and to recognise the novel and experimental dealings of Mr. and Mrs. *Richardson* with Mrs. *Richardson's* interest in this property, either as to the leases or the receipt of rent, as if creating in a Court of Common Law a sort of quasi-separate estate or interest in a married woman—and as if, in fact she were a *feme sole*.

Consequently, after carefully perusing these affidavits, I am unable to find any ground for holding that under the circumstances of this case Mrs. *Richardson* has made out any right at Common Law within the intent and meaning of the 123rd section of the Common Law Procedure Act of 1853, to the benefit of that section—at least during her coverture and as against her husband's official assignee.   As the last and most important English authority on this section of the Act, *Butler* v. *Meredith* (f), quoted by me in my former judgment in

(a) Dougl. 329.   (b) Cowp. 232.
(c) pp. 276, 316, edition, 1856.   (d) 6 Bing. 689.
(e) 11 Q. B. 916.   (f) 11 Exch. 89.

this matter, clearly establishes that the Judge to whom these applications are made, is bound to exercise his discretion in considering the affidavits, and to satisfy his own mind as to the legality of the application, and that the affidavits are sufficient to constitute the legal right to the order, I am bound to say that my mind is not so satisfied, and, therefore, that this application ought to be dismissed. And as the official assignee applies for his costs, I do not see how I can refuse these costs.

I think it right also to point out that the present affidavit in support of this application is made by Mr. *Richardson* alone, and that the allegations in that affidavit appear to me to be scarcely reconcilable with his previous sworn evidence in the Court of Insolvency.

Ex parte McIntosh (*a*).

THIS was an application to set aside an *ex parte* order to tax an attorney's bill of costs, on the grounds—First, that the order ought not to have been made *ex parte ;* and secondly, that it was not regularly obtained under the 11 Vic., No. 38.

The arguments sufficiently appear in the judgment which was delivered by

HARGRAVE, J. His Honor after stating the nature of the application, continued—

It was contended by Mr. *Darley* that this *ex parte* order, if granted under the first section of the Act, should have been applied for within one month after the delivery of the bill; and then that the order should have been made by the Prothonotary or other officer of the Supreme Court, with an order of the Judge restraining the attorney, under the conclusion of the first section, from commencing any action, &c., &c. The order was obtained on the 9th August, the bill of costs having been delivered on the 27th June, and it was contended that,

(*a*) In Chambers.

1865.

SEMPILL
v.
RASHLEIGH.

August 25.

The Rules of Practice directing that " during the half-yearly vacation no time shall run for pleadings or the doing of any other thing at Law or in Equity," do not apply to the month within which an application for an appointment to tax a bill of costs under the first section of the Attorneys Act must be made ; and an *ex parte* order having been obtained after the expiration of the month, was discharged by *Hargrave*, J.

as the action for the bill of costs was pending against Mr. McIntosh before the application of the *ex parte* order was made, such order was irregular, by omitting any direction to tax the costs of this action, or otherwise imposing terms and conditions if the order was made under the 2nd section of the Act.

On the other hand, Mr. *McIntosh* (on his own behalf) contended that under the 33rd General Rule of the 1st March, 1856, and the 10th General Rule of 26th August, 1856, directing that "during the half-yearly vacation no time shall run for pleadings or the doing of any other thing at law or in equity," the vacation time, from July 10th to July 31st, did not count as part of the "month" mentioned in the first section of the Act, and, therefore, that he was in full time on the 9th August to obtain an *ex parte* order under that section.

I am of opinion, however, that the " such month " mentioned in the first section of the Act is the month which must elapse after the delivery of a bill of costs before the attorney can bring his action, and as that month is clearly a statutory period independent of any rules or practice, and cannot be indirectly enlarged by any such Court rules, so the application for any of these *ex parte* orders under the first section must be made within the same time. The order, therefore, cannot be maintained as being issued under the first section of the Act.

With regard to Mr. *Darley's* second argument, that this *ex parte* order is not sustainable under the second section of the Act, it is to be observed—firstly, that the second section contains no express words limiting this section to orders on summonses ; and secondly, that the order contains no " directions," " conditions," or " restrictions," affecting the attorney's rights in the action, nor showing any *prima facie* necessity for any summons.

Mr. Darley referred to *Archbold's* Practice (*a*), and the volume of Forms (*b*), from which passages the

(*a*) Vol. I., pp. 104, 120.   (*b*) Nos. 48, 49, p. 30.

practice would certainly seem to have been to grant these orders usually upon summons and notice to the attorney; if the month has elapsed from the delivery of the bill, and if the action is sought to be restrained, or any other conditions or terms sought to be imposed on the attorney. But as I can find no express decision that *ex parte* orders without such terms or conditions are illegal under the second section, I am compelled to decide the present question upon a consideration of general principles applicable to the point for decision, and upon the true construction of the second section.

Limiting, therefore, my decision to this point alone, I am of opinion that this *ex parte* order is not necessarily irregular under the second section, for I think that this section, like the corresponding section (37) of 6 and 7 Vic., c. 73, confers (as all the Barons of the Exchequer held *In re Barber*) (a), a complete statutory general jurisdiction to order taxation of attorneys' bills of costs; and I, therefore, think that such jurisdiction includes a power to grant *ex parte* orders as well as orders on summons, and consequently that Mr. *McIntosh* had a perfect statutory right to obtain this order.

Nevertheless, as the order will be only partially efficient, for the purposes of complete justice as between these parties in relation to this bill of costs, and as I am unwilling to create a precedent for a new and inefficient practice in such matters, I shall discharge the order; but I discharge it without costs—1st, because the 33rd General Rule of this Court, of the 1st March, 1856, already referred to, has probably, and I think on a not unfair construction of that rule by an unprofessional person, misled Mr. *McIntosh* to think that he was within the month mentioned in the first section; and my second reason for discharging the order without costs is, because upon the true construction of the second section I cannot say that the *ex parte* order was illegal under that section, or otherwise absolutely irregular, under the circumstances stated in the affidavit; but only that it is incom-

(a) 14 M. & W. 720 ; 3 D. & L. 244.

N—4

plete for full justice between the parties in this matter, and I think it is undesirable for a single Judge at Chambers to introduce such new practice into these matters.

HICKEY *against* TOOTH (a).

A. agreed with *B.* for the sale to him of 46,000 sheep, more or less with a station, at 17s. 6d. a head. It appeared that several weeks before the contract *B.* had shown to *A.* a certain return, furnished by his superintendent, of the sheep on the station; and about the same time a flock of 1668 maiden ewes, mentioned in the return as being on the station, had been sold and removed. There having been a short delivery, *A.* sued *B.* ; the first count of the declaration setting out the agreement and alleging non-delivery, and

THIS was an action by a purchaser against the vendor of 46,000 sheep, more or less, together with certain stations, at 17s. 6d. a head, to be delivered on the 15th of June, 1861.

(*b*) The first count of the declaration set out the contract, and alleged as a breach a non-delivery of the whole number of the sheep sold. The second count was for the conversion of the sheep. The third count alleged that the defendant contracted that he had done no act whereby he precluded himself from delivering the sheep according to the contract. Breach, that before the time of the sale the defendant had precluded himself from delivering the sheep, according, &c.

The defendant pleaded to the first count—1. That he did deliver the sheep sold, &c., according to the agreement ; to the second count—2. Not guilty ; 3. That the sheep were not the plaintiffs as alleged ; to the third count—4. *Non assumpsit*; 5. That he had not precluded himself from delivering the sheep according, &c. Issue thereon.

At the trial before *Wise*, J., in November 1864, the evidence proved a contract for the sale by the defendant to the plaintiff of 46,000 sheep, more or less, with certain stations, at 17s. 6d. per head, and that the plaintiff only obtained delivery of 42,445—there being no more, in fact, at the time of the contract on the station.   The

the second count alleging a breach of a contract by the defendant that he had done no act whereby he had precluded himself from delivering the sheep according to the agreement.   The jury having given damages as for the non-delivery of these 1668 maiden ewes, the Court granted a new trial.

Quære (per *Stephen*, C. J.), whether the return ought in this action to have been received in evidence.

(*a*) Before *Stephen*, C. J., *Hargrave*, J., and *Cheeke*, J.

(*b*) The counts will be found set out at length in 2 Sup. Ct. R., C. L. 98.

real subject of dispute was the non-delivery of 1668 maiden ewes, which, according to the plaintiff's evidence, were the most valuable portion of the flock, and worth much more than the average price agreed to be given for the sheep. It appeared that, before the contract, the defendant thought that there were two flocks of maiden ewes on the station, and the return of the flocks furnished to him by the superintendent, and which, at the time of the negotiations a few weeks before, he had shown to the plaintiff, would seem to show this; but, in fact, only one flock was on the station when the contract was made, and only one flock was delivered; the maiden ewes in question having been sold ten, and delivered five, weeks before the contract. It was not disputed that the deficiency of 3555 head was too large; but it was argued that, as the plaintiff was only to pay for the sheep, together with the station, according to the number of sheep he received, the greater the deficiency, the less he would have to pay. The plaintiff had paid for 46,000, and it was conceded by both parties that he was entitled to receive back 17s. 6d. for every deficient sheep. The learned Judge told the jury that on the question of damages they were not entitled to take into consideration this particular flock of maiden ewes. But the jury found that there was a breach of contract, inasmuch as this reduced number was not a delivery of 46,000, "more or less;" and they gave damages for the non-delivery of the 1668 maiden ewes at 5s. each sheep with interest, estimating the value of each of these missing sheep at 22s. 6d.—that is, 5s. more than the contract price.

Stephen, for the defendant, now moved for a rule *nisi* for a new trial. It is contended that the plaintiff cannot possibly have sustained any damage whatever, because, in truth, the fewer the number of sheep delivered the less he would have to pay for, and so he might acquire the station for nothing, or next to nothing, since he was to pay only for the sheep which he received. But at any rate the jury had no right to estimate the value of the deficient sheep by the value of the 1668 maiden ewes, which it is said ought to have been delivered and were not, which, nevertheless, it is clear that they have done, although told by the Judge that those particular sheep were out of the question.

Rule *nisi* granted upon three points—1. That the damages ought to have been nominal only ; 2. That if not, that the damages were, at all events, excessive ; and 3. That the damages were calculated improperly, by reference specifically to the maiden ewes.

August 28.

Sir *W. Manning* and *Sheppard* showed cause. It is submitted that the jury were justified in estimating the damages by the highest value of all or any of the 46,000 sheep agreed to be delivered, or of the sheep on the station actually delivered. [*Stephen*, C. J. But what was that value ? What had these particular maiden ewes to do with the question ? Should it not have been average value ? That could not have been much above ten shillings, for the station was given in.] The return shown by the defendant to the plaintiff contained this flock as part of the sheep on the station ; the jury have found that they were worth 22s. 6d. a head, and therefore the damage the plaintiff has sustained by their non-delivery, is the difference between that value and the contract price. It was also a question for the jury whether, in a sale of so large a number of sheep, a certain proportion of maiden ewes ought not to have been found ; and the damages may have been estimated by them, not as the price of any particular flock, but as the price of a more valuable kind of sheep, of which there was a deficiency.

The plaintiff is also entitled to retain his damages on the third count. The defendant has prevented himself from fulfilling the contract he made. It was a contract for the sale and delivery of sheep accustomed to, and habitually on, the station. The defendant warranted that there were about 46,000 on the station, and by the return showed by him to the plaintiff, and by which it appeared that these 1668 maiden ewes were on the station, he warranted that they were the sheep that he sold. The sheep sold were not any sheep, but sheep referred to in this contract, and evidence, therefore, was admissible to apply the contract, and identify the specific subject matter; just as in *Macdonald* v. *Long-bottom* (a), the evidence of conversations and letters antecedent to the contract were allowed to explain the expression "your wool," which was used in the contract, and to point out the wool referred to. The sale may be likened to the sale of a non-existing chattel, in which there is an implied warranty that the vendor has done nothing to preclude himself from delivering it. In *Couturier* v. *Hastie* (b) *Parke*, B., says, "by selling a cargo the purchaser undertakes that the vendee shall have it if it exists, and that he himself had not before sold it to another." So here the defendant sold the sheep mentioned in the return. [*Stephen*, C. J. If the defendant sold these sheep, there might be a covenant like that mentioned in the third count; but the question is, whether there can be such a covenant if he did not sell them.]

The depreciation in the value of the sheep, that is, by the delivery of 42,000 inferior sheep instead of 46,000 good ones, may be such as to entail an actual loss. [*Stephen*, C. J. But it is admitted that if 46,000 had been delivered, the contract would have been fulfilled.]

Martin, Q. C., and *Stephen* contra. The evidence clearly was, that this particular flock of 1668 maiden ewes had been sold by the defendant ten weeks, and delivered five weeks, before this sale to the plaintiff. And the jury have given damages on a wrong principle, namely, that these particular maiden ewes ought to have been on the station. The contract was for the sale of sheep habitually on a particular station, and the returns referred to were no part of the contract. If there were

(a) 29 L. J. Q. B. 256 ; see *Shore* v. *Wilson*, 9 Cl. & F. 365.
(b) 22 L. J. Ex. 103, 301 ; S. C., 5 H. L. C. 673. See also *Aulton* v. *Atkins*, 18 C. B. 249.

sheep which had been removed from the station before the contract, those sheep were not sold. It is admitted that the plaintiff must obtain a verdict if the deficiency is greater than can be covered by the limitation of "more or less;" but he is not entitled to recover damages, because some particular sheep which were not the subject of the contract were not delivered. The complaint on the record is that among the 46,000 sheep, the subject of the contract, were in fact some which were not delivered, and which the defendant had put it out of his power to sell. If the sheep returns were admissible at all, it would be to show what in fact were the sheep on the run at the time of the contract. But these 1668 maiden ewes were not in fact then on the run, and so they did not pass by the contract. If, however, the returns were received to show what the defendant represented to be on the run, the evidence goes to support, not this action of tort, but an action for deceit or breach of warranty. The jury could not, without reference to these 1668 sheep, have given damages for the non-delivery of sheep of greater value than 17s. 6d. a head, especially as that price included the station. The only contract was for the sale of 46,000 sheep, or rather the defendant sold all the sheep on the station, estimating them at 46,000. There had been a representation, but it was not embodied in the contract. It is clear that interest was not recoverable. *Higgins* v. *Sargent* (a), and the 5 Vic., No. 9, sec. 23 (b) was referred to.

STEPHEN, C. J.   I am clearly of opinion that the jury cannot give damages for the non-delivery of these sheep, by reference to the value of this particular flock of maiden ewes, and that, therefore, the rule for a new trial must be made absolute.

If the defendant sold these 1668 ewes, it may be (although it is not necessary to decide the point, and we do not so decide) that he would have been liable as on a warranty that he had not previously

(a) 2 B. & C. 349.	(b) Sup. Ct. Pr. 19.

disposed of them. But, in fact, he sold only such

sheep as were at the time of the contract on the station, guaranteeing nothing as to the sex, quality, or age of any of the animals, beyónd this, that the total number should be "about" 46,000. As the actual number was considerably less, although by how much less we do not know, the plaintiff was entitled to damages for the non-delivery of the deficient number. We will assume the deficiency to have been about fifteen or sixteen hundred; say 1668. But the jury were not entitled to assume that the deficient sheep were in worth more than the average value of the others. And certainly they were wrong in estimating the animals by the value of the missing 1668 maiden ewes, with which the jury had nothing to do. It is indeed clear that the jury gave damages specifically as for these ewes, thinking that they ought to have been delivered. But the defendant never sold or undertook to sell these ewes to the plaintiff. If he represented at or before the sale that they formed part of the flocks, he might be liable as for a breach of warranty, or for fraudulent representation, but not in this action which is founded on a different view of the matter. And for myself, I may add, that it seems to me very questionable, for the reasons I have just stated, whether the returns of the sheep shown as they were to the plaintiff several weeks before the sale, ought in this action to have been received in evidence. The rule for a new trial must be made absolute with costs to abide the event, unless the plaintiff shall consent to take a verdict for nominal damages with the costs of the action (not to include the costs of this motion), in which case the verdict will stand with such nominal damages for the plaintiff.

HARGRAVE, J., and CHEEKE, J., concurred.

Judgment accordingly.

June 23.   THE QUEEN *against* SAUNDERS (*a*).

Recent pos-
session of
stolen bank
notes, of
which the
prisoner could
give no satis-
factory ac-
count, is
evidence
either that he
stole them, or
that he re-
ceived them,
knowing
them to have
been stolen,
according to
the other cir-
cumstances
of the case.

SPECIAL case under the 13 Vic., No. 8.

"This prisoner was tried before me at the late Goulburn Assizes, on an indictment containing two counts; the first, charging him with stealing some bank notes, which were taken from the Cooma mail; and the second, with feloniously receiving the same.

"It appeared in evidence that the mail had been stopped and robbed on the night of Tuesday, the 6th of December, between Queanbeyan and Bungendore, by two men who had their faces blackened, and could not be identified. The evidence against the prisoner was, that on the night of the 28th December he was arrested at Major's Creek, with six of the notes in his possession. Major's Creek is about six miles from *Burke's* public-house, at Gingamona, and twelve miles from Braidwood. The prisoner had endeavoured to pass one of the notes at Gingamona, and at first denied (to the constable) that he had any in his possession. He gave two inconsistent accounts of the mode of his acquiring these notes— neither of which was in accordance with probability.

"During the trial it was shown that the prisoner had been already tried for and acquitted of the robbery at the Braidwood Quarter Sessions. The Crown thereupon entered a *nolle prosequi* on the first count, and the case went to the jury on the second.

"In my charge to the jury on this count, I told them that in this particular case, having regard to the dates and the character of the property—passing from hand to hand, readily, in the neighbourhood—the ordinary legal presumption of larceny in the prisoner would not necessarily determine the case; but that if they thought that the prisoner really was not the thief, and had received the property from either a person who was so, or

(*a*) Before *Stephen*, C. J., and *Wise*, J.

from some other to whom the thief had delivered it—he knowing that it was stolen—the prisoner might be found guilty as a receiver.

"I, nevertheless, reserved the question for the Court, whether I was right in this charge.

" The prisoner was found guilty, and I sentenced him to twelve calendar months' imprisonment with hard labour.

ALFRED STEPHEN, C. J."

Sydney, 16th June, 1865.

Windeyer, for the Crown, referred to *R.* v. *Densley* (a).

No counsel appeared for the prisoner.

STEPHEN, C. J.   In *Langmead's* case (b) the prisoner was found in the recent possession of some stolen sheep, of which he could give no satisfactory account, and it might reasonably be inferred from the circumstances that he did not steal them himself; and it was held that there was evidence for the jury that he received them, knowing them to have been stolen.   It is there laid down that recent possession of stolen property is evidence, either that the person in possession stole the property, or that he received it, knowing it to have been stolen, according to the other circumstances of the case.   On the authority of that case, in which I entirely concur, this conviction must be approved.

WISE, J., concurred.

Conviction sustained.

(a) 6 C. & P. 399.   (b) 1 L. & C. 427 ; 10 L. T. N. S. 350.

PHILLIPS *against* WALMSLEY (a).

In an action of ejectment, it appeared that *D. B.* in 1826 died, seized of the land in question, then forming a part of a much larger property. He had several children, and *F.* an adopted daughter was brought up with them. *D. B.* died intestate; but leaving an unexecuted will, under which all his lands were to be divided, and *F.* was to have an equal share with *D. B.'s* children. After his death, all his children executed a memorandum, binding themselves to carry out their father's intentions.

EJECTMENT for a certain farm at Windsor. At the trial before *Wise*, J., in the sittings in November, 1864, it appeared that one *David Brown* was originally in possession of the land in dispute for several years, and that he devised (or rather intended to devise by a will prepared, but never executed) all his property, of which this land formed a portion, to his ten children. One *Margaret Fleming* was an adopted daughter only; but it was meant by *Brown* that she should share as a child with the others. *Joseph Brown*, his eldest son, by deed executed in 1828, reciting the father's intention, empowered his administrators to convey *Margaret's* share to her at the age of twenty-one. But this deed was so framed as not to convey the legal estate. By it the whole of *David Brown's* property was to be divided into eleven lots—and *Margaret Fleming* and the children of *David Brown* were to be put in possession of their respective portions; *Joseph Brown* himself retaining one share, and also taking all his father's personal property. No particular or separated lots were then appointed or specified. But in fact there were eleven

In 1826, *J. B.*, the eldest son of *D. B.*, on coming of age, executed—jointly with the administrators who were his brothers-in-law—an informal deed, by which he empowered them to apportion the lands, equally, among the intending devisees (*F.* included), and to convey their portion to each allottee on his coming of age. He undertook to join in the conveyances, and in the meantime the administrators were to hold the land, so to be allotted, in trust for or in conjunction with the parties. In consideration of the premises, the administrators made over to *J. B.* all the personal property. Soon after the execution of this deed, *F.* married the plaintiff's father—and, with him, occupied the land in question. She became of age in 1835. Her husband died in 1836. *F.* continued in possession until her death in 1838. From that time till 1864, except for about three years, during which some relation of *F.'s* collected the rent, as was said, on behalf of her children, nothing appeared in evidence respecting this farm. *J. B.* lived in the neighbourhood up to his death in 1862, without ever making any claim. The Judge declined to direct the jury, that they might presume the execution of a deed effectuating a partition of the land in accordance with the deed, or otherwise, conveying a legal title to the property to *F.*—and the plaintiff having been nonsuited, Held, on motion to set aside the nonsuit, that such direction was right, and that no such presumption legally arose.

(a) Before *Stephen*, C. J., and *Wise*, J.

farms; and before this *Margaret* was in possession of one of them, called Davies grant (the subject of this action), or in receipt of the rent of it by an agent who acted for her.   There was some evidence tendered of a casting of lots between the parties, before the execution of this deed, for their shares under some actual or supposed agreement; but the learned Judge refused to receive the evidence.   But at this time, that is, in 1828, *Margaret* was only about fourteen years old, and by the deed she was not to get a legal conveyance of her share or lot till she was of age.   In 1828 she married, and with her husband, *Phillips*, the father of the plaintiff, lived on *Davies* farm, till his death in 1836.   In 1835 she became of age, and continued to live there alone with three children, of whom the plaintiff is the only son and heir, until her death in 1838. . The plaintiff became of age in 1854, and the action was commenced within the ten years required by the statute.

The plaintiff relied on the possession of *Margaret Fleming* for twelve years, and his heirship to her. It appeared that her brother, of the same name of *Fleming*, was in possession for some years after 1838, on behalf (it was said) of her children—of whom the plaintiff was one, then about five years old, under some actual or supposed will in her favour made by her husband.   The plaintiff was not shown to have been in possession.   The defendant showed no title, but relied on the defect in that of the plaintiff.   *Joseph Brown* lived in the neighbourhood close by the farm, and had not, as far as the evidence went, made any claim on the land.

The learned Judge nonsuited the plaintiff, on the ground that he had failed to show any legal title ; that his mother's possession was referable to no title at all, as it was then shown to be in *Joseph Brown*.

Darley, for the plaintiff, obtained a rule *nisi*, on the ground that there was evidence to go to the jury from which they might have presumed a conveyance from

1865.

PHILLIPS
v.
WALMSLEY.

November 29, 1864.

Brown or his trustees, they having been empowered by the deed to execute one for him.

Sheppard and *Salomons* now showed cause. Possession is, it is admitted, *prima facie* evidence of title, and no other interest appearing in proof, is evidence of seisin in fee. But if the legal estate is shown to be in anyone else, the presumption arising from that possession is got rid of. In *Doe d. Carter* v. *Barnard* (a), it appeared that the plaintiff's husband had been in possession for eighteen years, when he died leaving a son (not a party to the action), and that the plaintiff then possessed and remained in possession for thirteen years ; and it was held that the plaintiff was rightly nonsuited, because the possession of her husband before her for eighteen years was *prima facie* evidence of his seisin in fee, and as he died in possession and left a son, it was also *prima facie* evidence of the title of his heir, against which the plaintiff's possession for thirteen years could not avail. So here the plaintiff has by his own showing proved the title to be in *Joseph Brown*, of which the defendant is entitled to take advantage. [*Wise*, J. There was no evidence that the defendant was in possession, but only that the plaintiff was out of possession.] The possession also having been out of *Margaret Fleming* and her descendants for some years, weakens any inference that might have been drawn from the evidence of her possession so long ago. The deed recites an arrangement by which the heir at law gave up the property to which he was then entitled, and agreed that it should be divided among his father's children and *Margaret Fleming*. But that was a mere voluntary agreement by the heir; and the doctrine of Courts of Equity as to family arrangements, where there is a doubtful right, has no application. In the present case there was no duty on the heir at law to carry out this arrangement, and it could not have been enforced by *Margaret Fleming*; *Stapelton* v. *Stapelton* (b) and the notes thereto. It is submitted that from all the circum-

(a) 13 Q. B. 945.   (b) 2 Wh. & T. L. C. 695.

stances, it is clear that the plaintiff's mother never obtained any conveyance from *Joseph Brown*, the only legal owner, and her possession, therefore, goes for nothing. There has been no such enjoyment of any right (which could have had no lawful origin except by deed), that in favour of such enjoyment the existence of such a deed must be presumed; *Lyon* v. *Reed* (a). There has been no dealing with the property in such a manner as reasonable men of business would not have dealt with it, unless there had been a conveyance; *Garrard* v. *Tuck* (b). There was no duty in the administrators to convey, and no trust in them. No presumption can arise in a case like this, that a deed of conveyance has been executed by the heir, or by these administrators; *Taylor* on Evidence (c). It arises in favour of long and uninterrupted possession only, and of a perfect title only incomplete for want of some technicality. "No case can be put," says Chief Justice *Tindal*, in *Doe* v. *Cooke* (d), "in which any presumption has been made, except when a title has been shown by the party who calls for the presumption, good in substance, but wanting some collateral matter necessary to make it complete in point of form. In such case, where the possession is shown to have been inconsistent with the existence of the fact directed to be presumed, and in such case only has it ever been allowed." The presumption arises when it is the declared duty of trustees to convey; for it is reasonable to presume that they performed their duty; *England* v. *Slade* (e), *Doe* v. *Sybourn* (f), *Doe* d. *Rees* v. *Williams* (g). *Joseph Brown* died only two years before the action was brought. There is a great injustice in any such presumption, except in aid of a clearly equitable title; and the plaintiff must, in order to succeed in ejectment, show a good legal title; *Cottrell* v. *Hughes* (h), *Goodtitle* v. *Jones* (i), *Roe* v. *Read* (k), *Doe* v. *Staple* (l), *Roscoe* on Evidence (m).

(a) 13 M. & W. 285.   (b) 8 C. B. 231 ; 18 L. J. C. P. 338.
(c) § 115. (d) 6 Bing. 179. (e) 4 T. R. 682. (f) 7 T. R. 2.
    (g) 2 M. & W. 749, 757 ; See *Doe* v. *Davies*, Id. 513.
(h) 15 C. B. 533 ; 24 L. J. C. P. 107.   (i) 7 T. R. 47.
(k) 8 Id. 118.   (l) 2 Id. 684.   (m) p. 683.

Sir *W. Manning*, Q. C., and *Darley* contra. The evidence as to drawing lots by the children of *Brown* and *Margaret Fleming*, should not have been excluded ; but that was one circumstance from which the jury should have presumed a conveyance from *Joseph Brown* to *Margaret Fleming*. This presumption was strengthened by the evidence that *Margaret Fleming* went into and remained in possession for some time, and received the rents. The evidence would have shown that the family arrangement between *Brown* was supported by a valuable consideration. For it appears that certain cattle and all the personal property were given up to the heir at law, and that he thereupon agreed to divide the land in accordance with the expressed intention of his father ; *Ellison* v. *Ellison* (*a*).

The question whether such a conveyance had been executed should have been left to the jury ; and they should have been told that they might presume a conveyance to *Margaret Fleming* in 1835, when she came of age. She was in actual possession for ten years ; and as the administrators of *Brown*, who were her trustees, were her brothers-in-law, it is most probable that she would have asked them to convey to her in 1835, or between that time and 1838, during all which time she was in possession of the land. *Bartlett* v. *Downes* (*b*), *Doe* v. *Passingham* (*c*), *Doe* v. *Sybourn* (*d*), and *Doe* v. *Wrighte* (*e*) were referred to.

August 18.

STEPHEN, C. J., delivered the judgment of the Court in this case as follows :—

This is an action of ejectment, for a small farm near Windsor, called *Fleming's*, brought by the eldest son of *Margaret Phillips*, deceased, formerly *Fleming*. At the trial, after rejecting evidence of a certain alleged actual partition, Mr. Justice *Wise* declined to direct the jury to presume, or tell them that they might presume, the execution of a deed effectuating such partition, or otherwise, conveying a legal title to the property—whereupon

(*n*) 1 Wh. & T. L. C. 199.	(*b*) 3 B. & C. 616.
(*c*) 6 B. & C. 305.	(*d*) 2 T. R. 2.
(*e*) 2 B. & A. 710.	

the plaintiff was nonsuited. And the question is, whether that nonsuit under the circumstances was right.

The original owner of this farm, then forming part of a much larger property, was *David Brown*, who died in 1826. He had several children, and *Margaret Fleming* was an adopted daughter, brought up with them. *Brown* died intestate ; but he left an unexecuted will, under which all his lands were to be divided, and *Margaret* was to have an equal portion with the rest. The entire family, accordingly, it seems, on his death, (although most of the children were then under age), signed a memorandum or document of some kind, binding themselves to act on and carry out the father's wishes ; and the widow, as also apparently one or two of the daughters, took possession of separate farms shortly afterwards. It is supposed, that at or about the same time all the farms in fact were allotted. But, in 1828, the eldest son Joseph, on coming of age, executed —jointly with the administrators, who were his brothers-in-law—a deed of a most peculiar and bungling character, by which he empowers them to apportion the lands (equally, as far as practicable) among all the intended devisees, *Margaret* included, and to convey the selected land to each allottee on attaining majority. He undertakes to join in the conveyances, and in the meantime the administrators are to hold the lands, so to be allotted, in trust for or in conjunction with the parties. In consideration of the premises, the administrators made over to *Joseph* all the personal property.

Soon after the execution of this deed, *Margaret Fleming* married the plaintiff's father ; and, with him, entered into or retained possession of the farm in contest. She became of age in 1835. The husband died in 1836, leaving her in sole possession, but having executed a will, not produced in evidence, dealing or affecting (it is supposed) to deal in some way with the property. *Margaret* continued in possession, until her death in 1838 ; when the plaintiff was five years old only. From that time until 1864, except for about three years, during which some relation of *Margaret's* collected the rent, on

behalf (it was said) of her children, nothing appeared in
evidence respecting this farm. But *Joseph Brown*, to
whom in law it belonged if not to *Margaret*, or to some
one claiming under her, lived in the immediate neighbourhood up to his death in 1862—without, it appears,
ever having made any claim. This acquiescence alone,
it was urged, strengthened the presumption that he had
at some time (and, if so, probably in 1835 or thereabouts), executed a conveyance to her of the property.

The previous question is, however, did any such presumption legally arise ; and we are of opinion, after
looking into the authorities, that it did not. It had
occurred to me, when the rule in this case was granted,
that the evidence as to the allotting should have been
received. But, according to the deed of 1828, the
selection (by lot or otherwise) was to be a subsequent
matter ; whereas the evidence proffered and rejected was
of an operation some years previous. I assume that an
allotting did in fact take place, as alleged ; for, notwithstanding the terms of that deed, there must, before the
widow and daughters took possession, have been some
selection—and probably for all the claimants. It by
no means follows, however, that *Margaret Fleming's* lot
was afterwards duly conveyed to her, or to her husband
in her right.

The former alone, of course, was the presumption contended for ; since it is the only one, which, if any, the
law would raise. As a matter of mere fact, all things
being considered, the likelihood is quite as great, or
greater, that no conveyance to either was executed.
Both would probably have been under the impression,
that they were already sufficiently secure ; but, if they
thought a conveyance necessary, and had obtained one,
their attorney would assuredly have taken care to get it
registered. Considered as a matter of mere legal or
artificial presumption, no case shows that one could
justifiably be made, by reason merely of a possession
extending over three years (or six, if we include the two
or three succeeding *Margaret's* death), after the time
when the supposed conveyance might have been exe-

cuted. Nor by reason of a possession embracing ten
years (during seven of which confessedly *Margaret* could
have had no title), followed by twenty-five or more,
throughout which possession has apparently been—from
whatever cause—in some one else. The plaintiff here
became of age in July, 1854, and brought his action
barely within the ten next years, which the statute
allowed him.

In the absence of all means of knowing the defence,
we could not assume that there is none, beyond that of
mere possession. But if the defendant has no other title,
he may rely on it as sufficient until the plaintiff has
established his own. The latter on the other hand may
have, and we will suppose at present that he has,
equitable or moral claims unjustly denied him. But, to
maintain an ejectment he must possess a legal title ; and
if a jury could (in his favour) presume the existence of
such a title, in a case like this, because apparently the
plaintiff ought to have (or his mother ought to have
had) one, it will be difficult to say in what case, presenting equitable claims merely, the jury may not make a
similar presumption.

It will sufficiently appear from *England* v. *Slade* (a),
Doe v. *Sybourn* (b), and *Keene* v. *Deardon* (c) that the
presumption of a deed having been executed is made,
only, in favour of persons having a clear beneficial title :
an *estate*, in point of fact, although perhaps equitable
only. The title, according to the judgment in *Doe* v.
Cooke (d), must be good in substance, but defective
because of some collateral matter, necessary to complete
it in point of form. In such cases, where the form alone
of a conveyance is wanting, which it was the plain duty
of some one (a trustee for instance) to execute, the presumption may be a reasonable one (although I confess
myself unable to see anything but fiction in the process)
that such a conveyance actually was executed. But here
the claim of the plaintiff's ancestor, however strong
morally, falls far short of the necessary conditions. The

(a) 4 T. R. 682.   (b) 7 T. R. 3.
(c) 8 East 263.   (d) 6 Bing. 179.

o—4

administrators could not have conveyed a legal title to
his mother, if they would ; the arrangement of 1828,
however honourable to the heir, could not have been enforced against him by her ; since no consideration, regarded by the law as such, moved to him from her—or
was at any time, on her behalf, paid or given.   See
Ellison v. *Ellison* (a), and the cases there cited.
According to the deed, under which a trust is supposed
to have been created, the farm itself was not then ascertained. In short, she had no "estate" known to the law;
but only a claim, which doubtless she and others at the
time regarded as equivalent.   She was, practically, in
the position of a beneficiary owner; but she was not one.

In *Doe* v. *Reed* (b) it appears to be clearly laid down,
that the question whether a conveyance conferring title
has been executed, however long the possession of the
party seeking to establish the presumption, is after all
one of fact. The Court there observes, that the grant of
a right of way is presumed, after long user, simply
because no portion of that user could be reasonably accounted for, unless there had been originally such a
grant. *Abbott*, L. C. J., adds, that the cases as to presumption had already gone far enough, and ought not to
be extended.   But the difference between the user of a
right of way, and a grant to support it, and the case of
a presumed conveyance to confirm, or create a title, is
obvious.

For the several reasons given, we are of opinion that
the nonsuit in this case was right; and the rule obtained
by the plaintiff for setting it aside, therefore, is discharged.

(a) 2 W. & T. E. L. C. 178, 182.   (b) 5 B. & A. 236.

1865.

KINGSTON *against* GALE (a).

EJECTMENT for a small parcel of land at Padding-
ton, by a landlord against his tenant, under a building lease—for breach of covenants contained in such lease.

The case was tried before *Stephen*, C. J., in May
1865. The lease which contained the covenants in
question was dated the first of July, 1858. The habendum was "unto the said lessee, his executors, administrators, and assigns, from the first day of July now
instant, for the term of ninety-eight years thence next
ensuing, yielding and paying, &c."

The covenants alleged to have been broken were as
follows:—"And also that he the said lessee, his executors, administrators and assigns, will and shall, within
six years from the commencement of this demise, lay out
and expend on the said parcel of land, exclusive of
internal painting and decoration, the sum of £150 at
the least, in erecting upon the said land a brick or
weatherboard house—to be well and substantially built;
and will and shall within three calendar months next,
after the expiration of the said period (or after the said
sum shall be so expended, as the case may be), render to
the said lessor, his heirs or assigns, or to his surveyor or
agent, the several bills, documents, and other evidence
requisite to prove to his satisfaction that the aforesaid
sum, at the least, was expended and laid out; and thereupon the said lessee, his executors, administrators or
assigns, shall be entitled to a certificate that the same
sum hath been duly expended as aforesaid. And also
will and shall, during the continuance of the term hereby
granted at his and their own costs and charges, keep the
same premises and every part thereof—with all erections

A lease pur-
ported to
have been
made on the
1st July, 1858,
habendum to
the lessee
"from the
first day of
July now
instant, for
the term of
ninety-eight
years thence
next ensuing."
It was proved
that the deed
was not exe-
cuted till May
1859. *Held,*
that the term
commenced
on the 1st
July, 1858.
The lessee
covenanted,
that, within
six years
"from the
commence-
ment of this
demise," he
would expend
£150 in erect-
ing on the
demised land
a house—to
be well and
substantially
built; and
that he would
produce
vouchers, to
prove the ex-
penditure of
that sum.
And also that
he would,
during the
continuance
of the term,

keep the premises—"with all buildings to be erected thereon"—in good repair; and
would insure "the buildings to be erected" to their full value, and keep the same so
insured during the term. *Held,* that these covenants bound the lessee to insure, as
well as keep insured, whatever buildings might be erected by him on the land, at
any time during the term.

(a) Before *Stephen*, C. J., *Hargrave*, J., and *Cheeke*, J.

and buildings to be erected thereon—in good and substantial repair and condition." And also, " and that the
said lessee, his executors, administrators or assigns, shall
and will, at his and their costs and charges, insure the
buildings, to be erected on the ground hereby demised,
to the full value of so much thereof as can be destroyed
by fire, in some public insurance office in Sydney aforesaid, and keep the same so insured during the term
hereby granted; and upon the request of the said lessor,
his executors, administrators or assigns, or his agents,
produce to him the receipts for the premiums for such
insurance for the current year." The lease was executed
in point of fact early in 1859; the evidence being conflicting as to the precise month, but pointing rather to
the month of May.

The action had been commenced on the 4th November, 1864.

It was proved that the defendant had erected on the
land two tenements—one of brick, and the other of
weatherboard; but several witnesses were called, who
deposed that they were of the most flimsey construction,
and that neither of them separately, nor even that both
taken together, could have cost £150. There was no
evidence called for the defence; but the jury, by the
consent of both parties, inspected the premises. A
certificate, also, alleged to have been given to the defendant by two builders, who were not called, and which
stated that they had examined the houses, and found the
value of them to be £800, was before the jury.

It appeared also that the defendant had never produced any vouchers of the outlay, and had not insured
the premises; the omission as to each of these particulars was suggested to have been the result of mere
oversight.

The learned Judge directed the jury, on the question
whether there had been a breach of the covenant to expend £150 in building a substantial house, " within six
years from the commencement of this demise," that as
the date was the 1st July, 1858, and the habendum
" from the first of July now instant," the commencement

of the demise must be taken to be the 1st July, 1858,
although the execution was not till May 1859, and that
therefore the action was not premature; that with regard
to the building covenant, the question was what had
been the actual outlay; and that whether the buildings
erected were of the required value or not, the defendant
was bound to insure, and keep insured what he did put
up—at all events where, as here, he insisted that the
buildings erected were of the full value.

The jury found that the lease was executed in May
1859, and gave a verdict for the defendant, expressing
as their opinion that the six years contemplated by the
lease had not expired, and that it was not necessary to
insure until the expiration of those six years. They also
found that a house had been erected by the defendant of
the required value.

Stephen, for the plaintiff, now obtained a rule *nisi* for
a new trial, on the grounds—first, that the verdict was
against evidence and the ruling of the Judge; and
secondly, that the defendant had broken his covenants
in the lease: (1) because he did not, within the six
years mentioned therein, lay out and expend on the said
land £150 in erecting a brick or weatherboard house,
well and substantially built; (2) that he did not within
three months render to the plaintiff the bills, documents,
and other evidence requisite to prove to his satisfaction
that that sum had been expended; (3) that he did not
insure the buildings erected on the demised ground, or
keep the same so insured during the term; (4) that he
did not at the request of the lessor produce to him the
receipts for the premiums for such insurance for the current year. Thirdly, that the verdict was against evidence and the ruling of the Judge, because the jury
found that the six years mentioned in the lease had not
expired at the commencement of the action.

Sir *W. Manning*, Q. C., showed cause. It is clear,
as the jury found, that the lease was executed in May
1859. Leases operate from the date of their execution.

"All deeds do take effect from, and therefore have relation to, the time, not of their date, but of their delivery" (a). In *Steele* v. *Mart* (b) a lease purported on the face of it to have been made on the 25th March, 1788, habendum from the 25th March now last past, and it was proved that the deed was not executed for some time after the date; and it was held that it took effect from the time of delivery, and not from the date of the date. It is laid down by *Eyre*, C. J., in *Wyburd* v. *Tuck* (c), as a point on which there could be no doubt, that "the habendum can only be considered as marking the duration of the lessee's interest, and its operation as a grant is merely prospective;" *Smith's* Landlord and Tenant (d). It is submitted, therefore, that now instant must be taken to mean now next. [*Stephen*, C. J. I have no doubt that the word "next" was inserted originally where the word "instant" is used now, and the word "May" where "July" is now found. But as this would make the term commence from the 1st July, 1859 only, whereas the defendant was already in possession, and had paid one, if not two, quarters rent; this clumsey arrangement was made by altering the date to July, 1858, and so giving about 5½ years only as the time in which the houses were to be built. Six years from the 1st July, 1859, would of course not expire till 1st July, 1865.]

It is also contended that the defendant was not bound to insure until the term had expired, or at any rate until the building covenant had been satisfied. If the defendant had put up a temporary hut while the house was being built, was he bound to insure that? The plaintiff, at all events, cannot say that he was so bound, as the plaintiff's case is that the house erected was not of the required value. If so, why should the defendant insure? He is only to insure the building "to be" erected, that is, buildings worth the stipulated sum; and not then until after the expiration of the six years (e).

(a) Shep. Touch. 72.   (b) 4 B. & C. 272 ; S. C., 6 D. & R. 392.
(c) 1 B. & P. 464 ; See *Shaw* v. *Kay*, 1 Exch. 412.   (d) p. 83.
(e) See *Doe* v. *Peck*, 1 B. & Ad. 438 ; and *Doe* v. *Ulph*, 13 Q. B. 204.

On the question of fact, whether there had been the required outlay on the house, the jury by the consent of both parties during the trial inspected the premises, and their opinion, therefore, was quite equal to any evidence.

Stephen in reply. Leases may commence in interest at a date different from that of the computation of time. Mr. *Smith* says (*a*), "A lease may be so worded as to run from one date in point of computation, and from another in point of interest. For instance, I may make a lease to hold for ten years from the 1st of January last, and it will begin in interest from the day of making, but in computation from last January ; or I may even make a lease for ten years from the date, but not to commence till the expiration of a lease for five years now existing in the premises, and it will begin in computation from the date, but in interest from the expiration of the out-standing lease." Citing *Enys* v. *Donnithorne* (*b*). So here this lease was to take effect in interest in May, although for the purpose of computation it was to begin in July, 1858. The Court may look at the then surround-ing circumstances to discover the meaning, as was done in *Bainbridge* v. *Wade* (*c*), to explain the nature of a written guarantee. The plaintiff is himself only a tenant, and probably with building covenants as stringent as those of the defendant. On the defendant's construction he has no legal title till the following July. And, therefore, although in possession in May, since it was shown that he paid his rent from the 1st of April, yet he would have had no estate, but was a trespasser till the following 1st of July. The words "commencement of this demise," in the building covenant, can only mean from the 1st July, 1858, for the term then commenced. But the covenant was to pay rent from the time of the commence-ment of his interest, and no other.

The defendant is clearly bound to insure the building, as it is erected. For if the defendant be not bound to insure, he is not bound to repair, and so for a large pro-

(*a*) Smith's L. & T. 85.   (*b*) 2 Burr. 1190.
          (*c*) 20 L. J. Q. B. 7.

portion of his tenancy, as for instance, three or four, out of the six years, the premises might remain unrepaired and uninsured.   The covenant to rebuild is no sufficient protection to the landlord, as the tenant might be too poor to fulfil such a covenant.   The defendant also states that he has fulfilled his building covenant ; and also endeavours to get rid of his obligation to insure, on the ground that he has not fulfilled it.

On the question whether there had been the requisite expenditure upon the house, all the evidence was one way, and as unfavourable to the defendant's case as was possible.   The defendant also was present in Court during the trial and was not called, although he alone could give the true state of the case to the jury ; and the latter, therefore, had no right to form an opinion in direct opposition to that evidence.

Cur. adv. vult.

September 15.

The Court now gave judgment as follows :—

STEPHEN, C. J.   This is an action of ejectment, brought by a landlord against his tenant—for breaches of covenant by the latter, in not erecting a substantial house to a stipulated amount within six years, and for not insuring the buildings erected; as also for not producing vouchers of the outlay, and receipts for such insurance.

It appeared at the trial, that the defendant had erected on the land two tenements, one a brick and the other a wooden structure, after (or one, it seems, before) the execution of the lease.   There was evidence for the plaintiff, however, that both united had probably not cost one hundred and fifty pounds (the fixed sum); and very strong evidence that neither, singly, could have cost so much ; as also that each was by no means substantial, but of the very slightest materials.   There was no evidence for the defence; but the jury, by consent of both parties, inspected the premises.   A certificate also purporting to be signed by two builders, was before the jury, declaring the " value " of the houses to be three hundred pounds ; but neither of these individuals was called. Neither was the defendant, who alone could have proved the actual outlay. I told the jury, that this was the true question. It is probable, that the two houses together (though not one merely) did cost one hundred and fifty pounds. But the jury found, saying nothing as to the cost, that "a house" was erected of that value.

It was not pretended that the defendant had ever produced vouchers of the outlay, or had insured the buildings; but the omission, as to each of these particulars, may have been the result of mere oversight. The jury, however, in the face of a direction from me to the contrary, expressed their opinion that the six years contemplated by the lease had not expired, and that it was not necessary to insure, until after the expiration of those six years. They consequently, on the whole case, returned a verdict for the defendant.

There never was a stronger illustration, probably, of the adage that hard cases make bad law, than that finding. Without fuller inquiry, however, into matters not in issue, and on which neither party was entitled to give evidence, we do not feel justified in saying authoritatively that this was a hard case on the defendant. But, be this as it may, the law—of which the jury were not constitutionally the judges—remains the same. We will assume, for the sake of argument, that the prescribed period of six years had not expired, but that a house to the stipulated cost (taking that as the fact meant to be found) was erected on the premises. So far, then, the defendant performed his contract. Five years elapse, however, after such erection, and he does not insure the building. During all that time, therefore, neither he nor his landlord has the security which insurance would have afforded, in case of its destruction by fire. The tenant, it is true, may possess the means of rebuilding; but, to the extent of the cost, his means have been expended—and they may be exhausted. The jury conceive, nevertheless, that, because the six years are not expired, he need not insure. Well, a few days before this expiry the premises are consumed. Where would be the landlord's security then ? and where the tenant's fund for their reinstatement ?

The defendant covenanted that, within six years "from the commencement" of the demise, he would expend one hundred and fifty pounds, at the least, in erecting on the land a house—to be well and substantially built; and that he would produce vouchers, to prove the expenditure of that sum. Also that he would, during the continuance of the term, keep the premises—"with all buildings to be erected thereon"—in good repair; and would insure "the buildings to be erected" to their full value, and keep the same so insured, during the term. It appears to us, that these covenants (reading them in connection with each other) bound the defendant to insure, as well as keep in repair, whatever buildings might be erected by him on the land, at any time during the term. If not bound to insure any such, erected for example during the first year, until after expiration of the sixth (for which construction we discover no reason), neither would the defendant be bound to repair any such buildings, until after that time. In this respect, his liability must be the same under either covenant.

The defendant here was allowed to put up, if he chose, a mere house of weatherboards; and it seems almost absurd to suppose, that such a structure—erected perhaps within the first few months—might be left at the tenant's option wholly without repair, for five years afterwards or more. If the house erected was of the required cost and value, there was every reason for stipulating that it should, thenceforward, be kept up to the value, by attention to repairs. But, whatever the value, or the description of the building, the reason for such a stipulation is equally cogent. A house (one house, costing a stated sum), is to be erected; but, "all buildings" of whatever kind are to be repaired—and insured, and kept insured. And this the defendant is to do by the terms of his contract, "during" the term. The meaning surely is not, that he is to insure the buildings during a portion of the term only.

It would be a strange defence to a tenant, under such

covenants as these, that he need neither insure nor repair the buildings, because they had cost perhaps ten pounds less than he ought to have expended on them. But here the defendant maintains, that the house has been wholly completed; and still, that he was not bound to insure.

On the whole we are of opinion, therefore, as to this point, that—even if the six years had not expired at the time of action brought—the defendant broke his covenant to insure the buildings ; and so, that the verdict cannot be sustained. We have next to consider whether it is or not wrong, also, on the other grounds taken ; and we are of opinion, that it is on both those grounds.

Without deciding, that a jury viewing premises may in no case unexceptionably form a conclusion of their own, as to matters in controversy respecting them, we cannot accede to the position that it may (except by express consent of the parties) supersede—much less be violently in conflict with—the sworn testimony. Respecting the substantiality of the buildings in this case, an independent conclusion might perhaps reasonably be drawn. But the actual cost, as distinguished from the value of those buildings, could have been shown conclusively by the defendant only ; and, as he was not called, even to contradict evidence respecting conversations with him, there was a great preponderance of testimony in the plaintiff's favour, on that point, which ought not to have been disregarded.

The question of law, on which our decision respecting the six years lapse of time must depend, is not free from difficulty ; but we all think that my direction on it was right. The lease (nearly the whole being printed) was evidently intended to bear date in May, and it was executed in fact about the 4th of that month, in the year 1859. But the actual date, as the instrument now stands, is the 1st day of July, 1858; and the habendum is from the "1st day of July now instant." It was executed in duplicate, and the term filled in was ninety-eight years " thence next ensuing." The writing shows, that the words originally inserted were now next; but, as this (according to the plaintiff, not contradicted by the solicitor who attested the execution) was a mistake, the words " now instant " were then and there substituted.

The suggested explanation of this was, that the plaintiff was himself similarly a lessee, sub-letting the premises; that there had been already an under-tenant, evicted only a few months before; that the plaintiff's own term was probably ninety-nine years; and that ninety-eight, reckoned from the 1st July, 1859, would have extended beyond any interest which he had to give.   But the expedient adopted for preventing that blunder, it is obvious, making the computation commence from the year previous, had the effect of shortening proportionally the six years, limited for the building of the defendant's house. It may be that this was not observed at the time; or that the result was immaterial, practically—or was thought so by the defendant, as his building was then already in progress.   Or it is possible that the alteration was altogether a fraud.   But the last supposition is improbable in the highest degree : for each counterpart exactly corresponds with the other; the manuscript dates, contrasting with the printed portions, must have attracted instant attention ; and the defendant himself, had the time agreed on really been six years from July 1859, would assuredly have set up this as his answer, when called to account in 1864 for not having fulfilled his contract.   His case was, however, even at the trial, not that the six years commenced in July, but in May 1859 ; and this, not because of any fraud or mistake, but simply because in point of law (as his counsel insisted) the time ran from the execution of the deed only.

Now it is clearly settled, that a lease may commence —and in practice such deeds often do—at one day in point of computation, and at another in respect of occupation or interest ; Bac. Ab. Lease E., and *Enys* v. *Donnithorne* (a). This lease is dated the 1st July, 1858. It was not executed till May, 1859.   But the term created by the instrument is ninety-eight years (that is

(a) 2 Burr. 1195.

to say, the defendant is to hold for that term), from the
1st day of July instant. That date, consequently, was
the commencing one of the term, for all purposes of
computation; and, from the commencement of the demise
or term, it is clear that the six years are to be reckoned.

Thus considered, there is no embarrassment created,
merely by the fact of an inconsistent period of execution.
The commencement in point of interest, or occupation,
would be the latter ; and rent, therefore (under the deed,
at all events), might be payable from the 4th May only.
But, as "May" cannot have been meant by the word
July, the term created must begin from some 1st day of
July. The month of July 1859, however, could not
have been intended by the words July instant, in a lease
bearing date the 1st July, 1858. To hold this would
be, as urged on the argument, to postpone the defendant's interest and right of entry, as well as the commencing point of computation, to July then next ; and
so, to replace the very words which both instruments had
rejected. The words " July instant," consequently can
only be understood of the date ; and the fact of the execution having been in May has no effect on them.

The case of *Steele* v. *Mart* (a) does not militate
against this conclusion. There, the lease was dated the
25th March, 1783, to hold from the 25th day of March
last. Unexplained, that would of course mean March
1782. But the rent was made payable quarterly ; and
the " first " payment was to be on the 24th June next
after the date. The instrument was executed, it appears,
in May 1783 ; and the Court held, that the term commenced from the 25th March then preceding. It will
be observed, that on the face of that deed there was an
inconsistency; and on the existence of this, mainly, not
alone the fact of the execution having been in May, the
decision was founded. The word " last " was reasonably
construed, under the circumstances of that deed, to mean
last before its execution. But there is no inconsistency
in the lease here, either as to days appointed for payment
of the rent, or otherwise.

(a) 4 B. & C. 274.

The case of *Styles* v. *Wardle* (a) is much more in point with the present. There a certain thing was covenanted, by a lease, to be done within twenty-four months after the date of the deed; but the instrument was not executed until above three months after that date. That Court held, that the computation ran from the date, and not the delivery, notwithstanding the lapse of so much of the agreed time in the interval. Mr. Justice *Bayley* observes, that there are cases in which it may be necessary, *ut res valeat*, to construe " date " as meaning delivery; but that, ordinarily, where a day is mentioned, it is the guide for purposes of computation—adding, that it would be very dangerous to allow a different construction.

There must, therefore, be a new trial in this case; and, since the verdict is wholly wrong, and was against the direction of the Judge, the costs of this motion only, and not the costs of the first trial, will be costs in the cause; so that the defendant will not get his costs of that trial, in any event.

HARGRAVE, J. I only wish to add to the reasons given by His Honor the Chief Justice—

1. As to the first branch of the judgment, viz., the construction of the covenants to repair and insure, extending during the first six years of the term, it must be remembered that the formal part of the lease containing the general and operative words of covenant immediately preceding all the details of the covenants necessarily and clearly commence exactly *co instanti* with the execution of the lease, and cannot be limited to any less period except by equally clear words postponing such general words to the end of the six years.

2. It is also the general law, as laid down by Lord *Ellenborough* and other Judges in numerous cases, upon the construction of covenants to repair and insure, that these covenants are always to be construed strictly in favour of the lessor. See *Woodfall's* Landlord and Tenant (b).

(a) 4 B. & C. 910.   (b) pp. 444, 492.

3. With reference to the second branch of the judgment—viz., as to the construction of the word "instant"
in the habendum of this lease—I would point out that
even independently of the authorities quoted by the
Chief Justice, it is plain that the parties to this lease by
obliterating the word "next," and inserting in lieu
thereof the word "instant," manifested their intention
clearly to be not the July "next" after the execution of
the lease, and therefore necessarily intended the July
next before such execution—*i.e.* in this case, July 1858.
I consider this circumstance perfectly conclusive upon
the construction of this covenant.

4. Lastly, with reference to the hardship of this case,
it must be remembered that this lessee can defend himself against the forfeiture of his lease under these covenants, by availing himself of the equitable jurisdiction
of the Court under the well established cases in that side
of the Court; and that the sections 5 to 9 of the recent
colonial statute, 26 Vic., No. 12, was passed by the
Legislature expressly to provide against such forfeiture
for non-insurance.

THE COMMERCIAL BANK *against* GIBBONS (a).

A CTION by indorsee of an overdue promissory note   Wherebankers
for £250 at two months, made by the defendant   discounted for
a customer a
in favour of *William Broughton*, or order, and endorsed   note given,
as they knew,
by *Broughton* to the plaintiffs.   for his accom-
modation by
Pleas 1. That the note was made by the defendant for   the defendant,
the accommodation of the payee, *Broughton*, and without   which was
any consideration to the defendant for the acceptance or   dishonoured,
and they were
payment thereof, as the plaintiffs at and after the time of   afterwards re-
quested or
the indorsement hereinafter mentioned well knew; and   directed by
the said *W. Broughton* indorsed the said note to the   the customer
to look to him
plaintiffs; and before the commencement of this suit,   for payment,
Held, that
they were not bound to appropriate in payment of the dishonoured note, any partial
payments or credits less than the amount of the note.

The bankers would be, under such circumstances, bound so to appropriate in case of
an equal or greater amount coming into their hands. *Marsh* v. *Houlditch* (b) considered.

(a) Before *Stephen*. C. J., *Hargrave*, J., and *Cheeke*, J.
(b) Chitty, 10th ed. 283.

and upon maturity of the said note, and at the place of presentment thereof for payment, the said *W. Broughton* paid the amount of the said note, and of all claim thereon to the then holders of the said note, to wit, to the plaintiffs; and thereby then satisfied and discharged the said note, and all claims thereon, whether against the defendant or any other person, by payment to the plaintiffs; and the plaintiffs accepted and received such payment in such satisfaction and discharge. 2. On equitable grounds, that the defendant made the said note at the request and for the sole accommodation of *W. Broughton*, as his surety only to secure a certain sum of money then to be advanced, and which was advanced by the plaintiffs to the said *William Broughton*, solely, and save as aforesaid, there never was any value or consideration for the making the said note; and the said note was endorsed and delivered to the plaintiffs, and accepted by them upon an express agreement between the plaintiffs and the defendant, that the defendant should be liable thereon as surety only for the said *W. Broughton;* and the plaintiffs, at the time when the said note was indorsed to them as aforesaid, had notice and knowledge of the said note having been so made as aforesaid. Averment, that the plaintiffs, while holders of the said note, without the knowledge or consent of the defendant, for a good and valuable consideration, gave the said *W. Broughton* time for the payment of the note beyond the time when the same became due, and forbore to enforce payment during that time upon and for the consideration aforesaid; and that the plaintiffs could and might, had they not given such time as aforesaid, have obtained payment from *W. Broughton* of the note and all moneys due thereon; and that by means of the premises the defendant hath been greatly prejudiced and damnified, and hath been and is wholly discharged from all liability to pay the amount due upon the said note. Issue thereon.

The case was tried at the Goulburn Assizes before *Stephen*, C. J., when it appeared that the action was brought to recover the amount of the principal and interest due on the promissory note declared on. The plaintiffs had a branch bank at Yass, of which one *Pearson* was the manager. The defendant was a storekeeper, and *Broughton* a squatter, in the neighbourhood. *Broughton* was a customer of the bank, with which he had had some large discount transactions. The note sued upon was a renewal of a former note given by the defendant for the accommodation of *Broughton*.

It appeared that a promissory note of defendant's in *Broughton's* favour, dated on October, 1863, at one month's date, was discounted by the latter in October, and the proceeds placed to his credit. In November, another similar note was given to retire the former one, and *Broughton* was debited with the former, and credited with the proceeds of the latter note. The same thing was done in December. In January, when the December note fell due, the defendant gave the note sued upon. It appeared that about that time the following correspondence took place between *Pearson* and *Broughton*. On 23rd November *Broughton* wrote to *Pearson* (enclosing the note above referred to); after stating that he was surprised that *T. B. Gibbons'* promissory note had been paid, he continued:—"It was my intention to have got a renewal from *Gibbons* before the 1st of December. I now enclose a promissory note at one month, which I hope you will discount and pass proceeds to credit of my account." On the 24th November *Pearson* replied, "Your favour of the 23rd instant is to hand, as also *T. B. Gibbons'* promissory note at one month, for £250, which has needful attention by crediting your account with proceeds, say £248 9s. 4d. It is to be regretted you did not adopt the usual course of authorising us by letter not to pay, when presented, your acceptance to *T. B. Gibbons*, recently charged to your account. *Gibbons* would then have applied to you to carry out the original arrangement, namely, that of renewing." On the 19th December *Pearson* wrote to *Broughton*, " *T. B. Gibbons'* promissory note bearing your endorsement for £250, and discounted for you, matures 26th instant." On the 24th December *Pearson* wrote to

P—4

Broughton, "*Gibbons'* acceptance for £250 to hand, and has been discounted, and proceeds have been passed to your credit. I presume the first bill of £250, maturing 26th, drawn by *Gibbons* in your favour, is to be charged to your account." On January 25th, 1864, *Broughton* wrote, "I have got a chance of sending the enclosed in to you for discount;" to which *Pearson* replied on the 26th, "I have duly received your favour of yesterday's date, enclosing bill, *T. B. Gibbons'* favour of yourself for £250, as a renewal of that maturing the 27th, to-morrow." On April 23, 1864, *Pearson* wrote to *Broughton,* "*Gibbons'* bill to you for £250 is still unpaid ; pray lose no time in retiring this also." Letters were also written on the 5th and 9th of May, by *Pearson* to *Broughton,* drawing his attention to his liability on the defendant's overdue note, and begging him to retire it.

The defendant was called, and stated that he had given the renewals to retire the overdue notes, and that he did not know the note now sued upon had not been paid at maturity, until *Pearson* told him so in June. It appeared that in the same month of June he had sued *Broughton* for the balance of a store account.

It appeared that after the dishonour of the note various sums had been paid into *Broughton's* credit. and drawn out by his cheques on the Bank ; and the amounts paid in were, taken together, more than the amount of the note ; but there was never a balance in his favour in a larger amount than the note.

It was contended that the plaintiffs were entitled to recover, as the sums paid in were specifically to be appropriated for other purposes, as indicated by the cheques drawn by *Broughton.*

His Honor asked the jury whether the Bank was cognisant that the defendant was a mere surety at the time of the discount, and at maturity, of the note. He ruled that a promise to regard the defendant as a surety was unnecessary. On the first plea he asked them whether the Bank was directed or requested by *Broughton,* after maturity of the promissory note, to look to him for payment, and to pay the amount out of funds coming to the hands of the Bank to his credit, and not otherwise specifically appropriated, that is, sums paid in and remaining to his credit over and above all sums drawn. And if so, did any moneys not so appropriated at the time of their being paid into *Broughton's* credit, come to the Bank's hands?   And his Honor directed the jury that if they so found, they were to deduct all sums coming within that category from the £250.   The jury found, in answer to certain specific questions submitted by his Honor—1. That the defendant was a mere accommodation party to the note as surety for *Broughton*; 2. that the Bank knew this at and before the maturity of the note; 3. and that knowing this, was requested by *Broughton*, after maturity of the note, to look only to him; 4. and that thereupon *Broughton* desired the Bank to pay all monies coming to its hands to his credit (and not absorbed by previous debts, and not when paid in specifically directed to be appropriated to some other purpose), in liquidation of that note.

They also found, on the second issue, that the Bank knowing that the defendant was such surety only, agreed without the defendant's consent to give to *Broughton* time to pay the note; but that such giving of time was not founded on, or in pursuance of, any binding contract or engagement.   His Honor thereupon directed the verdict to be entered for the defendant on the first issue, and for the plaintiffs on the second.

Isaacs now moved for a rule *nisi* to set aside the verdict on the first issue, and to enter it for the plaintiff or for a new trial, on the grounds—1. That there was no evidence of any request by *Broughton* to the Bank to look only to him to pay the promissory note. 2. That if there was such evidence, there was none of such assent by the Bank so to do. 3. That the Judge should have told the jury that, in the absence of such assent, the Bank would not be bound to appropriate *Broughton's* funds in payment of the note. 4. That even if the

June 19.

1865.

The
COMMERCIAL
BANK
v.
GIBBONS.
August 31.

Bank had been bound to appropriate, there was not money enough to meet the whole amount.

Rule accordingly.

Darley and *Butler* show cause. The note was never meant as a continuing security to the Bank, but merely as a temporary accommodation to relieve *Broughton* from the then dishonoured note. There was an arrangement or contract between the Bank and *Broughton*, that this defendant should not be looked to ; in other words, that *Broughton* alone should be considered liable to pay the note. This arrangement might be reasonably implied from the circumstances, and from the correspondence and the subsequent dealings between the parties. The letter of 24th November to *Broughton*, after stating that his account would be credited with the proceeds of the note, continues, " it is to be regretted that you did not adopt the usual course of authorising us not to pay, when presented, your acceptance to *Gibbons*, recently charged to your account." That letter shows the dealings between these parties, and is evidence of an understanding or agreement with the Bank, that if *Broughton* did not direct them to dishonour *Gibbons'* notes, that they would charge them to *Broughton*, and not look to *Gibbons*. It was equivalent to the Bank saying that in all similar transactions, unless directed by *Broughton* not to do so, that they would charge him with the amount. So all the subsequent correspondence must be considered with reference to that letter, and to the manifest understanding between the Bank and *Broughton*, that the latter was to be considered liable. Otherwise, it is clear that *Pearson* would have written to say that as *Broughton's* funds were insufficient, he should look to those primarily liable. The correspondence and dealings between the parties are sufficient to justify the finding of the jury.

In point of law there was a duty in the Bank as between it and *Broughton*, having evidently resolved to look to him, to appropriate the moneys paid in to the payment of the note as the earliest item. This was a case of a banking account, where all the sums paid in form one blended fund. In such a case as is laid down in *Clayton's* case (*a*), by Sir *William Grant*, there is no room for any other appropriation than that which arises from the order in which the receipts and payments take place, and are carried into the account. Presumably, it is the sum first paid in that is first drawn out. It is the first item on the debit side of the account that is discharged or reduced by the first item on the credit side. The appropriation is made by the very act of setting the two items against each other. And although that presumption may be varied by the particular mode of dealing, or any stipulation between the parties, as in *Henniker* v. *Wigg* (*b*), in this case the evidence was all in favour of the ordinary presumption. In *Hammersly* v. *Knowlys* (*c*) the note of *A.* was deposited by *B.* at his bankers as a security for money, the bankers knowing that it was an accommodation note, and *B.* afterwards paying in money generally without any specific appropriation, the money thus paid in was held to go in discharge of the then existing debt; and the banker was not allowed to make *A.* responsible for more than the balance remaining due at the time of such payment, although he afterwards allowed *B.* to increase his indebtedness. The same principle is recognised in *Field* v. *Carr* (*d*). In the absence of any agreement, that this note should be considered a continuing security, the plaintiffs were bound without any directions to apply the first money paid into *Broughton's* credit to the liquidation of this amount. *Marsh* v. *Houlditch* (*e*) is an express authority on the point. It was an action by the indorsee against the acceptor of a bill of exchange, accepted for the accommodation of the drawer, and indorsed by him to the plaintiff. The drawer's evidence at the trial was, "I told the plaintiff that the bill was an accommodation from the defendant to me; that I should take it up, and requested him not to apply to the de-

1865.

The
COMMERCIAL
BANK
v.
GIBBONS.

(*a*) Wh. & T. L. C. on Merc. Law 14   (*b*) 4 Q. B. 792.
(*c*) 2 Esp. 665.   (*d*) 5 Bing. 13.
    (*e*) Cited in Ch. on Bills 283, in nota.

fendant. He said very well, and requested me to take
it up as I could. I said he might depend on me. He
said he should look to me and not to him. The bill
was due the 1st October; I paid in £104 at the time of
the conversation; shortly afterwards the balance was in
my favour, &c." *Abbott*, J., to plaintiff's counsel,
"unless you can alter the fact of the conversation, it is
an answer to the action. The banking account of the
drawer with the plaintiffs having, at one time after the
bill was due, been in his favour to a larger amount than
the bill, the plaintiffs were bound to apply the balance
in discharging that bill, and could not keep it as a security
for a fluctuating balance, which might ultimately become due to them;" and the plaintiff was nonsuited.
There was no specific, that is opposing, direction by
Broughton to appropriate the sums placed to his credit
shown; and, therefore, every sum which came in to his
credit was applicable to pay the defendant's note.
There was no necessity for any assent by the Bank to
his request. But even if there were, there is ample
evidence of such assent. The arrangement was complete in June, and consequently no steps taken in that
month, or in July or August, to press *Broughton*.

It was also contended that in a harsh claim like this,
the defendant having by the laches of the Bank lost
all chance of getting payment from *Broughton*, the
Court would not grant a new trial. *Macron* v. *Hull*
(a), *Edmonson* v. *Machell* (b), and *Wilkinson* v. *Payne*
(c) were referred to.

STEPHEN, C. J. Should not the question, whether
there was any assent by the Bank to the arrangement,
have been put to the jury? On this point we should
like to hear argument.

Darley. In the first place the answer given by the
jury shows that they found that there was such an assent
in effect, although not in terms; for they found that
the bank, knowing that the defendant was a surety only,

(a) 1 Burr. 11.   (b) 2 T. R. 4.   (c) 4 T. R. 468.

agreed without the defendant's consent to give to *Broughton* time to pay the note. If they gave time to *Broughton*, it must be clear that they were only looking to him. At all events the Judge should have been asked to put the question in terms to the jury; and, therefore, the objection cannot now be taken (*a*).

Isaacs and *Salamons* contra. It has been attempted to extract an assent to an agreement out of this correspondence; but it is clear that all the letters to *Broughton* show that no such assent occurred (refers to letters of the 23rd April, the 5th and 9th May). So long as the defendant's renewals were to hand, the amount was charged to *Broughton*; but when in February there was no renewal, defendant was treated as liable, and charged with the amount. Then the bank pass-book shows that there were not sufficient assets to pay the amount of this bill. According to *Simson* v. *Ingham* (*b*) the pass-book is an admission by the customer, when communicated to him. "If," says *Bayley*, J., "a book had been kept for the common use of both parties as a pass-book, and that had been communicated to the opposite party, then the party making such entries would have been precluded from altering the account." In *Marsh* v. *Houlditch*, that has been relied on, there had been an amount to the defendant's credit, larger than the amount of the bill; and, therefore, at that moment the bank was paid. But the Bank is not to be paid by instalments. This bill has never been charged to *Broughton*, and the defendant has never been relieved from his liability.

STEPHEN, C.J. There must be a new trial on the first issue; costs to abide the event. In the first place, there was not, in my opinion, any assent by the Bank to the supposed direction or request by *Broughton* to look to him only for payment. It is clear that the plaintiffs

(*a*) On this see *Toms* v. *Wilson*, 32 L.J.Q.B. 33; *Hooler* v. *Carpenter*, 27 L.J.C.P. 1; *Holden* v. *Mordach*, 27 L.J. Ex. 27; *Martin* v. *Great Northern R. Co.*, 24 L.J.C.P. 209; *Jones* v. *Provincial Insurance Company*, 26 L.J.C.P. 272; *Morish* v. *Murrey*, 13 M. & W. 52; *Hardman* v. *Bellhouse*, 9 M. & W. 598.

(*b*) 2 B. & C. 73.

did not wish to press the defendant, and were willing to oblige *Broughton,* so far as was consistent with regard to their own interests; but there is no evidence to justify a finding that they agreed to look to *Broughton* alone; nor was there any consideration to support such an agreement. In the second place, there was no sufficient evidence of any such direction or request. Thirdly, I am further of opinion, although no point was taken as to any misdirection on this point, that even if there had been any such direction or request, the Bank was not bound to appropriate any partial payments or credits. For if so, the Bank would have been bound to debit the note at once, thereby *eo instanti* releasing *Gibbons,* even although they should never be afterwards paid at all. The Bank would be bound only in case of an equal or greater amount coming into their hands, which would be full payment. I have considered the case of *Marsh* v. *Houlditch,* and am prepared to abide by it. But I do not think it should be extended beyond its terms. In order to bring this case within that decision, it would be necessary to show an agreement that *Broughton* only was to be looked to.

HARGRAVE, J. I quite concur. *Marsh* v. *Houlditch* does not establish the proposition that a Bank must, in a case like this, when from time to time particular sums are paid in to the credit of the customer's account, write them off against the amount due on any note by such customer, without taking into account amounts paid out by the Bank under the authority of his cheques. Such a doctrine would be subversive of all banking arrangements. A bank, on the contrary, is bound to honour the cheques of its customer, so long as there are funds in hand to meet them; and it was not until there was a sufficient balance in hand at any one time to cover this note, that the Bank would be bound to charge it against the customer. If there were a distinct agreement between the parties to that effect, the payment of the customer's cheques by the Bank would be in their own wrong.

CHEEKE, J., concurred.

BLACKMAN *against* MYLECHARANE.

*B*UTLER moved, on behalf of the defendant, for a rule calling on the plaintiff to shew cause why the Prothonotary should not review his taxation in this case.

It was a squatting action in which the plaintiff having obtained a verdict with 40s. damages, the Court granted a new trial (*a*), on the ground that the verdict was against evidence. On the 31st May the defendant, under the 91st section of the Common Law Procedure Act of 1853 (*b*), gave notice to the plaintiff to bring on the cause to be tried. But instead of doing so, on the 9th of June the plaintiff gave notice to the defendant that he discontinued the action.

On the taxation of the defendant's costs before the Prothonotary, the latter disallowed all the costs for advice on evidence, instructions for brief, attendance at the public offices, examining and taking copies of documents, &c., drawing briefs and copies for counsel, &c., in fact all the costs of preparing for the trial.

The question is whether a party can by discontinuing deprive the other side of the costs. By the 16th section of the Common Law Procedure Act of 1857 (*c*), when a new trial is granted, on the ground that the verdict is against evidence, the costs of the first trial shall abide the event, unless the Court shall otherwise order. The 42nd rule (*d*) directs that "where the costs of the first trial are ordered to abide the event, such costs will not be allowed to the finally successful party, unless he succeeded on both trials. The costs of the motion will, in all cases, follow the event of the second trial, unless the Court shall otherwise order." Here the discontinuance was the event; and it is submitted that the plaintiff is entitled to all the costs which were common to the two trials; and the defendant is to be considered in the same

The plaintiff obtained a verdict, which was set aside, and a new trial was granted ; he then discontinued the action. Held (Hargrave, J., dissentiente), that the defendant was entitled to all the costs of the action, except those only of the first trial.

(*a*) *Ante*, p. 43.   (*b*) 17 Vic., No. 21.
(*c*) 20 Vic., No. 31.   (*d*) Sup. Ct. Pr. 9.

position as if the parties had gone down to a new trial, and the defendant had failed. In the words of *Bayley*, J., in *Howarth* v. *Samuel* (a), discontinuance is a mode of terminating a suit by the act of the plaintiff himself; and it must be attended with the same consequences as to costs, as if the event of the suit had been determined by the verdict of a jury. The same principle is recognised in *Gray* v. *Cox* (b). In the recent case of *Daniel* v. *Wilkin* (c), the defendants having obtained a verdict, and a new trial granted, the plaintiff gave a fresh notice of trial, and afterwards gave notice of discontinuance, and the cause was not again tried. On taxation, the costs of certain searches for documentary evidence, which would have been available if the cause had been tried again, were held to have been properly allowed. *Pollock*, C. B., says, "The costs for these inquiries and searches ought to be allowed as part of the costs of preparation for the second trial. In reality all the defendants' loss, in consequence of the first trial having been set aside, are the costs of the day." And *Alderson*, B., says, "The parties ought to be placed in the same situation as that in which they were before they proceeded to trial on the first occasion. As the defendants were entitled to make their preparations, on the supposition that the second trial would proceed properly, all their costs in so doing must be paid by the plaintiff if he discontinues the action." Even where a party succeeding on a second trial is not entitled to the costs of the first trial, he is entitled to such costs of the first trial as are available for the second; *Lambert* v. *Lyddon* (d). [*Stephen*, C.J. May not the defendant be entitled to the costs of the motion for a new trial, on the ground that it was successful ?]

Salamons showed cause. Where the plaintiff has succeeded on the first trial, and a new trial has been granted, the defendant cannot take any other step with regard to the new trial until he has received notice of trial, than give notice to the plaintiff to proceed, and

(a) 1 B. & A. 567.   (b) 5 B. & C. 459.
(c) 8 Exch. 156; 22 L.J. Ex. 73.   (d) 4 D. & L. 400.

then sign judgment, as provided by the 91st section of the Common Law Procedure Act (*a*). In England he can take down the cause for trial by proviso ; sect. 116 of the English Common Law Procedure Act of 1852. Neither party has any right to charge the other with the costs of preparing for trial, until notice of trial has been given ; and, therefore, where the plaintiff discontinues without having given notice of trial, the defendant is not entitled to the costs of his briefs; *Doe* v. *Neale* (*b*); and in *Daniel* v. *Wilkin* (*c*), which has been relied on by the other side, notice of trial had been given. But no case can be cited where—after a verdict for the plaintiff at the first trial, and a new trial granted—the defendant has been held to be entitled to the costs of preparing for the second trial, unless he has received notice of trial. [*Stephen*, C. J. But does that rule as to notice apply to a second trial ?] If the plaintiff had gone to trial the second time, he might have succeeded, and in that case would have been entitled to the costs of both trials; but the defendant could not have been so entitled in any event. It is submitted that the costs of the second trial, to which the defendant is entitled, are only the costs of the day. The authorities are unanimous, that where the plaintiff has discontinued without notice of trial, the defendant is not entitled to the costs of preparation for trial ; not even although under terms of taking short notice, *Cooper* v. *Boles* (*d*), *Curtis* v. *Platt* (*e*) ; nor the plaintiff either, although the defendant by obtaining orders for time to plead has so prolonged the period, as to necessitate such preparations being made by the plaintiff before issue joined, in order to be able to try the cause at the assizes ; *Freeman* v. *Springham* (*f*). But there is one authority which is precisely in point, and which it is submitted must govern this case. In *Reynolds* v. *Hickman* (*g*) there was a verdict for the plaintiff on a first trial, and a new trial ordered. Nothing was done for more than a year. The

(*a*) Sup. Ct. Pr. 20. (*b*) 2 M. & W. 782.
(*c*) 8 Exch. 156; 22 L.J.Ex.73; see *Jolliffe* v. *Mundy*, 4 M.& W.502.
(*d*) 5 H. & N. 188; 29 L.J. Ex. 141. (*e*) 33 L.J.C.P. 255.
(*f*) 14 C.B.N.S. 197; 32 L.J.C.P. 249. (*g*) 9 L.T.N.S. 757.

defendant then gave a month's notice of his intention to proceed and take the case down for trial by proviso. The plaintiff then discontinued; and it was held that the defendant was not entitled to costs beyond the period when issue joined.   He also referred to *Rigby* v. *Okell* (a), *Earl of Macclesfield* v. *Bradley* (b), *Evans* v. *Robinson* (c), *Eccles* v. *Harper* (d), *Bird* v. *Appleton* (e), *Peacock* v. *Harris* (f), and *Gray* (g) and *Marshall* (h) on Costs.

Butler replied.

Cur. adv. vult.

Their Honors gave judgment in this case as follows:—

STEPHEN, C.J.   We have looked into all the authorities, which are numerous, on the question as to review of taxation in this cause; and the result arrived at by us, notwithstanding the case of *Reynolds* v. *Hickman* (i), is—that the defendant is entitled by the discontinuance to all the costs of the action, except those only of the first trial.   The rule laid down in *Daniel* v. *Wilkin* by Chief Baron *Pollock*, and concurred in by Baron *Parke*, is adopted by us; that the successful party, in cases of this kind, cannot obtain the costs of any proceeding or matter, which was exclusively applicable to the abortive trial—but that the costs of all matters, which are equally available for the second trial, or would have been so had the cause proceeded to a second, are allowed him.   All that is lost by the setting aside of the verdict is the costs of the day.   In the language of Baron *Alderson* in the last mentioned case, all which took place at the first trial is wiped out; and the parties are put in the same position as to costs, that they were in before they began it.

With the exception of the case in the *Law Times*, not reported elsewhere, so far as we can ascertain (although the supposed decision was in November, 1863), the authorities appear to us to have settled the

(a) 7 B & C. 57.   (b) 7 M. & W. 570.   (c) 24 L.J. Ex 212.
(d) 14 M. & W 248.   (e) 1 East 111.
    (f) 5 A. & E. 449; *Lee de Rutzen* v. *Lloyd*, Id. 456.
(g) p 265.   (h) p. 88.   (i) 9 L. T. 757.

law, respecting the right to costs in cases of this kind, as follows.

In the first place, where the plaintiff discontinues his action before giving notice of trial, the defendant is not entitled to the costs incurred by him, if any, of preparing for trial. The reason for this rule, although in practice it occasionally operates somewhat harshly, is obvious. But all costs of that nature, incurred by a defendant after such notice, and before countermand or discontinuance, invariably are allowed. The collection of evidence, and the preparation of briefs, for example, are within the category; and (assuming the pleadings to remain the same) such briefs and evidence will be equally serviceable on a second, or any subsequent trial, if ordered by the Court, as at the expected first trial. The work is done, in other words, for the purposes of the cause; and not for one trial merely, should that one be unsuccessful. The conclusion naturally follows, that, if the first verdict be adverse to the defendant, and set aside for any reason at his instance, he is allowed the costs of those proceedings, in case of eventual success—in the same manner as he would have been, had that verdict been in his favour.

But, for a reason equally cogent, the costs of the first trial itself are never allowed, under any circumstances, to the party then failing. He who—owing to whatever mistake or cause of miscarriage—is unsuccessful at a trial, cannot throw the costs of it on his victor.

A litigant who twice succeeds, however, may or may not—according to the circumstances—obtain those costs. A verdict for the plaintiff, for instance, may be set aside for some irregularity or error, in which he had no share. Or, on the contrary, that verdict may have been won by his misconduct, or that which the law deems such. It will depend on the particular facts, therefore, or the nature of the case, whether he shall (although eventually succeeding) be allowed the costs of both trials. The Court consequently, in its discretion, either gives or withholds the costs of the first trial. And the rule now is, that, unless the Court otherwise directs, the twice

prevailing party gets the costs of the first trial, where
the verdict was set aside as being against evidence; but,
in all other cases, he will not be entitled to those costs,
unless the Court, by the terms of its order, shall have
expressly allowed them to him.   The defendant, however, in the case supposed, would never obtain the costs
of the first trial—although succeeding on the second;
for this would be to receive the costs of his own failure.

Before the Common Law Procedure Act, the costs of
the first trial were not allowed in any case (whatever
the ground on which the verdict was set aside), notwithstanding a second concurring verdict, unless the Court
had so ordered.   And then, as now, the allowance was
technically expressed by the words " costs to abide the
event "—meaning, ordinarily, the result of the second
trial ;—that is to say, a verdict finally sustained, and
followed accordingly by a judgment.   An award, however, has under circumstances been holden to be equivalent to such a trial.   The discontinuance of the action
necessarily has the same effect.   In *Howarth* v. *Samuel*
(*a*), Mr. Justice *Bayley* thus states the rule :—" Discontinuance is a mode of terminating the suit, by the
act of the plaintiff himself ; and it must be attended
with the same consequences as to costs, as if the event of
the suit had been determined by the verdict of a jury."
But, as already shown, the only costs which that event
affects are those of the first trial ; in other words, the
costs of the day.   And these costs—it will be remembered—are demandable only by a party who has succeeded on each occasion.   If the second is in conflict
with the first verdict, the costs of the earlier trial are
allowed to neither party.   But the general costs of the
cause, being common to both trials, remain unaffected
by any question touching, alone, the costs of that which
has been " wiped out " or put aside.

Bearing all this in mind, the case presents no other
difficulty than that which is introduced into it, first by
the fact that in *Daniel* v. *Wilkin* there had been a
notice of trial given ; and, secondly, by the reported

(*a*) 1 B. & A. 566.

decision in the *Law Times*. The plaintiff here obtained a verdict which was set aside. He then, without any further step, discontinues the action. The effect of this is, to place the defendant in the same position as he would have been in, had the cause proceeded to a second trial, and the event of the suit been then determined in his favour. The defendant, in that event, would not have been entitled to the costs of the first trial; and therefore he cannot get them now. But a plaintiff cannot, by preventing the case from going down to a second trial, deprive his opponent of an already vested, though merely inchoate right. The defendant is not in a better, but he must not be placed in a worse position, by the discontinuance. He is still entitled, because he always has been so—from the time of his having prepared for trial, after the notice originally served on him—to all the costs of that preparation.

It is unreasonable to suppose that a second notice of trial can be necessary so to entitle the defendant. The only effect of such a notice could be, to confer an additional right on him; namely, that of again making preparation, and of supplementing his former briefs by newly obtained evidence. But, as to all that he did in consequence of the first notice, if still available, why should the costs of this not be allowed him? And (it may further be asked) if the defendant does nothing in the way of preparation after the second notice, why should this latter confer a new right, as to costs incurred only under the first?

The right to them is not placed by the Court, in *Daniel* v. *Wilkin*, on the circumstance of a second notice having there been given; and we think it demonstrated, that nothing can depend on that fact. In *Reynolds* v. *Hickman*, no doubt, if that case be rightly reported, the decision (overruling one by Baron *Bramwell* in Chambers) is the other way. But the reasonableness of the party's claim, and the weight of authority in its favour, induce us to suspect that the solitary case opposed to it is a misconception.

It will be observed, that this judgment is not in any

degree founded on the circumstance, that the costs here are by the order of the Court, or by virtue of the Common Law Procedure Act, to abide the event. For, as the costs thus indicated are (confessedly) those of the trial only, which the defendant for reasons already given cannot claim, that circumstance is at present wholly immaterial. But it obviously would be an essential feature, in any case the converse of this ; for example, had the first verdict been for the defendant. Because there, had the plaintiff discontinued his action after getting that verdict set aside, his adversary would have twice succeeded—and then, possibly (though we do not so determine), the defendant might have got the costs of the trial also. The want of attention to this distinction, probably, has occasioned much of the misapprehension, which seems to prevail on this often litigated subject.

CHEEKE, J. I concur in the judgment now delivered by his Honor the Chief Justice, and I wish to make this remark, that I consider this judgment is not only founded on law, but on justice. The plaintiff obtained a verdict against evidence ; a new trial was granted by the Court upon that ground, and after that decision the plaintiff discontinued his action. Is it fair, therefore, between the parties that this course should be adopted to the detriment and disadvantage of the defendant ? The plaintiff, by the very fact of his discontinuance, admitted the insufficiency of his evidence in support of his case, and consequently feared the result of a new trial.

HARGRAVE, J. I much regret that I cannot concur in the judgment just delivered, and must be expected to give very sound reasons to defend such difference of opinion. I admit that if the expressions used by Baron *Alderson* in *Daniel* v. *Wilkin* (a), to the effect that "all which took place at the first trial is wiped out," are to be adopted to their full extent, the successful party will lose all advantage of the first verdict ; and conse-

(a) 8 Exch. 158.

quently when the plaintiff is such successful party, and he discontinues the action after the rule for the new trial, such discontinuance would of course entitle the defendant to the costs of the cause, so far as they would have been available, for the second trial. But all the authorities and practice hitherto both here and in England show that granting a new trial has not hitherto been supposed to assert any such extended power. It also seems to me that when the Court grants a rule for new trial, the first verdict is only set aside or suspended so far as such verdict interferes with the second trial, and so far as it entitles a party to receive costs; but that so far as regards the liability to pay costs up to that date at all events, the successful party in such first trial cannot be made liable to pay any costs by force of or authority of such rule for a new trial. It is obvious that the Legislative authority alone can impose such liability which has been done as far as is just by the 16th section of the Common Law Procedure Act of 1857, which directs the costs of the first trial to follow "the event" that is to await the result of the second or even third trial. With regard to discontinuance, I cannot concur in Mr. *Butler's* argument that the "discontinuance" by the plaintiff is in any sense "the event" contemplated by the Legislature in this section, and it is plain that the words "costs of the first trial" will not extend to "costs in the cause."

In *Howarth* v. *Samuel,* cited in the judgment of the Chief Justice, Mr. Justice *Bayley* is speaking of discontinuance by a plaintiff before obtaining a verdict in his favour.

I would further add that as by the English practice the plaintiff cannot discontinue without an order, this order is accompanied by imposing the terms or conditions of paying costs. It is plain that discontinuance *per se* has not any effect whatever as to costs; and as a plaintiff can in this colony discontinue without order, the Court or Judge has no such opportunity of imposing costs as a condition for discontinuance; and it is admitted the standing order of this Court does not apply

q—4

to such case as this ; or if it does, that it does not specify "what costs," the point of difficulty now under consideration.

With regard to the authorities, these chiefly relate to cases where the plaintiff has given notice of trial; by which conduct, however, he obviously alters his own position by his own act, and then by the reported cases, and upon principle also, he makes himself liable for costs ; and his subsequent discontinuance of the action will have relation of course to such new position in which he has placed himself by his own act.

This seems to be the admitted state of the authorities as collected in *Marshall* on Costs (a), *Gray* on Costs (b), *Chitty's* Practice (c), and *Lush's* Practice (d), all of which authorities place the liability to costs on the having given notice of trial ; and upon these authorities the Prothonotary states that he has for twenty years acted in the taxation of bills of costs in this Court; and the only exception to such practice appears to be an extract from the Prothonotary's book, in a case which specifies nothing but that discontinuance was ordered with costs, obviously, therefore, by order of the Court, as a condition for discontinuance.   In the recent case of *Reynolds* v. *Hickman*, reported in the *Law Times* (e), November 1863, the Barons of the Exchequer have also expressly sanctioned the same principle ; which I must assume, therefore, has also been the English practice, until unsuccessfully attempted to be altered by the application, similar to the present, made but refused in *Reynolds* v. *Hickman*.

My reasons from differing from the Chief Justice, and Mr. Justice *Cheeke*, in this matter, may, therefore, be shortly stated thus :—

1st. The order for a new trial cannot *per se* create a liability to pay costs.

2nd. The discontinuance by the plaintiff, according to the colonial practice, without order or condition, cannot create such a liability.

| (a) p. 88 | (b) p. 266 | (c) pp. 1471-2, 1530. |
| (d) p. 494. | | (e) 9 L. T. N. S. 75. |

3rd. The giving of notice for trial by the plaintiff is stated in the English authorities and books of practice to be essential to create liability in the plaintiff.

4th. The express authority of the very recent case of *Reynolds* v. *Hickman* is quite sufficient to overweigh and explain any general expressions in previous English reported cases.

5th. The uninterrupted "practice of the Court" here ought to become in such matters the "Law of the Court."

6th. I may also add that it appears to me to be contrary to the principles of our colonial statute, 15 Vic., No. 17 (Mr. *Wentworth's* Act), whereby the Judges of this Supreme Court were deprived of all power to fix the amount of fees mentioned in that Act; and that to assume such a power, as in any way connected with the power to grant new trials, would be altogether unconstitutional, and against the Statute of Gloucester (a), which plainly, while giving costs to the successful plaintiff, never contemplated the possibility of any less power than the Legislature assuming to create any general liability to costs. Upon sound principles in such matters, therefore, upon the printed books, upon express authority, and upon established practice of this Court, and with every respect to my learned brothers, there remains not the slightest doubt in my mind that these costs have been properly disallowed.

With reference to the cases mentioned as within the Chief Justice's knowledge, I have already on several occasions, in Chambers, informed both counsel and attorneys of my objections to treat any such private memoranda as authorised "law;" but I will now adopt the words of an eminent conveyancer and law author, when remonstrating against all such unreported cases as necessarily increasing "the glorious uncertainty of the law." Mr. *Watkins*, in the preface to his "Principles of Conveyancing," says:—"Is the Law of England to depend upon the private note of an individual, and to which an individual can only have access? Is a Judge

(a) 6 E. 1, c. 1.

to say, ' Lo ! I have the law of England on this point in my pocket ! Here is the note of a case which contains an exact statement of the whole facts, and the decision of my Lord *A.* or my Lord *B.* upon them. He was a great, a very great man; I am bound by his decision. All you have been reading was erroneous; the printed books are inaccurate. I cannot go into principle. The point is settled by this case.' Under such circumstances who is to know when he is right or when he is wrong. If conclusions from unquestionable principles are to be overthrown in the last stage of a suit, from private memoranda, who can hope to become acquainted with the Laws of England ? And who that retains any portion of rationality would waste his time and his talents in so fruitless an attempt? Is a paper evidencing the law of England, to be buttoned up in the side pocket of a Judge, or to serve for a mouse to sit upon in the dusty corner of a private library."

STEPHEN, C. J., mentioned that there were two cases in which the same decision had been pronounced as in the present, viz., *Baldwin* v. *Elliott* in September 1856, and *Mortimer* v. *Mort* in October 1860.

THE ATTORNEY GENERAL *against* THE BANK OF
NEW SOUTH WALES.

THIS is an action brought by *John Hubert Plunkett,* Esq., her Majesty's Attorney-General for the colony of New South Wales, on behalf of her Majesty the Queen, against the Bank of New South Wales, a corporation aggregate carrying on business as Bankers in the colony of New South Wales, to recover the sum of £400, claimed to be due and payable to the use of her Majesty, as and for penalties incurred under and by the four several Schedules of Duties hereto annexed, or for or in respect of the parchment or paper upon which the same respectively shall be written," and "at the several rates set down in figures in the schedule."

The third section of the Stamp Duties Act of 1865 enacts, that duties shall be paid "for and in respect of the several matters described or mentioned in this Act, and

The schedule was as follows:—" BILLS OF EXCHANGE—Inland bill of exchange or promissory note for the payment to the bearer, or to order, or on demand, of any sum of money not exceeding £50—*one shilling.* Foreign bill of exchange or promissory note drawn in, but payable out of the colony of New South Wales—*the same duty as on an inland bill of the same amount and tenor.* Bill of exchange, draft, or order drawn or indorsed out of the colony for payment of money on demand—*the same duty as on an inland bill of the same amount and tenor.* Draft or order for the payment of any sum of money to the amount of forty shillings and upwards to the bearer, or to order on demand—*one penny.*"

A promissory note made in the colony by *G. R.,* in favour of *H. T.* one month after date, payable in the colony, *Held* not liable to duty.

A promissory note made in the colony by *J. J.,* payable one month after date, in favour of *S. G.* or order, *Held* liable to duty.

A promissory note made in Queensland by *T. C.,* in favour of *A. P.* or order, one month after date, and payable in the colony, *Held* not liable to duty.

A bill of exchange made in Sydney by the Bank of New South Wales, payable at Maitland to the order of *J. C.,* three days after sight, *Held* liable to duty.

A bill of exchange drawn by the Bank of New Zealand, in the colony of New Zealand, payable to *J. H.* or his order at the Bank of New South Wales, in Sydney, fifteen days after sight, *Held* not liable to duty.

An instrument in the following form, "Tarong, Queensland, August 1, 1865, £10. Pay *J. B.* or order the sum of ten pounds stirling, on account of *Henry Wallis.* To Messrs. *S., H.,* and *Co.,* Sydney," *Held* liable to duty.

An instrument in the following form, "Bank of N. S. W., Maitland, 6th September, 1865. £149 16s. 3d. Pay to the order of Messrs. *A.* and *B.* one hundred and forty-nine pounds sixteen shillings and three pence, for value received.—*J. M. S.,* Manager. To the Bank of New South Wales, Sydney." *Held* liable to duty of one penny, as a draft for the payment of "forty shillings and upwards" to order on demand.

The schedule also contained the following item—"Receipt or discharge given for any sum of money for forty shillings and upwards—*one penny.* Exemptions from the preceding duties on receipts. Acknowledgment given for money deposited in any banks to be accounted for."

The bank of New South Wales having received from *J. E. C.* £114 on fixed deposit, repayable to *J. E. C.* twelve months after date, gave to him a memorandum as follows—"Bank of New South Wales, &c. Due 29th July, 1866, £114. Sydney, 29th July, 1865. Received from *J. E. C.* the sum of one hundred and fourteen pounds at a fixed deposit for twelve months, to bear interest at the rate of six per cent. per annum for that period from the date hereof. For and on behalf of the Bank of New South Wales—*C. M. P.,* Manager." *Held* liable to a penny duty as a receipt.

1865.

The
ATTORNEY
GENERAL
v.
THE BANK OF
NEW SOUTH
WALES.

virtue of the Stamp Duties Act of 1865, by the Bank of New South Wales, by reason of the said Bank having paid in the colony of New South Wales certain bills of exchange and promissory notes, and drafts or orders, which have severally and respectively been drawn and issued, or made and issued, as hereinafter mentioned, since the first day of July last; and also by reason of the said Bank having issued, or caused to be issued in the said colony, certain other bills of exchange, drafts, orders, or instruments as hereafter also mentioned, without the said bills of exchange, drafts, orders, or instruments having been stamped, for denoting the duties which the said Attorney-General alleges were by the said act charged thereon, which said bills of exchange, promissory notes, drafts, orders, and instruments are of the descriptions hereinafter mentioned, that is to say—

1. On the 4th day of July last, one *George Russell*, at Sydney aforesaid, made his promissory note, and thereby promised to pay to one *Henry Turner* the sum of £147 10*s.*, one month after the date thereof, and made the same payable at the Bank of New South Wales, Sydney; and that the said Bank of New South Wales, at Sydney, paid the same without the said promissory note having been stamped. The said Attorney-General alleges that the said promissory note should have been stamped with a stamp of the value of three shillings, to denote the duty payable thereon, and claims that the said Bank of New South Wales became liable to pay a penalty of £50 in respect thereof. And the said Bank alleges that the said promissory note was not liable to stamp duty.

2. On the 4th day of September instant, the said Bank of New South Wales paid a promissory note, made in the colony of New South Wales, bearing date the first day of August last, for the sum of £50, by *John Jones*, payable one month after date to *Stephen Graham*, or his order—which said promissory note, at the time it was so paid, was not stamped. The said Attorney-General alleges that the said promissory note should have been stamped with a stamp of the value of

1865.

The
ATTORNEY
GENERAL
v.
THE BANK OF
NEW SOUTH
WALES.

one shilling, to denote the duty payable thereon, and claims the sum of £50 as a penalty incurred by the said Bank of New South Wales, and payable to her Majesty herein by reason of the said Bank of New South Wales having paid the said promissory note. And the said Bank of New South Wales alleges that the said promissory note was not liable to stamp duty.

3. On the 14th day of July last, one *Thomas Collins*, at Queensland, made his promissory note, and thereby promised to pay to *Alexander Powell*, or order, the sum of £320, one month after the date thereof, and made same payable at the Bank of New South Wales, Sydney, and the Bank of New South Wales, at Sydney, paid the same, without the said promissory note having been stamped. The said Attorney-General alleges that the said promissory note should have been stamped with a stamp of the value of one shilling, to denote the duty payable thereon, and claims that the said Bank of New South Wales became liable to pay a penalty of £50 in respect thereof. And the said Bank alleges that the said promissory note was not liable to stamp duty.

4. On the 18th day of August last, the Bank of New South Wales, at Sydney, made a certain bill of exchange for the sum of £45, payable at the Bank of New South Wales, Maitland, to the order of one *James Capper*, three days after sight, and issued the said bill of exchange to the said *James Capper*, without affixing any stamp thereto for denoting the duty chargeable thereon. And the said Attorney-General alleges that the said bill of exchange was liable to a stamp duty of one shilling, and claims, in respect of the same having been issued without a stamp, that a penalty of £50 is payable by the said Bank. And the said Bank alleges that the said bill of exchange was not liable to duty.

5. The said Bank of New South Wales, on the 6th day of September instant, paid a certain bill of exchange drawn by the Bank of New Zealand, in the colony of New Zealand, bearing date the 13th day of August last, for the sum of £48, and payable to *James Hall*, or to his order, at the Bank of New South Wales in Sydney,

1865.

The
ATTORNEY
GENERAL
v.
THE BANK OF
NEW SOUTH
WALES.

in the colony of New South Wales, fifteen days after sight, without the said bill of exchange having been stamped.   The said Attorney-General alleges that the said bill of exchange should have been stamped with a stamp of the value of one shilling, to denote the duty payable thereon, and claims the sum of £50 as a penalty incurred by the said Bank of New South Wales having paid the said bill of exchange.   And the said Bank of New South Wales alleges that the said bill of exchange was not liable to stamp duty.

6. On the 28th day of August last, the said Bank of New South Wales, at Sydney, paid a certain draft or order drawn by one *Henry Wallis*, at Queensland, in the words and figures following—

Tarong, Queensland, August 1, 1865.
No. 72.   £10.
Pay *John Brown* or order the sum of ten pounds sterling, on account of
Henry Wallis.
To Messrs. *Scott, Henderson, and Co.*, Sydney.

without the same having been stamped.   And the said Attorney-General alleges that the said order should have been stamped with a stamp of the value of one penny, and claims that the said Bank of New South Wales became liable to pay a penalty of £50 in respect thereof. And the said Bank alleges that the said order was not liable to duty.

7. On the 5th day of September instant, the Bank of New South Wales, at Maitland, made and issued to one *Thomas Lindsay* a paper writing in the words and figures following, that is to say—

The Bank of New South Wales, incorporated by Act of Council.
Established 1817.
Maitland, 6th September, 1865.
No. 98694.   £149 16s. 3d.
Pay to the order of Messrs. *Allen* and *Bowden* one hundred and forty-nine pounds sixteen shillings and three pence, for value received.
John M. Saunders, Manager.
Edward D. Day, pro Accountant.
To the Bank of New South Wales, Sydney.

and before issuing the same affixed thereon a duty stamp of the value of one penny and no more.   And the said Attorney-General alleges that the said paper writing was liable to a stamp duty of one shilling, and claims, in respect of the same having been issued without being sufficiently stamped, that a penalty of £50 is payable by the said Bank. And the said Bank alleges that the said paper writing was sufficiently stamped.

8. On the 29th day of July last, the Bank of New South Wales received from one *John E. Curphy* the sum of £114, on fixed deposit, repayable to the said *John E. Curphy* twelve months after the date thereof, and gave to the said *John E. Curphy* a memorandum of deposit in the words and figures following :—

1865.
———
The
ATTORNEY
GENERAL
v.
THE BANK OF
NEW SOUTH
WALES.

The Bank of New South Wales, incorporated by Act of Council.
Established 1817.
Due 29th July, 1866.
No. 6936.   £114.   Sydney, 29th July, 1865.
Received from Mr. *John E. Curphy* the sum of one hundred and fourteen pounds as a fixed deposit for twelve months, to bear interest at the rate of six per cent. per annum for that period from the date hereof.
· For and on behalf of the Bank of New South Wales,
Charles M. Palmer, Pr. Manager.
Entered, *John T. Evans*, pro Accountant.

And the said Attorney-General claims that there is due to her Majesty, as stamp duty payable upon the said paper writing, the sum of three shillings, and that a penalty of fifty pounds is also due to her Majesty by the said Bank in respect thereof. And the said Bank alleges that the said memorandum of deposit was not liable to stamp duty.

The questions of law which the said Attorney-General, suing on behalf of her Majesty, and the said Bank of New South Wales, desire to submit for the determination of this honourable Court, are—

Whether the Bank of New South Wales is — by reason of the payment of the promissory notes set out in paragraphs 1, 2, and 3 of this case, and of the payment of the bills of exchange set out respectively in paragraphs 4 and 5, and of the payment of the order set out in paragraph 6, and of the issuing of the paper writing set out in the paragraph number 7—liable to pay the penalties claimed to have been incurred by such payments having been made, and by reason of such issue as aforesaid? And whether duty is payable to her Majesty upon or in respect of the Bank having made and issued the paper writing set out in paragraph number 8?

1865.

The
ATTORNEY
GENERAL
v.
THE BANK OF
NEW SOUTH
WALES.
September 23.

Sir *W. Manning*, Q. C. (*Stephen* with him), for the Crown. This is a special case to decide the question of liability to the Stamp Act of certain instruments (*a*).

1. 3. As to the instruments mentioned in clauses 1 and 3, very little argument was offered.

2. 4. With regard to those mentioned in clauses 2 and 4, it is submitted that though not payable "on demand," the instruments are subject to duty. By the first schedule to the Act " an inland bill of exchange or promissory note for the payment to the bearer or order, or on demand, of any sum of money," is liable to certain

(*a*) The third section of the Stamp Act provided that, "from and after the commencement of this Act there shall be levied, collected, and paid for the use of her Majesty, and to form part of the Consolidated Revenue Fund, for and in respect of the several matters described or mentioned in this Act, and in the four several schedules of duties hereto annexed, or for or in respect of the parchment or paper upon which the same respectively shall be written, the several duties or sums of money, and at the several rates set down in figures, against the same respectively, or specified and set forth in the said schedules of duties; and the said schedules and the several provisions, regulations, and directions therein contained, with respect to the said duties, and the instruments, matters, and things charged therewith, shall be deemed to be part of this Act, and shall be applied, observed, and put in execution accordingly."

Schedule I. annexed to the Act was as follows :—

	£	s.	d.
BILLS OF EXCHANGE—Inland bill of exchange or promissory note for the payment to the bearer, or to order, or on demand, of any sum of money not exceeding £50	0	1	0
And where the same shall exceed £100, then for every £50, and also for any fractional part of £50..................	0	1	0
Foreign bill of exchange or promissory note drawn in, but payable out of the colony of New South Wales.			
If drawn singly or otherwise than in a set of three or more..	The same duty as on an inland bill of the same amount and tenor.		
Bill of exchange, draft, or order drawn or indorsed out of the colony for payment of money on demand	The same duty as on an inland bill of the same amount and tenor.		

*   *   *   *   *   *   *   *   *   *   *

	£	s.	d.
Draft or order for the payment of any sum of money to the amount of forty shillings and upwards, to the bearer, or to order on demand.............................	0	0	1

*   *   *   *   *   *   *   *   *   *

	£	s.	d.
Receipt or discharge given for any sum of money, for forty shillings and upwards	0	0	1

Exemptions from the preceding duties on receipts—

Acknowledgment given for money deposited in any banks to be accounted for. Provided that this exemption shall not extend to receipts or acknowledgments for sums paid or deposited for or upon any letters of allotment of shares or in respect of calls upon any scrip or shares of or in any joint stock or other company, or intended company, which said last mentioned receipts or acknowledgments by whomsoever given shall be liable to the duty charged upon receipts.

duty. It is submitted that every such bill or note must be stamped, when payable to the bearer, or to order, or on demand. It will be contended that all instruments payable otherwise than on demand, are not within these words, and that according to any other construction the words, "or on demand," are superfluous. But it is clear that such a construction excludes all bills of ordinary currency and frequency, which would yield a revenue; and includes bills of such rare occurrence as to be worthless for the purposes of revenue. A promissory note payable on demand to *A. B.* will satisfy all the words. Such a construction also requires the word "or" to be omitted. The Court will take notice of the general object and intent of the statute.

5. The fifth clause sets out a foreign bill of exchange, payable in the colony to order, and not on demand. It is admitted that it is not liable to duty, unless the words "foreign bill of exchange" can be held not to be qualified by the words "drawn in and payable out of the colony," which follow the words "promissory note." This construction is supported by the consideration that there is no reason why a foreign bill, payable a few days after sight, should be exempt from duty, especially as this is the most ordinary form of foreign bills. A foreign bill of exchange, payable on demand, is hardly known. The 13th and 14th sections of the Act also favour this argument (a).

6. An ordinary station order drawn in Queensland, and payable in the colony, is clearly liable either as a bill of exchange payable at sight, and therefore not requiring acceptance, or as a draft or order.

7. A draft drawn by a country branch bank on the head office, payable to order, is within the Act. This is

1865.
—————
The
ATTORNEY
GENERAL
v.
THE BANK OF
NEW SOUTH
WALES.

(a) The thirteenth section enacts that the duties in respect of bills of exchange drawn out of the colony shall be payable upon all such bills, if, and when paid, indorsed, transferred, or otherwise negotiated within the colony, wheresoever payable, and the duties shall be denoted by adhesive stamps.

The fourteenth section enacts that the holder of any bill drawn or purporting to be drawn out of the colony, shall, before he shall present the same for payment, or indorse, transfer, or in any manner negotiate it, affix a proper adhesive stamp for denoting the duty chargeable thereon, and, &c.

1865.

The
ATTORNEY
GENERAL
v.
THE BANK OF
NEW SOUTH
WALES.

in the form of a bill of exchange, and is only stamped with a penny as a draft or order. It is submitted that the Legislature has, in this Act, made a distinction between bills of exchange and drafts or orders, and that this instrument is taxable as a bill of exchange, and not a draft or order; *Whistler* v. *Forster* (a).

8. The eighth clause contains a fixed deposit receipt to bear interest; and the question is whether it is a receipt or discharge for a sum of money. It is submitted that it is not an acknowledgment given for money deposited in a bank to be accounted for; but that those words only relate to ordinary deposits to be drawn against. *Dwarris* on Statutes (b) was referred to.

Martin, Q. C., for the defendant. 1. As to number 1, which has now been given up, it is clearly established by numerous authorities that a promissory note payable a month after date to *A. B.*, is not payable to bearer, or to order, or on demand; *Cheetham* v. *Butler* (c), *Dixon* v. *Chambers* (d), *Byles* on Bills (e), *Chitty's* Statutes (f).

There are certain rules laid down for the construction of statutes. 1st. All statutes *in pari materia* are to be construed as one system. Lord *Mansfield*, in the case of *The King* v. *Loxdale* (g), thus lays down the rule— " Where there are different statutes *in pari materia*, though made at different times, or even expired, and not referring to each other, they shall be taken and construed together as one system, and as explanatory of each other." This principle was recognised in construing the Bankrupt Act; *Ex parte Copeland* (h), the County Court Act in *Waterlow* v. *Dobson* (i), the Lottery Acts in *R.* v. *Smith* (k), *Bacon's* Abridgment (l), *Palmer's* Case (m), *Dwarris* on Statutes (n).

2. Statutes are to be construed so that no clause, sentence, or word should be void or insignificant. Thus, in *Loaring* v. *Stone* (o), where by a turnpike Act a toll

(a) 14 C. B. N. S. 284 ; 32 L. J. C. P. 161.   (b) pp. 582, 685.
(c) 5 B. & Ad. 837.   (d) 1 C. M. & R. 845.
(e) p. 91.   (f) 3 Vol. 1296.
(g) 1 Burr. 447.   (h) 2 De G. M. & G. 919.
(i) 27 L. J. Q. B. 55.   (k) 4 T. R. 419.
(l) 7 Vol., p. 454.   (m) 1 Leach 354.
(n) p. 569.   (o) 2 B. & C. 515.

of 4½d. was imposed upon every horse or other beast
drawing any coach or other carriage; for every horse
drawing singly any carriage, the same toll; for every
horse drawing any waggon or other such carriage drawn
by two horses, or more, the sum of 3d.; for every horse
laden or unladen and not drawing, the sum of 1d. The
statute then provided that no person should be liable to
pay toll more than once in any one day at any toll gate,
for passing and repassing in any one day with the same
horses and carriages through the same; but all persons
having paid toll once, and producing a ticket denoting
the payment of such toll, were afterwards to pass and
repass with the same horses and carriages, toll free
during the same day. A stage coach drawn by four
horses passed through a gate erected under this Act and
paid the toll. In the evening of the same day a different
coach called by the same name, belonging to the same
proprietor, driven by the same coachman, and drawn by
the same four horses, but carrying different passengers
and different parcels for hire, passed through the same
gate; and it was held that a second toll was payable in
respect of this carriage and horses. It was admitted
that the toll was paid for the horses and not for the
carriage; but the Court said that if so construed, no
effect would be given to the word carriage in the proviso.
So also in *R.* v. *Berchet* (a), where in commenting on
the words of 42 Ed. 3. c. 3, that "no man shall be put
to answer without presentment before justices, or matter
of record, or due process of law," it is argued that it is
clear that there is some other legal way to charge a man
with a crime besides by presentment; for what else mean
those words, "or matter of record, or due process of
law?" After referring to the canon referred to, it continues, "if the construction be right, that nothing but
presentment be meant, then all the rest is nonsense,
because it hath no meaning;" cited in *Viner's* Abridgment (b), *Bacon's* Abridgment (c). And in *Churchill*
v. *Crease* (d), *Best*, C. J., in construing the words of

1865.

The
ATTORNEY
GENERAL
v.
THE BANK OF
NEW SOUTH
WALES.

(a) 1 Show. 107.   (b) 19 Vol., p. 528.
(c) 7 Vol., p. 452.   (d) 5 Bing. 180.

1865.

The
ATTORNEY
GENERAL
v.
THE BANK OF
NEW SOUTH
WALES.

6 G. IV., c. 16, s. 82, that "all payments really and *bona fide* made, or which hereafter shall be made by any bankrupt," shall be valid, says, "now, unless the expression 'payments made' refer to a period anterior to the passing of the act, the expression 'hereafter to be made,' is altogether nugatory." See also *In re Scott (a).* So here, what can be the use of introducing the words "or on demand?" The words payable to order or bearer include all kinds of instruments; and the words "or on demand" could only have been introduced to limit the preceding words. [*Stephen*, C. J. If the words payable to order or bearer or on demand were omitted, all instruments would be included.] It is submitted that the words, "or on demand," relate to the time of payment; the words "order" or "bearer," relate to the party entitled to be paid. The clause, therefore, is confined to these two classes of payees, and therefore where the payee is designated by name only, without the words "or bearer" "or order," as in the instance suggested, the instrument is not liable under the act.

Thirdly, in order to impose a duty or tax, clear and unambiguous language is necessary. In *Tomkins* v. *Ashby (b),* where a memorandum—"Mr. *T.* has left in my hands £200"—was held not to be a receipt within the Stamp Act, Lord *Tenterden* says, "Acts of Parliament imposing duties are so to be construed as not to make any instruments liable to them, unless manifestly within the intention of the Legislature." The instrument must be manifestly within the contemplation of the statute, and the Court leans against the construction which imposes a burden on the public; as *Maule,* J., says, in *Portsmouth Floating Bridge Company* v. *Nance (c),* "If people intend to impose tolls, they should speak out." The same kind of language is used in *Denn dem.* v. *Diamond (d), The Leeds and Liverpool Canal* v. *Hustler (e), Gildart* v. *Gladstone (f), Brittain* v. *Cromford Canal Company (g), Stockton and Darlington R. Co.* v. *Barrett (h).* The

(a) 4 M. & W. 261.   (b) 6 B. & C. 541.   (c) 6 Sc. N. R. 831.
(d) 4 B. & C. 243.   (e) 1 B. & C. 425.   (f) 11 East 685.
(g) 3 B. & A. 139.   (h) 11 Cl. & F. 607.

language used must be clear beyond a reasonable doubt ;
and the intention must be ascertained from the words of
the statute, and not from any general inferences to be
drawn from the nature of the objects dealt with by the
statute ; *Fordyce* v. *Bridges* (*a*). And even where a
statute was supposed to have been founded on the report
of certain commissioners, it was held that that report
could not be referred to as a guide in construing a
statute ; *Martin* v. *Hemming* (*b*), *Ewart* v. *Williams* (*c*),
Haworth v. *Ormerod* (*d*), cited in *Dwarris* (*e*), *Philpott*
v. *St. George's Hospital* (*f*). Fifty words may be trans-
posed or even varied to meet the sense or clear intention;
as for instance, the word " and " for " or," if necessary,
as in *Waterhouse* v. *Keen* (*g*).

Bearing all these in mind, the words " or on demand "
must be construed to mean "and on demand." It is most
unreasonable to suppose that the Legislature meant by
these words to introduce a third class of payees. In the
English Act, which may be referred to as being in *pari
materia*, the words are either on demand or otherwise
than on demand. That shows the intention clearly, and
excludes all doubt. If it was intended to include all
bills of exchange and promissory notes, the words "on
demand" ought to have been omitted, as in the schedule
to the 17 and 18 Vic., c. 88, when referring to foreign
bills of exchange.

3. A foreign promissory note payable in the colony
one month after date, is clearly not within the Act.
The 13th and 14th sections only refer to bills of exchange, and the schedule contains no reference to any
such instrument payable in the colony.

5. A foreign bill of exchange, payable in the colony
five days after sight, is not within the schedule which imposes a duty only on such instruments when payable on
demand.

6. 7. It is also submitted that the drafts or orders
liable to duty, are those drawn in the colony and

(*a*) 1 H. L. C. 1.　　　　　　(*b*) 10 Jur. 1004.
(*c*) 3 Drew. 24.　　　　　　　(*d*) 6 Q. B. 307.
(*e*) p. 595.　　　　　　　　　(*f*) 6 H. L. C. 362.
　　　　　　(*g*) 4 B. & C. 209.

1865.

The
ATTORNEY
GENERAL
v.
THE BANK OF
NEW SOUTH
WALES.

payable on demand, and that, therefore, neither station orders drawn in Queensland, or drafts drawn by a country branch bank in the colony, but made payable to order, are liable.

8. The instrument referred to in number 8 is not liable as a receipt, *Tomkins* v. *Ashby* (a); and if considered as a promissory note, it is not liable as not being payable on demand.

Sir *W. Manning*, in reply, abandoned 1 and 3, but not the instrument mentioned in the eighth clause, because it is a writing entitling to the payment of money. [He was stopped as to the other point.]

Cur. ad. vult.

September 29.   The judgment of the Court was now delivered by

STEPHEN, C. J.   We have considered the authorities cited by Mr. *Martin* in this case, as establishing the general principles of construction on which he relied—but of which none are disputed by us.   We are not prepared to admit, however, that the well known rule as to statutes *in pari materia* applies, except as to enactments by the same Legislature.   It would be unreasonable to hold, that laws passed in England for revenue purposes afford a guide for ascertaining the sense of a given statute passed—although for a purpose of the same kind—in this colony.   But, with this exception, on which nothing in the case appears to us to turn, we entirely recognise the several well known propositions or canons of construction, which he quoted to us.   The opinions which we are about to express, are, as we conceive, in harmony with them.

On the first question, we are of opinion that the promissory note there described is not liable to any duty.   It is a non-negotiable instrument, and therefore is not payable either to bearer or to order; and, being at a stated time after date, it is not payable on demand.   Neither, although made payable at a bank, is it a "writing or demand" entitling to payment by a bank,

(a) 6 B. & C. 541.

or banking company. Still less is it a " bill, draft, or order," for any such payment.

On the second question, we are of opinion that the promissory note there described is liable to duty; that is to say, the amount payable not exceeding fifty pounds, a duty of one shilling. The instrument is not payable on demand, but to order, that is to a named payee, or his order, at a stated time after date. The argument was, therefore, that such an instrument—according to the rules of sound legal construction, did not come under the words of the schedule; which, it was insisted, includes bills or notes payable "on demand" only.

Now those words embrace, in terms, all promissory notes and bills payable "to the bearer, or to order, or on demand." But the defendants contended, that the last word "or" should be read as "and"—in effect should be eliminated; whereby, said they, the natural sense of the context would be preserved. By the last words, it was urged, there is no third class of instruments, or of payees, introduced; but an entirely different subject matter. The words "bearer or order" indicate parties to the instrument. The words "on demand" relate alone to the time of payment; and were intended to show, therefore, that instruments not payable on demand are exempt from duty.

It must be admitted, that these words do introduce a difficulty; which, if susceptible of application only to bills and notes payable to the bearer, or to order, it might perhaps be impossible to overcome. But the entire words may be read, we think, as if written thus:— " To the bearer, or to order, or on demand to neither order nor bearer." And, by this construction, which at least does no violence to the language, every word in the sentence operates; and no word is left out, or changed in intrinsic meaning. The conclusion appears to be supported, moreover, by reference to a subsequent part of the schedule; in which bills payable to the bearer, or to order, on demand, are specifically provided for as "drafts" or orders—and subjected to a much smaller amount of duty. Promissory notes, payable

R—4

1865.

The
ATTORNEY
GENERAL
v.
THE BANK OF
NEW SOUTH
WALES.

1865.

The
ATTORNEY
GENERAL
v.
THE BANK OF
NEW SOUTH
WALES.

on demand to the bearer, are also separately provided for.

There is this additional reason, for so understanding the enactment; that bills and notes drawn or made here, but payable abroad, are on the same footing with inland instruments of the same tenor. But bills and notes of that class, we apprehend, payable to order or bearer, are in fact never made payable on demand. We do not rely much, however, on this argument—though a practical one.

On the third question, we are of opinion that the promissory note there described is liable to no duty. Either designedly, or by oversight, bills of exchange only—or drafts or orders—drawn or indorsed out of the colony (and, we presume, paid, accepted, or negotiated here), *not promissory notes* made out of the colony, are taxed. Moreover, as will be seen by our answer to the fifth question, it would not be liable to duty even if a bill, or draft, or order—because it is not made payable on demand.

On the fourth question, we are of opinion that the bill of exchange there described,—the same being by the Sydney office on one of its branches, for forty-five pounds, payable at a stated time after sight, to the order of a payee named,—is liable to duty; that is to say, the sum of one shilling. The case is within the second category disposed of; and such a bill is not the less taxable, because drawn by a bank on another establishment of its own.

On the fifth question, we are of opinion that the bill there described is not liable to duty :—for, although a bill of exchange drawn out of and paid within this colony, it is not for the payment of money on demand.

But, on the contrary, the bill (or draft or order) described in the sixth question is liable to duty; namely, the duty of one shilling. It was drawn out of, and made payable to order within, the colony ; and it was payable on demand, because, as no time for payment was specified, the law made it payable immediately.

On the seventh question, we are of opinion that the writing there described is liable to a duty of one penny only. For, although certainly it is in strictness a bill of exchange, yet, as it was (for the reasons given in the last paragraph) payable on demand, and it is also made payable to order, the instrument does not fall within the classes, or either of them, specified in our answer to the second question. It is a "draft" for the payment of "forty shillings and upwards" to order, on demand; which description of bill, the schedule indicates as taxed (whatever the amount) one penny. Liability to the higher or scale duty is incurred only, as we have already decided, when the instrument is payable to the bearer, or to order, otherwise than on demand.

On the eighth question, being the last submitted by the special case, we are of opinion that the writing there described is within the meaning of the statute, not a promissory note—although possibly it might be so declared on in an action—but simply a receipt, and subject, therefore, to a duty of one penny only.

It is not very clear, that the words "receipt or discharge" in the schedule, standing alone, would have included a mere acknowledgment of this character. For, undoubtedly, the document is not in any sense a discharge, and, in the ordinary sense, it is not a receipt for money. But the Legislature, it must be inferred, meant the word receipt to embrace acknowledgments; for one particular kind of acknowledgment,—that is to say, for money deposited in a bank to be accounted for,—is exempted specifically from duty. We conceive that this must be taken to indicate, not money deposited as here for a fixed period, on a special contract to pay interest for the loan during that time, but deposits made in the usual course of banking business, and which may be withdrawn at any moment. The latter are to be accounted for, in the ordinary or proper sense of the expression; but moneys within the former category are "accounted for" already.

The penalties incurred by the defendants, supposing any to be desired, are easily ascertained—and judgment can be entered up for them. No penalty seems payable for the omission to take, or to give a receipt; but the

1865.

The
ATTORNEY
GENERAL
v.
THE BANK OF
NEW SOUTH
WALES.

1865
The
ATTORNEY
GENERAL
v.
THE BANK OF
NEW SOUTH
WALES.

bank is liable to three penalties of fifty pounds, in respect of the other instruments. We understood, however, that the only object was to obtain the opinion of the Court; and that the suit was really a friendly one, instituted for that purpose.

ROBERTSON *against* BLOXSOME (a).

There being disputes between two contiguous occupants of Crown Lands, it was agreed in 1841 to refer the question of boundary to the Commissioner of Crown Lands. That officer accordingly went on the ground in the presence of both parties, and then and there fixed the boundary. In an action of trespass between the same parties in 1865, in which the same boundary line came in dispute, evidence of the reference and the result was held to be rightly received.

TRESPASS for breaking and entering a sheep station, known as Wellington Vale, in the district of New England, between the 1st August, 1861, and the commencement of the action.

Plea 1, not guilty; 2. not possessed; 3. that the lands were the defendant's lands; 4. a plea alleging that the plaintiff's occupation was unlawful. Issue thereon.

This was a squatting action tried before *Stephen*, C. J., in February, 1865. The dispute was with regard to a triangular piece of ground consisting of about 320 acres, between the plaintiff's station called Wellington Vale, and the defendant's station, Ranger's Valley. At the trial the learned Judge received evidence of the result of a reference by the then contiguous occupants to the Commissioner, under the 10th section of the 2nd Vic., No. 27. It appeared from this evidence that there being disputes between the shepherds of these parties, the plaintiff's brother, then in possession of Wellington Vale to the north, and the defendant's superintendent for the defendant who possessed land, now known as Ranger's Valley, to the south, agreed to refer the question of boundary to the Commissioner; this agreement was in 1841. That officer accordingly went on the ground in the presence of both parties, and then and there fixed the boundary, and it was sworn by the plaintiff's witnesses that the boundary was ever afterwards till of late years acquiesced in and acted upon. But the defendant himself swore that although he heard of the

(a) Before *Stephen*, C. J., *Hargrave*, J., and *Cheeke*, J.

reference, he himself always ignored it. He said, "I always left these matters to my superintendent."

His Honor told the jury that the question was on the main issues, which of the two parties was in actual occupation at the period in contest, namely 1860–63. The jury having found a verdict for the plaintiff.

Martin, Q. C., now obtained a rule *nisi* for a new trial on the ground that the evidence of the decision of the Commissioner was improperly received.

Sir *W. Manning*, Q. C., and *Windeyer* showed cause. The question of prior occupation was rightly left to the jury, and they were made aware that there was no question of right affected by the reference and award or decision therein. It is submitted that the evidence of a decision or award resulting from a reference by both sides was rightly admitted. Where by a memorandum between *A*. and *B*., it was agreed that a question of boundary should be referred to *C*., although the lessees of *A*. and *B*. were not parties to the agreement; it was held that the agreement was evidence for the lessee of *A*. against the lessee of *B*., after proof that the lessee of *B*. had applied to *A*. for a lease of the lot in dispute, in case the decision should be against *B*., and that he was present when the boundary was staked out by *C*. The conduct of the lessee of *B*. was sufficient evidence that he assented to the setting out of the boundary line by *C*.; *Taylor* v. *Parry* (a). The decision also was acquiesced in, so that in all probability there was a continued occupation in accordance with the decision. A decision by any person upon a reference by two parties to a dispute as to the possession of land might be evidence explaining the subsequent occupation of these parties, and what was intended by them to be occupied.

Martin, Q. C., and *Isaacs* contra. Our objection was and is that evidence was received of a "decision,"

(a) 1 M. & G. 604.

that is, a *quasi* judicial act. [*Stephen*, C. J. I never
received it as a judicial act, but as something that had
been acted on]. The decision might have taken place
in the absence of the party, for the section (a) enacts that
as often as any complaint shall be made to the Commissioner by any person licensed to occupy Crown Lands as
aforesaid, that any dispute has arisen, the Commissioner
shall, being required so to do, visit such station and
enquire into the matter of the said complaint, and shall,
being thereto required by the parties in dispute, or
either of them, so to do, by writing under their or
either of their hands, hear and finally determine the
matter of the said complaints. What was said by the
Commissioner amounted to a valid and formal decision,
or no evidence of it was admissible, whereas there was
no evidence of any such request in writing to him.
The statutory provisions were not shown to have been
complied with.

There was no reliable evidence of any acquiescence by
the defendant, and none whatever of any previous reference by him to the Commissioner, so that *Taylor* v. *Parry*
does not apply. [*Stephen*, C. J. But I received the
evidence on the assumption that there was some evidence
that the party had beforehand said that he would be
bound;—that there was acquiescence by a previous
agreement.] It is submitted that there was no evidence
of any such previous agreement.

Cur. adv. vult.

STEPHEN, C. J., now delivered judgment as follows:—
The question was whether evidence was receivable of a
conversation between the plaintiff's predecessor and the
defendant's superintendent, and the Commissioner of
Crown Lands, with reference to the boundaries between
the stations of the plaintiff and defendant. It appears
that some reference was made—we cannot tell whether
under the statute, or by some private arrangement—and
the Commissioner was called, in to give an opinion as to

(a) 2 Vic., No. 27, s. 10.

the proper boundary between these stations. The plaintiff says that it was agreed to refer, and afterwards there was an acquiescence in the decision. The defendant says, I never assented or acquiesced in what took place; I ignored it. It is clear that an overseer has no power to cut off a portion of his master's station. But if the master does leave to the overseer to manage his station generally, and do all that is necessary to prevent trespasses, it strikes me that the master is so far bound by a reference of this kind that the parties can refer to it as a part of the *res gestæ*, and as throwing light upon the transactions between them. I have stated that I received the evidence on the ground that it was in the nature of a reference to settle disputes between the parties. In summing up I told the jury that the evidence was not received as evidence of a judicial act. No doubt it was pressed as a judicial act upon the jury, and they may have so thought, if they did not attend to my direction; but I do not think that we can assume this to be the case. In my opinion the evidence preponderated in favour of the other side; and it may be that the evidence referred to may have led to injustice; but as I cannot clearly see that this is so, the verdict cannot, it seems to me, be disturbed.

HARGRAVE, J., and CHEEKE, J., concurred.

Rule discharged.

1865.

November 26.

WILSON *against* O'CONNEL.

A bill of sale absolute in its terms was made subject to a verbal defeasance. It was *held* that under the second section of the Secret Bills of Sale Act (19 Vic., No. 2), such defeasance should have been written on the same paper or parchment on which the bill . of sale was written, before the time when the latter or a copy thereof was filed; and the bill of sale alone having been filed, was considered void as against a judgment creditor of the grantor of the bill of sale (a).

THIS was an interpleader issue, sent down for trial at the Tenterfield District Court. The question was whether certain goods, which had been seized by the sheriff under a writ of *fi. fa.* in an action by the defendant against *Cowper*, were at the time of their seizure the property of *Wilson*, or of the execution debtor.

It appeared at the trial before Mr. *Sheppard*, the acting District Court Judge, that the plaintiff claimed under a bill of sale from the execution debtor. The bill of sale was, in its terms, absolute, and has been registered under the provisions of the Secret Bills of Sale Act. But the evidence showed that there had been a parol agreement between the plaintiff and the execution debtor, that the property was to be reconveyed to the latter when the amount due from him to the former was paid. This parol defeasance was not registered under the Act. The learned District Court Judge was of opinion that although the bill of sale appeared to be in its terms absolute, as the evidence showed that it was conditional, it was void as not having been duly registered in accordance with the Act (b).

Stephen, for the plaintiff, now moved for a rule *nisi* for a new trial. It is submitted that the learned Judge was wrong. The Act only contemplates the cases of a defeasance under seal. A mere parol agreement, whether written or verbal, cannot control an instrument under seal. Here the bill of sale was absolute in its terms, and

(a) *Quære*—If an execution debtor has an equitable interest in goods by virtue of a secret stipulation attached to a bill of sale, is not the sheriff authorised to sell that interest under the 5 Vic., No. 9, s. 81?

(b) The second section of the Secret Bills of Sale Act, 19 Vic., No. 2, enacts that, "if such bill of sale shall be made or given, subject to any defeasance or condition, or declaration of trust not contained in the body thereof, such defeasance or condition, or declaration of trust, shall, for the purposes of this Act, be taken as part of such bill of sale, and shall be written on the same paper or parchment on which such bill of sale shall be written, before the time when the same or a copy thereof respectively shall be filed, otherwise such bill of sale shall be null and void, to all intents and purposes, as against the same persons, and as regards the same property and effects as if such bill of sale, or a copy thereof, had not been filed according to the provisions of this Act.

being registered as such, the requirements of the Act have been fulfilled.

STEPHEN, C. J. I am of opinion that the learned District Court Judge was right. The Act is strangely drawn; for if it had said that no defeasance should be in force unless it were in writing and also attached to the bill of sale, no difficulty could have arisen. It seems to me that where there is a parol defeasance, it must be registered with the bill of sale, and that this was the correct construction is shown by the provision as to "declaration of trust" which clearly need not be in writing. Where there is a bill of sale to a person who orally agrees with or promises the assignor thereupon that the property shall be restored on certain conditions, such last mentioned agreement must be in writing. If not in writing, it cannot be endorsed on or annexed to the instrument of sale, as the statute requires. The bill of sale itself, by such omission, becomes void, notwithstanding due registration in other respects under the statute. If a debtor can concoct a bill of sale and have a secret agreement controlling that bill of sale, which need not be registered, the object of the Act could be frustrated.

Ex parte WOODFORD.

SIMPSON moved to make absolute a rule for a prohibition under the Justices' Acts, to restrain certain parties from further proceeding in a certain conviction, whereby the applicant had been convicted of deserting from a British ship in the port of Sydney. The depositions clearly show that the ship has changed owners since the articles were signed, and the contract of service is therefore at an end. It is immaterial that there has been no change of the Captain, and that he is now the agent for the new owners as he was of the former ones. The original agreement was put an end to by the change of ownership.

When the change of ownership took place, the former owners disabled themselves from performing their part of the agreement with the applicant, and therefore the latter was absolved from performing his part also. He had a right to rescind the contract; *Planche* v. *Colburn* (a), *Jesse* v. *Roy* (b). The principle contended for has been expressly held to apply in a case like the present. In *Robins* v. *Power* (c), there was a change of ownership in a British ship by sale in England while she was in a foreign port, and the Court held that the contract under which the crew shipped was quoad the new owner at an end. *Cockburn*, C. J., says, "Admitting that a seaman engaged for a voyage must complete the same before he can sue for his wages, I am of opinion that no such question arises here, because the original contract was at an end, and so any service done by the plaintiff on board the vessel was not due under such contract." Mr. *Maclachlan* (d), in referring to this case, says, "If new articles are signed, the seaman's right to wages for the residue of the voyage is under them; but if the seaman leaves the ship as he lawfully may do before hearing of the change, or some time after, without entering into a new engagement, there is evidence from which a jury may infer a contract with the new owner to pay him *pro rata* for his services in the mean time." [*Stephen*, C. J. In that case there was a change of captains.] It is submitted that as the new owner would be entitled to discharge the men bound by the former articles, the latter were justified if they pleased in leaving the ship.

Windeyer showed cause. It is submitted that the change of ownership is utterly immaterial, and that the contract of service which is between the master and the crew (e), remains a contract notwithstanding such change. There are various justifications of desertion mentioned in *Abbott* on Shipping (f), but not any like this. The 205th section of the Merchant Shipping Act contemplates the possibility of a change of ownership; and that it was intended that the contract should continue notwithstanding a sale of the ship.

(a) 8 Bing. 14.
(b) 1 C. M. & R. 316; See *Sands* v. *Clark*, 8 C. B. 762; *Keys* v. *Harwood*, 2 C. B. 805.
(c) 4 Q. B. N. S. 778; 27 L. J. C. P. 257.   (d) On Shipping, p. 209.
(e) Merchant Shipping Act, s. 149.   (f) p. 135.

STEPHEN C. J. I am of opinion that the conviction must be sustained, although I have come to this conclusion not without difficulty, for the opinions expressed by the Judges of the Common Pleas in *Robins* v. *Power* apparently sanction the doctrine that a mere change of ownership entitle the seamen to throw up their contract entered into with the previous owners; but the only point decided in that case was that there was a new contract with the new owners. Moreover in that case the master was changed also, and the sale was in a foreign port, for the ship was lying at Suez. Here the same master continues, and the new owners must be taken to have adopted his contract. The sailors could sue the master, and the former owners could not put an end to that contract. That contract at all events continues in force, and by the Merchant Shipping Act of 1854, it seems to me that the master cannot discharge any of the sailors in case merely of change of ownership, and on the other hand, the new owners on the termination of the voyage will be compellable to pay the wages. If so, the seamen are bound, by the same statute, as I conceive, to continue on board, and desertion from the ship is consequently punishable. It would be most dangerous to say that there is a dissolution of the contract upon every change of ownership.

CHEEKE, J. I concur. The articles in my opinion still remain in force, and the seaman cannot be discharged without the certificate of the master.

FAUCETT, J. There is a difficulty in the case, but I think the decision now arrived at is the best for all those interested. The articles are an agreement not merely between the owners of the ship and the crew, but the master is a material party to the agreement, and as the sailors can enforce their rights under it against the captain, the latter should, I think, be able to rely upon it as against the sailors.

Conviction sustained.

1865.

LANG *against* FAIRFAX and another.

In an action of libel, the defendant pleaded (under the 11 Vic., No. 13, s. 4) the truth of the facts alleged in the libel, and that it was for the public benefit that the matter complained of should be published, &c. The jury having found that the publication was not for the public benefit; *quære*, whether the verdict will be disturbed.

Considerations upon which the question of whether the publication of defamatory matter is for the public benefit should depend.

Quære, how far the damage ought to be affected in an action of libel by the mere truth of the matters alleged in such libel,

THIS was an action against the proprietors of the *Sydney Morning Herald* for libel. The declaration, after stating that whereas before the committing of the grievances hereafter mentioned the plaintiff had, by public advertisement, convened a meeting of the constituency of Sydney West, and the citizens of Sydney generally, at which meeting it was by the said advertisement announced that the plaintiff would deliver an address in the Temperance Hall, on a certain day therein named, on certain matters of public importance, and the said meeting was accordingly held, and at that meeting the plaintiff appeared and delivered such an address; and after the day of the said meeting, to wit, on the 3rd day of January, A.D. 1863, the defendants falsely and maliciously printed and published of the plaintiff, in a newspaper called the *Sydney Morning Herald*, the words following, which contained the libel *in extenso* :—

"Dr. *Lang's* appearance at the said meeting, in one of those performances for which he is so celebrated, shews that time and age have not affected his memory, nor diminished the vivacity of his spite. His advertisement was in the approved style of play bills of the second order. It did not teach us to expect a minister of religion expounding the principles of morality, or a politician explaining the constitution of his country, or a steward giving up his account; but it was the note of a performer rehearsing an old drama, reproducing under new names old characters, quoting lines which have done duty upon innumerable occasions, but which seem almost to have lost their relevance in their accomplishment.

assuming that the publication of those matters was not for the public benefit.

Held, by *Stephen*, C. J., and *Wise*, J., that the question whether the publication was for the public benefit, is examinable by the Court.

When on such an occasion and in such an assembly we hear the Doctor repeat—

1865.

LANG
v.
FAIRFAX
and another.

> For freedom's battle once begun,
> Bequeathed from bleeding sire to son,
> Tho' baffled oft, is ever won.

We begin to ask how long the fight will continue, and when that happy child will be born whose experience is to be crowned by the victory so often foretold. It seems to us that already not only 'freedom's battle' has been won, but that its old mercenaries have turned their arms against it, and that above their drunken orgies we hear the last words of Madame *Roland*, as she mounted the scaffold, and turned to the statue of liberty beside it, 'Oh liberty, what crimes are committed in thy name!' Freedom, however, is indeed a generous possession. It expands the intellect, it nerves the arm, it cements the social fabric, it gives double sweetness to family enjoyments, it is the best heirloom from fortunate ancestors, and the best inheritance of happy children. But that freedom is not to be always found in the cause or in the circles of which Dr. *Lang* is the exponent or the leader and guide. Like all theatrical performances of the Doctor, he is himself the subject of his play. Like *Matthews* at home, he keeps up the dialogue, and makes his own achievements and resentments so much his topic, that we might fancy he stood alone in the world as the admired of all admirers.

"Let not the Doctor, however, confound notoriety with honour, or exult with puerile joy, over the reputation which he infers from the rebuffs and reproaches he incurs. Men can easily make themselves conspicuous. One man burned down a temple that his name might be immortalized, and even the power of a king could not deprive him of this prize, but the perpetuity and wide diffusion of a name is not always to be envied. *Jonathan Wild* and Mrs. *Brownrigg*, are names which still come before the public in all kinds of publications and with all kinds of references and illustrations, while the Judges who tried them and even the victims they sacrificed are totally forgotten. It is possible for men with a moderate share of intellect and great physical energy, to make themselves disagreeable to thousands of people by indefatigable mischief, and to command a larger observation than they could possibly attain by the most eminent virtue and useful toil. But this is only like the crackling of thorns under a pot. Dr. *Lang* is less talked of and considered now, because all his puns are punned, all his jokes are joked, and all his satire is spent, because his poetry is stale, and his anecdotes are known by the first word. What he says of one to-day, he has said of others innumerable times before. It seems that Dr. *Lang* had in the last session a little bill of his own: like many other bills with which he has been acquainted, it has unfortunately not been discounted. Having calculated upon its proceeds, he is greatly mortified to find his bill would not pass. He cannot practice upon himself in reference to a Parliamentary bill, the illusion which is said sometimes to have operated in the case of a gentleman giving bills of another description, who handing over a promissory note with the gaiety of a French Marquis, said with vivacity, 'Thank God that is settled!' Perhaps this species of gratitude is natural to people who have found relief for three or four months by so simple a process, and who by giving bills and rarely paying them, have come to mistake them for cash. The Doctor's Parliamentary bill has not been even of this avail, for after much waiting upon the ministry and great docility on his part, with the full expectation that a large debt would be converted into a free grant by the complaisance of the Government, still the anticipated day is far distant. The object of the meeting was to set out the qualities of Mr. *Piddington,* to whom he has given the very useful office of 'Parliamentary detective.' Addressing an honest auditory, one would suppose that such a functionary would really be popular, but the Doctor fancied that such a name would be odious to his audience, and could present to them no image more offensive than that of a detective. These men are indeed a nuisance to many self enjoying people—one pops into the midst of a jovial company and says to the most rollicking, 'Come, I want you.' Another is found in the lobby of Parliament, rummaging among old papers, asking awkward questions, and otherwise disturbing the happy arrangements of men, who having served the public on the hustings, hope to serve themselves by an exchange of their votes. We mean to go a little into this Parliamentary bill. Our tranquil times will give an opportunity to pay attention to many a small matter of trifling account, which might in the great transactions of troublous times escape us. We suspect we shall find that the Doctor is at the present moment enjoying a larger income directly from state aid than any clergyman under a Bishop in the colony of New South Wales. Dr. *Lang* has associated the *Sydney Morning Herald* with the Congregational body in a manner which that body would by no means be inclined to admit. We do not profess to represent any religious sect, much less the extreme opinions which may be sometimes ascribed to it. We have at any rate for the last eight years given our moderate but constant support to every rational movement for the equitable settlement of our ecclesiastical difficulties. We are not so enamoured of voluntaryism not to be fully conscious of the defects of its working, and the utterly worthless character of many who are vociferous for its universal adoption. Our concern in it arises from far wider views and deeper considerations than its bearing upon particular denominations. Accordingly we suspect that our opinions upon the subject have been only tolerated by the voluntaries of this city, and we cannot claim in any sense to have been the organ of their party. But is Dr. *Lang* the man to take us to task? He continued to receive the direct support of the state as long as it was convenient to himself. When he had made over his salary for some time, in order that he might release himself from difficulties in England, by a document of course of no value except as it was sustained by his honourable adherence to its stipulations, he came to this colony, and then and there resigned his stipend upon conscientious scruples—stood out before the public as the representative of voluntaryism, and thus simultaneously disappointed his creditor, and

1865.

LANG
v
FAIRFAX
and another.

obtained from his congregation in virtue of his sacrifice new pecuniary support. These things no doubt will be laughed at by his adherents as examples of the Doctor's wonderful cleverness, but in our opinion it was a piece of wonderful charlatanism, and merited a distinguished reward over the water."

Pleas 1. As to the prefatory matter, that the plaintiff had not, before the committing, &c., convened a meeting of the constituency of Sydney West, and the citizens of Sydney generally, nor was it announced that the plaintiff would at such meeting deliver an address on certain matters of public importance, nor was such meeting held, nor did the plaintiff appear and deliver such an address thereat. 2. Not guilty. 3. As to so much of the said declaration as complains of the printing and publishing by the defendant, of the words following, that is to say— "But is Dr. *Lang* the man to take us to task? He continued to receive the direct support of the State as long as it was convenient to himself. When he had made over his salary for some time, in order that he might release himself from difficulties in England, by a document, of course of no value, except as it was sustained by his honourable adherence to its stipulations, he came to this colony, and then and there resigned his stipend upon conscientious scruples, stood out before the public as a representative of voluntaryism, and thus simultaneously disappointed his creditors, and obtained from his congregation in virtue of his sacrifice new pecuniary support," the defendants say that the several statements and allegations therein contained were and are true, in fact; and the defendants further say that it was for the public benefit that the matters charged and contained thereby and therein, should be and were so printed and published. And the defendants further say that before the said printing and publishing thereof the plaintiff had been and was a minister of religion, that is to say, the senior minister of the Scotch Church in Sydney, in this colony, and as such minister of religion had been and was for many years in receipt of direct pecuniary support from the State, that is to say, a salary

of £300 a year, which he received and was entitled to
receive from the Government of New South Wales as
such senior minister of the Scotch Church as aforesaid,
so long as he continued to hold that office, and to perform the duties thereof; and that the plaintiff being
such minister as aforesaid, and whilst he was in the
receipt of such salary as such minister as aforesaid, and
whilst he was entitled to continue in the receipt thereof
as aforesaid, became and was indebted to a certain firm
consisting of divers persons, that is to say, *Robert
Ewing, Robert Angus, John Litt,* and *Ritchie Angus,*
carrying on business as merchants, in copartnership,
under the firm of "*Ewing, May and Company,*" at
Glasgow and Greenock, in Scotland, in a certain sum of
money, to wit, the sum of £764 6s. 8d.; and the said
firm, to wit, on the 5th day of September, A.D. 1840,
commenced an action against the plaintiff in the Court
of Queen's Bench, at Westminster, in England, where
the plaintiff then was, in which said action the plaintiff
was arrested under a Judge's order, and committed to
the custody of the Marshal of the said Court of Queen's
Bench. And the plaintiff thereupon proposed to the
said firm to execute an assignment to them, or a trustee
of their nomination of the said salary of him (the plaintiff), as such senior minister of the said Scotch Church
at Sydney, as aforesaid, together with a power of
attorney to persons to be mutually agreed upon between
the plaintiff and the said firm, to receive on behalf of
the said firm or their trustee the said salary, and also to
sign an authority addressed to the Colonial Treasurer of
New South Wales, requiring him to pay the said salary
to the attorneys so to be nominated as aforesaid, and also
to sign and deliver to the said firm or their trustee a
bill of exchange on *Andrew Lang,* Esquire, of Sydney,
landholder, the brother of the plaintiff, for the said sum
of £764 6s. 8d., and interest thereon, and the said firm
agreed to accept and accepted the said proposal, and it
was agreed between them and the plaintiff that the said
assignment of the said salary of the plaintiff as such
senior minister of the said Scotch Church, at Sydney,

aforesaid, should be made to one *James McClelland,*
as a trustee for the said firm, and that the said power of
attorney should be made in favour of and addressed to
James McArthur, Esquire, at Sydney, aforesaid, then
one of the members of the Legislative Council of the
said colony, and to *Kearsay Cannan,* then of Sydney,
aforesaid, surgeon, and the plaintiff in pursuance of the
said agreement, then by an indenture of mortgage under
his hand and seal, bearing a certain date, to wit, the
14th day of October, A.D. 1840, made or expressed to be
made between the plaintiff of the first part, the said
Robert Ewing, Robert Angus, John Litt, and *Ritchie
Angus,* of the second part; the said *James McClelland,*
of the third part ; and the said *James McArthur* and
Kearsay Cannan of the fourth part, did by the direction of the said firm, assign unto the said *James
McClelland* all that the said salary or sum of £300 per
annum, or any other sum or sums of money then due,
owing, and payable, or to become due, owing, or payable
to him the plaintiff, as such senior minister of the Scotch
Church, at Sydney, as aforesaid, by the Colonial
Government of New South Wales, aforesaid, to hold
the same and all arrears thereof, and all future payments
to become due on account thereof, unto the said *James
McClelland,* his executors, administrators, and assigns,
absolutely, subject to a proviso therein contained, for
making void the said indenture of mortgage and the
power of attorney therein contained, on payment by the
plaintiff to the said *James McArthur* and *Kearsay
Cannan* or the survivor of them, their or his executors
or administrators of the said sum of £764 6s. 8d., with
interest as in the said indenture mentioned on a certain
day, to wit, the first day of March, A.D. 1841, and the
plaintiff in and by the said indenture did constitute and
appoint the said *James McArthur* and *Kearsay Cannan*
jointly, or the survivor of them, the attorneys or attorney
irrevocably of the plaintiff, to demand, recover, and
receive of and from the Honorable *Campbell Drummond
Riddell,* Esquire, then Colonial Treasurer of New South
Wales aforesaid, or the Treasurer for the time being of

the Government of the said colony, and from all persons

who were or should be liable to pay the same the said
salary of £300 per annum, and all arrears thereof, and
future payments to become due in respect thereof, and
the plaintiff did also in pursuance of the said agreement,
to wit, on the 14th day of October, A.D. 1840, address
to the said *Campbell Drummond Riddell*, or to the
Treasurer for the time being of the said colony of New
South Wales, an order or authority in writing, signed
by the plaintiff, authorising the said Treasurer to pay
on behalf of the said firm to the said *James McArthur*
and *Kearsay Cannan*, the sum of £25 sterling, being
the salary of the plaintiff as such minister as aforesaid,
for the month immediately succeeding the presentation
by the said *James McArthur* and *Kearsay Cannan*, of
the said order, and to continue the said payment, on
account or in respect of the plaintiff's said salary as such
minister as aforesaid, of the sum of £25 monthly to the
said *James McArthur* and *Kearsay Cannan* till they
should surrender the said order or otherwise declare that
the aforesaid debt by the plaintiff to the said firm was
paid, and the plaintiff did then, to wit, on the 14th day
of October, A.D. 1840, in pursuance of the aforesaid
agreement, sign and deliver to the said *James
McClelland*, as such trustee for the said firm as aforesaid, a bill of exchange in writing, addressed to the said
Andrew Lang, in Sydney, aforesaid, whereby the
plaintiff requested the said *Andrew Lang*, at three
months after sight thereof, to pay to the order of the
said *James McClelland*, the sum of £764 6s. 8d., with
interest thereon, from the date of the said bill, at the
rate of five per centum per annum, and the said *James
McClelland* thereupon endorsed the said bill to the said
James McArthur and *Kearsay Cannan*, or the survivor
of them, of which the plaintiff had notice, and the
plaintiff upon his executing the said indenture of
mortgage and signing the said order and signing and
delivering the said bill of exchange as aforesaid, was by
the authority of the said firm released from the said
custody of the said Marshal of the said Court of

1865.

LANG
v.
FAIRFAX
and another.

Queen's Bench, and the said indenture of mortgage, and the said order, and the said bill of exchange were duly transmitted to the said *James McArthur* and *Kearsay Cannan*, at Sydney, aforesaid, for the purpose of the same being acted upon in pursuance of the terms thereof ; and the said bill of exchange was afterwards, to wit, on the 3rd day of September, A.D. 1841, at Sydney, aforesaid, duly presented to the said *Andrew Lang,* who refused to accept the same, whereupon the same was duly protested for such non-acceptance, of all which the plaintiff had notice, and the plaintiff having returned to Sydney, aforesaid, continued to act as such senior minister of the Scotch Church at Sydney, as aforesaid, and did receive and continue to receive from the state, that is to say, from the said Government of New South Wales, by virtue of his office as such minister of religion, as aforesaid, his said salary of £25 per month for a long period of time, that is to say, until the month of March, A.D. 1842, during all which time the said debt to the said firm, the payment whereof was so secured as hereinbefore mentioned, continued and was wholly due and unpaid by the plaintiff, together with a large arrear of interest thereon, and the defendants say that the plaintiff whilst he was so indebted as aforesaid, and whilst the said mortgage by him of his said salary was in full force and wholly unsatisfied, did resign and discontinue his connection with the State or Government of New South Wales as such minister of religion as aforesaid, and the receipt of and the right to receive his stipend, that is to say, his said salary, as such minister of religion as aforesaid, and did allege to his congregation that he resigned the same upon conscientious scruples, and did notify and state to the public that he was a representative and advocate of voluntaryism, that is to say, of a system by which all state aid in support of religion should be abolished, and the plaintiff did thereupon and thereby obtain from his congregation new pecuniary support ; and the defendants further say that it was for the public benefit that the matter complained of by the plaintiff and in the introductory part of this plea mentioned, should be published by reason of the following facts, that is to say—(1) the subject of state aid to religion by the Government of New South Wales had been and was at the time of the printing and publishing of the said matters complained of, a matter of great public interest and importance to the inhabitants of the said colony and others Her Majesty's subjects, and—(2) the plaintiff had been and then was a member of the Legislative Assembly of the said colony, and had been and was a prominent advocate as well in his Legislative capacity as otherwise, of the abolition in the said colony of state aid to religion. Issue thereon.

The cause came on for trial before *Wise,* J., and a special jury of twelve, in the May sittings, when it appeared that the plaintiff, who is a member of the Legislative Assembly, has been for many years a Presbyterian minister in Sydney. He arrived in the colony in 1823, and was up to 1842 receiving as such minister a salary of £300 a year from the Colonial Treasury. He left the colony on a visit to Europe in 1839, and when in England in 1840, was arrested for a debt by certain Scotch creditors, Messrs. *Ewing* and *May,* under a *ca. re.,* and lodged in the Queen's Bench. He obtained his release from prison by assigning to one *McClelland,* as trustee for the detaining creditors there, his government salary. He also gave an order on the Colonial Treasurer for his salary, and a collateral security by a bill of exchange drawn on his brother, Mr. *Andrew Lang,* in the colony. Messrs. *McArthur* and *Cannan* were appointed the agents in the colony for *McClelland.* The former, however, declined to act, and endorsed the bill on Mr. *Andrew Lang* without recourse to *Cannan.* In point of fact the creditors did not avail themselves of the order upon the Colonial Treasurer, for the plaintiff himself received his salary several months after the order was sent out to this colony—in fact, up to the time of the surrender of the salary.

It appeared that the plaintiff arrived in the colony

in or about May, 1841, and that the bill on his brother was protested for non-acceptance on the 3rd of September in that year. The plaintiff in February, 1842, announced that in consequence of the opinions he had formed with regard to the iniquity of state aid to religion, he should relinquish his salary, and in April, 1842, he actually relinquished it. It appeared that he had formed his opinions on the subject during his travels in America, in 1840. It was shown that the plaintiff afterwards executed a second mortgage of some house property belonging to him in Sydney, to one *Bryant*, to secure the amount due on the above dishonored bill with interest. This property had already been mortgaged to the Loan Company on the 19th June, 1841. The mortgage to *Bryant*, which was prepared by Mr. *Norton*, on the face of it purported to have been executed on 21st September, 1841, and the great question at the trial was whether it was executed on that day, or not, as was contended by the defendant, till the 3rd September, 1842. The plaintiff went into the box, and swore distinctly that the deed was executed in September, 1841, and stated that he had no doubt whatever on the matter; although when pressed in cross-examination, he admitted that his recollection was to some extent based on the fact that the date so appeared on the face of deed. He stated that he had seen *Bryant* on the matter before its execution in June or July, 1841. He stated that he believed it was a few weeks before he executed the deed that he saw *Bryant*. On the part of the defendants, evidence was called to show that the execution must have been in September, 1842. The deed itself was not registered till the 22nd September, 1842. This second mortgage was also assigned shortly afterwards, and the funds thus obtained were paid over to *Bryant*.

A model deed was put in evidence containing skeleton drafts of the different parts of various mortgage deeds prepared in Mr. *Norton's* office. The parts were arranged consecutively, and evidence was given by Mr. *Josephson*, who was at that time a clerk in Mr. *Norton's*

office, that he knew from a memorandum made on the
model deed, that the mortgage to *Bryant*, which was
the fourth in order of those contained in the model deed,
was not executed till September, 1842. The inferences
to be drawn from the model deed are sufficiently shown
in the judgments that follow, and need not be here
more particularly referred to. It also appeared that Mr.
Cooper Turner was the then solicitor for the Loan
Company, who were the first mortgagees of the property,
and that therefore the abstract of the title was by the
plaintiff's direction prepared by him. Mr. *Cooper
Turner* became the solicitor for the Loan Company, in
July, 1841, and Mr. *Iceton*, who was clerk to Mr.
Cooper Turner at that time, swore that the abstract
was not prepared till the 16th of July, 1842, and copied
on the 19th. This abstract itself also contained an
abstract apparently of a deed executed in 1842. It
appeared that the plaintiff had subsequently visited
England, and not been harassed by these creditors.
The learned Judge put the following questions to the
jury :—

"As to the special plea—1. Are the facts alleged
proved? 2. Was it for the public benefit that they
should be published?

"If either of these questions are answered in the
negative, the verdict will be for the plaintiff generally;
and, if so, what damages?

"If both these questions are answered in the affirmative, the verdict upon that plea will be for the
defendants?

"If so, then the question will be, Is the rest of the
article complained of a libel? and, if so, what damages?

"If not a libel, then a verdict for defendants?"

The jury found by 9 to 3 that the facts alleged on
the plea of justification were not proved, and by 11 to 1
that the publication was not for the public benefit.

Darvall, Q.C., now moved for a rule *nisi* for a new
trial. The verdict is clearly against evidence on the
plea of justification. The plaintiff was at the time a

member of Parliament, and a minister of the Scotch Church, and he had himself brought before the public the subject of state aid to religion, and his opinions and conduct with reference to that subject. It is clear that the mortgage to *Bryant* was not executed till September, 1842, and that as alleged in the libel he had after the surrender of his salary left his creditors without any security; and, as he admitted on cross-examination that his opinions on the question of state aid had been formed in America in 1840, it was a fair inference that when he gave the security to obtain his release, he must have formed the intention of abandoning his salary and thus defeating his creditors. If the deed had been executed in 1841, or the transaction had been founded on an arrangement made in 1841, the fact might have been proved by *Bryant* who is accessible in Melbourne. The plaintiff admitted that he directed an abstract of title to be prepared by Mr. *Cooper Turner,* who was the solicitor for the then mortgagees, and became so on July, 1841. Mr. *Iceton,* who was then his clerk, swore that the abstract was not prepared till July, 1842, so that the mortgage to *Bryant* could not have been executed till after that date. And in support of this date, it appears on reference to the abstract, that one of the deeds therein abstracted was not executed till 1842. Mr. *Josephson* also proved by a memorandum made on the model deed, which was prepared in 1842, that he must have prepared, and did prepare, the said mortgage from the model in 1842.

Lastly, there was a clear and satisfactory reason for making the deed purport to be dated on 21st September, 1841, because from the date on which the bill was protested, the amount of the bill together with the expenses was to bear interest, and for this reason the date from which the united amount would bear interest, was filled in before execution.

Rule granted on the ground that the verdict on the plea of justification was against evidence.

September 4.   *Dalley* and *Windeyer* show cause.   Mr. *Bryant,* Mr. *McArthur,* and Mr. *Cannan,* all persons who could have disproved the plaintiff's statement that the deed was executed on the day it bore date, were alive, and the defendants were bound to call them. The plaintiff's reasons for swearing to the date of the execution and the circumstance fixing it on his memory are, that he arrived in the colony in March, 1841, and did not relinquish his stipend till April, 1842. The plaintiff always intended .and told *Bryant* that he intended to substitute this mortgage for the assignment of his salary, and in payment of the bill of exchange given in Europe. The assignment of this second mortgage was executed immediately after its execution, and out of the proceeds of this mortgage the English creditors were paid.

Although Mr. *Josephson* said that he drew the deed in 1842, yet he said this from other materials which led him to this conclusion, and he had not, and did not pretend to have, any independent recollection whatever on the subject. In like manner, Mr. *Iceton* had no independent recollection, and only swore to the facts after looking at some paper of which the Court and jury can know nothing. The plaintiff's debt to his English creditors was paid, and it was paid out of the assets obtained from the assignee of, and shortly after, the mortgage. The libel therefore was shown to be false, for the creditors were not injured. The plaintiff has subsequently visited Europe, and if the creditors had not been paid, he would have been harassed. Although even if they had not been paid, or if the mortgage was not executed till 1842, it is clear that the plaintiff intended all along to pay them out of the proceeds of the money obtained by the mortgage, and in this view of the case also the libel was shown to be false. If the plaintiff always intended to pay, the abandoning this salary was not under the circumstances dishonest.

On the question of public benefit, it is submitted that the jury were entitled to look at all the circumstances in order to form their opinion on the question. It is submitted that the mode in which these matters are handled by the defendants, and the ex-

posure made of these private affairs of the plaintiff could
not possibly have produced or been calculated to produce
benefit to the public.   At all events the question was
for the jury, and the Court cannot say that they were
palpably wrong.   This particular question was intended
by the statute to be particularly within the province of
the jury.   Their decision is conclusive.   How can the
Court know as well as the public at large, as represented
by the jury, what publication is for the public benefit.
The libel imputes swindling to the plaintiff, and alleged
that he gave up his salary in order to cheat his creditors,
and that is shown to be false.   His creditors did not
care to touch his salary, for for several months he
received it with his own hand after this assignment.
It is also submitted that the Court will not grant a
new trial, even although of opinion that the verdict is
wrong on the plea of justification.   The damages shall
be referred to the good cause of action : *Doe dem.*
Lawrie v. *Dyeball* (a).

Per Curiam.   We are clearly of opinion that if the
verdict is wrong, we have no alternative to the granting a new trial, for we cannot tell what part of the
damages has been given for the portion of the libel
covered by the plea of justification, and what part for
the portion uncovered.

Martin, Q.C., and *Isaacs* contra.   The bill of
exchange which was dated the 14th of October, 1840,
and was at three months sight, was protested for non-
acceptance on the 3rd September, 1841.   The plaintiff
saw *Bryant* just about July, 1841, as he says, with the
power of attorney; if that be so, and the arrangements for
the mortgage were then made, why was the bill presented
and protested in September afterwards?   The abstract
of the title furnished by the Loan Company according
to the evidence of Mr. *Iceton*, was prepared on the 16th
of July, 1842, and copied on the 19th; it is also
manifest that the abstract could not have been prepared

(a) 8 B. & C. 70.

in 1841, for it recites a deed executed in May, 1842. Moreover, the date of the mortgage is filled in at the time in the handwriting of the same copyist. It is also proved by Mr. *Josephson*, that the deed was not prepared till 1842. The draft also had internal evidence that it was not prepared till 1842, and not even till after July in that year, for the draft preceding this in the model deed was of the latter date. The deed also was not registered till September, 1842, but it was essential by the then law, that the registration should be within thirty days, for otherwise by the 6 Geo. IV., No. 22, s. 2, it lost its priority. This argument is conclusive. [*Stephen*, C.J. The 6 Geo. IV., No. 22, s. 2, was repealed on 3rd January, 1842, by the 5 Vic., No. 21, s. 11.] The argument is the same, for if the deed was executed in 1841, the former Act, 6 Geo. IV., No. 22, was then in force. In 1842, by the 5 Vic., No. 21, the deed operated from the time of registration. But the plaintiff stated that the negotiations with *Bryant* preceded the execution of the deed only a few weeks, so that he in fact surrendered his salary and disappointed his creditors before even Mr. *Iceton* had prepared for him the abstract of title.

On the question of public benefit, it is submitted that any value that might have attached to the finding of the jury on this point is got rid of by the grossly wrong finding on the other. When the plaintiff talked at the public meeting of his sacrifices and efforts on behalf of the abolition of state aid, and the truth was that he got more by giving up his salary than he had before, was it not for the public benefit that the truth on such a point and of such a man should be known and commented on in reference to the state aid question ? In *Hedley* v. *Barlow*(a), the law is laid down by *Cockburn*, C.J., as follows: "Public men in every position must be prepared to go through the ordeal of criticism, and if they meet with comments which are merely unpleasant, they must endure it manfully without rushing always into actions. The right of

(a) 4 F. & F. 229.

1865.
LANG
v.
FAIRFAX
and another.

public discussion on matters of public interest is important, and it requires for its beneficial exercise that it should be exercised fully and freely, without being subject to too hard or strict a limitation. And so long as it is exercised fairly and honestly, it is protected or excused, even although it may, incidentally, involve the publication of defamatory matter. But, at the same time the comments must be fair, that is, conceived in a fair spirit, in the spirit of fair discussion, and not in a spirit of reckless or inconsiderate imputation. That which is recklessly defamatory can hardly be deemed fair; strong feelings may often arise in the course of the discussion of a public question, and, though there must be allowed the fullest freedom in such discussions, yet it is a freedom which must not be abused for the purpose of reckless imputations, and must be confined to fair comments, that is, comments which the jury consider 'fair' in spirit and intention, judging from the language used;" *Bayles* v. *Laurence* (a), *Hearne* v. *Stowell* (b). But the issue taken by the replication is only on the facts alleged as our ground, and not on the question of whether it is or is not for the public benefit. The latter is a question of law only. If the facts alleged showed no case of public benefit, the objection should have been taken on demurrer. [*Stephen*, C.J. The plea does not mention that the plaintiff attended a public meeting.] It is submitted that when the plaintiff talked of his sacrifices for the cause, it became for the public benefit that all men should be able to judge for themselves how far this champion had made any sacrifices, and whether his change of opinion on the question was sincere, and really owing to conscientious scruples, or was owing to a desire to promote his own interests. It would seem that the jury must have misunderstood the question and thought that the question for their consideration was whether the defendants published the matter for the public benefit. *Wilson* v. *Reed* (c), and *Paris* v. *Levy* (d), were referred to.   *Cur. adv. vult.*

(a) 11 A. & E. 925.   (b) 12 A. & E. 732.
(c) 2 F. & F. 149.   (d) 30 L.J.C.P. 15.

Their Honors gave judgment in this case as follows:—
STEPHEN, C.J.   The libel published by the defendants commences by commenting with much severity on an address, delivered by the plaintiff at a public meeting convened by him in Sydney, consisting of his constituents and sundry other citizens, and on him in reference to that address and other matters.   The article then charges him—he being a clergyman, formerly in the receipt of a Government salary as such,—with having continued to receive that salary, so long as it suited his own convenience to do so; and only having resigned it "on conscientious scruples" as the advocate of Voluntaryism (or opposition to any pecuniary aid from the State), because he had made over that salary as a security for debts contracted in the mother country—the plaintiff by the relinquishment under such circumstances doubly profiting, since he at once defeated his creditor, and obtained from the congregation on account of his "sacrifice" new pecuniary support.   The defendants then characterise this operation as a piece of charlatanism, meriting in their opinion, transportation.   Such I conceive, the expression used must be taken to mean—or nothing.   The following, however, are the exact words:—

" But is Dr. *Lang* the man to take us to task ?   He continued to receive the direct support of the State, as long as it was convenient to himself.   When he had made over his salary for some time, in order that he might release himself from difficulties in England, by a document, of course of no value except as it was sustained by his honourable adherence to its stipulations, he came to this colony, and then and there resigned his stipend upon conscientious scruples; stood out before the public as the representative of voluntaryism, and thus simultaneously disappointed his creditor and obtained from his congregation, in virtue of his sacrifice, new pecuniary support.   These things, no doubt, will be laughed at by his adherents as examples of the Doctor's wonderful cleverness, but in our opinion it was a piece of wonderful charlatanism, and merited a distinguishing reward over the water."

1865.

LANG
v.
FAIRFAX
and another.
September 27.

The defendants, omitting in their plea this last sentence,justify the remainder of the quotation by declaring that the matters stated are true : and, secondly, that the publication of them was for the public benefit. The jury, by a majority of nine to three have found against the former allegation, and by eleven to one against the latter. Both these conclusions are complained of. It becomes, therefore, the duty of the Court,first to inquire into the propriety of each, and then to determine whether they are so clearly and obviously wrong, (both or one of them,) as to call on us—in justice to the defendants,—to send the case down for a second trial. I proceed, then, in the first place, to consider the finding on the matters of fact.

The plea contains the following allegations. That the plaintiff, as senior minister of the Scotch Church in Sydney,received for many years,and was entitled still to receive, State support, that is to say, a salary of three hundred pounds a year ; that, while so entitled, he became indebted to Messrs. *Ewing, May,* and Company, in Scotland, in the sum of £764, for the recovery of which they, in October 1840, arrested him, the plaintiff being then in London—and that he procured his release, by executing an assignment of the aforesaid salary, and signing a document addressed to the Colonial Treasurer, authorising its payment, to certain agents monthly,as it should fall due, until liquidation of the debt. That by the deed of assignment two gentlemen resident in the colony, nominated mutually by the plaintiff and the firm, were constituted attorneys to receive the money, and carry out the arrangement. That the plaintiff also drew, and gave to *Ewing* and *May*, a bill of exchange on one *Andrew Lang*, in Sydney, for the amount; but which bill,on presentation eventually to that gentleman, was refused acceptance. The plea then states, that the plaintiff returned to the colony,and continued to receive his salary monthly until March 1842 ; when the debt to *Ewing* and *May* remaining wholly due, with interest thereon, and the assignment for securing its payment being still in full force, the plaintiff discontinued his connection with the State as a minister, and resigned his salary as such—asserting to his congregation that he did so upon conscientious scruples, and notifying to the public that he was an advocate of voluntaryism; in other words, of the abolition of all State aid to Religion—whereupon, and whereby, says the plea, he obtained from the congregation new pecuniary support.

Now, of these several allegations all were admitted, or proved beyond dispute, except this—the essential one—that at the time of the plaintiff's relinquishing his public salary, its assignment as security to his creditors continued in operation. The deed itself and power of attorney, the plaintiff's order on the treasurer, the bill of exchange and its protest after presentment, were produced at the trial. The power is as usual an irrevocable one, and he covenants not to do any act at any time, by which the receipt of his salary shall be prevented. The plaintiff returned to this colony in April 1841, but when those documents reached the gentlemen selected as agents, or were transferred by deputation to their own nominee, did not appear. The bill on Mr. *Lang*, however, was formally presented on the 3rd day of September 1841, at which date the debt with interest and charges amounted to £809—none of which, it appeared, had (up to February 1844 at all events) been paid. In March 1842, the plaintiff renounced all connection with the State, and consequently his salary; having himself, up to that time, continued to receive it. The announcement of his intention was in February, and its consummation was on the 1st April. That he thereupon obtained more than an equivalent for the surrender, by voluntary contributions from his congregation was conceded. So that upon the plea the question was,—the assignment becoming by such surrender utterly frustrated and useless,—whether the plaintiff had, at any time before the act, given to his creditors a substituted security. If not (unless he could conclusively have shown, that the renunciation without actual security was by their distinct assent), the act itself was clearly a proved fraud on the arrangement —such as it is quite unnecessary to characterise.

To establish, consequently, and on the side of the defendants to refute, the fact or assertion that such a security—in substitution of the assignment,—had been given before April 1842, was the main contest at the trial: In proof of the affirmative, a mortgage by the plaintiff to *Stevenson Atkin Bryant* (the deputed attorney) was produced, dated the 3rd September 1841, for the £809 then due, over some houses in Jamison-street, which mortgage, the plaintiff swore, was executed at or about that date. He was repeatedly pressed as to this fact—upon which, of course, the whole question depended; but, misled either by the date or his own impressions, he adhered to the statement.   Against this positive assertion, however, there was the following direct and circumstantial testimony; the united force of which, notwithstanding the verdict, it seems to me impossible to resist.

In the first place, the presentment and protest having been on the 3rd September 1841, the mortgage would not improbably have been prepared bearing that date. But the date of a deed, as every day's experience shows, is no real test of the time of its execution.   The total amount due up to the day of dishonour, including notarial charges, would naturally be filled in as of that day, and interest be made to commence, on the whole, from the same day.   So that, whenever executed, the deed would equally operate to carry out the arrangement. Secondly, there is the test or extreme probability afforded here by the date of registration. The property had been mortgaged by the plaintiff, so recently as the 21st June, for no less a sum than £1500 to the Loan Company, who therefore held the title deeds.   The mortgage to *Bryant*, consequently, being a second one, its speedy registration was of the utmost importance, and moreover, in 1841, deeds registered within a month after execution took effect from that time—whereas, if registered afterwards, they operated from the day of registration only. *Bryant's* mortgage was not registered, however, until the 22nd September 1842.   Thirdly, the plaintiff admitted that, before agreeing to give the mortgage, he had been threatened by *Bryant* with legal proceedings. This adds to the probability (the presentment and dishonour of the bill having only been in September 1841), that the mortgage was not executed in the same month. But, fourthly, the attesting witness to the execution, now a barrister, happened to have himself prepared the draft; and he not merely swore, but showed conclusively, that such draft itself did not exist until 1842.

This paper was produced in evidence, and I have it now before me. The document comprises, in fact, twelve drafts—prepared in one common form. They run in regular sequence, written alternately in red and black ink, and the first in order is dated June 1842. The third is dated 12th June, 1842. The fourth is *Lang's* to *Bryant* and filled in—exactly as in the engrossment, where the date evidently was contemporaneously copied —as 3rd September, 1841, while the next two drafts are dated respectively 1842, and 30th September, 1842. The common form itself, the model for all the drafts, is marked 1842.

Lastly, there is the evidence supplied by the abstract of title. The witness added, that he must have prepared this mortgage (the plaintiff's title being recited in it), from some abstract furnished for the purpose. Such an abstract was produced, from the office of Mr. *Bryant's* then solicitor, now deceased, having his handwriting on the document; and a solicitor, at that time a clerk to the Loan Company, or to the trustees representing them, swore that he prepared that abstract of title in July, 1842. And the document bears internal evidence, that it could not have existed at an earlier period; for two deeds are there mentioned, the stated execution and registration of which are the 21st May and 19th July, respectively, in that year.

It is thus demonstrated, that the mortgage in question was not executed, or even prepared, until some time after the last-mentioned date; and the only disputed allegation in the plea, therefore, that the plaintiff relinquished his salary before giving any other security to Messrs. *Ewing*, was established. In other words, his

T—4

assignment of the salary ·continued in force, at the
moment of, and for months after, the surrender of that
salary. And it is necessary to remember, in connection
with this proved state of things, that the Government
salary was an all-important security to the creditors. If
enforced, the income would have liquidated their claim
in three years. But the mortgage, accepted when that
security had been destroyed, might have been valueless.
Mr. *Bryant* appears to have sold it, in February, 1844
(if the consideration stated in his conveyance to *Breillat*
was the true one), at a sacrifice of the then accrued
interest; and, when transferred to *Wallis* in 1855, the
debt had by arrears increased to £1200 and upwards.

It was suggested on the argument, as at the trial, that
—assuming the mortgage not to have been executed
until after July, 1842,—the negotiations for and *Bryant's*
consent to accept it were in 1841. And the plaintiff
stated, most positively, that there was such a consent in
that year. No one will doubt that there must have been
negotiations of some kind between the parties, and that
at some time there was such a consent. But when this
took place, and whether it was simply to accept a
mortgage, because the salary had ceased to exist, or to
accept it instead of a salary still secured and available, is
another question. The plaintiff, in fixing the date of
such consent, refers evidently to that of the mortgage;
which he believed to be identical, it is clear, with the
time of its execution. He says as follows : " On my
giving Mr. *Bryant* to understand that a mortgage would
be prepared in his favour for the whole amount owing,
he agreed to accept it. This took place about June or
July, 1841. It was distinctly stated by myself, and
understood by him, that he was to be paid the amount
by a mortgage ; and he was actually so paid, in full, on
the 3rd September, 1841." Accordingly, in another part
of his examination—having thus stated the execution of
the deed to have been in 1841—the plaintiff expresses
his belief that the negotiations with *Bryant* preceded it
by a few weeks only. Again, " I am positive that the
transaction with Mr. *Bryant* was closed on the 3rd of

September, 1841 ; that satisfaction was then given, *and* the deed signed.*" But the plaintiff afterwards states, that the bill was presented to Mr. *Lang*, he knows *before* this mortgage. Then he admits some doubts as to the date of the execution, thus, " I will not state positively that the deed was finally executed in 1841, but I am positively certain that the debt was *virtually* cancelled then." Eventually the plaintiff adheres to his first declaration ; saying, at the close of his evidence, that he was confident the mortgage was executed in 1841—he had "no doubt, whatever," on the subject.

To all this, the following considerations have to be opposed. 1st. That the time of the execution being undoubtedly August or September, 1842, the negotiations would (on the plaintiff's own showing) have been in June or July of that year, and not 1841. 2nd. That if, before the 3rd September, 1841, all was arranged between the parties, there seems no conceivable reason why the bill of exchange should have been presented on that day, and a formal protest for non-acceptance drawn up. Those steps were necessary, in order to give a right of action against Dr. *Lang*; but they are apparently inconsistent with the idea of a then pending arrangement, much more a completed settlement between the parties. 3rd. That, if there was such an arrangement at that time, or any time in 1841, there could have been no reason for not at once carrying it into effect. The plaintiff obtained a conveyance to himself of the property, in June 1841. He mortgaged it in the same month to the Loan Company ; and his delay in executing the second mortgage, therefore (on the plaintiff's hypothesis of a virtual settlement with *Bryant* in 1841), is unintelligible. 4th. That since the plaintiff is conclusively shown to be mistaken as to that execution, notwithstanding the most positive allegations, his impressions respecting the time when he negotiated for the mortgage, and when Mr. *Bryant* assented to that arrangement, may not improbably be equally erroneous.

But, be this how it may, the result is, that, as the case now stands, the facts alleged in the plea were proved. The plaintiff's case was, that he substituted an *actual mortgage* for the assignment; and not a mere agreement to mortgage, which in itself was no better than any other agreement. If he desires now to amend that case, by saying that there was specifically such an agreement, and that the agent accepted it, at or about the period stated, in lieu of the then existing and tangible security, an opportunity ought to be afforded the plaintiff of raising that issue. But then, what date will be ascribed to such acceptance? What will be the evidence of it? and if not in writing, how could it be enforced? Such an arrangement must be relied on, as being itself (whether enforceable or not) an abandonment of the salary, both accruing and to accrue after such abandonment;—and then one naturally asks why, if so, the plaintiff's order on the Treasury was not, in testimony of his restored right, forthwith given back to him? Mr. *Bryant*, however, it was stated, is in a neighbouring colony; and unexceptional testimony may be adduced, perhaps, by his assistance, to sustain the plaintiff's explanation.

So much for the matters of fact. The next point for examination is, the finding of the jury on the question of public benefit. On such a question—whether it was for the public benefit, in any given case, that the particular facts alleged should have been published,—opinions may reasonably be expected to differ. There can be no demonstration as to this. And yet, as the reasons for or against the proposition, in every case, must be appreciable alike—supposing the capacity to be equal—by all right-minded men, and depend on no deductions from evidence, of which juries are constitutionally though not irresponsibly the judges, I conceive that a Judge of this Court cannot disclaim the duty, when appealed to on a motion for a new trial, of forming and expressing a perfectly independent opinion, on the propriety of the finding by the jury. But, on such a point, if differing from them, I would desire to do so with becoming respect, and free from overweening or presumptuous confidence. Now the grounds relied on in the plea, in support of the affirmative of the proposition in this case, are these—that the question of state-aid to religion (that is, I presume, of affording to its ministers, or certain classes of them, pecuniary support from the Treasury), was one of great public interest and importance, at and long before the time of the publication ; and that the plaintiff was a member of the Legislature, and as such, and otherwise, had been and was a prominent advocate for the abolition of that aid. In other language, the plaintiff was a public character, and in an elevated position—a clergyman, and a member of Parliament ; for years, while occupying that position, the strenuous opponent of State support to ministers of religion :—the continuance or abolition of that system, at the time of the defendants' publication, continued to be a question of great importance to the community ; and it was for the public interest, therefore, that the circumstances or motives which led to, or influenced that opposition, should be universally known.

That is the main proposition. It is a question of social polity—or of ethics, in the larger sense of the term,—to be determined irrespective of the other, but equally important, question of fact ; that is, whether the matters relied on in exposition of the plaintiff's motives are true. And, upon that abstract question, I cannot hesitate in my opinion. Surely, if a distinguished or prominent man becomes the advocate, as a member of the Legislature and otherwise, for the abolition of State support to ministers of religion, he moreover being himself one, and therefore to all appearance adversely interested, the public—who may be vitally affected by the measure—have a fair right to inquire, and it is for their benefit to be truly told, what that advocacy is really worth. In every discussion, doubtless, the strength of argument is the same, whatever the motives or the interest of the reasoner. But in the discussion of such a question, as of many others, personal character and position add weight to an opinion ; and it is beneficial to the public, therefore, in a view to the formation of their own, in such cases, to be enabled rightly to appreciate both.

The plaintiff put in evidence the report of his address, at the public meeting mentioned in the libel ; on which occasion, he introduced that question of State-aid ; and eulogised the recently passed measure, then under consideration of her Majesty's advisers at home. In that address, he appears to have dwelt on his own exertions in the cause, and to have introduced the defendants' newspaper, in connexion with them. It was to these circumstances, consequently, we may infer, that the libel alluded. Thus:—" It was one of the sayings of *Lamartine*, that every truth must have its Calvary ; and he (Dr. *Lang*) considered it a great honour his fellow-colonists had done him, by making him the victim for the establishment of this great truth in Australia, that the support of religion and its ministers did not require the aid of the State."   And again :—" Twenty years hence it would scarcely be believed, that, during the struggle for so long a period in this colony, no helping hand was held out until the eleventh hour, when the struggle was virtually terminated, and the great battle won ; and that, as far as that distinguished journal the *Sydney Morning Herald*, and the Congregational body in general were concerned, we who were engaged during those dreary years, here and elsewhere, had to fight as it were single-handed and alone."

In my opinion, therefore, the plea of justification—on both points—was established. And since, upon the facts, the verdict was demonstrably erroneous, I think it our duty to send the case to a second trial—although, as to the question of public benefit, the proper conclusion is confessedly a debateable one. It may be said, that certain passages in the publication were not justified. But the only (or undoubtedly the most) important of these is inseparable from the question, on which the majority of the jury so clearly miscarried ; and I cannot conceive it to be just, under such circumstances, to allow a verdict for large damages—founded on that misapprehension—to remain undisturbed.

Even assuming the eleven to have been right, in their opinion, that the grave charge made was not for the public benefit, the same damages would not have been given, we must suppose, had the jury thought that charge a true one. Many of them, moreover, may not improbably have considered, that the publication of a false charge never could be beneficial; and so, on the assumption of its falsehood, have concurred in the opinion. But, however this may be, it is clear to my apprehension that as on the main point the verdict was wrong, it ought to be wholly set aside, in order that both points—and the question of damages, as dependent on them, but more largely on the former—may be re-considered. I am unable to see the formal difficulty suggested, that the defendants have not specifically objected to the damages; because, as I understand the motion, if the verdict as to the facts be right, the damages are not complained of.

I have to report the judgment of Mr. Justice *Wise* as follows. A few days before his departure from Sydney, he sent me a short note stating his opinion; but his state of health was such, that he could attempt no elaboration, and no reasons are given. It was, however, after a conference with both Mr. Justice *Hargrave* and myself, at which our then views of the case were fully expressed. His Honor thinks that, as to the facts, the verdict was clearly against the evidence. But, on the second question, he conceives that—although much doubting whether he should have formed the same opinion—there ought not to be a new trial on that point. His Honor observes, that there was no motion to disturb the verdict for excess of damages; but only because it was against the evidence, on the special plea—and that the Court cannot know, on what parts of the libel the damages were given. I have already expressed my opinion on these points, with the reasons for that opinion. But, as Mr. Justice *Hargrave* agrees substantially with our colleague—on the question of damages, at all events—the result is that the verdict will stand, and the rule obtained by the defendants be discharged with costs.

HARGRAVE, J. I was not a Judge of this Court when the rule *nisi* was granted upon which a new trial has been asked for in this case, and shall confine my remarks to the arguments of the counsel in moving for the rule, and also to the judgment we have just heard. I have read the printed report of the trial, and the various documents, and I do not discover the slightest ground to interfere with the verdict of the jury. His Honor then proceeded to examine the two principal grounds taken by the counsel for the defendants—namely, that the jury were demonstrably wrong on the first issue, and that they were unfit to be trusted in regard to their finding on the second issue. His Honor thought that there was a continuous fallacy throughout the first ground of defendants' argument, namely, that the jury found the mortgage to have been executed on 3rd September, 1841. The verdict was not founded upon any particular date as the one upon which Dr. *Lang* executed this deed. The Judge's summing up and the questions, put by him to the jury, were equally general; the whole of the facts were placed before the jury, and upon these the jury found that Dr. *Lang* had not " disappointed his creditors," or been guilty of that dishonourable conduct which had been imputed to him by the defendants' libel. They came to this conclusion upon the whole of the evidence before them; their finding was legitimately within the scope of the whole evidence, and they endorsed their verdict with very moderate damages. The jury cannot be assumed, therefore, to have found on one particular fact alone. His Honor then proceeded to comment upon the details of the defendants' documentary and parol evidence, more especially with reference to the mortgage deed, the abstract of title, and what was called "the model deed; " and after stating that in his opinion the jury were quite right in apparently rejecting the parol testimony of the defendants' witnesses with reference to the particular dates of minor transactions twenty-five years, as against the written contents of *Bryant's* mortgage—and after commenting on the detailed contents of the defendants' documents, especially the abstract of title and the " model deed," as to which his Honor wholly disagreed from the conclusions arrived at by the Chief Justice—his Honor stated that, upon the facts in evidence before the jury on the first issue, his Honor was quite satisfied that the verdict of the jury was right

Upon the second issue, that the publication of these matters was for the public benefit, his Honor said, in my opinion the jury were right in their finding upon this issue also, because it cannot be fair to require men to preserve exact dates of such negotiations and pecuniary arrangements for so many years. It cannot be useful to hunt up attorneys' offices for these materials after twenty-five years' silence of the creditors, and no accusations meantime from any other person. Even if I were not able to point out the fatal errors in the evidence, to which I have directed attention, I should think the jury were clearly right. The reason is plain and manifest. It is this : if we are to have our properties protected by the Statute of Limitations, are we not to have our honour preserved ? As an Irish Judge once said, " time mows down with relentless scythe all our evidences of title. Parchments fade, and writings become illegible, but the common sense of all nations raises up statutory periods of time, beyond which titles cannot be impugned." So also with our characters and our honour, and the character and honour of those who are dead and gone. Is Dr. *Lang's* honour to be dependent on his recollection or on any other person's recollection of a particular date ? So far from thinking the damages in this case small, I feel no hesitation in saying that, if I had been on that jury, I should have given Dr. *Lang* every farthing of the damages he asked for. The way in which his venerated character was held up to scorn in a public newspaper of large circulation here and in England, such as this, fully entitled him to very heavy damages. It is to me clear and indisputable that the verdict of the jury was perfectly right upon both points.

1865.

December 1.   THE QUEEN *against* DICKSON and another (*a*).

The prisoner being indicted for stealing and receiving certain horses, was acquitted of the stealing, but found guilty of receiving. After the verdict of guilty had been pronounced and minuted by the clerk, the jury said that they recommended the prisoner to mercy, on the ground that they thought that she believed herself to have some claim to the property. The Court held that under the circumstances the verdict was wrong, and that the prisoner ought not to have been convicted. Practice as to the amendment of a criminal case reserved under the 13 Vic., No. 8.

THE prisoners, together with one *Gaven*, were tried before *Hargrave*, J., in October, on an information for stealing certain race-horses. There was also a count for receiving. *Gaven* was acquitted. It appeared that while the horses in question were being exercised, they had been seized by the prisoners; the jockeys made to dismount; the equipments of the horses stripped off and thrown down, and the horses themselves led away. They were then locked up and painted. It was also shown that enquiries for the missing animals had been made by the police, and that the prisoners had denied that they were in their possession. It appeared that the horses had formerly belonged to the prisoner *Dickson*, and that she still claimed them as her property, and that she had directed what had been done for the purpose of obtaining possession of them.

It appeared that after the verdict of guilty of receiving the horses had been pronounced, the prisoners being acquitted of stealing them, and had been minuted by the clerk, the jury said that they recommended the prisoner *Dickson* to mercy, on the ground that she believed herself to have some claim to the property. The prisoner's counsel thereupon submitted that the verdict returned by the jury was equivalent to a verdict of acquittal, and that the Judge ought so to direct it to be entered, or to direct the jury to retire and reconsider their verdict. The question for the consideration of the Court was whether that statement of the jury did not amount to a verdict of acquittal; and that, therefore, the jury ought thereupon immediately to have been so told.

Isaacs, for the prisoner, first asked that the case should be amended.

(*a*) Before *Stephen*, C. J., *Cheeke*, J., and *Faucett*, J.

Per Curiam. Where a case appears on the face of it, or upon the argument, to be imperfectly stated, it will be remitted to the Judge before whom the trial took place for his amendment. Where it is suggested that the case is wrongly stated, either by something having been omitted which ought to have been inserted, or something inserted which ought not to have been inserted, we are clearly of opinion that the proper course is to apply in the first instance—it may be on affidavits —to the Judge who tried the case ; and the Judge is entitled to say that he adheres to the case as stated ; and in such case the Court must take his statement as final. The Court must take the facts from the Judge who is the proper person to state them.

The Court then called on the counsel for the Crown to support the conviction.

Butler for the Crown. Whatever ground there may be for a recommendation for pardon, it is submitted that the circumstances are no ground in point of law for the objection. For the recommendation to mercy is no part of the verdict in any case. It is submitted that the words of Lord *Campbell*, in *Trebilcock's* case (*a*), are in point. " I am not aware that what a jury may say in recommending a prisoner to mercy, is to be taken as any part of the verdict." In that case the prisoner with whom a plate chest full of plate was deposited for safe custody, broke it open, and pledged the plate for a sum which he could not repay. The jury found him guilty of stealing the plate, but recommended him to mercy, on the ground that they believed he intended ultimately to return the property. The Court supported the conviction. In *Crawshaw's* case (*b*) the jury returned a verdict of guilty, but recommended the prisoner to mercy, on the ground that perhaps he did not know that he was acting contrary to law ; and the Court considered the verdict as perfectly valid nevertheless. These authorities show that the verdict and recommendation are distinct, and one does not qualify the other. He also referred to

(*a*) 1 Dears. & B. 575 : 27 L. J. M. C. 103.
(*b*) Bell, C. C. 303 : 30 L. J. M. C. 58.

1865.
___
The QUEEN
v.
DICKSON
and another.

Reg. v. *Meany* (a). But further, it must on the special case be taken that there was a larceny by some person; and if so, this prisoner may have imagined that she had "some claim" to the animals, and yet have been guilty of receiving. The Court will endeavour to make the recommendation consistent with the verdict.

STEPHEN, C. J. If the jury rightly or not were of the opinion that the prisoner *Dickson* believed, when she received the horses, that she had some claim to them, she could not have been lawfully found by them guilty of felony; and the legal conclusion, which the jury drew from the circumstances of concealment, denial, &c., that there was a felonious receiving, was therefore wrong. It may be that this fact of the prisoner *Dickson* believing herself to have some claim, led the jury to acquit her of the stealing; for that she took the horses, there is no manner of doubt whatever. But having acquitted the prisoner of larceny, the jury were equally bound to have acquitted her on the same ground of the felonious receiving also. The conviction was consequently wrong, and it is, therefore, unnecessary to consider whether, in point of form, the jury ought to have been told to reconsider their verdict, or whether their verdict already pronounced was in effect one of acquittal, and so that the Court ought to have directed it to be entered at once as such. We all are of opinion that the verdict and the recommendation having been *uno flatu*, the latter ought to be considered by us. Great reliance has been placed on what Lord *Campbell* said in *Trebilcock's* case, to the effect that the recommendation ought not to be considered as any part of the verdict. But in that same case the Court went on to consider the point, and to show that the conclusion drawn by the prisoner's counsel was unfounded. So also in *Crawshaw's* case in 1860, the Court took the recommendation into their consideration, and says that it did not invalidate the verdict, because ignorance of a statute is no excuse if the statute is violated. I think,

(a) 32 L. J. M. C. 24.

therefore, it is our duty to see what the jury's verdict meant; and it is quite clear to my mind that no other would satisfy their finding than a verdict of acquittal.

CHEEKE, J. The jury have found the prisoner guilty, and recommended her to mercy, on the ground that she believed herself to have some claim. But if there was any claim of right there could be no stealing, and therefore no receiving of property feloniously stolen.

FAUCETT, J. The prisoner *Dickson* was charged with specific acts of larceny and receiving. It is plain that she was present at the act charged as larceny, guiding and directing what was being done. There was evidence enough to support a verdict of guilty, if the jury had chosen so to find. But the jury acquit her of larceny, and therefore they must have considered that in what she did she was not actuated by any felonious intent. If she was not guilty of stealing these animals, how can she be guilty of receiving them having been feloniously stolen? It seems to me that they returned as their verdict that she was guilty of receiving, with a rider showing that they must have been mistaken in that verdict. For if she believed that she had some claim, she could not have had the felonious intent.

Prisoner discharged.

December 16.

In the matter of an arbitration between WARBY and ROSE (a).

A submission to arbitration stated that it was agreed that certain disputes between A. and B. should be referred to certain arbitrators therein named, and it was amongst other things agreed that the costs of preparing and executing the reference and a duplicate thereof should be in the discretion of the said arbitrators. The award adjudged that B. should pay the sum of fifteen guineas, being the costs of the arbitrators in making their award, and that he should bear all his own costs and expenses in relation thereon. The Court set aside the award, on the ground that the arbitrators had not determined by whom and to whom the costs of preparing and executing the reference and a duplicate thereof should be paid.

*M*ARTIN, Q. C., moved to set aside the award in this case, on the ground amongst others that the arbitrators had failed to award who should pay the costs of preparing and executing the submission, and a duplicate thereof. As to this they made no award. They also made none as to the costs of the reference, except that *Rose* should pay all his own and their charges for the award, which they fixed at a stated sum.

The submission, after reciting that disputes and differences had arisen between *Rose* and *Warby*, respecting the liability of the latter to erect certain premises at Wagga Wagga, stated that it was agreed for the final ending of all such disputes that the same should be referred to certain arbitrators therein named; and it was amongst other things agreed that the costs of preparing and executing the said reference and a duplicate thereof should be in the discretion of the said arbitrators.

The award, after determining the question of damages, adjudged that *Rose* should "pay the sum of fifteen guineas, being the costs of the arbitrators in making their award, and that he shall bear all his own costs and expenses in relation thereto;" but did not make any award respecting the costs of preparing and executing the said reference and a duplicate thereof.

Rose's affidavit stated that the reference and a duplicate thereof were prepared and witnessed by his attorney, Mr. *Miller*, whom he had paid for the same; and therefore, he continued, "in directing me to bear my own costs, the said award virtually directed me to pay such costs of preparing and executing the said reference."

Blake showed cause. It is submitted that *Warby* cannot complain of the not determining the costs of the

(a) Before *Stephen*, C. J., *Hargrave*, J., and *Cheeke*, J.

submission. The whole expense was incurred by *Rose*, and he asks nothing for this, as he states in his affidavit. The inference, from the silence of the award, is that each party is left to pay his own costs throughout, except the costs of the award, which are to be paid by *Rose* alone.

Martin in reply. As to the costs of preparing and executing the submission, there may have been and there were other costs besides the mere preparation of the document. On this portion of the reference the award is silent, and therefore is bad. There is nothing to show that if this point had been considered by the arbitrators they would not have given these costs to *Warby*.

STEPHEN, C. J. As the arbitrators have omitted to decide a matter submitted to them, the award must be set aside. They had power to determine by whom and to whom the costs should be paid of preparing and executing the submission. They have not done this, and the Court cannot tell what the amount may be. In this respect the award is, in my opinion, and I say it with great regret, fatally bad. The award must be set aside without costs.

HARGRAVE, J., and CHEEKE, J., concurred.

Ex parte BRADLEY (a).

When upon the plaintiff not appearing a case is struck out under the 63rd section of the District Cour'. Act, the action is at an end, and a District Court Judge has no jurisdiction to restore to the list a case so struck out.

FOSTER moved to make absolute a rule for a prohibition granted on the 29th of August, to restrain the District Court Judge of Sydney, the registrar, and the plaintiff, in the case of *Love* v. *Bradley*, from further proceeding in the said action. In the sittings of the Metropolitan District Court in July, the plaintiff not being present, the case was struck out. Afterwards, the plaintiff asked the Judge to restore the case to the list, and this application was refused. In the sittings in August, the plaintiff applied to another Judge of the same District Court to restore the case, and this application was granted. The question is, whether that Judge had jurisdiction to make the last mentioned order? or whether the case by being struck out was not at an end? It is submitted that the case was at an end, and that the striking out was not merely from the cause list, but from the minute book which is the only record or entry of the case. In August the Court had no jurisdiction over the case at all. There is no provision in the statute enabling the case, when once struck out under the 63rd section, to be restored; and unless empowered by statute, inferior Courts cannot even grant new trials; *Great Northern R. Co.* v. *Mossop* (b). In that case a prohibition issued, because a county Court Judge, after he had once heard and disposed of an application for a new trial, re-heard the case at a subsequent Court. *Jones* v. *Jones* (c) was referred to. On the face of the minute book the entry is that the plaintiff did not appear, and the case was struck out. It is submitted that the minute

(a) Before *Stephen*, C. J., *Cheeke*, J., and *Faucett*, J. The case had been already argued before *Hargrave*, J., and *Cheeke*, J.; but judgment had not been delivered, although there had been an intimation of opinion in favour of the application. The respondent asked that the point, which was an important point of practice, might be re-argued before three Judges. It may be added that the same application had been made in Chambers before *Hargrave*, J., and was refused.

(b) 17 C. B. 138.   (c) 5 D. & L. 628.

book and not the plaint book is the record, and that the
entry in the minute book is conclusive that the case is at
an end. No inconvenience can arise from so construing
the 63rd section, as by the 65th the Judge can grant
time, or adjourn the trial upon such terms as he may
think fit. The 46th and 71st sections of the Act, and
rules 5 and 8, were referred to.

Darley showed cause. First, the case has not been
lawfully struck out, under the 63rd section of the District Courts Act. [*Stephen*, C. J. But the minute
book so states the judgment.] It is submitted that the
words "struck out" have no more stringent or other meaning than the same words in the Supreme Court Practice,
and merely mean struck out from the cause list. The
decision in *Great Northern R. Co.* v. *Mossop* does not
apply ; for in that case the application had been fully
heard, and the matter was *res judicata*. But here the
attempt is being made to prevent any hearing at all.
Can it be supposed that the plaintiff was meant to be
put to a new action, and all the expense of one and the
loss of time thereby caused ? The cause is only struck
out from the minute book, and not from the plaint book.
But it is submitted that the latter only is the record book.

Foster replied.

STEPHEN, C. J. I am of opinion that the prohibition
must go. After the striking out of the case in the
month of July, the Court in August had no jurisdiction,
simply because the action was at an end. The 63rd
section provides what is to be done when the plaintiff
does not appear. When the defendant appears, but
does not admit the demand, the Judge may give him the
costs of the day—to recover which the defendant would
be entitled to bring a separate action. But he does not
get the costs of the action, as in the case of a nonsuit.
Why should there be this provision as to costs, if the
action was to go on? For if the action went on, these
costs could have been taken into consideration on the
taxation. Why should the defendant bring a separate

u—4

1865.

Ex parte
BRADLEY.

action for the costs, unless it was supposed that by being struck out the case was at an end ?   The rules provide that there shall be a plaint book ; this book contains a record of what occurs before the trial.   But the record or quasi record of what occurs at the trial is contained in the minute book.   As the respondent *Lore* has, by his opposition, rendered a second argument necessary, although he was told the Judges were against him on the first argument, he must pay the costs of such second argument.   There will be no costs of the first argument.

CHEEKE, J., and FAUCETT, J., concurred.

HINKLE and wife *against* SCHONBEIN.

A notice signed by the plaintiff's attorney, calling on the defendant to admit a paper to be a copy of a convey-ance "made between *J. P.* of the one part, and the defendant of the other part, original in the possession of the said defendant," is some evidence for the jury of the existence of an executed con-veyance to the effect mentioned.

A husband takes a free-hold interest during the joint lives of himself and his wife

EJECTMENT.   The plaintiff's title at the trial before *Cheeke*, J., in July, 1865, was founded upon a grant from the Crown to the female plaintiff after her marriage, in consideration of money paid by the plaintiff, her husband.   After the plaintiff's case was closed, the defendant tendered in evidence a notice to admit, signed by the plaintiff's attorney, notifying that the plaintiffs proposed to adduce in evidence at the trial the several documents thereunder specified, and that the same might be inspected, &c., calling on the defendant to admit, that "such of the said documents as are specified to be originals were respectively written, signed, or executed, as they purport respectively to have been, and that such as are specified as copies are true copies," &c.   There were then enumerated in the notice—1. a Crown grant to the female plaintiff; 2. a demand of possession; 3. copy of a writ of execution "issued out of the District Court, holden at Grafton, by one *Thomas Fisher*, against the lands tenements and hereditaments of the above named plaintiff, *Gaspar Hinkle*, and signed by *James Page*, as Registrar of the said Court, holden at Grafton,"

land granted by the Crown to the wife after her marriage, in consideration of money paid by the husband, and such interest can be seized and sold under an execution against the husband under the 78th and 79th sections of the District Court Act.

dated, &c.—the original in the possession of *James Page*, Registrar of the District Court, holden at Grafton; 4. copy of an indenture of conveyance or bargain and sale of the land and premises in dispute between the parties in this action, made between *James Page*, as Registrar of the District Court holden at Grafton, of the one part, and the above named defendant of the other part— original in the possession of the above named defendant. The learned Judge rejected the evidence; and the jury having found a verdict for the plaintiff,

Rogers now obtained a rule *nisi* for a new trial, on the ground that the notice was receivable as an admission by the plaintiffs of the existence of the documents specified in the notice, and of the contents thereof.

Darley, for the plaintiff, now showed cause. The question is whether a notice signed by the plaintiffs' attorney, calling on the defendant to admit a paper to be a copy of a " conveyance made between *J. P.* of the one part, and the defendant of the other part; original in the possession of the said defendant," is, or is not some evidence for the jury of the existence of an executed conveyance to the effect mentioned. It is submitted that it affords no such evidence. The admission in *Holt* v. *Squire* (a), where, in an action against the acceptor of a bill, his attorney had served notice on the plaintiff. to produce all papers relating to the bill declared upon, " which said bill " the notice went on to state, " was accepted by the said defendant " was an admission of a specific fact, namely, of its acceptance. So in *Marshall* v. *Cliff* (b), the undertaking, which was as follows—" I hereby undertake to appear for Messrs. *T.* and *M.*, (the plaintiffs) joint owners of sloop Arundel, &c.," was an equally specific admission of ownership. But here there was nothing said as to the execution of this document. But in the next place, if it were otherwise, yet the conveyance (it having been from the registrar of a District Court, under the 79th section of the District Courts

1865.

HINKLE and wife v. SCHONDEIN.

August 28.

December 6.

(a) Ry. & Mood. 282. (b) 4 Camp. 133.

Act) should have been shown to have been duly registered. That section provides, that no such deed of
bargain and sale (executed by the registrar) "shall
operate and be effectual" as a conveyance of the estate,
right, title, and interest of the person named in the *fi.
fa.*, "until the same shall have been duly registered in
the proper office for the registration of deeds, and be in
the index book thereof, in the name of the person whose
interest in such lands and hereditaments is intended to
be thereby conveyed." But it is also submitted that
such a conveyance on a *fi. fa.* could not convey the
wife's estate. The Crown grant was to her after
marriage, in consideration of money paid by the plaintiff,
her husband. This was in law good as a seisin in her.
The same words in a conveyance to husband and wife,
which would make a joint tenancy in other persons, gives
the entirety to them, and the husband as against her
cannot pass any right, title, or interest. The wife
cannot be a trustee for her husband, therefore she is no
trustee at all, and therefore, where there is a purchase
by the husband in the name of his wife, the presumption
exists that it is intended as an advancement to her alone.
The money is an advancement to the wife. In *Kingdom*
v. *Bridges* (a), a married man purchased a walk in a
chase, and took the patent to himself and his wife, and
J. S. for their lives and the life of the longest liver of
them. And the Lord Chancellor held that this should
be presumed an advancement and provision for the wife.
And the same point is decided in *Back* v. *Andrew* (b).
He referred to *Robertson* v. *Norris* (c), *Devoy* v. *Devoy*
(d), Co. Litt. 187 b. ; 1 Cru. Dig. 402, and 1 Ro.
Abr. 271.

Stephen contra. All freeholds of which the wife is
seized at the time of the marriage or afterwards, are by
law vested in the husband and wife, during the coverture,
in right of the wife. During their joint lives the husband
is entitled to the profits, and has the sole control over it.

(a) 2 Vern. 67.   (b) 2 Vern. 120.
(c) 11 Q. B. 916.   (d) 26 L. J. Ch. 290.

Steph. Comm. (*a*). This is a different case from that of a joint estate in the husband and wife. If this land had been purchased by a third person in the wife's name, the husband would clearly have had a life estate in the property. Why not now? If the land had descended to her, the case would be the same. Why not also in a case like this? As to advancement, that consideration had nothing to do with the question. The advancement means merely that after the husband's death the land will be hers, and not belong equitably to the representative of the husband. He referred to *Glaister* v. *Hewer* (*b*).

STEPHEN, C. J. I am clearly of opinion that the notice to admit was some evidence for the jury of the existence of an executed conveyance to the effect mentioned in the notice. It was for the jury to decide whether it was or was not sufficient.

I am also of opinion that the male plaintiff was and is (irrespective of the sale under the execution) seized of the estate during his wife's life, and that estate, assuming the sale to have been established, was and is by such sale transferred to and vested in the purchaser, that is, the defendant. If the law were otherwise, a man by purchasing land in his wife's name would be able to defeat his creditors.

CHEEKE, J., and FAUCETT, J., concurred (*c*).

(*a*) 2 vol. 274. (*b*) 8 Ves. 199.
(*c*) See *Greeneley's* case, 8 Rep. 71 b; *Doe* v. *Parrat*, 5 T. R. 654; *Green* v. *King*, 2 Bl. Rep. 1211.

GOLDING and another *against* HUMBLE and another.

In an action for an infringement of a patent, the invention of a gold amalgamator, with a count in detinue for the machine, a Judge had granted ex parte an injunction, under the Common Law Procedure Act, restraining the defendants from using the machine. On motion to dissolve the injunction—the defendants' case being that they purchased the machine from a third person authorised by the plaintiffs to sell it—the Court dissolved the injunction, on the ground that whether it was an infringement of a patent or not, it was not a case for an injunction.

December 15.

MARTIN, Q. C., moved for and obtained a rule to dissolve an injunction granted under the 47th section of the Common Law Procedure Act of 1857 (a), by *Hargrave*, J., in Chambers, restraining the defendants from using a certain engine for extracting gold, &c., from ores.

An action had been brought for the infringement of a patent right, the invention of a gold amalgamating machine, granted by the Governor, under the 16 Vic., No. 24, to the plaintiffs. There was also a count for the detention of such a machine.

The defendants' case was that they had purchased the machine in question from one *Minehan*, with whom it had been left by the plaintiffs as collateral security for certain advances made to them by *Minehan*, and that the latter had authorised the sale in case of non-payment. The defendants did not claim any right to use the invention, or to imitate it.

The plaintiffs admitted some of the advances, but denied that *Minehan* had any lien over the machinery, or any authority to sell it.

Martin, Q. C., and *Salamons* now moved to make the rule absolute. It is submitted that the injunction ought not to have been granted *ex parte*. The proper practice is to grant a rule to show cause only in the first instance ; *Gittens* v. *Symes* (b). The present case is merely a dispute about the property in the particular machine, and is not a proper one for an injunction. The Court cannot issue an injunction ordering the defendants not to detain this machine, for the right to detain is the specific point to be tried. This injunction enjoins the defendants not to use property which they claim as their own.

(a) 20 Vic., No. 31.　　　　(b) 15 C. B. 362.

Butler showed cause. *Gittens* v. *Symes* only shows the practice which the Court of Common Pleas have thought fit to adopt. He referred to *Mayall* v. *Higbey* (a). It is submitted that this is a patent of a particular subject matter—of a particular machine which the plaintiffs have an exclusive right to use.

Salamons, in reply, referred to *Carnes* v. *Nesbitt* (b).

STEPHEN, C. J. I am of opinion that the injunction ought to be dissolved. Assuming this to be a case of the infringement of a patent, which in my opinion is doubtful, it is not a case in the exercise of a sound discretion for an injunction. It is a question of disputed property. The defendants say that they bought the machine from a person who had a right to sell it; and that vendor and his wife say that they had a right to sell it. But the plaintiffs say that the vendor had no such right, and that as it is a patented article, the defendants have been guilty of an infringement of their patent. I give no opinion whether this is a case of an infringement of a patent. I think it safer, in order to prevent ruin to the defendants without doing any good to the plaintiffs, to dissolve the injunction. Ought the machine to remain idle, after the defendants have paid money for it? The Court must consider the balance of inconveniences; and it seems to me that the injunction is likely to cause more inconvenience to the defendants than convenience to the plaintiffs. The costs of this motion to be costs in the cause generally.

CHEEKE, J., concurred.

FAUCETT, J. I guard myself from any expression of opinion whether this is an infringement of a patent.

(a) 31 L. J. Ex. 329.   (b) 30 L. J. Ex. 348.

Ex parte McLaren.

The Court
will not, on a
summary ap-
plication,
order the
town agent of
a country
attorney to
pay over to
the client
money be-
longing to
the latter,
received by
the agent
under in-
structions
from the
country attor-
ney, unless
there be some
fraud or neg-
ligence, or
other special
circumstance.

December 9.

A RULE had been obtained calling on a town agent of a country attorney to show cause why he should not pay over to the client certain money belonging to the latter, and received by the town agent under instructions from the country attorney.

The town agent claimed a right to retain the amount, because, as he alleged, the country attorney was then and still is indebted to him for business generally in a larger sum. This indebtedness was denied by the country attorney, who swore that the respondent had promised to render an account, and had not done so.

Martin, Q. C., now moved to make the rule absolute. In *Hanley* v. *Cassan* (a), the town agent of the attorney for the plaintiff in a suit received the sum sued for from the defendant, and at the request of the plaintiff's attorney set it off against advances in an account between them. The Court compelled the town agent to pay the amount *de novo*, he not showing that there was an account between the plaintiff and his attorney, with a balance in favour of the latter. *Alderson*, B., saying that the agent must be treated as agent for the party to the action.   This case is referred to and distinguished in *Robbins* v. *Fennell* (b), where it was held that for want of privity the client could not bring an action for money had and received against the town agent, in respect of the proceeds of the cause which the latter may have received in the ordinary course of his business. The present is a summary application, as in *Hanley* v. *Cassan*, and it is not necessary, therefore, to show any contract as in the case of an action. In *Moody* v. *Spencer* (c) the town agent having received money in the course of the suit from the opposite party, was held to have received it to the use of the client.

(a) 11 Jur. 1188.   (b) 11 Q. B. 248.   (c) 2 D. & R. 6.

Foster having referred to *Robbins* v. *Heath* (a), *Cobb* v. *Becke* (b), and *Ex parte Jones* (c), was stopped by the Court.

STEPHEN, C. J. The rule must be discharged. The town agent cannot be made responsible to the client, for there is no privity between them, unless there be some fraud or negligence, or other special circumstances (such as perhaps that he is clearly indebted to the country attorney, although as to this case I should entertain very great doubts), to fix a personal liability on him. But, as here, the respondent has not shown clearly that the country attorney is indebted to him; and as he has repeatedly promised to render an account, and has not done so, we discharge the rule without costs.

CHEEKE, J., and FAUCETT, J., concurred.

STOCKDALE *against* HAMILTON and another.

December 5.

THE first count stated that for a long time, before and at the time of the commencement of this suit, the plaintiff was and from thence continually has been and now is seized of and entitled to, at law and in equity, in fee simple, and was and is lawfully and rightfully in the actual, peaceable, and exclusive possession, occupation, and enjoyment, by himself and his tenants, of certain land in this colony (to wit), 2000 acres of land at *The first count of a declaration framed under the 23rd section of the Real Property Act, alleged that the plaintiff was seized and was in possession of land, and that* the defendants knew these facts, but that the defendants, notwithstanding, falsely alleged themselves to be seized and in possession, and thereupon applied for a title under the Act. The second count omitted the allegation that the plaintiff was seized, and the allegation that the defendants knew of the plaintiff's title. The third count alleged both seisin and possession, but omitted the statement that the defendants knew either fact. The fourth count alleged only possession in the plaintiff. In all other respects, every count was the same as the first. The acts complained of were stated in exactly the same terms, and so was the resulting damage. On motion to strike out three of the four counts, the Court confined the plaintiff to the first count, on the ground that the four counts were founded on the same cause of action, and in violation of the Reg. Gen. T. T., 1853 (Pl.) r. I.

(a) 11 Q. B. 257 in notn. (b) 6 Q. B. 936.
(c) 2 D. P. C. 161.

Brisbane Water; that the defendants, after the time
when the "Real Property Act" came into operation,
falsely claimed, pretended, alleged, and declared to the
Registrar General of the said colony and otherwise, that
they were the persons in whom the fee simple of the said
land was vested in possession, at law or in equity, and
that they were jointly seized of an estate of inheritance
in fee simple, in the said land, and took proceedings and
made application to the said Registrar General, and
otherwise, to bring the said land under the provisions of
the said act, and to obtain a certificate of title under the
said act that they were the persons in whom the fee
simple of the said land was vested in possession as aforesaid, and that they were seized of an estate of inheritance
in the said land, and in and by such proceedings and
application falsely alleged and declared that they were
seized of an estate of inheritance in fee simple, in the
said land; that whilst the plaintiff was so seized of and
entitled to and was in such possession and occupation of
the said land as aforesaid, as the defendants well knew,
they, the defendants, so as aforesaid, falsely claimed,
pretended, alleged, and declared, and continued to
falsely claim, pretend, allege, and declare to the said
Registrar General and otherwise, that they were the
persons in whom the fee simple of the said land was
vested, in possession at law or in equity as aforesaid, and
that they were jointly seized of an estate of inheritance
in fee simple in the said land, and carried on and made
and continued to carry on and make the said proceedings
and application to the said Registrar General and otherwise, to bring the said land under the provisions of the
said act, and to obtain such certificate of title as aforesaid
under the said act, that they were the persons in whom
the fee simple of the said land was vested in possession
as aforesaid; and whilst the plaintiff was so seized and
entitled to, and was in such possession and occupation of,
the said land as aforesaid, as the defendants well knew,
caused the said Registrar General and other official
persons in that behalf, to take and continue and carry on
proceedings for bringing the said land under the pro-

visions of the said act, and for granting to, and in favour of, the defendants such certificate of title in and by them to the said land as aforesaid, whereas the defendants were not and never were persons in whom the fee simple of the said land was vested in possession, or otherwise at law or in equity, and were not and never were seized of an estate of inheritance in fee simple in the said land, but on the contrary never had, and have not, any right, title, or interest whatsoever at law or in equity, or otherwise in or to the said land, as they well knew; by means of which said wrongful acts of the defendants the plaintiff has been put to great trouble and expense in defending and protecting himself and his right, title, estate, and interest in and to the said land, and to the possession and occupation thereof, and against the said application and attempts of the defendants to bring the said land under the provisions of the said act, and to obtain such certificate of title in them to the said land as aforesaid, and has been otherwise greatly injured. Averment, that within the period of three months before the commencement of this suit, he duly entered and lodged with the said Registrar General a caveat, in pursuance of the provisions of the said act, forbidding the bringing of the said land under such provisions; and he has brought this suit to establish his title to the said land, and his said right, title, estate, and interest therein and thereto, and to obtain from this honorable Court an order and injunction restraining the defendants and the said Registrar General from bringing the said land under the provisions of the said act, as well as to recover damages from the defendants for the injury he has sustained by and in consequence of their said wrongful acts. Averment, that within three months from the receipt by the said Registrar General of the said caveat, the plaintiff in pursuance of the provisions of the said act, duly gave notice in writing to the said Registrar General of this action, and of the nature and purpose thereof.

The second count omitted the allegation that the defendant was seized, and the allegation that the defendant knew of the plaintiff's title.

The third count alleged both seisin and possession, but omitted the statement that the defendant knew either fact.

The fourth count alleged only possession in the plaintiff.

In all other respects every count was the same as the first. The acts complained of were stated in exactly the same terms, and so was the resulting damage.

(a) *Darley* now moved to strike out three out of the four counts of the declaration, on the ground that all the four counts were founded on the same cause of action; that they were in contravention of the first Pleading Rule of Trinity Term, 1853, and of the 21st General Rule of the 12th April, 1856. He also asked that the count not sought to be struck out should be amended as being embarrassing. These counts were framed under the 21st and 23rd sections (b), in connection with the 13th section of the Lands Transfer Act. They are all clearly framed on the same subject matter. He referred to *Mercer* v. *Stanbury* (c), and *Day's* Common Law Procedure Act (d).

Isaacs showed cause. The words, same cause of action, does not mean the same state of facts. The test whether the counts are not distinct, is whether they would not each require different evidence to support them.

(a) A summons had been taken out returnable in Chambers, but the matter had been by consent referred to the full Court.

(b) 26 Vic., No. 9, sec. 21 enacts—"Any person having or claiming an interest in any land so advertised as aforesaid, or the attorney of any such person may within the time by any direction of the Commissioners for that purpose limited, lodge a caveat with the Registrar General in form B, of the schedule hereto, forbidding the bringing of such land under the provisions of this Act, and every such caveat shall particularize the estate, interest, lien or charge claimed by the person lodging the same, and the person lodging such caveat, shall, if required, deliver a full and complete abstract of his title."

Sec. 23 enacts—"After the expiration of three months from the receipt thereof, every such caveat shall be deemed to have lapsed, unless the person by whom or on whose behalf the same was lodged shall, within that time, have taken proceedings in any Court of competent jurisdiction to establish his title to the estate, interest, lien or charge therein specified, and shall have given written notice thereof to the Registrar General, or shall have obtained from the Supreme Court an order or injunction restraining the Registrar General from bringing the land therein referred to under the provisions of this Act."

(c) 25 L. J. Ex. 316.   (d) p. 387.

In *Gilbert* v. *Hales* (a), counts stating the cause of
action to have arisen out of the law merchant, other
counts stating it to have arisen out of the law of France,
and a third set of counts out of an agreement between
the parties, were allowed to remain together on the
record. In *Miller* v. *Ross* (b), this Court decided that
the Court or Judge might allow any number of counts,
which the circumstances of the case rendered it reasonable for the plaintiff to have. In this case it is a new
kind of action arising under the Real Property Act, for
a new injury. The plaintiff has duplicate counts for
injury done to him as the owner of the freehold, or failing to prove freehold, as being in lawful possession; in
one case alleging that the defendants knew his title; in
the other, omitting such allegation. Unless the Court is
now prepared to say that the *scienter* is immaterial,
these two series of counts will be allowed. If the plaintiff
were to fail through any technicality in this action, he is
left altogether without remedy, as the three months
within which he must take proceedings are passed.

STEPHEN, C. J. I am of opinion that the plaintiff
must be confined to the first count. That count alleges
that the plaintiff was seized, and was in possession of
land, and that the defendant knew these facts; but that
the defendant, notwithstanding, falsely alleged himself
to be seized and in possession, and thereupon applied for
a title under the act. If all these facts were made out,
it would still be a question whether an action would lie.
That question would arise either on demurrer or in
arrest of judgment. In this state of things the defendant
may deny the plaintiff's title or his possession; or the
defendants' knowledge of either the one or the other; or
lastly, he may allege that he did not know that he
himself had no title. The plaintiff might then reply by
questioning the materiality of either of these issues
tendered by the defendant. He might say it is immaterial whether I have a freehold title; possession is
sufficient. Or my possession is immaterial; it is suf-

(a) 2 D. & L. 227 ; 13 L. J. Ex. 333.   (b) 1 May, 1863.

ficient that I have a legal title, and that you know it. Or the plaintiff might demur to the sufficiency of the fourth issue, and say, "you knew you were not in possession, and therefore had no *locus standi* to take these proceedings before the Registrar General."

Further, if the plaintiff were to take issue on these allegations of the defendants, the case might go to trial; and then the Court having before them the finding of the jury on all these facts, would be able to decide the whole question. In my opinion this result can be more satisfactorily arrived at by one count. The Legislature also has said that there shall not be two counts for the same subject matter of complaint. There is no doubt the language of the 23rd section is difficult to construe; and that it would have been better to have enacted that proceedings should have been stayed until a specific issue, as for instance, whether *A* or *B*. were entitled, should be determined. The count does not seem to be framed so as to embarrass the defendant.

CHEEKE, J., concurred.

FAUCETT, J. The first count seems to me to be sufficient. If the plaintiff does not succeed on that count, he cannot do so on any of the others. The defendant can plead, and when the issues are found the Court can say whether the action will lie or not.

Order accordingly.

MILLER *against* HENNESSY (a).

December 16.

D^{ARLEY} moved to rescind an order made by Hargrave, J., in Chambers, referring the plaintiff's bill of costs, for which this action was brought, to be taxed. The bill, which was for £34 16s. 4d., had been delivered on the 27th March, 1865. The summons issued on the 20th September, and was served on the 4th October in the Albury district. An appearance was entered on the 17th October. The declaration was filed the following day, endorsed with notice to plead in twelve days. The time to plead, therefore, expired on the 30th October, and judgment was signed on the 1st of November. On the same morning the defendant's attorney asked the plaintiff's attorney to wait till he took out a summons to tax. It was sworn that if taxed the bill would probably be reduced "much below" £30. A summons in Chambers for a reference was granted on the 3rd of the same month, and on the 9th the order now complained of was made. It is submitted this order ought not to have been made. The second section of the Attorneys Act (b) provides that no such reference shall be directed upon an application by the party chargeable after judgment signed, after such bill shall have been delivered, "except under special circumstances to be proved to the satisfaction of the Supreme Court or a Judge thereof, to whom the application for such reference shall be made." The learned Judge thought that the circumstance, that the amount might be reduced below £30, was a special circumstance within this section. He referred to *Cowdell* v. *Neale* (c), and *In re Whicher* (d).

Plaintiff sued for the amount of an attorney's bill, and signed judgment for £34 15s. 6d. It was sworn by the defendant's attorney that if taxed the bill would be reduced much below £30; and also that on the same morning on which and before judgment was signed, he asked the plaintiff's attorney to wait till he could take out a summons to tax. *Held* (*Hargrave*, J., *dissentiente*), that these were not special circumstances under the proviso of the second section of the Attorneys Act, enabling a Judge to order a reference to taxation.

Butler, on the other side, referred to *In re Dearden* (e).

(a) Before *Stephen*, C. J., *Hargrave*, J., and *Cheeke*, J.
(b) 11 Vic., No. 33.   (c) 26 L. J. C. P. 37.
(d) 13 M. & W. 549.   (e) 23 L. J. Ex. 14.

STEPHEN, C. J.   The question is, what are "special circumstances" under the proviso of the second section of the Attorneys Act?   The judgment was signed for £34 16s., and it is sworn that if taxed the bill will probably be reduced below £30.   The defendant's object is to deprive the plaintiff of the costs of the action. Another "special circumstance" relied on is, that before the judgment was signed, that is, on the same morning, the defendant's attorney asked the plaintiff's attorney to wait till he could take out a summons to tax.   I am of opinion that neither of these matters is a special circumstance within the meaning of the statute.   It appears that the bill was delivered eight months before the summons issued ; and the defendant, therefore, must have had perfect knowledge of what he was sued for.   On the morning when judgment was signed, the plaintiff's attorney was asked to wait till the other side could get an order to tax.   He said "no, your object is to prevent me suing in the Supreme Court," and he signed judgment.   Why is the Court to deprive him of advantages given him by law, there being no irregularity in his proceedings ?

HARGRAVE, J.   I differ with great respect from the judgment of the Chief Justice.   It seems to me that the Legislature, by using the words "special circumstances," and leaving that question to the discretion of the Judge, has not limited the exercise of that discretion to any particular class of circumstances.   A latitude is left by the Legislature to the Judge.   The bill itself, in this case, was not before me.   But there was evidence, which was uncontradicted, that if taxed the bill would be reduced below £30.   In such case the plaintiff would not get his costs of suing in the Supreme Court without a Judge's certificate.   That seemed, and still seems to me, a special circumstance.   There had been a quickness in the plaintiff's proceedings with a view to obtain money, that is, these costs, to which it would seem he was not legally entitled.   Another circumstance was the great distance of the defendant's residence, which was near the Murray.

The action was brought in Sydney. The proceedings, therefore, especially as the plaintiff had been lying on his oars for eight months—and after such long delay started into sudden activity—ought not to be hurried on. The defendant also had not put the plaintiff to any trouble by pleading. All these things taken together amount, in my opinion, to such special circumstances as the statute requires.

CHEEKE, J. I concur in the opinion of the Chief Justice, and think that there are not any special circumstances in this case.

Rule absolute.

1865.

MILLER
v.
HENNESSY.

KEEP and another *against* BENJAMIN (a).

December 1.

SALAMONS moved to set aside an order of *Hargrave*, J., to hold the defendant to bail, and all subsequent proceedings, on the ground that the affidavit upon which the order was made did not sufficiently show that the action was likely to be defeated.

The affidavit in question stated that the defendant was a storekeeper, carrying on business in Brisbane, in the colony of Queensland, and had been in Sydney for about ten days; and that the deponent was informed that the defendant had that day gone to the plaintiff's attorney's office, and stated that he was going to Brisbane the next day. The plaintiffs are Sydney merchants, who have supplied the defendant with goods. The words of the section (b) are, "that such action will be defeated," and that has been construed to mean the defendant not being within the jurisdiction of the Court at the time of final judgment therein, so as to be then taken in execution; *Bank of Australasia* v. *Dunlop* (c). But the section was never intended to apply to cases like

An affidavit to hold to bail stated that the defendant was a storekeeper, carrying on business in Brisbane, in Queensland; that he had been in Sydney for ten days, and had stated to the plaintiff's attorney that he was going to Brisbane the next day. *Held*, insufficient.

The affidavit must either state that the action will be probably defeated in the words of the statute, or must state

circumstances from which that result can reasonably and naturally, and not by conjecture merely, be deduced.

(a) Before *Stephen*, C. J., *Cheeke*, J., and *Faucett*, J.
(b) 3 Vic., No. 15, s. 2. (c) *Steph*. Sup. Ct. Pr. 125.

v—4

the present, when the liability is incurred by a person resident out of the jurisdiction to a person within it. The word "remove" implies that there must have been a previous residence. The onus of showing that the action will be defeated lies on the plaintiffs, and there is nothing to show that the defendant has not property in this colony.

Darley showed cause. The decision of the learned Judge was right. The facts disclosed were sufficient to induce him to believe that the defendant, resident in Queensland, would not be in this colony at the time of final judgment. No facts are alleged which would lead to the inference that the action will not be defeated. Any irregularity in the affidavit has been waived by the defendant putting in special bail; *Greene* v. *Glassbrook* (a), *Holliday* v. *Lawes* (b), *Mammatt* v. *Mathew* (c).

Salamons in reply. In this colony the proceedings for the arrest and in the action are quite collateral. If special bail were not put in, an action would immediately be brought on the bail bond.

STEPHEN, C. J. .I am of opinion that the meaning, under the now existing state of the law, of an action being "probably defeated" must be taken to be that the plaintiff will not be able eventually to obtain satisfaction in this colony for his debt. It seems to me, therefore, that the affidavit of debt in support of the arrest must either state this probable result in the terms used in the statute, or must state circumstances from which that result can reasonably or naturally, and not by conjecture merely, be deduced. Here it is stated that the defendant is residing in Queensland, and carrying on business there. It may seem probable; therefore, that he will not come back to this colony. But is that the only inference to be drawn? The affidavit does not say that he has no property in, or that he is not likely to return to, this colony. I do not think the affidavit

(a) 1 B. N. C. 516.   (b) 3 B. N. C. 541.
                (c) 10 Bing. 506.

sufficient. We set aside the order, and direct the special bail bond to be cancelled with six guineas costs.

CHEEKE, J., and FAUCETT, J., concurred.

Order accordingly.

THE QUEEN *against* CYRIL CECIL.

September 8.

S*ALAMONS* obtained a rule calling upon the defendant to show cause why an information should not be exhibited against him, for writing and sending through the post to *N. J. Crocker* a libellous letter. The letter was as follows:—

Sydney, 22nd July, 1865.

SIR,—You called at my house this afternoon. Do not call there again; if I find you there I will kick you out of it. I have now discovered what those who have known you many years knew long ago, viz., that you are a dastardly mean coward. None but an infamous villain could be so base as to insult me in my present position, in the way you have done. You told my wife an impudent falsehood, when you said that I avoided you this morning. You know as well as I do that I came out of one door in Messrs. *Richardson* and *Wrench's* Auction Room expressly for the purpose of meeting you, thinking there was another opening into the room in that side of the building in which you were. If ever I avoided you, it was not on account of the money I owed you, but because you were a *thing* too loathsome to come near.

I have had business transactions with people of all nations, but never have I met with a more detestable wretch than yourself. I bitterly repent having got into your debt. But no one knows better than yourself that it has been utterly out of my power to repay you. You well knew at the time you were menacing me that for many months I have been doing nothing. You shall have all the money I owe you, and at the same time all the contempt and scorn I can heap upon you. Rest assured of this. In one thing I shall be honest and constant in my hatred of yourself. I hate you well. I hate you honestly.—Yours,

C. *Cecil.*

The affidavit of the prosecutor (who was a person engaged in mercantile pursuits) in support of the rule, after verifying the letter, denied that there had been anything in his language or conduct which could have misled the defendant in applying to him such offensive language; and stated that an apology had been demanded, but not made. He also deposed that he

Where the defendant sent by post to A. (a person engaged in mercantile pursuits, but not occupying any public position) a letter containing a libel upon him, couched in the most gross and offensive terms, and calculated to cause a breach of the peace, the Court discharged a rule for a criminal information, on condition that the defendant paid the costs of the motion.

believed that the libel was calculated and intended to excite to a breach of the peace.

Affidavits in answer by the defendant and his wife having been filed, making several counter charges, *Salamons* who now moved to make the rule absolute, asked for leave to file affidavits in reply to the new matter set up by these affidavits, under the eighteenth section of the Common Law Procedure Act of 1857 (a). This practice has been allowed in order to prevent the necessity of a second application where the first has been rendered ineffectual by perjured testimony, as in *R.* v. *Eve* (b).

Isaacs, for the defendant, relied on this new matter in defence, and opposed the application for leave to file affidavits in reply, on the ground that the Common Law Procedure Act did not apply to criminal proceedings. No case will be found in which such leave has been granted.

Per Curiam. Let the argument proceed on the affidavit now filed, and it may not be necessary to give any opinion on the present point (c). ·

Isaacs showed cause, and contended that enough was disclosed by the affidavits filed in answer to prevent the Court granting this extraordinary remedy.

Salamons replied.   •

STEPHEN, C. J. I am of opinion that the present rule must be discharged, but on the condition only that the defendant shall pay the costs of the motion. He ought to pay the costs, because the offence is clearly established, and the libel is couched in the most gross and offensive terms. The defendant also was asked to

(a) 20 Vic., No. 31. This section enacts that, "upon motions founded upon affidavits, it shall be lawful for either party, with leave of the Court or a Judge, to make affidavits in answer to the affidavits of the opposite party, upon any new matter arising out of such affidavits, subject to all rules as shall hereafter be made respecting such affidavits.

(b) 5 A. & E. 780.
(c) See *Grady* and *Scotland's* Cr. Pr. 21 ; Corner Cr. Pr. 170; 1 Ch. Cr. L. 861.

withdraw it, and ought to have done so; but he has
refused to do so, and has sought to justify the language
appearing in this paper by counter charges, which we
cannot regard as justifying or excusing such a letter.
Nor, since the prosecutor has not been allowed to
reply to these charges, and the matters charged are
entirely new, and could not reasonably have been anticipated by him (for the letter in no way refers to them),
can we say that they show conclusively matters of
extenuation ? But, unless the defendant shall compel the
further prosecution of the case by refusing to accept the
condition, we refuse the information. This is an unusual and peculiar mode of prosecution, and demands
extraordinary circumstances to call for its interference;
but here, in the first place, the libel affects no public
person, or person in high station, in whose character the
community generally can have an interest—or any
question or matter in itself of public interest or importance. Nor is the offence (however gross as it affects
the prosecutor) of that heinous kind to call for either
speedy or unusual interference. The prosecutor, therefore, should be left to the ordinary remedy and course of
procedure, by application to the magistrates as in other
cases of misdemeanor, or direct application upon affidavit
to the Attorney-General as the quasi grand jury.

1865.

The QUEEN
v.
CYRIL CECIL.

Rule discharged on payment of costs by the
defendant ; otherwise, rule absolute.

December 20.

BUCKLEN against KAY (a).

Drawer and payee against the acceptor of a bill of exchange, dated 10th December, 1864, and payable to the plaintiff's order three months after date. Plea, that by a contemporaneous agreement in writing the money was not to be paid until the expiration of six months from the date of the bill. Averment, that the agreement and the acceptance constituted and were one and the same contract. Replication, that the agreement mentioned in the plea is one and the same agreement, and was and is in the words and figures following, &c. It then set out a mortgage, dated the 9th December, 1864, of a share in a claim for £150,

ASSUMPSIT by drawer and payee against the acceptor of an overdue bill of exchange for £150, dated 10th of December, 1864, and payable to the order of the plaintiff three months after date.

Plea, that at the time of the alleged acceptance it was agreed in writing between the plaintiff and the defendant, as part of the same contract with the acceptance of the said bill, that the money in the said bill mentioned should not be payable by the defendant to the plaintiff, nor should the defendant be called upon to pay the same, or any part thereof, to the plaintiff, until the expiration of six months from the date of the said bill; and the defendant accepted the said bill on the terms of the said agreement, and not otherwise; and the said agreement and the said acceptance always constituted and were one and the same contract and inseparable parts thereof. Averment of the fulfilment of all conditions precedent, and that by reason of the premises the time for the payment of the money in the bill mentioned has not, according to the said agreement, yet elapsed.

Replication, that the agreement mentioned in the plea is one and the same agreement, and was and is in the words and figures following, and not otherwise. The replication then set out at length an agreement between the plaintiff and defendant, which, after reciting that the defendant was entitled to one-half share in a prospecting claim near Albury, and had applied to the plaintiff for £150, which the latter had agreed to advance upon the repayment being secured out of the said one-half share of the said claim, witnessed that in consideration of with a proviso that should the defendant repay the £150, together with interest, "within six months from the date hereof," the agreement should be void.

Held, on demurrer, that if it sufficiently appeared on the record that the loan was the sole consideration for the bill, and that there was only one transaction, it would be a good defence at law; and the pleadings were allowed to be amended to raise this defence.

(a) Before Stephen, C. J., Cheeke, J., and Faucett, J.

£150 then paid by the plaintiff to the defendant, the latter transferred to the former all his right, title, and interest in the one-half share of the said claim, with a proviso that should the defendant repay the said sum of £150, " together with interest thereon, at the rate now chargeable at the Bank of New South Wales, Albury, within six months from the date hereof, then this agreement shall be null and void, otherwise it shall remain in full force and virtue. In witness whereof the parties aforesaid have hereunto signed their names and affixed their seals this ninth day of December, 1864." The replication then alleged the identity of the parties.

Demurrer and joinder.

Darley in support of the demurrer. It is submitted that the agreement relied on by the defendant is an inseparable part of the bill sued upon. The replication shows that its legal effect is correctly stated in the plea. *Wake* v. *Harrop* (a) is an authority that although the bill cannot be altered by parol evidence, a contemporaneous agreement may be efficient to control its meaning. There a defendant having on the face of a written document contracted as a principal, the Court held that it was competent to him by way of equitable plea to an action against him, to show that, in fact, he signed as agent for a third party, and that the plaintiff verbally agreed that he should not be responsible as a principal.

Salamons in support of the replication. Verbal evidence is not admissible to contradict or vary the absolute engagement on the face of a bill or note; *Hoare* v. *Graham* (b). Although this rule does not apply to a contemporaneous agreement in writing between the parties, *Brown* v. *Langley* (c), yet in such case the agreement must be parcel of the contract, and not collateral; *Webb* v. *Spicer* (d), *Spiller* v. *Westlake* (e). But here there is no allegation identifying the bill sued upon with the amount mentioned in the mortgage. There is nothing to show that that bill is the amount

(a) 30 L. J. Ex. 273.   (b) 3 Camp. 57.   (c) 4 M. & G. 466.
(d) 13 Q. B. 86.   (e) 2 B. & Ad. 156.

referred to in the agreement, *Brill* v. *Crick* (a), and extrinsic evidence is not admissible for that purpose. The bill is also a day later in date than the date of the mortgage.

Darley in reply. It must be taken on these pleadings to be admitted that the agreement set out in the replication is the agreement on which the defendant relies in his plea. Before the Common Law Procedure Act, the plaintiff would have craved oyer of the deed, thus making it part of the previous pleading, and demurred; but now the documents set out are to be taken to be part of the pleading in which they are set out. [*Stephen*, C. J. What is there on the record to show that there was not some other agreement by which this bill should be given? There is also no averment that the consideration for the bill was no other than the loan secured by the mortgage. Is it, moreover, anything more than an equitable plea?]

STEPHEN, C. J. On the whole, I am of opinion that the defendant has a defence to this action, if the necessary facts appeared on the record to show that the loan was the sole consideration for the bill, and that there was only one transaction between these parties. The defence, therefore, is good at law. I think, however, that the defendant must amend. I have had some doubt whether the words, " the said agreement and the said acceptance always constituted and were one and the same contract and inseparable parts thereof," are sufficient. But it is clear that, as by the bill the amount is payable to the order of the plaintiff, and on the 13th of March; whereas by the mortgage, the amount is payable to the plaintiff himself, and on the 9th of June, the contracts are not one and the same, although it may be there was only one transaction. The plea is also incorrect, for alleging that it was agreed that the bill should not be payable until the expiration of six months from the date of the bill; whereas the words of the agreement are " within six

(a) 1 M. & W. 236.

months from the date" of the agreement. The demurrer, therefore, must be overruled, with costs to be paid by the defendant; but we give leave to the defendant to amend without payment of costs. Costs of the amendment to be costs in the cause.

BUCKLEN
v.
KAY.

CHEEKE, J., and FAUCETT, J., concurred.

Judgment accordingly.

LEVY against SMITH.

THE first count of the declaration stated that the defendant, on the 6th of August, 1863, by his promissory note now overdue, promised to pay to one *S. Ashlin* or order the sum of £237 8s. 1d., four months after the date thereof; and *S. Ashlin* then indorsed the said note to the plaintiff, but the defendant did not pay the same. There was a second count for another promissory note of £251 17s. 3d.

Action by the indorsee against the maker of two promissory notes, payable to S. A. or order, and by him indorsed to the plaintiff.

Plea—that after the de- livery of the promissory notes to *S. A.*, and while they remained his property and part of his estate, he was indebted to the plaintiff and divers other persons; and that *S. A.* indorsed and delivered the notes, he being at the time insolvent, within sixty days before his sequestration; and that such indorsement and delivery had the effect of preferring the plaintiff, being a creditor as aforesaid, to others of his then existing creditors. The plea also alleged the fact of the due sequestration of *S. A.*'s estate, and the appointment of an assignee thereof; and that by him, since the commencement of this suit, the election had been made to avoid the transaction, on behalf of the insolvent's creditors—and to claim the instruments as part of the assets belonging to the estate. *Held* good.

Replication—that *S. A.* was indebted to the plaintiff, long before and at the time of the indorsements in question, for services as an attorney; and that he lent *S. A.* money, on two occasions, upon security of the notes, which were accordingly deposited with and agreed to be held by the plaintiff, as security for the repayment of such loans with interest—both such loans, and the consequent deposit, being more than sixty days before the sequestration. It then alleged that eventually *S. A.* sold him the notes, and thereupon indorsed them without recourse, for a stated sum (such sale and indorsements being within the sixty days), the plaintiff deducting therefrom the amount due to him for services, and for the two loans and interest thereon; which deduction, it was then agreed between the parties, should be taken as payments of those amounts. Averment—that the plaintiff was not at the time aware, nor had he notice, that such payments were voluntary preferences by *S. A.* over other creditors, or that the latter was then insolvent, or rendered thereby insolvent, &c.—negativing the other matters mentioned in the enactment. The replication also alleged that the transaction was not a fraudulent preference; and that it had not the effect of a preference as alleged in the plea. *Held* bad—that the transaction between the plaintiff and *S. A.*, as disclosed on these pleadings, was one of a transfer and delivery of chattels, void as against *S. A.*'s assignee, under the 8th section of the 5 Vic., No. 17, and could not be deemed a payment within either the 12th section of that Act or the 1st and 2nd sections of the 25 Vic., No. 8.

Plea to both counts—that after the promissory notes were made by the defendant, the same were respectively delivered to the said *Spencer Ashlin*, and by virtue of such making and delivering thereof respectively, the same became and were the property, estate, goods, and effects of the said *Spencer Ashlin ;* that afterwards and before the commencement of this suit, by an order duly made under and in pursuance of the laws of this colony in that behalf, the estate and effects of the said *Spencer Ashlin* were duly placed under sequestration, according to law, as insolvent—and *J. P. Mackenzie*, one of the official assignees of insolvent estates in this colony, was by the same order duly appointed official assignee of the said estate and effects, and has ever since been and now is such official assignee, and the sole assignee thereof ; that after the said promissory notes were respectively so made and delivered to the said *Spencer Ashlin* as aforesaid, whilst the same were in his possession and were part of his property, estate, goods, and effects, and before the commencement of this suit, and before the said sequestration of his estate and effects as aforesaid, the said *Spencer Ashlin* being then insolvent, and then being in contemplation of surrendering his estate as insolvent, and within sixty days preceding the making of the said order for the sequestration of his estate, did indorse the said promissory notes, the same respectively being then part of his property, estate, goods, and effects, and deliver the same to the plaintiff—the plaintiff and divers other persons then being respectively creditors of the said *Spencer Ashlin ;* that the said indorsements and deliveries by the said *Spencer Ashlin* to the plaintiff of the said promissory notes had the effect of preferring the plaintiff, so being such creditor of the said *Spencer Ashlin* as aforesaid, to others of the said creditors of the said *Spencer Ashlin*, which indorsements and deliveries of the said promissory notes respectively, by the said *Spencer Ashlin* to the plaintiff, are the respective indorsements of such promissory notes respectively mentioned and alleged in the said counts ; that after the commencement of this suit, the said *J. P. Mackenzie*, as such

assignee of the said estate and effects of the said *Spencer*
Ashlin as aforesaid, has elected to treat and has treated
the said respective indorsements and deliveries by the
said *Spencer Ashlin* to the plaintiff of the said promissory notes respectively as void, and has duly declared
the same to have been and to be void, and has duly
avoided the same to the intent, and so that the said
promissory notes so being such property, estate, goods,
and effects of the insolvent estate of the said *Spencer*
Ashlin, and all rights of action and suit in respect
thereof might respectively be, and whereby the same
respectively became and were and are vested in, and
became and were and are the property of, the said *J. P.*
Mackenzie, as such assignee as aforesaid, whereby and
by reason of all which premises the said indorsements
and deliveries by the said *Spencer Ashlin* to the
plaintiff of the said promissory notes respectively,
became and were and are absolutely void; that after the
said *J. P. Mackenzie*, as such official assignee as aforesaid, so elected to treat the said indorsements and
deliveries by the said *Spencer Ashlin* to the plaintiff of
the said promissory notes respectively as void, and after
he so as aforesaid avoided the same, he duly gave notice
thereof to the defendant, and also to the plaintiff; that
afterwards the said *J. P. Mackenzie*, as such assignee as
aforesaid, duly gave notice to the defendant not to pay
any moneys whatever to the plaintiff, or to any other
person than himself, on account or in respect of the said
promissory notes, or either of them, and that he holds
the defendant liable to him, as such assignee as aforesaid,
for the amounts due upon the said promissory notes
respectively, and all rights of action and suit in respect
thereof, as estate, goods, and effects vested in and absolutely belonging to him as such assignee as aforesaid.

Demurrer and joinder.

Replication—that at the times of certain loans of
money by the plaintiff to the said *Spencer Ashlin*, and
of the indorsements to the plaintiff of the promissory
notes as hereinafter mentioned, the plaintiff was the
attorney for the said *Spencer Ashlin*, and at the said

times the said *Spencer Ashlin* was indebted to the plaintiff, for certain services performed by the plaintiff for the said *Spencer Ashlin*, as an attorney on the retainer of the said *Spencer Ashlin*, and the said *Spencer Ashlin* continued so indebted from the time of the said deliveries to the time of the said indorsements of the said promissory notes respectively ; that after the time of the making of the said notes respectively by the defendant, and previously to the time of the indorsements thereof by the said *Spencer Ashlin* to the plaintiff, and at periods respectively of more than sixty days from the date of the sequestration of the estate of the said *Spencer Ashlin* as insolvent, it was agreed by and between the plaintiff and the said *Spencer Ashlin* that in consideration of the plaintiff lending the said *Spencer Ashlin* a certain sum of money, to wit, the sum of £30, the plaintiff who then had the said notes in his possession should hold the said notes as a security for the said loan and interest, and the plaintiff then lent to the said *Spencer Ashlin* the said sum of £30 ; and afterwards, before the time of the indorsement of the said notes respectively, and at a period of more than sixty days from the time of the sequestration of the said *Spencer Ashlin's* estate as insolvent, the plaintiff lent to the said *Spencer Ashlin* a further sum of £25, on the agreement with the said *Spencer Ashlin* that the said notes should be held as a security for such further loan ; and it was afterwards agreed, by and between the plaintiff and the said *Spencer Ashlin*, that the plaintiff should purchase of the said *Spencer Ashlin* the said promissory notes for the sum of £122 10s., that the said *Spencer Ashlin* should sell the same to the plaintiff, and should indorse the said promissory notes respectively to the plaintiff without recourse, and that the plaintiff should deduct from the said sum of £122 10s. the sum of £55, being the amount of the aforesaid loans, with the sum of £5 for interest thereon, and also the sum of £10 10s. due from the said *Spencer Ashlin* to the plaintiff, for professional costs, and that the said deductions should be and should be taken as payments by the said *Spencer*

Ashlin of the said debts; that the said agreement so

made as aforesaid was executed and performed by the
plaintiff and the said *Spencer Ashlin*, according to the
terms thereof; that the said agreement by and between
the plaintiff and the said *Spencer Ashlin* for the purchase
of the said notes, was made, executed, and performed by
both parties thereto, at one and the same time; and that
neither at the times of the said loans of money by him to
the said *Spencer Ashlin*, nor at the time of the purchase
(*sic*) of the said promissory notes respectively by the
said *Spencer Ashlin* to the plaintiff, nor at any other
time until the time of the sequestration of the estate of
the said *Spencer Ashlin* as insolvent, was the plaintiff
aware, or had he notice or knowledge, that the said
Spencer Ashlin was at any of the said times insolvent,
or was by payment of the aforesaid debts rendered
insolvent, or that the said *Spencer Ashlin* contemplated
surrendering his estate as insolvent, or that legal proceedings for causing his estate to be sequestrated had
been commenced, or that the said *Spencer Ashlin* knew
that legal proceedings for obtaining an order for the
sequestration of the said *Spencer Ashlin's* estate as
insolvent had been commenced, or that the payment of
the aforesaid debts to the said plaintiff was a voluntary
preference by the said *Spencer Ashlin* of the plaintiff
over the other creditors of the said *Spencer Ashlin*.
Averment, that the said indorsements of the said promissory notes to him by the said *Spencer Ashlin*, were not
a fraudulent preference by the said *Spencer Ashlin* of
the plaintiff over other creditor or creditors of the said
Spencer Ashlin, and had not the effect of preferring the
plaintiff to other creditor or creditors of the said *Spencer
Ashlin*.

2. That before the time of the alleged election by the
said *J. P. Mackenzie* as official assignee of the insolvent
estate of the said *Spencer Ashlin*, to treat the said
respective indorsements and deliveries of the said promissory notes by the said *Spencer Ashlin* to the plaintiff
as void, and before the times of the said alleged declaration and notices by the said *J. P. Mackenzie*, as such

1865.

LEVY
v.
SMITH.

official assignee, of his treating the said respective indorsements as void, the said *J. P. Mackenzie*, as such official assignee, had sold and conveyed for valuable consideration, to a certain person (to wit) one *L. E. Threlkeld*, all the assets of the said insolvent estate, and the said alleged election was not made by the said *J. P. Mackenzie* for the benefit of the creditors of the said insolvent estate of the said *Spencer Ashlin*.

Demurrer and joinder.

Martin, Q.C., in support of the plea and the demurrer to the replications. As to the second replication, it is presumed the Court will overrule it, in accordance with its decision in *Mackenzie* v. *Barker* (a).

The first replication is founded on the assumption that the transaction is a payment. *Morris* v. *Flower* (b) is an authority that the delivery of a cheque is a transfer void under the 8th section; neither is it a payment protected by the 12th section and the recent Act (25 Vic., No. 8); *Morris* v. *Flower* (c). [*Wise*, J. That case was commenced before the 1st September, 1861, and was saved by the third section.] The first and second sections of the new Act (d) were only intended to apply to cases of payment under the 12th section of the 5 Vic., No. 17, leaving untouched all transfers under the 8th section. But the transaction disclosed on the face of these pleadings is clearly one of transfer of these promissory notes. It appears that the

●

(a) 2 Sup. Ct. R., C. L. 56.
(b) 2 Sup. Ct. R., C. L. 196.   (c) 3 Sup. Ct. R., App. 11.
(d) These sections are as follows:—"Every payment heretofore or hereafter made by any person before the sequestration of his estate under the Act 5 Vic., No. 17, to any creditor, for or on account of any just debt due at the time of payment, shall, except only in the cases hereinafter mentioned, be and be deemed to have been a valid payment, anything in the said Act notwithstanding.
Provided that such creditor or the person receiving payment on his behalf shall not at the time of payment have known that the debtor was then insolvent—or was by such payment rendered insolvent—or that he then contemplated the surrender of his estate as insolvent—or that proceedings for causing his estate to be sequestrated had been commenced—or that the payment was a voluntary preference of such creditor to other creditors. And notice to the creditor or person so receiving payment of any such matter by whomsoever given, if in accordance with the fact, shall be equivalent to and be deemed knowledge in such creditor or person."

plaintiff had a claim upon *Ashlin*, for services as an attorney, and that then the plaintiff lent two sums of £30 and £25 each to *Ashlin*, on the deposit of these notes as security, and that afterwards and within sixty days of *Ashlin's* sequestration, *Ashlin* having agreed to sell these notes to the plaintiff for £122 10s., endorsed them to him. The deposit of the notes did not operate as a transfer. But when the endorsement took place, the old debt for attorney's services was at all events paid to the plaintiff, who was thereby preferred; and, according to *Wilson* v. *Cobcroft* (a), if the transfer is for any past debt, however small, the whole security is invalidated.

Isaacs in support of the replications and the demurrers to the plea. It is submitted that the circumstances and matters alleged by the plaintiff in his replication, bring the case within the first and second sections of the new Act, 25 Vic., No. 8, as a transaction of payment, merely and simply. And this is the effect of the transaction— quite as much as if the plaintiff had paid the purchase money in cash in full to *Ashlin*, and the latter thereupon had handed over the amount of his debts to plaintiff in cash.

The plea is bad. It does not aver that the defendant had paid or offered to pay, or was ready and willing to pay, to the official assignee, the amounts of the notes. Neither does it allege or disclose circumstances that show any fraudulent intention on the part of *Ashlin* to prefer the plaintiff to his other creditors. In *The Bank of Australasia* v. *Harris* (b) the Privy Council say, " the better opinion is, that according to the true construction of the act the words, 'having the effect of preferring any then existing creditor,' indicate fraudulent preference, and were not intended to refer to any case of preference not fraudulent." In order to invalidate this transaction, as a transfer under the 8th section, there ought to have been an allegation in the plea that the preference relied on was fraudulent.

1865.

LEVY
v.
SMITH.

(a) 14 December, 1859.   (b) 1 Sup. Ct. R., App. 21.

1865.

LEVY
v.
SMITH.

Martin in reply. It is submitted that the deposit with the plaintiff by *Ashlin* of the two promissory notes, on an advance at the time of money by loan—although it is admitted such loan and deposit are themselves not affected by the Insolvent Act—does not take the case out of the eighth section, the indorsement and purchase of the promissory notes having been within the sixty days of the sequestration of *Ashlin's* estate, and o affected by that section. And, moreover, this purchase or indorsement—the same being in part a liquidation of the previous debt due by *Ashlin* to this plaintiff—amounted to a transfer of property, and had "the effect of preferring" the plaintiff to *Ashlin's* other creditors.

Cur. adv. vult.

December 30.

STEPHEN, C. J., now delivered the judgment of the Court as follows :—

This is an action by the indorsee against the maker of two promissory notes, payable to *Spencer Ashlin* or order, and by him indorsed to the plaintiff; the amount of one being £237, and of the other £251. The defendant disputes the validity of the indorsements, as against *Ashlin's* creditors :—the said *Ashlin* having become insolvent, and his assignee having elected on their behalf to avoid the transfer. And the question for decision by the Court is, in substance, having regard to section 8 of the Insolvent Act, and the two first sections of the late Amending Act, whether the transaction between *Ashlin* and the plaintiff, on the whole, was a transfer of property, void or voidable as a preference, under the first mentioned enactment, or is protected as a " payment " by the more recent statute.

There is a subordinate question raised on the pleadings, that is to say, on the third replication to the second plea—whether the election by the assignee at all events was effectual ; because of its having been made (as that replication alleges) after his sale of the assets to a third party. Since the filing of the demurrers, however, the issues of fact on the record have gone down to trial; and, it then clearly appearing that the election preceded such sale, and the jury having so found, this point was not argued. A considered judgment on it, therefore, is unnecessary ; but, in order to dispose of the costs on the demurrer to that replication, judgment will formally be entered thereon, in accordance with my present opinion, for the plaintiff. It is of course to be understood, if the question should again arise, that this direction will not be taken as a decision on the point.

The second plea—on which and on the second replication thereto the questions arise—alleges that after the delivery of the promissory notes to *Ashlin*, and while they remained his property and part of his estate, he was indebted to the plaintiff and divers other persons ; and that *Ashlin* indorsed and delivered the notes, he being at the time insolvent, within sixty days before his sequestration ; and that such indorsement and delivery had the effect of preferring the plaintiff, being a creditor as aforesaid, to others of his then existing creditors. The plea states formally the fact of the due sequestration of *Ashlin's* estate, and the appointment of an assignee thereof ; and that by him, since the commencement of this suit, the election has been made to avoid the transaction, on behalf of the insolvent's creditors—and to claim the instruments as part of the assets belonging to the estate.

The second replication sets up the following facts in answer ; that *Ashlin* was indebted to the plaintiff, long before and at the time of the indorsements in question, for certain services as an attorney ; and that he lent *Ashlin* money, on two occasions, upon security of the notes, which were accordingly deposited with and agreed to be held by the plaintiff, as security for the repayment, with interest—both such loans, and the consequent deposit, being more than sixty days before the sequestration. Then, that eventually *Ashlin* sold him the notes, and thereupon indorsed them without recourse, for a stated sum (such sale and indorsements being within the sixty days), the plaintiff deducting therefrom the amount due to him for services, and for the two loans and interest thereon ; which deductions, it was then

x—4

agreed between the parties, should be taken as payments of those amounts. Finally, in order to bring the case within the protecting clauses of the new statute, the replication avers that the plaintiff was not at the time aware, nor had he notice, that such payments were voluntary preferences by *Ashlin* over other creditors, or that the latter was then insolvent, or rendered thereby insolvent—and so on, negativing the other matters mentioned in the enactment. Moreover, the replication alleges that the transaction was not a fraudulent preference ; and that it had not the effect of a preference, as alleged in the plea.

The replication is demurred to—on the general ground, simply, that the matters there alleged constitute no answer, in point of law, to those stated in the plea ; but the question raised by this demurrer, in effect, is the one already mentioned. The plea on the other hand is demurred to, because it does not allege that the preference relied on was fraudulent ; an allegation, the materiality of which under section 8 of our Insolvent Act has never before, in this Court, arisen specifically for decision.

Now that section, so far as it in any degree touches the present case, enacts in terms as follows—that all alienations, transfers, deliveries, mortgages, or pledges, of any estate, goods, or effects, real or personal, made by any person being insolvent, or in contemplation of surrendering his estate as insolvent, or within sixty days preceding the sequestration of his estate as insolvent, and having the effect of preferring any then existing creditor to another, shall be absolutely void—that is to say, according to the decision of this Court in *Mackenzie* v. *Murnin*, in January 1860, followed by several other cases, void as against the insolvent's creditors. But the admitted facts here are, that, although there was no fraud or fraudulent preference (in the ordinary sense at all events of the word fraudulent) in the transaction, the insolvent holder of the notes sued on transferred and delivered them to the plaintiff, by sale, within the prohibited period before sequestration, partly indeed for cash, and in satisfaction of money advanced on their

deposit, but partly also in liquidation of a debt previously
due to the plaintiff, and unconnected with that deposit.
It seems to me vain to contend, that such a transaction
had not necessarily the effect, as to that previous debt,
of preferring one of the insolvent's creditors to every
other then existing creditor. If, therefore, it was in legal
construction a transfer and delivery of property, and not
a " payment " within the recent statute (questions to be
considered presently), I think that the sale and indorsement of those instruments was, at the election of the
insolvent's assignee, utterly inoperative and void—by
force of the 8th section above cited.

Such a transaction is not merely within the words of
that enactment. The object of the statute is (as with, I
apprehend, every other bankruptcy code) to secure an
equal distribution of the insolvent's assets, among all his
creditors having equal claims. It is made the primary
duty of the insolvent honestly to surrender all his estate
—in order that they, and the creditors entitled to any
preference in payment, by virtue of any lien or otherwise, may be paid as far as the assets will extend. By
the Amending Act of 1844, the principle is illustrated
and enforced, by making every insolvent punishable who
contracts any debt, which he has not a reasonable expectation of being able to pay; or who shall have given
to any creditor a preference, in itself fraudulent or unjust—thus drawing the distinction between a preference
simply, and one which may under the circumstances
have been morally wrong. But the object of equal distribution would plainly be defeated, and frauds be
facilitated if not encouraged, on the part of persons
contemplating or on the eve of bankruptcy, if they were
permitted to select favourite creditors, and pay them
preferentially to others. Every bankrupt law, therefore,
I believe, will be found to contain some provision, in
restraint of such preferences. Now it cannot be denied,
that there was such a preference in this case. The
plaintiff, by the transaction here impeached, was paid his
own debt in full—to the exclusion or injury of all those
other creditors, having an equal right to satisfaction out

of the same assets, whose sources of payment were thus absorbed or diminished. It follows, that this case is equally within the spirit of the clause, and the mischief which it was intended to remedy.

But other codes, it seems, in the endeavour to carry out the same object, use the term "voluntary" or "fraudulent" when legislating against acts of preference. And accordingly any threat to sue, nay even any demand of payment, not preconcerted by the debtor, however embarrassed at the time he may know himself to be, will relieve the transaction of payment from its real character of a preference. Every person of experience in such matters is aware, and there are cases enough on record to show, how easy evasion of the law is under such a system. Concert can rarely be brought home to the parties; and the most dulcet of applications may, according to the nature of the claim, be construed to render the preferential payment, even by a father to his son, involuntary. It is not improbable that the local Legislature, having its attention drawn to this state of things, deliberately adopted a less elastic phraseology; and thus intentionally avoided every transfer of property, by an embarrassed debtor, either actually insolvent or on the verge of declared insolvency, having the "effect" of a preference. The difference between such an expression and a preference fraudulent, voluntary, or in any manner dependent on intention, is too marked to have been the result of accident. It is to be observed, moreover, that the 8th section touches no case of payments—properly so called. These are the subject of a separate, though not a happily worded section—the 12th. The one under review affects only transfers, or deliveries, of land or chattels; not in ordinary estimation payments, although both alike must be meant so to operate. And the reason for this distinction is obvious; since a debtor, but especially one in trade, who can only satisfy his liabilities by transferring land or handing over goods, may reasonably be suspected of insolvency.

I trust, therefore, that presumption will not be imputed to me, for declining to act on the doubt expressed

by the Judicial Committee, in the *Bank of Australasia*
v. *Harris* (a), as to the meaning of the word preferring,
or the words having the effect of preferring, in our
Insolvent Act. By an express decision of their Lordships, of course, every Judge of this Court would be
bound; but, in the mean time, it appears to me to be
my duty to follow *Sempill* v. *Anderson* (b), determined
in September 1861, and the case of *Morris* v. *Flower*,
argued before my late colleagues and myself in April
1862, and decided in May following (c). Incidentally,
though not in terms, the question as to the ingredient of
fraud or voluntariness in the transaction is decided by
those cases.

The construction of section 8 cannot be affected by
the fact, that in this case the promissory notes were not
indorsed, exclusively, to satisfy a previously existing
debt; and that the other creditors entitled to payment
were not prejudiced, therefore, except as to a portion of
the purchase money. For if such an objection could
prevail, the law might be with facility evaded in every
case, by the creditor's receipt of a slightly larger amount
of property than will cover his debt; handing over the
price of the excess, in money, to the person preferring
him. The principle and the rule must be the same,
whatever may be the actual amount of that payment. I
am also of opinion, that the promissory notes transferred
in this case were property—part of *Ashlin's* personal
estate, goods, or effects—within the meaning of the 8th
section. They certainly were not money, nor were they
treated as money; but, having originally been deposited
without endorsement, as security for the plaintiff's
advances on them, the notes were sold like any other
chattel, and then endorsed and delivered to the plaintiff
accordingly. Their previous deposit, in consideration of
a loan then made on the notes, though *Ashlin* may have
been insolvent at the time, could not be affected by the
enactment; for questions of preference can only arise,
between creditors equally entitled to claim the transferred

(a) 1 Sup. Ct. R., App. 21.
(b) See Appendix to the present volume.
(c) 3 Sup. Ct. R., App. 10.

property. But it is clear that the creditors generally had no such right, against the plaintiff, except subject to that loan; nor could the deposit constitute a preference, as between him and *Ashlin's* other creditors, because—so far as that debt was concerned—they and the plaintiff were not co-existing in that character until after the loan itself had been made. It was the final indorsement of the notes, in liquidation of that and the previously existing demand, which has made the 8th section applicable.

The question yet remains, whether the transaction is protected, as a payment, by the new statute of 1861. The 1st and 2nd sections of that Act (25 Vic., No. 8) make every payment to a creditor valid, any thing in the Act of 5 Vic., No. 17, notwithstanding, provided such creditor did not know that his debtor was insolvent, or was by the payment rendered insolvent, or that he contemplated sequestrating his estate as insolvent, or that the payment was a voluntary preference of such creditor, to the person's other creditors.

These sections, therefore, obviously, were passed to correct or qualify some enactment in the original Act, relating—not to transfers of property—but to payments. And consequently I infer (necessarily, as it seems to me), that the section thus qualified and restrained in its operation was the 12th, not the 8th section of the last mentioned law. For, by that 12th section, every payment made to a creditor by a person not compelled to make it, if that person knew himself to be insolvent, or contemplated surrendering his estate as insolvent, is declared fraudulent and void. The improvidence, not to say harshness and injustice of that enactment, had long been felt by the trading community; and it has been wisely removed by the recent statute. But the effect sought in this case to be given to it, by holding every transfer of property—otherwise amounting to a preference under the 8th section—to be a payment, which the party preferred and his embarrassed debtor may choose to call a payment, would be to extend the enactment far beyond its natural scope, or what could have been intended by the Legislature. Every alienation or transfer of goods whatever, made by such a debtor, which shall have the effect of preferring one creditor to another, must inevitably be in effect a payment. But, in the language of Mr. Justice *Milford*, in *Morris* v. *Flower*, " it never could have been contemplated, that the same transaction might be treated either as a transfer, or a payment, at the option of the creditor receiving the goods in payment." It is clear to me, therefore, that the statutes must have meant by the word payment something which was not such a transfer. If not, the 8th section would be virtually repealed (a). .

For these reasons, I am of opinion with the late Mr. Justice *Wise*, that the transaction here was one of a transfer and delivery of chattels, void as against *Ashlin's* assignee, under the 8th section of the 5 Vic., No. 17 ; and cannot be deemed a payment, within either the 12th section of that Act, or the 1st and 2nd sections of the 25 Vic., No. 8. The judgment of the Court, therefore, will be substantially for the defendant. The formal entry of judgment on the several demurrers has already been notified (b).

(a) See *Jones* v. *Makenzie*, 13 Moore P. C. 6, 9 ; in which it seems to be taken for granted, that the *bona fides* of a transaction is not in question under section 8 of our Colonial Statute.

(b) There being a dispute as to the correct way in which the findings on the several issues ought to be entered on the record, an application was made, in Chambers, to *Stephen*, C. J., who, on the 29th March, 1866, delivered the following judgment :—

A verdict was entered in this case for the defendant, generally, subject to the opinion of the Court as to the propriety of my direction —and subject, also, in case that opinion should be in accordance with my own, to such distribution of the finding, on the several issues, as I should thereafter direct to be entered. The judgment being in favour of the direction at the trial (see the judgment delivered on the 30th of December last), I have now to make the necessary order as to that distribution.

The first issue is on the defendant's plea, setting up his assignment ; and it raises the question, whether the plaintiff was at the time of such assignment a creditor, not named therein. Now there is no doubt, on the evidence, that he was not so named, nor were the promissory notes there indicated. It is equally certain, that the plaintiff then held those notes. But the issue is not thus divisible ; as the plea, taken by itself—or the replication, taken by itself, is. It was not necessary to mention the notes, or at least to name the plaintiff, in *Smith's* assignment, because (according to the judgment of the Court) the indorsements were rendered void, by the operation of the Insolvent Act, on the assignee's election to avoid them ; and the plaintiff, therefore, in respect of those notes, was not a creditor of *Smith* at all. Consequently, a material allegation by the plaintiff being negatived, the whole replication fails as an answer to the plea. This first issue therefore must remain, as at present found, for the defendant.

On the second issue there seems more difficulty ; for it raises the question, whether the payee of the notes (*Ashlin*) did or not indorse them to the plaintiff. Now there was no dispute, that in point of fact *Ashlin* did indorse—that is to say, did actually sign his name on those notes, and deliver them, with intent to pass the property therein, to the plaintiff. But that delivery, and that act of indorsation, were (as already observed) voidable at the election of the assignee ; and, upon his making such election, the transfer or attempted transfer became invalid from the beginning. In other words, the indorsement and delivery alike were, on and after that election, by virtue of its retroactive operation, absolutely void. Consequently, in legal effect, *Ashlin* did not indorse (*i.e.* did not effectively transfer) the notes to the plaintiff ; and the issue, therefore, on this second plea also, must stand for the defendant.

Were it to be entered otherwise, there would be an inconsistency in the findings on the record. A plaintiff doubtless may be the legitimate indorsee of a note or bill, and yet, by some subsequent matter raised on the pleadings, not be entitled to recover. But here the defendant's case is, that the plaintiff never was such an indorsee ; or at any rate was not so, for the purposes of this action.

The third issue is on the defendant's plea, setting up the provisions of section 8 of the Insolvent Act. The plea alleges, that the indorsement relied on by the plaintiff was within sixty days next before *Ashlin's* insolvency ; and that it had the effect of preferring the plaintiff, then being a creditor, to the latter's other creditors ; and that the assignee afterwards (but after the commencement of the suit) elected to avoid such indorsement, and the delivery of the promissory notes consequent thereon ; the same being a transfer of property within the meaning of the enactment—by reason of all which premises, says the plea, such indorsement and delivery became void. Now the plaintiff, in his first replication to this plea, denied its several allegations ; in other words, traversed it generally. But, if the judgment of the Court was right, all those allegations were established ; and, so far as it respects the mere matters of fact, irrespective of their legal effect and value, it is indisputable that they were so.

The next issue is the fourth ; raised by a second replication to the same plea. The plaintiff here sets up in answer, in effect, the provisions of section 1 and 2 of the last Insolvency Amending Act ; which exempts certain "payments" from the operation of the previous law. He states in detail the circumstances, out of which the indorsement of the notes arose ; that he had previously lent *Ashlin* money on them, the latter being then the plaintiff's debtor for services rendered ; and that eventually an arrangement was made between them, whereby the instruments were to be taken in payment of the entire debt ;—and accordingly that they were so taken. The replication proceeds to negative all the exceptions contained in section 2 ; the material one being, that the plaintiff did not know that such payment was, on *Ashlin's* part, a voluntary preference.

Now the question is not, merely, on such a replication, if wholly traversed, whether the greater part of its allegations are established —but whether the whole (so far as they are material) are established. And the main contest here was, whether in legal effect and construction the notes, or their indorsement to the plaintiff, could be deemed a payment ; and so, whether the allegation was sustained that he took them in payment. On this point, the jury were instructed to find for the defendant ; and the Court has, in the judgment delivered by me, upheld that finding. The issue on this replication, therefore, must necessarily be so entered, although it be conceded that the plaintiff proved every other allegation in the pleading.

As to the fifth issue (raised by the third replication to the same plea), which denies that any election was made by *Ashlin's* assignee until after his sale of the assets, it is admitted that the fact was as stated in the plea. The defendant succeeds, consequently, on this last issue also.

1865.

Rouse and another *against* Nixon (*a*).

EJECTMENT for an allotment of land in Elizabeth-
street, Sydney—to defend for a portion of which
the defendant appeared.

At the trial before *Stephen*, C. J., in the November
sittings, the plaintiffs' title was shown as follows. On
the 30th November, 1840, the land was granted to
C. Roberts. On the 30th January, 1852, it was mortgaged by *Roberts* to *Plomer*. On the 20th April, 1863,
Roberts executed a mortgage of the same land to Messrs.
Rouse and *Terry*, and this mortgage had become vested
in the plaintiffs. On the 21st April, 1863, a receipt for
the mortgage money and interest was indorsed on the
mortgage of the 30th January, 1852, by *Plomer*, in
pursuance of the 16 Vic., No. 19, sect. 52.

The mortgage to *Rouse* and *Terry* of 20th April,
1863, and the receipt by *Plomer* of the 21st April, 1863,
were both registered on the same day (the former being
registered and numbered before the latter). It thus
appeared that the plaintiffs' mortgage was registered
before the registration of the first mortgagee's receipt
and indorsement on the latter's original mortgage. The
defendant had been in possession since 1862. There
had been no demand of possession, or notice to quit,
before action brought.

At the trial, it was contended that the plaintiffs could
not recover; first, because the defendant having been in
possession at and before the 20th April, 1863, must be
presumed to have been then a tenant, and not a trespasser, and could not, therefore, be ejected without
demand of possession or notice to quit; and secondly,
because the plaintiffs had no title. On the 20th April,
1863, the legal estate was in *Plomer*, and the plaintiffs
were mortgagees of the equity of redemption only. On

The 52nd
section of the
Trustee Act,
1852, enacts
that when
ever the per-
son entitled
to receive
payment of
any money
secured by
mortgage
upon land
shall endorse
upon the deed
of mortgage
an acknow-
ledgment
under his
hand, attested
by one wit-
ness of the
payment of
the mortgage
debt in full,
such indorse-
ment shall,
upon registra-
tion thereof,
&c., "operate
as a discharge
of the mort-
gage debt,
and a recon-
veyance of all
and singular
the heredita-
ments com-
prised in such
mortgage, to
the person or
persons who
shall, at the
time of such
payment, be
entitled to the
equity of re-
demption
thereof, ac-
cording to his
or their
respective
interests
therein."

Held, that the section applies only to the case of mortgagor and mortgagee, where
the former pays off the latter's mortgage.

(*a*) Before *Stephen*, C. J., *Cheeke*, J., and *Faucett*, J.

the 8th of May, 1863, the day of the registration, the title of *Plomer* was transferred to *Roberts*, as the person entitled to the equity of redemption, under the 52nd section of the Trust Property Act of 1852 (*a*). For the plaintiffs were not on that day, any more than on the 21st of April, entitled to the equity of redemption. Although the plaintiffs could redeem *Plomer's* mortgage, the person throughout entitled to the equity of redemption was *Roberts* alone. How then could there be, in the words of this enactment, a "reconveyance" by *Plomer* to any one else?

The learned Judge ruled, as to the first point, that every presumption was that the defendant was a tenant (if a tenant at all) to *Roberts*, since the defendant had come in long after 1852. But *Roberts* during all that time had no legal title, and the defendant therefore could have had none. On the second point his Honor refused to nonsuit, as he thought the point a doubtful one; as it was questionable whether the Legislature did not mean, by the words "person entitled to the equity," to indicate a mortgagee of such equity equally with the mortgagor. His Honor therefore directed a verdict for the defendant, reserving leave to the plaintiffs to move to enter the verdict for them, if the Court should think fit.

November 30.   A rule *nisi* accordingly having been obtained,

December 29.   *Blake* (*Salamons* with him) showed cause. The plaintiffs' mortgage was registered before the registration of the first mortgagee's (*Plomer's*) receipt and indorsement on the latter's original mortgage. The question, therefore, is, in favour of whom did such last mentioned registration operate—as a conveyance to the plaintiffs—or

(*a*) 16 Vic., No. 19. This section is as follows :—" Whenever the person entitled to receive payment of any money secured by mortgage upon land, shall endorse upon the deed of mortgage an acknowledgment under his hand, attested by one witness, of the payment of the mortgage debt in full, or of any less sum in satisfaction thereof, such indorsement shall (upon registration thereof in the manner provided by law for the registration of other instruments affecting land) operate as a discharge of the mortgage debt, and a reconveyance of all and singular the hereditaments comprised in such mortgage to the person or persons who shall, at the time of such payment, be entitled to the equity of redemption thereof, according to his and their respective interests therein."

as a re-conveyance to *Roberts* the mortgagor? If the latter, the legal estate is in *Roberts*, and so not in the plaintiffs. It is submitted that *Roberts* was the person entitled to the equity of redemption and not the plaintiffs, for they were only the mortgagees of his equity of redemption. The equity of redemption constitutes an equitable estate in the land, the old ownership being supposed to be continued; the mortgagee holding the estate only as a pledge for the money, in the repayment of which he is principally interested (*a*).   It may be granted and devised in the same way as might have been done with the estate before the mortgage was made ; *Spence* (*b*). It may itself become the subject of a mortgage again and again ; each mortgage or pledge being of the same character, except that by the first mortgage the legal estate passed.   Every such mortgagee as being a person claiming an interest, legal or equitable, in the property mortgaged, under or through the mortgagor, by privity of title, has a right to redeem the property, in order to make his own claims available, whether those having a prior claim to redeem are willing to proceed or not (*c*). He can redeem any prior incumbrancer on payment of the principal, interest, and costs due to him, such redeeming party being also liable to be redeemed by those below him, who are all liable to be redeemed by the mortgagor (*d*).   The mortgage debt being regarded as an interest of a personal nature secured on lands, each mortgagee in succession is a creditor of the mortgagor, and he can sue in debt for the money· secured by the mortgage.   But the equity of redemption, notwithstanding all these dealings, remains in the mortgagor, and he is the only person who is entitled to pay off all the other claimants.   The equity is realty, and goes to the heir; but the intermediate interests vested in the various mortgagees are personalty, and go to the personal representatives.   If, therefore, a subsequent mortgagee redeems a prior mortgagee, the mortgage thus redeemed is transferred to him ; but in such a case there is no

1865.

ROUSE
and another
v.
NIXON.

(*a*) See Burton 452.   (*b*) 2 Vol. 645 ; see Coote 26.*
(*c*) Id. 660.   (*d*) Id. 665 ; See Smith's Comp. 291.

re-conveyance, nor is any mortgaged debt discharged. It is only when the mortgage debt is liquidated and discharged that a re-conveyance is executed; and such re-conveyance can only be to the person who originally made the mortgage. Where a second mortgage is only made to pay off an existing mortgage, the proper course is to execute an assignment of the old mortgage. In the present case the plaintiffs ought to have obtained from *Plomer* an assignment of his mortgage. *Roberts* had never ceased to own and be entitled to the equity of redemption. Or they might have postponed their mortgage till *Plomer* was paid off, and the receipt registered. It is submitted that by the registration of the receipt the estate was re-conveyed to *Roberts*. The statute does not contemplate the case of several mortgages. The words, "the persons entitled to the equity of redemption thereof, according to their respective interests therein," must be intended to mean the heirs or devisees of the mortgagor. A second mortgagee has only a charge on the land. Suppose there has been a third and a fourth mortgage, and then that the first has been paid off and his receipt endorsed and registered, who would be at the time of such a payment entitled to the equity of redemption? This shows that the person so entitled is the mortgagor to whom alone a re-conveyance is possible. This section is found in a Trustee Act, in connection with various provisions for facilitating the getting in of the legal estate when outstanding, and was intended to apply only to cases where the legal estate could be re-conveyed. But it is inapplicable to cases of intermediate mortgages, where several persons, whose rights cannot be parcelled out, are entitled to obtain for themselves the entire fee, subject to redemption. The words "discharge of the debt, and re-conveyance of" the mortgaged premises, can only apply to cases where the object is to revest the estate in the mortgagor.

Martin, Q. C., and *Darley* contra. The equity of redemption is an estate in the land. *Roberts*, after the mortgage to *Plomer*, having that estate in the land, mortgaged it to the plaintiffs. The plaintiffs became purchasers, qualified owners of *Roberts'* estate, and were by their mortgage entitled to redeem *Plomer*, and so were persons entitled to the equity of redemption in right of *Roberts*. All he had the plaintiffs had. "The principle of the decision is," says *Wigram*, V. C., in *Frazer* v. *Jones* (a), "that the mortgage, as between the mortgagor and the mortgagee, is a mortgage of the mortgagor's entire interest, saving only the rights of prior incumbrancers;" *Spence* (b). It is submitted that the clause in question is not limited to a mortgage of the legal estate, but applies equally to all mortgages; and the estate which is re-conveyed by the indorsement and registration, is the estate vested in the mortgagee who is paid off. If such mortgagee has the legal estate, then that estate is re-conveyed; if an equitable estate, then such estate only is re-conveyed. For example, if a second mortgagee is paid off by the mortgagor, and the receipt for the payment is duly endorsed and registered, then the mortgagor does not get back the legal estate, but only the estate which was under mortgage to such second mortgagee, that is, the equity of redemption. The owner of the original equity of redemption is the second mortgagee, and is the person in whom the legal estate vests by the statute, on payment of the original mortgage, and due indorsement and registration. No doubt a mortgagor has a right to redeem a second mortgage as well as a first; but it is submitted that the right of redemption, which is meant by the statute, is the original right of redemption existing on the execution of a legal mortgage, and to that right the second mortgagee became entitled with all its privileges on the execution of his mortgage, just as much as if he had purchased it, and obtained a conveyance of it, because (subject to the right to redeem) every mortgage is a conveyance, absolute and complete; *Whitworth* v. *Gaugain* (c), *Spence* (d). The 53rd and 54th sections tend to show the correctness of this conclusion, that the

1865.

Rouse and another
v.
Nixon.

(a) 5 Hare 481.
(c) 3 Hare 427.

(b) 2 Vol. 657.
(d) 2 Vol. 638.

1865.

ROUSE
and another
v.
NIXON.

statute meant to include, or may include, the mortgagee as the party entitled to the equity of redemption. It could not have been intended that the mortgagor by paying off the first mortgage and obtaining the receipt should get back the legal estate ; but that the person obtaining the receipt should take the interest of the person who was paid off, whatever it might be.

STEPHEN, C. J. The 52nd section is applicable only to cases in which the registration of the mortgagee's receipt can operate as a discharge of the debt as well as a re-conveyance to the person entitled to the equity of redemption. But the plaintiffs never owed a debt to *Plomer,* and could not receive a "re-conveyance." They were, therefore, not the persons entitled to the equity of redemption within the terms or meaning of the enactment. They were indeed not in the proper sense so entitled at all, for they were not the purchasers or owners, but only the mortgagees of the mortgagor's equity of redemption. Moreover, if there had been four mortgages in succession—suppose that for his own protection the fourth paid off the second or the first mortgage—what would be the effect ? The receipt and registration might operate as a " conveyance" (though not a re-conveyance) of the lands in the one case, and of the mortgagor's equity of redemption in the other case ; but would it also operate as a discharge of the debt ? If not, the enactment would only operate for one of its declared purposes, instead of the two declared purposes. And if on the contrary the enactment would operate in such a case fully, and so discharge the debt, in what position would the unfortunate fourth mortgagee be ?

On the other hand, if it be said that the statute was not intended to apply to such a case, why should it be held to extend to a case where—merely by contrivance—the second mortgagee pays off the first out of the moneys advanced on the second mortgage ? In short, every consideration tends to show that the section applies only to the simple case of mortgagor and mortgagee, where the former pays off the latter's mortgage.

CHEEKE, J., and FAUCETT, J., concurred.

Rule discharged.

FOTHERINGHAM and another *against* O'BRIEN.

THE first count stated an agreement that in consideration that the plaintiffs would, by *W. H. Aldis* their agent, deliver to the defendant a certain valuable and negotiable instrument of the plaintiffs then current—that is to say, a bill of exchange for £264 10s., dated the 16th June, 1865, payable to *W. H. Aldis* or order five months after date, drawn by *Aldis* and accepted by the defendant, and indorsed by *Aldis* to the plaintiffs—the defendant promised and agreed with the plaintiffs by their agent that he would, upon the delivery to him of the said instrument, procure and deliver to the plaintiffs or their agent another bill of exchange to the same tenor and effect, that is to say, a bill of exchange for £264 10s. dated, &c. Averment of fulfilment of all conditions precedent. Breach, that defendant had not procured or delivered *modo et forma*.

The second and third counts were in trover and detinue.

Pleas to the first count—1. *Non assumpsit*; 2. Traverse that *Aldis* was the plaintiffs' agent: To the second count—3. Not guilty: To the third count—4. *Non detinet*; 5. Traversing plaintiffs' property in the bill. Issue thereon.

It appeared at the trial before *Cheeke*, J., in the November sittings, that the plaintiffs had discounted the bill in question for *Aldis*, and that they had afterwards given the bill back to *Aldis* to be exchanged for another, or to be discounted by him for the plaintiffs' benefit. It was supposed by the plaintiffs that the defendant had got the bill from *Aldis* and destroyed it, or returned it. The plaintiffs gave value for the bill, and then handed it back. In support of this case the plaintiffs produced, first, a letter written by them to the defendant as follows:—"We handed to our mutual friend Mr. *W. H. Aldis*, on Saturday, the

In an action brought to recover a bill of exchange for £264 10s. in favour of A., accepted by the defendant, and endorsed by A. to the plaintiffs, it appeared that the plaintiffs had discounted the bill for A., and had afterwards given it back to him to be exchanged for another. The plaintiffs' case was, that the defendant had got the bill from A. and tore it up. Plaintiffs wrote to the defendant stating these facts, and demanding a return of the bill; to which the latter replied. "I must refer you to your principals in the matter you allude to, and in which I have no interest." The defendant and A. were in Court at the trial, and neither of them were called for the plaintiffs. No evidence was called for

the defendant. The jury having found a verdict for the defendant, the Court granted a new trial on payment of costs.

29th instant, your acceptance in his favour, due 19th November, for £264 10s., which he undertook to discount, and hand us the proceeds. This instrument, he tells us, he gave to you to be exchanged (as it bore our endorsement erased) for one of the same tenor and date. We have repeatedly applied to Mr. *Aldis* to return it to us: his only answer is, that you tore it up. Now, as the bill is our property, we must request you will give it, or one like it, to Mr. *Aldis,* to hand back to us." To this, the defendant, replied, "I beg to acknowledge receipt of your note of the 12th instant; and in reply, to state that I must refer you to your principals in the matter you allude to, and in which I have no interest." This was the plaintiffs' case. But the defendant was in Court, and so was *Aldis,* and neither of them was called by the plaintiff. No evidence was called for the defendant. Under these circumstances the jury found for the defendant.

November 29.

Sir *W. Manning* obtained a rule *nisi* for a new trial, on the ground that the verdict was against evidence.

December 19.

Butler showed cause. Granting that the jury might have given a verdict for the plaintiffs, if they had thought fit, the present verdict for the defendant will not be disturbed, as the question was for them. It was more incumbent upon the plaintiffs than the defendant to call *Aldis*; and since the former chose to leave their case so very meagre and bare, they cannot complain that the jury have found a verdict against them on account of the want of the evidence of *Aldis.* Although where there is no evidence in itself to affect a defendant, the mere fact that he is not called as a witness is not sufficient to sustain a verdict against him: yet, if there is some evidence against him—as for instance, an implied admission on his part—then the circumstance that he is not called to explain it, has been considered enough to turn the scale and sustain the verdict; *McKewen* v. *Cotching* (a). He also referred to *Adams* v. *Midland Railway Co.* (b).

Sir *W. Manning,* Q. C., contra.

(a) 27 L. J. Ex. 41.   (b) 31 L. J. Ex. 35.

STEPHEN, C. J.   The defendant ought to have gone into the box to rebut the inference arising from his silence as to a charge so serious—he answering the plaintiffs' letter, but evading the charge altogether.   It is obvious that the defendant was the only person who could have proved the non-destruction or the non-receiving of the bill.   Why did he not go into the box? And the jury, as the case stood, might have justifiably found for the plaintiffs.   But the question was certainly for them, and it cannot be denied that *Aldis* might have been called by the plaintiffs, had they not suspected complicity with the defendant.   Yet the result is not a satisfactory one.   The truth has not been disclosed, or justice done, and the amount at stake is a large one. Moreover, if the defendant has destroyed the bill placed in his hands, knowing that he has no right so to do, his conduct deserves exposure.   Or if he has not done the act, the defendant can easily so state.   Therefore there must be a new trial.   But as the plaintiffs did not call *Aldis*, and might have done so, they must pay the costs of the trial, whether the omission was the plaintiffs' fault, or their misfortune only (*a*).

1865.

―――――

FOTHERINGHAM
and another
v.
O'BRIEN.

(*a*) See *Nixon* v. *Sharpe.*—8th October, 1863.

Butler showed cause against the rule for a new trial obtained last term—against a verdict for defendant.   Plaintiff sued for £50 on an account stated, and his only evidence was a letter signed by the defendant, and addressed "Mr. *Nixon*,"—in which the defendant says, "So soon as I receive advice from the office (*i.e.* of the writer's being allowed an 'advance' of £50), I will remit your £50 in full." There was no evidence whatever of the consideration for any debt, or of the existence of one, beyond what may be implied from the expression cited ; and the plaintiff was not put in the box, although his absence was unaccounted for, and it was suggested that he was in town at the time and easily accessible.   On the other hand, neither was the defendant called.   But (as it was said) he was in the far interior.   The question was whether the plaintiff had or had not proved his case ; or whether the letter merely amounted to this, that the defendant admitted his liability to pay out of a particular fund only, which as yet he had never received.   The following cases were referred to—*Hughes* v. *Thorpe,** *Fesenmayer* v. *Adcock,*† *Fryer* v. *Roe.*‡

Per Curiam.   We think the latter construction possible—although in our opinion it was not the probable one.   And we all think that as the plaintiff might have removed all doubt and difficulty as to the existence of the debt, if due, by simply becoming a witness, he cannot obtain a new trial except on payment of costs.   But we also think that he ought to have a new trial, as we can see clearly that justice has not been done.

* 5 M. & W. 667.   † 16 *ib.* 449.   13 C. B. 439.

Y—4

1865.

Ex parte CONN (a).

A. being in the occupation of an unlicensed house, in which several persons were found drinking spirits, was apprehended with those persons under the 51st section of the Sale of Liquors Licensing Act, and brought before the justices. Thereupon, evidence was gone into ; and, at its close, the further hearing of the case against *A.* was adjourned. On the day of adjournment, *A.* did not appear; and, in her absence, the justices convicted her (under the same section) of unlicensed retailing, and inflicted a fine. *Held* (*Faucett*, J., *dissentiente*), that the conviction was bad.

Held (per *Stephen*, C. J., and *Cheeke*, J.) also, that the provisions of the 11 and 12 Vic., c. 43, had no application to the case.

*W*ILKINSON moved to make absolute a rule for a prohibition under the Justices' Acts, to restrain further proceedings in respect of a conviction under the fifty-first section of the Sale of Liquors Licensing Act of 1862 (b). The applicant was brought up in custody by a constable, having been apprehended under the powers conferred by that section—there being no warrant or summons in the case—and was charged (under the same section) with selling liquor by retail in an unlicensed house. The evidence for the prosecution being closed, the hearing was adjourned at the request of the applicant; but the applicant was not committed, nor were any recognizances taken for her appearance. On the day to which the hearing was adjourned, the applicant did not appear, but sent a letter to the justices excusing her absence, and asking for a further postponement.

The magistrates, however, proceeded with the case, and convicted her. It is submitted that the applicant, who was brought up in custody (there being no warrant or summons), was not then bound to attend at the day to which the adjournment was made, and at all events could not be adjudicated against in her absence. The hearing had been adjourned when she was present ; but she was not again brought up, and being absent was convicted. The applicant was not proceeded against by information, complaint, or summons, but was brought up and prosecuted *in vinculis*. On the adjournment, therefore, she ought to have been again brought up. She could not be sentenced to any imprisonment legally in her absence. The defendant must be present in all cases when sentence is passed; and where the judgment is of corporal punishment, which imprisonment is, he must be present—the Court cannot dispense with his attendance ; *R.* v. *Hann* (c), *Templeman's* case (d),

(a) Before *Stephen*, C. J., *Cheeke*, J., and *Faucett*, J.
(b) 25 Vic., No. 14.   (c) 3 Burr. 1786.   (d) Salk. 56, 400.

2 Hawk., c. 48, s. 17. *Simpson's* case (a), in which it was held that a man might be convicted of deer stealing without appearing, if duly summoned, may be relied on by the other side; but the decision in that case, which was only arrived at after repeated arguments—the inclination of the Court being, at first, the other way—was, that if it were not allowed, the consequence would be that the offender would escape altogether. The justices at that time had no authority to issue a warrant. But that necessity does not now exist, as the justices can now issue a warrant.

1865.

Ex parte
CONN.

The question, however, is one of construction, and depends on the meaning of certain sections of Sir *John Jervis'* Act, with respect to summary proceedings (b). That statute draws a clear distinction between the cases when the defendant is summoned and when brought up on warrant. The third section provides that where a summons has issued, if the party fails to appear in obedience to the summons, and due service of the summons is shown, the justices may proceed *ex parte* to the hearing of such information or complaint, and "adjudicate thereon as fully and effectually, to all intents and purposes," as if there had been an appearance. But the sixteenth section, which authorises an adjournment to a certain time and place, and which ought to have regulated the justices in this case, after providing that the justices "may suffer the defendant to go at large, or may commit him, or may discharge him, upon his entering into recognizances," directs that if at the adjournment either or both of the parties shall not appear, the justices "may proceed to such hearing or further hearing as if such party or parties were present." In the one case the justices may adjudicate as fully and effectually, to all intents and purposes, as if there had been an appearance; in the other, the power given is only that they may hear and further hear. In the thirteenth section also, the words used are "hear and determine," where it was intended to give a plenary

(a) 1 Str. 44; 10 Mod. 250, 345.   (b) 11 & 12 Vic., c. 43.

1865.

Ex parte
Conn.

jurisdiction.   The authority of Mr. *Oke* (a) also supports the contention, that under the sixteenth section
the justices had no jurisdiction over a defendant who
appeared under compulsion, if they allowed him to go
at large ; for he says, quoting that section, " the justices
may suffer the defendant (who appears *not* on a warrant)
to go at large, or may commit, &c." It is submitted,
therefore, that the justices could hear the case, but
could not adjudicate or determine without having the
applicant brought before them on warrant, or issuing
process to make her appear for judgment.   It is clear
that there is no provision for continuing proceedings
after the person apprehended ceases to be in custody.

Cur. adv. rult.

December 12.

Judgment was now delivered as follows :—

STEPHEN, C. J.   The appellant, being in the occupation of an unlicensed house, in which several persons
were found drinking spirits (the adjudication is defective in sundry points, but I assume such to be the
facts, alleged as well as proved), was apprehended with
those persons under section 51 of the Act, and brought
before the justices.   Thereupon, without formal charge
or information exhibited, evidence was gone into ; and,
at its close—as an indulgence to this defendant, it would
seem—the further hearing of the case against her was
adjourned.   On the day of adjournment, she did not
appear ; and then, in the defendant's absence, the
Justices convicted her (under the same section) of unlicensed retailing, and inflicted a fine to the full amount
provided for that offence.

Mr. Justice *Cheeke* and myself—who, with Mr. Justice
Faucett, heard the case—are of opinion that the conviction cannot be sustained.   The proceeding throughout
is a peculiar one ; and the enactment, it appears to us,
which is of the most summary character, must be strictly
pursued.   Persons found drinking in an unlicensed
house, in which intoxicating liquors are sold by retail,
may be apprehended, and so may the person found in

(a) Synopsis Pt. 1, Ch. 1, s. 3.

charge of the house ; and, being taken before justices, all the parties may then be summarily proceeded against, convicted, and fined.   But, in such a case, in order to give the magistrates jurisdiction, it would of course be necessary to show all those facts ; the finding of the persons, that the house was unlicensed, that liquors were sold there, and so on.   In the absence of any record of such matters, what will exist, or appear to have existed, as the initiation or legal groundwork of the inquiry ? It is possible, that (as to this defendant, at all events, she having been the seller of the drink) another course might have been adopted—although we need not now so decide—on the bringing up of the several parties.   That is to say, she might perhaps have been proceeded against in the ordinary way, by a regular charge or information filed ; and, in that event, the several provisions of Sir *John Jervis'* statutes would have applied.   There would then have been an information, and a charge to meet— upon which a summons might have been issued.   Here, however, the proceedings are entirely of an anomalous character ; and Mr. Justice *Cheeke* and myself conceive, that those statutes have therefore no application to the case.

It is not necessary to hold, that the Justices could not legally adjourn the hearing, under any circumstances, after the bringing up of the parties.   Possibly there was such a power.   But it is quite clear, that the enactment does not contemplate, or at any rate does not provide for, the contingency of an adjournment.   It assumes an inquiry and decision, all the parties being found as it were in the very act, on their being brought up in custody.   No provision is made for their liberation on bail, therefore, before or pending the inquiry.   And it would seem to follow, that—if there were an adjournment—all must either remain in custody, or that, should they be admitted to bail, the remedy would be exclusively (as under sections 9 and 13 of *Jervis'* Summary Convictions Act) by the estreating of, or by action upon, the recognisance.   Section 16 of that Act, upon which the justices would appear to have acted, applies

solely—as the terms of that section clearly show—to the
hearing or further hearing of an information, or a complaint, exhibited under the statute.

Mr. Justice *Hargrave*, after conference with the other
Judges, agrees in substance with the opinions here expressed.   He thinks, also—on the assumption that the
said 16th section could be taken to include a case of this
kind—that the objection mainly relied on against the
conviction is fatal.   For, in that section, the power conferred in the absence of an accused, after an adjournment, is simply (in terms) to proceed further with the
hearing; whereas, in the cases provided for by the 2nd
and13th sections (*i.e.*, of non-appearance after summons),
the power is given to proceed to the hearing, and to
adjudicate—or, as expressed in the latter of those
sections, to hear and determine the case.   Whence it
appears that the Legislature bore in mind the distinction
between a hearing, merely, and the hearing and determining of the matter; and the inference is deducible,
therefore, that the distinction expressed was intended.

As to the case of the *Queen* v. *Simpson* (a), it appears
to us—with great respect to Mr. Justice *Faucett*—not to
affect the reasoning on which this judgment is founded.
It may be, that a defendant duly summoned (as in that
case) to meet an information, exhibited before justices,
and not appearing to answer the charge, could at
Common Law be proceeded against in his absence.
Whether all summary proceedings before justices, however, since the passing of Sir *John Jervis'* statutes, are
or not wholly regulated by them, and not by the Common Law, is questionable.   But not to dwell on that
objection, it is sufficient to rely on the answer, that this
is no case of proceeding by a summons, or charge or
information exhibited.   It is, as already shown, a proceeding of a very similar kind, against persons in
custody—created by statute, and highly penal throughout.   The jurisdiction over these persons arises out of
and is founded on that position; and no provision is
made in the statute for the continuance of the juris-

(a) 1 Str. 44.

diction so created—certainly not for its exercise in the party's absence—after the legal termination of that custody.

FAUCETT, J. The object of a summons is to give the magistrates jurisdiction, and to give the person charged notice of what he is charged with.

But by the 51st section of the Licensed Publicans' Act, under which the defendant in this case was convicted, the constable had power to apprehend the defendant at once and bring her before a magistrate. This being done, and the charge being made in the defendant's presence, the magistrate had jurisdiction, and the defendant had notice, as fully as if a summons had been issued, and the defendant had appeared to such summons. The case is then partly heard, and at the defendant's request is adjourned, and the further hearing is fixed for a future day. On the day appointed the defendant does not appear, and she is convicted in her absence and fined £30.

It is objected that this conviction is wrong.

The principal objection raised before me in Chambers was, as to the construction of the 16th section of 11 and 12 Vic., c. 43. Under that section the magistrates have power to adjourn the hearing of a case, and if at the time and place appointed for the further hearing the defendant does not appear, they have power to proceed to the hearing or further hearing, as if the party or parties were present. It was contended that, because the words "hear and adjudicate" are used in one section, and the words "hear and determine" in another section of the Act, and the word "hear" only is used in the 16th section, that, therefore, the magistrates have, under the latter section, no power to adjudicate or determine.

But—admitting the force of the argument—it appears to me that if this be the proper construction, the whole proceeding must be abortive, as there is no other provision under which, in such a case, the magistrates can adjudicate, or take any steps to bring about an adjudication. The proceeding, in fact, would stop short. I therefore think that as the statute gives power to proceed to a hearing as if the parties were present, it necessarily gives power to do all things that might be done if the parties were present, and therefore to adjudicate. Besides, the next sentence gives power—in the absence of the complainant—to finally dismiss the case, which appears to me to show that the Legislature contemplated a final termination in either event.

It is now, however, contended that the 16th section is entirely inapplicable to the present case, and on that point I am not prepared to dissent from the judgment just delivered, inasmuch as that section seems to provide for those cases only in which a summons has been issued.

But when I consider that the defendant in this case was duly brought before the magistrate, and duly charged with the offence for which she was apprehended, and that the adjournment took place at her own request, I am of opinion that as she did not appear at the time appointed, the conviction, in her absence, was good, irrespective of the statute 11 and 12 Vic., c. 43.

In *Rex* v. *Simpson* the defendant had been summoned, but it did not appear that he was ever before the magistrate, yet he was convicted in his absence, and the conviction was held good.

The case was argued several times, and is cited in the most recent authorities as good law. *Parker*, C. J., in giving judgment, says :—" We are of opinion the offender may be convicted without appearing. The statute is silent as to the method of proceeding, and the law of England, it is true, in point of natural justice, always requires the party charged with any offence to be heard before he be condemned in judgment; but this rule must have this exception, unless it is through his own default. Were it otherwise, every criminal might avoid conviction. The law being so, the magistrate is bound to give some opportunity to the party to appear; and if upon such notice he neither comes nor sends a sufficient excuse, the magistrate may proceed to judgment. If this was not to be allowed, the consequences would be that the offender would escape unpunished, because he would never appear purposely to be convicted, and that would be to make the execution of the law depend on the will of the offender."

Now, as the present case does not appear to come within any of the provisions of *Jervis'* Act, and as the statute under which the conviction took place is silent as to the mode of proceeding, I think it must be governed by the principle here laid down. And as all the proceedings that have taken place appear to me to be fully equivalent to the issuing of a summons, both as regards the giving jurisdiction to the magistrate and notice to the defendant, I am of opinion that this conviction ought to stand.

Prohibition granted.

McBean *against* Taylor (a).

December 19.

THIS is an appeal against the direction of *Isidore J. Blake*, Esq., Judge of the South-western District Courts, in an action tried before him and a jury in the Deniliquin District Court, on the 29th November, 1864, to recover damages for the neglect to return eleven bags of flour, the property of the plaintiff, taken possession of by the defendant on the 11th day of December, 1863, and converted to his own use, under the following circumstances as proved.

The particulars of the plaintiff's claim were—(1) trespass; (2) trover for the conversion of eleven bags of flour; and (3) that in consideration that the plaintiff delivered to you eleven bags of flour to be kept by you, and to be re-delivered by you to the plaintiff on request, or other flour to be delivered in exchange for the same or in lieu thereof, for reward to yourself, you promised the plaintiff to return the said eleven bags of flour, and re-deliver the same to the plaintiff, or to deliver other

The defendant, in January 1864, took out of a dray con-, veying flour to the plaintiff's station eleven bags of flour. The plaintiff thereupon agreed to forgive the abduction, on condition that the defendant would replace the quantity on demand. To this the defendant assented, but delayed sending any flour to the plaintiff. The latter remonstrating, but never peremptorily demanding

the flour till September, when flour had advanced considerably in price. The plaintiff having sued the defendant for the conversion of the flour, and also for a breach of the contract to re-deliver, *Held*, that the plaintiff was entitled to recover the value of the goods at the time of the demand in September.

(a) Before *Stephen*, C. J., *Cheeke*, J., and *Faucett*, J.

flour in exchange for the same or in lieu thereof, on request ; and afterwards the plaintiff requested you to re-deliver the said eleven bags of flour, and a reasonable time for the re-delivery thereof elapsed after such request, yet you did not re-deliver the said flour to the plaintiff, and did not deliver other flour in exchange for the same or in lieu thereof, whereby the same was wholly lost to the plaintiff, and the plaintiff had to purchase other flour and pay carriage of the same from Deniliquin to Woorooma Station.   There was also a claim for goods sold.   The particulars also, after claiming £25 6s. for eleven bags of flour purchased in Melbourne and de-livered at Deniliquin, claimed £50 " as damages sus-tained by the plaintiff in consequence of the defendant failing to return the said eleven bags of flour as promised."   The defendant pleaded not guilty, and not possessed to the first two counts, and traversed the promise and the request in the third count, and also that a reasonable time had elapsed.   He also, as to the last count, paid £25 6s. into Court in satisfaction thereof, with costs up to such time.

The case then continued as follows :—" The plaintiff is licensee of the Woorooma Station, on the Edward River, and in December, 1863, purchased fifty bags of flour in Melbourne for use on his said station, at the rate of £13 a ton, or £1 6s. a bag.   The carrier, on his way up with the flour, stopped at the defendant's Royal Hotel, in Deniliquin, and the defendant being in want of flour for his own use took eleven bags of the plaintiff's, being one bag over a ton, and of the value of £14 6s. without the carriage, and he gave notice thereof by a note written by *Alfred Key* (his clerk or book-keeper), and sent on by the carrier to the plaintiff's station, and addressed to one *Colvin*, the plaintiff's manager at his station.

The defendant having failed to replace the flour, the plaintiff demanded its return at the times and in manner proved at the trial by the documentary evidence herein-after set out."

On the 11th December, 1863, defendant wrote to the

plaintiff, stating that he had "borrowed" eleven bags of flour, and that the plaintiff would "get it by next drays, as he (the defendant) had written to Melbourne to start them." On the 13th June, 1864, the defendant wrote, "as to the flour I hardly know how to answer, as I wrote to the Melbourne firm for it to be replaced. However, I will write to *Adam* about it." On 9th July, 1864, the plaintiff wrote to the defendant, "I wish you would be good enough to let me know whether you can send down the flour on or before the end of this month; our stores are now getting short, and shearing time is now advancing, when large supplies will be required, so that we must have it, reason or none; and if you cannot find the means of sending it down at that time, I will be compelled to send my own team for it. Please, do not fail in returning me a definite answer by return mail." To this the defendant replied, "I am very busy just now, so you must excuse a short epistle. I fear there will be some bother about the flour; it should have been sent direct from Melbourne long back, and I assure you it was no fault of Mr. *Taylor's*. It would be rather too much to expect *Taylor* to give flour at the present price for what he received, and which should have been replaced long ago. I wish I could see you to explain matters." On 31st July, 1864, plaintiff wrote as follows:—"I am sorry to say that the time mentioned in one of my letters having now nearly expired without your sending the flour, and no satisfactory arrangement come to as regards it, we will be compelled to send our dray for it, and if you have not it to spare, we could buy it on Mr. *Taylor's* account at one of the stores—or, if you would prefer it, we could buy it in the Moulamein on obtaining the necessary order from you, and awaiting your immediate reply." In the following September the plaintiff's attorney wrote, applying for a return of the flour at the plaintiff's station, or payment for the same at present market price, with carriage added; and on the 8th November a formal demand was served.

The case continued—"It was proved also, on the part of the plaintiff, that flour had considerably advanced in price, and that plaintiff had purchased flour in Deniliquin (in the month of October, 1864), at £35 a ton, or £3 10s. a bag.

On cross-examination of one of plaintiff's witnesses, it was elicited on the part of the defendant that plaintiff had purchased flour in Melbourne, in March 1864, at £17 10s. a ton, or £1 15s. a bag, and that the cost of carriage thereof was £8 a ton. .

On this evidence the Judge directed the jury that the amount of damage the plaintiff had sustained was the difference between the price of the flour taken by defendant, and the cost of carriage, in the month of December 1863, and the price of flour and cost of carriage paid by plaintiff for that purchased by him in March 1864; and the Judge also directed the jury that a sum covering that difference had been paid into Court, and therefore their verdict must be for the defendant.

Under such direction the jury returned a verdict for the defendant.

Against this direction the plaintiff has appealed in point of law.

The question for the opinion of the said Supreme Court is—whether the measure of plaintiff's damage was the difference between the price of the flour taken in December 1863, with the cost of carriage thereof, and the price the plaintiff paid for the flour he bought in October 1864, being his first purchase of flour after his first demand of a return of the eleven bags taken by the defendant; or whether such damage was as the Judge directed the jury."

Isaacs, for the appellant, relied on *Eliot* v. *Hughes* (a), where it was held in an action for the non-delivery of certain goods—the price of which had been paid at the time of the purchase—that the measure of damages was the difference between that price and the price at the time of the trial, which was considerably larger. The third count claims special damages.

(a) 3 F. & F. 387.

Stephen for the respondent. In the case relied on the
action was for breach of contract, and the goods had
been paid for. But this is an action for the wrongful
conversion of the flour, and there was no contract
between the parties, and therefore the measure of
damages is the value of the goods at the time of their
conversion; *Mayne* on Damages (*a*). Why should a
man be allowed to sleep on his rights, and then be
entitled to the value of the goods at the particular time
he may elect to bring his action, when they may be ex-
travagantly high? Mr. Chancellor *Kent,* who favours the
doctrine contended for by the plaintiff, says that the
plaintiff can only be indemnified by giving him the price
of it at the time he calls upon the defendant to restore
it. If so, the damages in this case would be the value
in June, when the first demand was made. The provision in the 24th section of the 5 Vic., No. 9, that the
jury may give damages in the nature of interest over
and above the value of the goods at the time of the conversion, in all actions of trover, confirms the correctness
of the ruling of the learned District Court Judge.

STEPHEN, C. J. The facts of the present case appear
to me to be as follows :—The defendant, in or about
January 1864, took out of a dray conveying flour to the
plaintiff's station eleven bags of flour, then worth
(with the carriage here added, the flour having been
bought in Melbourne, and being then at Deniliquin on
its road to the station) about £18. The plaintiff was
then entitled to bring his action ; but he forgave or
agreed to forgive the abduction, on condition that the
defendant would replace the quantity on demand. The
defendant assented and promised accordingly, but delayed sending or purchasing any flour for the plaintiff ;
the latter in the interval remonstrating, but never peremptorily demanding the flour till the 20th September.
During all this time the price of flour was advancing.
These facts appearing at the trial, the learned Judge
ruled that the jury, notwithstanding, could not give as
damages the price of the flour at the last mentioned date

1865.

MᴄBᴇᴀɴ
v.
Tᴀʏʟᴏʀ.

(*a*) p. 204.

1865.

McBEAN
v.
TAYLOR.

with carriage added, but only the price in January, the
time of the taking—or the price in March, when the
defendant promised immediately to procure the flour. I
am of opinion that this ruling was incorrect, and that
the jury ought to ·be allowed to give the value of the
goods at the time of the demand in September. The
flour was taken tortiously; the right of action was
waived on the agreement that the flour should be returned on demand. This agreement was broken. There
must, therefore, be a new trial; as the defendant having
paid into Court the lower price, namely, that which pre-
vailed in March, obtained the verdict. The appeal,
therefore, must be sustained, and with costs; for,
although the error here was the direction of the Judge,
that direction itself was the result of the objection taken
by the defendant, and the arguments by which he supported that objection—so that there are no special circumstances to take the case out of the general rule.

The other Judges concurred.

RAYNER *against* LYSTER:

A. was tenant
to *B.* of a cer-
tain theatre,
under an
agreement
containing
the following
terms—" *A.*
shall allow
free access to
the persons
employed in
selling fruit.
A. also further
agrees not to
produce the
dramas of
" Faust" and
the "Corsican
Brothers."
A. to pay *B.*
the sum of
£60 per week
in advance,
for the use of
the theatre;

MONEY had and received and on accounts stated.
Plea, never indebted. Issue thereon.

At the trial before *Faucett*, J., in the October Sittings,
it appeared that the defendant was the lessee of the
Prince of Wales Theatre, Castlereagh-street, and that
the plaintiff (who is an actor and theatrical manager)
had become his under-lessee under the following agreement :—

Prince of Wales Opera House,
January 20th, 1864.

Mr. *W. S. Lyster* hereby agrees to let Mr. *Joseph Rayner* have the
use of the Prince of Wales Opera House for a term of fourteen
weeks, commencing April 18th, 1864, and terminating July 23rd,
1864, both dates inclusive. Mr. *Rayner* to have the use of the
scenery, properties, and wardrobe belonging to Mr. *Lyster*, with the
exception of such wardrobe and properties as Mr. *Lyster* will require
to take with him for the use of his Opera Company; also certain
scenes that Mr. *Lyster* will have painted during the ensuing Opera
season, which will be put away and not made use of by Mr. *Rayner.*
Mr. *Lyster* reserves for himself the right to receive the rents of the
fruit stalls, &c., for which Mr. *Lyster* undertakes that the front of the
house shall be kept clean, and seats, &c., covered every night.

also four weeks rent in advance, £240—the said sum to be retained by *B.* as the
last four weeks rent of this agreement. In the event of the rent not being paid
punctually, according to this agreement, *B.* to have full power to reenter, &c., and
the said deposit of £240 to be forfeited, in compensation to *B.* for the non-fulfilment of
the agreement." *A.* entered upon the tenancy and paid the £240. *B.* having re-entered
for non-payment of rent—there being nine days rent in arrear—relet the premises to
another tenant for the residue of the term mentioned in the agreement at the same
rent, and was paid his rent in full from the time of his re-entry. *A.* having sued *B.* for
the amount of the deposit less the rent due, *Held* that he was not entitled to recover.

Mr. *Rayner* shall allow free access to the persons employed in selling fruit, &c.

Mr. *Rayner* also further agrees not to produce or perform during the term of his occupancy, the dramas of "Faust and Marguerite" and the "Corsican Brothers."

Mr. *Rayner* to pay Mr. *Lyster* or his agent the sum of sixty pounds per week in advance, for the use of the said Prince of Wales Opera House, also four weeks rent in advance (£240)—the said sum to be retained by Mr. *Lyster* as the last four weeks rent of this agreement. In the event of the rent not being paid punctually, according to this agreement, Mr. *Lyster* or his agent is to have full power to re-enter and take possession of the said Prince of Wales Opera House, without let or hindrance on the part of Mr. *Rayner*, his agent or employees, and the said deposit of £240 to be forfeited in compensation to Mr. *Lyster*, for the non-fulfilment of the agreement.

(Signed)   *W. S. Lyster.*

Witness—*Charles Dillon.*

1865.

RAYNER
v.
LYSTER.

The plaintiff, on taking possession under the agreement, paid the defendant £240 ; £40 in cash, and the balance of £200 by cheque, which was afterwards honored. A week's rent was paid on the 25th April, and on 2nd May. Default being made on the 9th and 16th May ; the defendant re-entered on the 18th, and relet the theatre for the rest of the time mentioned in the agreement for the same rent, to the performers themselves. It appeared that the defendant had in fact been paid his entire rent in full from the time of the re-entry. The action was brought to recover back the difference between the £240 thus paid by the plaintiff to the defendant, and the amount due to the latter for the nine days rent. A verdict was found for the plaintiff for the amount of his deposit less the rent due, subject to the opinion of the Court as to whether the £240 is a forfeiture or a penalty.

A rule having been obtained accordingly,

Martin, Q. C., and *Salamons* showed cause. The agreement contains certain stipulations on both sides. The plaintiff promises to give free access to the fruit sellers; not to perform "Faust" and the "Corsican Brothers;" and to pay rent of £60 a week; also four weeks rent in advance—the said sum to be retained by Mr. *Lyster* as the last four weeks rent of this agreement. In the event of the rent being unpaid, the defendant is to be able to re-enter, and the said deposit of £240 to be forfeited in compensation to Mr. *Lyster*, for the non-fulfilment of the agreement. It is submitted that these words clearly show that it was the intention of the parties that the £240 was to be forfeited, not for the non-payment of rent, but generally "for the non-fulfilment of the agreement." The £240, therefore, is a penal sum ; and the case therefore falls within the rule, that where articles contain covenants for the performances of several things, and then one large sum is stated at the

November 29.

December 20.

end, to be paid upon breach of performance, that must be considered as a penalty ; that is, merely as a sum intended to cover any damage which may be actually incurred by a breach of the contract (*a*). It also appears that the £240 was the rent for the last four weeks, and yet it could not have been intended that it should have been altogether forfeited for the non-payment of the rent of the last two weeks. Even in *Horner* v. *Flintoff* (*b*), where the agreement used the words "liquidated and settled damages," *Parke*, B., says, "where parties say that the same ascertained sum shall be paid for the breach of every article of an agreement, however minute and unimportant, they must be considered as not meaning exactly what they say, and a contrary intention may be collected from the other parts of the agreement. The rule laid down in *Kemble* v. *Farren* was, that where an agreement contains several stipulations of various degrees of importance and value, a sum agreed to be paid by way of damages for the breach of any of them, shall be construed as a penalty and not as liquidated damages, even though the parties have in express terms stated the contrary." He also referred to *Sparrow* v. *Paris* (*c*), and the cases cited in *Chitty* on Contracts (*d*).

Sir *W. Manning*, Q. C. (*Stephen* with him) contra. The authorities cited are inapplicable to the present case. In those cases the action was brought for the penalty ; and it may be that if the defendant had been suing for the forfeiture, or if the £240 were to be forfeited indiscriminately by the performance of any one of various events, the Court might hold the contract to be one for a "penalty" strictly, and not for liquidated damages. But here the deposit was paid to the defendant as four weeks rent in advance, but to be "retained by the defendant as the last four weeks rent." [*Stephen*, C. J. In case of non-payment "punctually," the defendant might re-enter; and the deposit is to be forfeited to the defendant "in compensation for the non-fulfilment of the agreement," that is to say, by such non-payment.]

STEPHEN, C. J. I am of opinion that the verdict must be entered for the defendant. It is clear that the deposit never was meant to be paid back. In any event it was to be kept. But if the defendant should enter for non-payment of rent, then the deposit is to be retained as "compensation" for the default.

CHEEKE, J., and FAUCETT, J., concurred.

Verdict to be entered for the defendant.

(*a*) *Chitty* on Contracts, ch. 6.   (*b*) 9 M. & W. 679.
(*c*) 7 H. & N. 597 ; 31 L. J. Ex. 137.   (*d*) Ch. 6.

APPENDIX.

STEPHEN, C. J., having taken his seat (a), remarked that, before entering on the ordinary business of the assize, he desired to address some observations to the magistracy and inhabitants of the Southern circuit, in reference to the state of crime so long prevailing in these and the Western districts, and to recent legislative measures adopted for its repression. He then delivered the following Address:—

It had long been obvious to the Judges, as it has been to the police, made familiar with the subject by repeated investigation in the Courts, that the constant outrages on person and property of which the interior has for years been the scene, could not have continued unchecked during such a period, considering the efforts made to apprehend the criminals, unless these men received extensive and ready assistance, by shelter and information, calculated to enable them to elude capture, and thus also to commit further crimes. A recommendation emanated from this Bench, therefore, after a trial conspicuously exhibiting the inadequacy of the existing law, eighteen months ago, suggesting enactments of a comprehensive and more stringent character, against the harbourers and abettors of bushrangers; and to this, probably, in a greater or less degree, the late statute called the Felons' Apprehension Act is owing. Neither the responsibility nor the honour of this valuable enactment, however, as it now stands, is altogether mine; and, believing it to be a measure as just and (in the true sense of the word) merciful in its provisions, as these are likely to be beneficial to the community, I am not only glad of the opportunity of stating, but, if time will allow me, of vindicating them—by showing how entirely they are in accordance with the principles of our ancient English law.

There is a saying very popular among a certain class of declaimers, that a man cannot be made moral by Act of Parliament. But this is true in terms only. If the meaning intended to be conveyed is, that statutes are useless in the attempt to repress crime, the saying is false; and the impress of a law, for good or for evil, may be traced in the character of a nation for ages. The turpitude or the innocence of an action, indeed, and the degree of its criminality, will generally among the mass of men be estimated according to the light in which legislation appears to regard it. The English have always been celebrated among the nations as an order-loving, crime-hating people; and the result may be seen in the anxiety betrayed in their laws to put down crimes

(a) The Goulburn Circuit Court.

A—4

—those more especially of murderers and robbers—at all |hazards and at any cost. But of this very feeling among the community, implanted so thoroughly as it has been through centuries, much is traceable to the very laws themselves from the most early times enacted against those offences; requiring assistance from all persons whatsoever in pursuing the criminal, making the neighbourhood of the place in which committed responsible civilly for the loss, and in punishing those who, from indifference or a worse feeling, abstain from giving that assistance. In my humble judgment, therefore, the Legislature deserves grateful commemoration for the determined spirit in which it has manifested its will that this widespread evil of bushranging may at length be attacked, not in its source merely, but in all its ramifications among the depraved and dissolute—those who favour or help, and those who will not aid to put down the crime.

The provision of the first and second sections of the Act, so necessary in the actual state of things, will find an ample justification in the recital; that not only have these robbers remained long at large, being harboured by many persons, but that they have murdered officers of justice sent for their pursuit, and now are associated together in gangs mounted and armed, and prepared therefore to resist all opposers. The enactment accordingly is, that after certain steps cautiously and slowly taken (a Justice's warrant after oath of the crime, then an indictment by the officer representing here the grand jury, followed by process from a Judge and a solemn summons to surrender, to be published in every available way), the party accused and summoned may be made an outlaw. But this summons can only be issued, where the crime charged is capital; that is, one punishable by law with death. Then, after proclamation to that effect by the Executive, the outlaw may at any time—either by a constable or a private individual, and either with or without demand to surrender—provided he be armed or reasonably suspected of being armed, be shot dead.

It is evidently not meant by this, that the outlaw is needlessly and wantonly to be killed; for the words are, "may be taken alive or dead." But the object was, against men thus charged, and thus remaining at large, armed, desperate, and prepared at all points for resistance, to protect the well-disposed—officers as well as individuals—from the doubts and risks to which in the previous state of the law they were exposed, in the endeavour to arrest a supposed felon. A careful examination of the authorities will show that these doubts (in the case of a private individual at least) are of a very alarming character. And it is too much to expect, that persons encountering armed ruffians like these should, in addition to the risk of being themselves instantly killed, incur the danger of a charge of felony, for an act righteously meant—but perhaps not in strictness legally justifiable. The most humane will hardly contend. that the life of the honest man and good subject should be more liable to sacrifice than that of an accused and notorious practised robber; or that a proclaimed and armed felon of that stamp, who has set all law at defiance, may be allowed one more chance of his life, and of escape, by requiring a challenge—and so, giving him the opportunity of adding a murder (probably not the first) to his list of crimes.

The enactment, as I have thus explained, applies only to outlaws for some capital crime, proclaimed and armed, or reasonably supposed to be armed; and since this is so, if there be any truth or force in the observations with which I have accompanied the explanation, it may with all respect be questioned—unless there be no probability of bushranging ever arising again,—whether a law so wholesome should not be made perpetual.

By the ancient law of England, an outlaw for felony (all felonies being in those days capital) might be killed by any one; and although this barbarity, since the act might be done without pretence of the furtherance of justice, was put an end to by a very early statute, the power was still left to the sheriff—and so, I apprehend, the law remains at this day. By the same law, moreover, an outlawry for any such felony amounts to a conviction of the crime, as effectually as if the accused had been found guilty of it by a jury. But the process of outlawry, as it exists in England, though more slow, is not so careful of the accused's safety as that prescribed by the local enactment. For, as you have seen, he has here secured to him ample means of knowledge; and even then, if he be not armed, and so may be approached without danger to the taker's life, the colonial outlaw is (as to apprehension) on the footing of any other indicted person.

I have next to state the substance of the harbouring clauses of the Act; the fourth and sixth—which, although subordinate to the main object of suppressing robberies and their attendant crimes, is, as conducive to that object, the most important portion probably of the measure.

By the former of these sections, every person in any manner affording support or assistance, of any kind whatever, to a proclaimed outlaw, knowing him to be such—either by shelter, sustenance, or information, or by the gift or loan of anything intended or *tending* to facilitate his escape, or to enable him to commit further crime, is declared guilty of felony; and, besides forfeiting all his property, may be sentenced to hard labour for fifteen years. Moreover, the giving of false information to any constable in search of such outlaw, or withholding information if demanded, is made equally punishable. And, although the person may act thus under compulsion more or less, in respect to the assistance or support afforded, the fact will be no defence, unless he shall as soon as possible afterwards have gone before some justice, or officer of police, and stated on oath all the facts connected with such compulsion.

Such, in substance, is the enactment against the harbourers and abettors of an outlaw; and, by the aid of upright and intelligent juries carrying it into effect, we may hope that the great scandal and reproach to these districts, that so many of the inhabitants have aided murderers and robbers in their career, will at length be wiped away. There will of course be no offence committed, if the party received and relieved is not known by the receiver to be an outlaw; for such, I conceive, was clearly the meaning of the Legislature. But this knowledge need not, I apprehend, amount to *certainty* as to the fact. If, in his own mind, the person receiving or relieving an outlaw believes (or perhaps only even suspects) him to be such,—although on these points I pronounce no decided opinion,—the offence would probably be deemed complete. And certainly if there exist reasonable grounds, from the appearance and demeanour of the party, or other circumstances, and from the extensive circulation of the proclamation of outlawry in the district, for the entertaining of such a belief, there would be strong evidence to go to a jury of such knowledge.

The difficulties under the law as it stood, before the passing of this statute, were these: that to constitute harbouring an offence, the harbourer must have had knowledge of some particular felony having been committed, and by the party harboured—and the harbouring must have been with the proved intention to aid in the felon's escape. The harbourer then became an accessory to the felony. But, although he could be tried independently of the principal, the latter's guilt had to be proved on the occasion as well as his own. Finally, the punishment provided (except for the harbouring of a murderer) was wholly inadequate to the offence.

It remains only to be said of section 6, that it enables any justice or officer of the police force to enter into and search any house in which an outlaw is reasonably suspected to be harboured, either by day or by night—and there to apprehend any person reasonably suspected to be an outlaw, or to have harboured one. The power is confined, it will be observed, to justices or officers in the police, and is not possessed by any ordinary constable, unless acting in aid of such. It extends, however, to the case not only of an outlaw, as in the previous clauses, but to that of any accused and *summoned* person, before his actual outlawry.

On the other hand, under section 7, which authorises the taking of horses, equipments, and ammunition, for the purpose of pursuing any outlaw (compensation for the use being provided for by the enactment), any ordinary constable has the power. Such a power, it may be admitted, is liable to abuse. But so is every other power—and every privilege, created for the public good. Practically, I am persuaded that no evil will be found to arise from this provision. But, should a solitary instance or two of rash or needless exercise of the right occur in the hot pursuit of an outlaw, such as he has been here described as being, the temporary inconvenience will assuredly be regarded, by the well disposed among the community, as of little moment—in comparison with the all important object to be attained.

It may be well to observe with respect to the 6th clause, giving powers to be exercised on reasonable belief or suspicion, that this reasonableness, as in every similar case, must be judged of in the first instance, at his own peril, by the person suspecting. Should any question respecting it afterwards arise, however, he will be required to establish the reasonableness to the satisfaction of a jury.

Let us now consider what the powers are, respecting the pursuit and arrest of a robber by the ancient English law—recognised and enforced by statutes, passed at various times from the reign of *Edward I.* to that of the third *George* (a). It is this. Upon a "hue and cry" raised (in

(a) Among other ancient statutes, the following (3 Edward I., cap. 9 of Westminster 1st, A.D. 1275) may be cited:—"Forasmuch as the peace of this realm hath been evil observed heretofore for lack of quick and fresh suit making after felons in due manner, and mainly because of franchises, where felons are received; it is pro-substance an openly made complaint, or outcry, by a person set upon and robbed on the road, or in any wood, or the like), the supposed felon shall be pursued by horse and with foot, from town to town, till he be taken. The sheriff of the county is bound, on such a complaint, to raise such hue and cry; and so is the constable of the hundred—or it may be raised by the party himself who was robbed. Every person above the age of fifteen, able to bear arms, is compellable to join in the pursuit, on pain of fine and imprisonment; and any person refusing assistance, if required of him, is similarly punishable. It is accordingly held, for this reason, that every one so joining has the same power, and the same protection, that the sheriff or constable hath: so that he may break open doors, if necessary, and may kill the person flying, although innocent, if he cannot otherwise be taken. Lastly, if the robber be not arrested within forty days, the inhabitants of the hundred wherein the crime was committed are answerable to the party robbed for his loss. By the ancient law, moreover, in cases of homicide or dangerous wounding, if the offender escaped, the town or hundred in which the crime was committed was fined.

A private person, not joining in any such hue and cry, and not acting in aid of a constable—although entitled equally with a constable, on reasonable suspicion, to apprehend a supposed felon, where a felony has actually been committed by some one,—seems not to have the same power or protection that the constable possesses. For, says Sir *Matthew Hale*, he is only permitted, but in such a case is not enjoined, to make the arrest. If, however, the party pursued be really guilty, and the individual attempting his arrest knows, or is content to abide the risk of proving the fact, then it would appear that the private person is entitled to break doors (the felon being actually in the house broken), and, provided the robber cannot otherwise be taken, to kill him—as a constable may do, on reasonable suspicion only.

I wish to add yet a few remarks, naturally suggested by the subject. It is not supposed, and the suspicion would be most unjust if anywhere entertained, that the majority of the southern and western districts assist, or in any degree sympathise with the wretched men of whom I have spoken. Far otherwise. But, that there has been a large amount of sympathy with bushrangers prevailing, both here and elsewhere, however disgraceful the fact, cannot be disputed. It is not easy to determine to what unhappy circumstances this should be attributed. That in no small degree, however, the institution and the support of bushranging in this colony are owing to the lawlessness, and spirit of self-will, which commenced with the Burrangong riots, and culminated in the acquittals of March 1861, no observant and intelligent person will be able with truth to deny. I am myself, in every sense and feeling, a colonist; and refer to the history of those days with sorrow, and not in anger. It is impossible to forget, however,

vided, that all generally be ready and apparelled at the commandment and summons of sheriffs, and at the cry of the country, to sue and arrest felons when any need is, as well within franchise as without; and they that will not so do and thereof be attainted, shall make a grievous fine to the king; and if default be found in the lord of the franchise, the king shall take the same franchise to himself; and if default be in the bailiff, he shall have one year's imprisonment, and after shall make a grievous fine; and if he have not whereof, he shall have imprisonment of two years."—*Taylor's* Book of Rights, p. 56.

that in that year there were publications in the local journals almost without precedent in a peaceful country, insisting on the illegal expulsion of certain foreigners from our gold-fields, and openly avowing a determination to exclude them by force. The riots followed—above a thousand of the subjects of the Queen participating in them; and of the many, who were sworn by the constabulary—till then credited members of the community,—to have been concerned in those outrages, unworthy of a people calling itself civilised, all except two persons were pronounced not guilty.

In the history of individuals, it will generally be found that a desperate disregard of duty in one direction, unless under overwhelming temptation, leads rapidly to the contempt and violation of all other duties. The mob which commences with one illegal act, impelled by whatever object, soon rushes unchecked into other excesses, and ends by breaking open prisons, and burning or pillaging a city. So we here see in the outset law and order openly set at defiance ; the helpless despoiled and maltreated, and punishment invoked for the perpetrators in vain. And it is certain that in May 1861, there began the system so long successfully organised by *Gardiner*, and supported by numerous adherents in the country traversed by him, the results of which have been the demoralisation of large numbers of our youth, the loss of a vast quantity of property and much productive labour, the sacrifice of several lives, the entailment of great suffering on innocent persons, and the acquisition by us of a character in the eyes of other communities which half a century perhaps may not obliterate.

There are countries, in which systematic or very extensive robbery by violence has ere now existed, and occasionally with features from which as yet this colony has been free. Highway robberies were common for a time in England, in the reign of *William* the Third. They have been a scourge for centuries, to travellers and others in parts of Italy. But we stand alone, I fear, in this; that the professional robber is here without any pretence of excuse or palliation for his lawlessness; that he has had before him every inducement to honesty; that he is the victim in no single instance of oppression, or temptation to crime from poverty; but that all seem to have plunged into habits of pillage, from an innate love of wickedness; and that the worst of these ruffians, certainly the greater number, have been young men—some not of age.

It is worth while to notice, however, that of the many who within the last four years have taken to this way of life, scarcely one—I believe not one—has finally prospered in his vocation, such as it is, or succeeded in escaping arrest and conviction, except by death. *Lowry*, *O'Meally*, *Burke*, and *Morgan* were shot while engaged in their nefarious trade. *Piesley* and *Manns* have been executed. *Bow* and *Fordyce* were sentenced to death, and now remain at the mercy of the Crown. *Gordon* and *Gardiner* are sentenced to hard labour, each in effect for life. *Hill*, *Drynob*, and *Jones*, after a very short career, as also *Vane*, *Jamieson*, and *Dunleavy*, are all now suffering under sentences varying from ten to fifteen years. It would be well if those who are said to have followed, and all who are disposed to follow, the example of these unhappy men, would take warning by their fate.

The wholesale discrediting of any body of men, engaged however

APPENDIX.

humbly as assistants in the administration of justice, and the disparagement of them by unjust comments and obloquy, cannot but be injurious to the community which has to look to them for protection. I must be permitted to say, therefore, in conclusion, that (after ample experience and tolerably close observation) I believe the police of this colony, speaking of them of course generally, but with very few exceptions at any time coming under my notice, to be highly intelligent, faithful, zealous, active, and gallant public servants—little deserving the complaints sometimes still made against them. How unreasonable is it, for example, to complain of the constabulary, for inability to capture the bushrangers said to be now at large. If we may conjecture the movements of these men by those of their predecessors, the state of the interior over which they roam would alone go far to account for the failure. Those robbers traverse often, if not habitually, an extent of country nearly as large as that of Ireland, but having a population not one sixtieth that of Ireland; thickly wooded in most parts, and of a very broken surface in many others, along sixty or eighty miles of which there were probably not three houses in which a constable would obtain true information respecting these men, but throughout every portion of which the latter had friends, ready to assist them in every way. Add to this, that in almost every encounter, and every case of pursuit, the bushrangers have been mounted on fresh horses, easily procured at any time by a new robbery; while the horses of their pursuers, even if ordinarily equal in speed and power, were almost unfit for use from fatigue. Let due allowance be made for these things, and for this also, that the police have always had other duties to discharge, with little intermission to recruit their strength, and I am persuaded that blame on this score at least will hardly be attached to these functionaries.

But, gentlemen, my address has already extended much beyond the limits which I had proposed to myself, and I will occupy your time no longer.

ROBERTSON *against* DUMARESQ (a).

In a proceeding by way of petition of right against the Government for not granting an allotment of land pursuant to contract, it was proved that the Governor, in order to induce D. to settle there, promised him a grant of land at W. ; that D. gave up his claim to an allotment at W. in consideration of a promise to grant an allotment at H., which latter was not carried out.

Held, not to be necessary to prove as a condition precedent that D. had settled in the colony, the agreement implying only that he should settle when the grant was made.

Held, further, that the measure of damages for breach of such a contract is the highest value which such land as had not been allotted had acquired.

THIS (b) was an appeal from a judgment of the Supreme Court of New South Wales, refusing a new trial in a proceeding in the nature of a petition of right, brought by the respondent against the appellant, the Secretary for Lands and Public Works, nominated as defendant to represent the Government under the provisions of an Act passed in the colony, " To give relief to persons having claims against the Government of New South Wales." The respondent having, under the provisions of this Act, petitioned for and obtained leave to prosecute his claim, proceeded to file a declaration against the nominal defendant. A rule or order of the Judges of the Supreme Court made under the Act, rendered this form of proceeding necessary, which was of an untechnical nature.

The plaintiff, by his declaration, set forth his claim against the Government in substance as follows :—

" That in the year 1826, being a captain in the Royal Staff Corps serving in the colony, but with no intention of settling there, the then Governor-General *Darling* promised him, as an inducement to settle in the colony, and for other reasons, a grant of land at Woolloomooloo.

" That subsequently he gave up his claim to that land, in consideration of a promise from the Governor of another allotment in Hyde-park-gardens, near Sydney, which was about to be appropriated to grants.

" That relying upon this promise, he, in 1827, retired from active service, and settled in the colony, and also filled certain civil offices under the Government.

" That in 1831 the above promise was ratified by the Governor, but, that owing to some change in the plans, the allotment to him was from time to time postponed.

" That Governor *Darling* left the colony before his promise was carried out, and his successor, Governor *Burke*, in 1831, informed him, the respondent, that he could not have an allotment in Hyde-park, as it was not to be alienated, and offered him the choice of another allotment in an inferior position, and of less value, and otherwise less desirable, which he declined, and that from that time to the present he had failed to obtain a fair equivalent or compensation in lieu of the land promised to him."

To this declaration the defendant demurred and raised the question whether the declaration disclosed any sufficient contract on which a right of action could rest. The judgment of the Court on the demurrer was in favour of the plaintiff, thereby sustaining the declaration.

The action then proceeded on the pleas, which took issue on the above counts of the declaration, and the trial took place before *Milford*, J., and a jury. Both the Judge and the parties treated the issue and

(a) Present—The Right Hon. Lord CHELMSFORD, the Lord Justice KNIGHT BRUCE, and the Lord Justice TURNER.
(b) This case is reprinted from the 10 Law Times, N.S. 110.

the evidence admissible as of an exceptional character, and not so strictly as in an ordinary action. In summing-up he directed the jury that, if the Governor promised to give the plaintiff a piece of land if and on condition that he would settle in the country, and he afterwards, within a reasonable time, did so, the promise was binding from that time. If he did so with an intention to complete the contract, he could take advantage of his having done so; but if he did so without reference to the contract, he could not. There was no consideration moving from him, and the learned Judge put the question to them, " Did the plaintiff perform the condition? that is, did he settle with reference to the contract?" And with reference to damages, he told them that they were to be estimated according to the present value of the land. The jury found a verdict for the plaintiff £5000 damages. A new trial was afterwards moved for on the grounds that the verdict was contrary to law, and was against evidence, and the damages were excessive. The rule for a new trial was refused, whereon the present appeal was brought.

Sir *H. Cairns*, Q. C., and *W. Williams*, for the appellant, contended, first, that what passed between the Government and the respondent, as to the allotment, did not amount to a contract, for there was nothing definite and specific in the negotiation. Secondly, even if the promise had been specific, there was no legal consideration; there was merely an intention in a certain event, which did not happen, to make a grant of the land. Thirdly, even if there was a promise legally binding, it had been discharged by the offer of a third piece of land in lieu of the other. Fourthly, the damages were excessive, and ought not to have been estimated in the manner in which damages are estimated when stock is not delivered: *Hadley* v. *Baxendale* (a), *Logan* v. *Hall* (b), *Owen* v. *Routh* (c).

Bovill, Q. C., and *B. A. Fisher*, for the respondent, contended that the objections as to the indefiniteness of the contract had not been raised in the Court below, and it was now too late to insist upon them. The finding of the jury had cured any objection that might have been previously raised on that ground. As regards the damages, the true rule was that the highest value should be taken as the test of the loss, the principle being that whatever the party might have gained if the promise had been fulfilled was the measure of what he had lost.

LORD CHELMSFORD. With respect to the first proposed objection that the verdict was against law, it does not appear to have been raised upon the motion for a new trial, nor would it have been so. If the evidence of the contract offered at the trial showed that it was invalid for some reason which was not apparent upon the face of the declaration, the defendant should have applied to the Judge to nonsuit the plaintiff, and whether he took this course or not, it was competent to him to raise the objection upon a motion for a new trial. And yet, although the invalidity of contract was not (and could not have been) a point for the consideration of the Court, upon the argument of the

(a) 9 Ex. 341. (b) 4 C. B. 598. (c) 14 C. B. 327.

rule, it is assigned by the appellant as the first of the reasons for his appeal, and was insisted upon at some length by his learned counsel at the bar. The objections which they urged were that the contract was without consideration, and that it was uncertain and indefinite as to the extent of the allotment to be granted, and the character and cost of the building to be erected. But these objections not being open upon the present appeal, they have been wholly excluded from their Lordships' consideration, as, in forming a judgment upon the case, they have endeavoured to confine themselves (as they were bound to do) to the questions raised in and determined by the Court below. They use the word "endeavoured," because it is a little difficult to ascertain the exact shape in which the objections to the verdict were presented to the Court. The only points which appear to have been argued are, that the verdict was against evidence; that the Judge misdirected the jury as to the rule for estimating the damages; and that the damages were excessive. The ground upon which the verdict appears to have been objected to as contrary to the evidence was, the jury having found that the plaintiff had settled in the colony with reference to the contract; in other words, that he preformed the condition upon which he became entitled to the allotment of land. The appellant's counsel, however, objected to the verdict as against evidence upon another and a wider ground, and as their Lordships have no means of knowing whether the objection was or was not presented in this form to the Court below, they will not leave it unnoticed. The declaration alleges that the Governor promised the plaintiff, as an inducement for him to settle in the colony, to grant him a portion of Woolloomooloo; that the plaintiff gave up his claim to the fulfilment of this promise, in consideration of receiving a promise from the Governor of a grant of an allotment in Hyde-park-gardens; and that a portion of the land first promised to the plaintiff was granted to Dr. *Douglas* by the Governor. The appellant's counsel insisted that the respondent had entirely failed in proof of these allegations; that he never had a promise binding upon the Governor in respect of Woolloomooloo, and that, therefore, his relinquishment of his claim to an allotment in that district could not be the consideration for the promise of a grant in Hyde-park-gardens. And for this they relied upon the terms of a letter written by Dr. *Douglas*, which was in evidence in the case as a part of the proceedings of the Committee of Legislative Council appointed to inquire into the respondent's claim, in which, with reference to a particular portion of land in Woolloomooloo, he writes:—"I should have applied for it before had I not understood it was Captain *Dumaresq's* intention to have done so. I have since learnt from that gentleman that he has abandoned the idea." These expressions, however, are not at all inconsistent with the existence of a right at one time in the respondent to select an allotment in Woolloomooloo if he chose to exercise it; and the evidence seems to be quite sufficient to have justified the jury (if this question had been submitted to them) in finding that there was a binding promise of an allotment in the Woolloomooloo, and that it was relinquished for the promise of a grant of a portion of Hyde-park-gardens. Both these points appear to be fully established by the letter of the respondent of the 2nd June, 1830, and the answer of the Colonial

APPENDIX.

Secretary, on behalf of the Governor, of the 9th June, 1830. The respondent in his letter says:—"I beg leave to bring to your Excellency's recollection the circumstance of your implied promise, that I might have a building allotment in the neighbourhood of Sydney, and that on my renunciation of the land on Woolloomooloo Hills, afterwards given to Dr. *Douglas*, it was with the understanding that I should receive a portion of the Hyde-park-gardens in lieu thereof;" and he then requests the Governor to direct that an allotment may be measured off to him, and points out the one which, if permitted to select, he would prefer. The answer recites, in the usual official form, the purport of the respondent's letter, and not denying, and therefore virtually admitting, the statement it contains,—it informs the respondent that the Governor had directed his application to be noted, "in order to its being considered with those of other applicants when arrangements may be making for the location of Hyde-park." The promise thus admitted to have been given was more distinctly recognised by Governor *Darling* in a minute of the 15th October, 1831, made for the purpose of placing on record the claims of "the persons who were promised building allotments in Hyde-park," in which, arranging them in classes, he says, "The second class consists of *William Dumaresq*, Esq., promised by me some considerable time back, that he should receive an allotment as soon as the ground was measured, and he should have retired from the service." These letters and the official minute are amply sufficient to prove the allegations in the declaration, and if the case had been left to the jury upon this proof, and they had found for the respondent, their verdict could not have been disturbed. But, as already observed, the question seems to have been presented to the jury upon a narrower and different ground, viz., whether the plaintiff had performed the condition upon which he became entitled to the allotment. It appears that the learned Judge who tried the cause directed the jury that it was necessary for the plaintiff to prove that he had settled in the colony "with reference to the contract." But he afterwards agreed with the Chief Justice that the only material portion of the allegation in the declaration was that after the promise or offer the plaintiff in fact became resident, and that by so doing he performed the condition, and that it was not necessary to show a performance because and in consideration of the contract. The perplexity upon this part of the case seems to have arisen from the want of precision in the statement of the plaintiff's cause of action, and from a misapprehension of the real nature of his claim. If it is necessary in this proceeding in the nature of a petition of right to state the claim in a technical form, and to allege a consideration for the promise of an allotment, it is obvious that the true consideration was not the settling in the colony, but the agreement to settle if a grant were made, and if this had been thought of at the trial, an amendment of the declaration might have been made which would have obviated all difficulty. It is not easy to understand how the actual settling in the colony can be made a condition precedent to a grant of this description, because no proof of its performance can possibly be given, and the utmost that any declaration or act of the grantee prior to the grant can amount to, being an intention to settle when the grant is made. But as the case was dealt with throughout as one in which the plaintiff could only enforce the promise of the Governor by performing the condition, which was held to be the actual settling in the colony, the question is, whether, assuming this view to be correct, the evidence is not sufficient to support the verdict. It appears that there were two periods at which an intention on the part of the respondent to settle in the colony was manifested—first, when he had received an offer of a colonial appointment, and was, as he states, induced by it to go on half-pay, and afterwards, when having been placed on whole pay again, he determined upon selling his commission and settling in the country. It is to be observed that his evidence, that "it was not the promise of the land which induced him to go upon half-pay and settle in the country, but the prior offer of the office of Deputy Surveyor-General and other consequential advantages," relates to the land at Woolloomooloo, which he afterwards relinquished for the promised allotment in Hyde-park. As to this latter promise the respondent states in his evidence at the trial—"In selling my commission and determining on settling in the country, I was influenced not alone by the specific promise, but also by my knowledge of the regulations which entitled me to a town allotment, and a country allotment if I settled in the country." There is no proof of the exact time when the respondent sold his commission; but in the minute of the 15th October, 1831, to which reference has been already made, Governor *Darling* says, the allotment in Hyde-park was promised to him "as soon as the ground was measured, and he should have retired from the service," therefore the promise must have been made while he retained his commission, and if so, his retirement from the service was a performance of the condition. Even, therefore, if *Milford*, J., was right, at the trial, in saying that it was necessary for the plaintiff to show that he settled in the country with an invention to complete the contract, there was here ample evidence to establish that fact. But *Milford*, J., was of opinion that, if his mode of presenting the case to jury was correct, they were not warranted in finding that the plaintiff had performed the condition unless his settling in the colony was solely with a view to the contract, and to the exclusion of all other motives. But as he agreed with the Chief Justice that a residence in fact, after the promise, was all that it was material for the plaintiff to establish, he thereby admitted that he had left the case improperly to the jury. It may, therefore, be considered unnecessary to examine his opinion that, in order to show performance of the conditions upon which the promise was made, it was necessary for the plaintiff to prove that it was his sole motive for settling in the colony. But in order that no part of the case should appear to have been omitted from their Lordships' consideration, a few remarks may be made upon this opinion, and upon the opposite view of the Chief Justice. It may be asked, if the opinion under consideration shall be held to be correct, in what way could a person holding a permanent official appointment in the colony, who is promised an allotment, or a person who has already one allotment, and is promised another, show that he has performed the condition in the strict and exclusive manner required? It seems only necessary to consider the nature of these grants to be satisfied that such a rigid rule can never properly be applied to them.

When an application is made to the governor for an allotment of land, and a promise is obtained, the application always implies a promise on the part of the applicant to settle in the colony, because the grants invariably contain a condition to that effect. A continuance in the colony, therefore, till the grant of the allotment is made, is necessarily connected with the promise, as without remaining the applicant can never be entitled to the promised grant. In every way, therefore, in which this case either was or might have been presented to the jury, the evidence was sufficient to warrant the verdict. The only remaining question relates to the damages—whether the proper rule for their estimation was given by the judge, and whether they are excessive. Supposing the rule for the measure of damages properly given, they do not appear to have been excessive. The committee of the Legislative Council selected to investigate the respondent's claim reported that he should be allowed to purchase land at auction for £5000, a sum apparently fixed with reference to land granted to Sir *F. Forbes*, which was sold by auction in 1842 for that sum. It was contended on the part of the applicant, that the land of Sir *F. Forbes* had buildings upon it, and was therefore an improper standard of the value of land which the respondent was to receive under an obligation to build upon it. But it appears by the evidence that Sir *F. Forbes's* land had never been built upon, and that even at the time of the trial it remained in its original unimproved state. If, then, the present value of the land was the proper criterion of the measure of damages, no objection can justly be taken to the amount awarded by the jury. But upon what ground can it be alleged that the judge was wrong in telling the jury to find their damages upon the present value of the land? The cases which were cited as to the measure of damages upon contracts for delivery of goods and for the re-transfer of stock, have very little application. The distinction between these two classes of cases is said to be that, in the former the damages should be only of the value of the goods at the time when they ought to have been delivered, because the purchaser has his money in hand, and may go in to the market and purchase similar goods; but as to stock, that the borrower who neglects to re-transfer at the time agreed upon holds in his hands the money of the lender, and prevents him from using it. The principle upon which damages are estimated upon the breach of an agreement for the re-transfer of stock is more applicable to the respondent's claim than that which is applied to contracts for the sale and delivery of goods, but the right of the respondent to the highest value of the lands which he has not received in performance of the promise made to him seems to be even stronger than that of the lender of stock upon the borrower's omission to replace it. The owner of the stock might have the means of purchasing other similar stock at the day, but the allotment of land promised to the respondent was a thing which he could not obtain except by the performance of the promise. If he had received his allotment as he ought to have done, he would have it, with the benefit of the increased value which it might have acquired while in his possession. Of this the other party has deprived him by the breach of his promise; and whether he has obtained the benefit himself, or has hindered the respondent from enjoying it, it seems to

1884.

ROBERTSON
v.
DUMARESQ.

be equally just and reasonable that he should pay the full value of the property to the person from whom he has wrongfully withheld it. Their Lordships are therefore of opinion that the judgment of the court below is right; they will recommend to Her Majesty that it be affirmed, and the appeal dismissed with costs.

Judgment affirmed with costs.

Dec. 1, 1863.

VIVERS *against* TUCK (a).

A Court of Equity will not decree specific performance of an agreement more favourable to the plaintiff than to the defendant, involving hardship upon the defendant and damage to his property, if he entered into it without advice or assistance, and there be reasonable ground for doubting whether he entered into it with a knowledge and understanding of its nature and its consequences.

Suit for specific performance of a partnership agreement, prepared and written by the plaintiff, dismissed, and the plaintiff left to his remedy (if any) at law for damages for non-performance thereof; the defendant, an illiterate man, being at the time of the execution of the agreement considerably in liquor, without professional advice, and without knowledge of its nature and consequences, which were

THIS (b) was a suit for specific performance of an agreement for a partnership, which was resisted by the respondent upon the grounds of fraud, circumvention, mistake, and surprise.

In the year 1859, the appellant and respondent agreed verbally to enter into partnership, for the purpose of establishing and carrying on gas works at West Maitland.

These gasworks were at the time of such agreement in course of erection upon part of a block of land in Maitland, the property of the respondent, who had then recently returned from a voyage to England, which he had undertaken, among other things, for the purpose of procuring the necessary plant, &c. The respondent was at the same time engaged in furthering a bill in the Legislature, which shortly afterwards became law, authorizing him to light with gas the towns of East and West Maitland.

On the 27th of September, 1859, a written document under seal, purporting to be a memorandum of the agreement which had been come to between himself and the respondent, was drawn up by the appellant, and executed at the house of the respondent by both parties, in the presence of Mr. *Buchanan*, a coach-builder at West Maitland, who attested its execution in the usual manner. This document was as follows:—"Memorandum of an agreement made this 27th day of September, 1859, between *John Warn Tuck*, of West Maitland, in the colony of New South Wales, hotel-keeper, of the one part, and *Robert W. Vivers*, of King's Plains, Wellingrove, in the said colony, of the other part. The said *John Warn Tuck* hereby agrees to receive the said *Robert W. Vivers* as an equal partner and proprietor with himself of the West Maitland gas works, and plant and premises, consisting of one half that parcel or block of land on the south-west side of High Street, West Maitland, on which are situated the Commercial Hotel, the coach manufactory, and the said gas works and plant, that is, the south-east side or half thereof on which the said gas works are situated, and extending from the said High Street to the south-western end of the said block, or parcel of land, and all the buildings and improve-

highly favourable to the plaintiff, and the agreement with respect to the property affected by it being moreover vague and obscure.

(a) Present—Lord KINGSDOWN, the Lord Justice KNIGHT BRUCE, and the Right Hon. Sir JOHN TAYLOR COLERIDGE.
(b) Taken from 1 Moore P. C. N. S. 516.

ments contained thereon, and the gas-house, furnace, and fittings, the gasometer and fittings, the purifiers and fittings; and every other part of the said gas-works and plant. And the said *John Warn Tuck* agrees that the said *Robert W. Vivers* shall become proprietor of one-half of the above-named property on the following conditions: that is, the said *Robert W. Vivers* shall pay one half of the expenses justly and necessarily incurred in the erection of the said gas-house, works, and plant, and one-half of the expenses justly and necessarily incurred in the erection of the said gas-house, works, and plant, and one-half of the cost, freight, and commission, paid by the said *John Warn Tuck*, for all the fittings now used in the said works. And the said *John Warn Tuck* and *Robert W. Vivers* further agree to continue to invest equal amounts of capital for the completion of the said gas-works and the lighting up of the town of Maitland with gas, and to bear equally all other expenses reasonably and necessarily incurred for the manufactory of gas, and to receive equal shares of all the proceeds and profits thereof. And neither of the above-named parties shall have power to sell the whole or any part of his interest in the said gas works, plant, or premises, without the consent of the other partner; and if either party wishes to sell the whole or any part of his interest in the said gas works, he must give the other the option of purchasing from him; and if either party shall die, the surviving partner shall have power to claim, take, and enjoy possession of the whole of said gas works, plant, and premises, on payment to the heirs or assigns of the deceased partner the amount of capital invested by the said deceased which has not been realized by the profits of the investment. The above agreement shall come into force and take effect as soon as a bill authorizing the said *John Warn Tuck* to lay down the main gas-pipes in the streets and light up the town of Maitland with gas, shall have passed the Legislature of the Colony of New South Wales, and become law, and not sooner."

On the same day that the agreement was executed, the appellant paid to the respondent £2,000, in part performance, as he alleged, thereof, but for the repayment of which he took as security the title deeds of the property belonging to the respondent, and also his promissory note, upon which the appellant subsequently brought an action against the respondent.

Shortly after the execution of the above agreement, the respondent, who was an illiterate and uneducated man, discovered that the agreement he had executed was not at all in the terms of the verbal agreement he had previously entered into with the appellant, and, among other inaccuracies, contained stipulations regarding the right to sell, and also the right of survivorship, which had never been discussed between himself and the appellant, or assented to by him: under these circumstances, the respondent declined to act upon the agreement, or to admit the appellant into partnership, whereupon the appellant filed a bill against him in the Supreme Court, setting forth the above agreement, and alleging its due execution, and that it had been registered, and praying specific performance thereof, and for an injunction restraining the respondent from carrying on the gas works, &c., otherwise than in co-partnership with the appellant, and for the execution of a proper deed of co-partnership.

The respondent by his answer admitted that on the 27th of September, 1859, an agreement for partnership, and also for the purchase and sale of one moiety of the gas works at Maitland, was entered into between himself and the appellant, but stated that its terms were different from those embodied in the written agreement. The answer alleged, that the agreement entered into between the appellant and the respondent was to the effect, that the latter would receive the former as an equal partner and proprietor with himself in and of the West Maitland gas works, plant, and appurtenances, and the manufactory of gas there to be carried on, upon condition that the appellant should pay one-half the expenses which should have been incurred by the respondent in erecting the gas-house, providing the works and plant, and establishing the manufactory, such expenses to include as well the cost, freight, and commission on the gas fittings then in use, as the outlay incurred by the respondent in the voyage which he had made to England, and also the costs of the gas bill above referred to, and denied that the agreement in question was for the purchase and sale of any part of the land on which the gas works stood, or that the respondent ever agreed or intended that the appellant should become proprietor of a moiety or any other portion of such land. The answer further stated, that the respondent had great difficulty in reading, and did not read the document before signing it, or hear it read, and had no professional adviser to explain its legal bearing, and that having been drinking freely at that time, he was not in a condition to understand it, even if it had been read to him by the appellant; that he signed it on the assurance of the appellant that it truly represented the previous verbal agreement, but that such agreement did not truly express such verbal agreement in many important respects, especially as to the ownership of the land and payments to be made by the appellant, and the clause of ownership, and the respondent in his answer submitted that he ought not to be compelled specifically to perform the alleged agreement.

Evidence was entered into upon either side, and the appellant and respondent were both examined and cross-examined. The respondent's evidence was to the same purport as the statements contained in his answer. A Mr. *Goodall*, a surveyor, was examined, and he estimated the value of the respondent's property as being worth £7,830, without the gas plant, &c. Mr. *Buchanan*, the witness to the agreement was also examined, and he deposed to the fact of the respondent, although not drunk, yet as being under the influence of liquor at the time he executed the agreement. Mr. *Macdonald*, the manager of the Commercial Bank, who saw the parties a few hours after the execution of the agreement, said the respondent was then sober.

The cause came on to be heard on the 27th of November, 1860, before the Primary Judge (Mr. Justice *Milford*), when the Court decreed specific performance of the agreement, and ordered that a proper deed of partnership between the appellant and respondent, in pursuance of the terms of such agreement, should be executed by the parties (including in such deed a conveyance by the respondent of the land, plant, and premises, comprised in the said agreement) for the purposes of the co-partnership, and awarded the appellant costs of suit.

From this decision the present respondent appealed to the full Court, and that Court, consisting of Sir *Alfred Stephen*, Chief Justice, Mr. Justice *Wise*, and Mr. Justice *Milford*, principally on the ground of the vagueness and obscurity of the agreement relating to the appellant's block of land, reversed the decree of the Primary Judge, and dismissed the appellant's bill, without costs, directing that each party should bear the costs of the original suit and of appeal. Mr. Justice *Milford* dissented from the other two Judges.

From this decree the present appeal was brought.

The Attorney-General (Sir *R. Palmer*) and Mr. *Knox Wigram* for the appellant. As it is not in dispute that the agreement of the 27th of September, 1859, was properly executed by the respondent, the *onus probandi* was upon him to make out that such agreement did not express the terms of the contract, which it is admitted existed between the appellant and himself at the time of its execution, and this he has failed to do. Neither has he established by any satisfactory evidence the allegation in his answer that when he signed the agreement he was incapable from the effects of drink—which fact, if proved, would not be sufficient of itself to avoid the agreement, *Lightfoot* v. *Heron* (a)—or otherwise, of understanding what he was doing, as he was presumed to do; *The Marquis of Townsend* v. *Stangroom* (b). Neither the appellant nor respondent had any professional advice with reference to the agreement. It was agreed between them that the verbal agreement should be committed to writing by the appellant; not one word as to the necessity of professional advice was raised by either of them. There is nothing in the agreement itself which is unfair to the respondent, nor is the bargain so hard as to be set aside by a Court of Equity. Mere inadequacy of price is not sufficient to set aside the contract, *Griffith* v. *Spratley* (c), *Collier* v. *Brown* (d), nor is it incapable of being carried into effect. The respondent has altogether failed in establishing any pretext for resisting its performance. In reversing the decision of the Primary Judge the majority of the Supreme Court attached considerable weight to the supposed ambiguity in that portion of the agreement which relates to the division of the block of land abutting High-street, in one-half of which the appellant was to take an interest. This was a difficulty suggested by the full Court where none existed, and if there was any apparent ambiguity it admitted of satisfactory explanation. No objection of any kind was taken to the description of the block of land in the agreement by the pleadings, yet the Chief Justice and Mr. Justice *Wise*, contrary to the opinion of the Primary Judge, held that the entire description was ambiguous, and that the agreement could not be enforced.

Sir *Hugh Cairns*, Q. C., and Mr. *Bowring* for the respondent. A decree for specific performance is a matter of discretion with a Court of Equity, and such discretion was, in this case, properly exercised by the full Court refusing specific performance of the alleged agreement of

(a) 3 You. & Coll. 586.
(c) 1 Cox 383.

(b) 6 Ves. 328.
(d) 1 Cox 428.

B—4

the 27th of September, 1859, for want of mutuality and for obscurity, leaving the appellant to his remedy, if any, by an action at law; *Lord James Stuart* v. *The London and North Western Railway Company* (a). The memorandum, containing the alleged agreement, was prepared and written wholly by the appellant, and, certainly, did not embody the terms of the verbal agreement between the parties, but departed· in many important respects, in the appellant's favour. The respondent, an ignorant man, who could scarcely read, was induced to sign the memorandum without professional aid, when partially intoxicated, under circumstances of mistake and surprise, and such agreement cannot be supported; *Cooke* v. *Clayworth* (b). The agreement, however, is too vague, uncertain, and obscure to be enforced in a Court of Equity. As originally written the block of land was described as "one-half that parcel of land on the west side of the High-street, West Maitland, on which are situated the Commercial Hotel, the coach manufactory, and the said gas works and plant, that is, the south side or half thereof, on which the said gas works are situated, and extending from the said High-street to the western end of the said block, and;" whereas it now stands with the letters St. squeezed in before the words, "west side of High-street;" the word "east" interpolated between the word "south" and "side," and the letters "8th." inserted before the words "western end." The initials of the appellant, but not of the respondent or the attesting witness, are appended to the margin opposite the interpolated word "east." Such an agreement cannot safely be acted on.

The Lord Justice KNIGHT BRUCE. The question in this case is not whether an action can be maintained, or should be brought, on the agreement in dispute (that of the 27th of September, 1859), nor is it whether that agreement should be delivered up to be cancelled. Consistently with the decree under appeal, an action may be brought against the respondent by the appellant for damages for the non-performance of the agreement, and it would have been quite consistent also with it that, if the respondent had filed a bill for the purpose of having the agreement delivered up to be cancelled, that bill should have been dismissed. The question is only whether a Court of Equity shall decree a specific performance of it against the defendant.

The principles by which Courts of Equity are guided in cases of specific performance have long been established, and are well known; but there is (so to speak) this addition to the great and leading authorities, by which we are all more or less guided in controversies of this description,—that of late years the defendant has been examinable as a witness for himself; and, therefore, when he is so examined the practical value of his statements in opposition to the plaintiff does not rest merely upon his answer, which may or may not be used by the plaintiff; but his allegations are to be read as those of a witness,—a witness under a bias, no doubt, but possibly to be trusted, possibly to be believed, possibly a man whose testimony ought to be acted upon; and in this case the defendant has been examined and cross-examined as a witness. He states, in effect, that he did not understand the true

(a) 1 De G. Mac. & Gor. 721.   (b) 18 Ves. 12, 14.

nature and terms of the agreement as written; that he did not intend to bind himself by any such contract; and that the agreement, as prepared, is one highly disadvantageous to him and to a portion of his property not involved in the agreement. How, then, was the agreement obtained? The agreement was prepared and written by the plaintiff. The signature of the defendant was obtained to it without the presence or advice of any professional man, and without any advice whatever. The agreement, as far as mere property is concerned, independently of any particular value, if any, to be derived from the circumstance of having the plaintiff as a partner, is (perhaps it might be said on the very face of it, but certainly on the face of it combined with the evidence of Mr. *Goodall* and the evidence of the defendant himself) one much more favourable to the plaintiff than to the defendant; very favourable to the plaintiff and damaging to the defendant.

Their Lordships see no reason to distrust the evidence of Mr. *Goodall*, who appears to be a respectable and competent person, and who was not cross-examined; and whether his evidence be considered, or be not considered, their Lordships think that the language of the agreement with respect to the property affected by it is vague and obscure—too vague and obscure to be safely acted on. In the mode of viewing it upon which the plaintiff insists, Mr. *Goodall* declares specifically that it is highly disadvantageous to the property of the defendant. Their Lordships believe that statement.

It is not the habit of a Court of Equity to decree the specific performance of an agreement more favourable to the plaintiff than to the defendant, involving hardship upon the defendant and damage to his property, if he entered into it without advice or assistance, and there be reasonable ground for doubting whether he entered into it with a knowledge and understanding of its nature and its consequences. In these particulars the present agreement, in their Lordships' judgment, fails. The defendant had no adviser. The plaintiff drew the agreement and acted for himself. The defendant swears that he did not understand its terms, and that he did not mean what those terms import, whatever that may be. Their Lordships think that he thus swears with considerable probability of truth; and they are, upon the whole materials before them, satisfied that undue advantage was taken of a man without professional or other advice, who did not understand what he was doing, to the great detriment of his property.

Their Lordships come to the conclusion that the bill was properly dismissed, and they will, therefore, humbly advise Her Majesty that this appeal should be also dismissed, with costs.

September, 1861.

SEMPILL *against* ANDERSON.

B., being at the time in insolvent circumstances, and knowing himself to be so, purchased from the defendants some corn and flour. The goods were delivered without demand of cash, and so remained with the insolvent for a day or two. After a few days, the defendants having demanded from B. immediate payment for the flour and corn, or a return of the property, the latter paid the price of the corn, and returned the flour to the defendants. On the forty-sixth day following, B. sequestrated his estate. The official assignee having brought an action, under the 8th and 12th sections of the Insolvent Act, to recover the amount so paid, and the value of the goods so delivered. Held, that he was entitled to recover; the preferring by B. of the defendants to his other creditors, under such circumstances, being invalid equally with regard to the payment and re-delivery in question.

STEPHEN, C. J., delivered the judgment of the Court in this case as follows:—

This is the case of a motion for a new trial, which was made to and refused by the Court last term. It was then intimated, that a written judgment would be delivered at a future day; and I proceed now, with the concurrence of my colleagues, to carry out our intention at the earliest practicable period—by stating the circumstances out of which the question arose, and the grounds of our decision upon it.

The facts lie in a very narrow compass. One *Barron*, being at the time in insolvent circumstances, and (according to the finding of the jury) knowing himself to be so, purchased from the defendants some corn and flour. According to the latter it was a cash transaction; but, as sworn by the insolvent, nothing was said about cash—it was simply a sale at stated prices, with nothing whatever settled as to time of payment. Be this as it may, the goods were delivered without demand of any cash, and so remained with the insolvent for a day or two. It may be right to mention, also, that no fraud in obtaining the possession was imputed to him; and, at the trial, the imputation was distinctly disclaimed. After a few days, the price of flour rising in the market, the defendants called on *Barron*, and insisted on immediate payment both for it and the corn, or a return of the property. Thus pressed, he paid the price of the corn, and returned to the defendants all the flour; one sack only excepted, which had been sold. On the 46th day following, *Barron* sequestrated his estate; and the official assignee thereupon brought this action, to recover back for the benefit of the creditors generally—under sections 12 and 8 of the Insolvent Act—the amount so paid, and the value of the goods so delivered, by the insolvent.

The cause was tried before Mr. Justice *Wise*; and he told the jury that, on this evidence, the plaintiff was entitled to recover—even if they thought that, in the first instance, there had been a contract for cash. For, as the corn and flour had been delivered on (at all events) a contract of sale, the property in them passed to *Barron*; who, on his part, became thereby debtor for the price. At the time of the demand, therefore, the defendants were his creditors in that amount; and no more entitled to satisfaction, legally speaking, than any other contemporaneous creditors, there being in fact several, possessing equal claims. His Honor held, accordingly, that the preferring of the defendants to those other creditors, under such circumstances, was invalid under the statute—equally with regard to the payment and re-delivery in question. On this direction, a verdict was returned for the plaintiff for £80; of which amount, £25 was the sum paid as aforesaid.

We are of opinion that the direction was right on both points. With respect to the insolvent's delivery of the flour, valued by the jury at £55, the cases in this Court under section 8 have been so numerous, and the terms and meaning of the enactment are so very plain, that it is difficult to understand how, at this period, an argument on the point can be attempted. It was suggested, referring to decisions under the English statute, that no delivery of goods can be invalidated, as a preference, unless it was spontaneous, and with intent to prefer. But the words of section 8 admit of no such construction. Omitting portions of the enactment inapplicable to this question, they are these. All alienations, transfers, or deliveries, of any goods or effects, by any person being insolvent, or within sixty days "preceding the sequestration" of his estate, and having the effect of preferring any then existing creditor to another, are declared to be void. So that the only point for inquiry, in any case submitted for decision under this clause, is of the simplest character. It is not, what was the intention of the parties, or was the transaction one under pressure: but, what was the effect of that transaction. Did or did not the particular transfer, or delivery, the party being at the time insolvent, have the effect of preferring one co-existing creditor to another? If it did, the transaction is made void in express terms.

With the expediency or policy of such an enactment, it is hardly necessary to say that, as Judges, and for the purposes of construction, we have nothing whatever to do. As little can the decision be influenced, by considerations of real or alleged hardship in any particular instance. It is impossible to doubt that there was here a delivery and transfer, by an insolvent person, of goods clearly his own property at the time, in point of law, to persons who were at the same time his creditors, on account or in satisfaction of the debt then due to them. It is too clear for dispute, therefore, that the effect of such a transfer was, to prefer those creditors to all others at the time existing. Had the insolvent sold those goods, no lawyer can doubt that the sale would have been valid. Had the defendants sued him for the price, whether the goods were sold, or remained in his shop, no person would venture to say that the action was not maintainable. The flour, consequently, belonged to *Barron*; and the price to the defendants. The fact, then, can make no difference in the decision, that he delivered that flour in satisfaction, to the creditor from whom he had bought it, instead of selling the article to a third party, or handing it over to some other creditor, had there been one equally urgent.

As between these parties, the contest is one merely of legal right. It is not a contest between the defendants and *Barron*; but between them and the other creditors. The latter insist that, the defendants having sold and parted with the goods, and become creditors for the price, the insolvent had no more right to liquidate it by those goods than by any other part of his property; but that all the co-existing creditors, the defendants among them, should share that property alike—no one being paid preferentially to any other. And the question obviously is, not whether such a conclusion would operate harshly, as it is called, on one or the other of the litigating parties, but which of the two, on the construction of this enactment, is right.

The same or similar remarks apply, with equal force, to the question that arises as to the £25 payment. The 12th section, however, on which the validity or invalidity of that transaction depends, is framed in terms singularly embarrassing: and, had not the point on former occasions been before the Court, and twice deliberately determined, we should have thought it well deserving further discussion. But the cases of *Perry* v. *Hart*, in December, 1858, and *Wilson* v. *Beattie*, decided in the previous September, in each of which the question was fully considered, must now be taken to be conclusive. In the former case, the amount at stake was considerable, and the point was formally raised by demurrer; and I have always supposed, until the recent motion, that it was from the date of that argument accepted as settled. But, as the grounds of neither decision appear to have been reported, we feel it to be desirable to state the reasons, on which as it appears to us those cases ought to be upheld.

The section, omitting redundant words merely, is as follows. All payments made to any creditor, by any person not compelled by legal process to make the same, and knowing himself to be insolvent, or in contemplation of surrendering his estate, or knowing that proceedings for obtaining an order for sequestration of his estate have commenced, or that any such order has been made, are hereby declared to be fraudulent. But, all payments really and *bona fide* made by an insolvent, to a creditor, before any order for the sequestration of his estate is known to the insolvent, or to such creditor, shall be valid. In a subsequent sentence, every person receiving any payment therein declared to be fraudulent, shall be bound to repay it for the benefit of the creditors generally.

The enactment, therefore, is in effect this. If a person knows himself to be insolvent—or that an order has been made, or proceeding commenced for sequestration of his estate—he may not, except under compulsion by legal process, pay any creditor. He is equally restrained, of course, if he himself contemplates sequestration. Nevertheless, although such an order may have been made (which, in the case of a compulsory sequestration, may occur without his knowledge), if that order be not known to him, or to the creditor receiving payment, such payment, if really and *bona fide* made, will be valid.

The first portion of the clause, consequently, includes cases equally of intended voluntary surrenders, and of completed or commenced compulsory sequestrations. Apparently, however,—though the language is too obscure to justify a positive opinion—the order mentioned in this first portion is the primary one merely; where, up to that time, there has been no final adjudication. For, it will be observed, the debtor is not yet spoken of as an insolvent; but only as a person who knows himself to be in an insolvent state. Be this as it may, the second portion of the clause refers, alone, to cases where the person has been declared insolvent, and where an order of sequestration has actually issued. He is now, for the first time in the clause, termed an insolvent —substantively; and the case provided for is, a payment made pending his own ignorance of such an order, and the paid creditor's equal ignorance. In such a case, notwithstanding section 58, by which every order for sequestrating an estate instantly divests the insolvent of his property, the payment so made will stand good. But, in all cases,—at least before sequestration—the knowledge of the debtor only is the test of invalidity.

Whether in fact the 12th section, by those who originally framed, or by those who altered the clause, was intended to be thus construed, is a question which cannot affect the decision; and we have no means of determining it. But no other construction will satisfy the words used, so as to give effect to them all; and if the result should be injurious, as it may be, to the interests of the mercantile body generally, the fault lies in the enactment—and the remedy is not with us, but is in the hands of the Legislature. We are at least able to add, that not only Sir *John Dickinson*, who took part in the judgment in *Perry* v. *Hart*, but Sir *William Burton*, who had occasion to consider this clause soon after its passing, concurred in the construction here adopted. I have a copy of a note made by the latter at that time, and the following is an extract from it:—" The passage beginning with the words 'but all payments' seems at first a contradiction to what immediately precedes. But I do not think that it must be understood so. The words seem to have been introduced, to meet the case of a person not knowing himself to be insolvent, nor that proceedings for obtaining a sequestration have been commenced, but who nevertheless has committed an act of insolvency, which has enabled a creditor to obtain an order for sequestration against him, the making of which is not known to him, or to the creditor, paid under such circumstances by him. Construing the passage thus, there is no opposition between the first and second portions of the section. The second or enabling sentence is confined to those cases which do not fall within the terms of the first or disabling passage, and is not an exception to it, but to the 10th (quære) and 53rd sections."

The application of the enactment, thus explained, to the particular case before us, is attended with no difficulty. *Barron* was debtor to the defendants in £25, for corn sold and delivered to him by them; and, knowing himself to be insolvent, he pays them the amount—although not compelled by any legal process so to do. By the express terms of section 12, therefore, such payment may be recovered back from the defendants; unless it can be, by some means, brought within the second portion of the clause. But, for the reasons already given, it is not affected by that part of the enactment; which relates to payments made after sequestration only. The inference is inevitable, that the second portion contemplates exclusively payments so made; for the sole question under it is (supposing the payment to have been otherwise *bonâ fide*), whether the insolvent paying, and the creditor receiving the money, knew of the sequestration order. The existence in fact of such an order, consequently, at the time of the payment, is assumed.

To hold otherwise, would be to impute to the two portions of section 12 this absurdity; that the first invalidates payments by a debtor contemplating sequestration, or knowing himself to be insolvent, but the second protects such payments, if he and the creditor do not know, what could not possibly be known to them, or to anybody, that an order exists, which at the time has never in fact been made.

July, 1854.   RAMSAY *against* MAYNE.

By the statute
De Cattalis, sup-
posed to belong
to the reign of
Edward II., the
Crown has a
right to inspect
and take an
inventory of the
property of per-
sons arrested for
felony, and to
cause it to be
kept by sureties,
responsible to the
Crown and to the
accused, for its
custody and
appropriation.
A. was appre-
hended by a
constable on a
charge of felony.
He had on his
person at the
time some
money. The
constable took
the money from
him, and handed
it over to the
defendant as the
head of the
department of
police, and the
latter paid it to
the Colonial
Treasurer. *A.*
having made his
escape, and not
being re-taken—
and not having
been indicted,
nor any process
having been
initiated against
him, in a view to
outlawry—
demanded the
money from the
defendant, and
on his refusal to
return it, sued
for its recovery.
Held, that the
plaintiff was not
entitled to
recover.

STEPHEN, C. J., delivered the judgment of the Court in this case
as follows :—

This case has been several times considered by us, and we have found
it one of considerable difficulty; the question involved in it as to the
right of the Crown to secure the property of persons charged with felony
being very imperfectly dealt with by the text-writers, and its solution
depending on a portion of the law referred to, and on statutes which
(except as to points not now in controversy) appear never to have
received judicial interpretation.

The plaintiff was apprehended by a constable some months ago, on a
charge of horse stealing. He had on his person at the time a large sum
of money, which (it appears) a friend drew for him from the bank on
the day preceding. The constable (according to what is said to be the
ordinary practice), whether for the protection of the party in custody,
or in view to ultimate forfeiture on conviction, or because the property
might in some way be found to be connected with the charge, took the
money from him, and shortly afterwards handed it over to the defendant
as the head of the department of police; and the latter, on his part,
paid it into the Colonial Treasury. In the meantime the plaintiff
contrived to make his escape, and he has not since been re-taken. On
the other hand, neither has he been indicted; nor has any process been
initiated against him, in a view to outlawry—supposing such a result
to be attainable. In this state of things the plaintiff commissions a
person to act for him, who, by his authority, demands the money from
the defendant, and on his refusal to restore it, brings the present action
for its recovery.

Upon the authority of Sir *Matthew Hale*, who distinctly says (a) that
the seizure of an accused goods before indictment, though only is
custodiâ et causâ rei servandæ, is unlawful, I told the jury that their
verdict must be for the plaintiff. I gave leave to the defendant, however, to move for a non-suit, if the Court should be of a contrary opinion.
During the last term, accordingly, the case was argued; when, on
account of the importance of the question, and the long prevalence of
the usage, not after indictment merely, but upon arrest (as stated by
Lord *Hale* himself), to seize the goods of persons accused of felony, we
reserved our judgment.

It is remarkable that the only statute on this point mentioned in
Hale, is the 1 Rich. III., c. 8; which is there said to enact, under a
penalty of twice the value, that no person shall seize the goods of any
one arrested or imprisoned before he be convicted. The learned writer,
citing Lord *Coke*, lays it down accordingly, that even after indictment
the goods can only be seized for purposes of inspection, and the taking
a list of them—to assist in detecting eventually any fraudulent sale.
And this right, apparently, he speaks of as one existing at Common
Law; not as one given by statute. In conformity with that view of

(a) 1 P. C. 364, 367.

the law, there are several modern instances of decision or dicta by
Judges, denouncing the practice of seizing prisoner's property by
constables. See 7 C. & P. 489, and the cases there noted.

Upon searching into other authorities, however, and on referring to
the statutes at large (Com. Dig. *Forfeiture*, D. 4; Bac. Ab., same title,
E.; 2 Hawk. P. C. 645; and Vin. Ab. *Forfeitures*, O. and P.), we have
found it impossible to follow implicitly the commentary of Sir *Matthew
Hale.*

In the first place, the prohibitory enactment in 1 Rich. III., relates exclusively to persons arrested or imprisoned for " suspicion " of felony.
These four last words, it is said, were omitted from the text and trans-
lations anciently used. They are, at all events, not noticed in the commentary. But the distinction between an arrest for felony and for
suspicion of felony (though now scarcely known in practice), could
hardly have escaped the observation of a Judge so eminent, had the
terms of the enactment ever been presented to him. The distinction is
in fact an important one; and it is drawn, we believe, in all the
statutes relating to bail—certainly in those of *Philip* and *Mary*, and of
the 7 and 8 G. IV. The arrest in the present case was distinctly on a
charge of felony, and not on suspicion only. But independently of
this, Sir *M. Hale* himself shows that the words "seize or take," in the
statute of *Richard*, must be understood only in the sense of removing;
for the goods of the accused (he says) may, after indictment, be
inventoried; and how could this be accomplished, in many cases, without seizing or taking? The right to take an inventory—at all events
—before conviction, it thus appears, was not abrogated by that statute.
Whence then arose that right; or on what is it now founded?

We find that it arose from the express provisions of a statute, cited as
the "Statute *De Catallis Felonum*," supposed to belong to the reign of
Edward II. The provisions of that statute, therefore, according to
Lord *Hale*, could not have been repealed by the 1 Rich. III.; nor can
we discover any ground for holding that they were thereby repealed.
This statute *De Catallis* is wholly unnoticed, however, not in his commentary only, but in the abridgements of *Bacon* and *Comyn;* and it is
cited in that of *Viner* inaccurately. It enacts that no man arrested for
felony shall be disseized of his goods until conviction of the same
felony; but that as soon as he is taken, they may be inspected and inventoried, on the view (*per visum*) of the Judges and Sheriffs, or other
the King's bailiffs and lawful men, and be safely kept by sureties of the
accused—such sureties to be responsible for the goods, or their value, if
the party be convicted of the felony; but subject to his right to maintenance and necessaries for himself and his family in the meantime.

Conceiving that enactment, apparently so little known, to be the
foundation of the right to inspect and take an inventory of goods,
which Sir *Matthew Hale* speaks of as existing at Common Law, and
regarding the enactment in 1 Rich. III. as not inconsistent with it
(*Hale* himself declaring the latter to be but in affirmance of the Common Law, with the addition of a penalty), we are of opinion that the
plaintiff here cannot recover. For, assuming that the constable alone
had no right to seize, or the defendant to keep, the money claimed in
this action, yet the plaintiff cannot be entitled to its possession; for

1854.

RAMSAY
v.
MAYNE.

such a right would be incompatible with that of the Crown, to cause it (as may perhaps even yet be done) to be kept by sureties, responsible to the Crown and the accused alike, for its custody and appropriation. It is not alleged that the plaintiff requires the money for purposes of maintenance, or defence; and suretyship he neither offers; nor, it is clear, would it suit his object to give. But he cannot defeat the enactment, by refusing to provide sureties; and it is to them, and not to him, that the custody is assignable.

The power exercised by Courts of Oyer and Terminer, of directing the restoration of property to prisoners, to enable them to provide for their defence, is only in accordance with the right to necessaries, expressly reserved by the statute, and would appear to be incident to their jurisdiction, in the administration of justice between the Crown and persons at trial for crimes. But the question, how far constables may interfere, in preventing the property of such persons from being devoted, before trial, to purposes other than necessaries, cannot be considered as finally determined, while the provisions of the statute of *Edward* II. remain unnoticed, if not unknown, as at present they appear to be.

May 21, 1844.   THE QUEEN *against* JOHN HODGES and THOMAS LYNCH (a).

The Supreme Court has jurisdiction, after conviction and judgment for felony at a Court of Quarter Sessions, to remove the record of such conviction by *certiorari*, for the purpose of correcting errors of fact in matters not appearing upon the record.

ON the third of the present month (in term time), the Court ordered the return to the *certiorari* for bringing up the record of the conviction of these prisoners at the Quarter Sessions, holden at Parramatta in April last, to be filed; and thereupon the Court, at the prayer of the prisoner's counsel, made a rule for enlarging the term until Wednesday, the 8th of this month, in order that the matter of the return might be disposed of, and a writ of *habeas corpus* having in the meantime (namely, on the 6th) been issued to bring up the bodies of the prisoners to be present on the motion for reversing the judgment, they were accordingly on that day brought into Court by the keeper of her Majesty's gaol at Parramatta. The Attorney-General having suggested that he had had no time to read the affidavits filed on behalf of the prisoners, and no sufficient opportunity afforded him for taking the necessary steps to have them answered, the Court, at his prayer again, by rule for that purpose, enlarged the term until Monday, the 13th instant, and in the meantime remanded the prisoners to their former custody, and ordered them to be brought up again on that day under the same writ, the Attorney-General at the same time undertaking to allow the prisoner's attorney, as of grace, to take copies of such affidavits as were intended to be used in answer to the motion for reversing the judgment. Accordingly, on Monday, the 13th instant, the prisoners were again brought up, and the gaoler's return to the writ of *habeas* having been read, and on motion filed, and the return to

(a) Present—Sir *James Dowling*, Kt., C. J., *Burton*, J., and *Stephen*, J., in banco.

the *certiorari* already in Court being produced, the prisoner's counsel moved on affidavit, setting forth matters extrinsic of the record, that the judgment of the Court below be reversed. Cause was shown by the Attorney-General and the Solicitor-General on affidavits in answer to those filed on the part of the prisoners, and the arguments not being concluded on that day, the Court again by rule enlarged the term till the next day, and in the meantime committed the prisoners to the custody of the sheriff, and ordered them to be brought into Court on that day. Accordingly, they were brought up again on Tuesday, the 14th, and the argument was resumed, and the prisoner's counsel (Mr. *Foster* and Mr. *Windeyer*) having been heard in support of their rule, the Attorney-General claimed and was allowed, in virtue of his office, the general reply. Whereupon the Court ordered the prisoners to be remanded to Parramatta gaol, to be brought up again on this present 21st May, and, having made another rule for enlarging the term until this day, to hear such judgment on the matter of their application as the Court should be advised to pronounce.

The decision of the Court was now delivered by

Sir JAMES DOWLING, C. J. Although the Court had decided on a former day upon argument, that after conviction and judgment for felony at the Court of Quarter Sessions, this Court has authority to remove the record of conviction by *certiorari* for the purpose of quashing it (not for error on the record, but for facts extrinsic of the record), yet, if persuaded by the more elaborate second argument of the 13th instant (which the law officers of the Crown were permitted to enter into), that its first decision was erroneous, the Court could have had no hesitation in retracing its steps on more advised consideration. We confess that notwithstanding the proper jealousy which this Court ought to entertain of the introduction of novelties into the administration of the law, and with that becoming reverence which we trust the Judges in this remote dependency will ever entertain for the wisdom of Westminster Hall, our opinion has not been shaken by what was addressed to us in the recent very able argument as to the soundness of the principle on which the *certiorari* was granted.

Yielding respect to the weight of authority, that errors on the records of a Court, constituted by the course of the common law, could only be reviewed by writ of error, the Court would have denied the *certiorari*, in this instance, on that ground (except for the purpose of assigning errors of record); but constituted as the Courts of Quarter Sessions in this colony are, in one most vital and important integral part of their jurisdiction, in a manner contrary to the course of the common law, we were not fettered by any decision in refusing the *certiorari* for the purpose of showing matters *dehors* the record, and establishing, by extrinsic facts, that the whole proceedings against the prisoners were void in their inception.

The gist of the first objection to the judgment pronounced on the prisoners, is, that the information on which it was founded was not presented by an officer properly authorised by law for that purpose. If this were an objection apparent on the record, it is not now necessary to decide whether it must not be brought under review by writ of error.

The only use which could be made of such a defect on the record, would be as evidence confirmatory of the extrinsic circumstances, or at all events not negativing such circumstances.

Adverting to this objection, the first question to be determined is, whether the Courts of Quarter Sessions in this colony are instituted in all particulars according to the course of common law; secondly, if they are not, whether the deviation be of serious importance; and thirdly, whether the departure from the course pointed out by the Legislature can be taken advantage of in this Court by *certiorari* in a summary manner by affidavits, showing the departure.

1st. By the course of the common law of England no man can be put on his trial for felony, but on presentment by a Grand Jury, twelve of whom must concur in finding the indictment, not only on their own oaths, but on the oaths also of the witnesses to sustain the bill. By the New South Wales Act (9 G. IV., c. 83), the institution of Grand Juries in the administration of criminal justice is withheld, not only in the Supreme Court but in the Courts of Quarter Sessions, and in lieu thereof all crimes cognizable by these Courts respectively shall be prosecuted in the name of the Attorney-General or other person appointed for that purpose by the Governor of the colony. It is quite obvious, therefore, that the Courts of Quarter Sessions of the colony are not, in this particular, instituted after the course of the common law; although the subsequent proceedings after the presentment of an information by the Attorney-General or other person appointed for that purpose, may be conducted according to the course of the common law.

2nd. Is the deviation of importance? Whatever may be the diversity of opinions in modern times as to the utility or inutility of Grand Juries in the administration of criminal justice, the people of England have in all times regarded the institution with sacred reverence, as one of the best safeguards of life and liberty. Indeed to prevent the admission of improper persons on Grand Juries, various statutes have been passed to remedy the mischiefs which had arisen to innocent subjects from indictments found against them by improperly constituted Grand Juries, contrary to the course of the common law. The statutes 11 Hen. IV., c. 9, and 3 Hen. VIII., c. 12 (which were passed in times not remarkable for abstinence from the adoption of arbitrary principles), were amongst others ordained to remedy such evils. By the last mentioned statute, " our said Lord the King, for the greater ease and quietness of his people, willeth and ordaineth, that indictments so made, with all the dependence thereof, be revoked, annulled, void, and holden for none for ever. And from henceforth no indictment be made by any such persons but by inquest of the King's lawful liege people in the manner as was used in the time of his noble progenitors, returned by the sheriffs, &c., and if any indictment be made hereafter in any point to the contrary, that the same indictment be also void, revoked, and for ever holden as none." On the construction of this statute it has been held, that offences not capital are as much within it as indictments for treason and felony, and also that it applies to indictments before justices of the peace as much as to indictments before superior justices; Hawk. P. C., c. 25, ss. 24, 25. Lord *Coke* (a), in commenting on these statutes. says, " And these laws

(a) 3 Inst. 34.

made for indifferency of indictors, ought to be construed favourably, for that the indictment is commonly found in the absence of the party, and yet it is the foundation of all the rest of the proceeding." Regarding it therefore as a first principle of the common law of England, that no man shall be put in jeopardy for felony, but by the concurring oaths of at least twenty-four indifferent persons—*i.e.*, of twelve grand jurors to find the bill, and of twelve petty jurors to condemn him,—this Court, sitting in an English colony, founded by English people, cannot but deem the constitution of the Quarter Sessions in this colony as involving a most vital departure from the course of the common law.

3rd. It being incontrovertible then, that there has been a deviation from the course of the common law, and that such deviation is of vital importance, the next question is, whether any objection can now be made, in a summary manner on affidavit, of extrinsic circumstances, showing that the course pointed out by the Legislature in substituting a Crown prosecutor in lieu of a grand jury has not been followed; or in other words, that the person standing *in loco* of a grand jury has not been lawfully constituted to perform the duties of a grand jury.

If the person so appointed be not appointed according to the mode pointed out by the Legislature, we apprehend it to be too plain for argument, that the objection would be as available to a prisoner as if he had been indicted by a grand jury improperly impanelled. Indeed we may say that it would be *a multo fortiori* available, because of the wide departure from the common law, in the adoption of this anomalous contrivance to dispense with grand juries. The only difficulty that has arisen here is, whether these prisoners are not now out of time, the objection (if well founded and allowable to be proved by affidavit) not being made until after trial, conviction, and judgment.

In the construction of the statute 3 Hen. VIII., c. 12, it has been holden (2 How. P. C., c. 25, s. 26) "that a person arraigned upon any indictment taken contrary to the purview thereof, may plead such matter in avoidance of the indictment, and also plead over to the felony." Again, it is laid down "that a person outlawed upon any such indictment, without a trial, may also show in avoidance of the outlawry, that the indictment was taken contrary to the purview of the statute. But if a person, who is tried upon such an indictment, take no such exception before his trial, it may be doubtful whether he may be allowed to take such exception afterwards, because he has slipped the most proper time for it; except it can be verified by the records of the same Court, wherein the indictment is depending, as by an outlawry in such Court of one of the indictors, &c., in which case it is laid, that any one as *amicus curiæ* may inform the Court of it." (a)

Giving full effect to the proposition, that in ordinary cases a prisoner shall be estopt from making formal objections after arraignment, trial, conviction, and judgment, which is no doubt a sound principle, still, if by law it can be made to appear by affidavit, upon the return to a writ of *certiorari* into this Court, that from circumstances he was prevented by available means from making the objection in the Court below, it would be hard upon a prisoner if he were told that the time was gone by, no matter how palpable the error might be. Now, had these priso-

(a) 3 Inst. 34.

ners the means or opportunity of taking the supposed objection to the appointment of the gentleman, in whose name they were in fact prosecuted?

Assuming that we are at liberty to look to the affidavits filed on both sides in this case, it appears that on the 3rd January, 1844, Mr. *E. Rogers*, the Clerk of the Peace, received a commission from the Governor, appointing him to be Crown Prosecutor at the Parramatta Sessions, and on presenting it to the Chairman and other Justices assembled on that day, the Bench, after hearing counsel, and Mr. *Nichols*, an advocate, pronounced the commission wholly void, and Mr. *Rogers* did not act.

At that session an information was lodged against the prisoners, in the name of Mr. *Cheeke*, as Crown Prosecutor, he having a commission issued prior to that of Mr. *Rogers*, to which they pleaded without making any objection to Mr. *Cheeke's* acting. The trials of the prisoners were postponed until the following April Sessions, when another information was filed against them in the name of Mr. *Cheeke*, to which they pleaded, were tried, convicted, and sentenced, without any objection that Mr. *Rogers'* commission superseded Mr. *Cheeke's*, or that Mr. *Cheeke* had then no sufficient authority to act as Crown Prosecutor. At the trial, Mr. *Nichols*, the prisoners' now attorney, acted as their advocate. It may be that Mr. *Nichols*, as their advocate, might, at both sessions, have taken the objection that Mr. *Rogers'* commission superseded Mr. *Cheeke's*; but after it had been solemnly decided, that Mr. *Rogers'* commission was void, it would have been an idle ceremony to take the objection, he himself being one of the gentlemen who had, in the January sessions, contended for its invalidity. At the April sessions it was not known that no new commission had been issued to Mr. *Cheeke*, and it was not known, in fact, until the 24th of April, after the sessions had terminated.

Taking it as a sound rule, that the prisoners were bound to make the objection at the trial (if they knew it), it seems that it would have been unavailing to them after the sessions had adjudged Mr. *Rogers'* commission to be void, and as it was not known to them at the trial, either that no commission was issued to Mr. *Cheeke*, or that there was any supposed infirmity in his old one, we do not think that the prisoners could now be prevented from impeaching the judgment, if it can be impeached in the manner proposed.

The case of *Rex* v. *Dickinson* (a) is an authority for holding that an objection not known to the prisoner, or the Court, until after conviction, will not preclude him from the benefit of it, if it goes to the legality of his trial. There the prisoner had been convicted of cattle stealing; but, after conviction, it appeared that the witnesses had attended before the grand jury without having been sworn. The learned Judge (*Bayley*) thought the objection came too late, and therefore passed sentence upon the prisoner, but reserved the point for the consideration of the Judges; and the case being afterwards considered, they, without deciding as to the validity of the objection, recommended a free pardon. In that case the fact of the irregularity would not have appeared on the record, and could only have been got at by extrinsic

(a) R. & R. 401.

evidence; and, though it be not an authority for the mode of correcting the error in this case, by *certiorari*, yet it shows the cautious jealousy with which the Judges of England regard the due administration of justice. It might to some appear to be an unimportant objection that the witnesses were not sworn before they went before the grand jury, when they were afterwards sworn at the trial, and the prisoner righteously convicted by the petty jury on the merits of his case. Still the Judges must have held, that he was not lawfully convicted upon an indictment duly presented according to law, though presented by the grand jury on their oaths. In effect, the principle of the objection in the present case (if well established) resolves itself into the question, has this information been duly presented by a *quasi* grand jury, duly appointed in the manner prescribed by law?

Taking it that the objection could not availably be made at the trial —that it is not one appearing on the record—that it could only be established by extrinsic evidence—and that the mode of initiating the trial is contrary to the course of common law—has this Court the power of correcting the alleged error in the way proposed?

Conceding that a writ of error lies, and that the prisoners may assign errors of fact, and that an issue is the proper mode of trial by the country, what process have we for directing the trial of such an issue? The authorities cited in our former decision, show that the jurisdiction of the Quarter Sessions, being constituted, in a vital branch of its proceedings, contrary to the course of the common law, the judgment may be falsified by showing the special matter without writ or error. How then can this Court reach the special matter except upon affidavit? In a vast variety of cases, both criminal as well as civil, this Court is in the habit, necessarily, of determining facts, in incidental proceedings, upon affidavit; and on principle, there seems nothing repugnant to the course of justice in determining by affidavit, the question raised on these affidavits, whether, for the purpose of the validity of this judgment, the gentleman appointed to conduct this prosecution was duly appointed under the Act of Council by which he holds his commission.

We are not called upon to (nor would we upon a collateral issue of this kind) determine the right of this gentleman to hold the office he claims to hold. The proper legal mode of determining that question would be by writ of *quo warranto*, to which he would be a party, and, so far as his rights are concerned, they might then be solemnly determined. But for the purpose of this case, and as regards the position of the prisoners, the Court has authority to ascertain as a fact, whether his appointment is in pursuance of the power of appointment vested in the Governor under the local Act, and from whom he derives his commission.

Two objections were made to the validity of Mr. *Cheeke's* appointment, as Crown Prosecutor, prior to the 30th December, 1843; first, that it was superseded by the appointment of Mr. *Rogers*, in January 1844; and secondly, that supposing that Mr. *Rogers'* appointment had not that effect, Mr. *Cheeke's* original appointment was not conformable to the Act of Council under which he was appointed; and, no proper commission having been issued to him authorising him to act in pre-

1844.

The QUEEN
v.
JOHN HODGES
and
THOMAS LYNCH.

senting an information against these prisoners, the judgment was void, as being *coram non judice.*

We shall address ourselves to the latter objection in the first instance.

The local ordinance, 4 Vic., No. 22, s. 10, after reciting the statute 9 Geo. IV., c. 83, by which all crimes cognizable by the Supreme Court should be prosecuted by information in the name of the Attorney-General, or other person appointed for such purpose by the Governor, and that all crimes (not committed by transported felons) should be prosecuted and tried before the Courts of General Quarter Sessions in the colony, in the same manner and subject to the same rules in every respect as trials in the Supreme Court; and reciting the expediency of appointing separate officers to prosecute in all trials for crimes within the limits of Port Phillip and New Zealand (when it was a dependency of the colony), respectively, as well as in the Courts of General Quarter Sessions throughout the colony; proceeds to enact "that until grand juries be established therein, it shall be lawful for the Governor to appoint, from time to time, some fit and proper person for Port Phillip, and a like person for New Zealand [such persons being respectively barristers of England or Ireland], by whom and in whose name all crimes, &c.," cognizable in the Supreme Court of New South Wales, and in the several Courts of General and Quarter Sessions (save as excepted in the recited Act) shall be prosecuted within the aforesaid limits of Port Phillip and New Zealand respectively, "and also that it shall be lawful for the said Governor to appoint" (omitting the words from time to time) "any officer or officers by whom and in whose name all crimes, &c., cognizable in the several Courts of General and Quarter Sessions in all other parts of the said colony may be prosecuted, except as aforesaid; provided always, that nothing herein contained shall be construed to limit or control any authority vested by law in Her Majesty's Attorney-General for the said colony "

From this provision it appears that the power of appointing the officer or officers in whose name all crimes may be prosecuted at Quarter Sessions, is vested in the Governor absolutely, without any reservation of the pleasure of the Crown. This being a new office, and the power of appointment being conferred unreservedly on the Governor himself, and subject indeed to no condition whatever, the question is, whether the power has been exercised in the mode and manner in which it has been conferred?

We are now to look to the most material affidavit produced on this point—namely, that of Mr. *Cheeke* himself, from which it appears, that by a commission under the great seal of the colony, and the hand of the Governor, dated 2nd June, 1841, in pursuance of the Act, 4 Vic., No. 22, he was appointed "during the pleasure of the Governor, and subject to the approval of her Majesty, her heirs, and successors," to be, and act as such officer in the Act mentioned, and to be the person by whom, and in whose name, all crimes, misdemeanours, and offences, not being committed by transported offenders, cognizable in the several Courts of Quarter Sessions to be holden in all parts of the colony, save and except Port Phillip and New Zealand excepted, should be prosecuted;" which commission was duly enrolled in the office of the

Colonial Secretary, and also in the Supreme Court, and which commission he accepted, and in pursuance thereof took the necessary oath of office before one of the Judges. The affidavit goes on to state, that by warrant under the Royal Sign Manual, dated 11th January, 1842, he was confirmed in his office of Crown Prosecutor, and thereupon letters patent, under the great seal of the colony, and the hand of the Governor, were issued and duly enrolled, dated 2nd August, 1842, by which he was appointed Crown Prosecutor in the territory of New South Wales, "during the pleasure of her Majesty Queen Victoria." It is further sworn, that he had never been removed or suspended from, nor ever resigned, his office, and hath always acted, and still does act, as such Crown Prosecutor, under and by virtue of the first commission issued by the Governor, and under and by virtue of the warrant under the Sign Royal Manual, and under the second commission issued by the Governor. In conclusion the affidavit states, that on deponent's return from Maitland in January last, he had an interview with the Governor at his Excellency's request, and was then informed by the Governor, that he was fully authorised to conduct the prosecutions which he had so already conducted on behalf of the Crown, as well as any thereinafter to be conducted in the said several Courts of Quarter Sessions respectively.

The commissions under which this gentleman has been appointed have not been produced for inspection; but we must now take it from his own representation of their contents, that by the first he held the office, "during the pleasure of the Governor, and subject to the approval of her Majesty, her heirs, and successors," and by the second, not during the pleasure of the Governor, but during the pleasure of her Majesty Queen Victoria. If, as is sworn by Mr. *Cheeke*, that he is designated both in the Queen's warrant and in his second commission as "Crown Prosecutor," it is to be observed that the act under which he is appointed contains no such designation, the words being "officer by whom and in whose name all crimes, &c., may be prosecuted."

Disregarding this, however, as not a very material circumstance, can we say judicially that either of these appointments is not in pursuance of the authority under which the power is conferred by the Legislature? The local ordinance it is true, in terms, confers the power on the Governor himself alone, without any reservation, either of his own pleasure or that of her most gracious Majesty. As representative of the Crown, for ministerial purposes, the duty is properly imposed upon his Excellency of communicating the appointment, and taking the pleasure of her Majesty upon it; but we apprehend that the appointment itself should be in pursuance of the act of the legislature by which the office was created. If this be not so, what limit is to be put upon departures from the mode and manner in which the legislature confers powers? This may be said to be a very strict objection, to which perhaps too much weight ought not to be attached in the ordinary transactions of mankind; but when it concerns the validity of the lawful authority of a functionary to act in the place and stead of a grand jury, in the administration of a vital part of the criminal justice of the country, and who is armed with the power of saying in his discretion who shall and who shall not be put on trial by informations in

1844.
_____
The QUEEN
v.
JOHN HODGES
and
THOMAS LYNCH.

his name, the Court cannot shrink from the duty of looking upon it as
a most serious objection (if it can be maintained), involving much more
important consequences than the interests of the prisoners now before
the Court.

The jealousy with which, even in olden time, the legislature has
guarded against the unlawful constitution of grand juries, has been
already pointed out, and the strictness noted with which the Judges of
England, in *Dickinson's* case, gave a prisoner the advantage of an error
almost of mere form. These considerations warn this Court of the
necessity of seeing that justice is administered in this colony by
authorities properly constituted by law, and in such form only as the
law has provided.

On the argument of this case the prisoners' counsel prayed in aid
the record itself as confirmatory of the extrinsic evidence that Mr.
Cheeke had not been appointed in pursuance of the Act, for it was
urged that had he been so appointed, the record would have alleged
the fact. The information begins thus:—"Be it remembered that
Alfred Cheeke, Esq., who prosecutes for our Sovereign Lady the Queen
in this behalf, being present in the Court of General Quarter Sessions
of the Peace now here, &c., informs the said Court," &c. This certainly
does not give any notification that Mr. *Cheeke* is an officer by whom
and in whose name the crime may be prosecuted in pursuance of the
Act of Council. The Court could not take judicial notice that *Alfred
Cheeke*, Esq., was an officer so appointed. Of the Attorney-General and
the Solicitor-General, the Court are bound to take judicial notice as
known law officers of the Crown; but of a private individual by name,
without any designation of his authority to perform the functions of a
Crown Prosecutor, the Court cannot take such notice. They may
privately notice that the gentleman so named is competent for the
office, but not that he is a duly appointed officer to prosecute on behalf
of her Majesty, unless it is made so to appear.

The defect in the record thus pointed out, was not permitted to be
taken as matter of error, inasmuch as no notice had been specifically
given of it by the prisoners' law adviser; but reference to it was, we
think, properly allowed as a circumstance to be taken in connexion
with other evidence *dehors* the record. Whether on a writ of error (if
this be a case in which error lies), or by assignment of error, the record
being now before the Court, the objection would not be absolutely
fatal, we are not now called upon to determine. It is enough for us to
decide whether Mr. *Cheeke* had a sufficiently good commission from the
Governor to act as an officer in whose name all crimes may be prosecuted within the jurisdiction of the Courts of Quarter Sessions. Mr.
Cheeke swears that he has so acted under his first commission (which
has never been revoked), and under the warrant with the Royal Sign
Manual, and also under the second commission, or letters patent.

Upon full consideration, we are of opinion that Mr. *Cheeke's* commission of the 2nd June, 1841, sufficiently constituted him to be the
officer in whose name crimes were to be prosecuted at Quarter Sessions,
and that the power of the Governor has been exercised by him in a
manner not open to any objection available to the prisoners. It is true
that the commission appoints him "during the pleasure of the Gover-

nor, and subject to the approval of her Majesty, her heirs, and successors." Although the local ordinance does not contain either of these conditions, yet the introduction of them by the Governor, as representative of the Sovereign, does not, in our opinion, vitiate the commission, and they may be rejected as mere surplusage. They are but supplemental to the act of appointment by the Governor. There is certainly an informality in introducing the conditions, but as the Governor has in fact exercised the power conferred upon him by the Legislature in appointing this gentleman, the annexation of the conditions, though not imposed by the Act, cannot be held by this Court as rendering the commission void. Whatever defects there may be in the subsequent commission issued to Mr. *Cheeke*, founded on the warrant under the Royal Sign Manual, we think that as Mr. *Cheeke* has a good commission, not superseded, and under which he has acted, the second may be treated as inoperative. The mode in which the Governor has exercised his power, by importing into the commission conditions not contained in the Act, has certainly raised doubt and difficulty; but on the whole, we are satisfied that the commission is not void, though open to the objection of great irregularity.

Were we not satisfied on this point, the Court would have been greatly embarrassed in dealing with the other objection, namely, that supposing Mr. *Cheeke's* commission to have been properly issued, still it has been superseded by a subsequent commission issued to Mr. *Rogers* for the same identical purposes, and duly notified in the *Government Gazette*.

Mr. *Rogers* states in his affidavit, that whilst he was attending as Clerk of the Peace at the Parramatta Quarter Sessions, on the 3rd January last, a commission from the Governor, appointing him Crown Prosecutor, was forwarded to him from the Colonial Secretary's Office, without any previous intimation to, or request from, him, and without any emolument to be derived therefrom. Immediately, by order of the Court, he read the commission aloud; and thereupon it was objected by the barristers present, and by Mr. *Nichols*, attending as an advocate, that the commission was wholly void; and the matters objected being considered, the Court pronounced it to be void accordingly. The Court then adjourned till next day. On the next day, Mr. *Cheeke* performed the duties of Crown Prosecutor, and continued to do so during that and the subsequent session in April, when the prisoners were convicted. It does not appear that Mr. *Rogers* has surrendered his commission, and for anything to the contrary he still holds it. He does, however, state, that he has not claimed to execute, and has not executed or qualified by taking any oath of office or otherwise to claim or execute, the office of Crown Prosecutor, and has never been admitted an advocate at the Quarter Sessions: but, on the contrary, is and has been excluded therefrom by a rule of Court, made in pursuance of the Act, 4 Victoria, No. 22. From the affidavit of Mr. *G. W. Newcombe*, a clerk in the Colonial Secretary's Office, it appears, that according to the usual practice, notices of appointments are prepared and dated at the same time as the commission; and that at the time of issuing the commission to Mr. *Rogers* to act as Crown Prosecutor, there was prepared and sent to the *Government Gazette* a notice of such appointment, intended to appear on the 5th January last, but before the publication, he was informed, and believed that it was decided by the Governor, that Mr. *Cheeke* should continue to act as Crown Prosecutor; but from some oversight no order was sent to the *Gazette* office not to insert the notification of the appointment of Mr. *Rogers*, and the notification was therefore by mistake published on the 5th January. It does not appear, however, that this mistake has ever been corrected, and consequently it must be taken that Mr. *Rogers* still stands gazetted as Crown Prosecutor, and as not yet having surrendered his commission.

Much discussion took place before us as to the effect of Mr. *Rogers'* commission, and the publication of his appointment in the *Gazette*, as having the legal consequence of superseding Mr. *Cheeke's* commission. The latter gentleman swears that he never resigned his commission. If so, it would follow that until a vacancy was created, the Governor could not appoint any one in his stead. It was however argued by the Attorney-General that Mr. *Rogers'* appointment was consistent with that of Mr. *Cheeke*, for by the peculiar wording of the local ordinance, the Governor might appoint more than one Crown Prosecutor for the Quarter Sessions, for the words are "officer or officers;" but we think that these words must be read distributively, and do not import a power of appointing any number of officers for the same Quarter Sessions. It would seem that after Mr. *Rogers'* appointment, and before it was published, some communication took place between the Governor and Mr. *Cheeke*, and the Chairman of the Quarter Sessions respectively, in which an arrangement was made that Mr. *Cheeke* should continue to act as Crown Prosecutor under his commission. Still we have the somewhat anomalous fact of two persons holding commissions at the same time, from the same authority, for the performance of the same duty—an irregularity which has led to considerable embarrassment. It is true that the Quarter Sessions adjudged Mr. *Rogers'* commission to be void, and we are not prepared to say that, as a Court of Record, the sessions had not full power and authority to determine upon the fitness and qualifications of an officer presented to them for the conduct and despatch of such important duties as those of Crown Prosecutor, notwithstanding that Mr. *Rogers* held a commission for the purpose. To hold otherwise would, on public grounds, deprive a Court of Justice of a most important privilege, and lay it open to have perhaps the most unfit person thrust into an office concerning the administration of justice, for which he was wholly disqualified. Setting aside this consideration, there are the important facts, however, that Mr. *Rogers* was never qualified for the office, nor accepted it, but repudiated it.

Taking it now that the appointment of Mr. *Rogers* was a mere mistake, fallen into without due consideration of the legal consequences, and that Mr. *Cheeke* must still be regarded as the officer appointed by the Governor, in whose name crimes were to be prosecuted, we are bound to hold for the reason already given, that that gentleman's commission has been made in sufficient compliance with the Act of Council, although we cannot but think that his Excellency was ill-advised in issuing a commission with the supplemental conditions thereto attached. These conditions have given rise to the laborious discussion which has ensued, and which might easily have been avoided by adhering to the terms of the power conferred by the local legislature.

The second objection to the judgment on the prisoners, was, that they were tried at a Quarter Sessions holden simultaneously with a session of Oyer and Terminer and Gaol Delivery of the Supreme Court, and consequently that the jurisdiction of the Quarter Sessions was thereby superseded. It is sworn that on the 2nd April last, in pursuance of the Governor's proclamation, the Quarter Sessions at which these prisoners were tried, were holden at Parramatta, and adjourned from day to day, until the 4th April, when the trial took place, and that on the 1st, 2nd, and 3rd days of the same month, the Supreme Court was sitting at the Court House at Woolloomooloo, as a Court of Oyer and Terminer and general Gaol Delivery. These facts not being denied, we are called upon to determine that the Quarter Sessions had no authority to try these prisoners, pending the sittings of the Supreme Court in its criminal jurisdiction.

It was contended that although the prisoners were in fact tried on a day when the Supreme Court was not actually sitting, yet that made no difference; for in law, the sittings of the Quarter Sessions are but one day, and that if they had no power to sit on the 2nd, they had none on the 4th April, for which 2 Salk. 606 was cited—an authority not now questionable.

It is not to be denied that this Court, by the statute 9 G. IV., c. 83, which created it, has the jurisdiction of all the Four Courts of Westminster, and especially the Supreme Jurisdiction of the Queen's Bench over all criminal causes. By that statute it is at all times a Court of Oyer and Terminer and general Gaol Delivery; and if the principle (4 Bl. Com. 266) applicable to the Queen's Bench at Westminster can come into operation in this colony, it follows as a necessary consequence that no Court of Quarter Sessions can exercise its power in any part of the colony so long as this Court sits. If the actual sitting of the Supreme Court, as such, be the test, such a consequence cannot be gainsaid, inasmuch as this Court is sitting almost throughout the year alternately, in its several common law, equitable, criminal, and insolvency jurisdictions; for though but one Judge may sit in the exercise of the several jurisdictions at a time, still each sitting is in law a sitting of the Supreme Court. The mere sitting of the Court for criminal causes only, would not supersede the powers of the Quarter Sessions. The sitting of the Court for any purpose would have the like effect. The whole of the colony is in law but one county, as respects the jurisdiction of this Court. It is not divided into separate counties as in England. Nay, the Commission of the Peace is not directed to magistrates of any particular district or county, but the magistrates appointed by the Crown are justices for the whole territory, except for the city of Sydney and the town of Melbourne, into which separate commissions issue. If, therefore, the Supreme Court is to be regarded in the same light as the Queen's Bench at Westminster, its sittings at any time (which may be throughout the whole year) would give rise to the apparently insuperable objection that no Court of Quarter Sessions can exercise its powers in any part of the colony during any such sittings. Does, however, this most alarming and mischievous consequence follow? We apprehend not. The jurisdictions of the Supreme Court and of the several Quarter Sessions of this colony, are severally created by the same statute, and derive their authority from the same common source. The Supreme Court has the like jurisdiction as the Queen's Bench at Westminster, but it does not follow that it has exclusive jurisdiction over offences triable by the Court of Quarter Sessions. The same Act that institutes the Supreme Court, also institutes Courts of Quarter Sessions, and gives to these Courts the like jurisdiction as is vested in Courts of Quarter Sessions in England, as well as an extensive summary jurisdiction over transported offenders. The Supreme Court may have all the jurisdiction of the Queen's Bench, without becoming "the Queen's Bench;" and it may have every possible portion of·that jurisdiction to all intents and purposes, without its appropriating to itself also, the fiction upon which the supposed analogy is founded, that the Sovereign is actually present in person to preside over its administration. Were it not for this fiction (7 Bac. Abr. Title Court, K. B. 4 Blac. 265) it would be difficult to contend that even the sitting of the Queen's Bench in England would interfere with the power of any other Court. Supposing, however, that this Court is simply to be regarded as the Queen's Bench, we are of opinion that its sittings would not interfere with the sittings of the Quarter Sessions in this colony. The Courts of Quarter Sessions in England are not created by statute, neither are Courts of Oyer and Terminer. They sit in England in each county by virtue of the Queen's commission. It is true they sit quarterly by statute; and they have also by statute conferred upon them certain criminal jurisdiction; but still they derive their powers from the Royal Commission, issued to justices individually as Justices of the Peace. In this colony the several Courts of Quarter Sessions are instituted as "Courts" specially, by name, by virtue of the same statute which gives jurisdiction to this Court. Admitting, therefore, that this Court and the Queen's Bench have respectively the like jurisdiction, still the Quarter Sessions here have a concurrent jurisdiction in criminal cases, similar to that exercised by Quarter Sessions in England, notwithstanding the sitting of the Supreme Court, subject, however, to the superior and superintending control of this as the Supreme Court of the colony. By the statute 9 G. IV., c. 88, this Court is vested with the power of fixing the times and places at which it shall hold its sittings. Is then the jurisdiction of the Quarter Sessions over matters properly within their powers to depend upon the time and place at which this Court shall fix its sittings? This anomaly has been guarded against by the Legislature, in creating Courts of Quarter Sessions distinct and separate from the Supreme Court, quite independently of the principle on which Quarter Sessions exist in England. The power of fixing the time and place at which such Courts should be holden, was not in like manner provided for as the sittings of the Supreme Court, and hence it became necessary for the local legislature to interpose. Accordingly, by the 3 Will. IV., No, 3, s. 14, power is vested in the Governor to fix the times and places at which such sittings shall be holden, to be notified in the *Government Gazette*. It may be that there is no declaration that the sittings of the Supreme Court shall not operate as a supercession of

1844.

The QUEEN
v.
JOHN HODGES
and
THOMAS LYNCH.

the sittings of such Courts; but such a declaration, upon the plain construction of the statute which created them, was wholly unnecessary. All the fiction which is applicable in England to the. paramount presence of the Queen's Bench in a county into which a commission is issued, really falls to the ground, and is wholly inapplicable to the jurisdiction of the county (for such it must be regarded for the purpose of this argument) of New South Wales, which has two separate jurisdictions created by the statute, subject only to the control of the supreme over the separate inferior jurisdiction. We are not driven to arguments of convenience or inconvenience in so holding, but are bound so to determine, from the plainly expressed intention of Parliament in providing for the due administration of justice in New South Wales, in the Supreme Court, and the Courts of Quarter Sessions respectively.

It appears to us, therefore, that the seemingly cogent objection to the sittings of the Quarter Sessions in this case, concurrently with those of the Supreme Court in its criminal jurisdiction, is really without foundation. The Judges by rule of Court fixed its sittings for the 1st of April, without reference to the Quarter Sessions, and the Governor in virtue of the local Act, appointed the Quarter Sessions to be holden in Parramatta at the same time; but as he had the power of so doing, it appears to us that there is no analogy between the sittings of this Court and that of the Queen's Bench sitting in an English county into which a commission from the Crown had issued to justices or others to constitute a Court of Oyer and Terminer.

Admitting it to be argumentatively doubtful whether this Court has exercised lawful authority in granting a *certiorari* for the purpose of correcting errors of fact, alleged to have been committed by the Quarter Sessions in matters not appearing upon the record, these prisoners have had the advantage of a most elaborate investigation of their case, and after full deliberation, we are of opinion that in this mode of proceeding there is no ground for disturbing the judgment, and consequently they must be remanded in execution of the sentence of the Court below.

If they have any other remedy for disturbing the judgment, they must take such steps for that purpose as they may be advised.

Let the prisoners be remanded to her Majesty's gaol at Parramatta.

CASES

ARGUED AND DETERMINED

IN

THE SUPREME COURT

OF

NEW SOUTH WALES,

IN EQUITY.

BEFORE

HIS HONOR SIR ALFRED STEPHEN, KNT. C. B.,

The Primary Judge in Equity,

AND ON APPEAL TO THE SUPREME COURT.

1865.

June 18.

RUSSELL and others *against* BRUYERES.

THE plaintiffs were, in effect—by assignment from *Horatio Appleton,* the registered proprietor here, under the 16 Vic., No. 24—the patentees for New South Wales of a machine invented by *Eli Blake,* in the United States, for breaking stones. The defendant being desirous of erecting some quartz-crushing machinery, contracted with one *Mather* for its construction, and for the attaching to it of " an *Appleton's* stone-breaking machine"—at a stated gross sum for the whole work. *Mather,* in ignorance (as was alleged by the defendant) of the plaintiff's title, sent to Melbourne for, and imported thence, the last mentioned article; *Appleton,* it seems, having the sole right of making or vending *Blake's* invention in the sister colony. The machine, therefore, having been procured out of New South Wales, in apparent violation of the plaintiffs'

A. desiring to erect some quartz-crushing machinery, contracted with M. for its construction, and for the attaching to it of a machine, for which letters of registration had been granted within New South Wales, under the 16 Vic., No. 24. The machine having been procured out of New South Wales, was ready to be supplied by M. under his contract. On the application of the grantees of the letters of registration, the Court refused to grant an injunction to restrain A. from accepting it.

Quære, whether any restriction in a patent affecting or intended to affect the buyers of a manufactured article, made and sold in violation of the patent, can be supported.

A—4

local patent, was now ready to be supplied by *Mather* under his contract; and the plaintiff sought to restrain, by injunction, the defendant from accepting, or at least from using it (a).

Milford, for the plaintiffs, in support of the motion for an injunction, relied on the first section of the 26 Vic., No. 24, which enables the Governor to grant letters of registration for the exclusive enjoyment and advantage, for a period of not less than seven nor more than fourteen years, for all inventions or improvements in the arts or manufactures, to the author, designer, or his agent or assignee.

Blake for the defendant. The proper party to look to is *Mather,* who erected, or is about to erect, the machine for the defendant. No injunction will lie in cases of this kind. The defendant merely contracted with *Mather* for the procuring of such machine, and for its erection; and it was imported by *Mather,* and not by the defendant. It does not appear at present to be in the defendant's possession, or under his control. It is not unlawful for any person to import a patent article, or a copyright book for the private use of the importer. He might not be able to sell it to a third person; but why should he not import as the defendant, or rather *Mather* here has caused to be done? He also referred to *The Universities of Oxford and Cambridge* v. *Richardson* (b), and *Bythewood's Conveyancing, Title, Patent and Copyright* (c). It is nowhere alleged that the defendant has imported for purposes of sale; and there has been no application to the defendant not to use the machine.

Cur. adv. vult.

July 7.   The following judgment was now delivered by the PRIMARY JUDGE. This case was reserved by me for consideration, chiefly because I desired to discover some authority, on which the plaintiff's claim might be

(a) The defendant having appeared immediately to the bill, the motion was heard on notice.

(b) 6 Ves. 689.   (c) 7 Vol., pp. 511, 547.

sustained; for my impression then was, that it ought
to be supported, if possible, not merely against persons
who should infringe the patent by making or importing
the article, but against all who might purchase it from
them. But I can find no such authority; and am
satisfied on reflection, but especially under the circumstances, that the injunction asked for against this
defendant cannot be granted.

After stating the facts as above, his Honor continued—

As I assume, for the purposes of this judgment, that
the plaintiffs have all the rights which they could
possess if actual patentees, it is unnecessary to consider the effect of the wording, not very definite, of the
local enactment. This confers on the registered person,
within the colony, the "exclusive enjoyment and advantage" of the particular invention. But what do
the words mean? They convey no greater privilege
or protection, at all events, I apprehend, than letters
patent in England would to an inventor there. Now,
a patentee has, in the words of his patent, by himself and his agents or assigns, or such persons as
he or they shall agree with, the exclusive right to
"make, use, exercise and vend" his invention, whether
of a manufactured article or a process, within the limits
of his patent. It is clear, from the *Oxford* and *Cambridge* case *(a)*, and on the reason of the thing, that an
English patentee—having such a right in England,
but there only—could not lawfully cause the article
specified in his patent (in that case bibles and prayer
books) to be sold, nor could any purchaser from him
in England lawfully sell the article in Scotland, to the
prejudice of any patentee, having a similar exclusive
right in that kingdom. And conversely, of course :
that the Scotch patentee, or a purchaser from him
there, could not transmit or import from Scotland
for sale, and sell, in England, such specified article
—to the prejudice of the patentee there.

It would seem to follow, that the purchase in and
importation from Melbourne, for sale in New South

(a) 6 Ves. 708-9.

Wales, of the stone-breaking machine in question, and its sale or delivery under such a contract as that of *Mather*, constitute an infringement of the right of the plaintiffs—by themselves and their licensees—exclusively to have the "making, using, and vending" of such articles in this colony. But, in the absence of *Mather*, this position can only be taken to be assumed —not determined. The defendant, however, appears to me to be no party to that infringement. The bill charges, that the defendant imported the machine. But he merely stipulated with *Mather*, for the procuring of an *Appleton's* stone-breaking machine—which might and ought to have been procured in Sydney, from the plaintiffs. Does their right under the statute, to the exclusive "enjoyment and advantage" of *Eli Blake's* invention, extend to preventing the use of the article, by a purchaser, under the circumstances stated, from *Mather*? I can find no case anywhere, in which such a claim has been set up by a patentee. If the right exists, there would surely be—among the numerous instances of actions and suits for the infringing of patents—some trace of such a claim.

If the defendant had himself imported the article, or caused it to be imported, although for his own use, I should be inclined to doubt if he were protected. Lord *Eldon's* observation in the case of the Universities would only apply to this (as I understand it), on the supposition that *Mather*, or the defendant, being at the time in Melbourne, had there purchased the article, and for his own use; and afterwards brought it here, but not for sale. My opinion is founded on the fact, that the defendant was substantially no party to the importation. He contracted for the obtaining of a machine described; and it has been obtained, although wrongfully, and he has paid for it. If the defendant cannot use the article, because it has been so obtained, neither could any purchaser of a bible from the wrong patentee, in England or Scotland, as the case might be, have lawfully read the purchased book—or the buyer of articles in a market, wrongfully set up to the injury of another, be allowed to consume those articles. The purchaser of an article of dress, manufactured or improved by some patented but pirated process, could not be allowed to wear it. Many similar examples might be suggested. But I see no just reason, all things being considered, for extending the remedy so far. The plaintiffs here may restrain *Mather*, if there be the infringement complained of, from delivering the machine; or they may bring an action against him at law.

If it be urged, that the Act of 16th Victoria confers exactly the same privileges, and imposes precisely the same restraints, as an English patent—a construction which I have assumed, but not decided—and that, if so, the restriction extends in terms to the "using" of the invention, the answer has been in part already given. But the defendant will not use the invention, either literally, or (as I apprehend) within the meaning of the words referred to, by using the purchased pirated article. The prohibition was directed to the using of the invention itself, piratically and adversely to the inventor, in the manufacturing of the article, or the using of the process specified. The word cannot reasonably be understood, as prohibiting the use of the article by an innocent purchaser, after manufacture. The mode, or the process patented, the purchaser has had nothing to do with; he neither has made nor vended the pirated article. I doubt, indeed, whether any restriction in a patent, affecting or intended to affect the buyers of a manufactured article made and sold in violation of the grant (assuming the non-existence of complicity with the manufacturer or vendor), could be supported in point of law.

As the motion for the injunction has wholly failed, and on the merits, it must necessarily be refused with costs.

Frost *against* Healy and others.

A testator, whose property consisted of real estate, leasehold lands, and a squatting station fully stocked, and ready money, devised the whole to his wife, jointly with F. and H., their survivors and survivor, and the heirs and executors of such survivor, upon trust to permit her "to have the full benefit and enjoyment" of the property for life, and then upon trust to divide it among all his children—the boys at twenty-one, and the girls at that age or on marriage. *Held*, that the trustees had such an estate or interest in the personalty as would enable them to interfere, to protect the interests of those in remainder, and to prevent the commission of waste in respect to such interests.

A suit having been instituted by F. against H. and the testator's widow, who had married again, and against *Harford* her present husband, charging sundry breaches of trust by the two former defendants, and misappropriations by *Harford*—an injunction was granted against all the defendants, restraining them from further interference with the trust estate, and an order for the appointment of a receiver was made. A motion by *Harford*—denying the allegations of waste, and claiming personally a right during his wife's life to the enjoyment of the property—to dissolve the injunction as against him, and to discharge that order, was dismissed with costs, except as to the testator's real estate, respecting which the evidence of waste had failed.

Held also, that the Court would interfere, although the *cestui que trusts* were not parties to the suit.

THIS suit was instituted by one of three trustees and executors appointed under the will of *Samuel Elliott*, against the other trustees and executors—one being the testator's widow, who has married again—and against *Paul Harford*, her present husband, charging sundry breaches of trust by the two former defendants, and misappropriations by the defendant *Harford*; and it prayed, among other things, for an injunction against all the defendants, to restrain them from further interference with the trust estate, and for the appointment of a receiver and manager. The late Primary Judge, upon affidavits by the wife and the plaintiff substantiating the main charges, in February last, granted the injunction, and order for a receiver and manager; and the husband now, on his own behalf, denying the allegations of waste, and claiming personally a right during his wife's life to the enjoyment of the property, moved to dissolve the injunction as against him, and to discharge that order.

The testator's property consisted of real estate, some leasehold lands, and a "squatting" station (or two such stations adjoining each other), apparently fully stocked—besides ready money. He devised the whole to his wife, jointly with *Frost* and *Healy*, their survivors and survivor, and the heirs and executors of such survivor, upon trust first to permit her "to have the full benefit and enjoyment" of the property for life, and then upon trust to divide it among all his children—the boys at twenty-one, and the girls at that age or on marriage. There was no provision for the education or maintenance of the children, during the mother's life; but there was a clause, giving power to the trustees or trustee for the time being to secure those objects, after her death. There were the usual declarations making the trustees' receipts a discharge to all parties taking the same, and entitling the trustees to reimbursement for their expenses. This, with the addition of the clause appointing the trustees executors, and guardians of the children, constituted the entire will.

It appeared that Mrs. *Elliott* married *Harford* in 1859, about eleven months after the testator's death, and she had managed the property in conjunction with her present husband till of late, when he alone had collected the stock and sold great numbers of the cattle, and had bought sundry tracts of land with, it was said, the proceeds, and put his own cattle to graze on the testator's land. There were allegations also that *Healy* had been purchasing largely, although a trustee.

The children were not made parties to the suit.

Martin, Q.C., and *Milford* in support of the motion. During the wife's life the trustees had no legal estate whatever, and no duty or power to discharge or execute in respect of any part of the property. For where real estate is devised to one person upon trust to permit and suffer another to receive the rents, the beneficial devisee takes the legal estate, and not the trustee. And where the expressions to pay unto, and permit and suffer to receive, were both used, it was held that the words "permit and suffer" coming last, controlled the former trust "to pay," and that the same construction was applicable; *Doe* v. *Biggs* (a), *Gregory* v. *Henderson* (b), *Lewin* on Trusts (c), and *Jarman* on Wills (d). Therefore, the whole legal estate vested in the wife; and on her marriage, vested in her husband. It follows that

(a) 2 Taunt. 109.   (b) 4 Taunt. 772.
(c) (4th Ed.), p. 162.   (d) 2 Vol. 240.

this plaintiff has no *locus standi.* The use is executed in the party benefited, unless some duty is interposed in the trustee, or he possesses some power to intermeddle; *Shapland* v. *Smith* (a). But here there is not even a provision for the maintenance of the testator's children, till the wife's death.

On a suggestion of waste or danger the parties in remainder may come in to ask for security, but not for a receiver. Where a specific legacy is given to one for life, and after his death to another, there the legatee in remainder was formerly entitled in all cases to come into a Court of Equity, and to have a decree for security from the tenant for life, for the due delivery over of the legacy to the remainder-man. But the modern practice is, in such cases, only to require an inventory of the articles, specifying that they belong to the first taker for the particular period only, and afterwards to the person in remainder; and security is not required, unless there is danger that the articles may be wasted, or otherwise lost to the remainder-man; *Foley* v. *Burnell* (b), *Leeke* v. *Bennett* (c), *Richards* v. *Baker* (d), *Story's* Equity Jurisprudence (e). Here, however, there is no remainder-man or reversioner before the Court.

The "enjoyment" of chattels can, in many cases, only be by consumption; *Randall* v. *Russell* (f). Will it be said that a life estate in hay or corn, or in cows, is confined to the use of the thing itself, till it disappears? But the defendant has done nothing, except manage the bulk of the property in the usual and proper course; so that there is no waste, at all events, and no danger in this case. As to the realty there is not even a suggestion of waste, and there are two persons acting quite as much entitled as the plaintiff can be. The judgment of *Milford, J.,* in *Wentworth* v. *Tompson* (g), was referred to.

The only ground on which *Frost* can sue is this, that he may hereafter be liable to his *cestui que trust* by

(a) 1 Br. C. C. 75.	(b) 1 Br. C. C. 279.
(c) 1 Atk. 470.	(d) 2 Atk. 320.
(e) § 604. (f) 3 Meriv. 190.	(g) June 9th, 1859.

reason of the misconduct of his co-trustee. But as he has now no duty, he is at present not practically a trustee at all. A receiver should not be appointed to dispossess a legal holder; *Skinner's Company* v. *Irish Society* (a), *Story's* Equity Jurisprudence (b).

Gordon, for the plaintiff, in support of the injunction. How can the purposes of the entire trust be secured, if the legal state be not in the trustees? The rule is, that where a trust is created, a legal estate sufficient for the execution of the trust shall, if possible, be implied; *Lewin* on Trusts (c). Here, it is necessary that the trustees should be held to be the owners, in order to enable them to carry out the trust. If there be no trust, the plaintiff will be relieved from his responsibility. But if the two trustees are to be permitted to deal with the property as they please, it may all vanish. The statute of Uses has no application to personalty. It is submitted that *Frost* must have a right to come here, if only to secure for the trust the property which, at Mr. *Harford's* death, at all events will be, and is now the intended patrimony of the children. Mr. *Lewin* (d) says, " if one trustee be cognisant of a breach of trust committed by another and either industriously conceal it, or do not take active measures for the protection of the *cestui que trust's* interest, he will himself become responsible for the mischievous consequences of the act. A trustee is called upon, if a breach of trust be threatened, to prevent it by obtaining an injunction ; and, if a breach of trust has already been committed, to file a bill for the restoration of the trust fund to its proper condition, or at least to take such active measures as, with a due regard to all the circumstances of the case, may be considered the most prudential." The plaintiff is quite willing to rely on *Wentworth* v. *Tompson,* where, although by consent, a receiver was appointed.

Martin, Q.C., in reply. A devise of personal property must have the same construction as that of real estate,

(a) 1 Myl. & Cr. 162.   (b) § 836.
*(c) Ch. 11, s. 11 (4th Ed.), pp. 163, 167.
(d) Ch. 13, s. 17 (4th Ed.), p. 210.

where both kinds of property are referred to in the same will; *Dunk* v. *Fenner (a)*, *Browncker* v. *Bagot (b)*, *Spence's* E. J. *(c)*. There cannot be two different channels; but the same interest will pass as to each species of property. A trust to permit and suffer to take or receive interest or dividends, has been construed to give the absolute property. in stock in the funds to the *cestui que trust*, who was a married woman; *Wagstaff* v. *Smith (d)*. How could the wife "enjoy" the property, unless she has the legal interest in it? If the trustees can interfere in the management and the like, the wife will not be the owner, and cannot be said to "enjoy" the property. He referred to *Knight* v. *Ellis (e)*, and *Jarman* on Wills *(f)*.

As to the appointment of a receiver, the Court does not appoint them as against parties in possession, where there is no fraud or waste, or where the rights are doubtful; *Seton* on Decrees *(g)*, citing *Earl Talbot* v· *Scott (h)*. The waste, also, must be flagrant.

Cur. adv. vult.

July 14.   The PRIMARY JUDGE having recited the facts of the case as above set out, continued—

It has been contended for *Harford* that his wife took, under this will, the legal estate—in at all events the real property—for her life; that her interest in the personalty, since no reason existed for a different disposition, was of the same nature; and that, the entire enjoyment of both being in her, without any control or power of interference in any other person, the co-trustees had no duty cast on them, and so no right to ask the interposition of the Court; or that, if the plaintiff had such a right, it could only be on facts showing a clear case of actual or meditated waste, and then that the Court would at the most direct security to be given, that the property ultimately should be forthcoming.

I shall assume, for the purposes of my present decision, that, on the authorities—however strong the reasons

(a) 2 Russ. & Myl. 567.   (b) 19 Ves. 574 ; S C., 1 Meriv. 280.
(c) 2 Vol., 150, 155.   (d) 9 Ves. 520.
(e) 2 Br. C. C. 570   (f) 2 Vol. 479.
(g) 2 Vol., 1010.   (h) 4 Kay & J. 96 ; 27 L. J. Ch. 273.

which might be urged, if the point were new, against that construction—the devise here of the real estate, although in terms to the trustees, vested the legal as well as equitable interest therein, for her life, in the widow. Such would seem to be the result of the rule, that, where no "use" in a third person or active duty in a trustee is interposed, words permitting a beneficiary to "receive the rents and profits" of an estate (to which words a permission to "have the benefit and enjoyment" of the property is equivalent), will carry the legal estate, to the extent of his equitable interest, to such beneficiary. But this is an artificial rule, founded on the statute of Uses, which does not extend to personal property. In limitations affecting real estate, the statute "executes" the use or trust, as we know, in the party meant to be benefited; and the Courts have arbitrarily decided, that a trust for the beneficiary in so many words, or a trust to suffer the beneficiary to receive the profits, is in effect the same thing. There is no decision, however, that, in respect of personal property, unless perhaps of leasehold interests, the same technical rules equally and under all circumstances must prevail—so that the Court cannot, in a case of this kind, give effect to a testator's actual intention. And, if not, I shall feel bound to hold here, that a devise—not to the testator's wife, but to trustees—of money, and of live stock on a cattle station (and the station also, assuming it to be occupied as "squattages" usually are), with other chattels, on trust to "permit" her to enjoy such property for life, and then to divide it among his children, is in legal operation what it is in terms, and, we may certainly infer, was by him meant to be.

The cases relied on for the defendant *Harford*, to show that the disposition by will of personal estate, where the terms used are the same, will follow that of the real, were *Browncker* v. *Bagot* (a), and *Dunk* v. *Fenner* (b). The former decided (following *Coulson* v. *Coulson* (c) that a certain limitation of lands there

(a) 1 Meriv. 280.　　(b) 2 Russ. and Myl. 565.
(c) 2 Atk. 246.

created an estate tail; and that, therefore, the testator having afterwards given personalty " for the same estate, and in the same manner" as the real property, an estate tail therein was equally meant to be created—whereby the personalty so limited became, according to a similarly artificial but established rule of construction, vested in the donee absolutely. *Dunk* v. *Fenner*, following *Jesson* v. *Wright* (a), and *Donn* v. *Penny* (b), are to the same effect. Sir *John Leach* held, that the limitation of the realty in that case gave the first donee an estate tail therein; and, therefore, as to the personal property, that the same words—by force of the rule just mentioned, both the real and personal estate being given in the same terms—carried the latter absolutely. It was, says the learned Judge, the testator's plain intention that both classes should go together; and the words, therefore, must receive the same construction as to both.

Those cases appear to me, although the distinction may not be easily defined, to be distinguishable from the present; and I do not think that their application ought to be extended. In both the conclusion was inevitable, that if—although on a purely artificial rule of construction, or of law—a certain kind or extent of interest was created as to the real estate, the same (the testator being taken to have intended what the technical words expressed) was equally created, or meant to be created, by the same words, with respect to the personal. An estate tail cannot exist in chattels, however; and therefore, as to these the donee necessarily took the entire interest. But in this case, the trust or use declared becomes vested (or, as the law terms it, executed) in the beneficiary donee, as to the real estate, by force of a statute only—and that statute, as already noticed, has no reference whatever to personalty. Even if we concede, therefore, that the testator must be assumed to have known, such being the legal but very violent presumption, how his freehold lands would vest by virtue of that statute, I do not see why it should not equally be assumed, that he was aware of the inapplicability of the

(a) 2 Bligh 53.   (b) 19 Ves. 544.

statute, to the fleeting and precarious chattel property which he was leaving. The inference is surely not a forced or unreasonable one, that the testator—if the distinction was present to his mind at all—meant his wife to be legally seized of the immovable property, but intended to vest his stations and the cattle on them in trustees, whose duty it would be to prevent the dissipation, sale, removal, or undue diminution of the property, to the irremediable injury of his children· The cases cited, at all events, do not go beyond the particular point decided in them; they do not necessarily embrace, even by inference, the point now for decision; and there is nothing, therefore, so far as their authority is concerned, to restrain or pervert the natural meaning of the words used.

As to a portion of the personalty, that is to say, the furniture, if any, the dead stock (whatever that was), and some other articles, the difficulty may perhaps arise which was suggested on the argument; namely, that the wife has of necessity an absolute right to them, because the use of such articles inevitably involves, sooner or later, their consumption. But this is a very subordinate matter. No such question can exist, with respect to the large sum in cash lying unexpended at the testator's death, or the squatting station, and the live stock on that property. The interest of the money, and the legitimate annual profits of the stock and station, are all which the widow was entitled to; and her present husband, although appearing now to ignore the ultimate rights of her children, must have been well aware that such—and such only—whether legal or equitable, was her title. I do not finally decide, that the legal estate in those chattel interests is in the trustees; for, as at present advised, even assuming it to have been in the wife, and now to be vested in *Harford* in her right, I am prepared to hold that, on reasonable evidence of waste in the defendants, or either of them, the plaintiff as one of such trustees is entitled—on behalf of those children, who will or may otherwise be defrauded of their rights—to ask this Court to protect them.

1865.

FRONT
v.
HEALY
and others.

1865.

FROST
v.
HEALY
and others.

I have no doubt that the jurisdiction exists to afford that protection, in exactly the way in which it has been temporarily given ; and notwithstanding *Harford's* allegations in his answer, and all that has been urged for him, I am of opinion that there is preponderating evidence of such waste here. As already observed, he would be entitled to the fair annual profits of the personalty ; and all that can be considered of that character (a question which it will often not be easy to determine), *Harford* has the right—such have been the defects of the will, and the improvidence of the widow on her marriage—to appropriate exclusively to himself. I say nothing now of any claim which she may think fit to advance, to a settlement. It is of his rights, as they stand at present, that I speak. But it is clear to my apprehension, that the defendant has been grossly deteriorating the property—the station, and the stock belonging to it—and appropriating to his own use much more than their legitimate yearly proceeds. I, therefore, refuse to disturb either the injunction or the appointment of a receiver—except as to the testator's real estate, respecting which the evidence of waste fails. For the reasons already assigned, I conceive the legal interest in that portion of the devised property, during the wife's life, to be in *Harford* ; but I exempt that portion, on the ground above stated alone. I am willing, on the same ground, to exclude from the operation of both orders the leasehold estate at Mudgee. With respect to all the other parts of the property, the defendant's motion is dismissed ; and, since the principal object of it has failed, and he has by asking for too much compelled the plaintiff to oppose, the dismissal will be with costs as to the whole.

I have looked at all the cases referred to on both sides; but none exactly touches the point, for which I understood them to have been cited. The decision in *Wentworth* v. *Tompson* (for instance) was, that one trustee, although himself guilty of negligence, might compel co-trustees to make good losses, in diminution of the trust funds, arising from breaches of trust by them—notwithstanding that the *cestuis que trust* were not parties, and that no claim had been then made by them ou the plaintiff. In some respects that case resembles the present. None of the parties there, however, had rights or interests of their own; thè trustees had all, confessedly, active duties to discharge; the suit was for the plaintiff's protection alone; and (although this distinction perhaps is not material) the objects of the trust were directly, and not remotely or contingently only, interested in the funds.

It may certainly be said, that the children of the testator here are interested, even now, that the property which is eventually—after their mother's death, and on their attaining certain ages—to become theirs, should not unduly be diminished. But the objection remains, that the plaintiff in this case sues a person who is at present the sole beneficiary of the fund, in his own right or that of his wife, and who is not and never has been a trustee. It will be answered that this person knew of the trust, and the limited nature of her interest under it, before his wrongful appropriation of that fund; and so, that the proceeds in his hands may be followed. Considered as a stranger to and ignorant of the trust, *Harford* would—in respect of any excess of appropriation by him—be in the position of an ordinary wrong-doer; and *Wentworth* v. *Tompson* would not, as far as he is concerned, apply. It would be a strong thing to maintain, however, that a tenant for life of personalty, because of his legal title to possession, or of his ignorance of the rights of parties in reversion, could not be restrained by injunction from making away with that property—or could not be displaced by a receiver, if thought necessary, on his actually making away with portions of it, and appearing to be likely to commit similar acts of spoliation.

If this can be done at the instance of the reversioners themselves, may it not also be at the instance of a trustee—who, on the happening of the event, although having no legal title now, will have the duty cast on him of entering on the property, and preserving it for their benefit? As to this last point, however, no difficulty of course exists, if *Elliott's* trustees have in them the legal interest; since, in that case, *Harford* is a *cestui que trust*, and no more. The other trustees are equally defendants; and the order for the receiver, as well as the injunction, may be supported—in that view of the case—as necessary at all events against them.

Possibly, in either event, I would here suggest, *Harford* may eventually be allowed to become himself the receiver, on proper terms. The interests of the wife and her children, might perhaps—since her husband would then be under the superintendence, as well as the direct control, of the Court—be promoted by that course. But this will depend on circumstances, of which, at the present stage of the cause, and in the absence of fuller information, it would be premature, if not impossible, to judge.

ECCLESIASTICAL.
June 26.

In the goods of SIMONS, deceased (a).

The advertisement of intention to apply for probate to one of two executors named in a will, must mention the second executor, and state the intention to apply for probate with leave reserved to him.

WILKINSON moved that probate might be granted to one of two executors named in the will—leave being reserved to the other executor to come in and prove.

It appeared that the advertisement required by the Rules stated merely the intention to apply for probate to the applicant, "the executor named in the will," &c., without stating the intention to apply for probate with leave reserved to the other executor to come in and prove, or otherwise showing that there were two executors. *In re Owen Jones*, deceased (b), and *In re Henderson*, deceased (c), were referred to.

THE COURT (*Stephen*, C. J., *dubitante*) refused the application, being of opinion that the advertisement was calculated to mislead, and was not a sufficient compliance with the Rules.

(a) Before *Stephen*, C. J., *Wise*, J., and *Hargrave*, J.
(b) 1 Wyatt & Webb; I. E. & M. 14.   (c) March, 1865.

1865.

ALLIANCE BANK (LIMITED) *against* IRVING.

July 28.
August 1, 2, 3,
and 24.

THIS was a suit instituted by the Alliance Bank (Limited), an incorporated public company carrying on business in London and elsewhere in England, on behalf of themselves and all the other unsatisfied creditors of *Clark Irving* (deceased), formerly of this colony, but who at the time of his will and death resided in England. The defendant, *Adelaide Irving*, who is the testator's widow, resides also in England, and is the sole executrix appointed by the will of the testator, and the sole devisee and legatee of all his real and personal property, subject to the payment of his debts.

A testator possessing large, real and personal estate in New South Wales, died domiciled in England, largely indebted to several creditors—one of whom, residing in England, instituted a creditor's suit in the High Court of Chancery against the testator's widow, who also resided in England, and was the sole executrix and devisee appointed by his will. In this suit a decree had been obtained for adminis-

The bill was filed on the 5th of June by Mr. *Robert Johnson*, as solicitor for the plaintiffs, under instructions given him by an agent of the Alliance Bank appointed under seal. It stated that the testator, *Clark Irving*, died on the 13th January, 1865, and as the plaintiffs believed in embarrassed circumstances—that at the time of his death he was indebted to the plaintiffs in the sum of £100,000 and upwards, and was also largely indebted to several other creditors, English and colonial—that he

tration of the testator's estate, and for receivers to collect his assets in this colony and elsewhere ; but before their actual appointment the executrix, without obtaining probate or administration in this Court, had, by her son as agent, taken possession of part, and was proceeding to collect and realize the residue of the testator's property in this colony. The plaintiffs, who were also English creditors, now instituted here a suit of the same character against the widow, and served her son with the bill, under an order for substituted service, and subsequently, but before appearance entered for the defendant, and without opposition, obtained an order for the appointment of a receiver, and for an injunction to restrain the defendant from dealing with the estate. A motion to rescind this order and dissolve the injunction was granted by the Primary Judge, on the grounds principally that the bill was defective for the purposes of administration, as the defendant was not the administrator or personal representative in this colony of the deceased ; and that the testator having died domiciled in England, and the parties being resident there, the Court of Chancery, which had already made a decree for the administration of the testator's assets, and was competent by virtue of its jurisdiction over the persons of the parties to carry into effect the provisions of the will, for the benefit of the persons interested, was the appropriate forum for the creditors to resort to for satisfaction of their claims (a).

(a) This order was reversed by the full Court on appeal (*Stephen*, C. J., the Primary Judge, *dissentiente*). See *Post.*

B—4

was possessed of personal and real estate in this colony of considerable value—and that the defendant had, by means of *John Irving* (the testator's eldest son and heir at law, and who was acting as her agent under a power of attorney), taken possession of part, and was proceeding to collect and realize the rest, of the testator's personal assets in this colony, and was in receipt of the rents and profits of his real estate.

It was prayed that the trusts of the will might be carried into execution—that the testator's estate, real and personal, in this colony, might be administered under the direction of the Court, and that the defendant might be restrained by injunction from receiving or collecting the testator's personalty, and the rents of his real estate, and that a receiver might be appointed for these purposes.

On the 9th of June an order was made for substituted service of the bill on *John Irving*, and on the 7th of July the plaintiffs moved for an injunction to restrain the defendant from dealing with the estate. In the affidavits used on this motion, it was stated that Mr. *John Irving* (who arrived in this colony in March last) had sold, or permitted the sale of, a steamer named the " Florence Irving," part of the testator's assets—that he had executed a mortgage over some valuable city property of the testator to the Commercial Banking Company of Sydney, to secure a debt of about £10,000 due from the testator, and for the recovery of which a writ of foreign attachment had been issued against the executrix—that in this last transaction, as well as in all his dealings with the estate, the defendant's agent acted under the advice of his solicitor, Mr. *R. J. Want*, whose firm were the general solicitors for the Commercial Bank. It was also stated that Mr. *John Irving* was endeavouring to dispose of certain valuable squatting stations belonging to the testator—that the defendant's solicitor refused to give any pledge that nothing should be done in the estate to the prejudice of the creditors—and that the defendant claimed to be entitled to some interest in the squatting property, under a settlement executed by the testator on the day before his death. It also appeared that the defendant had proved the will in England, but that no letters of administration to the effects of *Clark Irving* had been obtained in this colony by her or any other person.

The defendant had not appeared to the bill within the time limited for appearance, and the plaintiffs had not entered an appearance for her. The present motion was not opposed on her behalf; but the Primary Judge refused to grant the injunction, unless the order embraced also the appointment of a receiver. The plaintiffs accordingly took the order for injunction and receiver.

It was now moved on behalf of the defendant (who had in the meantime appeared to the bill) to dissolve the injunction, and rescind the order for injunction and receiver. From the affidavits read in support of the motion, it appeared that previous to the institution of this suit, the Alliance Bank had instituted proceedings against the defendant, by administration summons in the Court of Chancery in England, and that the defendant had appeared and resisted these proceedings, in consequence of which they were abandoned, or the summons dismissed. It also appeared that one *Newton* had also instituted in the Court of Chancery a suit of the same character as the present, and that a decree had (on the 19th of April last) been made therein, directing the appointment of two receivers, with power to constitute agents in this colony, and providing for the execution by the defendant of all acts necessary for the collection or management of the estate. It was also proved that notice of this decree was published in the Sydney newspapers on the 1st of July. The allegation that the testator died in embarrassed circumstances was denied, and, it was averred, that *John Irving* had been dealing with the estate in a careful and proper manner. It also appeared that the solicitors who filed the bill, did so under authority from an agent duly appointed under the corporate seal of the Alliance Bank, and that such proceeding had been duly ratified by the Bank.

SUPREME COURT REPORTS.

Darley and *Milford* in support of the motion.   First,
ALLIANCE   the solicitors who filed this bill have done so without
BANK   sufficient authority, for they have not been appointed by
(LIMITED)
v.   the Alliance Bank under its common seal.   The bank
IRVING.   is a corporation, and has no power to retain an attorney
except under its corporate seal; *Story* on Agency (*a*),
Arnold v. *Mayor of Poole* (*b*), *Fariell* v. *Eastern
Counties Railway Co.* (*c*), *Sutton* v. *Spectacle Makers'
Co.* (*d*), *R.* v. *Justices of Cumberland* (*e*).   By the
English Act (27 and 28 Vic., c. 29, sec. 3) Joint Stock
Companies are empowered to have duplicate seals; but
an inspection will shew that the seal affixed by the agent
here to the appointment of the solicitor, is not such a
duplicate of the corporate seal.   The solicitors who filed
this bill have, therefore, not been properly appointed,
and the plaintiffs might repudiate the whole of their
proceedings.   There is nothing which could bind the
plaintiffs suing here, except the fact of their retaining
an attorney; and if the appointment here acted upon
were repudiated by the Bank, as it might be, great
injury might be inflicted on the defendant; *Robson* v.
Eaton (*f*), *Hubbart* v. *Phillips* (*g*), *Baker* v. *Roe* (*h*).
There must be a special authority under seal to file a
bill on behalf of a corporation; and the probability that
such a proceeding will subsequently be ratified, does not
justify the solicitor in instituting a suit; *Daniel's*
Ch. Pr. (*i*), *Wilson* v. *Wilson* (*k*), *Lord* v. *Kellett* (*l*),
Hall v. *Bennett* (*m*), *Hood* v. *Phillips* (*n*), *Ward* v.
Ward (*o*), *Martin* v. *Greenway* (*p*), *Bacon's* Abr. (*q*).
If, therefore, the suit was instituted without authority,
the relief prayed should not have been granted, and
the injunction should now be dissolved.

Secondly, the bill cannot be maintained, inasmuch as
there is no personal representative of *Clark Irving* before

(*a*) Sec. 149.   (*b*) 2 Dow. N. S. 574, 597.
(*c*) 2 Exch. 344.   (*d*) 10 L. T. Rep. Har. Dig. (1865) 11.
(*e*) 5 D. & L. 431.   (*f*) 1 T. R. 62.
(*g*) 13 M. & W. 702.   (*h*) 3 Dow. 496.
(*i*) 1 Vol., p. 202, 3rd Ed.   (*k*) 1 J. & W. 457. 459.
(*l*) 2 M. & K. 1.   (*m*) 2 Sim. & St. 78.
(*n*) 6 Beav. 176.   (*o*) 6 Beav. 251.
(*p*) 10 Beav. 564.   (*q*) 2 Vol., tit. Corp., B. 5, p. 265.

the Court ; and in the absence of such a representative, the Court can make no decree for administration ; *Williams* on Executors (*a*), *Moore* v. *Curtis* (*b*). This is a ground of demurrer, and on a motion to dissolve an injunction any such ground may be relied on ; for, as an injunction would not in the first instance be granted, if the bill appeared to be demurrable, so, if granted, it will be dissolved, upon this being shown. Every bill for administration must state the fact of probate, or administration having been granted, and must make the administrator or personal representative a party, for without this there can be no administration of the estate. The bill shews that the defendant has taken out probate in England ; but it does not shew that either probate or administration has been granted to her here. In point of fact no steps have yet been taken, in this colony, for the appointment of a personal representative of the deceased, *Clark Irving*. And it is not sufficient that the person made defendant is the personal representative in another country ; *Williams* on Executors (*c*), *Westlake* on International Law (*d*). The cases of *Tyler* v. *Bell* (*e*) and *Lowry* v. *Fulton* (*f*) establish that the taking out of probate or administration in another country, does not constitute the defendant the personal representative here, and that an administrator cannot be sued as such, except in the country where administration has been granted. Nor by appearing in this suit does the defendant assume the character of a personal representative. It may be contended that she is here treated as executrix *de son tort* ; but such an executrix is not a sufficient personal representative as a party defendant in an administration suit. A bill might possibly be filed against her in that character, for the preservation of the property ; but that is not the object of the present suit, and no trespass or waste is alleged against her ; *Penny* v. *Watts* (*g*), *Logan* v. *Fairlie* (*h*), *Calvert* on Parties (*i*), *Story's* Eq. Plead-

1865.

ALLIANCE BANK (LIMITED) v. IRVING.

(*a*) 2 Vol., p. 1829, 5th Ed. (*b*) 10th Oct., 1860.
(*c*) 2 Vol., p. 1831, 5th Ed. (*d*) p. 287.
(*e*) 2 My. & Cr. 89, 110. (*f*) 9 Sim. 104.
(*g*) 2 Ph. 149, 152. (*h*) 2 Sim. & St. 284. (*i*) p. 143.

ing (a), *Maclean* v. *Dawson* (b), *Humphreys* v. *Humphreys* (c), *Lowe* v. *Fairlie* (d), *Creasor* v. *Robinson* (e). As therefore the relief sought in this suit could not be granted for want of a personal representative, the order for injunction and receiver ought now to be rescinded.

Thirdly, there has been a suppression of material facts in the plaintiffs' bill, and the affidavits on which the order for injunction and receiver was obtained. The suit of *Newton* v. *Irving* was instituted in March last, in the Court of Chancery, in England ; and on the 19th of April a decree was made by *V. C. Wood* for the administration of *Irving's* estate, for the benefit of all his creditors, and appointing receivers with adequate powers for the collection of his personalty and the rents of his real estate, both in England and in this colony. Notice of that decree was advertised in the newspapers here, on the 1st of July. The plaintiffs, no doubt, knew of that decree having been made, before the departure of the mail which brought out their instructions to commence this suit, and their advisers here ought to be presumed to have known it also. We have alleged such knowledge on their part, and it has not been denied. But, however that may be, the plaintiffs come into Court on the 7th July, and on affidavits sworn that day, but which are silent as to the facts referred to, moved for and obtained an injunction. Neither do the plaintiffs inform the Court that their own administration summons had been dismissed ; a fact from which it might be inferred that their claims could be successfully resisted—as we allege in our affidavits it can be—in the Courts of the country where the witnesses to the transaction on which their claim is founded, reside. If these facts had been before the Court ; if it was made apparent that the granting of an injunction and receiver would bring the jurisdiction of this Court into direct conflict with that of the High Court of Chancery—that the plaintiffs were already entitled to the benefit of a decree made in the English suit—that applications suc-

(a) sec. 171.   (b) 28 L. J. Ch. 742 ; 5 Jur. N. S. 1091.
(c) 3 P. Wms. 349.   (d) 2 Madd. 101.   (e) 14 Beav. 589.

cessful here might be rendered nugatory by the Court of Chancery in the exercise of its jurisdiction over the persons of the parties—this Court would have paused, before making the order in question, on the unopposed application of the plaintiffs. And it is not necessary that the facts concealed or suppressed should be such as would compel the Court to dissolve an injunction obtained, as it were, by surprise; it is sufficient if they are such as might create a doubt as to the propriety of granting it. The facts here concealed were material— vital facts; and if they had been laid before the Court, the order for injunction would not have been granted; *Daniel's Ch. Pr.* (a), *Hilton v. Lord Granville* (b), *Dalglish v. Jarvie* (c).

The appointment of a receiver is a matter resting in the sound discretion of the Court, governed by a view of all the circumstances of the case; *Owen v. Homan* (d). One of these circumstances is the probability of the plaintiff being ultimately successful in the suit, which, as we have shown, cannot be the case in the bill framed like this, the personal representative not being made a party. And another matter which would influence the Court's discretion, is the fact that the powers and duties of the receiver appointed here would lead to an antagonism between him and the officers of the Court of Chancery. That Court has jurisdiction to appoint a receiver of property out of its territorial jurisdiction; and when the appointment is made, this Court will not interfere, as on the same principle it will not interfere with a foreign official assignee; *Seton* on Decrees (e), *Houlditch v. Marquis of Donegal* (f), *Barkley v. Lord Reay* (g), *Faulkner v. Daniel* (h), *Bunbury v. Bunbury* (i), *Earl of Oxford's Case* (k), *Keys v. Keys* (l), *Harrison v. Gurney* (m), *Jackson v. Leaf* (n), *Sill v. Worswick* (o). And the English Court can restrain parties within their

(a) 2 Vol., p. 1266.   (b) 4 Beav. 130.   (c) 14 Jur. 945.
(d) 3 M. & G. 378.   (e) 2 Vol., p. 1 38, 3rd Ed., by Har. & L.
(f) 8 Bl. N. S. 343.   (g) 2 Ha. 308.   (h) 3 Ha. 204 n.
(i) 1 Beav. 336.   (k) 2 Wh. & Tud. 522, 228, 531, 2nd Ed.
(l) 1 Beav. 425.   (m) 2 J. & W. 563.
(n) 1 J. & W. 232.   (o) 1 H. Bl. 665, 690.

jurisdiction from carrying on a suit in another country; *Beckford* v. *Kemble* (a), *Portarlington* v. *Soulby* (b), *Penn* v. *Lord Baltimore* (c), *Story's* Eq. Jur. (d), *Graham* v. *Maxwell* (e). On the ground, therefore, that facts have been suppressed, which might have materially influenced the discretion of the Court in this matter, the order for injunction and receiver should be set aside, and the injunction dissolved—for the injunction cannot stand if the receiver be discharged.

Fourthly, the plaintiffs have taken a mistaken, improper, and irregular course in their proceedings in this suit. In the first place the order for substituted service was *ultra vires*. For this being a suit respecting lands in this colony, is one of the cases which are regulated by the provisions of the Act, 13 Vic., No. 31 (and see 4 & 5 W. IV., c. 84, and 15 & 16 Vic., c. 86, sec. 5), and the plaintiffs should have entered an appearance for the defendant, under that Act, before proceeding to move for an injunction. It may be contended that the order for substituted service was made under the general jurisdiction of the Court, and that the plaintiffs were not bound to avail themselves of the statutory provisions referred to. No doubt, under the general jurisdictions, the Court might order substituted service on an agent residing within its jurisdiction, and who had been authorised to act in respect of the subject matter of the suit. See *Hope* v. *Hope* (f), *Hobhouse* v. *Courtney* (g), *Murray* v. *Vipart* (h), *Weymouth* v. *Lambert* (i), *Cooper* v. *Wood* (k). But in all those cases there could be no doubt that the agent was in communication with his principal respecting the suit, and it was reasonable to think that the latter was kept informed of the proceedings. In this respect, the affidavits filed on behalf of the plaintiffs are insufficient to support a motion for substituted service. In *Hope* v. *Hope* notice of each motion was given to the defendant, and it was clear that

(a) 1 Sim. & St. 7. (b) 3 Myl. & K. 104, 108.
(c) 2 W. & T. 767, 2nd Ed. (d) 2 Vol., sec. 744.
(e) 1 M. & G. 71. (f) 4 De G. M. & G. 328, 341.
(g) 12 Sim. 140. (h) 1 Phil. 521.
(i) 3 Beav. 333. (k) 5 Beav. 391.

he knew what was going on. And see *Smith* v. *Hibernian Mine Co.* (a), *Daniel's Ch. Pr.* (b), *Cookney* v. *Anderson* (c), *Foley* v. *Maillardet* (d). But in this case, even assuming the order for substituted service to have been granted under the general jurisdiction, what possibility was there that the defendant could have got notice of the proceeding for the receiver and injunction, between the 5th of June, when the bill was filed, and the 7th of July, when the order for injunction and receiver was obtained. But further, none of the cases in which the general jurisdiction has been resorted to, fall within the Act, 18 Vic., No. 31. Where that Act applies, the general jurisdiction is merged. The case of *Wilkie* v. *Fattorini* (e) is not an authority for the plaintiffs, because it did not fall under the Act—for the lands there in question were in Queensland, and the order was made under the general jurisdiction. The plaintiffs, therefore, not having entered an appearance for the defendant, and not having given her, or even her agent, notice of the motion, have obtained the order for injunction and receiver irregularly. But, further, there is no case in which a receiver has been appointed without notice to the parties; *Daniel's* Ch. Pr. (f), *Morgan's* Ch. Orders (g), *Metcalf* v. *Pulvertoft* (h). A motion for a receiver cannot be made *ex parte*, except where the defendant has absconded. It is only in cases of emergency that a receiver will be appointed before answer, and a case of extreme emergency must be shewn if the application is made before appearance. In no case whatever will it be granted without notice. Here, however, we have a receiver appointed before appearance, without any case of emergency being made out, and without notice. If the plaintiffs had moved the Court for leave to serve the defendant's agent with notice of the motion before appearance, it might have been sufficient, but nothing of the kind was done; *Hill* v. *Rimmell* (i), *Meaden* v. *Sealey* (k), *Dowling* v. *Hud-*

1865.

ALLIANCE BANK (LIMITED) v. IRVING.

(a) 1 Sch. & Lef. 238.
(c) 32 L. J. 305, 427.
(e) 1 W. & O. 32.
(g) p. 481.
(i) 2 My. & Cr. 641.

(b) p. 301, 3rd Ed.
(d) 33 L. J. Ch. 335.
(f) 2 Vol., p. 995, 3rd Ed.
(h) 1 Ves. & B. 183.
(k) 6 Ha. 620.

son (a), *Caillard* v. *Caillard* (b), *Tanfield* v. *Irvine* (c),
Supreme Court Rules Equity (d).

Fifthly, there is no case made by the bill, either for
an injunction or the appointment of a receiver. The
plaintiffs do not allege, and have not proved in their
affidavits, any waste or misconduct on the part of the
defendant or her agent. The defendant, as executrix of
the testator, has a perfect right to do all she is alleged
to have done. She has a right to deal with the property
in this colony without taking out administration here.
An executrix can do almost any act relating to her office
without taking out probate. It is only necessary to take
out probate when there is a suit, and the fact of execu-
torship is distinctly put in issue. In this case it was
unnecessary for the defendant to apply for probate or
administration here. There were no debts due from
the testator in this colony except one, and that has
been arranged. Besides, it is very unlikely that the
defendant, being entitled to the surplus of the assets,
would act wastefully or improvidently ; and our affidavits aver that the contrary is the fact. Now
Courts of Equity will not take the administration of a
testator's estate out of the hands of those to whom he
has confided it, unless upon proof of some misconduct
or waste, or probable danger to the interests of creditors.
To act otherwise, would be to appoint a new executor to
the will without any reason for displacing the person
whom the testator has entrusted with the administration
of his effects—and this is what the Court has done in
this suit by the appointment of a receiver. The Court
will not even remove an executor who is in indigent
circumstances, unless upon proof of some danger to the
fund. In the present case nothing has been alleged or
proved to justify the interference of the Court in
appointing a receiver ; and if there is no ground for a
receiver, there can be none for an injunction ; *Williams*
on Executors (e), *Williams* on Executors (f), *Daniel's*
Ch. Pr. (g), *Middleton* v. *Dodswell* (h), *Anonymous* (i),

(a) 14 Beav. 423.   (b) 25 Beav. 512.
(c) 2 Russ. 149.   (d) p. 13.
(e) 1 Vol., p. 205, et seq., 5th Ed.   (f) 2 Vol., p. 1844, 5th Ed.
(g) 2 Vol., p. 983, 3rd Ed.   (h) 13 Ves. 266.   (i) 12 Ves. 4.

Smith v. *Smith* (a), *Taylor* v. *Allen* (b), *Utterson* v. *Main* (c).

1865.

ALLIANCE BANK (LIMITED) v. IRVING.

Sixthly, this Court ought not to entertain this suit within its jurisdiction. It is not the appropriate forum for the administration of this estate. In the first place, the testator died domiciled in England, and as it is the law of the domicil which must govern the distribution, at all events of the personalty, this Court ought to refuse to administer it; *Williams* on Executors (d), *Pipon* v. *Pipon* (e). Further, this Court cannot effectuate its own orders for the collection of the estate, because if persons indebted should refuse to pay the receiver, he would have to sue in the name of the personal representative, and there is no person filling that character before the Court or in this colony. In the next place the Court of Chancery is already seized of the case, and has made a most comprehensive decree for the administration of all the testator's assets, for the benefit of all his creditors. In virtue of that decree the Alliance Bank is already in the position of a successful plaintiff, in a suit having the same object as the present; *Rouse* v. *Jones* (f). It would, therefore, be encouraging, unnecessarily, a multiplicity of suits, besides a breach of international comity to allow the plaintiffs to proceed here for a remedy which they have already obtained in England. The Court of Chancery possesses all the powers requisite for doing complete justice to all parties. The executrix is within its jurisdiction, and may be compelled to do all acts required from her for the collection of the testator's property. It has power to appoint receivers to collect the colonial assets, and can arm them with the powers necessary for that purpose. And it can effectually protect all persons interested in the distribution of those assets against the consequences of any misconduct or waste on the part of the receivers, by causing them to give sufficient security for the proper performance of their duties. So that it is difficult to see

(a) 2 Y. & C. Ex. 253 ; 10 Ha. App. 71.   (b) 2 Atk. 213.
(c) 2 Ves. Jun. 95-98.   (d) 1 Vol., p. 377 ; 2 Vol., p. 1501, et seq.
(e) Ambler 26-800.   (f) 1 Phil. 462, 466.

how the rights of the plaintiffs can be endangered by leaving them in the hands of the English tribunal.   On the other hand, should this Court assert its jurisdiction, and continue its receiver, there would inevitably arise a conflict between it and the Court of Chancery.   No Court will allow its own receiver to be interfered with, even although erroneously appointed.   The consequence will be that when the receivers of this and the English Court meet in the course of their duties, and find them incompatible, this Court will proceed to restrain or punish the English receiver, while the Court of Chancery acts in the same manner to the Alliance Bank.   Again, the defendant may be compelled by the English Court to do what she is forbidden to do here.   And the plaintiffs may be restrained from taking any further proceedings here, and so those which are in progress be rendered nugatory.   Under all the circumstances this suit should be left exclusively to the English Court.   Equity Courts act primarily *in personam* ; they seek to enforce the rights of parties principally by proceedings against the person.   Proceedings *in rem* are resorted to only as subsidiary to the primary jurisdiction—the exercise of which in the present case, by the Court of Chancery, is sufficient for the purpose of doing complete justice. The plaintiffs and the defendant are resident in England, and personally amenable to the jurisdiction of the Court there.   So also is every person who can give evidence in proof or disproof of the plaintiffs' claim. Before that claim could be established to the satisfaction of this Court, a commission to take evidence would have to be sent to England, and this would involve delay and expense.   A suit involving so many difficulties as the present, and liable to the objections pointed out, is not one in which the Court, in the exercise of its discretion, would appoint a receiver.   It is submitted, therefore, that on all the grounds now urged, the order for injunction and receiver should be discharged, and the injunction dissolved with costs.

Martin, Q. C., and *Gordon*, for plaintiffs, *contra.* The plaintiffs are large creditors of an estate, great part

of which is in this colony. The English Courts can
exercise no coercive jurisdiction here, and have, therefore, no direct and immediate power over the testator's
colonial property. The English executrix has no
authority to collect the colonial assets without a grant
from this Court of letters of administration, and for this
it appears she has no intention of applying. Meanwhile,
the person who is acting as her agent, and who is beyond
the reach of the English Court, is collecting, mortgaging, and selling the colonial property, and making
arrangements for the payment of colonial creditors,
without any authority from the Court of Chancery.
The plaintiffs ask that the property should be preserved,
pending litigation in England, and this is the only
Court in the world which has the power to do so; *Story*
on Conflict of Laws (a), *Preston* v. *Melville* (b), *Bayley*
v. *Edwards* (c), *Ostell* v. *Lepage* (d). The appointment by the Court of Chancery of a receiver to collect
the colonial assets will be ineffectual for the purpose.
For, as that Court has no territorial jurisdiction here,
how can it enforce obedience to its orders, or compel
persons indebted to the estate to pay their debts to its
receiver? How are the English receivers or their agents
to be coerced, if they turn out neglectful or disobedient;
Dillon v. *Alvares* (e). This is the only Court which
has territorial jurisdiction in this colony, and which
consequently possesses the requisite powers for preserving
the testator's colonial assets, and enforcing their due collection or realization. This Court, therefore, is not tied
up by the order of the Vice Chancellor. Any creditor
of the deceased, *Clark Irving*, has a right to come here
and ask for the preservation of the colonial assets. There
is no conflict of jurisdiction, but there is a conflict between the defendant and the creditors. She challenges
their rights, because she claims superior ones. The
person in possession of the property here is her son, and
is no doubt working for her interest, which is antago-
nistic to that of the creditors. His title to deal with the

1865.

ALLIANCE
BANK
(LIMITED)
v.
IRVING.

(a) sec. 514.   (b) 8 Cl. & F. 1, 12.   (c) 3 Swanst. 703, 710.
(d) 5 De G. & S. 95, 105 ; 16 Jur. 406.   (e) 4 Ves. 359.

property is no better than that of a mere stranger. Hence the necessity for applying to this Court to prevent him from intermeddling with the assets, and to appoint some person under the control of the Court to collect them. But we do not ask that the decrees of the English Court should be ignored, nor insist on the administration of the estate, or the proving of the debts here. We wish rather to have the orders and proceedings of that Court recognised and carried into effect. And even if this suit were merely in aid of the English decree, the appointment here of a receiver and the granting of the injunction were necessary.

As to the first point insisted on in support of this motion, Mr. *Johnson* (the solicitor who filed this bill) acted under the sanction of an agent duly appointed by the Alliance Bank, and empowered to institute suits in the Courts of this colony, and the retainer has been duly ratified by the Bank. Besides, if the bill was filed without authority, it was a contempt of the Court, and the course for the defendant to have taken should have been to move for the bill to be taken off the file, and the solicitor to pay the costs. But, in fact, all that an attorney requires to enable him to sue, is that he should have some authority by word or writing—something to show that he is not acting without authority; *Wilson* v. *Wilson* (a), *Dundas* v. *Dutens* (b), *Lord* v. *Kellet* (c). Acquiescence on the part of the corporation is sufficient to enable the solicitor to sue, and the circumstances here are such as to warrant the Court in inferring acquiescence. All the cases cited on the other side, with reference to the appointment of attorneys by corporations, were actions by the attorneys against the corporations. In *Arnold* v. *The Mayor of Poole* (d), it was only held that a corporation cannot generally be sued on a contract not under seal. That case does not prove that the legal proceedings instituted by the attorney were invalid; but only that he could not recover his costs against the corporation, because his appointment was

(a) 1 J. & W. 457.   (b) 1 Ves. Jun. 200.
(c) 2 M. & K. 1.   (d) 2 Dow. N. S. 597.

not under the corporate seal. He might retain money
in his hands belonging to the corporation, and pay himself for work done under their authority, although he
could not recover his costs by action. In *R.* v. *Town
Council of Lichfield* (a), a sufficient retainer was held to
have existed, although the appointment was not under
seal. The following cases also were cited and commented upon—*Faviell* v. *Eastern Counties Railway
Co.* (b), *State Fire Insurance Co.* (c), *R.* v. *Justices
of Cumberland* (d), *Baker* v. *Roe* (e). But even
were the retainer of the plaintiffs' solicitor insufficient,
it is not for the defendant to object. The only
person who can be prejudiced by the insufficiency
is the plaintiffs' solicitor himself. But the plaintiffs
having ratified his appointment cannot, as against him,
repudiate the authority under which he has acted, much
less, therefore, can they shake off any liability to the
defendant which may attach to them in consequence of
these proceedings.

As to the second point urged for the defendant,
it is submitted that a receiver and injunction may
be obtained without making the personal representative a party. There cannot, indeed, be a decree for
account or administration until such personal representative be brought before the Court. This point is not disputed, and it is all that the cases cited on the other side
establish. But there is nothing to prevent the Court
from making interlocutory orders and references, such
as for the appointment of a receiver, previous to the
decree. And where there is no personal representative
in possession of the property, the Court will protect
it, and appoint a receiver for that purpose as of
course. In this case it is necessary that the Court
should interfere. The defendant's affidavits show that
the executrix does not intend to take out probate or
administration here, and yet her agent is mortgaging and
selling the estate, and paying debts without any legal
authority ; *Lowe* v. *Fairlie* (*f*), *Atkinson* v. *Hen-*

(a) 10 Q. B. 534, 539.   (b) 2 Exch. 344.
(c) 32 L. J. Ch. 300 ; 9 Jur. N. S. 298.   (d) 5 D. & L. 431.
(e) 3 Dow. 496.   (*f*) 2 Mad. 101, 105.

1865.

ALLIANCE
BANK
(LIMITED)
v.
IRVING.

shaw (a), *Stier* v. *Stier* (b), *Rendall* v. *Rendall* (c), *Major* v. *Major* (d).   The object which the plaintiffs have in view, at present, is simply the protection of the testator's assets, which are being dealt with in such a manner as to render the plaintiffs and other creditors extremely apprehensive of danger to their interests. The person who has taken possession has no legal title to receive or pay a single penny.   The defendant, whose interests he has been sent to look after, has put forward claims adverse or superior to those of the creditors, and disputes that of the plaintiffs.   The Court is then asked to take this property out of the agent's hand—to prevent it from being made away with—to preserve it for the benefit of all parties interested—and for that purpose to place it in the hands of a person directly accountable to the Court. Is the Court to be incapacitated from doing this, because the defendant declines taking out administration, and thus avoides the responsibility which would attach to her as the personal representative of the testator in this colony?   Is her agent to be allowed to deal with the estate just as he pleases, uncontrolled either by this Court or the Court of Chancery?   A receiver will be appointed, on the very ground that there is no personal representative.   Wherever property is unprotected, the Court will take it under its own protection for the ultimate benefit of all who have a claim upon it.   But the administration of it is another matter, and cannot (we admit) be decreed until a personal representative is appointed. When that is done in this case the representative can be made a party, and the suit proceed to a decree if that be thought expedient; at present it is essential that the property, whether it is to be administered here or in England, should be preserved, and the Court will never refuse its interference for that purpose when the property is in danger; *Wood* v. *Hitchings* (e), *Portman* v. *Mill* (f), *Ball* v. *Oliver* (g), *Feucheres* v. *Dawes* (h).

Thirdly, the plaintiffs have not been guilty of con-

(a) 2 V. & B. 85, 92.   (b) 11 L. T. N. S. 502.
(c) 1 Hare 152.   (d) 8 Jur. 797.
(e) 2 Beav. 296.   (f) 8 L. J. Ch. 161.
(g) 2 V. & B. 96.   (h) 5 Beav. 110.

cealing or suppressing material facts. There is nothing to prevent a creditor from suing here as well as in England. The plaintiffs were under no obligation to mention the fact of the English suit, and therefore there has been no suppression. If the English Court has no jurisdiction to protect and collect the colonial assets, how can proceedings in that Court be material with reference to a suit instituted here on the very ground of that defect ? [*Per Curiam.* It is not necessary for the plaintiffs to argue this point. I do not think there was any impropriety in not mentioning the fact of the English suit.]

Fourthly, the defendant contends that the order for substituted service was improperly granted. But if so, the proper course would have been to move to set it aside. Until it is discharged it stands good. The general power of the Court to direct substituted service is left, by the Equity Process Act (13 Vic., No. 31), where it was before. That power is not exercised on the principle that no proceedings can be taken until it appears that the suit has come to the defendant's knowledge. The defendant's son was managing all her affairs here. He had a special power of attorney to act for her here in all matters relating to the estate of the testator, and was assuming to manage and administer it. Substituted service on him was, therefore, properly ordered ; *Hope* v. *Hope* (a), *Hobhouse* v. *Courtney* (b). In the next place a receiver may be appointed before appearance ; *T'anfield* v. *Irvine* (c), *Meaden* v. *Sealey* (d), *Aberdeen* v. *Chitty* (e), *Duckworth* v. *Trafford* (f), *Davis* v. *The Duke of Marlborough* (g), *Taylor* v. *Allen* (h), *Coward* v. *Chadwick* (i), *Smith* v. *Smith* (k), *Davis* v. *Duke of Marlborough* (l), *Vann* v. *Barnett* (m). The whole practice of appointing receivers is founded on the principle that when property, the subject of litigation, is in imminent danger, the first object of the

(a) 4 De G. M. & G. 342.
(b) 12 Sim. 157.
(c) 2 Russ. 149, & 634.
(d) 6 Hare 620.
(e) 3 Y. & C. 379, 381.
(f) 18 Ves. 283.
(g) 1 Swanst. 78, 84.
(h) 2 Atkins 212.
(i) 2 Rus. 150 n, 634.
(k) 10 Hare App. 71.
(l) 2 Swanst. 137.
(m) 2 Br. C. C. 157.

Court is to protect and preserve it, and it will do this if necessary before appearance, without service or without notice. In this case, moreover, the time limited for appearance had expired, and the defendant was in contempt for not appearing.

With regard to the fifth objection taken for the defendant the question is, were the facts shown upon the motion for injunction sufficient to justify the Court in granting it? It is submitted that they were. It was sworn that the defendant's agent had sold a steamer, part of the testator's estate—that he had mortgaged some valuable city property to the Commercial Bank to secure a debt, for which the Bank had proceeded against the executrix by writ of foreign attachment—that the defendant's solicitor, Mr. *Want*, through whom this transaction was arranged, and whose firm were also the solicitors for the Bank, refused to give any pledge that nothing should be done in the estate to the prejudice of the creditors—that the agent was endeavouring to sell large squatting stations which belonged to the testator—and lastly, that the defendant claimed an interest in the estate, in virtue of some marriage settlement said to have been executed by the testator shortly before his death, but which the plaintiffs contended was void as against the creditors. These circumstances, coupled with the fact that the defendant had no legal standing as representative of the testator in this colony, and that her agent had no legal title to deal with the assets, were sufficient to justify the Court in making the order. Besides, as the defendant has been herself displaced in England by the appointment of a receiver, how can she complain of being restrained by the injunction? And if a receiver be desirable (as the defendant confesses by her consent to that appointment), what is this Court doing but carrying into effect the very object which she and the creditors, who now seek to rescind this order, have had in view? The pendency of the other suit in England does not preclude the plaintiffs from asking the aid of this Court for the preservation of the property. This is the only Court which can effectually do so. If, however, the two suits should be unnecessary, one or the other will be stayed on proper application for that purpose. In the meantime there is no reason to disturb the order of this Court. The receiver appointed here should be retained—if only to assist the English Court, by preserving the estate with the view of having it administered in England, should that course ultimately prove the most convenient.

Lastly, it is submitted that the plaintiffs have a clear right to institute this suit, notwithstanding the proceedings in the Court of Chancery. That Court has no territorial jurisdiction here. It has no coercive power over the person who is at present dealing with the assets in this colony. It, no doubt, can imprison the defendant if her agent here be guilty of misconduct; but it cannot prevent such misconduct, or indemnify the plaintiffs from the consequences of it. This Court alone has the power of affording full protection to the Colonial property, and effectually preventing it from being wasted or misappropriated. This bill is not demurrable for want of Equity. If it had been filed in England, the plaintiffs would have been allowed to proceed with the suit; therefore, *a fortiori*, they will not be restrained from going on with it here.

Darley in reply. Mr. *Want* was not the attorney, or did not act as the attorney for the Commercial Bank in the matter of the mortgage executed by *John Irving*. And there was no preference given to the Bank in granting this mortgage. There were no other colonial creditors of the testator. The Bank had issued a writ of foreign attachment against the executrix, and was in a position to sell the testator's property in this colony. It was to avoid this sacrifice that the mortgage was given. And it could not prejudice the English creditors, because the colonial creditors are entitled to be paid in full out of the colonial assets before they are sent out of the jurisdiction; *Williams* on Executors (a), *Wilson* v. *Dunsany* (b), *Cooke* v. *Gregson* (c), *Story's* Conflict

(a) 2 Vol., p. 1503. (b) 23 L. J. Ch. 492.
(c) 23 L. J. Ch. 734.

of Laws (*a*), —— v. *Lindsey* (*b*). The transaction of the mortgage, therefore, did not injure any party, but on the contrary benefitted all, and it was done *bona fide* without knowledge of the English suit, for the bill in *Newton* v. *Irving* was filed on the 29th of March last, and the mortgage is dated on the 12th of April following.

The Vice-Chancellor has not acted *ultra vires* in appointing receivers of property in this colony. The jurisdiction he has exercised would, under like circumstances, be assumed by any Court of Equity. The cases cited on this point for the plaintiffs—*Preston* v. *Melville* (*c*), *Foster* v. *Vassal* (*d*), *Dillon* v. *Alvares* (*e*), *Bayley* v. *Edwards* (*f*), *Ostell* v. *Lepage* (*g*)—were referred to and commented upon. There can be no doubt that the decisions in these cases were right, but they do not touch the question here. In this case— 1st, the plaintiffs and defendant both reside in a foreign country; 2nd, the defendant is executrix of a testator who was domiciled in that country; 3rd, a full and perfect decree for administration has been made in that country, and receivers have been appointed to collect all the assets for that purpose. Will this Court not recognise the fact of such appointment; or will it, at the instance of a foreign creditor over whom it has no jurisdiction, interfere with the officers appointed by the tribunal of that foreign country? The cases are decisive on this point, and establish that Courts of Equity have always asserted the same jurisdiction as the Vice Chancellor has exercised in the English suit—a jurisdiction which does not claim to affect foreign property or to coerce foreign tribunals, but to affect and coerce the persons of its own subjects; *Hibbert* v. *Hibbert* (*h*), —— v. *Lindsey* (*i*), *Hinton* v. *Galli* (*k*), *Cockburn* v. *Raphael* (*l*), *Smith* v. *Smith* (*m*), *Houlditch* v. *Marquis of Donegal* (*n*). The case then stands thus:—The

(*a*) ss. 509, 510, 512, 513, 518.   (*b*) 15 Ves. 91.
(*c*) 8 Cl. & F. 1, 12.   (*d*) 3 Atk. 587.
(*e*) 4 Ves. 357.   (*f*) 3 Swanst. 703.
(*g*) 5 De G. & S. 95.   (*h*) 3 Meriv. 681.
(*i*) 15 Ves. 91.   (*k*) 24 L. J. Ch. 121.
(*l*) 2 Sim: & St. 453.   (*m*) 10 Ha. App. 71.
                    (*n*) 8 Bl. N. S. 301.

foreign Court has assumed the jurisdiction and appointed receivers. It has power over both plaintiffs and defendant in this suit; and this Court which has no jurisdiction over the one or the other, is asked to interfere with the receiver appointed by the tribunal, to which both are subject, and which can restrain either of them from proceeding here; *Price* v. *Dewhurst* (a), *Whyte* v. *Rose* (b), *Sill* v. *Worswick* (c), *Hunter* v. *Potts* (d), *Phillips* v. *Hunter* (e), *Bunbury* v. *Bunbury* (f), *Story's* Eq. Jur. (g).

With regard to the cases cited for the purpose of meeting the objection, that there was not a personal representative before the Court, those of *Major* v. *Major* (h), *Atkinson* v. *Henshaw* (i), and *Wood* v. *Hitchings* (k) were cases where the right to probate was in dispute in the Ecclesiastical Court, and a receiver was appointed *pendente lite*. In *Stear* v. *Stear* (l) there was no executor—no person had taken out administration, and the bill stated that the estate was in danger. The circumstances of this case are different from those in any of the cases cited by the other side on this point. As to the real estate of the testator, the defendant is entitled as devisee; as to the personalty she can take out probate when she sees fit, and there is no allegation of danger to the estate. The principle applicable to this case is laid down in *Williams* on Executors (m); and see *Rendall* v. *Rendall* (n). The receiver is appointed for the preservation of the property pending the administration. But there is no danger in this case, and therefore no grounds for appointing a receiver. This bill would be bad on demurrer for want of parties, and the Court would not allow an amendment. In *Tyler* v. *Bell* (o) the Chancellor dismissed the bill, refusing liberty to amend under circumstances similar to this. This case being an administration suit, cannot be

1865.

ALLIANCE BANK (LIMITED) v. IRVING.

(a) 4 My. & Cr. 76.
(c) 1 H. Bl. 691.
(e) 2 H. Bl. 403.
(g) 2 Vol., sec. 899.
(i) 2 V. & B. 85, 92.
(l) 11 L. T. N. S. 502.
(n) 1 Ha. 152.

(b) 3 Q. B. 493.
(d) 4 T. R. 182.
(f) 1 Beav. 318.
(h) 8 Jur. 797.
(k) 2 Beav. 289.
(m) 1 Vol. 435.
(o) 2 My. & Cr. 89.

brought but against a party whom the Court can compel
to account.   If the plaintiffs really wanted the relief
they profess to seek, they ought to have taken out letters
of administration here, or have got some one to do so.

As to the proceedings subsequent to the order for substituted service, it is submitted that the Act 13 Vic., No.
31, applies to this case, and the Court cannot act under
its general jurisdiction where the statute applies.   Here,
the plaintiffs have not entered an appearance for the
defendant according to that act, nor has the Court satisfied itself that the suit has come to the defendant's knowledge.   The defendant's son, though dealing with the
property, has not been shown to be the defendant's
agent for the purposes of this suit.   He might have
intermeddled in a right adverse to that of the defendant,
or as heir-at-law to his father.   The Court, therefore,
should not have held him bound to supply the defendant's place in this colony for the purposes of this
suit, unless it was made apparent that he had been
appointed the defendant's agent with reference to the
matter.   The receiver appointed in this case must consequently be taken to have been appointed without notice
to the defendant, and before appearance, which is contrary to the uniform practice of the Court; *Hope* v.
Hope (a).

We submit that the authority under which the
solicitor for the plaintiffs filed this bill was invalid.
A solicitor may, no doubt, be appointed by a private
person, either by word or writing; but a corporation
cannot appoint a solicitor except by writing under seal.
And the reason is obvious.   A private person can declare
his will by word or writing without seal; but in matters
like this a corporation cannot speak—cannot manifest
its intention in any way, except in writing under its
common seal; *In re State Fire Insurance Co.* (b).
And no subsequent ratification by the plaintiffs can, as
against the defendant, render valid *ab initio* a proceeding which has been commenced without authority, and
by which the defendant has been injuriously affected.

(a) 4 De G. M. & G. 328.   (b) 32 L. J. Ch. 309.

The ratification may estop the plaintiffs from repudiating the acts of their solicitor in any dispute between them and him, in regard to those proceedings; but it cannot retrospectively remedy the injury originally inflicted on the defendant, in being brought into Court ostensibly by parties who might afterwards have denied that they had authorised the suit.

1865.

ALLIANCE
BANK
(LIMITED)
v.
IRVING.

Cur. adv. vult.

Judgment was now delivered as follows, by the PRIMARY JUDGE. This is a creditors' suit, instituted by the Alliance Bank of London, for themselves and all his other creditors, English and colonial, against the executrix and devisee of *Clark Irving*, formerly of this colony, but who at the time of his will and death resided in England, praying that the trusts of that will may be carried into execution, that his estate real and personal in the colony may be administered, and for an injunction to restrain the defendant, and her agents here (she being absent), from collecting or disposing of the same, and that a receiver may be appointed for those purposes.

Upon affidavit that the defendant is represented in this colony by her son, who was dealing extensively with the property, both real and personal, and paying (or making arrangements to pay) certain colonial creditors preferentially, to a large amount, under her authority, an order was made for substituted service on her son; and afterwards, on motion, upon proof of such service, and that he continued in the management or control of the property, which is of very great value, but believed to be wholly unequal to the testator's debts, and moreover that the defendant personally claimed an interest in the estate under a marriage settlement—no appearance being entered, and her solicitors stating, after the time limited for such appearance, that none would be entered —and irremediable mischief to the creditors' interests being sworn to be apprehended—I granted an *ad interim* injunction, and by the same order directed a receiver to be appointed. It should be added, that (although not stated in the bill) it appeared that the

August 24.

defendant had proved the will in England, but that no probate or administration had been obtained here.

The defendant now moves to rescind that order, and dissolve the injunction, on the following grounds:— 1. That the suit was instituted in the name of a corporation ; but their solicitor has not been constituted, or authorised to act for them, under the corporate seal. 2. That there is not before the Court, for want of colonial probate or administration, any legal personal representative of the testator. 3. That material facts (hereinafter mentioned) were known to the corporation when the injunction was applied for, but were concealed from the Court. 4. That, having reference to the Equity Process Act of 1849, my order allowing substituted service was wrong ; or that, if right, a formal appearance should have been entered for the defendant —and that her agent was entitled to notice of the subsequent motion. 5. That no case had been established for the plaintiff, of waste or other misconduct in the defendant, or her agent, justifying an injunction or the appointment of a receiver. 6. That, on the facts now appearing, the whole subject matter, and the entire administration of the estate, should be left in the hands of the English tribunals ; and that this Court, assuming it to have the power, ought not to interfere with and supersede the receivers, who (it was shown) have already been appointed by the Court of Chancery, in a suit there instituted and pending, having the same ostensible objects as the present, and to which the corporation was, in effect, with every other English creditor—or might, if it chose become—a party.

On all these points, but especially the fourth and first, a very great number of authorities were cited on both sides ; the larger portion of which, however, the conclusion about to be expressed renders it unnecessary for me now to consider. The new facts brought before me were these:—1. The Alliance Bank had itself instituted, before (it seems) the suit just alluded to, a proceeding against this defendant in the Court of Chancery, by administration summons, in respect of this very debt;

which proceeding, after appearance by her, had been discontinued or dismissed. 2. One *Newton*, an English creditor, has instituted there against the executrix a suit of the same nature as the present (on behalf therefore of all the creditors), in which a decree has been made by Vice-Chancellor Sir *W. Page Wood*, in terms of the prayer ; and two receivers have been appointed—with power, subject to the approval of the Judge, to constitute agents in this colony—to get in the testator's estate. Advertisements moreover have been published, in pursuance of the decree, in the London and Sydney newspapers, calling on the creditors to appear in November next, and prove their debts. 3. The testator was domiciled, and died, and the debt to the Alliance Bank, if any—but which is altogether disputed—was contracted, and the defendant herself wholly resides, and that bank has its principal establishment, in England. 4. The suggestion as to undue dispositions of the property by the defendant's agent, is, in my opinion, satisfactorily met; and I see no reason to suspect waste, or irremediable mischief to the estate, in his proceedings. By what legal authority, however, he sells, or can otherwise appropriate the chattel property, it is not easy to discover.

Under these circumstances, it appears to me that I am bound to discharge the recent order. The objection that the plaintiff's attorney has not been properly appointed, may perhaps be dismissed on both the grounds suggested. Firstly, the Bank has duly constituted an agent in this country, by deed under the corporate seal, for the express purpose of instituting suits, and that agent has appointed the attorney. Secondly, whatever value there might be in the objection, for some purposes, the defendant can hardly be deemed competent to take it. I do not find sufficient evidence, that the Bank knew of Vice-Chancellor *Wood's* decree and order, before applying for the injunction—although there may be strong reason for suspecting that they did. It is unnecessary to inquire further, therefore, what validity there might be in the defendant's third objection. And I shall

1865.

ALLIANCE BANK (LIMITED) v. IRVING.

assume for the purposes of this judgment, without affecting to decide the point, that there is nothing in her fourth ground of exception—as to the substituted service, and the supposed irregularity of the subsequent motion. But I am of opinion that, on the sixth objection taken, if not also on the second and fifth, the defendant is entitled to succeed in this application.

With respect to the two last mentioned—that, as to the colonial property, the only subject matter of this suit, there exists no personal representative of the testator, and that there has been a failure to establish, under the circumstances, any ground for interference by injunction—the case stands simply thus. Here is a Bank established in London, suing in respect of an enormous debt there contracted, and seeking to have the colonial assets administered, both real and personal estate being equally liable, and the testator's creditors paid thereout; but there is no person in the colony entitled by law to administer, or (unless it be the receivers appointed in England, or their agents), to collect the personalty, and no one consequently against whom a decree could be made, to compel such administration. The defendant is the deceased's personal representative in England only, and she is there resident. Her agent in this country, moreover, although dealing with the assets, is not shown to be wasting or misapplying them; and not only is the right to administration here not in litigation—which might have furnished a ground for interposition pending the contest—but no colonial grant of administration appears to have been applied for. Where is the foundation, then, for the plaintiffs' right to the interference of this Court? It might be a strong thing to hold, that such an agent (or his principal), assuming authority to dispose of a testator's colonial assets, could under no circumstances be restrained, as an executor *de son tort*, from meddling with them. But it seems clear from the authorities—I will mention one only in addition to those cited, *Creasor* v. *Robinson* (a), following *Penny* v. *Watts* (b)—that in a suit of this kind no decree can be

(a) 14 Beav. 589.   (b) 2 Phill. 152.

made, in the absence of the legal personal representative.

The sixth objection, however, appears to me to be the strongest, and I think it fatal to the plaintiff. The testator was, it is conceded, not a temporary resident only, but domiciled in England, where his will was made, and where he died ; and both the plaintiff and the defendant, as well as the other creditors who act in concert with the plaintiff, reside there. All these persons, consequently, are amenable to the jurisdiction of the English Court; and, a decree to account and for administration of the assets having been made, the plaintiff can be restrained by that Court from suing the defendant (as executrix, at all events), in any other. The decree professes to deal with the colonial as well as with the English property, not on the supposition that there is any control over the former, locally, or over individuals here, vested in the Court of Chancery, but on the ground of that jurisdiction over the parties, to which I have just referred, and of its exclusive jurisdiction to construe and carry into effect the provisions of the will, and distribute the assets among such persons as that Court—being the Court of the deceased's domicil, and therefore the appropriate forum—shall find entitled thereto. See, among the numerous authorities quoted on the argument, the case of *Enohin* v. *Wylie* (a), before the House of Lords. And it is for this reason that the decree confers (or assumes to confer) power on the receivers, personally or by their agents, to collect the assets real and personal in New South Wales.

There may, no doubt, be great difficulties in the way of carrying out any such power; for how, in case of resistance in the colony, is the order of the Court to be enforced ? No small difficulty might be found to arise, moreover, in the event of administration being obtained here, followed by a suit in this Court by colonial creditors, seeking payment out of the local assets. For, although any such administration would be auxiliary only, and subordinate to the original or domiciliary one, yet it is equally clear that the duty of administering

(a) 31 L. J. Ch. 405.

such assets does, ordinarily, belong to the local tribunal —still, in the discharge of that duty, being as a general rule guided by the law of the domicile. I say as a general rule ; because, in the marshalling of the assets, the local law would seem to prevail. And it would be strange if colonial creditors were to be remitted to a distant jurisdiction, without the sight of realising their demands on the spot, out of the property trusted by them.

Nevertheless, it appears to be settled that local creditors have no exclusive or preferential claim on the property covered by the secondary administration: *Story's* Conflict of Laws (a), *Story's* Eq. Jur. (b). So that, if there were here an administrator of the colonial assets, and no previously obtained decree in the Court of the domicil, this Court could not have declined the exercise of its jurisdiction, but would have administered the assets (although very possibly without the intervention of a receiver), for the benefit equally of the English as of the colonial creditors. Or the Court might, perhaps, even in such a case, abstain from final actual distribution—and cause the assets to be transmitted, as circumstances should seem to require, to the place and forum of the domicil, to be distributed there.

Under the circumstances of this case, however, I feel after consideration no difficulty as to the proper course. Whatever means there may be of enforcing here the English decree, in respect of the authority or powers, practically, of the receivers appointed under it, I am of opinion that the Alliance Bank has no claim, in any way—but at all events none in the way sought, and at present obtained—to the interference or assistance of this Court. I think the Bank bound by that decree; and that it would be most inexpedient, if not indecorous, for this Court to sanction a second suit for the same purpose, after such a decree by the domiciliary Court, at the instance of a creditor resident within its jurisdiction ;—thus inducing a rivalry of receivers, a second set of accounts and claims, with perhaps conflicting re-

(a) ss. 518-524.   (b) ss. 584-589.

sults on the two investigations (to say nothing of the difficulties of proving or disproving a debt here, which was contracted, if any where, at the other side of the globe), and eventually the risk of directly opposing decisions on the same rights.

My conclusion is, that the order made in this cause for the injunction, and for the appointment of a receiver, be rescinded. And the application to discharge it must be granted with costs—not as a punishment to the plaintiff, but as a matter of justice to the defendant, an executrix, wrongly brought here.

1865.

ALLIANCE
BANK
(LIMITED)
v.
IRVING.

Sept. 18, 19,
26, and 27.

THE plaintiffs having appealed from the order above reported of the Primary Judge, the case came on to be argued before the full Court (a); first (by arrangement between the parties), on those points only on which his Honor's decision was founded. The other members of the Court then intimated their opinion that the defendant—so far as those points were concerned—had failed to sustain her opposition to the original order ; that the case was a proper one, notwithstanding the arguments then urged, for an injunction and the appointment of a receiver in this suit; and consequently, that unless she could succeed on some other of the objections taken, that order ought to be restored. The case was, therefore, subsequently argued fully on the defendant's other grounds of objection—with the exception of that as to the corporate seal, which point was abandoned.

On appeal from order of Primary Judge rescinding a previous order for injunction and receiver, on the grounds principally that under the circumstances of this case the Court of Chancery (in which a suit for the same purpose had been instituted, and within the jurisdiction of which all the parties resided) was the appropriate forum for the creditors of

the testator to resort to for relief, and that the defendant in this suit was not the personal representative of the testator in this colony (*Vide Supra*, p. 17).

Held by the full Court (*Stephen*, C. J., *dissentiente*) that the order for injunction and receiver ought to be restored.

Held also that this Court ought not to refuse, at the instance of any creditor of a testator, to exercise its inherent jurisdiction over his property situated in this colony, but ought to place all such property under the protection and management of officers appointed by this Court, more especially when the personal representative declines taking out administration here.

Held further, that the rights of creditors suing here are not diminished or affected by proceedings relative to the same matter in a foreign Court.

Held also that the absence of a legal personal representative of the testator is a matter of objection which may be cured at any time before hearing, and is without any effect on an application for a receiver and injunction *ad interim*.

(a) *Stephen*, C. J., *Hargrave*, J., and *Cheeke*, J.

1865.

ALLIANCE
BANK
(LIMITED)
v.
IRVING.

The argument and cases cited were substantially the same as in the Court below.

Martin, Q. C., and *Gordon* for the plaintiffs.

Darley and *Milford* for the defendant.

Cur. adv. vult.

October 31.

On this day judgment was delivered as follows (*a*):—
STEPHEN, C. J. (*b*)   After stating the previous proceedings in the case as above set forth, continued—

Since I adhere to the opinions expressed when making the order appealed from, my judgment is easily delivered. It appears to me, as it did then, that these plaintiffs have no right to come here; and that they make out no case, for the interference of this Court in their favour. If they were creditors really and truly seeking protection—if any one creditor in the colony (and therefore not subject to the jurisdiction of the domicile) had sued with them—if their stated object had been, however pretended the representation, to aid or control the English receivers, or merely to preserve the property from waste, by persons likely to prey on it without authority—or if even a decree had not been pronounced in the English suit, under which every creditor can come in and share equally in the assets, real as well as personal—I might feel hesitation respecting the course to be taken.   But here are English creditors, or persons assuming to be

(*a*) Before the delivery of the judgment
Darley, for the defendant, said it was his duty to call the attention of the Court to the fact that an injunction had been granted by the English Court of Chancery in the suit of *Newton* v. *Irving*, restraining the Alliance Bank from continuing any proceedings in this suit or commencing any other suit in this colony for the administration of the estate of the testator, *Clark Irving*.   He read an affidavit of this fact, and that notice of the injunction had been served upon the plaintiffs' solicitors, who had stated that by the advice of counsel they intended to take no step in violation of the same.   He therefore asked the Court not to deliver judgment in the present case, unless such judgment was actually prayed for.

Hargrave, J., said that in his opinion, and that of Mr. Justice *Cheeke*, nothing which had been said by Mr. *Darley* ought to delay the delivery of the judgment with which the Court was prepared.

(*b*) The Chief Justice being absent, his judgment was read by Mr. Justice *Faucett*, who had himself taken no part in the hearing or consideration of the case.

creditors—(it appears that they have obtained a judgment, but even that is not mentioned in their bill)—who have themselves commenced an administration suit in England, from which they have withdrawn; and there is a decree pronounced in another suit there, under which they are not only entitled, but bound, to come in and prove, and be paid their just demands. These plaintiffs can even be ordered by that Court, as doubtless they soon will be (they being wholly amenable to its jurisdiction), not to institute any rival proceedings here. Every effort is made, in and by means of that suit, to collect the colonial property—and cause it to be remitted, under the control of the English Court, for due distribution among the creditors. There is no reasonable ground for supposing, that there either is or will be foul play in this colony. In point of fact, if we except the arrangements made about the steamboat, and with the Commercial Bank—transactions which are satisfactorily explained—nothing in the defendant's management here is complained of. No dissipation of the property is suggested in the bill; no want of power to administer or collect that property. There is no statement that the administration is contested—and so, that there is danger to the estate from non-collection, or collection by improper hands. Receivers giving large security are appointed in England, to be represented here by agents approved of by the English Court, these also giving large security.

In this state of things, the plaintiffs institute the present suit—openly and avowedly to administer the estate; that is, to do in the colony what their own Court is actually doing, and has a clear and indisputable right to do, as between them and the executrix, in the country of the testator's domicile, where both parties alike reside. And this suit is instituted, moreover—and a decree therefore "to administer" is sought—against a person who actually at this moment has not the power; for the defendant, as yet, is not in this colony the testator's legal representative. I do not insist much on this, however, as influencing me at present. I regard the present

suit, under the circumstances, as foundationless, unnecessary, and vexatious; certainly not as one in any
way to be encouraged.

It was said on the argument that the English suit is a
friendly one; that it has been instituted by *Newton* at
the instance of the executrix, for the purpose of enabling
her to defeat other creditors. I am not a little surprised
at such an observation. A very large proportion of administration suits, as every practitioner knows, are of a
friendly character; and it is possible that one of
Newton's objects may be, in that suit, to defeat a claim
which he supposes to be unfounded. It is obviously his
interest, if (as is alleged here) the estate be insolvent, to
oppose that claim; and, so far, the widow's interests
and his are doubtless identical. But these plaintiffs,
residing on the spot, can have nothing to apprehend.
They have only to prove a just debt, and no litigant can
deprive them of their rights. Every creditor will share
equally in the assets, and the plaintiffs must know it.
If the Commercial Bank has been unduly preferred, the
executrix can be made answerable at home for her misconduct. The friendliness of the plaintiff there, should
the Alliance Bank complain, could not stifle the inquiry.
And it is quite open to these plaintiffs, in aid of that
suit, I apprehend, or otherwise (making proper persons
parties to the bill), to proceed against the favoured
creditor—if there be anything wrong in the transaction—
here. But to compel the executrix, or *Newton*, to
litigate here the claim of an English bank, on transactions to an enormous amount occurring in England,
where all the parties interested (and presumably the
witnesses also) reside—and this, after a decree in a suit
there pending, having exactly the same object—appears
to me, I confess, to be rather a strong measure.

It will be understood that I am far from surrendering
the jurisdiction of this Court. There may be many
creditors here, who are or may become entitled to institute such a suit as this—notwithstanding the decree in
the English suit. I am far from holding that creditors
beyond the jurisdiction of the English tribunal (those

especially, perhaps, domiciled in this colony, who may naturally look to the colonial assets for payment), are to be sent there to obtain justice. Nor do I say that these plaintiffs, although within that jurisdiction, and bound by that decree, might not obtain an injunction and a receiver—certainly an injunction in aid of the English receivers—under certain circumstances, and on a bill aptly framed. But the plaintiffs here have put on the record no such bill, and have no claim whatever, under the circumstances, to the order—or eventually to the decree—sought by them.

In addition to all other reasons, I must again advert to the difficulties and inconveniences, practically, looking at the matter as one of discretion, which must attend the appointment of rival receivers in this colony. Pending this appeal, the appointment of two agents to the English functionaries, approved of by the Vice Chancellor, has been received. The decree of the Court having been on the 16th April last, and the order appointing these receivers the 12th May, the sanction to the appointment of their agents was on the 22nd May; all prior to the institution of this suit, whether the plaintiffs then knew of that decree or not. I have never been insensible to the difficulties, which those agents may experience here, from the want of any coercive power (within this colony) in the tribunal which assumed to give them the authority. But I conceive that—as between the parties before us— the colonial Court ought to recognise that authority, and do all that may be possible to enforce it—or at least to assist the receivers in its exercise. I see much more difficulty in indulging these plaintiffs with rival officers; thus defeating effectually the English decree, although one confessedly (or at least indisputably) binding on the plaintiffs, as well as on the defendant.

This being my view of the case, I need offer no opinion on the other objections raised to my first order. If any one of them be fatal, the appeal of course fails. But it is not necessary for me, nor do I feel called on (except in the event of any difference of opinion between my colleagues) to enter into any question respecting them.

D—4

1865.

ALLIANCE
BANK
(LIMITED)
v.
IRVING.

HARGRAVE, J.   The first and most important point in this case for the consideration of the Appellate Court is as to the jurisdiction of the Supreme Courts of the colony, over property situate in this colony ; and my brother Mr. Justice *Cheeke* and myself consider it to be of extreme importance that this Court should firmly maintain its supreme jurisdiction ; and that not the less strenuously because the defendant here attempts to oust the colonial jurisdiction chiefly on the ground that the estate of the late *Clark Irving* will be more properly administered by persons out of the jurisdiction of this Court, and by persons assuming to act in this colony under decrees and orders alleged to be issued by the English Equity Courts.

It appears to us to be a self-evident abnegation of the clearest functions of our own Supreme Court to refuse to exercise its inherent jurisdiction on the grounds insisted on by the defendant, more especially as this defendant has refused to submit herself up to the date of this appeal (by probate of the testator's will or otherwise) to the ordinary jurisdiction and control of our colonial Courts, even in the mere administration of the personal assets of the testator without suit.

Such being our opinion as to the jurisdiction of this Court, and as to the plaintiff's *locus standi* in this suit, it follows that the plaintiff's rights must in our judgment be primarily considered as wholly irrespective of any English proceedings, or any statements or allegations as to any such proceedings.

It must also be observed that the present contention being only as to the appointment of a receiver and manager of the estate of the testator, and for an injunction, it is obvious that no English proceedings could, under the circumstances, nor without considerable delay, afford effectual protection against local malversation, extravagance, or other misconduct.

 · It has, however, been argued, secondly, against the chief point in this appeal, that there exists in this case certain special reasons or collateral grounds for our con·sideration, which should induce this Court to refuse the exercise of its jurisdiction to this plaintiff; and the following points and facts have been suggested and argued, with a view to disentitle the plaintiff accordingly, viz.:—

1st. The testator was domiciled in England at the time of his death.

2nd. The plaintiff in this case is out of the jurisdiction of our colonial Court.

3rd. The plaintiff has instituted proceedings of some kind in England in this testator's affairs, which proceedings have been stayed, dismissed, or abandoned.

4th. The plaintiff may possibly be restrained in England from taking or prosecuting the present or other proceedings in this colony.

5th. The colonial creditors are invited by the English decree to go in and prove their debts before the Chancery Court in England.

After attentive consideration of these several points, we have failed to discover any sufficient ground to induce this Court to refuse its jurisdiction to the plaintiff.

1st. The domicil of the testator at his decease being in England may, indeed, guide the marshalling of his debts or the distribution of his assets ; but cannot exclude the jurisdiction of our Courts over his colonial assets, more especially when the application is for a receiver and injunction for the protection of such colonial assets. As Lord Chancellor *Cottenham* said, in *Preston* v. *Viscount Melville* (a), "The domicil regulates the right of succession, but the administration must be in the country in which possession is taken and held, under lawful authority, of the property of the deceased."

2nd. The circumstance of the plaintiff being out of the jurisdiction can at most only create some liability to give security for costs, and cannot in any degree diminish or affect his right to the equitable jurisdiction.

3rd and 4th. It is impossible to understand how any past or future failure of the plaintiff in an English suit can exclude him from his rights in this colony ; such a doctrine would be pregnant with the most mischievous results.

(a) 8 C. & F., p. 12 (1841).

The fifth ground of objection also seems wholly beside the present application.   The property being protected by this Court under its own jurisdiction, the colonial and English creditors can hereafter direct the administration of the assets both in this colony or in England, with due regard to all the rights of the several creditors *inter se.*

We now consider, in the third place, the six grounds of objection, upon which the defendant succeeded, before the Primary Judge, in rescinding the *ex parte* order for the receiver and injunction.

1. The first objection, viz., as to the corporate seal, is now abandoned by the counsel for the defendant.

2. The second objection, as to the absence of a legal personal representative of the testator, clearly is a mere technical objection, which may be cured at any time before the hearing of the suit ; and, upon the established authorities, is without any effect upon the present application for a receiver and injunction.

3. The third objection, viz., as to the concealment of material facts from the Primary Judge on making the *ex parte* application, appears to us not to have extended to mislead the Court, nor to have amounted to any wilful suppression or concealment of material facts affecting the equities of the parties to the suit ; and therefore cannot affect the equitable right of the plaintiff to the relief which he may be entitled to in this suit.

4. Nor do we see any force in the fourth objection —viz., that the order for substituted service is irregular under 13 Vic., No. 31, either in its inception, or in its not being followed up by entering a formal appearance for the defendant, or by giving notice to the defendant of the subsequent motion.   It seems to us that the plaintiff had, as against a defendant out of the jurisdiction, a perfect right to apply for the order *ex parte*; and that under the present circumstances this *ex parte* order cannot be considered irregular or void under 13 Vic., No. 31, or as contrary to the inherent jurisdiction of the Court.

5. With regard to the fifth objection, we are of opinion that considering the allegation in the bill as to the insolvency of the testator's estate, and the other allegations in the affidavits as to the dealings of *John Irving* with the steamship Florence Irving; considering also the proceeding as to the actions upon the testator's promissory note with the Commercial Banking Company and the settlement of that action by a mortgage by *John Irving* to that bank; considering also the attempt to sell the pastoral property of the testator; and lastly considering that the defendant claims a separate personal interest as against the creditors under an alleged post-nuptial settlement alleged to have been made about the date of the will, and just before the testator's death—the plaintiffs have fully made out their right to a receiver and manager of the estate and to the injunction prayed; more especially as against an executor who has up to the date of this appeal refused to prove the will in our colonial jurisdiction; we also think that the refusal of the attorney of the defendant to enter into any undertaking with the plaintiff's attorney, is a circumstance not to be disregarded, indicating the probable course of defendant's conduct in dealing with the testator's assets; and consequently creating, with the other circumstances above mentioned, ample ground for the equitable interference of this Court.

With regard to the sixth and last objection, viz., that this Court ought not to interfere with the English receivers or their agents in this colony, by granting any order which would "*clash*" as it is said with their English authority; we think on the contrary, that, considering not merely our own supreme jurisdiction, which ought not to be "denied" to any suitor in this Court, whether in proceedings at Common Law or in Equity, and which jurisdiction we are bound neither to surrender nor impair, and considering also the peculiar nature of all colonial property, both real and personal, and considering especially the large pastoral properties of the colony, and the special nature of such properties, it is of the utmost importance that the law should be

1865.

ALLIANCE
BANK
(LIMITED)
v.
IRVING.

clearly laid down and firmly maintained by this Court,
—in exercising its own primary jurisdiction over all
colonial property, and in placing our own colonial
officers exclusively in the possession, control, and
management of such property, when subjected to any
litigation—whether in a common creditor's administration suit like the present, or otherwise. We also think
that any other course would be in effect simply nugatory
as regards all practical protection of such property, if
they were thus to be abandoned to a jurisdiction only
existing at the other side of the globe, and incapable of
the slightest practical beneficial effect in the case now
before us, either for the creditors of the deceased or any
other parties interested in his colonial property.

We think, therefore, that this appeal is right upon
all its grounds, and that the motion to discharge the
order for the receiver and injunction ought to have
been refused, with costs; but there can be no order for
costs of this appeal on either side.

CHEEKE, J. I concur fully in the reasons given by Mr.
Justice *Hargrave* with reference to the matters of this
appeal.

June 27, 28,
and 29, 1864.

Reversal in
part by full
Court of
decree of Pri-
mary Judge
in redemption
suit. Bill for
redemption—
filed by the

BROUGHTON *against* RODD and others (a).

THIS was an appeal by the plaintiff from the decree
of the Primary Judge, directing the redemption of
certain mortgages, and that in taking the accounts the
considerations mentioned in the deeds should be taken as
the principal moneys due on the mortgages respectively.

purchaser of the assets of insolvent mortgagor—charged that the consideration in
some of the deeds was not paid at the time of their execution, nor so large a sum
ever paid, and prayed besides usual accounts, an account of all moneys paid by
defendants.

Answer set up special agreements as to the consideration to be inserted in the deeds.

Held (reversing decree of Primary Judge), that with respect to one of the deeds, the
special agreement was not proved by the evidence, and that the deed ought to be
taken as an incumbrance to the extent only of the sums actually advanced.

(a) *Coram,* full Court.

The facts of the case, arguments of counsel, and judgment of the Primary Judge, are reported *supra*, Vol. III. (a).

Martin, Q.C., and *Milford* for plaintiff and appellant.

Sir *W. Manning*, Q.C., for defendant *Gregan*.

Broadhurst, Q.C., for defendant *Graham*.

On this day (b) judgment was delivered as follows :—
STEPHEN, C. J. After stating that this appeal—
owing to differences of opinion on the Bench, followed
by the death of Mr. Justice *Milford*—had been twice
argued, and the decision further delayed in consequence
of the death of Mr. Justice *Wise* while it was under
consideration, continued—

It will be seen that the judgment of the Court is in
effect a reversal of the learned Primary Judge's decree,
on the most material point in contest; although Mr.
Justice *Hargrave* and myself do not, I believe, concur
altogether in that result on the same grounds.

The bill is filed to redeem three mortgages—or instruments dealt with as such—executed by one *Roberts*;
the two first before his insolvency in 1859, and the last
immediately after the release of his estate in the same
year. As to the earliest in date of these (that to the defendant *Rodd*), there is no question; and the greater
part, if not the whole, of the amount due on it has been
satisfied. The second, the mortgage for £1500 to the
defendant *Gregan*, we are agreed, cannot now be impeached. However suspicious the circumstances attending that security, in its inception, it has been too often
recognised by the insolvent, and the amount claimed
under it admitted by him to be due, to be at this late
period, at the instance of any one, brought into controversy. But the third instrument, purporting to be an
incumbrance to the defendant *Graham* for £2400,
stands on a different footing; and the question raised

(a) 3 W. & O., Eq. 52.
(b) The decree was directed to bear date as of the 1st February,
1866 ; January being vacation.

has been not merely as to its precise character, whether really a mortgage or a deed of trust, but for what sums it shall in either event be deemed a security. The plaintiff is neither a creditor of the insolvent, nor does he represent the latter, or his assignee ; and, if he did, the suit is not instituted to set this deed aside. The plaintiff is a purchaser, merely, of the assets in *Roberts's* estate, under his second insolvency in 1862; that is to say, all real or personal assets then the property of the assignee. It appears to me, therefore, that the plaintiff wisely abstains from any attempt to defeat *Graham's* conveyance, as such—and, admitting its validity as an incumbrance, intended and operating to secure the repayment of moneys due by the insolvent, disputes the extent of the debt only. For, subject to the liabilities stated (and to one other, not now in question), the property conveyed or mortgaged belongs to Mr. *Broughton* by virtue of his purchase ; and he is clearly interested, accordingly, in cutting down their respective amounts.

Now, the origin of the transactions between *Roberts* —a person obviously of the most facile temperament— and the defendants, *Gregan* and *Graham*, is involved in no obscurity. The difficulty is to ascertain, amid several conflicting and some confused statements, what was in truth their agreement, or that of *Roberts* and *Graham*, as to the £2400 ; in other words, what amount of indebtedness that sum really represents. The facts are these : In January, 1859, being then much embarrassed, *Roberts* mortgaged his only property (a life interest in a farm and in some houses) to *Gregan* for £1500 ; of which, for the reason already given, it is now useless to inquire how much was actually advanced or due—and, within a month afterwards, he was compulsorily declared insolvent. The property would then, as a matter of course, have been sold, and probably sacrificed ; for the insolvent's life, at that period, was a precarious one. It therefore became an object of importance to him, to procure the release of his estate from the sequestration ; and this could only be effected, obviously, by compounding with his creditors. The amount due to these, as

Gregan and *Graham* declare, and I see no reason to doubt, was about £2400 ; and several were conferred with and a meeting duly convened took place, on the subject of such a compromise.

Graham, before that meeting, had been *Gregan's* attorney; but, at and from that time, he certainly (according to my understanding of the evidence) acted equally as attorney for the insolvent. And here begins the dispute as to the facts between these parties. According to *Roberts*, *Graham* or *Gregan* was to compromise with the creditors, for whatever portion these would accept—and the full amount due was to be inserted, in a mortgage to *Graham* ; but that security was to stand for such sums, only with interest, as one or the other (both sharing the task) should eventually advance. In confirmation of this version, some of the creditors—although stoutly contradicted on this point—assert that they were assured by *Gregan*, if not by *Graham*, that the composition proposed was on the behalf, and for the benefit of the insolvent. That is to say, if the representation meant anything, that the portion of debt abandoned was not to be transferred to a third party. Two of these persons add, indeed, that *Gregan* expressly said he was to get nothing, beyond interest for his advances, by the arrangement. But, according to *Gregan* and *Graham*, supported by repeated though loose admissions of *Roberts* himself, (as testified by a witness of undoubted veracity) any amount of reduction, which might thus be effected, was to be for the *latter's* benefit—or, rather, for their benefit jointly. In other words, the whole £2400 was to be paid to them, or one of them ; the difference between it and the composition going into their own pockets.

Mr. *Graham's* counsel urged on us, that this assertion was far more likely to be the truth. In the first place, *Roberts* could be no more prejudiced by a liability to pay *Gregan* or *Graham* the £2400 in question, than to pay the same amount to the supplanted creditors. But, by the aid of those two individuals, he obtained time, and avoided the sacrifice of his property. Secondly, in was improbable in a high degree, that *Gregan* and *Graham*, the one as attorney, the other a mere money lender, would have undertaken all the trouble of solicit‑ ing that composition, and the risk of advancing so much money, for the mere reward of a not very unusual interest rate.   There is much force in these arguments. On the other hand, it seems scarcely credible—even in the case of so weak a man—that this insolvent should have agreed to pay such an enormous premium, for services which would have been amply remunerated by a tithe of the amount.   The composition proposed at the meeting was ten shillings in the pound only ; and many of the creditors accepted it, although a few were paid in full, and some twelve shillings or more in the pound. *Gregan* and *Graham* were partners in the operation, although the security was (as we have seen) to the latter alone ; and they admit, that the total amount paid by both has not exceeded £1700.   So that these gentlemen, according to their own account, were to receive at least, £700 profit—to be considered as capital ; on which, as well as on the moiety actually paid, they were to get 10 per cent. per annum from the date of that security.   The value of *Roberts'* interest, in the various properties mortgaged to the defendants, stated by him in a very loose way, was, as I collect, considerably over £1000 a year.

How it came to pass that the estate was released, after the meeting of creditors mentioned, I am unable to understand ; for nothing definitive was then settled, and many of them, it appears, were not paid, even if they had agreed to accept the composition ultimately taken by them, until some time after that release.   All the creditors, however, we may conclude, must in some manner have acquiesced in the order made, or the Court would have had no materials for that adjudication.   I cannot find, however, that the defendants ever came under any obligation to the creditors, on *Roberts'* behalf, to pay a composition to them.   Be this as it may, on the 15th April, 1859, the insolvent's estate was released ; and, on the 16th, or shortly afterwards, he executed to

Graham the conveyance—be it mortgage or trust deed —on which the question now under consideration arises. By this instrument (attested, by the way, solely by *Gregan*), it is recited that *Roberts* was indebted to several persons in sums amounting to £2400, which *Graham* had agreed to advance him for the purpose of paying them, taking a conveyance of his property "*upon the trusts hereinafter declared*," to secure the repayment of that sum, with interest. It is then witnessed, that, in consideration of that sum of £2400, " in hand paid by *Graham*," as *Roberts* thereby admits, the latter conveys the several estates, &c., subject to the existing mortgages thereon—to hold the same, during the life of *Roberts*, upon the several trusts following. Of these the first is, to receive the rents and profits—and they are to be applied, after payment of taxes, repairs, commission for collecting, and such sums as *Graham* might expend in insuring *Roberts'* life, in satisfying interest on the sums of £2000, £1500, £700, and £2400 (due to *Rodd*, *Gregan*, *Driver*, and *Graham*, respectively), and then to the reduction half-yearly of the principal moneys. Provision is made, also, for the repayment of any further advances by *Graham* : and, on all sums *thereafter* paid, he is to receive interest at ten per cent. The rate payable, therefore, on any sums already advanced by him or *Gregan*, does not in terms appear to be expressed.

My conclusion, on the whole, as to the agreement which this deed was framed to carry out, is, that *Gregan* and *Graham* (both or either) were to be paid only what they should actually advance, with ten per cent. interest thereon. There are difficulties, of course, in arriving at an opinion either way—but, without reference to the position of the parties, which might possibly in a suit differently framed, have defeated the defendants' claim altogether, that which I have now expressed seems to me, on the balance of testimony, to be the sounder one. It was no small matter for *Gregan*, the prime mover in this business, to secure his equivocal incumbrance, and acquire the certain means of its liquidation. As to *risk* in the new transaction, there was little or none ; for *Graham* had power to insure the borrower's life, and the rents were sufficient (apparently) to keep down all current charges, and afford a surplus towards reduction of the principal.   I do not indeed see —as already observed,—what there was to compel payment to the creditors, to any extent—whether £1700 or £1200.

On admissions made by *Roberts*, such as those deposed to in the affidavits, little value can be placed.   The exact words used, the conversation which led to these, all the circumstances in short accompanying them, are not before us.   But the statements of *Gregan*, by which his co-partner is equally bound, are strongly corroborative of *Roberts'* sworn evidence.   And the examinations of the same defendant before the Insolvency Commissioner, not merely as to his accounts, but the whole of the negotiation, tend little to induce superior belief in his representations.   I impute intentional false swearing to no one ; for daily experience shows me, how testimony is unconsciously warped and perverted by the interest of the speaker.   But the defendant *Graham*, for himself and his comrade, was bound—the assertion in their deed as to the sum lent having been falsified—to furnish the most conclusive evidence in their favour as to the true consideration ; and in this, in my opinion, they have failed.

If satisfied that, in point of fact, *Roberts* had agreed to give these defendants as a premium, or reward for their exertions and skill, the excess over any composition effected by them, and to secure the amount of that premium, as well as their actual payments, by this mortgage or trust conveyance, I should have felt no difficulty in upholding the arrangement.   It does not appear to me, with deference to my colleague, that the rule which prevails in Courts of Equity, as to collateral advantages sought to be secured by mortgagees over their mortgagors, applies to a bargain of that kind— made prior to the mortgage, and forming part of the previously-agreed mortgage money.   The case of *Broad*

v. *Selfe* (a), following *Webb* v. *Rorke* (b), and other authorities cited, is supposed to be decisive against the allowance to a mortgagee, under colour of his security, of any distinct collateral advantage whatever. But a mortgagee is not restricted from stipulating for any such ˙advantage; as, for instance, that he shall be employed to sell the property, or to collect the rents, or dispose of the yearly proceeds. On the contrary, the commission allowed mortgagee merchants, on the sale of West Indian produce, shows that there may be stipulations collateral to a mortgage, beneficial to the lender. The substantial decision in *Broad* v. *Selfe* was, that a mortgagee cannot bargain for his employment as agent to sell, or to have a commission on the value of the property, if paid off without a sale. But the mortgagee was nevertheless allowed a compensation for his services, and all expenses incurred by him in respect of the intended sale.

It may be, that the mortgagee in that case (a redemption suit) could not have obtained a reference to the Master, to ascertain the amount of those items, without the aid of the then recent enactments—not yet adopted in this colony. But the circumstances here, for the reason given, are I conceive essentially different. In *Broad* v. *Selfe*, the stipulation related to matters which could not arise, until after the relation of mortgagor and mortgagee should have commenced. It was, therefore, strictly a collateral advantage; whereas, in the present case, the reward supposed to have been bargained for was, or would have been, a portion of the agreed mortgage money—the consideration for which, always supposing the agreement itself to be not fraudulent or sinister in its object, the parties were on each side competent to settle for themselves, before the security would have existed. Such an agreement, it appears to me, is in its nature no more collateral to or connected with a mortgage, or the relation of mortgagor and mortgagee, than any other bargain would be—the performance of which should afterwards be secured by a mortgage.

(a) 9 Jur. N. S. 886.   (b) 2 Sch. & Lef. 668.

The result of this judgment is, that the decree appealed from must be upheld as to *Gregan's* mortgage; but it is reversed, as far as *Graham's* is concerned. Instead of a declaration sustaining the £2400 therein mentioned, the latter instrument will stand as a security for such sums, only, as shall be shown to have been advanced under or in reference to it, by those defendants or either of them—to the insolvent or to his creditors. On all such sums, interest will be calculated at ten per cent. from the day of payment. *Gregan's* costs of suit (so far as they relate to the £1500 mortgage), are necessarily allowed him. But *Graham* must bear his own costs; for he has resisted improperly the claim made by the bill, as to the £2400 deed, and failed to establish the case set up by him in his defence.

HARGRAVE, J. There can be no doubt that every mortgagor is entitled not only to a re-conveyance of his estate on payment of principal and interest, but also to an account of rents and profits while the mortgagee has been in possession, extending even to wilful default. The whole jurisdiction of Equity in mortgage transactions recognises these rules, and the established decrees in such transactions have now fixed beyond all dispute the equitable rights and liabilities of mortgagor and mortgagee in taking the mortgage accounts, whether in redemption or foreclosure suits.

Upon the general equity of this bill it is therefore clear that the plaintiff, as representing *Roberts'* estate and interest as mortgagor, is entitled to the usual accounts and directions as adapted to the three mortgages mentioned in the pleadings, and as directed by the late Primary Judge Mr. Justice *Milford*, in the decree now under appeal; and that the only point fairly open to argument is as to the special declaration inserted in the decree—that the sum of £2400, though neither covenanted to be paid by the mortgagees, nor paid, as alleged in the mortgage deed, nor, in fact, ever paid at all, except as the accounts may hereafter show, is to be taken as the basis of the payments to be allowed to the mortgagee.

With reference to this declaration, I am clearly of opinion that both upon the equity and the facts of the case, this declaration should be omitted from the decree, thereby leaving the accounts to extend: 1st, to the sums actually paid by the mortgagees in discharge of the debts of the mortgagor, as mentioned in the mortgage deed; 2, to all other payments by way of commission, interest, insurance, or otherwise, also as mentioned in the deed; 8, to all "just allowances," according to the established meaning of those words in mortgage decrees.

I consider that the established decisions of the English Equity Courts from *French* v. *Baron* (a), before Lord *Harkwicke*, in 1740; *Webb* v. *Rorke* (b), before Lord *Redesdale* in 1806; *Chambers* v. *Goldwin* (c), before Lord *Eldon* in 1804; *Langstaffe* v. *Fenwick* (d), before Sir *W. Grant* in 1805; and numerous other subsequent cases now recently followed in *Broad* v. *Selfe* (e), by the present Master of the Rolls, have clearly established that it is not competent for a mortgagee to claim, under colour of his mortgage, any collateral advantage beyond principal, interest, and the usual equitable allowances.

The last mentioned authority is especially useful as pointing to the statutory remedy now provided in England by Sir *Hugh Cairns'* Act (21 and 22 Vic., c. 27), extended by Mr. *Rolt's* Act (25 and 26 Vic., c. 42), for the trial in equity of questions of fact, with or without a jury, and otherwise amending and extending the equity procedure, and conferring common law powers and jurisdiction upon the Equity Courts. But it will be seen, on referring to the two reports of this case, that the Master of the Rolls in no degree questioned the equitable maxim above stated, but merely, under the statutory power recentlyconferred upon the English Court, directed an inquiry as to the value of the mortgagee's "services."

With references to Sir *W. Manning's* remarks upon *Webb* v. *Rorke*, and the effect of the repeal of the Usury

1866.

BROUGHTON
v.
RODD
and others.

(a) 2 Atkyns 120.   (b) 2 Sch. & Lef. 668.
(c) 9 Ves. 260.   (d) 10 Ves., 405.
(e) 9 Jur. N. S. 886 ; 2 New Reports 541-3.

Laws upon the established authorities above quoted as regulating the equities between mortgagees and mortgagors, I refer to Lord *Brougham's* judgment in *Leith* v. *Irvine* (a), in which it is distinctly laid down (as in fact it had been frequently laid down before), that the foundation of this branch of equity is "altogether independent of usury or any tendency to usury," and is "to *prevent imposition and oppression, by one person having an obvious advantage over another*;" and that this equitable jurisdiction is founded on the maxim that it is " *contrary to public policy* " to support or recognise such collateral agreements between such parties as mortgagor and mortgagee.

In fact, this protection of mortgagor against mortgagee, is only one branch of that larger equity which in the relation of attorney and client, and in many other relations of life, surrounds all persons in a position of inferiority against the pressure of the superior influence, and which applies to " *all the relations in which* dominion may be exercised by one person over another;" words which were used by Sir *Samuel Romilly* in his celebrated argument of *Huguenin* v. *Baseley* (b), and adopted by Lord Chancellor *Cottenham*, in 1837, when delivering judgment in *Dent* v. *Bennett* (c), and which no Court of Equity will now either impugn or unsettle.

Without entering further into the principles of Equity bearing upon this case, I am further of opinion that the deed now under consideration, though treated by all parties as a mortgage deed, appears to me to be more in the nature of a trust deed, there being on the one hand neither proviso for redemption nor covenants by the "mortgagor" to pay mortgage money, nor covenants for title; nor, on the other hand, any covenants by the "mortgagees" to pay the £2400, nor to pay the debts mentioned in the mortgage deed. It is in fact impossible to contend that the mortgagees could have filed any bill for forclosure in this case; and, therefore, the relation of trustee and cestuique trust was, in my opinion, the real

(a) 2 M. & K. 227.   (b) 14 Ves. 273.
              (c) 4 M. & C. 277.

and primary relation constituted by this deed between Mr. *Roberts* and the defendants, *Gregan* and *Graham*.

The right of the defendants, therefore, as trustees to any personal benefit from their transactions as to the trust matters becomes still more contrary to equity than when considered as between mortgagor and mortgagee ; and the declaration under appeal still more necessary to omit from the decree as irregular between trustees and their cestuique trust.

Finally, I may also mention that after carefully perusing the evidence in this case, both in the answers of the defendants in the (three) sets of affidavits, I differ altogether from the late Primary Judge as to the effect of that evidence, and think the value of the defendants' evidence, as against the plaintiff's evidence, is by no means sufficient, in my opinion, to establish the fact of any such agreement for remuneration as set up by defendants, *Graham* and *Gregan*, and still less sufficient to establish an agreement to charge *Roberts's* estate with any such remuneration.

For these reasons I concur in the judgment for reversing the decree to the extent I have mentioned.

E—4

November 13, 1865.

VICKERY against MARR.

Reversal by full Court of decree of Primary Judge granting an injunction to prevent nuisance. The plaintiff *V.* was owner, since 1838, of certain lands, whereon he was erecting buildings and excavating cellars. He complained that *M.*, the owner of land and premises adjoining, allowed sewerage to flow from his land into the cellars so excavated, and prayed that *M.* might be distrained from continuing the nuisance. The sewerage ran through a drain crossing the land of *V.*, but which *M.* claimed a right by prescription to use for such purpose.

THIS was an appeal by the defendant to the full Court from the judgment of the Primary Judge, granting an injunction in terms of the prayer of the bill.

The suit was instituted by *Ebenezer Vickery* against *Henry Marr*. The bill stated that the plaintiff was the owner of certain land fronting Pitt-street, and extending thence eastward to land belonging to the defendant in Castlereagh-street, Sydney—that the plaintiff had commenced to erect on his said land certain buildings of great value, intended to be used as stores, warehouses, and mercantile and other offices, and was excavating large cellars under the buildings in course of erection— that one of the buildings on the defendant's land adjoining was occupied as a manufactory of cordials, soda and ærated water, and ginger beer—and that a steam engine was erected on the premises, and was kept in constant use in connection with the manufactory. The bill further stated that in consequence of such occupation and user of the defendant's said piece of land, a large quantity of sewerage and other foul and offensive matter and water mingled therewith, were collected on the said land, and that the defendant allowed the same to pass off from his land upon that of the plaintiff, and that the same flowed into the cellarage excavated by him, to his serious injury. The defendant, by his answer, admitted the flow of water and sewerage as alleged, but not their offensive character, and he set up a right to discharge the same over the plaintiff's purpose.

Held (*Stephen*, C. J., *dissentiente*), that as *V.* and his predecessors had so long acquiesced in the user of the drain as a sewer, he was not entitled to the interposition of a Court of Equity for the purpose of preventing the nuisance.

Held also that his remedy, if any, under the circumstances, was by action at law under the Common Law Procedure Act.

Quære—whether, as there can be no such thing, strictly speaking, in this colony as "time immemorial," and the Prescription Act (2 and 3 W. IV., c. 71), not having been adopted here, the rules of law applied in England prior to that Act, as to the presumption of lost grants of casements, ought to be followed in this colony.

ground into the public sewer in Pitt-street, by virtue of user of a drain and watercourse on that ground, "during time whereof the memory of man nameth not to the contrary," which drain had been enjoyed by him and those through whom he claimed as an easement belonging to his land during such period peaceably and without interruption or opposition, and openly and as of right. And the defendant further alleged that if the plaintiff had suffered any annoyance, or his premises any detriment, by the said sewerage, the same was occasioned by the plaintiff's own act in cutting through the sewer referred to. The defendant had also offered to contribute towards the expense of connecting the sewer through his premises with drains on the premises of the defendant.

The cause came on for hearing on motion for a decree. From the evidence (which was given on affidavit) it appeared that the drain in question had existed many years, and that in excavating the cellars it had necessarily been cut into, whence the overflow from it on the plaintiff's premises. Originally, before the existing title of the present parties, and before the formation of Castlereagh-street, or any of the streets farther to the east, a natural streamlet (called by the witnesses a creek or watercourse) traversed them all, from Macquarie-street. From that which is now Castlereagh-street, the little creek entered the defendant's land, and thence ran westerly over the plaintiff's allotment, and across Pitt-street, into what is called the Tank Stream. Its precise direction over these lands at the early period mentioned, namely from 1800 to 1802, or thereabouts, was not clearly shown, but appeared to be very nearly the direction of the present watercourse and drain on the plaintiff's land. The original streamlet had for many years disappeared. Three streets eastward of the plaintiff's allotment now cross what was once its bed, and in the most westerly of these, its waters, should any trace of them remain, are (as the plaintiff stated) intercepted and lost in a common public sewer there formed. The watercourse and drain in question appeared however to have continued in existence for an indefinitely long period both before and since the year 1838, when the grant of the plaintiff's land issued, and to have been used by the defendant or his predecessor and their tenants, as well as others up to the commencement of this suit, and that not for the passage alone of water naturally flowing in that direction, but latterly also of water brought to and adulterated on the defendant's premises, and for many years, of sewerage there produced of every description.

Some of the facts stated in the affidavits are more particularly specified in the judgments delivered by their Honors.

On the hearing the Primary Judge granted the injunction prayed for by the bill (a).

(a) On the hearing his Honor the Primary Judge, after stating the facts as above, delivered judgment as follows :—

The question in this case is whether the defendant is entitled to the continued use of the drain or watercourse, for the purposes for which it has lately been employed or for any purposes.

I am of opinion that he is not. Had the ancient or any other natural stream there continued to flow—the existence of an artificial or covered drain along portions of its course, by whomsoever constructed, could never have entitled the defendant, or any other riparian proprietor, to pollute the waters of the stream, by transmitting offensive matters through that drain. The plaintiff and his predecessor, in common with every other proprietor on the banks or edge of the stream, would have had a right to the use of those waters, in their natural state—or at least free from any such added matters. But, as already noticed, the creek once flowing exists no longer ; and the drain has since, except as to the added pollutions, received only water falling into it from higher land levels, not from any stream or natural continuous source. So that the defendant's claim must amount to this—that because the drain (in common with others along the bed of the creek more eastward) existed very many years above twenty, while it formed partially the passage for a natural stream, and because, after the extinction or diversion of that stream, its former bed or course on the plaintiff's land, including the drain, has for many years up to the time of this contest been used to convey other waters, and among these falling and refuse water from the defendant's land—throughout which entire periods all the proprietors eastward of the plaintiff's allotment (the defendant being one), have habitually caused sewerage to be cast into that stream, or into its bed and course since its extinction, and consequently to flow over the plaintiff's land into the drain in question, *therefore* he (the defendant) can insist on the continued use of that bed or course, and drain, for these purposes, for ever.

The defendant's case is, by his answer, that he or his predecessor has always been accustomed to discharge sewerage there ; and, although the evidence does not quite establish this (in terms, at all events), I shall assume the fact to be so. In his affidavit *Marr* says that the "creek" was used as a drain by all persons eastward of the plaintiff's land, ever since he can remember. He ought to have added, if the fact were so, that the drain itself on that land was a *sewer*, and always so used. The defendant should also have stated

The defendant having appealed, the case came on to be argued before the full Court (a).

how long he has used the land since the diversion of the creek; and whether any water passes down now to his premises, from lands eastward of his own. But he makes no allusion to the extinction of that creek, or says what then became the drain or sewer. *Cunningham* speaks of the same creek, as passing forty years ago along a covered drain above Castlereagh-street, to Elizabeth-street (eastward both of the plaintiff's and the defendant's land), through which a man once groped his way to a water-closet. And that drain, he states, continued through the defendant's land to the plaintiff's—conveying thence the waters of the creek to Pitt-street. *Tuckwell* identifies the drain now on the plaintiff's ground, as the Pitt-street portion; and says that, for above twenty years next succeeding 1799, the "creek" running in it was used for all the purposes of a drain. But neither *Tuckwell* nor *Cunningham* makes any statement, specifically, as to user of the drain since the disappearance of that creek—or indeed (except in a very loose way, or as to belief) since 1824.

The continued existence and use of the drain, however, for a great number of years as a sewer, may reasonably be concluded. If permitted to introduce my own observation on the ground, since the argument, I may testify that the bed or course of the water across that ground, from the commencing point, is undoubtedly used as a sewer now. But throughout the upper or eastern portion of its course, the water runs sluggishly *upon*—not under the plaintiff's land, or in any covered passage whatever. Whether a trace remains of the ancient creek, it may not be so easy to say; and, as the only affidavit to the fact of its disappearance was filed in reply, I should be prepared even now to direct, or allow to either party, the adduction of further evidence on that point, if I thought it material. But, although the reception of the affidavit was objected to, no suggestion was made that the fact is otherwise. And the point appears to me to be immaterial, because the defendant's case—in the view which I take of it—fails either way. If the creek still sends its waters along the course indicated, the defendant commits unquestionably a nuisance by turning sewerage into them. On the other hand, if (as I believe the truth to be) the creek has wholly ceased to flow there, the defendant's right would rest on a claim to send sewerage down the course, after the extinction or diversion of the stream, simply because sewerage was always so sent while that stream existed. But, obviously, the defendant can have no greater right now, than he possessed then; and we need not inquire, therefore, whether a previously vested right, if he had one, would have been affected by the creek's disappearance.

It is clear to my apprehension, consequently, that the defendant must make out his claim by user, simply irrespective of any question connected with the stream. In other words, since there can be no such thing in this colony, in strictness, as *immemorial* usage, and we have no enactment here giving title by prescription, founded on a user for twenty years merely, the defendant must establish a case calling on the Court, either as a fiction of law or as matter of fact, to presume or infer from that user the execution of a *grant in his favour*, of the right to discharge this sewerage. Not alone a right to discharge it into the creek, so long as that stream should continue, by the waters of which the filth might be carried down, but into and over the course of that creek in all time coming, whether it should cease to flow or not.

There is no legitimate ground, I conceive, for any such conclusion. To escape inundation of his dwelling, some predecessor of the plaintiff's may have constructed the drain in question, a covered

(a) Sir *A. Stephen*, C. J., *Hargrave*, J., and *Faucett*, J.

1865

VICKERY
v.
MARR.

Sir *W. Manning*, Q. C., for appellant, cited *Bright v. Walker* (a), *Jenkins* v. *Harvey* (b), *Bealey* v. *Shaw* (c),

passage underground near the street (though by whom constructed we had no evidence), thereby concealing and facilitating the exit there of the stream—without any intention of permitting his neighbours, what perhaps he could not easily prevent, to cast sewerage or impure water into the uncovered portions. Such a grant must be by deed; and, until 1838, none could have been effectually executed. And why should the proprietor have granted such an easement to any one? No consideration, no inducement, is suggested for it; no stipulation that the drain should be repaired, or cleansed, at the grantee's expense—or that the latter should contribute to those objects. But his supposition is, that because the plaintiff's predecessor, or his tenants (in perhaps a weatherboarded structure, for no other is mentioned) suffered the then existing creek, the natural course of which they could not legally divert, to be polluted for so many years by the passage therein of sewerage, therefore he, in or soon after 1838, granted that privilege along the same course, the drain included, irrevocably, and without restriction, to every one. I say this, because it is plain from the case set up, that whatever the plaintiff or his predecessor allowed to this defendant, he has equally allowed to every other easterly neighbour.

The question remains, as to the power and duty of this Court in such a case to interfere by injunction—but especially without a previous trial at law. As to the jurisdiction, I entertain no doubt whatever. If annoyance to the inmates of a dwelling by the ringing of bells, to an extent destructive of their comfort, if the obstruction of ancient rights, or nuisance by carrying on an offensive trade, can be restrained by injunction (as to all which examples there are well known decisions), why may not a nuisance like the present? The foundation of this jurisdiction is not necessarily an irremediable, but a *material* injury; some considerable mischief or annoyance, touching health or personal comfort, requiring prevention as much as the remedying of the evil. It would be idle to contend that the sending down of sewerage—the scourings of yards, and overflowings of privies—is not the infliction of a serious evil on the person whose land is so polluted, destructive of all comfort to the residents, and materially injurious to the value of any buildings erected, or to be erected there.

I have looked into the authorities. and I do not find that the course has been uniform, as to sending the question (whether of legal right, or of fact merely, as for instance whether nuisance or not) for inquiry at law. In a case like this, where the plaintiff's title is clear to the perfect enjoyment of his land, until the defendant shall have established an equally clear right to obstruct that enjoyment, and the nuisance itself is in its character indisputable, the Court would, I think—even before the alteration introduced by s. 62 of the statute of 1852, adopted by our Equity Practice Act, s. 49—not have hesitated to interfere without the aid of a jury. In *Emherst* v. *Spencer*[*] the Lord Chancellor *Cottenham* appears to have thought that questions of nuisance ought invariably to be decided in a Court of Law. This, however, was in the year 1849. In 1856, shortly after the new enactment, Lord *Cranworth* observes that "the old practice" was to require a trial at law; but, he adds, "by reason of the recent alteration that is now not necessary" although, in the particular case, he refused an injunction without such a trial, the evidence being very conflicting. *Broadbent* v. *Imperial Gas Company*.[†]

On the whole, therefore, my duty appears clearly to be to grant the injunction in this case. And not merely to restrain the defendant

[*] 2 M'N. & G. 51.   [†] 7 De Gex M'N. & G. 448.

(a) 1 Cr. M. & R. 211.   (b) 1 Cr. M. & R. 877.   (c) 6 East 208.

Weld v. *Hornby* (a), *Attorney General* v. *Mayor, &c., of Kingston upon Thames* (b).

Gordon, for respondent, cited *Hunt* v. *Peake* (c), *Bonomi* v. *Backhouse* (d), *Solomon* v. *Vintner's Co.* (e), *Cocker* v. *Cowper* (f), *Mounsey* v. *Ismay* (g), *Stevens* v. *M'Clung* (h).

Sir *W. Manning*, Q. C., in reply.

On this day the judgment of the Court was delivered as follows :—

STEPHEN, C. J. I retain the opinions already expressed by me. The small watercourse or streamlet, flowing for so many years over both the plaintiff's and

from sending down sewerage, but also any refuse or waste water, on the plaintiff's land; although, had the injunction been applied for only as to the latter, it would perhaps have been refused. But, for the reasons assigned, I recognise no more right in the defendant, upon the evidence, to use the land for one purpose than for the other. I shall nevertheless give no costs; first, because of the defendant's long user of the land for these purposes, without molestation, and secondly, the apparent acquiescence in that user by the plaintiff, or those under whom he claims, throughout that period. To these reasons a third may be added, namely, the defendant's readiness to meet the demand of abatement made on him, by orders of compromise—not altogether unreasonable, in a hard and apparently doubtful case.

(a) 7 East 195.   (b) 11 Jur. N. S. 596.   (c) 29 L. J. Ch. 785.
(d) 27 L. J. Q. B. 378.   (e) 28 L. J. Ex. 370.
(f) 1 Cr. M. & R. 418.   (g) 34 L. J. Ex. 52.
(h) STEVENS *against* M'CLUNG.*—This was an action of trespass for breaking down a dam, belonging to the plaintiff, on the Bombala River.

The plaintiff and defendant both held land on the Bombala River—that of the defendant being situated higher up the river than that of the plaintiff. Defendant had erected a dam and built a mill, but ere it had commenced to work plaintiff constructed his dam. This caused a back flow of water by which, as was asserted, defendant sustained injury in the manner already mentioned. Several legal questions as to the relative rights of riparian proprietors were raised and discussed, during the progress of the trial.

His Honor the Chief Justice told the jury that, although in England the rights connected with the appropriation of flowing waters were regulated by the Prescription Act, there could be no prescription in this colony, in as much as there could be no immemorial possession. His direction was that, if the jury should be of opinion that defendant had appropriated the water to his own and a beneficial use (and for this purpose it would not be necessary that his mill should be actually at work), the defendant, having first erected his dam, would be legally entitled, if it was injured by that of the plaintiff, to abate the nuisance created by the latter.

The jury returned a verdict upon the several issues, which substantially amounted to one for the defendant.

* Sup. Ct., N. S. W., 12th Nov., 1859.

the defendant's allotments, while in other hands, and pending the slow process which converts a collection of frail tenements into solid structures and a formed city, has long—though it is uncertain how long—ceased to exist. As I understand the facts, the drain (if by this is meant a covered passage) never existed, at any time, throughout the course of that stream; but was formed in certain portions, only, of the bed. Thus, the stream flowed in a covered way above the defendant's land, for a distance more or less great—but, at or near the spot where that stream and its impurities entered the plaintiff's ground, in its downward course, the flow was on the surface. There existed another portion of the stream, still lower (that is to say, near the Pitt-street boundary) which again was covered; doubtless because a dwelling of some kind was placed there. And it is into this last mentioned portion, being unquestionably at present a drain, and nothing more, that the plaintiff has necessarily cut in erecting his warehouses. But the fact of that cutting, it seems to me, under such circumstances, affords no answer to the plaintiff's claim. What he complains of is, that the defendant sends ordure and other offensive matters over the allotment, *above* (and thence into) that covered passage, which latter would, but for the intrusion, convey nothing—for there would be nothing to convey—and so could be productive of no injury.

That the act of transmitting such matters over or into land, on which the owner is erecting a habitation and other buildings, is the commission of a nuisance—of the serious character which a Court of Equity will restrain, if in other respects the case be a fitting one for interference, I can entertain no doubt. Two questions, nevertheless, yet remain; first, whether the defendant has a right to commit the nuisance—and, secondly, whether the Court in any event ought to interpose, considering the length of time during which the defendant, or his predecessor, has in fact been allowed to commit it.

On this latter point, opinions may not unreasonably

differ, and the plaintiff, if his claims had appeared to me more questionable, would assuredly have found no disposition on my part to assist him.   But it struck me at the hearing, as it does still, that—if the defendant has after all no right to do the thing complained of, the plaintiff is entitled to have the nuisance abated, whatever may be the inconvenience of this result to the wrong doer.   And I confess myself not to be without alarm, at the legalization by mere permissive user, too often only another term for apathy as to filth—of nuisances like these in a now populous city.   While land continued unoccupied, or was scantily tenanted, and covered by dwellings of the lowest order, such as are still visible in this very street, drainage would scarcely be thought of, or was impracticable.   And the stream, here and there covered in and built over, then again passing openly over the soil, may in those early days and afterwards have brought in its course (as the evidence shows that it did) many abominations.   But who was to interfere ?   Against whom would have been the remedy ?   Now, however, the flow of water has ceased, and the plaintiff, whose ownership commenced last year only, desires to be relieved from the substituted soil.   That is to say, he asks that his buildings may not be rendered uninhabitable, by the continued transmission over his allotments,—not of the *stream* such as it used to be, but of refuse and used water, artificially brought to the defendant's premises, and ordure mingled therewith.   In point of fact, transmitted (probably) over the dry or derelict bed of that stream, but there left either to escape or remain as accident may determine.

Unless the defendant has a legal right to do this, the plaintiff would be entitled at law to damages for the injury.   But these would not arrest it ; and every additional act, day after day, would be a new trespass—for which the plaintiff might again bring an action.   This Court, therefore, since it is appealed to, ought in my opinion to afford at once the only effectual remedy.

As to that legal right, it can only exist in one of the following ways.   By license, which the plaintiff was entitled to revoke. User—from time immemorial—which implies the existence originally of a grant. Or by statutory prescription—which the Legislature, doubtless for good reasons, has not thought fit to introduce. These failing, nothing is left the defendant but the fiction of a lost grant, which we must imagine to have existed, if at all, in or since the year 1838. The existence of such an instrument may no doubt, in some cases, and under certain circumstances, be presumed. But for the reasons given in my former judgment, I am of opinion that in a case like the present—all the considerations suggested being taken into account—no Court or jury would be entitled to make such a presumption. The foundation for it is, the difficulty of accounting in any other manner for the exercise, originally, of the particular easement :—the argument being, that in all probability the claimant or his predecessor would not have been permitted, in the first instance, to enjoy such a privilege (whatever it may be) in derogation of the rights of his neighbour, unless the latter had in fact granted it formally to him. Here, however, the original passing down of the stream, with its gradually increasing impurities, requires no such explanation. Or, if applied to the impurities alone, the presumption of a grant cannot reasonably extend to their continuing passage after the extinction of the stream itself—and, therewith, of the means of carrying down the matters so transmitted.

I wish to add a few words, as to my personal inspection of the premises. In reference to a similar proceeding by the present Master of the Rolls, Lord *Westbury* says (a), that the Court must nevertheless determine, in every case, not on conclusions drawn from its own observation, but on the evidence only. We have, ourselves, in the recent case of *Kingston* v. *Gale*, with respect to the inspection of certain buildings by a jury, expressed the same opinion. The legitimate object of a view—as it is more technically called—is simply that the tribunal may the better understand and apply the evidence ; not to obtain materials for controlling, or

(a) 10 Jur. N. S. 689.

perhaps even of supplementing it. I inspected the place because the facts—as stated on the affidavits, loose and meagre as they are—were not sufficiently intelligible to me, without the aid of ocular observation. My conclusions are drawn, however, from that evidence only; and, indeed, the matters on which I rest them are scarcely, if at all, in dispute.

HARGRAVE, J. The circumstances of this case are peculiar and novel, and the evidence very meagre and unsatisfactory, and does not appear to me to entitle the plaintiff to the injunction granted by the Primary Judge.

First. Taking into consideration only the plaintiff's affidavits, it appears that he admits that a "watercourse formed by nature might have existed as alleged by defendant;" "that the portion of plaintiff's land across which the drain flowed was excavated for the new cellars of plaintiff's houses;" "that the plan annexed to plaintiff's affidavit shows the course of the drain through defendant's premises, and also as it existed on plaintiff's land;" "that the drainage passing through defendant's land, is or has been for many years, discharged on plaintiff's land;" and that in "plaintiff's land the drain had been covered over with a few stones" until destroyed recently by the plaintiff's excavations and buildings (a).

Under such a state of admissions by the plaintiff's own affidavits, I am unable to understand how he can have acquired by his own acts and conduct in thus excavating cellars and destroying the drain through his own land any equity to come to this Court for an injunction against the defendant—the object of which injunction can only be to compel the defendant also to destroy the drain so far through his land, or otherwise provide for the new state of circumstances which, by the plaintiff's own affidavits, has only recently arisen, and from the plaintiff's own conduct. Among all the numerous cases of injunctions of this class, I do not find any reported case at all similar in its facts to the present;

(a) His Honor made references here to the paragraphs in the affidavits.

nor do I see how any claiming under such circumstances as these for our equitable interference can be supported without greatly extending our equitable jurisdiction.

Secondly. As to the manufactory, this is admitted by the plaintiff in his first affidavit (par. 8) to have been used as at present for ten years past; and I cannot see any satisfactory proof upon the affidavits that a jury would find the waste water from this source to be either a "nuisance" or even offensive; consequently no injunction can be granted upon that ground until the verdict of a jury has been obtained by the plaintiff; *Attorney-General* v. *Cleaver* (a), *Crowder* v. *Tinkler* (b), *Elmshirst* v. *Spencer* (c).

The *third* ground of equity set up by the plaintiff that he has acquired a right to compel the defendant to stop up his drain by the circumstance that public sewers have been constructed in Macquarie-street, Phillip-street, Elizabeth-street, or Castlereagh-street, into which sewers some of the owners of land higher up this drain have transferred their sewerage, so as not to come down the old drain, either to the defendant or plaintiff, does not deserve notice as a ground of equitable relief. Upon consideration, therefore, of the plaintiff's affidavits only, I do not think this injunction can be maintained.

But if we consider the defendant's affidavits and claim of easement, whether by prescription or by long user, sufficient to protect him from the extraordinary interference of this Court by way of injunction, until the plaintiff has obtained a verdict in a Court of common law, the plaintiff appears to me to be still less entitled to the injunction, without very much extending the usual limits of Chancery jurisdiction in such matters.

Upon this second branch of the argument, "I do not see any necessity to enter into any consideration of the authorities, further than to state that I concur in the position maintained by Sir *W. Manning*, viz., that the well-known authorities and established rules of law as to the presumption of grants, surrenders, and documents in support of possessory titles, apply to this colony as rules

(a) 13 Ves. 210.   (b) 19 Ves. 617.   (c) 2 M. N. & G. 45.

of evidence in Courts of Law and Equity before the
Prescription Act, 2 and 3 W. IV., c. 71—although that
statute has not been adopted in this colony. The rules
of law, however, as to presumption of various kinds, in
support of possessory titles and long user and enjoyment,
have been so long established beyond all question, that
to throw a doubt (as mentioned in *Taylor* on Evidence) (a) upon such important principles of Jurisprudence, would, in my opinion, be most dangerous to every
branch of our law of property.

Besides the objections to the plaintiff's bill we have
the equitable doctrine established by the cases already
cited as before Lord Chancellor *Eldon,* and recognised
beyond all doubt. By such cases as *Earl of Ripon* v.
Hobart (b), before Lord Chancellor *Brougham* ; *Squire*
v. *Campbell* (c), before Lord Chancellor *Cottenham*;
and recognised in numerous other cases, that equity will
not interfere by injunction in favour of a plaintiff who
has slept upon his alleged rights, or been guilty of any
laches or neglect himself, but will leave such plaintiffs to
their usual remedies at Common Law ; more especially
where it appears upon all the evidence, as in this case,
that the plaintiff has not recovered any verdict at Common Law, and that the alleged nuisance may be easily
remedied by the construction of a sewer in place of the
drain through both the properties, and therefore the
injury complained of cannot be said to be irremediable.

If, therefore, I had felt any hesitation as to the want
of equity of the plaintiff on his own affidavits, I should
have felt no doubt that the claim of the defendant to the
easement in question, under all the circumstances of the
case upon these affidavits, ought to have been a sufficient
answer to the plaintiff's application for the perpetual injunction which has been granted on this bill.

Lastly. If the plaintiff considers himself aggrieved in
any way, all the other remedies of the law, especially an
application under the 44th section of the Common Law
Procedure Act, 1857 (20 Vic., No. 31), for a Common

(a) Part 1, chap. 5.   (b) 3 Myl. & Keen. 169.
            (c) 1 Myl. & Cr. 459.

Law injunction, are open to him ; but having considered
this case in all its hearings, I am of opinion that this
plaintiff has failed to bring himself within any of the
rules of the Court of Equity with reference to injunctions of this class ; and I therefore think the Court
of Appeal is bound to reverse the order of the Primary
Judge, and to dissolve the injunction.

With regard to costs, as I think this bill almost
entirely an experiment upon the Court—and as the defendant does not appear to have done any act to render
this suit necessary, and appears also to have offered
before the suit to pay £60 towards the construction of a
drain through the plaintiff's land, I think the bill ought
to have been dismissed with costs.

FAUCETT, J. I do not question the jurisdiction of the
Court as to its power to grant an injunction without the
intervention of a jury, provided it is satisfied that the
matter complained of is a nuisance, and that the plaintiff
is in other respects entitled to relief. And I am of
opinion that the matter complained of in this case is
sufficiently shown by the evidence to be a nuisance.

I am also inclined to think that the plaintiff has made
out his right to enjoy his land free from this nuisance.

If the plaintiff brought an action at law against the
defendant for causing or continuing the nuisance, what
defence could the defendant set up ? According to the
evidence he could only say that he is entitled to an easement over the plaintiff's land.

But a right to an easement can only be supported by
an Act of Parliament, or by a licence or a grant from
the predecessors of the plaintiff or from plaintiff himself.

There is clearly no Act of Parliament; and if a
license had been given, such a license I should think
would be revokable at any time. Then is there any evidence of a grant ? I can see none ; unless continual and
uninterrupted user for a long period of years is by a
fiction of law to be deemed such evidence. But I am
not quite satisfied that in this country, or at all events in

this case, such a fiction would be held to exist. I will,
however (in favour of the plaintiff) suppose that such a
fiction would not be held to exist, and consequently that
the plaintiff's legal right as against the defendant would
be clear.

Assuming this then, the question still remains—is the
plaintiff entitled to the equitable intervention of a Court
of Equity ?

Now I have always understood it to be a leading
principle of Equity that a person seeking the equitable
assistance of the Court must come speedily, and not
sleep on his rights ; at all events that he ought not to
delay so long as to allow the evil complained of to grow
by user almost into a right, or into the appearance of a
right.

But what do we find here ? The defendant has
enjoyed this easement in one form or another ; and I do
not think it is of much importance whether there was
originally, and still continues, a flowing stream of water
into which the offensive water passed and still passes,
and by which it was and is still carried away ; or
whether the stream has ceased to flow in the whole course
or in part, leaving a channel or drain through or over
which the matter passes, the evidence appearing to me
to show that the line or course—whether there is a
stream now or not—over which the matter flowed ten,
twenty, or thirty years ago, is the same—so far as
regards this suit—as that over which the matter now
complained of flows. The defendant, I say, has thus
enjoyed the easement for many years, certainly for ten
years, so far as Mr. *Henfrey* is concerned, and, as may
be fairly gathered from the evidence, for a period altogether of fifty years and upwards.

I do not collect when the large buildings now on the
defendant's land were erected ; but since their erection
they have enjoyed the benefit of this easement without
any objection or interruption from the plaintiff's predecessors. There is even reason from the evidence to suppose with their knowledge and acquiescence ; and this

state of things has continued for a short time since the plaintiff has come into possession.

After the plaintiff's predecessors and the plaintiff himself have thus so long lain up, and the plaintiff himself, although for a short time, now when the plaintiff wishes to turn his property to more beneficial purposes, and for that reason desires to abate this nuisance, which I admit, at least for the sake of argument, he is entitled to do, has he any claim to the equitable assistance of the Court?

With the greatest respect for the opinion of his Honor the Chief Justice, I am of opinion that he has not. On this part of the case alone I differ from his Honor, and on this point I found my judgment.

I am further, however, induced to come to this opinion, because in my opinion the plaintiff can now obtain full relief at law. He may commence an action at law, and under the Common Law Procedure Act claim a writ of injunction to prevent the repetition or continuance of the nuisance. An injunction obtained in such an action would, in my opinion, be perpetual.

I think, therefore, the injunction ought to be dissolved with costs.

No costs of the appeal.

1865.

FROST *against* HEALY and others.

November 21, 22, 1865.

THIS suit now came on for hearing on motion for a decree. The facts and principal questions involved in it are reported *ante*, p. 6, and the testator's will is set forth *in extenso*, in the judgment of his Honor the Primary Judge.

Gordon, for plaintiff, cited *Jarman* on Wills (*a*), and *Frost* v. *Healy* (*b*).

Martin, Q. C., and *Darley* for defendant *Paul Harford*, cited *Lewin* on Trusts (*c*), *Lester* v. *Biggs* (*d*), *Shapland* v. *Smith* (*e*), *Adams* v. *Adams* (*f*), *Wagstaff* v. *Smith* (*g*), *Benn* v. *Dixon* (*h*), *Spence's* Equitable Jurisdiction (*i*), *Dunk* v. *Fenner* (*k*), *Donn* v. *Penny* (*l*), *Browncker* v. *Bagot* (*m*), *Garth* v. *Baldwin* (*n*), *Coulson* v. *Coulson* (*o*), and *Richards* v. *Baker* (*p*).

Blake for defendant *Elizabeth Harford*, cited *Osborn* v. *Morgan* (*q*), *Tidd* v. *Lister* (*r*), *Seton* on Decrees (*s*), *Scott* v. *Special* (*t*), *Greedy* v. *Lavender* (*u*), *Vaughan* v. *Buck* (*v*), *Wilkinson* v. *Charlesworth* (*w*), and *Bate* v. *Hooper* (*x*).

Darley for defendant *Healy*, cited *Cafe* v. *Bent* (*y*), *Howe* v. *Lord Dartmouth* (*z*), *Neville* v. *Fortescue* (*aa*),

A testator devised the whole of his property, consisting of real estate, leaseholds, and a squatting station fully stocked, and also ready money, to his wife, jointly with *F*. and *H*., their survivors and survivor, and the heirs and executors of such survivor, upon trust to permit her " to have the full benefit and enjoyment " of the property fo^r life, and then, upon trust, to divide it among all his children—the boys at twenty-one, and the girls at that age, or on marriage. *Held*, that the legal estate in all the real and personal property of the testator was vested in the three trustees, but that the wife was entitled to the enjoyment of the whole *in specie* during her life.

In a suit instituted by *F*. against *H*. and the testator's widow, who had married again, and against *Harford* her present husband, charging sundry breaches of trust by the two former defendants, and misappropriation by *Harford*, an order was made on motion before the hearing for an injunction to restrain the defendants from further interference with the trust estate, and for the appointment of a receiver (*ante*, p. 6.) At the hearing the injunction was dissolved, and the receiver discharged, on the ground that according to the true construction of the will the dealings of the defendants were not breaches of trust, the wife being entitled to enjoy the property specifically.

(*a*) 2 Vol., p. 239, 242, 251.	(*b*) Supra, p. 6.	(*c*) p. 162.
(*d*) 2 Taunt. 109.	(*e*) 1 B. C. C. 75.	(*f*) 6 Q. B. 860.
(*g*) 9 Ves. 520.	(*h*) 10 Sim. 636.	(*i*) 2 Vol. 150, 155.
(*k*) 2 R. & M. 567.	(*l*) 19 Ves. 545.	(*m*) 1 Mer. 280.
(*n*) 2 Ves. 646, 661.	(*o*) 2 Atkins 246.	(*p*) 2 Atkins 321.
(*q*) 9 Hare. 432.	(*r*) 10 Hare. 140 ; 3 De G. M. & G. 857.	
(*s*) 2 Vol. 22, 23.	(*t*) 3 McN. & G. 599.	(*u*) 11 Beav. 417.
(*v*) 7 Jurist 338.	(*w*) 10 Beav. 324.	(*x*) 5 De G. M. & G. 338, 345.
(*y*) 5 Hare. 24.	(*z*) 7 Ves. 137, 141.	(*aa*) 16 Sim. 333.

1865.   *Pickering* v. *Pickering* (a), *Foley* v. *Burnell* (b), *Leeke*

FROST   v. *Bennett* (c), *Durham* v. *Crackles* (d), *Tidd* v.
v.   *Lister* (e).
HEALY
and others.

Gordon, in reply, referred to *Williams* on Executors (f).

December 1.   On this day, judgment was delivered by the
             PRIMARY JUDGE.   In this case the first point for the
             consideration of the Court is to declare the true con-
             struction of the testator's will, at least so far as such
             declaration is necessary, either to give the plaintiff any
             relief on this bill, or to establish the legal and equitable
             position of the parties of this suit towards each other in
             relation to the trusts of the late Mr. *Elliott's* will up to
             the present time.
                 The will was in the following words, all of which must
             be carefully considered before construing the clauses,
             more especially in dispute in this case :—" This is the
             last will and testament of me *Samuel Elliott*, of the
             Macquarie River, in the district of Bligh, and colony of
             New South Wales, grazier : I give, devise, and bequeath
             unto my dear wife *Elizabeth* (since married to *Paul Har-
             ford*, and who are both defendants in this suit)—and to
             Henry Frost, of Mudgee, in the county of Wellington,
             and colony aforesaid, licensed victualler (the plaintiff), ·
             —and *John Healy*, also of Mudgee, aforesaid, butcher
             (one of the defendants)—all and singular the lands and
             tenements, houses, runs, stations, cattle, horses, moneys.
             securities for money, household goods and furniture, and
             other goods, chattels, and effects, of what nature or kind
             soever, and wheresoever situate, of which I may die
             seized or possessed of, to hold the same unto my said
             wife *Elizabeth*, *Henry Frost*, and *John Healy*, and the
             survivors and survivor of them, and the heirs, executors,
             and administrators of such survivor, according to the
             respective natures thereof; but upon the trusts neverthe-
             less, and subject to the several declarations hereinafter

(a) 2 Beav. 31.   (b) 1 B. C. C. 274, 279.
(c) 1 Atk. 471.   (d) 32 L. J. 111.
(e) 10 Hare. 140.   (f) 2 Vol. 1628.

contained, of and concerning the same ; that is to say, upon trust to permit and suffer my said wife *Elizabeth* to have the full benefit and enjoyment of all my said property, estate, and effects, for and during the time of her natural life, and from, and immediately after, her decease, upon trust, to pay and divide all my said property, estate, and effects, unto, and equally between, all and every the child or children of me, the said testator, who, being a boy, or boys, may attain the age of twenty-one years, or being a female or females may attain that age or first marry, in equal shares and proportions. And in case only one child of me, the said testator, being a boy, shall attain the age of twenty-one years, or being a female shall attain that age or first marry, then I give, devise, and bequeath the whole of my said property, estate, and effects unto such only child, his or her heirs, executors, administrators, or assigns, for ever. I hereby authorise and empower the trustees or trustee for the time being of this my will, to apply the yearly income to be derived from the share or shares to which any child or children of mine, being a minor or minors, shall be entitled to under this my will, for and towards her, or their maintenance, education, or benefit, during his, her, or their respective minority or minorities." Then follow the usual clauses as to trustees, receipts, and reimbursements, and the will concluded as follows :—" I hereby make, nominate, constitute, and appoint my said wife *Elizabeth*, and the said *Henry Frost* and *John Healy*, joint executrix and executors of this my will, and guardians of my children during their respective minorities." In the first place, I am clearly of opinion that as this will contains no words, which, either expressly or by implication, can be construed as giving any estate-tail to the testator's widow, now Mrs. *Harford*, there can be no ground for applying the cases cited in argument on that head as to this will; and therefore no ground for conferring on Mrs. *Harford* any absolute interest in the personalty, as seems to have been successfully contended on the former hearing as to continuing the injunction of this case.

1865.

FROST
v.
HEALY
and others.

In the second place, I am also clearly of opinion that the words of general devise and bequest of all the testator's real and personal property upon the trusts of his will, are sufficient to convey and vest the legal estate in all such property in the three trustees of his will, and that the subsequent words as to the testator's widow "having the full benefit and enjoyment of all the said property, estate, and effects, for and during the time of her natural life," in no way divests the trustees of such legal estate, either as to real or personal property during Mrs. *Harford's* life.

Thirdly, I am of opinion that Mr. *Darley's* construction of the testator's will is the right one ; and that this case comes within the authorities of *Pickering* v. *Pickering* (a), and on appeal before *Lord Cottenham* (b), *Whiting* v. *Whiting* (c), and other cases.

It is well known that of late years the Courts have extended the scope of these cases, and that the intention to give a tenant for life the right to enjoy in specie may be gathered from the whole will ; and further, it has even been laid down in *Hinners* v. *Hinners* (d), that Courts now favour the construction which will give enjoyment in specie, if within the fair words of the will.

Now considering (1) that in this will the freehold lands are included in the general devise ; 2, that the direction to divide is not to operate till after Mrs. *Harford's* death; 3, that the directions for maintenance and education are also subsequent to Mrs. *Harford's* death ; 4, that the will contains no powers of sale or conversion; and 5, observing that in *Harvey* v. *Harvey* (e) the words "full and entire enjoyment" were held to give enjoyment in specie, I feel no doubt whatever but that Mrs. *Harford* is entitled for life to the full benefit and enjoyment of all the testator's property, according to the full meaning of the words of the testator's will.

At this stage of the cause, I do not think I am in a position, upon this will and this evidence, to declare any

(a) 2 Beav. 31.   (b) 4 Myl. & Cr.   (c) 5 Jur.
(d) 3 Hare 609.   (e) 5 Beav. 134, 18.

further construction of this will, more especially in the absence of the *cestui que trusts* in remainder; and this is the less necessary, as I would hope that the parties to this suit will now be enabled to proceed amicably in carrying out the trusts of the will, upon the footing of the declaration I have made as to the construction of the will with all the usual directions as to accounts asked by the bill, which seem to me necessarily to follow from such construction, upon the evidence before me.

Of course, upon this construction, the dealings of Mrs. *Harford* and the defendants as to the cattle on the station are not breaches of trust, as might have appeared if the trustees had been entitled to the absolute ownership of the station property, clear of Mrs. *Harford's* right to " enjoy specifically."

The injunction, therefore, should be dissolved and the receiver discharged, without prejudice to what may hereafter appear on the accounts as to whether the defendants, Mr. and Mrs. *Harford*, have dealt improperly with the cattle. Liberty to apply. Reserve further directions and costs.

1866.

February 2,
1866.

In re the trusts of the will of HENRY USHER, deceased,
and the Trust Property Act of 1862.

A testator charged his real estate with an annuity, and after payment thereof and meanwhile subject thereto made several specific devises of the property—some in fee, others for life with remainders in fee over. The trustees were directed to distribute the surplus rents, when they amounted to £1000, among the devisees, "rateably and in proportion to the relative value of the properties respectively devised to them."
Trustees (seeking advice of the Court as to the distribution) *directed* to cause the

THIS was a petition under the 30th section of the Trust Property Act of 1862, by *William Woodeson Rowe, Joseph Clarkson*, and *Thomas Goodyear Hill* (the trustees of the will of *Henry Usher*, deceased, late of Newcastle, in this colony), for the " opinion, advice, and direction " of the Court, as to the administration of a portion of the trust property, which was subjected by the testator to a very unusual and troublesome clause of distribution among the devisees of his will.

It appeared that the testator, after bequeathing an annuity of £200 to his sister, Mrs. *Bevington*, and charging the same on all his real estate at Newcastle, devised certain freehold lands, houses, and hereditaments, subject to the said annuity, and from and after full payment and satisfaction of the same up to the death of the annuitant, to certain specific devisees, viz. :—(1) Certain allotments and buildings to *Thomas Goodyear Hill*, in fee ; (2) certain other allotments and buildings to *Joseph Clarkson* and *Mary Ann Clarkson*, his wife, for life estates, with remainder to the said *T. G. Hill*, in fee ; (3) certain other allotments and buildings to *John Standley*, of Whitechapel, London, for life, with remainder to his children as tenants in common in fee ; (4) certain other allotments and buildings to the said *J. Clarkson* and *M. A. Clarkson*, his wife, for life

several properties to be valued—to divide the fund into as many parts as there were devises—each part of the fund bearing the same proportion to the whole as the corresponding devise, and where the devise was in fee simple to pay to, or invest for the benefit of the devisee, the whole of such allotted portions of the fund ; but in the case of life interests, with remainders in fee, to cause the relative values of the same to be calculated, and the portion of the whole fund corresponding to such devise subdivided according to such valuation, and the parts respectively allotted to the life devisee and the devisee in remainder paid to them, or invested for their benefit respectively.

Held, that the general valuation of the properties devised should be used in all future distributions.

Held that the words "to permit *A.* to live rent free and without molestation," during the life of an annuitant, in a dwelling-house, charged with payment of the annuity, and specifically devised after satisfaction of the same, confers no transferable interest on *A.*, nor diminishes the legal estate of the specific devisee.

CASES IN EQUITY. 87

(5) a certain other allotment and buildings, being the
testator's dwelling-house and premises, and also a piece
of land adjoining the same, used as a garden by testator,
unto *Fanny Maria Ferm*, in fee, for her sole and separate use, &c.; (6) a portion of an allotment, with buildings, to *Andrew Henry Ferm*, in fee; (7) a certain
other allotment with buildings, to *William Woodeson
Rowe*, in fee; (8) certain other allotments and buildings
to *Clarence Hewson Hannell*, in fee; and (9) certain
other allotments and buildings to *James Edward
Hannell*, in fee.

The will then contained the following directions :—

" And I do hereby will and direct that the said *Joseph
Clarkson* and his said wife and each of them shall be
allowed to live in my said dwelling-house rent free, and
without molestation during the life of the said annuitant,
and until the same shall be handed over to the said
Fanny Maria Ferm, the devisee thereof, or to some
person duly authorised by her to take possession thereof.
And I do hereby will and declare that the residue of the
rents, issues, and profits of my said real property after
payment and satisfaction of the said annuity, and after
paying for all necessary repairs and other outgoings in the
care and management thereof, shall, when and so often
as the same shall accumulate to the sum of one thousand
pounds or upwards, be divided by and between my above
named devisees, rateably and in proportion to the relative
value of the properties respectively devised to them by
this my will, by my trustees and executors herein
named."

The petition stated that the annuitant and all the
devisees and legatees survived the testator. Some of
them resided in England, and two of them were infants.
Joseph Clarkson and his wife were, in accordance with
the authority to that effect contained in the will, in occupation of the residence devised to *F. M. Ferm*. The
trustees had accumulated nearly £1000, as to the distribution of which, under the above provision, they now
sought the advice and direction of the Court.

1866.

In re the trusts of the will of HENRY USHER deceased, and the Trust Property Act of 1862.

1866.

In re the trusts
of the will of
HENRY USHER
deceased,
and the Trust
Property Act
of 1862.

February 9.

Blake for petitioners.

Gordon for *Clarence Hewson Hannell.*

The PRIMARY JUDGE, after stating the facts as above,
continued—

No authorities have been cited to the Court as bearing
upon the construction of such a clause as that in regard
to which my advice is sought.   I must, therefore, interpret the words of the testator according to the well-
established general rules of construction of such instruments, so as to give to all the words used their ordinary
meaning, and also so as to give to every expression some
effect, and so as to form one consistent construction in
relation to every part of the will.

Firstly, it appears to me that the trustees should obtain
a proper and certified valuation from competent and dis-
interested surveyors or other professional persons, of the
value of the nine several " properties," included in each
of the above mentioned devises, according to the testator's
freehold or other interest therein, and as devised under
the nine several devises above mentioned ; and the £1000
should in the first instance be divided into nine several
portions, according to the proportion which each of such
valuations bears to the £1000 ; but this direction is subject to my remarks as to Miss *Ferm's* interest.

Secondly, the whole of any such amount or portion
may be paid to or invested for any of the devisees where
the devise is in fee simple; but where the devise is subdivided, or consists of a life interest only to one devisee,
with remainder to another devisee in fee simple, then the
trustees ought to take the opinion of some actuary or
other competent valuer of life interests and reversions, and
as to the proportionate share which such life estate and
such remainder or reversion in fee bears to the whole
value of such subdivided devise ; and the alloted amount
or portion appropriated to such devise should be subdivided according to such valuation, and these two
amounts should be paid, or invested for the benefit of
such life devisee, and devisee in remainder respectively.

Thirdly, with reference to the fifth of the above devises which is subject to a direction that *Joseph Clarkson* and his wife, and each of them, should be allowed to live, as the petition states they have lived, in the testator's dwelling-house rent free, and without molestation, during the life of the said annuitant, and until the same should be handed over to the said *Fanny Maria Ferm*, the devisee thereof, or to some person duly authorised by her to take possession thereof—I am of opinion that this permission to occupy rent free confers no transferable interest to *Joseph Clarkson* or his wife, nor diminishes the legal devise of the life estate to *Fanny Maria Ferm*; but it must nevertheless be taken into consideration in the valuation of this particular devise, and in the following manner:—The ages of *Joseph Clarkson* and his wife must be taken, and the age of the annuitant, and an actuary must calculate the aggregate value, since the death of the testator, of the annual rent of the dwelling-house during the life of *Joseph Clarkson* and his wife, subject to the contingency of the annuitant dying before the death of the survivor of *Joseph Clarkson* and his wife; another aggregate value must be deducted from the relative value of this fifth devised property, before making the general proportionate division of the £1000. There will be no difficulty in ascertaining such valuation of this right of occupation, the duration of which I also think must be construed according to the plain meaning of the words as used—viz., as extending to *Joseph Clarkson* and his wife, or the survivor of them, and during the life of the annuitant, and even beyond such life, until the devisee (*Fanny Maria Ferm*) takes possession. This right of occupation being a life interest will be less than the aggregate actual rental during the period since the testator's death to the end of the accumulation. If *Joseph Clarkson* and his wife cease to occupy at any time, the value of this property will be *pro tanto* increased; but I think that this fact of the "dwelling-house" not having contributed anything to the £1000, as alleged in the petition, is a matter quite dehors the construction of the will; and I do not think that the

1866.

In re the trusts of the will of **Henry Usher** deceased, and the Trust Property Act of 1862.

1866.

In re the trusts
of the will of
HENRY USHER
deceased,
and the Trust
Property Act
of 1862.

valuation of *Fanny Maria Ferm's* devise should be diminished, except in the manner I have stated.

Lastly, the general " valuation " of the properties devised must be used for all future distributions, as I think the general rule as to the will "speaking" at the death of the testator, must apply in this respect. Of course, this will not apply to the successive valuations of Mr. and Mrs. *Clarkson's* right of occupation, which will diminish in value as they grow older.

Under the proviso at the end of the 30th section of the Act, I direct the costs of the trustees and of the parties appearing on this petition to be paid by the trustees out of the accumulations before dividing £1000, the same being, in my opinion, a separate fund set apart by the testator, and as to which alone these difficulties arise.

Sept. 20, 21,
and 25, 1865.

SEMPILL, assignee, &c. *against* LEE and others.

L., in 1843,
settled certain
real property
on two un-
married
daughters,
one of whom
M. subse-
quently
married *B.*
L., after the
settlement,
continued in
possession of

THIS was an appeal by the plaintiff to the full Court, from a decree made in this suit by his Honor Mr. Justice *Milford*, the Primary Judge in Equity, on the 2nd of March, 1865.

The bill was filed by *Robert Hamilton Sempill*, the official assignee of the estate of *James Brady*, one of the defendants, against *William Lee*, the said *James Brady* and *Maria* his wife, *John Dargin*, *Thomas Kite*,

the property, and *B.* knew nothing of the settlement until 1859. On 15th March, 1861, *B.* was sued for a large sum—and a verdict being obtained on the 30th May against him, he became insolvent on 1st June following. On the 26th March, *L.* having discovered that *B.* was entitled to a life interest in the property settled on his wife, and which was worth about £4000, and not being then aware of the action, offered *B.* £500 for his life interest, for the purpose of settling the property on *B.'s* wife free from her husband's claims. The offer was accepted. Part of the £500 was, on the 8th of April, handed by *L.* to his solicitors for payment to *B.*, on the execution of the conveyance settling the property on the wife. The conveyance was executed on the 20th of April, and part of the £500 was returned to *L.* in payment of a prior debt.

Held, that under the 7th section of the Insolvent Act the deed was void as against *B.'s* creditors, the consideration not being such a valuable one as would give validity to the conveyance under the Act.

Held also, that as against the creditors under *B.'s* insolvency, and under the circumstances, his wife was entitled to a settlement of not less than one-half the annual income of the property.

George Lee, and *John Lee,* praying that an indenture by which *James Brady's* life interest in certain land had been conveyed to trustees for Mrs. *Brady,* the daughter of *William Lee* and wife of *James Brady,* and other deeds by which the land so conveyed to trustees for Mrs. *Brady* was conveyed by her in trust for herself for life, with remainder to her children, might be set aside as having been given fraudulently and without adequate consideration, and for an account of the rents and profits of the land received by the defendants. The facts of the case as appeared from the pleadings and evidence were as follows :—

In the year 1843, *William Lee* was possessed of considerable real estate, and being desirous of settling part of it on his wife and two daughters, *Maria* and *Elizabeth,* he by indenture dated the 27th of October, 1843, conveyed several parcels of land to the defendants *John Dargin* and *Thomas Kite,* their heirs and assigns, to hold the same unto, and to the use of the said *John Dargin* and *Thomas Kite,* their heirs and assigns, upon trust to pay the rents and profits to his wife, *Mary Lee,* till his said daughters should respectively attain the age of twenty-one years, or marry ; and then as to one moiety thereof for his daughter the said *Maria Lee,* her heirs and assigns, and to convey the same to the said *Maria Lee* and her heirs.

Maria Lee married the defendant, *James Brady,* on the 14th of June, 1847, but whether she was of age before she married did not appear. No settlement was made on the marriage, which was had against the wish of the father, *William Lee.* *James Brady* did not know of the deed of 1843 till about twelve or eighteen months before his insolvency, and *William Lee* continued in possession of the property after the deed of 1843, but gave his daughter a house to live in for seven years before the year 1861, and paid her £100 a year for part of the time between 1843 and 1861, and £50 a year during the rest of that period.

In the year 1860, *Brady* had become liable on a bill of exchange which he had accepted for the accommodation of *J. E. Dargin*, drawn in favour of Messrs. *Cohen and Co.*, for the sum of £3,275, and payable on the 28th September, 1860. Messrs. *Cohen and Co.* brought an action against *Brady* on this bill, on the 15th of March, 1861, to which he appeared on the 2nd of April. The trial was had on the 30th of May, and a verdict then given against *Brady* for £3,449 13s. 4d. The Judge who tried the case directed execution to go in six days.

William Lee, on the 4th of March, 1861, instructed his solicitors—Messrs. *McIntosh* and *Pinnock*—to prepare a settlement of his money in favour of his children, and left with them many deeds relating to his property, and amongst others the deed of October, 1843. On the 26th of March, *William Lee* had an interview with his solicitors in reference to the interest of *Brady* under this deed, when he instructed the solicitors to offer him £500 for his interest, in order that a settlement might be made free from *Brady's* interest. The offer was made on that day, and accepted by *Brady*. On the 8th of April, *William Lee* gave his solicitor a cheque for £500 to pay to *Brady*, and a conveyance was executed, dated the 5th of April, by which *Brady* conveyed his interest to the defendants *Dargin* and *Kite*, who were to hold the fee simple of the moiety of the said land, upon trust for such persons as Mrs. *Brady* should appoint, and in default for her separate use.

On the 12th of June, 1861, Mrs. *Brady* and *Dargin* and *Kite* conveyed the before-mentioned premises, and *William Lee* conveyed other premises, to the defendants *John Lee* and *George Lee*, and their heirs, upon trust for Mrs. *Brady* for life, for her separate use, and after her death for *A. J. Brady*, *A. H. Brady*, *E. S. Brady*, and *E. H. Brady*, and other children of Mrs. *Brady* in fee.

It appeared that in March 1861, *Brady* had little or no property besides the life interest in the premises comprised in the deed of 1843, but there was no evidence shewing that he was then indebted to any person besides *William Lee* and Messrs. *Cohen and Co.* He was indebted to *William Lee* in £360, on a note which had been given by *Lee* to *Brady* for his accommodation, and by him discounted and paid by *Lee* when due. When *Brady* was paid the £500, the consideration for the deed of the 5th of April, after his execution of it, he was asked to pay the debt of £360 due to *William Lee* out of it, which he did, so that he retained in fact only £140. The income arising from the property was about £400 a year, or more.

It was stated that *Brady* was a man of intemperate habits, about forty-six years of age, and that he did not enjoy good health.

According to the evidence, if *Brady's* life had been of an average probable durability, his interest would have been worth about £4000 ; but on the other side, it was alleged that he was a confirmed drunkard, and subject otherwise to disease, and that his life was not an insurable one.

On the hearing, it was contended on the part of the plaintiff that this sale of the interest of *Brady* for £500 was void under the 13th Eliz., c. 5, and under the 6th, 7th, and 8th sections of the Insolvent Act ; and that it, together with the deed of the 12th of June, 1861, ought to be set aside so far as they prevented the creditors of *Brady* from obtaining payment of their debts.

The defendants contended that the estate was subject to Mrs. *Brady's* equity to a settlement which made £500, if not the full value of his life interest, yet sufficient under the circumstances to constitute a *bona fide* and valuable consideration—that the deed was not therefore void or liable to be set aside, but if it should be, then that *William Lee* was entitled to be repaid his £500—and that Mrs. *Brady* was entitled to a settlement made on herself and children before the creditors could have any part of the property applied in payment of their debts.

On the 16th February, 1865, the Primary Judge made a decree dismissing the bill with costs (a).

1865.

SEMPILL, assignee, &c.

v.

LEE and others.

(a) The reasons given by his Honor for the decree made by him on the hearing, are contained in the following extract from his judgment :—

"By the 13th Eliz., c. 5, all alienations of lands and hereditaments made for the intent or purpose to delay, hinder, or defraud creditors,

Gordon and *Milford* for plaintiff.   The question here is not between *Brady* and *Lee,* but between *Lee* and *Brady's* creditors, whether the former shall be allowed to deprive the latter of all *Brady's* property.   Between the father-in-law and the son-in-law a property worth £4,000 is disposed of for £500, out of which the creditors of the latter get only £140, and that at a time when *Brady* was hopelessly insolvent.   The transaction took place, and the balance of the £500 was paid back to *Lee* at a time when *Brady* could have had little doubt but that he would fail in the action brought against him by

and others, of their just debts, shall be taken (only as against those persons whose debts shall be hindered, delayed, or defrauded) to be clearly and utterly void.   By the 6th section, the Act is not to extend to any estate made or conveyed upon good consideration, and *bona fide* lawfully conveyed to any person not at the time having any manner of notice or knowledge of such fraud or collusion as aforesaid. By the 6th section of the Insolvent Act, every alienation of real estate made by any person who at the time is actually insolvent, or who by such alienation shall be rendered insolvent without valuable consideration, is declared to be fraudulent and void.   By the 7th section, all alienations of real estate made by any person after he has contracted any debt, and within twelve months preceding the sequestration of his estate, or preceding any time at which it shall be made to appear by proof that he was actually insolvent without valuable consideration, is liable to be set aside on a summary application to, and by order of, the Supreme Court, at the instance of any creditor of the insolvent whose debt was contracted prior to the making of such alienations, in so far as such creditor would thereby be prevented from receiving the full amount of his debt.

By the 8th section all alienations of real estate made by any person being insolvent, or in contemplation of surrendering his estate, or within sixty days preceding the making of any order for sequestration, and having the effect of preferring any then existing creditor to another, shall be void.

First, as to whether this case comes within the statute of *Elizabeth.* If *W. Lee,* in the terms of the 6th section of the Act had not, at the time of the conveyance to him, any knowledge or notice of the fraud, if such there were, contemplated by *Brady,* for there was a valuable consideration given, it does not.   I must say that I do not see anything in the evidence to shew that *Lee* had such notice.   *Brady* was not on good terms with his father-in-law, *Lee.*   It may be, that the position of *Brady* would point to the probability of his being anxious to seize any opportunity that might offer to escape paying this debt of £3275 to Messrs. *Cohen and Co.,* which he conceived some other person ought to pay, and for which he had received no consideration, but I do not see that there was any communication between *W. Lee* and *Brady.*   *W. Lee* says he knew nothing of the action having been brought against *Brady.*   He must, however, have known that he was in difficulties, for he had not paid him the £360 he owed him, and he (better than anybody) must have known what the life interest which he purchased was worth.   The circumstance that the offer which he made was not of the full value of the interest intended to be purchased is not enough to fix him with the knowledge that the sale was made by *Brady* to defraud his creditors, it is simply the case of a person knowing another to be in difficulties, and taking advantage of that to make a good bargain.   The offer came from *Lee,* not from

Cohen and Co. Lee says that he did not know of the action against *Brady* till after the 5th of April; but the question is, did he know of it before the 20th April, when the conveyance was completed? It is difficult to believe that *Lee* did not know of *Brady's* circumstances at the time of the transaction. The conveyance was a plan to withdraw the property from the reach of *Brady's* creditors, and would therefore be set aside in their favour, even although a valuable consideration had been given for it.

Brady. Upon examination it is found that the sum of £500 is not a great way from the value. The life of *Brady* could not be insured, or, if it could, only at a ruinous rate ; this might reduce the value one-half. Then there was the right of Mrs. *Brady* to her equity of settlement, which is usually half the income, and perhaps in this case might be more, as the property had been hers, and no settlement or provision for his wife had ever been made by *Brady* ; besides, nobody would like to invest money in the purchase of such an interest unless he could make a large profit. It would therefore be difficult to get a purchaser at near the estimated value in the tables shewing the value of a life interest of a man aged forty-six.

The conclusion which I draw from these facts is that Mr. *Lee*, knowing that *Brady* was in difficulties, but not knowing of the precise position he held with regard to his creditors, nor forming any plan for defrauding them beyond getting the property for a low price, was anxious to preserve for her benefit the life estate in the property which had been settled on his daughter by the deed of 1843, and consulted his solicitors on the subject, who devised a scheme by which that might be effected. They proposed the purchase for £500 from *Brady*, possibly expecting to be able to induce him to pay to *W. Lee* the £360 he owed him, though of this there is no evidence. Part of the plan I cannot but think was on the supposition that it was doubtful whether the mere purchase for £500 would render the transaction valid against creditors, that another deed should be executed by which Mrs. *Brady* should, for valuable consideration, emanating from Mr. *Lee*, convey her interest, together with other property settled by Mr. *Lee* to herself for life, for her separate use, with remainder to her children.

No fault can be found with this plan as fraudulent, in the common acceptation of the term, or as morally wrong, the only question is whether it can stand as against *Brady's* creditors. I have not considered *Brady* as a party to this arrangement, nor is there any evidence that he was in any way connected with it. All that the evidence enables me to say is, that he (*Brady*) knew of the claim upon him by Messrs. *Cohen and Co.*, and that but for, or perhaps with his interest under the deed of 1843 he was insolvent. He owed £360 to Mr. *Lee*, and £3275 to *Cohen and Co.*, and he does not appear to have had any other property. Did he by selling his future interest in the property for £500 defraud his creditors ? and, if so, how are Mr. Lee, and Mrs. *Brady* and her children, affected by his fraud ?

Supposing *W. Lee* to be a stranger to *Brady* in this transaction, which, in fact, he was, I see no reason why *Lee* should not endeavour to make a good bargain with *Brady* for the purchase of his life interest. He does not commit any act of fraud as against the creditors, by doing this. There is no rule of law or equity to prevent such transactions—*Gwynne* v. *Heaton*,[*] *Abbot* v. *Sworder*[†]—even if *Brady*, for

* 1 Bro. C. C. 8.   † 4 De G. & Sm. 448.

But can the consideration here be considered as a valuable one? A valuable consideration, according to Mr. Justice *Story* (a), is "something equivalent to the grant." Is £500 an equivalent for a life estate in a property worth £4,000? Under ordinary circumstances this would surely not be so in the case of a person of *Brady's* age. It is sought, however, to depreciate the value of his life interest, by representing his life as not insurable. But this is not clearly shewn to be the fact. It does not appear that it was ever tried to insure his

reasons known to himself, were willing to sell his interest at a low price. There is no evidence of extortion being practised by *Lee*—the offer is made and accepted. If *Brady* were willing to do this in fraud of his creditors that could not affect *Lee*, and he would, notwithstanding, be a *bona fide* purchaser for valuable consideration without notice. When we consider the position of *Brady* as to his health and habits of life, and the circumstance that Mrs. *Brady* was entitled to her equity of settlement, I do not see that the price *Lee* gave was so inadequate as to imply any fraud on his part, or to prevent the purchase being one for valuable consideration. That Mrs. *Brady* was entitled to this equity is clear; the legal estate was outstanding in *Dargin* and *Kite*, and a purchaser could not obtain his full legal rights without the intervention of this Court; *Sturgis* v. *Champneys*,* *Hanson* v. *Keating*.† And Lady *Elibank* v. *Montolieu*‡ shows that if a wife has such a right as a defendant, she may file a bill to enforce it.

If I am right in the view of the case which I have taken with regard to the statute of *Elizabeth*, I do not see that it is affected by the Insolvency Acts.

So far as relates to the 6th and 17th sections, what I have said shows that I am of opinion that there was a valuable consideration given for *Brady's* interest in this property; and as to the 8th section, the purchase had no effect in preferring *Lee* to any other creditor, for the evidence shows that the payment to *Lee* by *Brady* of £360 was a totally different transaction from the purchase (perhaps constituting a fraudulent preference) which had been completed before the payment was made.

This being my opinion of the purchase itself, I need not consider the effect of the deed of June, 1861; but clearly there was a purchase from Mrs. *Brady* by *Lee*, in consideration of his conveying a house for the benefit of her children.

I have now to consider whether the plaintiff has a right to have an account directed of the rents and profits belonging to *Brady* between the time of his marriage and his executing the deed of the 5th of April, 1861. *Brady* being so entitled, *Lee* took the rents. Now the proper course would have been for the trustees, *Dargin* and *Kite*, by *Brady's* direction, to have brought an action of trespass against *Lee*. *Lee* had no more right to enter on the land than I had, and surely if I had done so no suit for an account would lie against me in a Court of Equity. It was simply a legal right to be enforced in a Court of law. On the whole, I am of opinion that this bill must be dismissed, with costs. Although the case called for inquiry, that ought to have been made in the Insolvent Court before this bill was filed, and the result of such inquiry being the ground work for the suit, and that being instituted with knowledge, or presumed knowledge, of the facts and failing, the plaintiff must pay the costs.

* 5 My. & Cr. 97.   † 4 Hare 1.   ‡ 5 Ves. 737.

(a) 1 Eq. Jur., sec. 854.

life. But in any case it is difficult to bring in this as an element in the calculation of what should be considered as an equivalent to the grant. If *Brady's* life was insurable, the consideration given was not an equivalent; if it was not insurable, how could the value of his life interest be calculated, and the equivalent ascertained? Again, it is sought to depreciate the value of *Brady's* interest by supposing Mrs. *Brady* entitled to an equity of settlement out of it. *Lee* says, in his answer, that he took this alleged right of Mrs. *Brady* into consideration before he made the offer; and the learned Primary Judge seems to have allowed this as one of the grounds on which the consideration should be held sufficient. But it is submitted that Mrs. *Brady* had no equity to a settlement out of the life estate of her husband, in the case of a sale of it to a particular assignee; *Tidd*. v. *Lister* (a), *Durham* v. *Crackles* (b), *Gleaves* v. *Paine* (c), *Elibank* v. *Montolieu* (d), *Perry* v. *Muir* (e). [*Per Curiam*. Suppose it shown to the satisfaction of the Court that the husband had not maintained or contributed to the maintenance of the wife.] It does not appear from the proceedings that *Brady* was not maintaining his wife at the time when this transaction took place, April 1861. [*Per Curiam*. How does a purchaser know that the possessor of a life interest is maintaining his wife?] He must take his chance of that. If at the time this deed was executed *Brady* had deserted his wife, or was not supporting her, *Lee* might have made her right to a settlement an element in the calculation of the value of *Brady's* life interest. But, under the circumstances of this case, there was not such right. And if this point had been brought before the notice of the Primary Judge, there is no doubt that his views as to the sufficiency of the consideration would have been materially altered. The consideration, therefore, not being valuable—that is, not an equivalent to the grant—the conveyance must be held void under the 6th, 7th, and 8th sections of the Insolvent Act. A Court of

1865.

SEMPILL assignee, &c. v. LEE and others.

(a) 3 De G. M. & G. 857, 868.   (b) 32 L. J. Ch. 111.
(c) 32 L. J. Ch. 182.   (d) 1 W. & T., L. C. 341.
(e) 2 W. & O., Eq. 1.

G—4

Equity will take from third parties what they have got through the fraud or undue influence of others; *Hugue-nin* v. *Baseley* (a).   And this is what the Primary Judge supposed to be the case here, when he says that Mr. *Lee*, knowing that *Brady* was in difficulties, endeavoured to get the property settled on Mrs. *Brady*.   In any event this bill should not have been dismissed with costs.   In *Holmes* v. *Penney* (b), *Thompson* v. *Webster* (c), and *Hale* v. *M. S. O. Company* (d), the transactions were held *bona fide*; but as the circumstances appeared suspicious, the bills were dismissed, but without costs.   As to the right of the plaintiff to an account of the rents, we submit that the Court has power to follow these into the hands of *Lee*, and now that he is before the Court to make him account for them; *Lewin* on Trusts (e).

Sir *W. Manning*, Q. C., and *Darley* for defendants. It is sought in this suit to set aside a deed as fraudulent, and also under certain clauses in the Insolvent Act.   We must distinguish between *Brady* and *Lee*.   It is quite consistent to suppose that *Brady*, when he made the bargain, might know that he would be insolvent, and meditate a fraud in the transaction, and *Lee* be entirely innocent of such fraud, and know nothing of the action. There is no allegation in the bill of *Lee's* debt, or that *Brady* gave him a preference.   The return of the £360 was not at all proposed to *Brady* when the £500 was offered for his life interest.   The two payments were quite distinct.   It was only after the £500 was paid and the transaction completed that *McIntosh* spoke to *Brady* about the promissory note.   We admit it may appear that *Lee* was getting a preference.   But the transaction would have been quite the same if *Brady* had got the £500 by the sale of cattle, or otherwise.   It cannot be said that the consideration of the deed was affected by the promissory note.   Therefore the question of fraud cannot be put, on the ground that the consideration was only £140.   We submit that whatever fraud there might

(a) 2 Wh. & T. 462.   (b) 26 L. J. Ch. 179.
(c) 28 L. J. Ch. 700.   (d) 28 L. J. Ch. 777.
                (e) p. 580 seq.

have been, if *Lee* was not a party to it, the deed cannot be set aside as regards him ; *Twyne's* case (a), *Hale* v. *Metropolitan Saloon Omnibus Co.* (b). If a person purchases property with a title *bona fide*, and for value, a Court of Equity will not set aside the deed against the purchaser, although there might be equitable grounds against the seller. *Brady* having the power to convey, his deed is *prima facie* good, both in law and equity. It may indeed be set aside for fraud, but the *onus probandi* as to the fraud lies upon the plaintiff. Now it is clear from the evidence that the transaction in question did not originate from anything connected with *Cohen's* action. It was a month before *Cohen's* action that *McIntosh* discovered that *Brady* was entitled to a life estate. The untowardness of the dates—the 26th of March and the 5th of April—is no doubt *prima facie* suspicious, but it is perfectly well explained by the evidence of Mr. *Lee* and Mr. *McIntosh*. *Lee* acted *bona fide* throughout the whole transaction. He knew nothing of *Cohen's* action when the contract was made. He had no communication with *Brady*. He had no intention whatever to defeat *Brady's* creditors ; his only intention was to save his own property, which he had at first designed for his daughter, from her dissipated husband. It was very natural that *Brady* should conceal from his father-in-law the fact of his having given the accommodation indorsement for £3000, as he might hope to get out of it without any of his family knowing about it. Putting the case most strongly·—if *Lee* made the agreement on the 26th of March, and only after that became acquainted with *Cohen's* action—was he not justified in saying " I will not mind that, but will stick to my contract." Was there any fraud in such conduct as that ? As to the inadequacy of price, it must be such as to demonstrate gross imposition. And it is not the absolute value of the property that has to be considered, but what the parties thought it was worth. Now here, as Mr. *Lee* had been in possession for eighteen years, *Brady* might have thought his own title so precarious that £500 would

1865.

SEMPILL
assignee, &c.
v.
LEE
and others.

(a) 1 Smith L. C. 10.   (b) 28 L. J. Ch. 777.

1865.

SEMPILL
assignee, &c.
v.
LEE
and others.

be a good price for it. And who could know whether Mrs. *Brady* had or had not an equity to a settlement, until the fact should be decided in a Court of law. The very doubt respecting it would depreciate the value of the property. It may be admitted that *Brady* was at the time maintaining his wife, and also that she might not at that time be able to assert her right to a settlement; but she had an inchoate interest which she might assert on the contingency of his deserting or ceasing to maintain her, or becoming insolvent. The Primary Judge was right as to the costs. Although *Brady* might not be entitled to costs, Mr. *Lee* who did no wrong was entitled to them, and still more Mrs. *Brady* and the trustees; *Barrow* v. *Barrow* (a), *Harrison's* Trusts (b), *Holmes* v. *Penny* (c).

Gordon in reply.

November 10.

On this day, judgment was delivered as follows:—

STEPHEN, C. J.   This is an appeal from a decree by the late Primary Judge, dismissing the bill with costs. The suit is by the assignee of *James Brady*, an insolvent, to set aside a conveyance of his life interest in certain property, executed by him on the 20th (but dated the 5th) April, 1861, to the defendant *William Lee;* the plaintiff maintaining that the same, with a conveyance executed by *Lee* and Mrs. *Brady* in June following, consequent on the arrangement of 20th April, is void against the insolvent's then creditors—both under the statute 13th *Elizabeth*, and the 6th and two following sections of our Insolvent Act—as having been made to defeat those creditors, and without valuable or good consideration.   Mr. Justice *Milford* thought, on the evidence, that the consideration for the impeached deed was under the circumstances sufficient, or, at all events, was not grossly inadequate, although confessedly in any view of the matter very small; and he therefore dismissed the bill.

We have in conference considered all the facts of this case, and the arguments urged on both sides at the hear-

(a) 24 L. J. Ch. 267.   (b) 22 L. J. Ch. 69.
(c) 26 L. J. Ch. 179.

ing of the appeal; and we are constrained to dissent, 1865.
although on my own part not without hesitation, from SEMPILL
the conclusion arrived at by his Honor. The defendant's assignee, &c.
counsel were relieved by us, from arguing the question of v.
LEE
actual fraud; and, for myself, I acquit the parties—as and others.
did the late learned Primary Judge—unreservedly, of all
fraud or fraudulent intention whatever. The principal
defendant, as a father, did in my opinion no more than
what he believed to be his duty, in securing a provision
for the wife and children of a dissipated and perhaps embarrassed man. There is no proof that he knew of
Messrs. *Cohen's* claim, at the time of his bargain with
Brady ; and he denies (as to his belief at all events) that
he had that knowledge when the latter executed the conveyance. The insolvent himself expected to be relieved
from it; for he was a surety only, and had reason to
believe that the principal—out of funds set apart for the
purpose, and which failed only by accidental circumstances—would have taken up his bill. But, be this
how it may, and whatever his object, Mr. *Lee* senior has
obtained a transfer or alienation, which we cannot regard
as having been for value, within the reasonable construction of the enactments referred to; and therefore, as
against those creditors, it is void.

The facts are shortly these. In 1843, for some reason
not explained, Mr. *Lee* spontaneously settled certain
landed property on two unmarried daughters (the now
wife of *Brady* being one), and their heirs respectively, in
equal moieties; the conveyance being to trustees for that
purpose. *Lee* seems, nevertheless, from the time of the
settlement, to have treated it as waste paper; and *Brady*,
who married in 1847 the elder daughter, knew nothing
of it until the year 1859, or thereabouts—and even then
he appears to have a vague notion, only, of its nature.
The trustees never entered into possession, or received
the proceeds of the property. They were collected exclusively by *Lee*; the latter allowing his daughter a sum
yearly, and occasionally the use of a house in which she
and her husband lived. In the meantime, according to
the evidence (as I understand and accept it), the latter

had gradually become of greatly intoxicated habits; he had suffered from *delirium tremens*, and other serious ailments—and his life is said not to have been, in the early part of 1861, an insurable one.

I mention these matters, as essential in my opinion to the right understanding of the case; and with the less reluctance, because the period has long passed—and with it, doubtless, the state of things thus spoken of. Now, in February 1861, the insolvent had incurred his liability to *Cohen and Co.*; but no action at their suit was commenced until the 15th March. On the 4th March, *Lee* consulted his solicitor as to making arrangements, generally, for his family; and then the latter discovered from the deeds laid before him, and brought to his client's notice, that the daughters had each the interest mentioned —and consequently that *Brady*, in right of his wife, there being issue of the marriage, had an equitable life estate in the property. The result was that *Lee* instructed his solicitor on the 26th (the father and son-in-law not being on speaking terms) to offer *Brady* £500 for the latter's life interest.

The offer was made on the same day, and accepted. The conveyance in question—settling the property wholly on the wife, or as she should direct, freed from that incumbrance, so to call it—was prepared; and on the 8th April, *Lee* placed the amount in the solicitor's hands, to be paid on the execution of the instrument. But, on the same occasion, he also instructed his solicitor to obtain from *Brady*, if possible, on such execution, payment of an overdue bill for £360 due to himself—the purchaser, out of the purchase money. On the 20th, as already mentioned, the conveyance was signed; and *Brady* then, at the solicitor's request, after formally receiving the £500, handed back the amount of *Lee's* claim—retaining the difference only.

At this time, *Brady* had doubtless reasons of his own for accepting a very small sum, in exchange for that property; and it is possible (though I by no means say that such is the fact), that he wished to preserve it specially from Messrs. *Cohen's* claim. On the 2nd April he had appeared, and on the 15th pleaded, to the action at his creditor's suit; and, on the 22nd—although the cause was not tried till the 30th May—the cause was at issue. He must have been conscious that the estate was simply transferred to his wife; and that, if he failed in the pending action, and the expectations formed by him in connexion with it, all his own rights would pass to the successful plaintiffs. But, whatever *Brady's* views, an innocent purchaser for value would of course not be prejudiced by them. In the result, the verdict was against *Brady* for the large amount claimed; and he immediately afterwards, that is to say, on the 1st June, sequestrated his estate.

Now, there can be no doubt that, whether *Brady* was or not " actually insolvent " at the time of the alienation in question, he was thereby " rendered " insolvent; so that—irrespective of any provisions in the statute of *Elizabeth*—that conveyance was absolutely void (or, at least, voidable at the election of his assignee), by the express terms of section 6 of the Insolvent Act, unless it was in fact for valuable consideration. And, by section 7 of the same Act, since the alienation was within twelve months before sequestration, it would as against all then existing creditors, if without valuable consideration, be liable to be set aside. It therefore becomes necessary to consider, first, what is the legal meaning of those words; and then what is the evidence, and the reasonable and just conclusion, as to the value of the interest alienated.

As to the first point, it is obvious that the term valuable consideration cannot, without involving an absurdity, be taken to mean or include any and every pecuniary advance or payment, whatever the amount. It would be admitted, that no conveyance founded on a payment or consideration merely illusory, for instance, could be supported. On the other hand, the fact simply of inadequacy cannot be the test. If it were, every advantageous bargain might at the instance of disappointed creditors be defeated. The question will be, therefore, whether—in cases of that kind—the consideration is so grossly and violently inadequate, so entirely out of proportion to the value of the property acquired, as at once to strike the mind. It will often be a most difficult task, in examples neither of fraud in the buyer, nor imbecility in the seller, to draw the line. But, in every case of startling disproportion, if the money consideration be such as irresistibly to suggest the idea, that some other inducement than this caused (and not merely influenced) the act of alienation, such consideration cannot, in my opinion, be deemed a "valuable" one, within the intent and meaning of this enactment.

What, then, was the price paid here? Five hundred pounds, for an interest which is proved to have been— estimated by the average duration of life—worth above four thousand. I say "above" four thousand; because the valuation was taken, I observe, on the assumption of a rental of £400 a year—whereas the actual rental appears to have been £450 or more. The learned Primary Judge considered that half of this ought to be deducted, in estimating the value, for the proportion which would probably have been set apart, on any purchaser from the husband coming to this Court (as it would be necessary to do) to obtain the benefit of the purchase, for the use of the wife. But we all agree, that—in the absence of any evidence of *Brady's* not having maintained, or been in a position to maintain his wife, at that time—Mrs. *Brady* could not have claimed any settlement out of his life interest. The authorities cited are quite conclusive as to this; *Tidd* v. *Lister* (a), and *Durham* v. *Crackles* (b). Was £500, then, a valuable consideration for the undiminished property? My colleagues are of opinion that it was not. The case is, however, as it appears to me, by no means free from difficulty; for the life of a man like *Brady*, such as he is described as having been in 1861, may have been marketably worth little. I should have liked therefore fuller inquiry, before deciding such a point. But, on the whole, taking the evidence as it stands, and being compelled to regard the opinions of the trustees, and others interested, as open necessarily to some disparagement, I concur with the other members of the Court.

(a) 32 L. J. Ch. 249.   (b) 32 *Ibid* 112.

The fact of Mr. *Lee's* own debt having formed a portion of the consideration (not originally, but by the arrangement made on the occasion of the execution of the deed), does not materially affect the case—if at all. For, since *Brady's* life interest was worth, confessedly, much more than the amount of that debt, or, as the plaintiff maintains, more than the united amount of both *Lee's* and *Cohen's* debts, the £360 cannot be regarded as either a bad or doubtful claim. It was due on a dishonoured bill, and immediately enforceable. On the assumption, therefore, that it in effect formed part of the purchase money, this debt was equivalent to cash between the parties. If, on the other hand, the settlement of that debt formed no part of the consideration, but was a subsequent matter, the question of value is obviously unaffected by the transaction.

As the conveyance is void, if at all, by section 6 of the Insolvent Act, we need not consider the case in connection with the statute of 13th *Elizabeth*. The conveyance would also, under section 7 of our Act, having been within twelve months before the sequestration, be liable to be set aside. The plaintiff's counsel contended, however, that the conveyance—irrespective of any question as to value—was void against creditors, under the same Act, section 8 ; because, being within sixty days before sequestration, it had " the effect of preferring one then existing creditor" (to wit, Mr. *Lee*) to the insolvent's other creditors. The question, whether the alienation— looking at all the circumstances—had or not that effect, might admit perhaps of doubt ; although my present impression is, I confess, adverse to the defendants upon the point. And the question on this section, it will be observed, is not one of actual preference or of intention, but simply as to the " effect " of the transaction.

But I am of opinion that this last question does not arise on these pleadings ; for the point is not taken by the bill. The charge is, exclusively, that the conveyance of 1861 was without value or valuable consideration; and therefore, being an alienation by a person actually insolvent, or contemplating the surrender of his estate, and within sixty days before sequestration, or twelve months before actual insolvency or sequestration, was either wholly void or voidable against his then creditors. But this is nothing to the purpose. To have made the 8th section available, it was necessary to charge or state that the alienation had (as matter of fact) the effect of a preference : whereas the bill does not even allege that *Lee* was a creditor, much less a creditor preferred or paid.

I may add that the bill does not even charge, that by the alienation in question *Brady* was rendered insolvent. The charge is, that he was actually at the time insolvent. Now, while owner of the life interest, he had ample means to pay every creditor. The case, therefore, as stated by the plaintiff in his bill, had the objection been insisted on, might altogether (I apprehend) have failed, but for the seventh section.

The result is, however, as already intimated, that, under the seventh—if not also the sixth section of the Insolvent Act, the conveyance of the 5th (executed on the 20th) April, 1861, must be declared void as against the plaintiff ; and the conveyance or settlement of 12th June following will, of course, share the same fate. The parties to this suit will bear, severally, each his own costs of the appeal. But the costs of the plaintiff, up to the original hearing inclusively, must be paid by the principal defendant.

I am of opinion that the decree must be limited to the receipts of the rents and profits by the trustees, respectively, under those deeds—and therefore to the period since April the 5th, 1861. It appears to me that we have nothing to do with the rents, which were received by *Lee* senior in derogation of *Brady's* rights, at any time before the conveyance or settlement of that date. The suit was instituted, exclusively, for the purpose of impeaching that conveyance. So far from having sought redress in respect of receipts by *Lee*, the plaintiff in his bill states (paragraph 5) that the rents and profits, from *Brady's* marriage up to the time of that conveyance, were duly received by the latter. The prayer is, accordingly, that such conveyance may be set aside ; and, until the amendment of the bill, no account was sought except against the trustees and *Brady*. By that amendment, the trustees of the settlement of 12th June, 1861 (mentioned in Mr. Justice *Milford's* judgment), were introduced as defendants ; and an addition was made to the 16th paragraph, simply, that the latter and *William Lee*, as well as the first named trustees, had received the rents and profits. But, as the 5th paragraph was left untouched, and no charge is made against those trustees in respect of the settlement of 1843, that they either had themselves received and not accounted for, or had wrongfully permitted *Lee* to receive and retain, the rents and profits since 1847 and before 1861,—I think that such addition (if directed at all to the last-mentioned receipts, which I much doubt), is too loose and vague to include them.

I concur, moreover, in the opinion of the late Primary Judge, that, as against the said *William Lee*, the principal defendant, in respect of the rents admitted to have been received by him, this proceeding is not the plaintiff's appropriate remedy. He had either a right to receive and retain them, as his own, or he was in receiving them a stranger and a trespasser ; and we are not now to anticipate his defence. He may perhaps meet the claim, partially at least, by the statute of limitations. In any case, he is not a trustee as to those rents, and there is nothing respecting them to be set aside. On the other hand, the trustees having confessedly received none of those rents, have nothing to account for respecting them.

One question only remains, as it appears to me ; and that is, what allowances ought to be made to the trustees, in taking the accounts of the rents and profits received by them under the conveyance and settlements of 1861. And as to this, I am of opinion, that they should have not only the ordinary just allowances, but also a proper sum—to be ascertained by the Master, not exceeding one half of the annual net income—for the maintenance of the wife and children, since the date of the insolvency. The Court is asked to give the insolvent's creditors, as

1865.

SEMPILL
assignee, &c.
v.
LEE
and others.

against the trustees of those settlements (and therefore against the wife, who is the object and meritorious cause of the settlement), the power to appropriate his life interest in the property, I conceive that, on the ordinary principle of equity, and according to the authorities, we ought not to do this—since the husband is insolvent, and therefore the exact circumstances have arisen, on which (in the case of a life interest) the equity of the wife to a settlement depends—without securing to her in effect such a provision.

I do not think the Court called on, all the circumstances being considered, to make any order for the return of Mr. *Lee's* purchase money.

HARGRAVE, J.   Several most important allegations of this bill are so contradicted by the evidence in the cause, especially as to the receipt of the rents previous to the deeds of 1861, and several other allegations of this bill are so vague and loose in their terms, that it is in my opinion impossible to give the plaintiff any other relief than as mentioned by the judgment just delivered by the Chief Justice ; and I also think that such relief can only be given on the grounds mentioned, viz., that the deeds of 1861 must be declared void under the sixth and seventh sections of the Insolvency Act.

Such being the opinion of the Court, it does not seem to me to be either necessary or desirable to enter into any consideration of the various other topics introduced into the argument, and not necessary to support the decree now made ; further than to state that Mr. *Brady*, in my opinion, beyond all doubt, executed the conveyance now set aside, not merely for the consideration of the £500, but for the consideration that the same instrument was a settlement of his property on his wife and children.   This circumstance, however, that this conveyance was in fact a *quasi* family arrangement on Mr. *Brady's* part, quite as much as on Mr. *Lee's*, places the conduct of both those gentlemen in their proper light ; but it is plain that the validity of the conveyance as against Mr. *Brady's* creditors must depend upon the substantial sufficiency of the money consideration, which, as stated in the Chief Justice's judgment, cannot be considered as adequate to give validity to the conveyance under the Insolvency Act.

The only other point in this decree upon which I have felt some difficulty is, as to the direction to the Master to settle the amount of Mr. *Brady's* equity to a settlement out of the rents to be accounted for by the trustees; but considering that the plaintiff's counsel very properly admitted that he could only oppose that claim, though fairly stated on her answer, upon the technical ground of the frame of this suit;—and as such objection seems to me to be sufficiently answered by the circumstances, first, that the deed is set aside on the ground of Mr. *Brady's* insolvency—secondly, that Mrs. *Brady's* claim is, therefore, substantially correlative with the plaintiff's equity—and thirdly, that the present decree, without this reservation, would be in effect a decree against Mrs. *Brady*—I am prepared (under the circumstances of this case) to carry the usual form of a decree in this class of suits further than has been heretofore done, by directing the reference on Mrs. *Brady's* behalf.

CHEEKE, J. I concur generally in the judgment now pronounced by the Chief Justice and Mr. Justice *Hargrave*. On the main points of this appeal, with reference to the deed of the 5th April, 1861, and the conveyance or settlement of the 12th June following, I consider that under the 6th section of the Insolvent Act, and equally in regard to the 7th section of the same Act, both deeds must be declared void as against the plaintiff in this suit on behalf of the creditors.

1865.

November 24.   YEO and wife *against* ROTTON and another.

Trustees are liable for the loss of trust moneys, if, in investing them on lands of permanent value, they lend more than two-thirds the value, or if they lend more than one-half on houses or buildings of fluctuating value. Considering the nature of colonial property, the Court is more inclined to narrow than enlarge this rule.

THIS was a suit instituted by *James Yeo* and *Eliza Yeo*, his wife, against *Henry Rotton* and *James Ingram Burfitt*. The defendants were the trustees of certain property, to a share of which the plaintiff (*Eliza Yeo*) was entitled. A sum of money to which the said plaintiff was entitled had been lent by the defendants on mortgage, which the bill alleged was wholly inadequate for its repayment; and the plaintiffs charged that the defendants, previous to the investment, had not taken proper measures to ascertain the value of the property taken as a security, and in particular had not employed a competent person to make a valuation of it. The mortgagor had absconded without paying the mortgage money, which was consequently lost, and it was prayed that the defendants might be ordered to make it good.

The words of the trust were "to invest upon mortgage of fee simple lands, or upon the security of Government debentures."

It appeared by the evidence that under a settlement dated October, 1852, and by an account signed and approved on 7th September, 1857, Mrs. *Yeo* (then *Eliza Burfitt*), became entitled to the sum of £203 9s. 10d., with interest, from 7th September, 1857; and that she had only received from the defendants (her trustees) £20 on account of interest. They alleged that they were unable to pay the principal money to Mrs. *Yeo* or her husband, the co-plaintiff, by reason of the depreciation in the value of the security in which it was invested by them in September, 1857. It appeared also that the plaintiff's fund of £203 9s. 10d., with two other funds of the same amount, was lent by the defendants to a person named *Lewis* upon mortgage of certain freehold land, a cottage, and outbuildings, situated in Bathurst. The chief question was whether the circumstances of that loan were such as to relieve the defendants from their liability to pay the fund which it appeared beyond all question could not be realised without great loss on the security.

Gordon, for plaintiffs, cited *Lewin* on Trusts (a), *Macleod* v. *Annesley* (b), *Stretton* +. *Ashmall* (c).

Sir *W. Manning,* Q. C., and *Darley* for defendants, referred to *Jones* v. *Lewis* (d), *Lewin* on Trusts (e).

Gordon, in reply, referred to *Lewin* on Trusts (f).

On this day judgment was delivered as follows by the PRIMARY JUDGE. After stating the facts of the case, his Honor continued—

December 1.

The general rule established by such cases as *Rider* v. *Bickerton* (g), *Stickney* v. *Sewell* (h), *Philipson* v. *Gatty* (i), *Jones* v. *Lewis* (k), *Macleod* v. *Annesley* (l), *Stretton* v. *Ashmall* (m), *Vickery* v. *Evans* (n), and *Norris* v. *Wright* (o)— as a guide to trustees in selecting freehold investments—is, that they must not lend more than two-thirds the value upon freehold agricultural or other lands of a permanent value; and that upon free-hold houses or other buildings of a fluctuating value, they must not advance more than one-half of the value.

This rule is so simple and so unquestioned, and is also so consistent with business habits and common prudence —it has also been so long an acknowledged guide to the legal profession, and to all persons in the position of these defendants—and, moreover, is of so much importance for the protection of all trusts and family settlements in this colony no less than in England, as a restraint on speculative or careless dealings with trust property—that I cannot hesitate for a moment to maintain authority in this Court against all trustees who place themselves clearly within its scope. In fact, considering the more fluctuating value of colonial property than English property, I should rather be inclined to

(a) p. 345.   (b) 16 Beav. 600.   (c) 24 L. J. 277.
(d) 4 Chit. 355.   (e) p. 597.   (f) p. 775.
(g) 3 Swanst. 80 (1743). (h) 1 Myl. & Cr. 8 (1835).
(i) 7 Hare 516 (1848).   (k) Chitty's Eq. Ju., p. 3555 (1852).
(l) 16 Beav. 600 (1853). (m) 3 Drew 9 ; 24 L. J. 277. (1855).
(n) 10 Jur. N. S., p. 30, (Jan. 1865).   (o) 14 Beav. 291.

narrow than to enlarge this rule, as applicable to colonial trusts.

In this case, it appears to me upon the evidence to be clear that, considering (1) that the trust expressly allowed investments in Government debentures, or that the house property selected yielded no actual rent at the time of the loan ; and (2) that the security was property of a very speculative value as house property ; and observing that the borrower employed the trustees' solicitor—I am of opinion that the trustees ought to have obtained clear and distinct value at the time of the loan of the substantial adequacy of the security proposed, or that they ought now to have produced conclusive evidence to the same effect ; and having failed so to do—for not even the defendants' own witnesses can bring themselves to value the security nearly up to the required amount, while the plaintiffs' witnesses fall still further short of such adequacy of value —I am of opinion that the trustees did not at the time of the investment use due diligence or proper prudence in performing their trust, and in obtaining an adequate security for the trust fund according to the rule I have mentioned, and that they are consequently now liable for the loss.

As to the second part of their defence, viz., that there has been subsequent acquiescence by the plaintiffs in this breach of trust, this also seems to me wholly to fail upon the evidence ; and I am therefore compelled to decree that the defendants make good the loss of the trust fund according to the prayer of the bill.

With regard to costs, although there is nothing to impeach the honour or *bona fides* of the defendants, yet, as they clearly erred in the performance of their trust, and as they refused to comply with the very lenient offer made to them by the plaintiffs before the suit—viz., that plaintiffs would accept the trust fund of £203 9s. 10d., and would forego their just claim for interest, the plaintiffs have been thereby compelled to come into this Court, and the defendants, therefore, must pay the plaintiffs costs.

AN INDEX

<small>TO THE</small>

PRINCIPAL MATTERS IN THE CASES

AT COMMON LAW.

A—4

CRIMINAL INFORMATION. 1. Where the defendant sent by post to A. (a person engaged in mercantile pursuits, but not occupying any public position) a letter containing a libel upon him, couched in the most gross and offensive terms, and calculated to cause a breach of the peace, the Court discharged a rule for a criminal information, on condition that the defendant paid the costs of the motion. *R.* v. *Cyril Cecil* 323

CROWN LANDS OCCUPATION ACT OF 1861. 1. The 28th section of the Crown Lands Occupation Act of 1861 provides, that it shall be lawful for any party to an action of trespass upon Crown lands, of which no lease from the Crown shall be in force, "to plead and put in evidence any promise, engagement, or contract from or with the Crown, or its agents lawfully authorised, for the granting under the orders in Council, or under this Act, for any term unexpired, of a lease of such lands; and such promise, &c., shall, as between the parties in such action, have the same effect as if a lease from the Crown of such lands had been duly issued, in pursuance of such promise, &c., to the party entitled thereunder to such lease." *Held*, that this section gives effect only to promises, &c., made after the order in Council came into operation.

In a squatting action it was proved that A. occupied 68,500 acres of land, called by the general terms of G., from 1838 to 1848, when he applied in the usual way for a lease of G. by the ascribed limits, and stating in his application that the quantity of land was only 16,000 acres. This application was advertised in the *Gazette*. A license in the usual form, to occupy certain lands "known as G.," was afterwards issued, and rent was for several years paid by A. as for 16,000 acres. After some years the Government discovered that the quantity of land actually occupied was much larger than 16,000 acres, and thereupon, in 1856, it promised a lease of about 30,000 acres out of the entire area to B. In an action of trespass by A. against B., for trespasses on the land included in the promise to B., the latter pleaded a promise of a lease under the 28th section of the Crown Lands Occupation Act of 1861, and A. replied a previous promise under the same section. *Held*, that even assuming that the application for a lease, and its publication in the *Gazette* in 1848, coupled with the subsequent licenses and payments of rent, were unitedly some evidence of a promise to A. as to 16,000 acres—they were no evidence of such a promise as to 68,500 acres; and a verdict which had been found in favour of A. was set aside. *Blackman* v. *Mylecharane* 43

2. The sixth section of the Crown Lands Occupation Act of 1861 enacts, that where two or more persons entitled to leases claim the same land, "the lease shall be granted to the person whose right thereto may have been or may be established, after due enquiry, to the satisfaction of the Governor or the minister;" and where the right shall not have been so established, "it shall be lawful for the minister to require such right to be enquired into and determined by arbitration, and the lease may be granted in accordance with the award of such arbitration." The fourth paragraph of the 23rd section says, that "the award of any arbitrators appointed in pursuance of the Act, shall be binding, final, and conclusive upon all parties to the arbitration, for all intents and purposes whatever." *Held*, that it is discretionary with the Crown to issue a lease to the party in whose favour the award is made or not.

The eleventh and fourteenth paragraphs of the 23rd section provide that any submission to arbitration under the provisions of the Act, may be made a rule of the Supreme Court on the application of either party, and that no award shall be set aside for irregularity or error in matter of form. *Held,*

the plaintiff, being a creditor as aforesaid, to others of his then existing creditors. The plea also alleged the fact of the due sequestration of S. A.'s estate, and the appointment of an assignee thereof ; and that by him, since the commencement of this suit, the election had been made to avoid the transaction, on behalf of the insolvent's creditors—and to claim the instruments as part of the assets belonging to the estate. *Held* good.

Replication—that S. A. was indebted to the plaintiff long before and at the time of the indorsements in question, for services as an attorney ; and that he lent S. A. money, on two occasions, upon security of the notes, which were accordingly deposited with and agreed to be held by the plaintiff, as security for the repayment of such loans with interest—both such loans and the consequent deposit being more than sixty days before the sequestration. It then alleged that eventually S. A. sold him the notes, and thereupon endorsed them without recourse, for a stated sum (such sale and indorsements being within the sixty days), the plaintiff deducting therefrom the amount due to him for services, and for the two loans and interest thereon ; which deduction, it was then agreed between the parties, should be taken as payments of those amounts. Averment—that the plaintiff was not at the time aware, nor had he notice, that such payments were voluntary preferences by S. A. over other creditors, or that the latter was then insolvent, or rendered thereby insolvent, &c.—negativing the other matters mentioned in the enactment. The replication also alleged that the transaction was not a fraudulent preference—and that it had not the effect of a preference as alleged in the plea. *Held* bad—that the transaction between the plaintiff and S. A., as disclosed on these pleadings, was one of a transfer and delivery of chattels, void as against S. A.'s assignee, under the 8th section of the 5 Vic., No. 17, and could not be deemed a payment within either the 12th section of that Act, or the 1st and 2nd sections of the 25 Vic., No. 8. *Levy* v. *Smith* — 329

JUSTICES. 1. A. being in the occupation of an unlicensed house, in which several persons were found drinking spirits, was apprehended with those persons under the 51st section of the Sale of Liquors Licensing Act, and brought before the justices. Thereupon evidence was gone into ; and, at its close, the further hearing of the case against A. was adjourned. On the day of adjournment A. did not appear, and in her absence the justices convicted her (under the same section) of unlicensed retailing, and inflicted a fine. *Held* (*Faucett*, J., *dissentiente*), that the conviction was bad.

Held (per *Stephen*, C. J., and *Cheeke*, J.), also that the provisions of the 11 and 12 Vic., c. 43, had no application to the case. Ex parte *Conn* — 354

LARCENY. 1. Recent possession of stolen bank notes, of which the prisoner could give no satisfactory account, is evidence either that he stole them, or that he received them, knowing them to have been stolen, according to the other circumstances of the case. *R.* v. *Saunders* — 200

2. The prisoner being indicted for stealing and receiving certain horses, was acquitted of the stealing but found guilty of the receiving. After the verdict of guilty had been pronounced and minuted by the clerk, the jury said that they recommended the prisoner to mercy, on the ground that they thought that she believed herself to have some claim to the

A bill of exchange drawn by the Bank of New Zealand, in
the colony of New Zealand, payable to J. H. or his order, at
the Bank of New South Wales, in Sydney, fifteen days after
sight, *Held* not liable to duty.

An instrument in the following form—"Tarong, Queensland, August 1, 1865, £10. Pay J. B. or order the sum of ten
pounds sterling, on account of *Henry Wallis*. To Messrs. S.
H. and Co., Sydney." *Held* liable to duty.

An instrument in the following form—" Bank of New South
Wales, Maitland, 6th September, 1865. £149 16s. 3d. Pay
to the order of Messrs. A. and B. one hundred and forty-nine
pounds sixteen shillings and three-pence, for value received.—
J. M. S., Manager. To the Bank of New South Wales,
Sydney." *Held* liable to duty of one penny, as a draft for the
payment of "forty shillings and upwards" to order on
demand.

The schedule also contained the following item—"Receipt
or discharge given for any sum of money, for forty shillings
and upwards—*one penny*. Exemptions from the preceding
duties on receipts. Acknowledgment given for money deposited in any bank to be accounted for."

The Bank of New South Wales having received from J. E.
C. £114 on fixed deposit, repayable to J. E. C. twelve months
after date, gave him a memorandum as follows—"Bank of
New South Wales, &c. Due 29th July, 1866, £114. Sydney,
29th July, 1865. Received from J. E. C. the sum of one
hundred and fourteen pounds, at a fixed deposit for twelve
months, to bear interest at the rate of six per cent. per annum
for that period, from the date hereof. For and on behalf of
the Bank of New South Wales.—C. M. P., Manager." *Held*
liable to a penny duty as a receipt. *The Attorney-General* v.
The Bank of New South Wales   245

CASES IN EQUITY.

INJUNCTION. 1. A. desiring to erect some quartz crushing machinery, contracted with M. for its construction, and for the
attaching to it of a machine, for which letters of registration
had been granted within New South Wales, under the 16 Vic.,
No. 24. The machine having been procured out of New
South Wales, was ready to be supplied by M. under his contract. On the application of the grantees of the letters of
registration, the Court refused to grant an injunction to
restrain A. from accepting it. *Russell* v. *Bruyeres*   1
See PATENT.

2 A testator possessing large and real and personal estate in
New South Wales, died domiciled in England, largely indebted to several creditors—one of whom residing in England
instituted a creditor's suit in the High Court of Chancery
against the testator's widow, who also resided in England, and
was the sole executrix and devisee appointed by his will. In
this suit a decree had been obtained for administration of the
testator's estate, and for receivers to collect his assets in this
colony and elsewhere; but before their actual appointment
the executrix, without obtaining probate or administration in
this Court, had, by her son as agent, taken possession of part,
and was proceeding to collect and realise the residue of the
testator's property in this colony. The plaintiffs, who were
also English creditors, now instituted here a suit of the same
character against the widow, and served her son with the bill,
under an order for substituted service, and subsequently, but
before appearance entered for the defendant, and without
opposition, obtained an order for the appointment of a receiver,
and for an injunction to restrain the defendant from dealing
with the estate. A motion to rescind this order and dissolve
the injunction was granted by the Primary Judge, on the
grounds principally that under the circumstances of this case
the Court of Chancery was the appropriate forum for the
creditors of the testator to resort to for relief, and that the
defendant in this suit was not the personal representative of
the testator in this colony.

Held, by the full Court on appeal (*Stephen*, C.J., *dissentiente*),
that the order for injunction and receiver ought to be restored.

Held, also, that this Court ought not to refuse, at the
instance of any creditor of a testator, to exercise its inherent
jurisdiction over his property situated in this colony, but
ought to place all such property under the protection and
management of officers appointed by this Court, more
especially when the personal representative declines taking
out administration here.

Held further, that the rights of creditors suing here are not
diminished or affected by proceedings relative to the same
matter in a foreign Court.

Held, also, that the absence of a legal personal representative of the testator, is a matter of objection which may be
cured at any time before hearing, and is without any effect
on an application for a receiver and injunction *ad interim.*
Alliance Bank (Limited) v. *Irving*   17 45

3. The plaintiff V. was owner, since 1833, of certain lands,
whereon he was erecting buildings and excavating cellars.
He complained that M., the owner of land and premises adjoining, allowed sewerage to flow from his land into the
cellars so excavated, and prayed that M. might be restrained
from continuing the nuisance. The sewerage ran through a
drain crossing the land of V., but which M. claimed a right by
prescription to use for such purpose. *Held* (*Stephen*, C. J.,
dissentiente), that as V. and his predecessors had so long
acquiesced in the use of the drain as a sewer, he was not
entitled to the interposition of a Court of Equity for the
purpose of preventing the nuisance.

Held, also, that his remedy, if any, under the circumstances, was by action at law under the Common Law Procedure Act. *Vickery* v. *Marr* 66
See PRESCRIPTION.

4. A testator devised the whole of his property, consisting of real estate, leaseholds, and a squatting station fully stocked, and also ready money, to his wife, jointly with F. and H., their survivors and survivor, and the heirs and executors of such survivor, upon trust to permit her to have the full benefit and enjoyment of the property for life, and then, upon trust, to divide it among all his children—the boys at twenty-one, and the girls at that age, or on marriage. *Held*, that the legal estate in all the real and personal property of the testator was vested in the three trustees, but that the wife was entitled to the enjoyment of the whole *in specie* during her life.

In a suit instituted by F. against H. and the testator's widow, who had married again, and against *Harford* her present husband, charging sundry breaches of trust by the two former defendants, and misappropriation by *Harford*, an order was made on motion before the hearing for an injunction to restrain the defendants from further interference with the trust estate, and for the appointment of a receiver. At the hearing the injunction was dissolved, and the receiver discharged, on the ground that according to the true construction of the will the dealings of the defendants' were not breach of trust, the wife being entitled to enjoy the property specifically. *Frost* v. *Healy* 6, 81

NUISANCE.
See INJUNCTION, 3.

PATENT. *Quære*, whether any restriction in a patent affecting or intending to affect the buyers of a manufactured article, made and sold in violation of the patent, can be supported. *Russell* v. *Bruyeres* 1
See INJUNCTION, 1.

PERSONAL REPRESENTATIVE.
See INJUNCTION, 2.

PLEADING.
See INJUNCTION, 2.

PRESCRIPTION. *Quære*—whether, as there can be no such thing, strictly speaking, in this colony, as "time immemorial," and the Prescription Act (2 and 3 W. IV., c. 71)—not having been adopted here, the rules of law applied in England prior to that Act, as to the presumption of lost grants of easement, ought to be followed in this colony. *Vickery* v. *Marr* 66

PROBATE.
See ADVERTISEMENT FOR PROBATE.

REDEMPTION. Bill for redemption—filed by the purchaser of the assets of insolvent mortgagor—charged that the consideration in some of the deeds was not paid at the time of their execution, nor so large a sum ever paid, and prayed besides usual accounts an account of all moneys paid by defendant.

Answer set up special agreements as to the consideration to be inserted in the deeds.

Held (reversing decree of Primary Judge), that, with respect to one of the deeds, the special agreement was not proved by evidence, and that the deed ought to be taken as an incumbrance to the extent only of the sums actually advanced. *Broughton* v. *Rodd* 54

SETTLEMENT. L., in 1843, settled certain real property on two unmarried daughters, one of whom M. subsequently married B. L., after the settlement, continued in possession of the property, and B. knew nothing of the settlement until 1859. On 15th March, 1861, B. was sued for a large sum—and a verdict being obtained on the 30th May against him, he became insolvent on 1st June following. On the 26th March,

1

Lightning Source UK Ltd.
Milton Keynes UK
UKHW010752280219
338010UK00004B/293/P